Demystifying the Internet

A deep dive into the Building Blocks, Applications, Security, Protocols and Hidden Secrets of the Internet

by

Kevin Curran

1

Foreword

The Internet is a complex beast. However it can be understood. It is simply a combination of standards based protocols intereacting with applications and devices. The common denominator of the Internet is the Internet Protocol (IP). Every device which connects to the Internet must run IP. This book is an attempt to examine in depth various aspects of the Web.

There are no shortcuts to true knowledge and insight can only come from understanding principles and facts surrounding a subject area. This book does not dwell on the history of the Internet. Suffice to say that it was a combination as usual of military demands and industry/university collaboration. I doubt however that many of those involved back then could have foreseen the impact that early bandwidth limted network would have on society in the future. Interestingly however, the building blocks have not changed much since the initial days. Protocols are crucial to providing functionality and their standardisation enables widespread adoption.

This book is divided into six sections.

In section 1 – The Network underneath, we examine protocol stacks, standards and issues, what causes delays in the network, mesh networking & wireless sensor networks. We also look at disruption tolerant networking, streaming audio and cognitive radio.

In section 2 - Internet Building Blocks – Protocols and Standards, we examine computational GRIDS, web operating systems and really simple syndication (RSS). We then look at Javascript, XML, E4X and AJA, the semantic web, voiceXML and web services.

In section 3 - Internet Trends, Applications and Services, we examine web 2.0, electronic surveillance, mobile social software, the long tail, cyberterrorism, podcasts and blogging and web accessibility for users with disabilities.

In section 4 – The Mobile Internet, we look at WiMAX, hybrid web applications, browsing the Web through a Phone, in vehicle computing, body area networks, mobile IP and cellullar IP and mobile adaptive applications.

In section 5 – Internet Security, we examine cryptography, universal authentication, honeynets, wireless (WiFi) security, email SPAM, hacking and Internet fraud.

In section 6 – The Hidden Web, we look at the invisible web, digital watermarking & steganography, vertical search engines, location positioning, web intelligence and ambient intelligence.

Table of Contents

1 Introduction

On the 22nd May 1973, a young man named Bob Metcalf authored a memo that described "X-Wire", a 3Mbps common bus office network system developed at Xerox's Palo Alto Research Center (PARC). It was also called the Alto Aloha Network protocol but it became more commonly know as *Ethernet*. There are few networking technologies from the early 70's that have proved to be so resilient. Metcalf deservedly went on to everlasting fame in the networking community (Metcalf also founded the global company 3COM) and his story should have ended here. However, in 1995, he predicted that the Internet would self-destruct from overload[1]. His argument was that network load (messages, packets) are growing exponentially, while network bandwidth (fiber capacity, switch performance) is growing linearly and at some point, these two curves cross and the result being that demand will exceed capacity. To cut a long story short – he was wrong. The Internet is still around and so is Bob but somehow his *Future of Networking Predictions* are not now taken quite as seriously by those in the industry. This anecdote is used here not to ridicule a great man such as Bob Metcalf but rather to serve as a warning to those of us who think that they know how a complex beast such as the Internet is about to behave in the days ahead. You'll be pleased to hear that I keep my predictions to a minimum in the remaining pages.

On a different note, mention to a young person that the Internet was not around "when you were young" – and you can visibly see their face change as they attempt to comprehend how on earth a race of people could survive without it. I personally remember my epiphany concerning the power of the web back in the early nineties when I was reading a book outside enjoying the sunshine when I was stung by a wasp. I simply got up after the shock and without any serious thought I returned to my office and entered the query "sting wasp cure". It was later that day that I realised that the web had become an extension of myself. Today, of course a student seeking answers from a park bench can quite easily look it up on their iPhone.

There are no shortcuts to true knowledge and insight can only come from understanding principles and facts surrounding a subject area. This book does not dwell on the history of the Internet. Suffice to say that it was a combination as usual of military demands and industry/university collaboration. I doubt however that many of those involved back then could have foreseen the impact that early bandwidth limted network would have on society in the future. Interestingly however, the building blocks have not changed much since the initial days. Protocols are crucial to providing functionality and their standardisation enables widespread adoption.

Mobile communications is a continually growing sector in industry and a wide variety of visual services such as video-on-demand have been created which are limited by low-bandwidth network infrastructures. The distinction between mobile phones and personal device assistants (PDA's) has already become blurred with pervasive computing being the term coined to describe the tendency to integrate computing and communication into everyday life. The new g-phone with the Android operating system from Google labs and the iphone from Apple are the start of the newer generation of smart phones. We often forget that quite a sizeable portion of the earths population are still not on the internet and that many of these are likely to be accessing the web from a mobile device rather than the usual desktop model. It is little wonder then that many of the large corporations such as Microsoft, Google and Apple are concentrating so much on this space.

This book is divided into sections which allow a reader to dip straight into. Perhaps some readers will be mostly interested in aspects of network security, therefore section 5 will be of most appeal. Others may find the aspect of mobility and the web to be of most interest therefore they are referred to section 4.

Section I – *The Network Underneath* provides an overview of protocols and how they provide the necessary functionality to move packets of information from source to destination. It discusses the problems of delay and what happens when packets become corrupt. This section introduces wireless networks and the model of mesh networks. It also provides an insight into cognitive radio and streaming multimedia over the web. Internet traffic is essentially the load on the network, or the amount of packets of data traversing the network. When the Internet was first developed, it was never visualised as being a public service, so the increase in network traffic was no real cause for concern. Indeed, the growth rate of Internet Traffic has posed sever problems for measuring this traffic, which is essential to the understanding of Internet Congestion. A common complaint about traffic measurement studies is that they do not sustain relevance in this environment where traffic, technology, and topology change faster than we can measure them. So then, future proposals on Internet congestion can only estimate the actual load on the network at any particular time. Internet traffic in general is

---

[1] Metcalf, B. (1995). Predicting the Internet's Catastrophic Collapse and Ghost Sites Galore in 1996, *InfoWorld*, Dec 4, 1995

said to be "Bursty", that is, that bursts of traffic rather than a steady flow are transmitted. The most serious effects of congestion are seen in the form of congestion collapse. This section discusses such issues in depth.

Section 2 Internet Building Blocks – Protocols and Standards provides an overview of Computational GRIDS, Web Operating Systems, Really Simple Syndication (RSS), Javascript, XML, E4X and AJAX, the Semantic Web, VoiceXML and Web Services. Computational GRIDs offer a degree of resource sharing that could surpass even the Web as they will not only change the way in which data is accessed but also how this data is produced, consumed and stored. The online community steadily grows each year and with this escalation, the number of services provided increases in an attempt to meet the demands of a computer literate audience. There is a progression from a human-oriented use of the web to an application driven concept referred to as web services. We discuss the factors leading to this development and the inspiration behind web services and we also detail the languages, platforms and systems involved in these services.

Section 3 - *Internet Trends, Applications and Services* introduces Web 2.0, Electronic Survelllence, Mobile Social Software, Long Tail, Cyberterrorism, Podcasts and Blogs and Web Accessibility for users with disabilities. Web 2.0 is a social phenomenon referring to an approach to creating and distributing Web content itself, characterized by open communication, decentralization of authority, freedom to share and re-use and "the market as a conversation. Web 2.0 is about making sure that users add value to a site as a side effect of what they are actually using the site for. In effect, web 2.0 is making use of the long tail such as Amazon when it collects user reviews of their products. Most of us are used to software being developed, packaged, picked up in the store and kept updated through downloaded and installed patches. In the web 2.0 world, applications are run online, with no installation, updates are constant and continuous and access is instant from any computer with a browser. This section provides a clearer definition of web 2.0 and the technologies and web sites which utilise web 2.0 principle along with related areas such as web accessibility and electronic survelllence.

Section 4 – *The Mobile Internet* introduces WiMAX, Hybrid Web Applications, Browsing the Web through a Phone, In Vehicle Computing, Body Area Networks, Mobile IP and Cellullar IP and Mobile Adaptive Applications. The Mobile Web refers to the World Wide Web accessible to mobile devices such as cell phones, PDAs, and other mobile devices connected to a public network. Accessing the Mobile Web does not require a desktop computer and since it can be accessed with a number of mobile devices, the Internet can be accessed in remote places previously unconnected to the Internet. Currently, the mobile visitors browsing the web with wireless mobile devices like PDA and Smartphones become the fastest growing community of web users. We also outline here the quest to provide mobile devices with the abiltity to detect and respond appropriately to changes in network connectivity, network connection quality and power consumption in addition to other topics.

Section 5 – *Internet Security* provides an introduction to Cryptography , Universal Authentication , Honeynets, Wireless (WiFi) Security, SPAM, Hacking and Internet Fraud. Wired networks have always presented their own security issues, but wireless networks introduce a whole new set of rules with their own unique security vulnerabilities. Most wired security measures are just not appropriate for application within a WLAN environment; this is mostly due to the complete change in transmission medium. However, some of the security implementations developed specifically for WLANs are also not terribly strong. Email has become very useful and practically universal. However, the usefulness of email and its potential for future growth are jeopardized by the rising tide of unwanted email, both SPAM and viruses. This threatens to wipe out the advantages and benefits of email. An important flaw in current email standards (most notably SMTP) is the lack of any technical requirement that ensures the reliable identification of the sender of messages. A message's domain of origin can easily be faked, or 'spoofed'. This section investigates the problem of email spam and provides an overview of methods to efficiently minimize the volumes along with other such issues of security.

Finally, section 6 – *The Hidden Web* introduces the Invisible Web, Digital Watermarking & Steganography, Vertical Search Engines, Location Positioning, Web Intelligence and Ambient Intelligence. A web crawler or spider crawls through the web looking for pages to index and when it locates a new page it passes the page on to an indexer. The indexer identifies links, keywords, and other content and stores these within its database. This database is searched by entering keywords through a interface and suitable web pages are returned in a results page in the form of hyperlinks accompanied by short descriptions. The Web, however, is increasingly moving away from being a collection of documents to a multidimensional repository for sounds, images, audio, and other formats. This is leading to a situation where certain parts of the web are invisible or hidden. The term known as the "Deep Web" has emerged to refer to the mass of information that can be accessed via the Web but cannot be indexed by conventional search engines. The concept of the Deep Web makes searches quite complex for search engines. This section provides an overview of the 'invisble web' along with related topics such as steganography.

2   Internet Protocols

Kevin Curran

This chapter introduces the problems of streaming media to mobile resource constrained multimedia devices due to a variety of factors including monolithic protocol stacks, bloated middleware and fluctuating conditions in the underlying network infrastructure. The problem to be addressed is introduced along with existing approaches to the problem and the proposed solution put forward by this body of work.

Introduction

In the early days of computing every time a new communications application was developed, a set of communications routines for handing the communications hardware had to be developed. The result was that even when these routines did work, they did not work very well when they did actually work. There were simply too many types of communications hardware for every application to be able to work on every machine. There were also too many opportunities for errors to creep into the code handing the communications hardware. The solution was to develop a set of routines built into the system for each piece of communications hardware attached to the computer. The applications could then access these routines via a set of standardised calls. Doing this meant that applications could be moved from one computer to the next without substantial change. Furthermore, since the routines only needed to be written once for each piece of communications hardware, any software errors could be detected and fixed more quickly (Tannenbaum, 2004). Once the concept of assigning different levels of controls to different sets of standardised routines caught on, network designers developed *reference models*. Reference models are standard ways of breaking the task of communications into different *layers*. Each layer performs tasks for the layer above it and calls upon the layer below it to perform certain tasks for it in turn. The International Standards Organisation have developed a network model that contains 7 layers. Internet Protocol (IP) is a connectionless protocol that gateways use to identify networks and paths to networks and hosts. In other words, IP handles the routing of data between networks and nodes on those networks. TCP is an end-to-end protocol that is used for push and pull communication via a point-to-point link. TCP is the primary transport protocol in the Internet (as well as Intranets and Extranets) suite of protocols providing reliable, connection-oriented, full-duplex streams and uses IP for delivery. RTP is a real-time transport protocol providing supporting applications transmitting real-time data over unicast and multicast networks (Camarillo, 2005). We discuss here these major building blocks of the Internet.

Background

When a user launches a browser and requests an action to be performed the browser interprets the request. It sends information to the appropriate site server where the requested information is stored and this site server sends the information back. The Internet is actually a packet switching network which sends requests via packets of data (datagram's). Each packet contains the IP address of sender and receiver, and the information being requested. On any one request there can be more than one packet. This is because each packet is of a fixed size and some requests may need more than this. This means the request must be broken up into the appropriate number of packets. The route taken to obtain the requested information depends on the sender's geographic location and that of the receivers. If there are a lot of packets along a certain route they will all be queued or find a different route until they reach their destination. The destination cannot send any information until all the associated packets have been received. When all the packets have been received the destination sends the requested information back in packets via routers to the sender. Again the same problem arises in relation to routes and bandwidth (Saiedian & Naeem, 2001). The Transmission Control Protocol (TCP) is a communication protocol which enables two hosts to establish a connection and exchange streams of data. It sends information to a client/server and must receive a response or it will send the information again. The client TCP breaks down the information into smaller packets and numbers it. The server TCP then reconstructs it so the original data can be viewed. When a user types in a URL into the address box and presses "go" a DNS lookup is performed. When the DNS lookup is complete the client connects to the server via a TCP connection. The request is broken down into equal sized packets. Each packet, containing the IP address of the destination server, is then passed through the internet via routers. Each router resolves the next router in line using a routing algorithm. This process is repeated by every router until the destination server is reached with the request. The server then responds to the requesting client in the same way until the request has been fulfilled (Xilinx, 2005). Between the server and the client is the most likely place for a congestion to occur. This is why it is so important that the size of the information the user has requested should be as small as possible.

The *ISO* (International Standards Organisation) have developed a network model which represents a different level of abstraction with each layer performing a well-defined function with minimum information flowing across layer boundaries (as described above). Another principle was that there should be a manageable number of layers (Ji, 2003). Figure 1 shows the structure of the 7-Layer OSI (Open Systems Interconnection) Reference Model. The Network Access Layer has between broken up into three separate layers comprising the Network Layer, the Data Link Layer and the Physical Layer. Two additional layers have been placed between the Application Layer and the Transport Layer: the Presentation Layer and the Session Layer. The Application Layer provides interfaces for using high-level network protocols such as the File Transfer Protocol (FTP) and the Hypertext Transfer Protocol (HTTP).

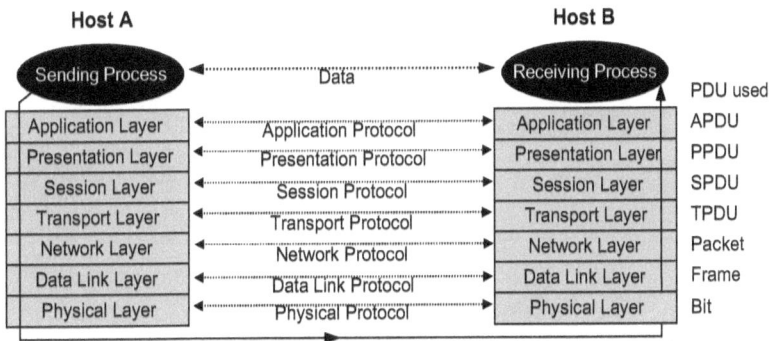

Figure 1: The 7-layer OSI Reference Model

Each layer is regarded as talking to its layer in the destination host (indicated by the dotted lines). The PDUs used by the Network Layer are more specifically referred to as *packets* in the OSI Reference Model where a packet contains a fragment of the data being transmitted rather than all the data. Sending packets rather than all the data at once allows the network to be shared more evenly between hosts. The 7-layer OSI Reference Model passes the data from one layer down to the next where each layer typically adds its own header information to the data before passing it down (Kyas, 2002). The layers below regard the combined header and data as a single block of data adding their own header to the beginning.

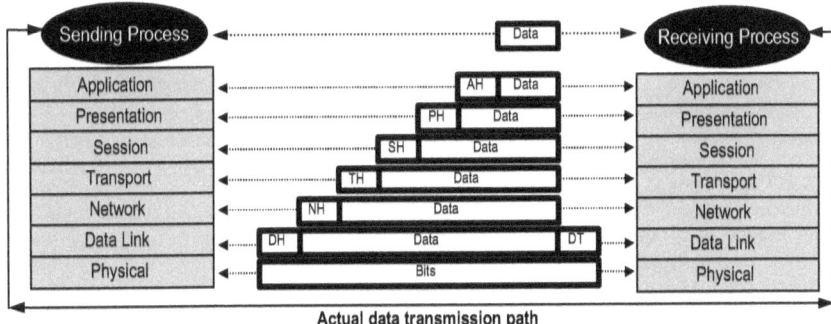

Figure 2: Each layer parcels the data received from the layer above into a PDU

In Figure 2 the header added by the Application Layer is indicated by AH (Application Header), the header added by the Presentation Layer is indicated by PH (Presentation Header), and so on. The Data Link Layer adds both a header (DH) and a *tail* (DT), which contains a checksum. The Physical Layer then transmits this as a sequence of bits. When the data arrives at the receiving host, the equivalent layer in the receiver strips of the header information. The remaining data is then passed up to the layer above and this is repeated until the receiving process is given the data originally sent by the sending process (Stallings, 2005).

Internet Protocols

Internet Protocol (IP) (Tannenbaum, 2004) is a connectionless protocol that gateways use to identify networks and paths to networks and hosts. In other words, IP handles the routing of data between networks and nodes on those networks. In addition to defining an address scheme; IP also handles the transmission of data from an originating computer to the computer specified by the IP address. It does so by breaking up larger chunks of data into easily manageable IP packets that it can deliver across the network in a connectionless fashion. In an effort to better manage network traffic, IP specifies the protocol for breaking single messages into a slew of portions. Each portion is responsible for finding its way across the network based on changing traffic congestion and the IP protocol. Each time a message arrives at an IP router, the router decides where to send it next. There is no concept of a session with a pre-selected path for all traffic. Routers can send data along the path of least resistance regardless of local network traffic congestion. Packets are sent across the Internet from subnet to subnet via gateways or routers as illustrated in Figure 3.

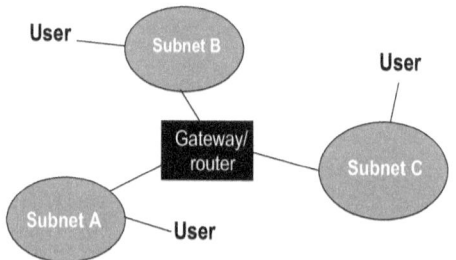

Figure 3: Gateways and subnets combine to form the Internet.

The Internet gateway is designed to be transparent to the end-user application in the host computers and the subnet it is attached to. The gateway routes the IP packets to the appropriate subnet. Routing takes place in the Internet layer of the gateway that enables TCP/IP to work on different types of LAN using different media and different protocols. The Transmission Control Protocol (TCP) usually resides in the Transport Layer and provides a reliable end-to-end communication service that uses acknowledgements to ensure that packets have been delivered. A different protocol called UDP can be used instead of TCP. The User Datagram Protocol (UDP) sends IP packets but does not use acknowledgements (and is therefore unreliable). This type of service is more suitable for status information, video conferencing and voice communication applications where the loss of the occasional packet can be safely ignored (Hofmann, 2005). Each application process must identify itself by a *port number*. The port number is equivalent to the service access point (SAP) found in the OSI model. Typically, ports 1-1023 are reserved for system use. Applications may use any of the other ports as long as no other application is currently using them. Multiple programs may communicate with a single application via a port but a port can be used only once on any host. In addition to ports, TCP/IP-base protocols use an identifier called a *socket*. A socket allows an application to communicate with a particular machine via a port using low-level read/write commands (in the same way as it would communicate with files) (Matthur, 2003). TCP/IP (Transmission Control Protocol/Internet Protocol) is a two-layered protocol. The *higher layer*, Transmission Control Protocol, manages the assembling of a message or file into smaller packets that are transmitted over the Internet and received by a TCP layer that reassembles the packets into the original message. The *lower layer* (network layer), Internet Protocol, handles the address part of each packet so that it gets to the right destination. TCP is an end-to-end protocol that is used for push and pull communication via a point-to-point TCP link (Halsall, 2005). TCP is the primary transport protocol in the Internet (as well as Intranets and Extranets) suite of protocols providing reliable, connection-oriented, full-duplex streams and uses IP for delivery. TCP's reference model differs from the OSI 7-layer model as can be seen in Figure 4.

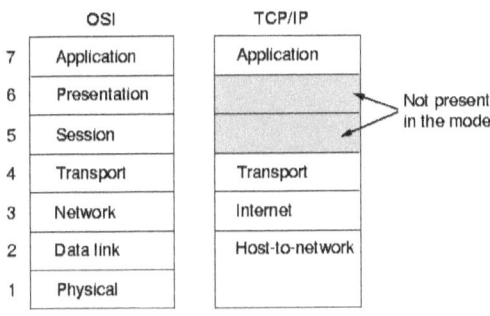

Figure 4: The differences between the OSI and TCP/IP reference models.

The TCP/IP model traditionally has 4 layers (the Data Link Layer and the Physical Layer are combined into a single layer called the Host-to-Network Layer but it is also common to show these layers separately). There is no session layer or presentation layer in the TCP/IP model (if necessary, their tasks are made the responsibility of the application layer). The TCP/IP layers that exist are essentially the same as those in the OSI reference model. The *host-to-network* layer is responsible for sending bits across the network and for link error control and link flow control (i.e. data link layer and physical layer combined). The *Internet* layer switches packets around the network and places packets on (or removes them from) the network using a packet format called IP (Internet Protocol). The *transport* layer accepts data (and instructions) from the application layer and breaks the data up into packets. It also reassembles received packets into data streams and passes that data to the appropriate port number (e.g. port number 1066) and is also responsible for end-to-end flow control. Finally, the *application* layer contains all the higher-level protocols such as TELNET, FTP and SMTP that are used by applications.

TCP supports functionality such as adaptive retransmissions, deferred transmissions and delayed acknowledgements that can cause excessive overhead and latency for real-time applications (Schmidt, 2002). Likewise routing protocols like IPv4 lack functionality (such as packet admission policies and rate control) that can lead to excessive congestion and missed deadlines in networks and end systems (Rosenberg, 2002). A limitation for running multimedia applications over TCP/IP is the problem of delay. IP does not allocate a specific path or amount of bandwidth to a particular session. The resulting delay can vary widely and unpredictably, posing serious problems for real-time applications. For most organisations today, committing to IP is a given. The question is how far that commitment can be taken in an application sense. So far, the thrust of vendors in dealing with real-time IP has been to provide quality of service (QoS) control has been to implement forms of mapping IP flows to ATM virtual circuits to provide service guarantees or using an IP-based reservation protocol such as Resource ReSerVation Protocol (RSVP). Unfortunately, these solutions ignore the fact that TCP is not well suited for real-time applications (Hofmann, 2005).

RTP is a real-time transport protocol providing supporting applications transmitting real-time data over unicast and multicast networks (Perkins, 2003). RTP is used in MBone audio/video tools in addition to numerous commercial implementations (Roussopoulos, 2003). RTP services include payload type identification, sequence numbering, and time stamping. Delivery is monitored by the closely integrated control protocol RTCP. While RTP provides end-to-end delivery services, it does not provide all of the functionality typically provided by transport protocols therefore RTP generally resides on top of UDP to utilise its multiplexing services. End-to-end support includes multi-party functions, such as synchronisation of multiple streams, and reconstruction of streams based on timestamps. Sequence numbers allow the identification of packet positions in a stream that may arrive out of order (e.g. to aid in video decoding). RTP bridges can act as synchronisation points along a path to transcode data into a more suitable format for the destinations that they serve (Balasubramanian, 2003).

Each RTP data packet consists of an RTP packet header and payload. The packet header includes a sequence number, a media-specific timestamp, and a synchronisation source (SSRC) identifier while the RTP control protocol (RTCP) provides mechanisms for data distribution monitoring, cross-media synchronisation, and sender identification. The control information transmission interval (sent to all participants) is randomised and adjusted according to the session size to maintain the RTCP bandwidth below some configurable limit. RTCP's primary function is to provide session feedback on data distribution quality, which is useful for diagnosing failures and monitoring performance, and can be adopted by applications for dynamic adaptation to congestion. Monitoring statistics such as Sender Reports (SR) include the sender's cumulative packet count and cumulative byte count while the Receiver Reports (RR) statistics include cumulative count of lost packets, jitter, short-term loss indicator, and round-trip time estimation time-stamps. RTP's design is based on the IP multicast group delivery protocol where data sources broadcast to a group's multicast address without knowledge of the actual group membership. Real time applications such as adaptive audio or video conferencing tools are often based on RTP so that they can work in loaded networks so long as a minimal amount of bandwidth is available. Real time applications make use of RTP's support of intra and inter-stream synchronisation and encoding detection with RTP being frequently integrated into the application software rather than being implemented as a separate layer. In accordance with the ALF principle, the semantics of several RTP header fields are application dependent and several profile documents specify the use of RTP header fields for different applications (e.g. the marker bit of the RTP header defines the start of a talk spurt in an audio packet and the end of a video frame in a video packet) (Tsarouchis, 2003). That is, RTP "will often be integrated into the application processing rather than being implemented as a separate layer" oblivious to whether IPv4, IPv6, Ethernet, ATM, or another communication mechanism is being used. It normally runs on top of UDP, using its framing services such as multiplexing and checksum.

Application Level Framing (ALF) is a protocol which explicitly includes an application's semantics in the design of that applications protocol (Yan, 2004). ALF promotes the breaking down of data into aggregates, which are meaningful to the application and independent of specific network technology. These data aggregates are known as Application Data Units (ADUs). The lower network layer should preserve the frame boundaries of ADUs so that applications are able to process each ADU separately and potentially out of order with respect to other ADUs. This ensures that ADU losses do not prevent the processing of other ADUs. In order to express data loss in terms meaningful to the application RTP data units carry sequence numbers and timestamps, so receivers can determine the time and sequence relations between ADUs. As each ADU is a meaningful data entity to the receiving application, the application itself can decide about how to cope with a lost data unit (e.g. real-time digital video might choose to ignore lost frames, whereas FTP applications may request the resending of lost packets) (Wu, 2002).

The RTP specification is designed to follow the principles of ALF and Integrated Layer Processing (ILP), that advocates a tight integration of the network and codec processing into the application. Thus, an application can take advantage of the feedback information provided by RTP and adapt as needed to the condition and behaviour of the network. A corollary of this principle is that each application needs to have intimate knowledge of both network and codec behaviours. Existing RTP based audio/video applications such as vic (An MBone video conferencing tool) (Perkins, 2003) use the principles of ALF and ILP to such an extent that RTP support is not easily extractable. There are no libraries so that RTP software cannot be reused for integration with existing applications, neither can new applications be designed to cleanly utilise the existing functionality thus the addition of new codecs and payload handlers is non trivial. ALF was later extended with a lightweight rendezvous mechanism based on IP multicast, aimed at receiver-based adaptation for real-time applications (e.g. audio and video conferencing). This is known as Light-Weight Sessions (LWS), and has been very successful in the design of wide-area, large-scale, conferencing applications.

Caching and its architectures

Caching is a technique used to store popular documents closer to the user. It uses algorithms to predict user's needs for specific documents and stores documents it deems important. Caching can occur anywhere within a network, on the user's computer, at an ISP or at a server. Many companies also use web proxy caches to display frequently accessed pages to their employees. This can reduce the bandwidth the company requires which in turn can lower costs (Fan et al., 1999). Another example of caching can be seen on Google, one of the worlds most popular search engines, which uses caching to provide their users with the documents they need much faster than without caching (sometimes in under half a second). Web-cache performance is directly proportional to the size of the client community (Franklin, 2006). The larger the client community the greater the possibility of cached data being requested and therefore the better the cache's performance. The main drawback with caching is that in most cases cached documents may never be viewed again. Caching a document can also cause other problems. Most documents on the internet change over time as they are updated. Static and Dynamic Caching are two different technologies which use caching to combat this problem in order to reduce download time and congestion. *Static Caching* stores the content of a webpage which does not change. There is no need to repeatedly request the same information over and over again as this just wastes time. This is an excellent approach to combat congestion. *Dynamic Caching* is slightly different. It determines whether the content of a page has changed by checking for updates. If the contents have changed, it will then store the updated version (Saiedian & Naeem, 2001). This unfortunately can lead to congestion and so is possibly not a very good approach as it does require checks to be performed on the source of the data to establish whether or not an update is necessary. If used properly these two technologies can work together to reduce latency and congestion. Prefetching is an intelligent technique used to reduce perceived congestion. It tries to predict the next page or document a user might want to access (Fan et al., 1999). For example, if a user is on a page with many links the Prefetching algorithm will predict that the user may want to view associated links within that page. The Prefetcher will then request the pages it predicts the user will try to access next and stores them until the user does actually request them. It will then display the page significantly faster than if the user requested the page without Prefetching. The only real drawback is that if the user does not request the pages the Prefetcher algorithm retrieves, congestion may have been caused needlessly.

Future Trends

As networks become more advanced, they tend to become more complex and increasingly difficult to maintain. To complicate matters further, there has been and for the foreseeable future, will be a scarcity of IT professionals to install, configure, optimize and maintain these complex systems. The aim of autonomic computing is to reduce the amount of maintenance needed to keep systems working as efficiently as possible, as much of the time as possible. i.e. it is about making systems self-managing (Murch, 2004). Another trend is introspection, which provides run-time system information allowing applications to examine their environment and act accordingly. Autonomic computing systems can provide an infrastructure for building adaptive applications that can deal with drastic environment changes. The introduction of mobility will also increase the complexity due to the proliferation in possible actions. A key goal for next generation networks is to provide a principled means of allowing the underlying infrastructure to be adapted throughout its lifetime with the minimum of effort thus the principles of autonomic computing provides a means of coping with change in a computing system as it allows access to the implementation in a principled manner

Car makers are adopting generalized protocols, such as CAN, which are experiencing high implementation rates in the small cars market. However, to support the several new and advanced control, telematics, and infotainment applications that are fast emerging in the automotive market, there is a rising demand for application-specific networks including FlexRay, MOST, and LIN that are developed for supporting a select set of applications. In the next generation of cars, multiple network technologies and protocols are expected to co-exist, supporting several advanced and futuristic features and applications (Frost & Sullivan, 2005).

Conclusion

The International Standards Organisation has developed a network model that contains 7 layers. Internet Protocol (IP) is a connectionless protocol that gateways use to identify networks and paths to networks and hosts. In other words, IP handles the routing of data between networks and nodes on those networks. TCP is an end-to-end protocol that is used for push and pull communication via a point-to-point TCP link. TCP is the primary transport protocol in the Internet (as well as Intranets and Extranets) suite of protocols providing reliable, connection-oriented, full-duplex streams and uses IP for delivery. RTP is a real-time transport protocol providing supporting applications transmitting real-time data over unicast and multicast networks. We discuss here these major building blocks of the Internet.

References

Balasubramanian, V., Venkatasubramanian, N. (2003). Server transcoding of multimedia information for cross disability access. ACM/SPIE Conference on Multimedia Computing and Networking, ACM/SPIE, 2003.

Camarillo, G., Garcia-Martin, M. (2005). The 3G IP Multimedia Subsystem (IMS): Merging the Internet and the Cellular Worlds, Second Edition John Wiley and Sons Ltd, December, 2005

Fan, L., Jacobson, Q., Cao, P. and Lin, W. (1999) Web prefetching between low-bandwidth clients and Proxies: Potential and Performance, ACM Press, 1999

Franklin, C. (2006) How Routers Work, HowStuffWorks.com, http://www.howstuffworks.com/router.htm

Frost & Sullivan (2005). Strategic Analysis of North American In-Vehicle Network Technologies and Protocols, The Info Shop, December 2005

Halsall, F. (2005). Computer Networking and the Internet, 5th Edition, Addison Wesley; 5th Edition, March 2005

Hofmann, M. Beaumont, L. (2005). Content Networking: Architecture, Protocols, and Practice, ISBN 1-55860-834-6, 2005

Ji, P., Ge, Z., Kurose, J., Towsley, D. (2003). Applications, Technologies, Architectures and Protocols for Computer Communication archive. Proceedings of the 2003 conference on Applications, technologies, architectures, and protocols for computer communications table of contents, Karlsruhe, Germany, pp.251-262, ISBN: 1-58113-735-4, 2003

Kyas, O., Crawford, G. (2002) ATM networks. Prentice Hall Publishers, ISBN: 013093601, 2002

Matthur, A. and Mundur, P. (2003). Congestion Adaptive Streaming: An Integrated Approach. DMS'2003 - The 9th International Conference on Distributed Multimedia Systems, Florida International University Miami, Florida, USA, September 24-26, 2003

Murch, R. (2004). Autonomic Computing. IBM Press, Prentice Hall PTR, ISBN: 013144025X

Perkins, C. (2003) RTP – Audio and Video for the Internet. ISBN – 0672-32249-8, Pearson Education, June 2003

Rosenberg, J., Schulzrinne, H., Camarillo, G., Johnston, A., Peterson, J., Sparks, R., Handley M., and Schooler, E. (2002) SIP: Session Initiation protocol, RFC 3261, Internet Engineering Task Force, June 2002

Roussopoulos, M., Baker, M. (2003) CUP: Controlled Update Propagation in Peer-to-Peer Networks. Proceedings of the 2003 USENIX Annual Technical Conference, San Antonio, Texas, June, 2003

Saiedian, M. & Naeem, M. (2001) Understanding & Reducing Web Delays. IEEE Computer Journal, Aug 2001

Satllings, W. (2005). Data and Network Communications, 7th Edition, Prentice-Hall, 2005

Tanenbaum, A. (2004). Computer Networks, Fifth Edition, ISBN: 0-13-066102-3, Prentice Hall, May 2005

Tsarouchis, C., Denazis, S., Kitahara, C., Vivero, J., (2003) A policy-based management architecture for active and programmable networks, IEEE Network, Vol. 17, No. 3, May-June 2003, pp. 22 - 28.

Wu, W., Ren, Y., Shan, X. (2002). Providing Proportional Loss Rate for Adaptive Traffic: A New Relative DiffServ Model. citeseer.nj.nec.com/wu02providing.html

Xilinx (2005) Transmission Control Protocol/Internet Protocol (TCP/IP), http://www.xilinx.com/esp/optical/net_tech/tcp.htm

Yan, B and Mabo R. (2004). QoS Control for Video and Audio Communication in Conventional and Active Networks: Approaches and Comparison, IEEE Communications Surveys & Tutorials, 2004

3   What causes delay in the Internet?

Kevin Curran, Derek Woods, Nadene McDermot

Congestion is increasingly becoming a major problem for the Internet, making many types of file transfer both unstable and unreliable. This chapter outlines the main issues surrounding congestion on the Internet.

Introduction

Congestion in a packet-switching network is a state in which performance degrades due to the saturation of network resources such as communication links, processor cycles, and memory buffers (Yang, 1995). Congestion in the Internet is becoming an ever-increasing problem today. Even though the technology surrounding the Internet has improved significantly, it seems that file transfer times continue to increase, with no real solution in sight. So then, it is important to understand firstly how congestion occurs and how it is measured, and subsequently, what mechanisms are in place to control this congestion. It is argued that three main factors--incompatibility of the newer applications with the Internet's architecture, massification of the Internet, and privatisation and concomitant commercialisation of the Internet--are responsible for an inherent change in the Internet's dynamics (Sarkar, 1995).

Internet Traffic is essentially the load on the network, or the amount of packets of data traversing the network. When the Internet was first developed, it was never visualised as being a public service, so the increase in network traffic was no real cause for concern. However, Internet Traffic has grown at an alarming rate, "When seen over the decade of the 1990s, traffic appears to be doubling about once each year" (Odlyzko, 2000). Indeed, the growth rate of Internet Traffic has posed sever problems for measuring this traffic, which is essential to the understanding of Internet Congestion. A common complaint about traffic measurement studies is that they do not sustain relevance in this environment where traffic, technology, and topology change faster than we can measure them. So then, future proposals on Internet Congestion can only estimate the actual load on the network at any particular time. In fact, no single organization is truly measuring global Internet behaviour, because the global Internet is simply not instrumented to allow such measurement (Murray, 2001). Internet traffic in general is said to be "Bursty", that is, that bursts of traffic rather than a steady flow are transmitted.

The most serious effects of congestion are seen in the form of Congestion Collapse. This is a condition, which occurs when "a sudden load on the net can cause the round-trip time to rise faster than the sending hosts measurements of round-trip time can be updated" (Nagle, 1984). Under these conditions the network can come to a complete stand still. "Informally, congestion collapse occurs when an increase in the network load results in a decrease in the useful work done by the network" (Floyd, 2000). Due to this increase in network traffic and the pressure it puts on the available bandwidth, the fairness of the Internet is also at risk. Fairness means that no user is penalised compared to others that share the same bottleneck links". This type of fairness has long been a measurement of a congestion control mechanisms worth to the Internet, as a public service all users should be treated equally. Unfairness in the Internet happens when congestion control techniques are not implemented, such as the AIMD method of control, which will be discussed later in this chapter. Flows that do not "back-off" when faced with congestion can greedily utilise all of the available bandwidth, leaving other flows fighting for their share.

Maximum Packet Size

A modern server uses Path Maximum Transmission Unit Discovery (PMTUD) heuristics to determine the Maximum Segment Size (MSS) which is the safe packet size that can be transmitted (Mogul et al, 1990). This technique was adopted to address the poor performance and communication failures associated with oversized packets which are fragmented at routers with small MTU (Kent et al, 1987). Today, the PMTUD concept is imperfect as it uses the Internet Control Message Protocol (ICMP) which some network administrators view as a threat and block them all, disabling PMTUD, usually without realising it (Knowles, 1993). This led to increased packets overheads due to retransmissions and eventually connection time-outs. Lahey (Lahey, 2000), suggested a workaround where after several time-outs, the server network should be reconfigured to accept an altered ICMP packet with the 'Do Not Fragment' bit disabled. Consequently the PMTUD feature is bypassed, but detection can take several seconds each time, and these delays result in a significant, hidden degradation of network performance.

DNS, Caching & Web Page Delays

DNS are the nub of the Internet infrastructure. They are responsible for translating domain names into an equivalent IP address needed by the Internet's TCP. The latency between DNS request and response is a random variable as the DNS lookup system uses the client's cache file, the hierarchical nature of the domain name and a set of DNS operating at multiple sites to cooperatively solve the mapping problem. A survey from Men and Mice (Menandmice, 2003) showed that 68% of the DNS for commercial sites (e.g. .COM zones) has some configuration errors, thus making them vulnerable to security breach and denial of service. They are normally handled by novices who do not fully understand the operation of DNS very well. An intelligent DNS management system was recently developed by Liu et al. (Liu et al, 2004) which offers administrators support in DNS system configuration, problem diagnosis and tutoring,

The network delay for Web page loading is dominated by the current version of the HTTP/1.1 standard. It is an application level protocol for transfer of Web contents between clients and servers. Due to increasing Internet traffic, HTTP/1.1 makes inefficient use of the network and suffers from high latencies for three reasons: (1) it takes time to transmit the unnecessarily large number of bytes, (2) TCP's three-way handshakes for opening a connection adds extra round trip time delay and (3) multiple parallel TCP streams do not share the same congestion avoidance state. Spreitzer et al. (Spreitzer et al, 2000), have composed a prototype for HTTP 'next generation' which should address these latency issues.

The caching mechanism is available ubiquitously. It exists on the client's local disk and is also provided by DNS, network servers and Internet Service Providers. Commercial providers such as Akamai (www.akamai.com) use cache server technology to help companies get their web pages faster to potential customers. Its rationale is to assuage congestion, reduce bandwidth consumption, improve retrieval times by temporary storing Web objects closer to the clients and reduce the burden on the site server as it handles fewer requests. Caching is often deliberately defeated as not all Web contents are cacheable. A modern day Web page contains both dynamic and static contents. Dynamic items are non-cacheable and typically they contain interactive and changeable items that provide a far richer experience for users, but they are not happy to wait for them (Nielsen, 1997). Cached components characteristically contain items that do not change, i.e. they are static. An intelligent cache engine has emerged recently that serves dynamic elements of Web page and reduces the latency time by 90% (Govatos, 2001). It works by estimating future client's behaviour at a site based on pass and present access patterns. The downside with caching is that if the user does not use the cached items, then congestion may have been caused needlessly.

Recommendations that were made to improve Web page designs have positive impact to page retrieval times as well as usability. The adoption of Cascaded Style Sheets (CSS) (Lie et al, 1996) and more compact image representations, Portable Network Graphics (PNG) (Libpng, 2004), have added value of reducing the file size and speeding up page downloads without sacrificing graphics design (Nielsen et al, 1997). PNG was designed to be successor to the popular GIF files, but it was not until the late 1997 when browser wars came to an end as many old browsers finally caught up and are able to read PNG formats. Another Web image format is JPEG which uses lossy compression and exploits known limitations of the human eye. Weinberger et al. (Weinberger et al, 2000) have created a new lossless/near-lossless image compression format called JPEG-LS. This standard is for continuous tone images and is currently awaiting approval from the World Wide Web Consortium.

Network connection quality can be described in terms of availability, latency, jitter, and capacity. Availability is the assurance that traffic will reach its destination successfully, and forms the basis of most service-level agreements. Latency is the delay that traffic experiences as it travels across the network while jitter is the change in this latency over time. Establishing a particular QoS level for a connection is a complex process, in part because of the stateless, best-effort paradigm upon which the Internet is based and the fact that one must balance all of the QoS parameters above (CISCO, 2000). There are two main approaches to QoS: the integrated services model (Crawley, 1998) and the differentiated services model (Fulp, 2001) . The integrated services model negotiates a particular QoS at the time it is requested. Before exchanging traffic, the sender and receiver request a particular QoS level from the network. Upon acceptance, the intermediate network devices associate the resulting traffic flow with a specific level of jitter, latency, and capacity. Resource Reservation Protocol (RSVP), a protocol for signalling QoS requirements for a particular traffic flow, is a key component. Differentiated services takes a different approach using traffic handling classes with various levels of service quality. These are established by the network administrator so when the sender needs a particular kind of handling, it marks each individual packet. Through the migration from resource-based to service-driven networks, it has become evident that the Internet model should be enhanced to provide support for a variety of differentiated services that match applications and customer requirements, and not stay limited under the flat best-effort service that is currently provided (Bernet et al, 2000).

Flow Control

Flow Control is the method of preventing network congestion and increasing fairness by making sure that a suitable amount of flows are transmitted so that the receiving devices are not flooded with data. It is convenient to divide flows into three classes:

- TCP- compatible flows,
- Unresponsive flows, i.e., flows that do not slow down when congestion occurs, and
- Flows that are responsive but are not TCP-compatible (Floyd, 2000)

The flow control mechanism of TCP uses slow start and congestion avoidance algorithms as a mechanism to control the data transmission rate (Floyd et al, 1999). This helps to reduce packets loss caused by congested routers. However, lost packets can be recovered using TCP's retransmission feature, but this incurs added delivery time. The aggressive behaviour of multimedia applications involving audio and video, in which developers employ UDP compounds the problem of congestion. UDP are not TCP friendly and they do not respond to packet drops which typically hint congestions. This aggressive behaviour degrades and even shuts out TCP packets such as Hyper Text Transfer Protocol (HTTP) and prevents them from obtaining their fair share of their bandwidth when they battle for bandwidth over a congested link. Lee et al. (Lee et al, 2002) examined the use of TCP tunnels at core routers to isolate different types of traffic from one another. Benefits include reduced TCP's retransmission per connected by over 500% and more packets can be processed using the same amount of memory resources. This concept is not used extensively on the current Internet infrastructure. Whilst TCP and TCP compatible flows are said to be responsive in the face of congestion, it is the unresponsive flows that cause network problems. These types of flows simply add to the congestion problem, as they are very high bandwidth flows. Unresponsive flows also promote unfairness in that whilst other flows decrease the data being transmitted, unresponsive flows aggressively hunt available bandwidth. There are three main techniques adopted to control the flows within a network. These are:

- Buffering – temporarily storing data until it can be dealt with.
- Source-quench messages – if a network device is showing signs of congestion (i.e. the buffer is full and packets are being dropped), then it will send Source-quench messages to the sending devices so that they will reduce the transmission rate at which they are sending data.
- Windowing – the sending device sends a certain number of packets to the receiver, but requires an ACK before any more data can be sent. When an ACK has been received by the sender then another set of packets can be sent. If no ACK is received then this is an indicator of congestion. The receiver has not received enough packets to send an ACK, so some packets may have been dropped, due to an overflowing buffer etc. The sender, on not receiving an ACK will then re-transmit the packets. This is, in essence, the AIMD congestion methodology.

Router Congestion Control

Routers have already been discussed in this book as being one of the key pieces of architecture of the Internet, so then it is important to consider the controls that are in place to effectively manage congestion at this point in the transfer of packets across the Internet. In the work of (Lefelhocz, 1996) the authors proposed a paradigm in order to maintain a fair routing system for Internet usage. The proposed design incorporated four controls for congestion management, which are widely implemented in the Internet today. These are Scheduling Algorithms, Buffer Management, Feedback and End Adjustment.

The two most popular scheduling algorithms are FIFO (First In First Out), which forwards packets according to their place in the queue, and WFQ (Weighted Fair Queuing), which attempts to allocate the available bandwidth fairly, thus protecting flows from unfairness on the part of others. The author feels that some form of Scheduling algorithm must be implemented in order to prevent bandwidth being "swallowed up" by greedy users. However this alone will not prevent packets from being dropped, so other measures must be implemented simultaneously. Buffering is required at a switch whenever packets are arriving faster than they can be sent out. This buffering should take one of two forms. The shared buffer pool method does not protect flows from one another, but forwards packets using the First Come First Use method. On the other hand, the Per-Flow allocation method uses a fairer method of packet forwarding where each flow is forwarded on merit and "well behaved" flows are serviced first.

Feedback is another important function at the router to control congestion. There are two types of feedback; Implicit feedback "requires the end user to monitor the performance of their data transmission for clues to the current network status" (Lefelhocz, 1996). An example of this type of feedback can be seen in the TCP slow start algorithm, where packet loss is the congestion indicator. Explicit Feedback takes the form of an indicator. This can be implemented in forward (FECN – Forward Explicit Congestion Notification) and reverse modes (BECN – Backward Explicit Congestion Notification). This type of congestion notification provides better control as it can be measured by the router in order to quantify the amount of congestion that is occurring.

The router relies on this end adjustment figure to give an accurate depiction of the amount of congestion that is occurring. This then controls the push of packets into the network, and thus the possible increase of congestion and pressure on the network. Routers manage traffic flow by using one of two methods: static routing or dynamic routing. Static routing is best implemented by small networks, where the topology and state of the network is known to be relatively stable. The routes taken by packets of data are hard coded by the network engineer manually and do not change unless the engineer becomes aware of changes within the network, such as a change to the network topology. Dynamic routing, on the other hand is used where the topology of the network is unknown and the route taken by packets of data is uncertain at the time of sending. Dynamic protocols are used to calculate the best path for the packets to take, considering many parameters. These dynamic routing protocols are used to discover the best paths for Internet traffic on a daily basis.

Gateway Protocols

Once dynamic routing has been chosen as the preferred method of path selection the actual protocol that will be used to implement the metrics and perform the calculations must then be considered. There are two main classes of gateway protocols: Interior gateway protocols and Exterior gateway protocols. Interior gateway protocols are used within autonomous systems, that is a set of routers under a single technical administration (Rekhter, 1995). Exterior gateway protocols are used to communicate *between* autonomous systems therefore providing the links between different networks, in order for them to work together as a single unit.

BGP v4 is the main routing protocol used in the Internet today. It is a Border gateway protocol that was designed for networks that implement TCP/IP. BGP is an exterior gateway protocol (EGP), which means that it performs routing between multiple autonomous systems or domains and exchanges routing and reachability information with other BGP systems. The protocol exchanges this information by using BGP speakers to communicate to the routers that directly neighbour it. These update messages can contain information such as withdrawn routes and Network reachability information. The protocol uses a number of variables to determine the best path for a packet. The following table outlines these variables and their metrics.

Next Hop	If it sees the next hop as being unreachable (down) that route is not considered
BGP Weighting	This is organised such that the larger the BGP weighting (cost) the greater the trustworthiness.
Same Weight	Highest local preference is used
Same Local Preference	Prefer route where originating traffic came from
No Originating route	Prefer route with least AS hop count

Same AS hop count	Prefer external route
All routes are external	Prefer lowest origin count
Same codes & AS	Prefer lowest MULTI_EXIT_DISC metric route. No metric=0
IGP Sync. Disabled	Prefer route through closest neighbour
Internal Paths Only	
All else fails	Prefer BGP route with router ID of lowest router IP address

Table 1 : BGP v4 metrics

As illustrated in Table 1, the BGP v4 protocol does not usually take the load on the network into account when choosing the best path. The load would constantly be changing as users went online and offline and there would be a lot of routing table updates to the extent that there would be just as much traffic being generated just to maintain the routing table.

The recent growth of the Internet has adversely affected the stability of routing in times of congestion. It has been proven that when a network is congested and packets are dropped, some of these packets could be the updated routing information of the network. Congestion in the network can hinder the propagation of routing information or peering refresh requests if the routing protocol messages are not isolated from data traffic (Shaikh, 2000). So then, it would seem that the very messages that are providing routers with information to stem the build up of congestion are at risk themselves (with both OPSF and BGP protocols displaying signs of unreliability under congested conditions). This can have great implications for routing and therefore Internet stability.

Proposals for alleviating congestion

Various suggestions have recently been made in order to improve upon the current TCP congestion control methods. These include the Limited Transmit method, which it is hoped will reduce unnecessary retransmit timeouts, and a SACK-based mechanism for detecting and responding to unnecessary Fast Re-transmits or Retransmit Timeouts (Bonald, 2000). In addition to this, another method for the improvement of the TCP congestion control technique is offered in the form of "General AIMD Congestion Control", (Yang, 2000). Yang proposes a window adjustment strategy where the window increase and decrease values are used as parameters, depending on the ACK's received or the packets lost. (Mo, 1998), propose the widespread use of an updated version of TCP Vegas, which they claim is fairer with regards to packet loss than its counterparts TCP Reno and Tahoe are, as it uses a complicated bandwidth estimation scheme.

(Mahajan, 2000) proposed a variation on the Random Early Detection method of congestion control in the form of RED-PD (RED with Preferential Dropping). They suggest several weaknesses that underlie the FIFO method of scheduling at routers, and aim to use the packet drop history at the router to preferentially drop the packets of high-bandwidth flows. The authors suggest that this will maximise fairness at the router. (Kumar, 1998) proposed the introduction of Gigabit routers onto the Internet Backbone provided by Internet Service Providers therefore as well as the increased packet forwarding speed, these routers will be able to provide enhanced service differentiation. It is technologically viable to incorporate mechanisms that can provide differentiated services even at very high speeds. These Gigabit routers have been be implemented by many ISP's on the Internet backbone. Some of The most controversial proposed methods for the alleviation of Internet Congestion involve the idea of using pricing methods. As with any other public service many believe that pricing the Internet would make end-users think twice about the amount of information that they download, which in turn would then help to decrease the amount of congestion that is occurring (Odlyzko, 1998).

References

Allman, M. (2008), "TCP Congestion Control", Request for Comments: 2581, Network Working Group, April 2008

Bonald, T. and Massoulie, l. (2000) "Impact of Fairness on Internet performance"

Bradley, C., "An Analytical Study of Internet Congestion", Msc Thesis, Computer Science Department, UCL, 2000

Floyd, S. (2000) "Congestion Control Principles", Request for Comments: 2914, Network Working Group, 2000

Floyd, S., (2001) "A Report on Some Recent Developments in TCP Congestion Control", IEEE Communications Magazine, April 2001

Key, P. (1999) "Congestion Pricing for Congestion Avoidance", Caltech Technical Report, February 1999

Kumar, V.P. (1998) "Beyond Best Effort: Router Architectures for the Differentiated Services of Tomorrow's Internet", 1998

Lefelhocz, C. (1996) "Congestion Control for Best-Effort Service: Why We Need a New Paradigm" IEEE Network, Volume 10, Number 1, January/February 1996

Mahajan, R. (2000), "Controlling High-Bandwidth Flows at the Congested Router", ACIRI, November 2000

Maurer, S.M. and Huberman, B.A., (2001) "Restart Strategies and Internet Congestion", Journal of Economic Dynamics and Control, 2001

Mo, J. (1998) "Analysis and Comparison of TCP Reno and Vegas", IEEE Networks, July 1998

Nagle, J. (1984) "Congestion Control in IP/TCP Internetworks", Request for Comments: 896, Network Working Group, January 1984

Odlyzko, A. (1998) "Paris Metro Pricing for the Internet", AT&T Labs – Research Internal Report AT823-23, 1998

Odlyzko, A. (2000) "Internet Growth: Myth and Reality, Use and Abuse", Information Impacts Magazine, available online from www.cisp.org, November 2000

Rekhter, Y. (1995) "A Border Gateway Protocol 4 (BGP-4)", Request for Comments: 1771, Network Working Group, March 1995

Sarkar, M. (1996) "An Assessment of Pricing Mechanisms for the Internet--A Regulatory Imperative", Presented at MIT Workshop on Internet Economics March 1995, The Journal of Electronic Publishing, May, 1996 Volume 2, Issue 1

Shaikh, A. (2000) "Routing Stability in Congested Networks: Experimentation and Analysis", SIGCOMM 2000: 163-17

Yang, C. and Reddy, V.S. (1995) A Taxonomy for Congestion Control Algorithms in Packet Switching Networks", IEEE Network Magazine, Volume 9, Number 5, July/August 1995

Bernet, Y., Ford, P., Yavatkar, R., Baker, F., Zhang, L., Speer, M., Braden, R., Davie, B., Wroklawski, J., Felstaine, E. (2000), *A Framework for Integrated Services Operation over DiffServ Networks*, IETF, ISSLL Working Group, RFC2998

Comer, D.E. (2000). *Internetworking with TCP/IP, Vol 1: Principles, Protocols and Architecture*. Upper Saddle River NJ: Prentice Hall

Crawley, E., Berger, L., Berson, S., Baker, F., Borden and M., Krawczyk, J. (1998) A Framework for Integrated Services and RSVP over ATM, RFC 2382, August 1998

Floyd, S. and Fall, K. (1999). Promoting the Use of End-to-End Congestion Control in the Internet. *IEEE/ACM Transactions on Networking*, Vol.7, No.4, 458-472

Errin W. Fulp and Douglas S. Reeves. (2001). Optimal Provisioning and Pricing of Differentiated Services Using QoS Class Promotion, Jahrestagung (1), pp. 144-150, 2001

Govatos, G. (2001). Accelerating dynamic Web site performance and scalability. *Chutney Technologies, Inc.,* Available at: www.caching.com/pdf/Preloader_final.pdf

Kent, C.A. and Mogul, J.C. (1987). Fragmentation considered harmful. *Digital Western Research Laboratory.* Research report 87/3, December. Taken from: http://research.compaq.com/wrl/techreports/abstracts/87.3.html

Knowles, S. (1993). IESG Advice from Experience with Path MTU Discovery. *RFC1435.* March. Available at: http://www.faqs.org/ftp/rfc/pdf/rfc1435.txt.pdf (March, 1993)

Lahey, K. (2000) TCP Problems with Path MTU Discovery. *RFC2923.* Available at: http://www.faqs.org/ftp/rfc/pdf/rfc2923.txt.pdf

Lee, B., Balan, R., Jacob, L., Seah, W. and Ananda, A. (2002). Avoiding congestion collapse on the Internet using TCP tunnels. *Computer Networks,* Vol.39, No.2, 207-219

Libpng (2004) http://www.libpng.org/pub/png/ (May, 2004)

Lie, H. and Bos, B. (1996). Cascading Style Sheets, level 1. *W3C Recommendation, World Wide Web Consortium,* 17th Dec 1996, revised 11th Jan 1999. Available at: http://www.w3.org/TR/REC-CSS1 (January, 2004)

Liu, C.L., Tseng, S.S. and Chen, C.S. (2004). Design and Implementation of an intelligent DNS management system. *Expert Systems with Applications,* 27:2, 223-236

Menandmice (2003) http://www.menandmice.com/6000/61_recent_survey.html (February, 2003)

Mogul, J. and Deering, S. (1990). Path MTU discovery. *RFC1191.* Available at: http://www.faqs.org/rfcs/rfc1191.html (November, 1991)

Nielsen, H.F., Gettys, J., Baird-Smith, A., Prud'hommeaux, H., Lie, H. and Lilley, C. (1997). Network performance effects of HTTP/1.1, CSS1, and PNG. *Computer Communication Review,* 27: 4.

Saiedian M.Z.H. and Naeem, M. (2001). Understanding and Reducing Web Delays. *IEEE Computer Society Press.* 34(12): 30-37

Selvidge, P.R., Chaparro, B.S. and Bender, G.T. (2002). The world wide wait: effects of delays on user performance. *International Journal of Industrial Ergonomics.* 29:15-20

Spreitzer, M. and Janssen, B. (2000). HTTP 'Next Generation'. *Computer Networks,* 33:593–607

Weinberger, M., Seroussi, M., and Sapiro, G. (2000). The LOCO-I Lossless Image Compression Algorithm: Principles and Standardization into JPEG-LS. *IEEE Trans. Image Processing,* Vol.9, August, 1309-1324

4   Mesh Networking

Kevin Curran, Derek Hawkes, Scott Hulme, Christopher Laughlin

Wireless MESH networks have evolved from a simple one channel radio to a three radio configuration, and now the technology itself seems to have reached a point of maturity where its uses have been brought outside of the military environment and have been implemented into everyday life. The main uses outside of the armed forces is offering broadband to the general public who live in areas with little or no broadband access or by people who are on the move in town areas. The topology seems to have been greatly affected by the increasing popularity of mobile wireless devices such as laptops, PDAs, phones and MP3 players.There are still several main issues that have to be addressed for MESH networking to reach its full potential. Obviously the privacy and security of those using the network needs to be taken into consideration as they are allowing others to view and connect to their computer. We examine here aspects concerning mesh networks, these include, what a mesh network is and how it differs from an ad-hoc network, which is a pre-mesh network.

Introduction

Mesh networks can be either wired or wireless, and is a way to design a network of nodes so that information such a data information, voice, video, instructions for nodes or any other type of information can be routed around a network without any interference, even when a node fails. Ad-hoc networks which are wireless have data forwarded by the nodes, depending on the connections within the ad-hoc network, also there is no central point within their topology, if the network is wired however then the function of forwarding data is carried out by the routers. Mesh networking has a topology that contains nodes that communicate with each other, via other nodes within the network or directly depending on the position of the source node to the destination node. Within the communication industry this type of communication between nodes is called hopping, and for this type of network to operate effectively each node must have at least two radio pathways to communicate with the other nodes.

The area covered by the mesh network of nodes is called a mesh cloud; this mesh cloud is only effective if the nodes are listening and communicating with each other. Mesh networks can be put into the category of ad hoc networks, which means that mesh networks and Mobile ad-hoc networking are closely related. However mesh networks do not have the problems associated with mobile ad hoc networks (MANETS), which is caused mainly by nodes moving around in different locations, and environments, but for today's demands the nodes within the mesh network must be capable of mobility, which puts more demands on the protocols of the network, as will be seen later in this essay. The main purpose of the wireless mesh network is to give connection between the mesh client and the wired backbone of a network, or back haul, this could be anything from providing the public within a residential area with access to the internet, to providing communication between units in the armed forces The mesh network can be randomly structured with no central point, and is not as geometrically shaped as other topologies, which are shown in Figure 5.

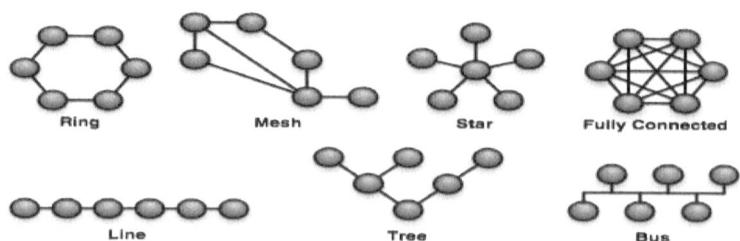

Figure 5: Different Network Topologies[1]

---

[1] http://en.wikipedia.org/wiki/Network_Topology

The mesh network can also be fully connected as shown in Figure 5. Within the wireless mesh network there are two types of nodes these include:

- Mesh routers: these devices forward data packets to each other within the mesh network, and have the capability to provide gateway/bridge functions, so that subnets (clients) can access the mesh network. Other than the routing capability for gateway/bridge functions as in a conventional router, a mesh router contains additional routing functions to support mesh networking.(Akyildiz Ian F 2005[1]) Mesh routers also can have numerous and different types of wireless interfaces, so that a variety of wireless technologies can access the mesh network for connection, into the wired backbone.

- Mesh clients: these devices do not have the capability of mesh routers, such as gateway /bridge functions. They are connected to the router either through a single wireless interface, or by wire through the Ethernet, if there are multiple mesh clients at one location then, a base station or access point will be connected to the clients, and from the base station a connection will made to the router/bridge within the mesh network.

The nodes in the mesh network execute the following sequence to achieve a route to the destination node as follows:

1. The source node sends out a route request packet to the whole mesh network.
2. Nodes within the network that receive the packet revise the information already stored by them, for use by the transmitting node or source node.
3. After updating the information, the nodes set up markers or pointers back to the source node through the route tables.
4. The wireless nodes also send back other active information such as IP address, the present sequence number for the request, and the identification number of the sources broadcast.
5. The other nodes within the mesh network will only answer the broadcast if they are either the destination or one of the nodes on the route to the destination.

Wireless mesh was originally developed for military applications, but has undergone significant evolution in the past decade[1]. These developments within mesh networking, which are used by the civilian population also, are of three stages, and are concerned with the configuration of the radio within the mesh network, which has improved reliability and adaptation of the network. This improvement is due to the reduced costs of radios, which in turn has lead to more radios being used in mesh networks, this allows the mesh network to use the additional radios to improve functions such as; client access, transmission between client and the mesh network, and radios specifically searching continuously for other nodes, to provide faster handover between nodes whenever the network is mobile. This early stage of technological development or innovation in wireless mesh is pre IEEE standard and is known as first generation wireless mesh.

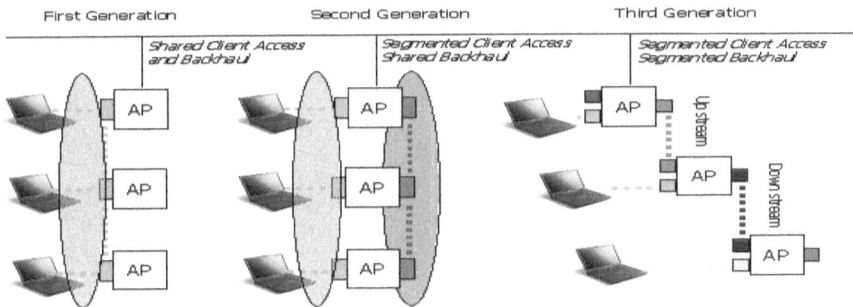

Figure 6: Three Generations of Mesh[2]

---

[1] http://en.wikipedia.org/wiki/Mesh_networking
[2] http://en.wikipedia.org/wiki/History_of_wireless_mesh_networking

The first mesh network generation used one radio channel to provide service to clients, and also the backhaul or transmission back to the mesh network. This type of radio configuration meant that when one node was transmitting, the other nodes in the mesh network were listening, therefore the nodes were transmitting, then receiving, then transmitting on the same channel. This intermittent stop-and-go behaviour adversely affects network performance especially if the destination is far away and the traffic has to be retransmitted ("hop") across many intermediate nodes first. A diagram of the first generation mesh network is shown in Figure 6.

The second generation of nodes in the mesh network improved on the performance of the mesh network by having two radios within the nodes, one radio would provide service for the client, and the other would be used for transmission to the mesh network or backhaul. But since a single radio mesh is still servicing the backhaul, packets travelling towards the internet share bandwidth at each hop along the backhaul path with other interfering mesh backhaul nodes- all-operating on the same channel. This causes degradation in the performance of the mesh network, however it is not as severe as the first generation mesh networks performance reduction. A diagram of the second generation mesh network is shown in Figure 6. The third generation of nodes used in the mesh network again improved on performance by having two radios in each node to service the backhaul, (uplink and downlink) and one to service the clients. This network controls the channels of the radios so that the radios are on separate channels, but have the same bands, therefore interference does not occur between nodes.

Wireless Mesh Network Architecture

The architecture of wireless mesh network has different types, these are as follows:

- Infrastructure/backbone uses mesh routers to form the mesh network, which have gateway/bridge functions that allow connection to other networks, such as the internet, or other subnets. The connection to the external networks can be either wired through the ethernet, if the client does not have a wireless network interface card or wireless if the client has a wireless network interface card. The radio technology used in wireless mesh networks is mostly IEEE 802.11, which is the original standard, developed by the IEEE, however wireless mesh network can use other radio technologies, such as Wi-Fi, WiMAX and fibber-optic technology, which can connect into the mesh network through access points(AP's) connected to the gateway/bridge mesh router. Figure 7 shows an Infrastructure/Backbone Wireless Mesh Network, this structure is also sometimes referred to as Infrastructure meshing.

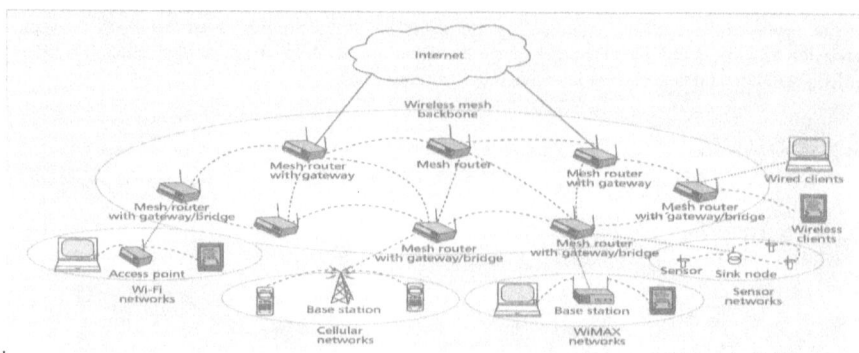

Figure 7: Infrastructure/Backbone WMNs (Akyildiz et al., 2005)

- Client meshing is where the client nodes provide the actual network functions, such as routing and configuration, as well as providing the applications required by the end user customer. Therefore this type of mesh network does not require mesh routers, because of this the functions and requirements of the customer's devices are much more extensive, compared to the infrastructure/backbone Wireless Mesh Networks. Client WMNs are usually formed using one type of radios on devices. A Client WMN is actually the same as a conventional ad-hoc network (Akyildiz, 2005).

- A hybrid wireless mesh network combines both infrastructure/backbone architecture and client mesh architecture. The infrastructure/backbone section of the hybrid mesh network provides connections to other networks, such as sensor networks, WiFi, WiMAX and the internet. With the client mesh section having functionalities such as routing and configuration, the connectivity and mesh cloud coverage within the wireless mesh network is improved. The characteristics of WMNs are outlined below, where the hybrid architecture is considered for WMNs, since it comprises all the advantages of WMNs (Akyildiz, 2005). Figure 8 shows the third type of wireless mesh architecture.

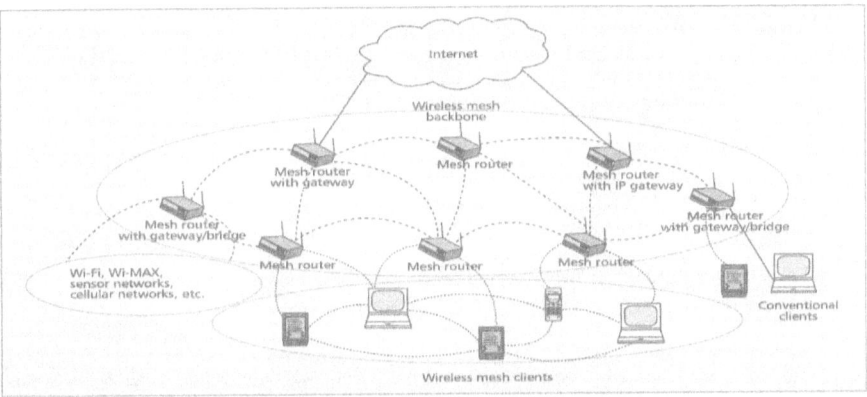

Figure 8: Infrastructure/Backbone WMNs (Akyildiz et al., 2005)

The hybrid mesh network, which comprises a combination of infrastructure and client meshing, gives the wireless mesh network hybrid the following characteristics:

- Wireless Mesh Networks are capable of forming themselves, re-routing around nodes that fail, self-organise and support ad-hoc networks.
- Mesh routers provide the infrastructure/backbone for the wireless mesh network, that are multi-hop.
- Mesh routers have limited mobility, and there function is routing and configuration mainly, this in turn reduces the number of mesh clients and other nodes that can be loaded onto a mesh router.
- Mobility of end nodes is supported easily through the wireless infrastructure.
- Mesh network routers can provide access for various types of different networks, including both wired and wireless, which means that integration of networks can occur.
- Power-consumption constraints are different for mesh routers and mesh clients (Akyildiz et al., 2005) .

Design of Wireless Mesh Networks

To improve radio communication, techniques such as directional and smart antennas have being suggested in the past. These antennas are very powerful both at transmitting and receiving signals in more than one direction, and have reduced interference from external sources, in comparison to dipole antennas. Other systems such as multiple input multiple output and multi-radio/multi-channel were considered. All these systems and techniques were suggested to improve capacity, and increase the adaptability of wireless mesh systems.

The wireless mesh networks can be further improved by increasing control of the higher protocol layers, using more advanced radio technologies; these could include reconfigurable radios, software radios, and frequency adaptable spectrum radios. Although these radio technologies are still in their infancy, they are expected to be the future platform for wireless networks due to their dynamic control capability (Akyildiz Ian F 2005[12]). By standardising the radio technology used by mesh networks it reduces the cost of the equipment required, and the installation of the equipment, and allows compatibility between different types of equipment such as PC's, and mobile phones. The organisation given the responsibility of ensuring compatibility between devices is the IEEE Standard Organisation. This organisation has being establishing different standards for new radio technologies for various levels of the mesh network, and upgrading these standards to accommodate new technologies coming into the forefront. These include the following standards:

- **IEEE 802.15.5** is the standard that deals with the defining of the Media Access Control layer and the Physical Layer, so that short range connections can be made between groups of devices that are moving, such as Laptops, mobile phones, and PDA's. The main problem with these devices is the power source capability, which does not allow for long range transmission, at high bandwidths. By using mesh technology were the communication is achieved by hopping from one node to another, the area covered by these devices is increased, and still maintains a high bandwidth because of the short distances.

- **IEEE 802.11s** is the standard that deals the Quality Of Service (QoS), handovers between nodes were the mesh client is mobile, and ensuring high speed bandwidth. This standard also improved on the infrastructure and protocols used in the nodes to make connections between each other, revise the topology of the network, and route configuration.

- **IEEE 802.16A** this standard addresses the problem of the interference with frequencies above 10 Gega-Hertz that occurred with the standard 806.16. The new standard 806.16A incorporates the Non-Line Of Sight (NLOS) operation, which is supported by the time-division multiple access (TDMA) in the Media Access Control layer.

- **IEEE 802.20** upgrades the previous standards to provide mobile wireless broadband, within the wireless mesh network, for both the indoor and outdoor environment.

Scalability is the amount of nodes that can be added to the mesh network, without compromising routing and transport protocols. If the number of nodes is increased, there is a possibility of more hops between nodes to achieve the destination of the data packet. However with each hop there is a certain percentage of loss in the bandwidth per hop, which can reduce the signal. To prevent this and ensure scalability in the Wireless Mesh Network, every protocol from the Media Access Control (MAC) sub-layer of the Open Systems Interconnection Basic Reference Model (OSI) to the application layer must be capable of adapting to increased number of nodes or be scalable. Initial mesh networks used a single radio, and for the source node to send the data packet to the destination node it may have several hops, as the data packet goes through each node or hop there is a certain percentage loss in the throughput. This percentage loss in throughput can reduce the distance of the transmission considerably. To overcome this problem multiple radios are added to each node, one being 802.11 and the other radio interface has a longer range, although the throughput is reduced, it remains at an acceptable level, for the increased distance gained.

The main advantage of wireless mesh networks is the ability of the network to forward data packets even if one or more of the nodes have failed. This is due to the wireless mesh network being able to self-organise, and having algorithms or protocols that can control the topology of the network, and routing of the data packets. These algorithms have to be based in the Media Access Control (MAC) layer so that they can control the physical layer or topology, and the routing protocols, by doing this the performance of the Wireless Mesh Network can be increased. Wireless Mesh Networks are used mostly for broadband applications, with different types of Quality of Service (QoS) needed for each application, this could include giving priority to one application over others, or ensuring a certain data rate flow. Thus, in addition to end-to end transmission delay and fairness, more performance metrics, such as delay jitter, aggregate and per-node through-put, and packet loss ratios, must be considered by the communication protocol (Akyildiz et al., 2005).

Security in wireless mesh networks from hackers and software viruses, and the authentication of various users within a network, has to be designed into the network, so that these elements do not interfere with the normal communication of the network. The problem with wireless mesh networks there is no centralized trusted authority, as the access points to the wireless mesh network can be numerous, therefore unauthorised access could be from various points. Ad-hoc networks has a certain amount of security solutions, which are being considered for wireless mesh networks, however they are not developed sufficiently to be implemented adequately for security purposes. Transit Access Points (TAP) can be compromised by an attacker. This could involve the actual removal or replacement of the device, so that it can be reprogrammed to change the topology of the network for the attackers benefit. The second form of attack is to access the device internally but make no changes to the devices, but simply monitor the traffic information passing ie secret information. This form of attack is very difficult to detect. The third form of attack is modifying the internal of the device; this type of attack is more easily detected, because of the use of a verifier by the Wireless Hot Spot (WHS). The fourth type is to build clones of the TAPs, these clones are then placed in various locations by the attacker, and used to download information by the attacker to corrupt the routing protocols. This again can be detected by the message authentication codes (MAC). If the routing mechanism is attacked, the adversary can change the topology of the network by increasing the route lengths. This in turn slows down the speed of the bandwidth to the mesh client. The attacker could be modifying the topology to improve the service for them, or to monitor traffic data, which could be for malicious use in future attacks. To prevent attack by this method the operator should use protocols that are secure. Some TAPs only serve one mobile client, whereas others serve two or more, therefore the TAPs with more than one mobile client, should perhaps get half as much again of the available bandwidth. The reason for this, is that the client connected to the TAP with more that one mobile client, will have reduced bandwidth due to the other client on the same TAP, even though they may be paying the same price as the only MC connected to a TAP. This situation can be adjusted by the attacker simply increasing the number of TAPs for the mobile client's information to travel through; subsequently this increases the number of hops, and decreases the bandwidth. To prevent this, the operator can reconfigure the wireless mesh network routinely, so that routes to TAPs from Mobile Clients can be optimised for traffic data.

The protocols of the network from the MAC sub-layer to the application layer of the OSI model, should be designed, so that the network will largely operate autonomously were possible. Also the management tools of the wireless mesh network, should be capable of maintaining constant operation, continually performance monitoring, and configure the wireless mesh networks parameters. These management tools with the protocols allow the network to operate autonomously, enables a wireless mesh network to be rapidly deployed. For the wireless mesh network to be effective, the wireless mesh network must be compatible with conventional; networks, such as computer networks, WiFi, Wi-max and various other wired networks. Therefore the mesh routers which are the Access Points (AP's) for these other networks must have gateways/bridges that are compatible with these mesh clients, and allow integration of the various types of networks.

Two of the technical challenges facing mesh networks are load balancing and routing. Load balancing is sending data packets through the mesh network so that the various paths have equal or almost equal amounts of data travelling along each, to reduce congestion, and prevent the slow down of data transmission. Routing is having a protocol that can decide which path or route to take through the mesh network, to prevent large amounts of data queuing in any one particular route or path. Existing solutions in mobile ad-hoc and sensor networks cannot be directly applied to WMN's due to the difference in traffic patterns, mobility scenarios, gateway functionalities and bandwidth requirements (Liang & Mieso, 2007). Therefore if most mesh clients wanted to access the internet, the data traffic will be travelling either towards internet gateways from the mesh client, or from internet gateways to the mesh client. The consequences of this, is a build up of data congestion on the routes leading towards the internet gateways, due to the mesh routers choosing the best path to the internet gateway. Therefore routing algorithms need to determine routes that will balance the data traffic across the mesh network, towards access points, and not simply the best path towards access points. Load balancing within the wireless mesh network can be accomplished by the following methods these include:

- **Path-Based Load Balancing**: Using this method the data traffic is spread across several routes of the mesh network.
- **Gateway-Based Load Balancing:** The data traffic load is balanced at particular internet gateways, or all of the gateways.
- **Mesh Routers:** Load balancing can also be carried out at the mesh routers over the wireless backbone (Liang & Mieso, 2007).

The protocols governing how the node should determine a path for data traffic in a mesh network, is called a routing metric, there are several types of routing metrics these include the following:

- **Hop count:** This metric determines the most suitable path by the number of hops required to achieve the destination node.
- **Expected Transmission count (ETX):** This metric takes into account the number of data packet losses and successful attempts ratio, along with the length of the path, which is determined by the number of successful transmissions from the Media Access Control (MAC) layer through the mesh network.
- **Expected Transmission Time (ETT):** This metric determines a route by considering the different transmission times for each possible route through the mesh network. It enhances ETX integrating the data transmission rate of each particular link into the routing metric. (Ma Liang [16])
- **Weight Cumulative Expected Transmission Time**: This metric considers the different bandwidths available in each route and the variety of paths available for the transmission.
- **Metric of Interference and Channel Switching** (MIC): MIC improves WCETT by catching both intra-flow interference within a path and inter-flow interference between adjacent paths. (Ma Liang [17]) This method takes into account the routes used in the current link, and the previous link, to achieve the

destination path. The MIC will set a larger parameter value when the current link to the destination is using the same route as the previous link; this is to take into account the intra-flow interference within each route. In order to capture inter-flow interference, MIC also catches the set of neighbours that the transmission on each current link interferes with (Liang & Mieso, 2007).This allows the data traffic to be routed through mesh routers which have less traffic flow.

Wireless Mesh Network Applications

Ad-hoc networks which are mobile were mainly design for either military or for special requirements in civilian applications. This however is changing with users wanting to access the internet or other more general applications, were high bandwidth is required for downloading to or from the internet or application. This has lead to the development of the ad-hoc network into a network with hierarchy, with some layers having wired or wireless connections, which is an extension of the wired infrastructure. This extension is called a mesh network, and has resulted in the ad-hoc network being part of a larger mesh network. The mesh network has many uses within the communication industry, which come under the following areas such as

Intelligent Transportation Systems: A mesh network could be set up within a city to implement the control systems for public transportation. An example for this application scenario is the Portsmouth Real-Time Travel Information System (PORTAL), a system that, as part of a city-wide public transportation communications network, aims at providing real-time travel information to passengers (Raffaele et al., 2005). This mesh network allows anybody at forty locations throughout the city to display real-time information regarding bus arrivals, destination and present location, and the system is installed in over 300 buses.

Public Safety: Due to the current social, political, economical and climatic trends within countries, the need for improved communication between emergency services within disaster areas has increased. The network for emergency services must be reliable, adaptive and have a bandwidth which is high, in the past the solution has being technologies such as mobile phones or radios, the disadvantage with these technologies is that the bandwidth is low, and therefore data rate transmission is slow. However they do allow high mobility and ubiquitous coverage of the network. An agency that uses mesh networks is the police. For instance the San Matteo Police Department in San Francisco Bay Area has equipped all its patrol cars with laptops, and motorcycles and bicycle patrols with PDAs, employing standard 802.11b/g wireless cards for communication.

Internet Access: Access to the internet has become increasingly important to the individual today, whether it is for private use or for work, the demand for access to the internet is increasing. With this increasing demand it brings problems for internet service providers, to provide access for subscribers no matter what their physical location is. The wireless mesh network provides a solution by having mesh routers located throughout either a urban or rural environment, and because the network is wireless the cost of installation is low and affordable to the subscriber. An example of this is the metro-scale broadband city network activated on April 2004 in the city of Cerritos, California, operated by Airmesh Communications Inc., a wireless ISP (WISP) Company (Raffaele et al., 2005). This network is built up with Tropos-based mesh technology and covers a city area as large as eight miles using more than 130 outdoor access points, less than 20 percent of them connected to a wired backhaul network.

Mesh Networks In Military Warfare: Military warfare in today's modern army does not only depend on weapons or intelligence, instead commanders want to see the situations in the battlefield in real-time, and assess them for strategic planning. The commander needs to be capable of viewing intelligence from vast distances, if this intelligence has data, voice and video capabilities, then the commander can make more informed decisions on troop his movements, battlefield terrain, enemy movements and locations, equipment and numbers. Therefore the communication system required for commanders must be able to maintain connection when highly mobile, highly robust to everyday usage, adaptable to the elements for various internal and external environments, low latency, real-time and have high security access authorisation. The first military network were ad-hoc and used nodes that had a single radio frequency, these nodes provided connections between adjacent nodes, by changing their function between mesh client and mesh router. This type of mesh network was slow and prone to interference, and in battlefield situations could leave the army with vulnerable areas for attack. This third generation of wireless mesh node has three radios, one for the mesh client, and two for the backhaul, the backhaul has a radio each for uplink, and downlink, and channel management of the radios, to prevent interference from other radios. In today's modern warfare having a central radio controller for all the communications can leave a troop squad vulnerable, if there communication moves out of there range. Therefore to prevent this occurring, if multiple wireless mesh nodes are deployed with troop squads, communication can be routed from one squad through the other squads nodes, to the intended command headquarters or squad commanders, the network must be scalable for this to operate successfully. For this communication between squads to be maintained, the network must be capable of changing topology continuously without the user being aware of it occurring. The nodes within the network should be able to connect with additional nodes, by searching for them automatically; the nodes within the network should be able to change frequencies in a co-ordinated simultaneous operation without having to get permission from a central node, to prevent interference from jamming. The network should be capable of being deployed on troops, and vehicles, to allow for continuous communication between sections of the army on the move, and allow nodes to connect directly with the upper hierarchy of the network when required, or hop between nodes to the upper hierarchy. Mesh networks provide the solution for modern warfare, as the mesh network can have an infrastructure with both wired and wireless connections; also the mesh network nodes because of there proximity to each other, allow a higher bandwidth for each mesh client so that latency time is reduced, and intelligence is processed faster by commanders in real time. The mesh network can also be increased to give a larger coverage area or mesh cloud in the warfare environment, due to their scalability, and the automatic detection of other nodes within range.

The mesh network and its different topologies are being used more commonly in modern day technology. One of the main places that the mesh technology has been deployed has been on the battle field. Many military units now use mesh networks to send and receive important data for surveillance. The military have become more efficient and power due to that fact that one unit could be connected to the mesh network miles away from the base unit and still be able to keep sending information such as video voice and data. The importance of networks in combat areas have become more and more relevant as the use of satellites, UAV's (Unmanned Aerial Vehicles) and a wide number of centralized and distributed information assets. The majority of these assets are controlled wirelessly with connections to wired networks for intelligence sources. The wireless connection must be stable to carry data, voice and increasingly video traffic. Mobility in the network is very important in both mobility of individuals and vehicles. To achieve this, the network hand offs between communicating devices must be coordinated to minimise data outages and reduction in performance. Theses hand offs also have to be transparent, to maintain session connectivity while in motion. In modern warfare the use of video streaming and storage of video has been growing rapidly. The mesh networks have been deployed to achieve the high bandwidth streams and low latency.

Mesh Network Installations

Wireless MESH networks have been seen as a solution to areas which have poor internet access, due to either being too far away from an exchange or having no ISP in the area. However, uses for wireless MESH networks have also been found in cities and business districts in order to provide access to the internet. This section details some MESH networks that have been implemented for the use of public and corporate communities.

MotoMESH

Motorola have recently undertaken a project called 'MotoMesh' which uses MESH network technology to provide broadband access to the public. The aim of the project is to enable users to be able to use broadband applications seamlessly anywhere, anytime even when on the move by foot or by vehicle. This has been done by using a form of wireless networking which is based heavily on the wired internet infrastructure. Using this technology a person is able to use broadband applications while they are on the move, even at speeds of up to 200mph. The technology is self-forming and self-healing which allows users to connect to either a pre-deployed network infrastructure or connect through other user's wireless devices within range. This means that there is no need for wireless broadband towers. The pre-deployed network infrastructure consists of a number of wireless routers, which can be attached to street lights and buildings among other things. An example of this equipment is shown in Figure 9.

Figure 9: Multi radio broadband system attached to a street light

These broadband systems are typically connected high on street lights as it offers the advantage of being out of the way of obstructions and also the street light offers a power supply. However if the user is out of range of one of these Multi radio broadband systems then the user's device will try and find a path though other users wireless devices such as mobile phones and PDAs until it does reach one of the systems.

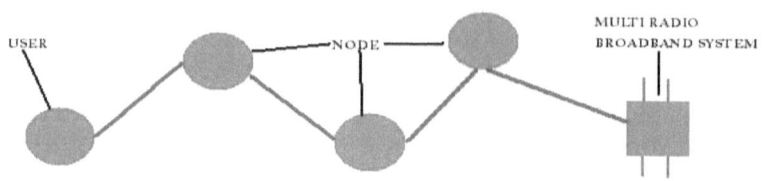

Figure 10: Node communication in a mesh

Figure 10 illustrates how a user that is out of range of the broadband system can connect to nodes within range in order to find a path to the broadband system.This system has already been deployed in the USA and was used to assist in the security during the Superbowl[1].

Meraki Roofnet

Meraki are a mesh networking company based in California funded by Google and Sequoia Capital. The company manufacture networking equipment, develop networking software and are currently working on a project called Roofnet. The organisation have developed software to aid in the setting up of MESH networks, the software is called 'Dashboard'. Dashboard uses a routing protocol called 'SrcRR' which uses two broadcasts. One broadcast determines the likelihood that a packet sent between two nodes will reach its destination. The second broadcast is used to build routing tables to try and find the best route to send the packet through. The company have created two different versions of their nodes; one version is for use inside while the other is for use outside. These nodes act as gateways whenever connected directly to the internet or as repeaters or boosters when they are not connected directly. The organisation has tested this software in real world conditions such as heavily populated areas and dense apartment blocks and believes that the combination of their hardware and software can offer people a high quality MESH networking service. The network allows for continuous growth and is able to handle large numbers of users with intelligent traffic queues and packet prioritisation[23].

London WI-FI MESH network

In 2007, the city of London took on a project to deliver a Wi-Fi MESH network called "The Cloud" in order to deliver internet access to a square mile of their financial district (Cellan-Jones, 2007). This network has been made available through the use of nearly 130 nodes attached to the city's street lights. This network has this time however not been aimed at the general public but at the bankers, traders, and brokers. This network is not

---

[1] http://www.motorola.com/mesh/pages/applications/intro_applications.htm
[2] http://meraki.com/oursolution/mesh/
[3] http://en.wikipedia.org/wiki/SrcRR

free to use, the user will actually have to subscribe through a provider who will charge fees in order to gain access. The main criticism of "The Cloud" is that it is a Wi-Fi based network and therefore it will work perfectly outside but will be limited to what buildings a user can gain access to while inside. A lot of the buildings in that area of London consist of very think walls which limit access indoor unless near a window. Therefore the question is, are the people working in the financial district going to use internet access while outside? Well surprisingly there are over 350,000 users registered to use the service, which would indicate that the network seems to be of some use[1].

Mesh for OLPC

OLPC (One Laptop per Child) was a project setup by members of the faculty at MIT Media lab; it was setup to oversee the children's machine project and the construction of the XO-1. This was a laptop that would cost $100, aimed at children in the third world. The project was setup in January 2005. The project creators had a set of principles child ownership, low ages, saturation, connection and free for open source. One of the main aims of the connection principle was that the laptops could connect in a class room even if there was no base station or server. This meant that all the laptops would need to use mesh technology. The hardware that the laptops used was a built-in wireless card that supported 801.11b/g, Marvell technology group also developed the wireless chip and crated the firmware and the drivers. The wireless antennas were placed like ears so that the laptop could get the best wireless coverage as shown in Figure 11. In most cases the wireless antenna is contained in the screen of the laptop, however noise from other electric components cause interference and can limit the wireless range. The Marvell card was designed with power saving in minds. The theory is that it takes one fourth the energy to send a signal half the distance, and if there is another laptop in the middle with will carry the signal for one fourth the energy data would be transmitted at half the energy than it would be if sending at full signal.

Figure 11: OLPC

The laptop was full of software that maximised the mesh network. The laptop was fitted with 802.11s which was a proposed wireless mesh standard from Intel, that was intended for small home or office use. The laptop was set to mesh whenever it's powered on. Each node would be operating in a peer-to-peer fashion with the other laptops. This meant that when one of the laptops had a connection to the internet, either directly or through another node, it would share with the other laptops so that they all would have the connection. The best example of the mesh is use with the laptops is the fact that it can share applications and file easily over the mesh.

---

[1] http://news.bbc.co.uk/2/hi/technology/6577307.stm

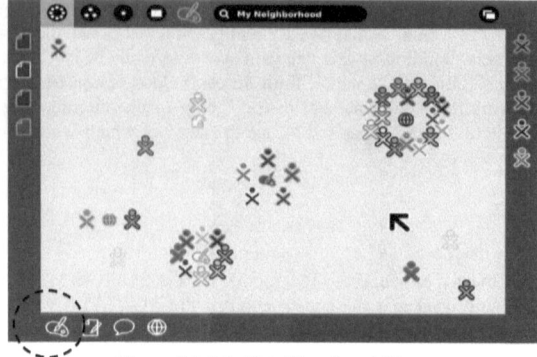

Figure 12: My Neighbourhood View

On the tool bar built into the Linux distribution that runs on the laptop is a share icon that lets the user share the file or application that they are using. Once they have chosen to share, the file or application appears in the neighbourhood view shown in Figure 12. Each cross with a dot on the top represents a node or laptop the node with the circle is sharing a browser page, as shown by the browser icon. The node beside it is the node that is sharing the browser page.

One of the main developments that may see the MESH network become even more popular in the near future is the development of the IEEE standard 802.11s. There are however other developments being made in the technology. For instance, in order to increase the through put using multiple radios, researchers at the Microsoft Corporation have developed what is called the 'MESH Connectivity Layer' (MCL). The MCL uses a 2.5 GHz routing protocol, which selects the best radio on each node and it also selects the best path between two nodes. This protocol has also been designed to assist in sending information over varied distances by changing the frequency the packets are sent. For example if the next node being hopped to is a long distance away then the frequency will be lowered, as lower frequencies travel further than high frequencies. In most current systems deployed on multi hop networks a node can only send or receive a piece of data at any one time. However a dual radio, multiple channel set up is now being developed, which means that a node will be able to send and receive a packet at the same time. This will increase the capacity of a multi-hop network greatly. Finally, Microsoft is currently researching the advantage of using MESH networks and researchers are in the process of developing a self organising wireless MESH network. The aim of this project is to connect neighbouring houses together using wireless technology. Microsoft claim that the advantages of such a network are that everyone using the technology will not need their own individual gateway, instead connect through gateways distributed throughout the community. This means that packets would dynamically find a route through the nodes in the community until they reach the internet gateway. This means that in less developed areas of the world where not everyone will have their own gateway would still be able to connect. It also means that there would be not need to lay cables to every house in order to receive an internet connect[1].

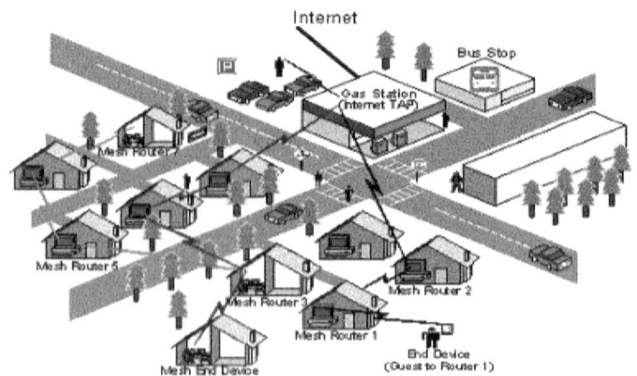

---

[1] http://research.microsoft.com/mesh/

Figure 13: Microsoft Mesh Network

Figure 13 illustrates a sole internet gateway located in a gas station. However all of the houses in the diagram are able to receive internet connectivity. Microsoft has however run into some problems with this project such as current wireless network range, customer's privacy and the security of their data, auto configurations. However these problems may be solved whenever the development of the new IEEE 802.11s standard is completed as some of these issues are being addressed within the standard.

Conclusion

Wireless mesh technologies are emerging as the most effective mode of communication structure for wireless networks. The mesh network itself has many different types of technology that can be implemented into the network to improve performance, such as broadband access to the internet, satellite communication for military warfare intelligence, communication network for controlling transportation system or production lines in factories using various sensors connected by a mesh network. The mesh network is also highly adaptable for today's modern dynamic environments, and can be upgraded easily by increasing the number of nodes, which increases the communication mesh with minimal loss of throughput. With new advances in radio technology, the mesh network nodes will have increased performances with regards to traffic data throughput, which should improve media output, such as video, data and sound. However it still remains that improvements can be made with regards to technical problems, such as load balancing, routing, protocols at the MAC, PHY layers, and scalability, so that the network is more efficient at providing a service for the user in communication of various media.

The cost of installing a mesh network is significantly lower in comparison to wired networks; this is due to the wireless back bone infrastructure. The number of connection points therefore required by the mesh network is significantly less, to achieve connection to the wired backbone. Wireless mesh networks can be easily and quickly deployed in any environment. This is due to the mesh nodes being able to re-organise and reconfigure themselves into the network, and search for all possible paths and other mesh routers available within the mesh network, for them to transmit and receive data, using the functionalities available to them. These functions are carried out automatically by the mesh node whenever they are powered up, and do not require user operation. The cost to subscribers that are connected to mesh networks is lower, in comparison to wired networks. Mesh networks are capable of maintaining high band widths over long distances. This can be maintained by increasing the number of nodes, which reduces the distance between nodes, and allows the transmission of traffic data at higher rates. By increasing and decreasing the distance the strength of the signal can be changed. If you reduce the distance by a factor of two, the resulting signal is at least four times more powerful at the receiver. The routers within the wireless mesh network that are not mobile can be used by the wireless backbone to carry out more sophisticated , with high demand for resources transmission techniques, than those that are implemented by user mesh client devices. The reliability of wireless mesh networks is due to the number of redundant routes or multiple paths that the wireless backbone provides for data traffic. This therefore increases the reliability of communication between end-points, against node failure along the transmission route. The scalability of the network allows for more bandwidth, as more devices are added to the network, however the number hops from source to destination should be kept low, as the data traffic. Mesh networks also offer high redundancy, which gives the nodes and mesh routers alternative routes to send data traffic, this therefore offers a stable communication system.

References

Akylidiz I.F, Wang Xudong, K. (2005) *A survey on Wireless Mesh Networks*, Georgia Institute of Technology, IEEE Radio Communications September 2005 Volume 43, Issue 9.

Cellan-Jones, R. (2007), Switch on for Square Mile Wi-Fi, BBC News, 23rd Aril 2007
http://news.bbc.co.uk/2/hi/technology/6577307.stm

Liang, M., Mieso, D. (2007): *A Routing Metric for Load Balancing in Wireless Mesh Networks,* Department of Computing and Information Science, University of Guelph Ontario, Canada, N1G 2W1, 21ST International Conference on Advanced Information Networking and Applications Workshops (AINAW07) IEE Computer Society

Raffaele, B., Marco, C., Enrico, G. (2005) Mesh Networks: Commodity Multihop Ad Hoc Networks, IEEE Communications Magazine March 2005

5   Wireless Sensor Networks

Kevin Curran, Gary Doherty, David O'Callaghan

Wireless sensor networks (WSN) are used in many applications including traffic control, military operations and health care. Sensor nodes can be of any size, and any cost. Most sensor nodes are very small and efficient. Wireless sensor networks are made up of a number of small sensor nodes and a main routing node. When a signal is received by a sensor node, it sends it to the main gateway node and performs the necessary operation. Wireless Sensor Networks present the potential of gathering, processing and sharing data via low-cost, low-power wireless devices. As society changes more opportunities for sensing equipment and applications materialise.This chapter provides an overview of wireless sensor networking technology.

Introduction

In 1901 Guglielmo Marconi transmitted signals across the Atlantic from Cornwall to St. John's, Newfoundland. Throughout the 20th century wireless transmission has advanced in a number of different technologies including radio, television, radar, satellite and mobile. As sensing, computing and communication are all following an exponential curve to zero in power, size and cost then it should make sense that wireless sensor nodes, which are a combination of sensor, computers, and communicators together in a small device, are also decreasing in size and cost. A sensor node is a node in a wireless sensor network that is capable of performing some processing, gathering sensory information and communicating with other connected nodes in the network. Wireless sensor networks are made up of many nodes, which are important in their functionality. The sensor nodes used for wireless networks in particular are much more adaptable and are capable of coping in more harsh environments which others cannot (Wilson, 2004).

WSNs also have the ability of wireless communication over a restricted area. Because of the fact they have memory and power constraints, they need to be well organised in order to be able to build a fully functional network. It is important that the nodes build up the network using their keys after distribution. To make sure that they are put in the correct places to get maximum coverage it is good to plan ahead on where they are to be placed as this will then allow a plan to be hatched for the handiest route for them to follow etc and it is also more secure when the node picks up on more than one other node as this allows the connections to be more spread and distribution of information to be spread further afield in case one failed. These are ideal for wireless sensor networks as they may are required to be in many types of environment. Sensor nodes in wireless networks for traffic control are required to deal with all types of weather. They are designed to cope with anything from snow to heavy winds. It is important that they are designed so they can accurately sense information and can send data (see Figure 14). Wireless sensor networks are often used for detecting chemical measurements in industry. Oil rigs use wireless sensor networks to control oil amounts and other chemicals. They are very important and the sensor nodes that are used have to be adaptable to these environments to ensure they function properly (Flury et al., 2007). Wireless sensor networks are used to measure radiation levels. This would mainly be done in hospitals and power plant industries. Smart Dust nodes are minuscule micro electromechanical sensors (MEMS) capable of detecting anything from light to vibrations. With breakthroughs in silicon and fabrication techniques, the size of these motes could eventually be as small as a grain of sand and be able to send data to other MEMS up to one thousand feet (Manges, 1999). Figure 14 shows how sensors have decreased in size and increased in performance over the last 5 years and the proposed size and frequency of sensors in 2012 (Mainwaring et al., 2002).

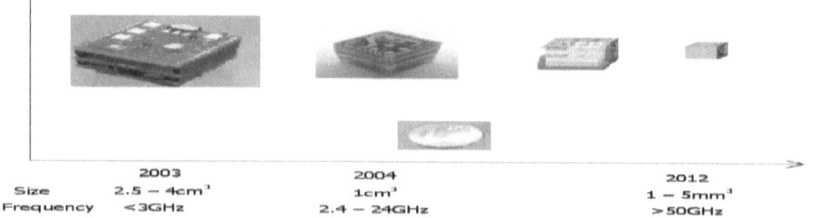

	2003	2004	2012
Size	2.5 – 4cm³	1cm³	1 – 5mm³
Frequency	<3GHz	2.4 – 24GHz	>50GHz

Figure 14: Evolution of sensor nodes

The military initially used WSN for applications by dropping sensors in an area from a plane and the sensors themselves formed the network, which enabled battlefield surveillance to take place. From here they developed into a cheaper and more powerful tool. Sensors are now being placed in very hostile areas where it would not be practical to install cables. High technology sensors the size of a grain of dirt are now being used by the military. These Smart Dust sensors are given a unique ID. The sensors are then aimed at the target from a plane and are very inconspicuous as they also look like dirt. It is believed that these sensors contributed to the death of Al Qaeda leader Abu Musab al Zarqawi (Anon, 2006). Figure 15 shows the development of sensor network applications (Khemapech et al., 2005).

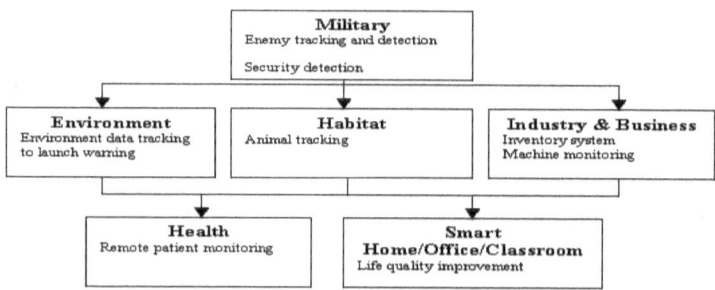

Figure 15: Sensor Network Applications Development

When referring to wireless devices people normally mention mobile phones, personal assistants or wireless laptops. Wireless sensor networks (WSN), unlike these devices, are inexpensive and do not depend on pre-existing infrastructures. A WSN is a network made up of multiple independent sensor nodes, which are usually referred to as motes, equipped with radio transceivers and a base station which monitor the surrounding environment for various conditions such as temperature, speed, motion or gasses. Formula 1 cars have sensors on different parts of the engine to monitor key conditions such as the engines performance, the brake temperature, the oil pressure and the tyre pressure. This data is fed back to the control centre where the engineers can see the status of the car on a PC. A wireless ad-hoc network is normally made up of sensors. Therefore each sensor operates a multi-hop routing algorithm meaning that the base station can receive data packets from a number of different nodes. Most people would have seen documentaries based in the animal world where a creature is captured and a collar is placed around their neck, which contains a sensor. The scientists use this data to monitor the movements of the animal, which enables them to trace its movements with a very high degree of accuracy. One of the advantages of a WSN is that again, unlike the 'traditional' wireless devices mentioned above, the more nodes available the better the network operation. If a large amount of nodes are in a small location then the network is even stronger again (Flury et al., 2007).

There are different network topologies that apply to wireless sensor networks. The Star network is a simple communications topology in which a single base can send and receive data and messages to a number of remote nodes. These remote nodes can only send signals through the single base and are unable to send them between each other. The advantage of this is in its simplicity and the ability to keep the remote nodes power consumption to a minimum. The disadvantage of this is that the base must be within range with the other single remote nodes.

They are unable to operate through each other, therefore the base is vital. The Mesh network allows any node within the network to communicate with and through each other. If a node is out of range from another, then it can send a message through an intermediate node to forward the message to the desired node. The advantage of this network is that if a node fails then another is available to forward any signal. This network can also operate in a longer range, where communication between nodes is generally unlimited. The disadvantage of this system is that it uses a lot of power and the more distance between communication of the nodes, then the longer it will take. Finally, the Hybrid Star-Mesh network is a more versatile network and maintains the ability to keep the power of wireless sensor nodes to a minimum. Nodes with the lowest power are unable to forward messages, therefore minimal power is maintained. However, nodes with more power in this network are able to forward these messages from those of low power (Wilson, 2004).

Wireless Sensor Hardware

Sensor nodes can vary in size from the size of a glove compartment to a grain of sand although the latter are yet to be released commercially, only for military use. The cost of a node varies also, from as little as a few euros to hundreds of euros. The price is dependent on the network size and the applications required. There are generally two types of sensor nodes used in a WSN. They are sensor nodes and gateway nodes. Sensor nodes gather required data from their surroundings by means of sensors that are attached to them. The node links with other nodes in the vicinity to transmit data to a data gateway. Sensor nodes need to know about the topology of the network to enable data to reach the gateway node. Gateway nodes are the interface to the system or control centre in the WSN. They are also used by the host when data is being requested from the WSN as shown in Figure 16.

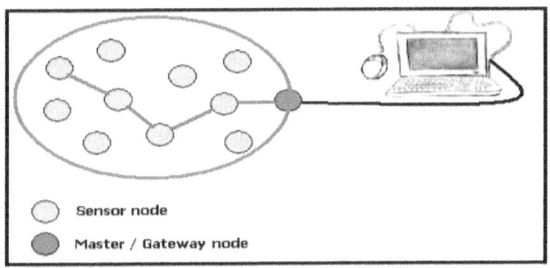

Figure 16: Sensor node and Gateway node

A sensor node is made up of a power source, a micro-controller, a transceiver, external memory and sensors (Figure 17). The sensor is the eyes and ears of the node and its main purpose is to sense or determine physical data from the target area. The sensor generates a signal, which represents a drop in temperature or the presence of a car for example. The wave that is generated goes through the analog-to-digital converter (ADC), which creates a digital signal. The binary signal is then sent to the micro-controller. More intelligent sensors such as MEMS have been made to determine a wider range of activities.

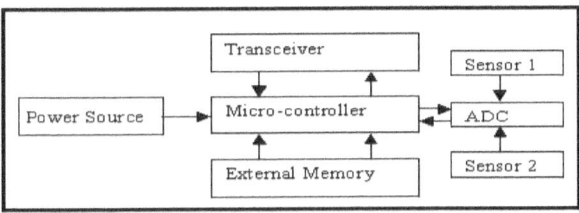

Figure 17: Sensor Node Architecture

Transceiver

All sensor nodes have a transmitter and a receiver. These components are both contained in a transceiver, which enables a node to receive data from another node and forward the data to another node as necessary. The operational states are Transmit, Receive, Idle and Sleep. When a radio is operating in idle mode it is absorbing almost as much power as it would in receive mode. Transceivers do not have a unique global identifier. Given the large number of sensor nodes manufactured worldwide it would be unrealistic to assign one to each node. The radio band used by sensor nodes is the industrial, scientific and medical (ISM) band that uses un-licensed frequencies. Components that use the ISM band need to be able to handle interference from other sources that may overlap. The frequency used by WSN's are between 433MHz and 2.4GHz. However, communication between medical devices may occupy multiple bands and use different protocols. To prevent interference in the excessively used unlicensed ISM band, biomedical devices may use the licensed wireless medical telemetry services (WMTS) band at 608 MHz (Stankovic, 2005). There are three modes of communication that could be used with sensor nodes. They are laser, infrared and radiofrequency (RF). As energy consumption is one of the major flaws with sensor nodes one would expect laser to be the preferred option as it uses less power than RF, does not need an antenna and is also robust when it comes to security. However, laser is very susceptible to atmospheric conditions. It also requires line of sight, which cannot always be guaranteed given the sometimes-covert nature of sensor node deployment. Although infrared doesn't need an antenna it has a restricted broadcasting capability. RF, which does need an antenna, is the easiest to use.

Microcontroller

The microcontroller processes the data that it receives from other components of the sensor node. Other options include microprocessors, and field-programmable gate arrays (FPGA). FPGAs are not very power efficient and do not work well with traditional programming techniques. They can be reprogrammed and reconfigured as necessary to eliminate deployment costs but this takes time and energy. Microcontrollers are a suitable choice for sensor node. They are the best choice for embedded systems. Because of their ability to connect to other devices, programmable, power consumption is less. This is because these devices can go to sleep state while part of controller is still active. The platform on the microcontroller needs to contain an instruction effective CPU, different HW interfaces, memory and a wake-up time. A power effective processor guarantees fast processing time and low power consumption. In order to keep expenses low and to prevent any further components being added to the already limited space the maximum number of feasible interfaces needs to be on a microcontroller. Microcontrollers and FLASH memory are the most applicable memory types given their amount of memory storage and price. The amount of memory needed depend on whether the memory is to be used for storing application data or for programming the device. The memory should generally be as little as possible as long as there is room for the application software and protocol. This will ensure that the cost and energy used are small (Zhao and Govindan, 2003).

Power Unit

Power consumption is one of the prime issues WSN have to deal with. There is more power required for communication than there is required for sensing or computing. The energy cost of transmitting 1 Kb a distance of 100 m is approximately the same as that for the executing 3 million instructions by 100 million instructions per second. Depending on the surroundings, two types of batteries are used, chargeable and non-chargeable as it would be impossible to change the battery in a hostile environment. Nowadays, sensors are being developed to recharge using solar power, thermogenerator or vibration energy. Another technology being used in sensor power units is Dynamic Power Management (DPM). This enables devices that are not being used to be switched off and on as necessary. This is performed with help from the operating system (Ruiz, 2005). Another power saving method is Dynamic Voltage Scheduling (DVS). In this method it is possible to reduce the power by a factor of four by varying the voltage with the frequency (Yu and Prasanna, 2003).

WSN Operating System

The operating system of a node is not as complicated as those of a standard PC. WSN applications have certain tasks that would not be used on a standard PC. User interfaces would be one example that would be used generally on a normal operating system but not on sensor nodes. The main characteristics of the operating system should be as follows:

- Small in size and energy efficient as sensor nodes are constrained in memory and power
- Ability to deal with packets in real-time and on-the-fly
- Provide a high degree of software modularity for application specific sensors
- Should be robust and reliable and able to workaround individual device failures

As hardware for wireless network systems are the same as traditional systems, operating systems such as eCOS and uC/OS can be used for wireless sensor networks. TinyOS is the operating system that was initially designed for sensor networks and was designed to be used in conjunction with the smartdust project. What is now known as the TinyOS Alliance started out as a project between University of Berkeley, California and Intel Research. It has been implemented by developers worldwide, on many platforms, for a wide variety of wireless sensor networks. It is written using the nesC programming language, which is based on the C programming language but aimed primarily at sensor networks where demands on concurrency and low power consumption are high but the hardware resources are limited (Levis et al., 2003). TinyOS is free and is used on the MICA2 platform. The fact that it is open source also means that many of the software components needed to use the platform are already written. This also makes it easier for the software to interface with different hardware. It is an event-driven operating system in that it is driven by external factors detected by the sensor. The core of the operating system is about 400 bytes which makes it suitable for every type of modern micro-controller. TinyOS has a two level scheduling structure i.e. its ability to perform extensive tasks which can be interrupted by an event. There are two interfaces, command and event. To smooth the progress of modularity, each component declares the commands it uses and the events it signals. The main tasks carried out are executing the main computation, calling lower level commands, signaling higher level commands and scheduling tasks within a component (Archer et al., 2007). The programming language used by TinyOS is nesC. This language is designed to detect race conditions between task and event handlers. As with nesC, there are also operating systems adaptable for the programming language C. These include MANTIS, BTnut, SOS, Contiki and Nano-RK. Nano-RK and MANTIS are based on multithreading, in which applications do not need to capitulate the microprocessor to other processes. Nano-RK is an operating system that allows tasks to be controlled, such as CPU time, networking and sensors. SOS and Contiki are also event driven operating systems like TinyOS. These are particular built for smaller modules and support the dynamism within these modules. BTnut is based on C programming and is a simple operating system.

Wireless Sensor Network Applications

There are numerous areas across many disciplines where a WSN could be deployed. It has been used in the farming industry for years using RFID technology. A farmer would use a WSN to keep track of cattle by placing nodes throughout the land and also placing a node on the animal. The node on the animal sends a signal to the node in the field and the farmer can see if any of the cattle are loose from the herd or in difficulty if the signal is coming from the same general area over a period of time. However, the agricultural industry could also use sensor for monitoring pH levels in the soil water. Modern smart buildings use WSN to monitor temperature and heat. However, this is a relatively new technology in this field and when it becomes more common there would be other areas in the building industry where WSN could be used such as in the health of the building itself. Sensors could be placed in certain areas of the structure during the building phase and a network could be setup that would provide stress or vibration readings from certain areas. The example in the introduction of this essay would be a prime example of what is to be expected from WSN.

Health services have introduced WSN monitoring in some areas in the US but again this is an emerging technology. Sensor nodes could be placed on patients in long term care to monitor their whereabouts. In the case of people who are recovering from an operation, if they had a node placed in strategic areas their conditions could be monitored from a central location and help sent if readings were abnormal, say blood pressure for example. It would also be helpful in an emergency involving numerous people where a monitor could be placed on all patients and those whose readings are worst could be dealt with first. Sensors can also be integrated into machinery, structures and the environment, along with accurate delivery of sensed information could provide many benefits. Some benefits would include conserving natural resources, fewer failures, improved manufacturing productivity, improved emergency response and enhanced security. An ideal wireless network sensor is networked and scalable and consumes little power. It should cost little money, reliable and easy to maintain. Recent advances have resulted in the ability to integrate sensors, radio communications, and digital electronics into a single integrated circuit. This enables networks of very low costs to communicate with each other using low power wireless data protocols. A key feature of a wireless sensor node is to reduce the amount of power consumed by the system. This sensor driven data collection model requires an algorithm to be loaded to the node to determine when to send data based on the event. The majority of WSNs that are energy efficient use multi-hop paths to keep transmission power low. Most WSN have just one gateway node which means that the nodes surrounding the gateway node are going to be used more often. These nodes are going to need to have their batteries replaced more often than the other nodes in the network as shown in Figure 18.

Figure 18: Batteries near gateway need to be replaced more often (Younis et al., 2003)

Multi-hop algorithms are used so that energy can be saved by sending packets of data to the nearest node. As the nodes closest to the gateway lose their power the network relies on the furthest nodes to perform the task of sending the data to the gateway. This uses more power and eventually the batteries need to be replaced. The whole network would eventually be brought down if this was to happen.

Conclusion

A sensor node, also known as a mote, is a node in a wireless sensor network that is capable of performing some processing, gathering sensory information and communicating with other connected nodes in the network. Wireless Sensor Networks are ideal for monitoring and analysing. Many shops use wireless sensor networks as a means to stop thieves. These sensors are equipped with alarms to ensure security levels are kept to a maximum. Wireless sensor networks are also suitable for monitoring movements in urban areas such as the desert and forests. It allows these areas to be monitored without the expense of labour. Wireless sensor networks are used to try and detect the risk of natural disasters as soon as possible and are fast to send data, giving people a chance to act. Security, using wireless sensor networks is one of the most important areas where it must be working correctly. In more urban areas there is less time dedicated to maintenance. Power must also be available to all security sensors at all times. A failure in power can result in high consequences if timing goes wrong. Some areas to indicate where wireless sensor networks can be used for security issues include monitoring disease, monitoring floods, vehicle tracking, monitoring volcanic eruptions, alarm signalling and forest fires.

Energy conservation is arguably the biggest issue facing sensor nodes as in some cases the batteries cannot be replaced due to the environment they are in and they need to be in operation for months. . If the network is proposed to do a lot more then more power will be needed to meet these requirements. Smart energy saving electronics with advanced power and rechargeable systems will provide a long term maintenance free wireless sensor network system. Security will also be an issue when nodes are being used in general everyday life. This could be fatal in medical monitoring so it is something that will have to be tested strenuously before being released to market. The future of wireless sensor networks is seen as being useful for road traffic accidents. These sensors can be used to indicate how serious the accident is and indicate how quickly the emergency services are to arrive. This could contribute to saving lives and is a useful method that can be employed. Areas such as health care and chemicals depend highly on wireless sensor networks to monitor and collect data which is essential to their activities. Other areas such as traffic monitoring and security are vital for communication. Wireless sensor networks provide to industry what it hasn't had before. The growth in technology has allowed the shift from an ordinary network to a wireless sensor network, and can perform operations such as monitoring the likelihood of a natural disaster. Wireless sensor networks also provide access to a wireless internet connection. This has become useful to many larger organisations and universities to enable everyone to have easier access to the Internet and be able to use laptops rather than being restricted to one area to have access to the Internet. Wireless sensor networks have enabled applications that were previously not practical. As new standards are being introduced and less powered systems are being developed, the growth and widespread deployment of the wireless sensor network will continue and will provide functions to people that has never been available previously.

References

Anon (2006) Smart Dust Stalked Zarqawi, StrategyPage.com, June 2006
http://www.strategypage.com/htmw/htecm/articles/20060610.aspx

Archer, W., Levis, P. and Regehr, J. (2007) Interface Contracts for TinyOS, *IPSN*, April 2007

Flury, R. and Wattenhofer, R. (2007) Routing, Anycast, and Multicast for Mesh and Sensor Networks, *Infocom*, May 2007

Khemapech, I., Duncan, I. and Miller, A. (2005). A survey of wireless sensor networks technology, Proceedings of The 6th Annual PostGraduate Symposium on The Convergence of Telecommunications, Networking and Broadcasting

Levis, P., Lee, N., Welsh, M. and Culler, D. (2003) TOSSIM: Accurate and Scalable Simulation of Entire TinyOS Applications., The First ACM Conference on Embedded Networked Sensor Systems (Sensys03), November 2003

Manges, W. (1999) It's Time for Sensors to Go Wireless. Part 1: Technological Underpinnings. Sensors Magazine., April 1999

Mainwaring, A. Polastre, J., Szewczyk, R., Culler, D., and Anderson, J. (2002) Wireless Sensor Networks for Habitat Monitoring, WSNA'02, September 2002

Ruiz, L., Braga, T., Silva, F., Assuncao, H., Nogueira, J., Loureiro, A. (2005) On the design of a self-managed wireless sensor network, IEEE Communications Magazine, Vol. 43, Issue 8, Aug. 2005 pp 95 – 102

Stankovic, J. (2005) Wireless Sensor Networks for In-Home Healthcare: Potential and Challenges in High Confidence Medical Device Software and Systems (HCMDSS) Workshop, Philadelphia, PA, June 2-3, 2005.

Wilson, J. (2004) Sensor Technology Handbook, Newnes Publishers, USA, ISBN:0750677295

Younis, M.; Bangad, M.; Akkaya, K. (2003) Base-station repositioning for optimized performance of sensor networks, Vehicular Technology Conference, 2003. IEEE 58th Vol. 5, Issue , 6-9 Oct. 2003, pp: 2956 - 2960

Yu, Y., Prasanna, V. (2003) Energy-balanced task allocation for collaborative processing in networked embedded systems, Proceedings of the 2003 ACM SIGPLAN conference on Language, compiler, and tool for embedded systems, June 11-13, 2003, San Diego, California, USA

Zhao, J. and Govindan, R. (2003) Understanding Packet Delivery Performance In Dense Wireless Sensor Networks, The First ACM Conference on Embedded Networked Sensor Systems (Sensys'03), November 2003

6   Disruption Tolerant Networking

Kevin Curran and James Knox

Disruption Tolerant Networking (DTN) is a technology that will provide network services for environments so extreme that no end-to-end path exists through a network. Disruption Tolerant Networking hopes to tackle the problem of communicating in areas where due to various factors normal means of communication have limited success and are unreliable. DTN is aimed specifically at networks which are subject to frequent and long lasting disruptions that destroy or severely degrade normal communications. This chapter provides an overview.

Introduction

Delay Tolerant Networking (DTN) is an approach to computer network architecture that seeks to address the technical issues in mobile or extreme environments that lack continuous network connectivity. In a DTN, asynchronous variable-length messages (called bundles) are routed in a store and forward manner between participating nodes over varied network transport technologies. Disruption Tolerant Networking is important due to the importance of managing network congestion. Congestion is caused by heavy traffic load which can result in long delays in data transmission due to retransmission because of data loss. Currently end to end congestion control is handled by the TCP protocol that prevents the network from collapsing but network degradation does occur when the network becomes congested. TCP/IP works well when there is no disruption to end-to-end communication. Disruption Tolerant Networking addresses weaknesses in TCP such as implementing congestion control mechanisms where each router can make decisions based on local information such as accepting a bundle of data from another router. This local information may include storage availability and the risk of accepting the data bundle based on previous experience, which may have had adverse effects on the network resulting in loss of data. This chapter provides a review of Delay Tolerant Networking.

Delay Tolerant Networking

Disruption Tolerant Networking allows messages to pass through the network with successive responsibilities, rather than the traditional end-to-end acknowledgement scheme (Riehn, 2004). The main thrust behind Disruption Tolerant Networking is survivability and resilience. The aim is to have a network that will work in environments where continuous end-to-end connectivity cannot be assumed. This could be due to environmental factors, underwater, in desert conditions, deep space, or during warfare. There are many benefits in such a system for example, in places that suffer from disaster or where normal communications are destroyed (Grover and Tipper, 2005). One of the problems with TCP is that it has a short time-out counter, therefore if no data is sent within a short period the circuit is shut down. This makes it unsuitable as a protocol in deep space as end-to-end connectivity would not be possible. Disruption Tolerant Networking is better suited as it is delay tolerant. Disruption Tolerant networking organises information flow into bundles. Messages pass through networks with successive responsibility unlike the current TCP structure that uses end to end acknowledgements. Intelligence is moved into the network to allow each network to make best choice on delivery of bundles via the optimal path.

Flow control is used to ensure that the destination can handle all incoming data. Congestion control is used when buffers in routers are under pressure due to the limitations of the buffer size. It limits the data loss within a network by inducing flow control which is automatically triggered when there is a difference in the arrival rate and transmission rate of data within the network. When the rates differ TCP will send an acknowledgement to the source which will reduce the transmission rate until transmission rate is equal to the arrival rate. This works well for the internet with end to end connectivity however where end to end connectivity cannot be guaranteed due to external factors this causes problems as automatic flow control and congestion control cannot work under the same set of rules. Unreliable connections make it difficult to ascertain when action is required to limit flow control or when to initialise congestion control (Grover and Tipper, 2005). The only way around this problem with DTN is to initiate congestion control by disregarding bundles due to resource depletion and returning bundles if, the management of local buffer space is under threat. In this case bundles would be returned to their destination address until the problem was rectified. The management of this system would require the sending application to issue differing TTLs with every bundle being sent depending on their importance and the conveyance of this bundle would be on the basis of the time to live being met. The downside of this would be to accept all bundles with a large TTL; however this has the disadvantage of depleting router buffer space for a long time and all the inherent problems this brings with it.

To help reduce the problems with TTLs and bundles being dropped, DTN implements a custodial transfer system to allocate preference to certain types of bundles that meet certain criteria, allowing for a more efficient system with the conveyance of high priority bundles at the expense of others. As high priority bundles would be forwarded faster than lower priority bundles it would mean that they would have a far better chance of reaching their destination before being timed out, this means that end to end latency would be lower allowing the added benefit of reducing the TTL at every point on the path and therefore increasing the delivery time, and reducing congestion. If a bundle meets the requirements of the congestion control algorithm which is applied to all bundles and if the inbound bundle is flagged for custody transfer then a custody acceptance message is sent back to the current custodian. This causes the bundle to be removed from the custodian's buffer freeing up buffer space and relieving congestion control (see Figure 19).

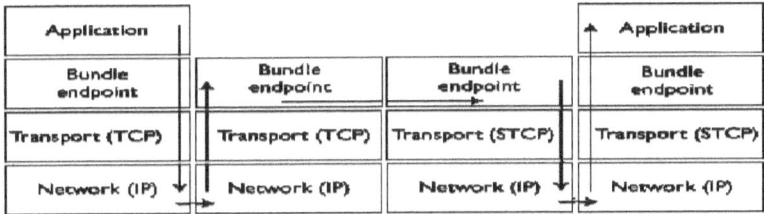

Figure 19: High priority

If a custody transfer bundle is refused then a custody refusal message is sent back to the current custodian along the originals sender route, this retriggers the resending of the bundle usually via a different route. At the same time, the absence of a custodial acceptance message triggers congestion control. Here congestion pressure at the current custodian remains unrelieved because the custodial bundle remains in the custodian's buffers, causing net space to increase over time (Burleigh et al., 2004). The problem with this is how one decides on the custodial timeout because unlike TCP/IP that has an end to end connection it is far harder to gauge the time of a round trip using the custodian method. However the benefit of the DTN based network systems is that unlike the protocol TCP/IP which requires a continuous end to end connection in order to work, the Custodial transfer system allows for breaks to occur in the connection of the end to end path which will not affect the data transmission as illustrated in Figure 20.

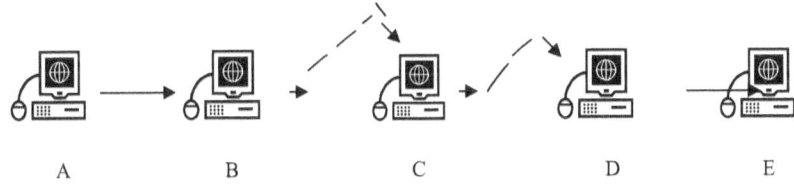

Figure 20: Custodial Transfer System

For example, if node A was trying to communicate with node E through nodes B,C and D then with the TCP/IP protocol this would not be possible as there is no continuous connection. However with DTN node C acts like a waterwheel first scooping the data from node B then releasing it to node D. This allows for there to be a break in connection between nodes C and D while the connection between B & C is open. Therefore it allows connections to be maintained even though connections to B & C and C & D were not opened concurrently. Thus the network integrity is maintained for bundle transfer to take place without the need for continuous end to end connection.

Conclusion

DTN based network systems are ideal for Interplanetary Networks which allow for long-haul communication capabilities where a continuous end to end link is not sustainable. Other places where DTN can be used include spacecraft, military/tactical, some forms of disaster response, underwater, and some form of ad-hoc sensor/actuator networks (Akyildiz, 2003). It may also include Internet connectivity in places where performance may suffer such as developing parts of the world.

References

Akyildiz, I., Akan, O., Chen, C., Fang, J., and Su, W. (2003) InterPlaNetary Internet: State-of-the-Art and Research Challenges, Computer Networks Journal, Vol. 43, Issue 2, pp. 75-113, October 2003.

Riehn, M. (2004). Disruption Tolerant Networking. Available at:
http://www.darpa.mil/sto/solicitations/DTN/proposers.htm Accessed [10th March 2007].

Burleigh, S., Jennings, E. and Schoolcraft, J. (2007) Autonomous Congestion Control in Delay-Tolerant Networks, American Institute of Aeronautics and Astronautics.
http://pdf.aiaa.org/preview/CDReadyMSPOPS06_1317/PV2006_5970.pdf [15th March 2007].

Grover, W. and Tipper, D. (2005) Design and Operation of Survivable Networks, Journal of Network and Systems Management, Special Issue on Designing and Managing Networks and Service Reliability, Vol. 13, No. 1, pp. 7-13

7   Streaming Audio on the Web

Jonathan Doherty, Kevin Curran, Paul Mc Kevitt

Streaming media across the Internet is still an unreliable and poor quality medium. Services such as audio-on-demand drastically increase the load on the networks therefore new, robust and highly efficient coding algorithms will be necessary. Packet delay from network congestion has been partially alleviated using routing protocols and application protocols such as real-time transport protocol (RTP). These have been developed to assign a higher priority to time dependant data. However, it is also the case that some servers automatically dump packets that are time sensitive, so streaming applications have had to resort to 'masking' the packets by using HTTP port 80 so packets appear as normal web traffic. This chapter provides an overview of the problems of maintaining a satisfactory quality of service when streaming audio over IP networks.

Introduction

Streaming media across the Internet is still an unreliable and poor quality medium. Current technologies for streaming media have gone as far as they can in regards to compression (both lossy and lossless) and buffering songs streamed from a web based server to clients. It is anticipated that in future we will witness the next revolution through telecommunications technology. In the past two decades the communications sector was one of the few constantly growing sectors in industry and a wide variety of new services were created. Digital and powerful communication networks are being discussed, planned or under construction. Services such as audio-on-demand drastically increase the load on the networks. The spread of the newly created compression standards such as MPEG 4 reflect the current demand for data compression. As these new services become available the demand of audio services through mobiles will increase. The technology for these services is available but suitable standards are yet to be defined. This is due to the nature of mobile radio channels, which are more limited in terms of bandwidth and bit error rates as for example the public telephone network. Therefore new, robust and highly efficient coding algorithms will be necessary. Audio, due to its timely nature requires guarantees that are very different in nature with regards to delivery of data from TCP traffic for ordinary HTTP requests. In addition, audio applications increase the set of requirements in terms of throughput, end-to-end delay, delay jitter and synchronization.

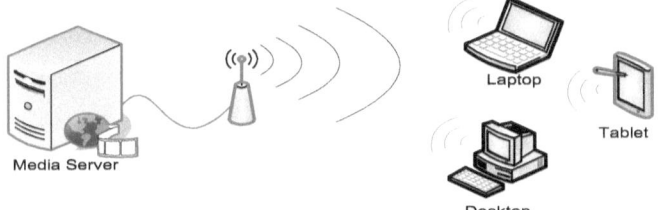

Figure 21: Streaming media across wireless networks

Applications such as Microsoft's Media Player and Real Audio have yet to overcome the problems attributed to using a network that is built upon a technology that does not rely on the order the information is sent, but more so the speed at which it travels. Despite a seemingly unlimited bandwidth, a Quality of Service protocol in place and high rates of compression, temporal aliasing still occurs giving the client a poor/unreliable connection where audio playback is patchy when unsynchronised packets arrive (see Figure 21). Traffic on a wireless network can be categorised in the same way as cabled networks. File transfers cannot tolerate packet loss but can take an undefined length of time. 'Real-time' traffic can accept packet loss (within limitations) but must arrive at its destination within a given time frame. Forward error correction (FEC) which usually involves redundancy built into the packets, and automatic repeat request (ARQ) (Perkins et al. 1998) are two main techniques currently implemented to overcome the problems encountered. However bandwidth restrictions limit FEC solutions and the 'real-time' constraints limit the effectiveness of ARQ.

The increase in bandwidths across networks should help to alleviate the congestion problem. However, the development of audio compression including the more popular formats such as Microsoft's Windows Media Audio WMA and the MPEG group's mp3 compression schemes have peaked and yet end users want higher and higher quality through the use of lossless compression formats on more unstable network topologies. When receiving streaming media over a low bandwidth wireless connection, users can experience not only packet losses but also extended service interruptions. These dropouts can last for as long as 15 seconds. During this time no packets are received and, if not addressed, these dropped packets cause unacceptable interruptions in the audio stream. A long dropout of this kind may be overcome by ensuring that the buffer at the client is large enough. However, when using fixed bit rate technologies such as Windows Media Player or Real Audio a simple packet resend request is the only method of audio stream repair implemented.

The latest addition to network protocols specifically addressing 'real-time' communication include Voice over Internet Protocol (VoIP), a technology that allows telephone calls using a broadband Internet connection across a packet switched network instead of a regular (or analog) phone line. The IPv6 header is a new format that is designed to keep header overhead to a minimum. This is achieved by moving both non-essential fields and optional fields to extension headers that are placed after the IPv6 header. The streamlined IPv6 header is more efficiently processed at intermediate routers. New fields in the IPv6 header define how traffic is handled and identified. Traffic identification in the IPv6 header allows routers to identify and provide special handling for packets belonging to a series of packets between a source and destination. Because the traffic is identified in the IPv6 header, better support for QoS (Quality of Service) can be achieved during transit for streaming applications.

One of the most recent additions to network communication is the inclusion of VoIP (Voice over Internet Protocol). This new technology allows users to make telephone calls using a computer to either another computer with an Internet connection, or a telephone (for the cost of a local call). VoIP converts the voice signal from a telephone/microphone into a digital signal that travels over the Internet and is converted back at the receiving computer. One of the driving forces behind VoIP is its cost; the Internet does not recognize state and country borders. With VoIP technology, the distinction between local, long-distance, and international calling largely disappears, and callers can save on long-distance and international charges. VoIP is not without its problems that are associated with real-time traffic across networks: packet delays/losses. One of the main issues Internet telephone applications such as Skype and Vonage face is the quality and reliability of communication via the Internet. The traditional public switched telephone network sets a high standard for IP telephony to match before mainstream acceptance. Both IPv6 and VoIP are important changes that have been made to current network communication protocols. Although the network reliability and overall QoS is greatly improved, there is still room for improvement. The core idea of the IPv6 header format shows the need for optional information to be included in packet headers. The VoIP protocol shows an area of time dependant communication, where error recovery is still in its infancy.

Audio Formats and File Compression

The number of audio formats has increased dramatically since the introduction of digital media. Previously when there was simply vinyl (LPs) and cassettes, audio was in an analogue format. With the introduction of digital storage a number of different formats have emerged, all serving a particular purpose. **Error! Reference source not found.** lists the most common of these:

File Extension	Origin/Name	Remarks
AU,SND,ULW	Sun Microsystems	Sun Microsystems file format
AIFF, AIF, AIFC	Audio Interchange File Format	File format for storing digital audio on Macintosh computers
GSM	GSM Audio File	Audio file used for GSM Supported devices
MIDI, MID, SMF	Musical Instrument Digital Interface	Protocol designed for recording and playback on digital synthesizers.
MP3	Moving Pictures Experts Group	MPEG 1 audio layer 3 compresses files to 1/12 of their size
WAV, WMA	Microsoft	Audio file that has become a standard PC audio format with CD level quality

The three main formats most commonly used by PCs are WAV, MP3 and MIDI. The Waveform Audio File format is the standard audio format for Microsoft Windows, but is now also supported by Macintosh computers.MP3 is the most popular audio format around, developed by the Fraunhofer Institute in Germany in 1991. MP3 files are able to produce good/reasonable sound quality and yet maintain small file sizes. By removing audio that the human ear cannot hear file sizes can be reduce by up to one twelfth of its original size. MIDI was developed for communication between electronic musical instruments. The file contains no audio information but instead commands for a series of notes (with information on their length and volume). MIDI files can be played on a MIDI player (application) using the available "instrument" sounds using a sound card on a PC or any other compatible device.

Compression and Mp3s

In order to make audio files more manageable it is necessary to reduce their size, and there are a number of ways in which this can be done. One method is to reduce the sampling frequency (Menin, 2002) of the recording system, however, this has some serious side-effects as far as sound quality is concerned, high-frequency content of the sound is lost, leading to recordings lacking in brightness and clarity. Mp3 compression uses a number of perceptual coding techniques to reduce file size and yet maintain quality audio. Through the use of lossy compression the sample rate of Mp3 files determines the level of quality. CD audio format uses a 16bit sample rate (samples measured every 44.1kHz or 44,100 slices every second) which equates to 5.2Mb per minute of recording. The sample rate is the number of times an audio is measured per second. Mp3 files can be sampled at the following levels:

- 1411 bitrate – CD Quality
- 192 bitrate – good CD quality mp3 files
- 128 bitrate – near CD quality.
- 64 bitrate – FM Broadcast quality.
- 32 bitrate – AM radio quality.

Most mp3 files are compressed to either the 128 bitrate or the 64 bitrate. An acceptable loss of quality is permitted for the advantages of the reduced file size. It is for this reason mp3 files are so popular within the Internet and networks. The last few years have seen an impressive growth in multimedia content on the Internet. One striking success in this area has been mp3 audio, which has led to the development of mp3 players, such as the iPod. Another recent area of growth is wireless networks, both in wide area technologies such as 2.5G/3G and local area technologies such as 802.11b.

Jitter control

Streaming audio over a network has one serious problem associated with it: Jitter. This is when media being played back starts and stops as the packets of the stream are sent inconsistently. Because of the nature of networks, it is possible for packets sent to arrive in a different order than they were originally sent. The receiving application then has to restructure these into their correct order. In the context of streaming this can be devastating as portions of audio may arrive too late to be played, leading to sections of the audio to be dropped altogether – making the audio sound jittery. This effect is compounded by the quality of the transmission; high quality audio signals require a large number of packets that in turn require a larger bandwidth (Bush et al., 2000). Jitter control can be managed at hops across the network. At each hop a packet is examined to determine its position relative to the rest of the stream. If packets are found to be 'lagging behind' they can be forwarded with priority over other packets in the same stream. Likewise, packets that have managed to jump the queue are 'slowed down' to allow others to catch up. Jitter occurs more frequently when streaming audio across wireless networks. The nature of wireless communication and its inconsistencies amplify the effects of packet loss when bursty packet losses occur. Streaming media players are almost indifferent to the format of an audio file before streaming, but results from analysis vary greatly depending on the format used. The quality of the audio signal received depends greatly on both jitter and file formats.

Aspects of Audio Analysis

Sounds are traditionally described by their pitch, loudness, duration, and timbre. The first three of these psychological perceptions are well understood and can be accurately modelled by measurable acoustic features. A number of different qualities of audio must be analysed before a complete picture can be gained.

- *Loudness*: Notes can be played with varying degrees of strength in that the same note when analysed will have very different signal strengths. It is computed by the signal's root-mean-square (RMS) level in decibels.
- *Pitch* is the perception of the frequency of a note and is often cited as one of the fundamental aspects of music. Pitch is estimated by taking a series of short-time Fourier spectra. For each of these frames, the frequencies and amplitudes of the peaks are measured and an approximate greatest common divisor algorithm is used to calculate an estimate of the pitch.
- *Frequency* is the physical measurement of vibration and is often confused with pitch. For example, to the human ear the note *A* above *middle C* is perceived to be of the same pitch as *middle C*, but is not at the same frequency.
- *Brightness* is a measure of the higher frequency content of the signal. Brightness is computed as the centroid of the short-time Fourier magnitude spectra and can change over the same range as pitch. However, it cannot be lower than the pitch at the same interval.
- *Timbre*: "The quality of a sound by which a listener can tell that two sounds of the same loudness and pitch are dissimilar" (ANSI, 1973). The definition of timbre is greatly debated but generally accepted as the combination of all the remaining attributes of music, i.e.: *melody, harmony, rhythm*, and *dynamics*.

Two inherent problems associated with MIR (Music Information Retrieval) are the complexity of audio and the complexity of the query (Downie, 2004). Music is a combination of pitch, tempo, timbre, and rhythm, making analysis of music more difficult than text. Structuring a query for music is made difficult owing to the varying representations and interpretations including natural transitions in music. Monophonic style queries usually perform better where simple note matching can be used whereas polyphonic audio files and queries simply compound the problem. Adding to the complexity of music structure and query structure is the method of analysis of audio. The format of an audio file limits its type of use, different file formats exist to allow for better reproduction, compression and analysis. Hence it is also true that different digital audio formats lend to different methods of analysis. Musical Instrument Digital Interface (MIDI) files were created to distribute music playable on synthesisers of both the hardware and software variety among artists and equipment and because of its notational style allows analysis of pitch, duration and intensity (Doraisamy & Rueger, 2004). An excellent tool for analysis of MIDI files is the MIDI Toolbox (Eerola & Toiviainen, 2004) which is based on symbolic musical data but signal processing methods are applied to cover such aspects of musical behaviour as geometric representations and short-term memory. Besides simple manipulation and filtering functions, the toolbox contains cognitively inspired analytic techniques that are suitable for context dependent musical analysis, a prerequisite for many music information retrieval applications. However, reproduction of a MIDI file can vary greatly on different machines simply from differences between the composers and listeners equipment and it is because of this it is not used for general audio playback. Pulse code modulation (PCM) is a common method of storing and transmitting uncompressed digital audio. Since it is a generic format, it can be read by most audio applications similar to the way a plain text file can be read by word-processing applications. PCM is used by Audio CDs and digital audio tapes (DATs). Support for WAV files was built into Windows 95 making it the de facto standard for sound on PCs. This format for storing sound in files in PCs was developed jointly by Microsoft and IBM.

Digital Signal Processing

Most forms of audio analysis using computers to identify its characteristics involves digital signal processing (DSP). A varied number of different techniques have been used to analyse audio for different qualities. The results required determine the type of analysis that is used. However, almost all forms of DSP are based on one core principle Fourier analysis (also known as spectral analysis, frequency analysis, or harmonic analysis). Fourier analysis is a mathematical technique for describing a series of waves in terms of repeated cycles of components. One of the core principals of Fourier analysis is that it is based on an infinitely repeating signal. Discrete Fourier Transform (DFT) transforms a series of discrete observations measured over a finite range of time into a discrete frequency-domain spectrum (Williams, 1997). The resultant output of DFT analysis is a continuous frequency spectrum that includes all the frequencies. It should be noted that results from Fourier analysis depends on the sampling interval used, a large sample interval can lead to information being missed.

The fast Fourier transform (FFT) is a discrete Fourier transform algorithm that reduces the number of computations needed. One of the shortcomings of the Fourier Transform is that it does not give any information on the time at which a frequency component occurs. One approach which gives information on the time resolution of the spectrum is the short time Fourier transform (STFT). STFT uses a moving window over the signal and the Fourier transform is applied to the signal within the window as the window is moved. One problem associated with DFT analysis is leakage. A DFT is calculated over a finite sample using a rectangular window where abrupt changes at the beginning and end of the window cause leakages. A window is applied to both the beginning and the end of the sample interval to smooth out to a single common amplitude value. The basic window used to smooth the signal is the triangle window, other windows that reduce leakage even more include the Hanning window and the Hamming window: similar to the Hanning window except raised on a pedestal (Lyons, 1997).

MPEG 7 and DSP

One of the most common formats for audio compression is mp3, defined by the Moving Picture Experts Group (MPEG). The mp3 format uses perceptual audio coding and psychoacoustic compression to remove all the audio the ear cannot hear. It also adds a modified discrete cosine transform (MDCT) that implements a filter bank, increasing the frequency resolution 18 times higher than that of its predecessor MPEG Layer 2. The result in real terms is mp3 coding shrinks the original audio signal from a CD (PCM format) by a factor of 12 without sacrificing sound quality, i.e. from a bit rate of 1411.2kbps of stereo music to 112-128kbps. Because mp3 files are small, they can easily be transferred across the Internet. MPEG 7 (Martinez, 2002) is a standardised description of various types of multimedia information. Where MPEG 4 defines the layout and structure of a file and codecs, MPEG 7 is a more abstract model that uses a language to define description schemes and descriptors – the Description Definition Language (DDL). Using a hierarchy of classification allows different granularity in the descriptions. All the descriptions encoded using MPEG 7 provides efficient searching and filtering of files depending on the search criteria. MPEG 4 replaces MPEG 3, which was incorporated into MPEG 2 rather than creating another standard. It should be noted that the MPEG 7 standard only specifies the format for descriptions of content, and not the algorithms to utilise its descriptions. Only recently have developers begun implementation of the standard. MPEG 7 classes and application developments have primarily been in the Java and C++ language formats by a number of researchers/institutes including the MPEG 7 Library by the Joanneum Research group (Joanneum, 2005) and an MPEG 7 Audio Encoder by Holger Crysandt (Wellhausen & Crysandt, 2005). The MPEG 7 Library is a comprehensive list of over 800 description schemes and descriptors using classes in C++, which allows developers to use the functionality of MPEG 7 in their own applications. Whereas the Java MPEG 7 Audio Encoder is a complete application for MPEG 7 analysis with the audio analysis results stored in the XML format. The Java MPEG 7 Audio Encoder can be launched from the web using Java virtual machine or on the local machine as a command line application. The audio encoder returns data in an XML format based on AudioPowerType, AudioSpectrumCentroidType, AudioWaveformType, AudioSpectrumEnvelopeType, AudioSpectrumFlatnessType and AudioSpectrumSpreadType. Although not as complete as other systems, it has already been used as an analysis tool by other researchers for similarity analysis and pattern recognition (Matushima et al., 2004). The descriptions encoded using MPEG 7 can provide efficient searching and filtering of files.

The AudioSpectrumEnvelope descriptor describes the short-term power spectrum of the audio waveform as a time series of the distribution of energy and can be used to generate a spectrogram to aid search and comparisons. The AudioSpectrumEnvelope descriptor describes the spectrum of the audio according to a logarithmic frequency scale resulting in a scalar output of values. The spectrum consists of one coefficient representing power between 0Hz and loEdge, a series of coefficients representing power between loEdge and hiEdge, and a coefficient representing power beyond hiEdge. To extract the AudioSpectrumEnvelope involves the use of a sliding window Fast Fourier Transform analysis. The spectral centroid measures the average frequency of a spectrum and is usually averaged over time. A spectral frame is some number of samples which is equal to the size of the FFT. The higher the centroid, the *brighter* the sound. The implementation of MPEG 7 using specific DSP techniques allows analysis of audio to be performed to an agreed standard, thereby removing the need for developers to re-invent the wheel.

Streaming Audio Approaches to Packet Loss

Solutions to the inherited problems within streaming audio have included research into a number of varying techniques. The probability of packet loss across bursty networks has been modelled where time delay is used to control the flow of packets and measure the difference between the current time and the time the packet arrives (Lee & Chanson, 2004). This technique can be used to predict network behaviour and adjust audio compression based on current network behaviour. Higher compression results in poorer quality audio but reduces network congestion through smaller packets. A variation of this theme has been used to create new protocols that allow scalable media streaming (Mahanti et al., 2003). Randomising packet order to alleviate the large gaps associated with bursty losses was implemented, where the problem was reduced by re-ordering the packets before they are sent and reassembled into the correct order at the receiver (Varadarajan et al., 2002). This reduced the bursty loss effect since packets lost were from different time segments. Although nothing is done to replace the missing packets, overall audio quality had improved through smaller gaps in the audio – albeit more frequent.

A number of techniques that use some form of redundancy where repetition is used to replace lost audio segments have been developed. Sending packets containing the same audio segments but with a lower bit-rate alongside the high bit-rate encoding increases the likelihood of packet arrival but at the loss of audio quality, as well as increasing the overall network bandwidth usage (Perkins et al., 1998). Another approach to using redundancy in the form of unequal error protection (UEP) was developed, where improvement is achieved with an acceptable amount of redundancy using advanced audio encoding (AAC) (Wang et al., 2003). Segmentation of the audio into different classes such as drumbeats and onset segments allows priority to be applied to more important audio segments with ARQ applied to high priority segments and reconstruction technique for the replacement of low priority segments based on the AAC received in previous segments. One of the most recent methods of interpolation of low bit-rate coded voice is used where observation of high correlation of linear predictors within adjacent frames allowed descriptions to be inserted using linear spectral pairs (LSP), and then reconstruct lost LSPs using linear interpolation (Wah & Lin, 2005).

Voice Communication

Traditional methods for interpolation between lost packets are still popular with Internet telephone applications where timing is critical with limited signal degradation is acceptable. State of the art research into forward error correction range from Waveform Similarity Overlap Add (Liang et al., 2003) where lost packets of a section of voice are merged based on pitch similarity rather than straightforward interpolation. WSOLA decomposes the input into overlapping segments of equal length, which are then realigned and superimposed to form the output with equal and fixed length. Using a windowing technique minimises the changes in signal strength of the two segments. This leads to increased processing overhead, but concealment is possible if packet loss is limited to one or two sections.

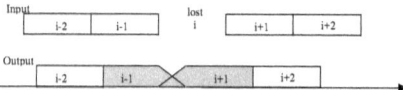

Figure 22: WSOLA Loss Concealment

FS-CELP (Lin & Wah, 2005) is an implementation of the Federal Standard 1016 Code Excited Linear Prediction, based on the principle of linear predictive coding. Linear Predictive Coding (LPC) is a powerful speech analysis technique, and one of the most common methods for encoding good quality speech at a low bit rate. LPC provides relatively accurate estimates of speech parameters. Using multi-description coding, FS-CELP allows multiple descriptions of the signal to be encoded into two streams - odd and even samples. Reconstruction of the original signal is possible if only one of the two streams is lost. Only with the loss of both odd and even streams is error correction not possible.

Building redundancy into packets is a popular method for FEC; FreePhone (Bolot et al., 1999) uses an adaptive approach where redundancy is coded depending on the loss characteristics of the network at that time (using RTCP feedback). Bolot justifies this by pointing out that there is little point in using high levels of redundant information encoded into the packets if there is little chance of it being used. The actual method for FEC used is a simple 'next packet scenario' where packet n is encoded with not only its own data, but a redundant version of packet *n-1*. In the event that packet loss occurs for packet *n-1*, the packet can be reconstructed using the information encoded into packet *n*. Using an adaptive approach minimises the extra network bandwidth required to carry the redundant data, thereby reducing the overhead required to use FEC.

Audio/Video Streaming

Many techniques used for error correction when streaming audio can also be applied when video signals are sent as well. Traditional ARQ methods have been improved with the use of Gap Detection in packets where a large number of packets in sequence are lost. Detection of large gaps allow for a retransmission request before buffer levels run low, thereby allowing sufficient time for the missing segments to be resent. Another approach is to use timeout detection where, packet loss is detected by estimating the arrival time of packets. If a packet hasn't arrived by a certain deadline, it is assumed to be lost and an ARQ is sent. Both these techniques have their merits under certain conditions, but a combination of these has been used to improve overall performance (Sze et al., 2001). One of the drawbacks of this approach is that there is no reduction in the buffer size. Techniques for correction of video frames very similar to audio approaches in that temporal concealment methods estimate the missing section based on interpolation between previous and next blocks of the frame (Pyun et al., 2003). The BMVT (Bidirectional Motion Vector Tracking) system is unique as it uses previous and future frames to predict the content of the missing segment rather than preceding and subsequent blocks within the current frame. Based on the principal that an average value can be taken of a similar segment of blocks between the previous and subsequent frames, a best possible match can be used for the missing blocks in the current frame. Where this approach is beneficial to video error correction (based on the similarity of continuous frames of video), audio does not follow the same linear path.

Utilising measurements of network congestion and delay has led some research into reduction of overall signal quality through more lossy encoding at the server, thereby alleviating traffic requirements. Adjusting the audio quality constantly in relation to network traffic increases the reliability of packets arriving within the time constraints. The main feature of the ZeroChain encoder (Leslie & Sandler, 2001) is the 'Bit Allocation' procedure which produces a chain of bits in which the most important information appears first, and the least important information appears last. This means that the ZeroChain (encoded audio) may be cut at any point, keeping the more important parts of the audio. Using this method allows audio quality to be scaled as network bandwidth constraints fluctuate. One of the problems that ZeroChain does not overcome is 'bit errors'. Packets can be dropped by networks when bit errors occur within packets, hence these losses cannot be compensated for. Research by Wyse et al. (2003) makes use of percussion repetition and encodes it separately in the signal. Using predictive techniques packet loss can be compensated in the audio signal by recreating the percussion based on the information coded in the other segments.

Conclusion

Solutions to the inherited problems within streaming audio have included research into a number of varying techniques. The probability of packet loss across bursty networks has been modelled where time delay is used to control the flow of packets and measure the difference between the current time and the time the packet arrives. In general, most streaming audio applications aim to improve reliability by meeting the constraints of the network rather than deal with multiple types of errors (Leslie & Sandler, 2001). Other systems apply the technique of randomising the order of packets prior to transmission (Varadarajan et al., 2002); this reduces the effects of bursty errors as the group of packets lost is spread evenly over a larger area.

References

ANSI (1973) American National Standard: Psychoacoustical Terminology. Technical Report, S3.20, American National Standards Institute.

Bolot, J. C., S. Parisis, and D. Towsley (1999) Adaptive FEC-Based Error Control for Internet Telephony. In IEEE INFOCOM, Volume 3, 1453–1460.

Bush, S. F., A. Kulkarni, S. Evans, and L. Galup (2000) Active Jitter Control. In 7th International Intelligence in Services and Networks Conference (ISN). Athens, Greece.

Doraisamy, S. and S. Rueger (2004) A Polyphonic Music Retrieval System Using N-Grams. Presented at the 5th International Conference on Music Information Retrieval, ISMIR 2004, Barcelona, Spain.

Downie, J.S. (2004) The Scientific Evaluation of Music Information Retrieval Systems: Foundations and Future. In Computer Music journal, Vol. 28, Issue 2, 12 – 23.

Eerola, T.and P. Toiviainen (2004) MIDI Toolbox: MATLAB Tools for Music Research. University of Jyväskylä, Kopijyvä, Jyväskylä, Finland. Available at http://www.jyu.fi/musica/miditoolbox.

Joanneum (2005) MPEG 7 Library: A Complete API to Manipulate MPEG 7 Documents. Joanneum Research. Available at: http://iis.joanneum.at/mpeg%2D7/ Site last visited 08/06/2005.

Lee, K.K. and S.T. Chanson (2004) Packet Loss Probability for Bursty Wireless Real-time Traffic Through Delay Model. In IEEE Transactions on Vehicular Technology, Volume 53, Issue: 3, 929 – 938.

Leslie, B. and M. Sandler (2001) Packet Loss Resilient, Scalable Audio Compression and Streaming for IP Networks. In The Second International Conference on 3G Mobile Communication Technologies. London, England. 119 - 123.

Liang, Y.J., N. Farber, and B. Girod (2003) Adaptive Playout Scheduling and Loss Concealment for Voice Communication over IP Networks. In IEEE Transactions on Multimedia, Volume 5, Issue 4, 532 - 543.

Lyons R.G. (1997) Understanding Digital Signal Processing. Reading, Massachusetts, Addison Wesley.

Mahanti, A., D.L. Eager, M.K. Vernon, and D.J. Sundaram-Stukel (April 2003) Scalable On-Demand Media Streaming with Packet Loss Recovery. In IEEE/ACM Transactions on Networking, Volume 11, Issue: 2, 195 – 209.

Matushima,R., D. Hiramatsu, and R. Melo Silveira (2004) Integrating MPEG-7 Descriptors and Pattern Recognition: An Environment for Multimedia Indexing and Searching. In Proceedings of the WebMedia and LA-Web 2004 Joint Conference 10th Brazilian Symposium on Multimedia and the Web 2nd Latin American Web Congress, Volume 10, 125-132.

Martinez, J.M. (2002) Overview of MPEG-7 Description Tools. IEEE Multimedia, Vol. 9, Issue 3, 83 – 93.

Menin, E. (2002) The Media Streaming Handbook. Upper Saddle River, New Jersey, U.S.A. Prentice Hall.

Perkins, C., O. Hodson, and V. Hardman (1998) A Survey of Packet-loss Recovery Techniques for Streaming Audio. In IEEE Network Magazine. Issue 5, Volume 12, 40-48.

Pyun, J., J. Lee, J. W. Jeong, J. H. Jeong, and S. Ko (2003) Robust Error Concealment for Visual Communications in Burst-Packet-Loss Networks. In IEEE Transactions on Consumer Electronics, Volume 49, Issue 4, 1013 - 1019.

Sze, H.P., S.C. Liew, and Y.B. Lee (2001) A Packet-Loss-Recovery Scheme for Continuous-Media Streaming Over the Internet. In IEEE communications Letters, Volume 5, Issue 3, 116 - 118.

Varadarajan, S., H.Q. Ngo, and J. Srivastava (2002) Error Spreading: a Perception-driven Approach to Handling Error in Continuous Media Streaming. In IEEE/ACM Transactions on Networking, Vol. 10, Issue 1, 139 – 152.

Wah, B. and D. Lin (2005) LSP-based Multiple-description Coding for Real-time Low Bit-Rate Voice Over IP. In IEEE Transactions on Multimedia, Volume 7, Issue 1, 167 – 178.

Wang, Y., A. Ahmaniemi, D. Isherwood, and W. Huang (2003) Content-Based UEP: A New Scheme for Packet Loss Recovery in Music Streaming. In Proceedings of Eleventh ACM International Conference on Multimedia, Berkeley, CA, USA. 412 – 421.

Wellhausen, J. and H. Crysandt (2003) Temporal Audio Segmentation Using MPEG-7 Descriptors. In Proceedings of SPIE Storage and Retrieval for Media Databases, Volume 5021.

Williams, G. P. (1997) Chaos Theory Tamed. Taylor and Francis Limited, London.

Wyse, L., Y. Wang, and X. Zhu (2003) Application of a Content-based Percussive Sound Synthesizer to Packet Loss Recovery in Music Streaming. In Proceedings of 11th ACM International Conference on Multimedia. Berkeley, CA, USA. 335 – 338.

8   Cognitive Radio

Kevin Curran, Gary O'Callaghan, Fionnuala McCullough

Cognitive radio (CR) can monitor, observe, and react to events in a specified environment. The fundamental benefits are the ability to self-adapt, self-manage, and self-optimize under normal conditions, and the ability to self-diagnose and self-heal when unusual problems arise e.g. base stations can automatically adjust operating range (e.g., by controlling transmit power, receiver sensitivity, data rate, frequency channel selection) to compensate for neighboring base stations that fail. In contrast to many wireless systems where static frequency channels are pre-selected in advance and tedious frequency planning is mandatory to minimize interference from equipment operating in adjacent coverage areas. CR can achieve a performance that is close to a licensed band even when using an unlicensed band due primarily to its inherent ability to switch to best channels. This chapter provides an overview of Cognitive Radio.

Introduction

Cognitive radio is where wireless devices are sufficiently computationally intelligent about radio resources and related computer-to-computer communications to detect user communications needs as a function of use context, and provide radio resources and wireless services most appropriate to those needs. Its roots came from the discovery by regulatory bodies in various countries which found that most of the radio frequency spectrum was inefficiently utilised. For example, cellular network bands are overloaded in most parts of the world, but amateur radio and paging frequencies are not. Independent studies concluded that spectrum utilization depends strongly on time and place. Moreover, fixed spectrum allocation prevents rarely used frequencies from being used by unlicensed users, even when their transmissions would not interfere at all with the assigned service.

The term cognitive radio (CR) was invented by Joseph Mitola (Mitola et al., 1999). CR refers to a software based radio system which is capable of sensing factors in its environment such as geographical location and the RF characteristics of other radio devices in the same locale, the CR device can then alter its power, frequency, modulation and other parameters to dynamically reuse available radio spectrum (Mannion, 2004). CR builds on the invention of Software Defined Radio (SDR), whereby for example the software in a cell phone defines the parameters of operation when the user moves from place to place. In the US the development CR is led by the Federal Communication Commission (FCC), who deal with commercial applications, and the Defence Advanced Research Projects Agency (DARPA), who deal with military applications (Mannion, 2004).

Cognitive radio can monitor, observe, and react to events in a specified environment. The fundamental benefits are the ability to self-adapt, self-manage, and self-optimize under normal conditions, and the ability to self-diagnose and self-heal when unusual problems arise e.g. base stations can automatically adjust operating range (e.g., by controlling transmit power, receiver sensitivity, data rate, frequency channel selection) to compensate for neighboring base stations that fail. In contrast to many wireless systems where static frequency channels are pre-selected in advance and tedious frequency planning is mandatory to minimize interference from equipment operating in adjacent coverage areas. CR can achieve a performance that is close to a licensed band even when using an unlicensed band due primarily to its inherent ability to switch to best channels (Devroye et al., 2006). This chapter will present an overview of cognitive radio but first we introduce the concepts of licensed and unlicensed frequency bands and software defined radio.

Licensed and Unlicensed Frequency Bands

It can be extremely difficult to locate radio spectrum and even harder to find spectrum that is available worldwide. Spectrum allocation in the international community is controlled by multiple regulatory bodies such as the FCC in U.S., MKK in Japan and CEPT in Europe). The Licensed bands are generally not prone to interference problems but premium licensed bands can be costly. For example, 2.5 GHz, 3.5 GHz (outside U.S.) and the 4.9 GHz (public safety) are popular licensed bands for wireless access e.g., Wi-Max, wireless DOCSIS. The license-free frequency bands however are widely employed and they provide dynamic, opportunistic access to spectrum for a limited time period. There are benefits such as large-scale frequency planning is avoided and ad-hoc networks also become possible. The 5 GHz band is increasingly used to support wireless backhaul transmissions e.g., multihop mesh networks. It is becoming increasingly deregulated and in the UK market forces are starting to have a bigger say in the use and allocation of radio spectrum e.g. the UK recently deregulated 865-868 MHz band for RFID use.

In the US the FCC assigns users to specific frequencies which include AM, FM radio, shortwave, citizens band, VHF and UHF for TV and bands for cellular phones, GPS, air traffic control, security alarms and radio controlled keys. With the development of new wireless devices the demand on the radio spectrum will only continue to increase (Ashley, 2006). Legacy hardware can exacerbate this shortage, for example vacuum tube TV sets in the 1950's forced new transistor based model to receive only VHF signals. Such hardware related inflexibility is now addressed by software based wireless designs. The next generation wireless technology called Software Defined Radio (SDR) uses embedded signal-processing algorithms to sift out weak signals and reconfigurable code structures to receive and transmit new radio protocols (Ashley, 2006). SDR code and other programmable radio frequency front end interface technologies on laptops could receive TV signals. If fitted with an SDR RF card, for instance, a laptop could then be used as a cellular handset or base station. CR advances this situation by allowing the SDR system to reconfigure its analog RF output, and incorporate self awareness, transmission protocols and etiquette. This would free the user a controlling network and their contract fees (Ashley, 2006).

In 2004, the FCC commissioned a Notice of Proposed Rule Making for how CR could be realized. This coincided with other work to open up new radio spectrum to commercial use, e.g. opening spectrum between 3.1 and 10.6 GHz to commercial use for ultra wideband signalling. In their Spectrum Policy Taskforce report of 2002 the FCC recommended a migration towards a "policy based" solution allowing an opportunity to seamlessly move across spectrum using policy engines to check whether this is permissible (Mannion, 2004). The FCC has identified much potential in allowing the 6MHz wide band in the UHF band currently assigned for television to be opened up for to secondary markets for last mile data access. This would give the 54 Mbps available with WiFi but the bandwidth delivered would be useful especially in rural areas (Mannion, 2004). It is worth noting that the entire radio spectrum up to 100 GHz only 5 - 10% is in use at any given instant (Bing, 2004). Software Defined Radio will allow the industry to find more creative and efficient use of the airwaves, which in turn, will continue to bring benefits to consumers however software must have sufficient controls so that devices cannot be modified to operate outside FCC-approved parameters. In September 2005, Cisco received the first FCC certification for 802.11a SDR.

Cognitive Radio

Software defined radio (SDR) is seen as a key technology for future wireless communications (Bing, 2004). SDR hardware is largely reconfigurable and reprogrammable by software. This opens the way for new services and prolongs the lifespan of wireless devices. A device with flexible radio hardware is capable of running different applications, much like PC hardware. A high degree of reconfiguration requires support for different system functionalities. Multi-band systems support more than one frequency band and multi-homing systems support more than one radio standard or service. An example of SDR technology is Motorola's Canopy product[1]. Cognitive Radio (CR) is a concept with which a network or wireless node changes its transmission parameters without interfering with licensed users. The alteration of these parameters is based on several factors found in the external and internal radio environment. Examples of these factors are the radio frequency spectrum, user behaviour and network state. The main functions that a Cognitive Radio can perform are:

- Spectrum Sensing – Detecting unused spectrum and sharing it without interference to others.
- Spectrum Management – Capturing the best spectrum to meet user requirements.
- Spectrum Mobility – a cognitive radio user exchanges the frequency of the operation.
- Spectrum Sharing – Provides a spectrum scheduling method.

Smart radio that leverages on SDR hardware to perform intelligent and opportunistic sharing of unlicensed radio spectrum employs real-time interaction with its environment to determine transmitter parameters such as frequency, power, modulation and learns when to operate and when to interrupt service. Smart radio must rely on intelligent protocols to adapt spectrum use in response to location and operating environment ultimately leads

---

[1] http://motorola.canopywireless.com/

to "plug and play" wireless systems which require minimum or virtually no manual intervention or frequency management during deployment.

Potential military applications for CR are being developed by DARPA in their XG (next generation communications) in order to allow multiple users to share spectrum in a way that coexists and complements sharing protocols used in WiFi technologies (Mannion, 2004; Bing, 2004). CR is capable of reconfiguring its communication functions based on prior experience, so in the case of car radio, CR would allow the device to build up a database of propagation characteristics, signal strength of different transmission bands throughout car journeys. It could then use this information to decide how best to transmit at different times of the day and in different places. This dynamic use of bandwidth will free up the radio spectrum and allow for more RF options which are more dependable and considerably cheaper than at present (Ashley, 2006).

In traditional wireless systems most of the intelligence to make the network operate efficiently resides centrally in the network. In CR by contrast this intelligence would reside in the handsets, laptops or wireless devices. A cognitive controlled subsystem controls the SDR allowing a CR unit to detect RF networking opportunities wherever it finds itself. It is envisioned that CR devices will exist in networks of other CR devices with each contributing to and taking information from a central database which contains the information necessary to transmit effectively in a particular location at a particular time (Ashley, 2006). Although the communications and wireless industries are now only beginning to take notice of cognitive radio, the U.S. government is already interested in the possibilities that CR offers. Cognitive radios are thought to be a powerful tool for explaining and solving general and specific spectrum access issues, an example of this is locating an open frequency and using it. It improves current spectrum use e.g. fills in the unused spectrum and leaves spectrum that is already in use alone and can improve wireless database performance with increased user throughput and system consistency. The FCC in the US is seeking to remove regulatory impediments in order to continue development and deployment of cognitive radios. Cognitive radios are a possible solution to interoperability issues that are present in public safety organisations especially first responders.

Conclusion

Cognitive radio has the potential to allow multidimensional reuse of spectrum in space, frequency and time and remove the spectrum and bandwidth limitations that slowed broadband wireless development around the world. This new software is closely related to Software- Defined Radio (SDR). SDR is the software found within a cell phone which operates in real time as the user goes from location to location. Cognitive Radio is more intelligent however as it is a radio that is aware of and can sense its environment; learn from its environment, and perform functions that best serve its users. Although Cognitive Radio can be described as software defined radio, there are problems in designing high quality spectrum sensing devices and algorithms for exchanging spectrum sensing data between nodes. Applications of spectrum sensing include emergency networks, Wireless LANs, higher throughput and transmission distance extensions.

Cognitive Radio is poised to take advantage of the increasing deregulation of radio spectrum to provide high-speed broadband services. It can potentially lead to virtually unlimited wireless bandwidth when spectrum is used and reused more efficiently and co-operatively and ultimately increase capacity and efficiency as a direct result of being able to switch between momentarily idle channels in different portions of radio spectrum for short period of usage. This will solve two key problems in multihop networks which are the ability to operate on multiple non-interfering channels removes the bandwidth penalty associated with single-channel multihop systems and the ability to sense for spectrum availability and switch to different channels dynamically provides an excellent solution to wireless Denial of Service (DoS) attacks and network intrusion problems. The technical foundations for Cognitive Radio have been established with the development of Wireless LANs, where dynamic frequency selection and transmit power control are core features. Software functions like filtering, band selection and interference mitigation need to be further developed into this model however many technical hurdles still remain to be overcome such as determining an acceptable level of interference with other radios in the same locale so that it can stay within an acceptable threshold.

References

Ashley, S. (2006) Cognitive Radio, Scientific American, Vol. 294, No. 3, March 2006

Bing, B. (2005) All in a Broadband Wireless Access Network, December 2005, ISBN: 0976675218

Devroye, N., Shyy, D. and Dunyak, J. (2006) Limits on Communications in a Cognitive Radio Channel, IEEE Communications Magazine, Vol. 44, No. 6, pp. 44-49 June 2006

Mannion, P. (2004) EETimes - Sharing spectrum the smarter way, 4th of May 2004 http://www.eetimes.com/showArticle.jhtml?articleID=18700443

Mitola, J. and Maguire, G. (1999) Cognitive Radio: Making Software Radios More Personal, IEEE Personal Communications, Vol. 6, No. 4, 1999.

9   Computational GRID Environments

Alan Bradley, Kevin Curran and Gerard Parr

Computational GRIDs offer a degree of resource sharing that will surpass even the World Wide Web (WWW) as they will not only change the way in which data is accessed but also how this data is produced, consumed and stored. Corporations are using computational GRIDs to improve their operations. Future GRIDs will allow an organisation to take advantage of computational GRIDs without having to develop a custom in-house solution. GRID Resource Providers (GRP) make resources available on the GRID so that others may use these resources. GRPs allow companies to make use of a range of resources such as processing power or mass storage. This chapter provides an overview of computational GRID environments.

Introduction

GRID computing aims to make all computing resources available constantly on a 24/7 basis. Many large corporations are currently using computational GRIDs to improve their operations. However future GRIDs will allow an organisation to take advantage of computational GRIDs without having to develop a custom in-house solution. GRPs will allow companies to make use of a range of resources such as processing power or mass storage. No matter how powerful the infrastructure behind a computational GRID is it will be nothing without software that allows users to take full advantage of the technology. Typically batch jobs which require a significant amount of processing will be best suited to take advantage of the GRIDs resources. Development of applications capable of running on the GRID will be required to run in a heterogeneous environment (Oram, 2001). Previous experience of distributed applications development has shown that Application Programming Interfaces (API), frameworks and middleware have facilitated the rapid development of distributed applications as they provide a level of abstraction that allow developers to concentrate on the application logic without concerning themselves how the application will use the underlying network. The successful and rapid development of GRID applications will require that the developer is afforded the same level of abstraction.

The Globus project is an effort to build a set of essential GRID services for the construction of computational GRIDs (Globus, 2003). These services cover key aspects such as security, resource location, resource management and communication. The toolkits provision of these key services greatly helps in the development of GRID applications as developers can make use of existing services and are thus free to concentrate on the implementation of application specific logic (Foster and Kesselman, 2000). The Globus framework is based on a layered architecture in which high-level services are built on top of an essential set of core local services. The Globus Resource Allocation Management (GRAM) provides the local component for resource management (Czajkowski et al., 1998). GRAM provides a consistent API which can be used by GRID tools and applications to exchange requests for the allocation of resources. The Globus toolkit uses the Nexus communication library (Foster et al., 1996). The Nexus libraries define a low-level API that is used to support a range of higher-level programming models such as remote procedure call (RPC) and remote I/O. The Globus toolkit has been designed to support a wide range of communication types that will be used within computational GRIDs. It comes equipped with the Nexus API that affords developers with a high degree of control over the mappings between high-level communication requests and the underlying protocol requests. The Globus Metacomputing Directory Service (MDS) maintains dynamically updated information on the underlying communications network, protocols, network bandwidth and latency. Higher-level applications and libraries can use this information to configure the communications system in the manner most suited to the current application. The Globus Metacomputing Directory Service (MDS) is a repository of information relating to the state of the components in the GRID. This information is updated dynamically and can therefore be used by applications to adapt their behaviour to changes in the GRID. MDS provides a set of tools and APIs for discovering, publishing and accessing information about the structure and state of a GRID.

Commodity GRID (CoG)

With the emergence of the Computing GRID Environment (CGE) new services are becoming available which go beyond those on offer in the current Internet. Although these new services are advantageous they come with challenges for applications as they may not be compatible with existing commodity technologies used to develop distributed applications. To integrate GRID technologies with existing commodity technologies the Globus project has developed Commodity GRID (CoG) kits[1] which allow developers to develop applications using various technologies and integrate with emerging GRID technologies. Currently CoG kits have been developed for a number of programming languages including Java, Perl and Python, each of these CoG kits provide interfaces for the appropriate language to interface with a GCE. Past experience of developing distributed applications has lead to a number of technologies such as CORBA (Vinoski, 1997) , RMI (Sun, 2008), JINI (Arnold et al., 1999) and DCOM (Rogerson, 1997) which facilitate the development of distributed applications by providing a framework that provides common services needed by all applications. As a result the development of distributed applications was simplified as developers were able to make use of frameworks that had already been tried and tested. Technologies such as those mentioned above have been classified as commodity computing (Von Laszewski et al., 2000). The distinction between this and GRID computing is commodity technologies tend to focus on issues of scalability, component composition, and desktop presentation, while GRID developers emphasize end-to-end performance, advanced network services, and support for unique resources such as supercomputers. The development of CoG kits has therefore been an effort to bridge the gap between these two aspects of computing and allow the wide variety of commodity applications to take advantage of GRID technologies and services through appropriate interfaces (Von Laszewski et al., 2000). CoG kits provide a mapping between commodity frameworks and computational GRID services. The use of CoG kits affords developers the ability to write applications in familiar programming languages and also take advantages of GRID services. CoG kits allow programming languages such as Java or Perl to make use of services provided in the GRID Fabric. In relation to the work here is the ability to access the Resource Management Services as they provide a means to discover resources on the GRID and also to find information on these resources.

Java has already proved to be a popular choice in the development of distributed systems since the Beta version was released in 1995; the widespread uptake of the language can be attributed to its cross platform capability and its inherent security due to the concept of a virtual machine (VM) (Boger, 2001) . The Java CoG kits are classified based upon their role. The low-level GRID interface components provide mappings to common GRID services such as MDS (Von Laszewski et al., 2000), which can be used to gain information about the state of resources on the GRID and which is of particular interest to a system such as that developed for this dissertation. Gregor von Laszewski et al (Von Laszewski et al., 2000), illustrates a piece of Java code that utilizes the functionality of the CoG kit to execute a job on the GRID. This illustrates the attraction to the various CoG kits as developers will have the ability to take advantage of existing skills in languages such as Java and extend their applications to take advantage of the GRID. Sun Microsystems's GRID Engine is a software solution that can be used to implement a computational GRID. It is available in a standard and enterprise edition. The later being capable of supporting much larger GRID implementations such as a global GRID. In fact Sun Microsystems's GRID Engine and the Globus Project have interfaces that allow the two systems to be interoperable (Ferguson, 2003).

GRID Applications

This section summarises some of the current applications that have been developed to take advantage of GRID computing. Currently many of the applications developed to take advantage of computational GRIDs have been designed for large commercial or research organisations, however there are now increasing applications being developed for the average consumer that take advantage of GRID computing. An early adopter of GRID technology was the North American Space Agency (NASA) they have used GRID computing to build the Information Power GRID (IPG) (NASA, 2003). The IPG is a network comprised of high performance computers, data storage devices, scientific instruments and user interfaces. Currently the IPG is being used as a test bed which links to systems at other test sites to form a heterogeneous GRID which is being used to test GRID software such as Globus. If the test beds prove fruitful this could be the future architecture of the GRID. Using the power of their internal company GRID IBM have created a Microprocessor design Gird which enables 80% utilization of resources for chip simulation, resulting in lower errors in microprocessor design and reducing the development cycle for chips (Dotinga, 2003). Boeing has used GRID clustering technology to help

---

[1] http://www-unix.globus.org/cog

in the aerodynamics analysis of their new set of rockets. After 16 months the system was found to perform better than expected and may become the standard for developing and deploying rockets (Smith, 2003).

Discovery of GRID Services

JINI is a technology developed by Sun Microsystems which aims to allow plug-and-play capabilities for network devices. Using JINI devices can be plugged into a network, discover the available services at runtime and therefore form what is referred to as a "community" in real-time without any planning by an administrator. This is the type of facility that will be required in global computational GRIDs where resources will be provided by third parties, therefore organizations will require the ability to dynamically discover the available services and form their own GRID based on these services. As JINI is an extension of the Java programming language it is therefore capable of running on any device equipped with a Java Runtime Environment (JRE) and would therefore be suitable for execution in an extremely heterogeneous environment such as a global computational GRID. Currently JINI is targeted at an environment capable of supporting multicast protocols (typically a LAN) however some work has been carried out to investigate the potential of integrating JINI technology into the infrastructure of a computing GRID. One of the advantages JINI has to offer is the fact that it is concerned primarily with the communication process and has therefore a layer of abstraction over the actual service. This abstraction is provided by an interface that defines the service, therefore the actual implementation of the service can be hardware or software. Although JINI is a powerful technology the work to integrate this technology with computational GRIDs is still in its infancy therefore this chapter will focus on discovering GRID services based on current GRID standard such as the protocols supported by the Globus toolkit.

The Metacomputing Directory Servcice (MDS) is provided by the Information Services component framework of version 3.0 of the Globus toolkit (Lee et al., 1998). The purpose of this framework is to provide information which can facilitate GRID resource discovery, selection and optimization. MDS gathers this information using the GRID Index Information Service (GIIS) and GRID Resource Information Service (GRIS). GIIS offers a means to obtain information on the entire collection of devices attached to the GRID, whereas GRID runs on the individual devices and allows clients to directly query the devices.

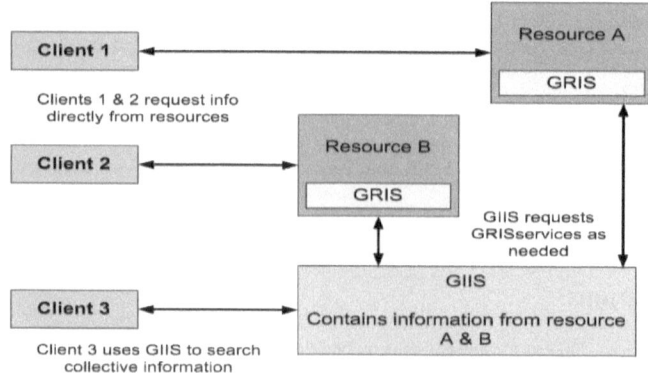

Figure 23: GRIS communication with clients (GRAM, 2003)

GIIS is designed to provide information about services in a GRID. Services can be in the form of software service such as OSGA or hardware resources such as MSS or high volume processing capabilities. With GIIS each service is represented as an object (Plale et al., 2002). Currently the service is provided by Lightweight Directory Access Protocol (LDAP) servers which provide a means to persistently store the attribute values of the objects. Therefore resource discovery is achieved by looking up the LDAP Directory Information Tree (DIT). In a GRID DIT, the root of the tree is marked by "0=GRID" to indicate it encompasses all components of the GRID. The next tier below this represents major GRID projects such as NASA's IPG and the Department of Energy's Science GRID (DoE, 2008). The tiers below this represent the various components that comprise each of the GRID projects. Using a DIT, resources can be discovered by following the appropriate sub paths from the root node.

Monitoring Services on the GRID

Monitoring services on offer within a GRID environment is important for a number of reasons. By conducting an analysis of the performance, the service could be tuned to improve the performance levels. Also more importantly within a GRID environment monitoring of performance levels allows for performance predictions and therefore allows administrators to ensure their site will be capable of meeting the current demand. Monitoring will also allow better decisions to be made by GRID schedulers responsible for deciding where a job should execute. The Globus project uses the GRID Resource Allocation Management (GRAM) protocol for the task of resource management. Figure 24 illustrates the problem of managing resources in a GRID environment, problems can stem from distributed users and resources, variable resources states, variable grouping and connectivity and the lack of a centralized scheduling policy (GRAM, 2003).

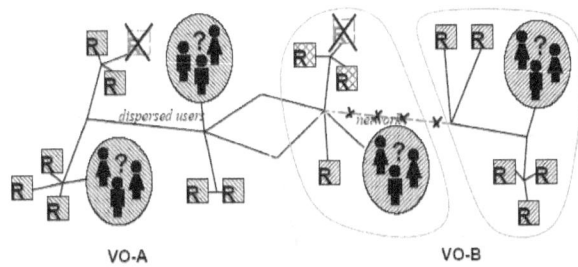

Figure 24: Resources in the GRID (GRAM, 2003)

Previous network technologies such as ATM have allowed users to negotiate a Service Level Agreement (SLA) that specifies the acceptable limits the user is prepared to accept from a system. SLA's also play a crucial role in resource allocation and provisioning in the emerging computational GRID infrastructure. The GRAM service in the Globus toolkit provides a means for monitoring resources attached to the GRID and supports three types of SLA.

1. Task Submission (TSLA) available in GRAM. This is based on the promise to perform a complex task.

2. Resource Reservation (RSLA). This implies a promise to make a resource available to the users

3. Lazy Task / Resource Binding (BSLA). This binds a resource capability to a TSLA. When the GRID receives a TSLA it uses resource binding (BSLA) to acquire necessary resources to perform the task.

Using the GRAM protocol an application has the ability to reserve the resources it needs so they are available when required. This is illustrated in
Figure 25. The Agent runs on the applications behalf and reserves the necessary resources.

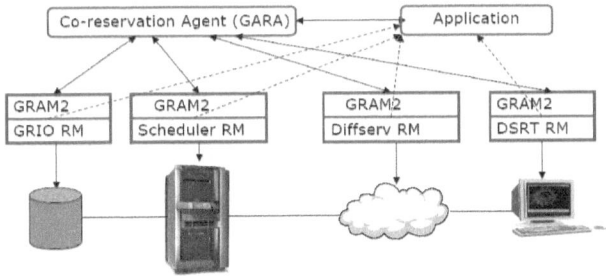

Figure 25: Application using GRAM (GRAM, 2003)

Reservation protocols for computational GRIDs allow GRID applications to reserve resources at various locations throughout the GRID in advance of actually making use of the resource.

Conclusion

GRID computing aims to make all computing resources available constantly on a 24/7 basis. Many large corporations are currently using computational GRIDs to improve their operations. However future GRIDs will allow an organisation to take advantage of computational GRIDs without having to develop a custom in-house solution. The Globus project is an effort to build a set of essential GRID services for the construction of computational GRIDs. Currently many of the applications developed to take advantage of computational GRIDs have been designed for large commercial or research organisations, however there are now increasing applications being developed for the average consumer that take advantage of GRID computing. An early adopter of GRID technology was the North American Space Agency (NASA) they have used GRID computing to build the Information Power GRID (IPG).

References

I. Foster and C. Kesselman. *The GRID: a blueprint for a new computing infrastructure.* Morgan Kaufman Publishers, New York, US, 2000

A. Oram. *P2P - Harnessing the Power of Disruptive Technologies.* O'Reilly, London, March 2001.

Globus Project. http://www.globus.org, 2003

K. Czajkowski, I. Foster, N. Karonis, C. Kesselman, S. Martin, W. Smith, S. Tuecke. *A resource management architecture for metacomputing system.* In Proc. IPPS/SPDP '98 Workshop on Job Scheduling Strategies for Parallel Processing, pg. 62-82, 1998.

I. Foster, C. Kesselman and S. Tuecke. The Nexus approach to integrating multithreading and communication. J. Parallel and Distributed Computing, 37(1):70-82, 1996.

Vinoski, S. *CORBA: Integrating Diverse Applications within Distributed Heterogeneous Environments,* IEEE Communications Magazine, Vol. 14, No. 2, February, 1997.

Sun Microsystems, Sun Microsystems GRID Technology, 2008, http://www.sun.com/GRID

K. Arnold, B. Osullivan, R. W. Scheifler, J. Waldo. *The Jini Specification. The Java Technology Series.* Addison-Wesley, New York, USA, June 1999.

D. Rogerson. *Inside COM - Microsoft's Component Object Model.* Microsoft Press, 1997.

G. von Laszewski, I. Foster, J. Gawor, *CoG Kits: A Bridge between Commodity Distributed Computing and High-Performance GRIDs.* ACM Java Grande Conference, pp. 97–106, San Francisco, CA, 3-5 June 2000.

M. Boger. Java in Distributed Systems, Wiley, ISBN: 0-471-49838-6 2001

A. Ferguson. *GRID Computing Is it really worth the hype?,* Linux Pro, March 2003.

NASA, *Information Power GRID,* 2003, http://www.nas.nasa.gov/About/IPG/ipg.html

R. Dotinga. *GRID Computing good for business.* Wired Magazine, January 16th 2003

Smith, R. *GRID CLUSTER BOOSTS BOEING'S DELTA IV ROCKETS.* GRIDtoday, Januaray 13, 2003: Vol. 2, No. 2 (Article online at http://www.gridtoday.com/03/0113/100949.html)

C. Lee, C. Kesselman, J. Stepanek, R. Lindell, S. Hwang, B. Scott Michel, J. Bannister, I. Foster, A. Roy. The Quality of Service Component for the Globus Metacomputing System. Proc. IWQoS '98, pp. 140-142, 1998.

GRAM: Globus Resource Allocation & Management. http://www.globus.org/training/toolkit-internals/06-ResourceMgmt.pdf. 2003

B. Plale, P. Dinda, G. von Laszewski. *Key Concepts and Services of a GRID Information Service,* Proceedings of the 15th International Conference on Parallel and Distributed Computing Systems, 2002

DoE (2008) Department of Energy, Science GRID. http://doescienceGRID.org/, 2008

10   WebOS – Moving the Operating System to the Web

Kevin Curran, Leanne Doak, Damien Armstrong

Operating Systems were developed to provide system services, such as I/O, communication and storage. The role expanded over time with the addition of multiprogramming and local area networks. The role of an operating system has been pretty standard until the arrival of the WebOS. WebOS is a term used to describe web operation systems. A WebOS in practice is a virtual desktop on the Internet. It is a simple, less featured and remotely accessible operating environment that runs in a browser delivering a rich desktop like experience, with various built-in applications. This term "WebOS" is not truly accurate, because it is not actually a real operation system like windows therefore some prefer to describe is as a 'Web Desktop'. This chapter outlines WebOS in greater detail.

Introduction

There has been an increase in the number of services that are available over the Internet. In keeping with this trend a new development has been a move towards web based operating systems known as WebOS. A WebOS is a framework for supporting applications that are geographically distributed, highly available and scalable (Vahdat, 1997). WebOS includes mechanisms for resource discovery, a global namespace, remote process execution, resource management, authentication and security. A WebOS framework enables a new concept for Internet services. Instead of being fixed to a single location, services can push parts of their responsibilities out onto Internet computing resources, and to the client. These dynamically reconfiguring and geographically mobile services provide a number of advantages, including:

(i)   Better end-to-end availability (service-specific extensions running in the client mask Internet or server failures),

(ii)   Cost-performance (moving information closer to clients, network latency, congestion, and cost can all be reduced while maintaining server control)

The growth of the Internet can be attributed to its lack of central control, making the concept of a WebOS a contradiction in some ways. This concept began with office applications and the first to launch a usable suite was a company called WebOS Inc. The application was called *HyperOffice*[1] and contained common desktop applications including Web email, document management and file storage, online calendars, online contact management, and project management tools. It was aimed at users who wanted constant availability and remote connectivity at all times. There are various advantages to using this kind of software especially in a business setting as the software is completely web-based so there is no need to download or install programs from the net or numerous CDs. It is user-friendly and easy-to-use with personal login details allowing for multiple users within the same company to gain access from any internet connected workstation regardless of browser or platform.

WebOS

Traditionally, Internet applications and protocols are developed and set up without the intervention of any centralized authority. WebOS broadens this to wide area applications running in a secure HTTP name space with the same interface, caching, and performance of existing distributed file systems. There are numerous advantages of integrating the file system with application controlled efficient wide area communication.

---

[1] http://www.hyperoffice.com

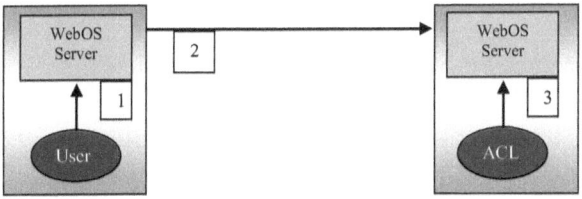

Figure 26: WebOS in Action

Figure 26 illustrates the architecture of WebOS. '1' is where the user transfers portions of their access to the server. 2 is where the WebOS serves Communication using SSl and 3 is where the emote server checks if proper credentials are stored in ACL's. WebOS defines a model of trust to support applications operating across organizational boundaries providing both security guarantees and an interface for authenticating the identity of principals. One core WebOS Application is *remote computer engine* which allows remote programs to be invoked in the same way as local programs. WebOS is used to address issues such as the identity of requesting agents. This is done through authentication and programs run in a restricted virtual machine isolated from other programs to protect the local system from unauthorised access.

The main argument at present against the WebOS approach is security. Many argue that the privacy, control and reliability issues prevent the WebOS from being an alternative to the standard OS. In addition, WebOS requires a fast and reliable connection to work correctly and has problems operating peripheral devices. Web applications rely on open source infrastructure and an array of technologies and formats - and these are constantly changing. Fred Oliveira of WeBreakStuff states "after service outsourcing and personal outsourcing, we're seeing a new age of web-service outsourcing. One with no regulations only expectations and hopes. Everything is based on trust, and trust sometimes fails….and the problem here is that even with web-services as a liability, there's no fallback mechanism, no alternative route, and no "competitor service" that can be plugged into an app in the timely manner like web 2.0 applications require. This proves that purely mash-up based applications have small foundations, and like a house with no foundations, they may fail to resist, should the unexpected happen." (Ezzy, 2006).

WebOS Implementations

Google have produced a number of web based products. Gmail was the first desktop client like email reader. There now is also Google calendar, spreadsheets and more. There are many OS like YouOS and EyeOS, they have been tackling WebOS for a long time which means that Google are not already working on their very own WebOS but may look to take up one them.

Figure 27: Google Desktop

Google had introduced the first iteration on their desktop search. It was a small web server that can insert data from a local machine into browsing pages. There are 3 main parts to the WebOS system:

- Browser – application interface, user views content and manages data locally and on Internet.
- Web Applications – Making web a richer environment for productivity e.g. Gmail
- Local web Server - Handles data delivery and display on browser.

YouOS is another attempt to bring the web and operating systems together to form a shared virtual computer. WebOS, according to YouOS, is liberation of software from hardware

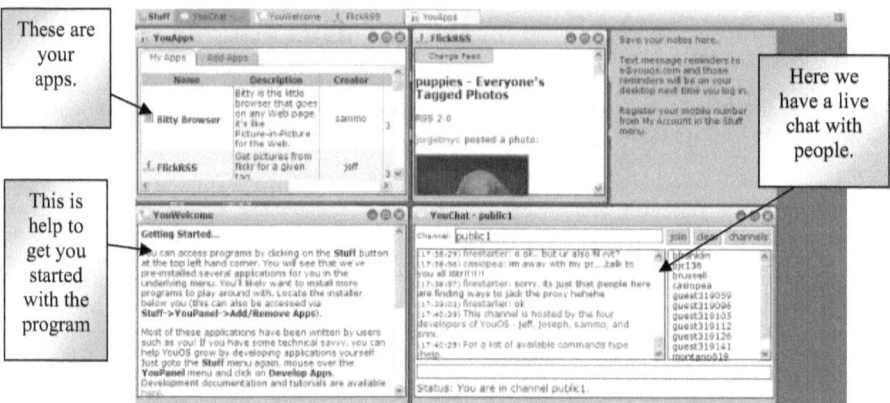

Figure 28: YouOS Screenshot

WebOS provides operating system services to wide area applications. On a single machine developers can rely on the local operating system to provide these abstractions. WebOS provides basic operating systems services needed to build applications that are geographically distributed and highly available. One such application that demonstrates the utility of WebOS is Rent-A-Server.

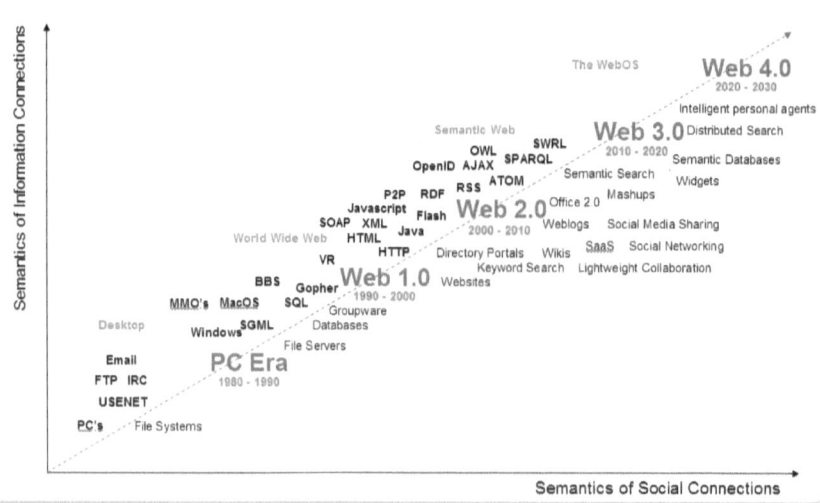

Figure 29: Semantics of Information V Social Connections (Source: www.radarnetworks.com)

Figure 29 illustrates the importance of keeping an eye on trends in Internet Technology Google, Yahoo, YouOS, Netvibes and WebTopOS have been among the main players on the scene to actually develop their vision of Web OS along with a host of other start-ups. Some are available already and others are still in their prototyping stages as illustrated in Figure 30.

Name	Developer	Engine	Free	Support external applications	Graphical User Interface
theWebtop	Atlantis Computing	AJAX	Yes (Beta)	Yes	Tab-based
DesktopTwo	Sapotek	Flash	Yes (Proprietary)	No	Windows-like
Edeskonline	eDesk Online Pvt. Ltd.	AJAX	For 3 months, then $24/year	Yes	Windows-like
EyeOS	eyeOS Team	AJAX	Yes (Open Source GPL)	Yes	Mac-like
Fenestela (French)	Websilog SARL	AJAX	No	Yes	Windows-like
G.ho.st	Ghost Inc	Flash	Yes	No	Windows-like
Goowy	Goowy Media, Inc.	Flash	Yes (Proprietary)	No	Windows+Mac-like
yourminis	Goowy Media, Inc.	Flash	Yes (Proprietary)	No	Tab-based
Ironbox	Oaesys Corp	AJAX	Yes/Subscription	Yes	Windows-like
Protopage	Protopage	AJAX	Yes	Yes	Tab-based
Purefect	Klorofil Project/Saltanera	PHP + AJAX	Yes (Open Source CPL)	Yes	Windows+Mac-like
Sea Drive	SEA Corporation	PHP + AJAX	Yes (Subscription Upgrades)	Yes	Windows+Mac-like
WebtopOS	WebtopOS Inc.	AJAX/J2EE	Yes (paid plan in development)	Yes	Windows-like
XinDesk	XIN	AJAX	Invitation Only (alpha)	Yes	Windows-like
YouOS	WebShaka, Inc.	AJAX	Yes (Proprietary)	Yes	OS/2-like
Netvibes	Netvibes Team	AJAX	Yes (Proprietary)	Yes	Tab-based
Oos	iCUBE Project	AJAX	Yes (Proprietary API: reBOX)	Yes	Windows-like
Orca Desktop	Team Orca/Fenestela	AJAX	Yes (Proprietary)	Yes	Windows-like
Virtual OS	Virtual OS	PHP	No	Yes	Tab-Based
DoxBoard	DoxBoard	AJAX	Yes	Yes	Mac-like
Desktop On Demand	Desktop On Demand	Java / NX	Yes (Beta, By Invitation Only)	No	Linux+Windows-like

Figure 30: Comparison of various Web desktops (Wikipedia, 2007)

A working environment which can be accessed from anywhere is always going to appeal to certain consumers, hence the rising popularity of the current software on offer. However web-based applications also offer a whole new range of security issues and the possibility of uninvited access by hackers to corrupt or extract information. As with all these applications security and data integrity are always top of the developer's agenda. Information stored on a network device can be vulnerable to attack and so must be made secure. It is worth keeping in mind that in this case, the web browser has access to your machine and can potentially quite easily interact with locally stored information and programs. A Web-based desktop needs a very high speed connection due to the fact that all code used for the visualisation such as .jss files, flash files, etc must firstly be stored on the workstation before it can be displayed. Coding also presents a problem. XHTML, Flash, JavaScript, CSS, etc are not as good at providing the functionality and user interaction of applications built using common desktop development tools such as C or Visual Basic. They were originally designed to create web pages, so to develop actual programs which run through the browser may be much more difficult or limited. (23/8/05, *kottke.org*)

Conclusion

The idea behind a Web Operating system (sometimes referred to as Web 3.0) is a virtual desktop or 'webtop' which can be accessed from anywhere, read through a browser with various applications similar to the basic ones available on an ordinary OS, such as filing systems and interacting windows. WebOS includes mechanisms for resource discovery, a global namespace, remote process execution, resource management, authentication and security. A WebOS framework enables a new concept for Internet services. Instead of being fixed to a single location, services can push parts of their responsibilities out onto Internet computing resources, and to the client. It may indeed be possible that the future holds a world which revolves on the web, a free standing machine with a Wi-Fi connection and a browser installed on its hard drive. It remains to be seen but for the present the traditional desktop and operating system is handling most of our domestic and business needs.

References

Ezzy, E. (2006) Webified Desktop Apps vs Browser Apps. Read/Write Web Magazine, September 2006
http://www.readwriteweb.com/archives/webified_desktop_apps_vs_browser_apps.php

Kottke, J. (2005) GoogleOS? YahooOS? MozillaOS? WebOS? August 2005,
http://www.kottke.org/05/08/googleos-webos

Vahdat, A., Eastham, P., Yoshikawa, C. WebOS: Operating system services for wide area applications. Technical Report UCB CSD-97-938, U.C. Berkeley, 1997. http://citeseer.ist.psu.edu/vahdat97webos.

11 Really Simple Syndication (RSS)

Kevin Curran and Sheila Mc Carthy

Email has been one of the major reasons for the broad acceptance of the Internet, and although email is still a vitally important communication tool, it suffers from an increasing number of problems as a medium for delivering information to the correct audience in a timely manner. The increasing volume of spam and viruses means that email users are forced into adopting new tools such as spam-blocking and email-filtering software which attempt to prevent the tirade of unwanted emails. This chapter provides an overview of Really Simple Syndication (RSS) standard which allows web content to be delivered to news readers in an active manner.

Introduction

Many users are also becoming increasingly reticent to divulge their email address for fear of an impending spam influx. Further to this, recent studies suggest that up to 38% of bona fide email messages are being erroneously blocked by filtering software. In reality this means that more than a third of emails, newsletters, special offers, and event announcements are not reaching their intended audience (Patch & McKinlay-Key, 2004). Therefore, the combination of email issues such as the increasing difficulties associated with multimedia downloads, such as delays, compression and data integrity maintenance could be seen as creating a demand for an alternate, effective and secure communication methodology. One such alternative technology is Really Simple Syndication (RSS) or previously known as Rich Site Summary. RSS allows some elements of websites, such as headlines, to be transmitted in unembellished form. When devoid of all elaborate graphics and layouts, such minimalist headlines are quite easily incorporated into other websites. In other words, third party websites can insert this content on their site through embedded RSS news readers and thus provide active news feeds quite easily to their clientele. RSS, termed a lightweight content syndication technology, offers many advantages over streaming and email, and for the consumer, no more difficult to access as the RSS readers are akin to email clients (Byrne, 2003). There is no question that the media is keen to adopt a new communications option, and RSS most certainly can comply.

RSS solves a myriad of problems webmasters commonly face, such as increasing traffic, and gathering and distributing news (BBC, 2008). RSS can also be the basis for additional content distribution services (Kerner, 2004). The real benefit of RSS, apart from the added benefit of receiving news feeds from multiple sites simultaneously in the viewer, is that all the news feeds (i.e. news items) are chosen by the user. With thousands of sites now RSS-enabled and more on the way, RSS has become perhaps one of the most visible Xtensible Mark-up Language (XML) success story to date. RSS formats are specified using XML, a generic specification for the creation of data formats. Although RSS formats have evolved since March 1999, the RSS icon ("⬛") first gained widespread use in 2005/2006.RSS democratizes news distribution by making everyone a potential news provider. It leverages the Web's most valuable asset, content, and makes displaying high-quality relevant news on a site relatively easy (King, 2004). It must be recognized however that RSS cannot entirely replace the primary function of email which is to provide person-to-person asynchronous communications but it does compliment it in some interesting ways.

History of RSS

RSS can be found as an acronym for, *Rich Site Summary, Resource Description Framework (RDF) Site Summary,* or indeed *Really Simple Syndication,* the latter is used here (Oasis-open, 2004). The RSS format was created to facilitate 'channels' on Netscape Netcenter (Netscape, 2005) and was made available to the general public in March of 1999. Channels were a 'pull' type mechanism where users requested certain information from various channels. The original RSS, version 9.0 was created by Netscape as a method of building portals to major news sites for news headlines. Portals are websites dedicated to specific topics. It was however, soon replaced by the 0.91 version which stripped out many of the less important features, as Netscape believed 0.90 proved simply too intricate for this undemanding task. The newly established 0.91 itself was promptly dropped by Netscape as their interest in the portal making business declined. The now obsolete 0.91 was swiftly adopted by the competition, UserLand Software and employed as the foundation for all its web-based concepts. Shortly after this, RSS version 1.0, new version based on Resource Description Framework (RDF), was developed by a third party spin off, a group of designers who built their version modeled closely on the concepts and framework of the initial, original 9.0 (prior to its simplification into version 0.91). The Resource Description Framework (RDF) integrates a variety of applications from library catalogs and world-wide directories to syndication and aggregation of news, software, and content to personal collections of music, photos, and events using XML as an interchange syntax. The RDF specifications provide a lightweight ontology system to support the exchange of knowledge on the Web (Van der Vlist, 2001; Nilsson, 2001). As a result of this, Userland, indignant at being omitted from the latest increment, ignored version 1.0 and continued to advance their own brand of RSS, developing versions 0.92, 0.93, 0.94 through to their current 2.0. In reality this means there are seven different formats to contend with. A feed aggregator, also known as a feed reader, news reader or simply as an aggregator, is client software or a Web application which aggregates syndicated web content such as news headlines, blogs, podcasts, and vlogs in a single location for easy viewing (Wikipedia, 2008). Aggregators must be flexible and comprehensive, and must be able to recognise and deal with all versions. RSS version 2.0 is currently offered by the Berkman Centre for Internet and Society, at Harvard Law School.

Really Simple Syndiation (RSS) Standard

RSS has rapidly developed into a prevalent means of sharing content between websites. Many sites already use RSS, and as word spreads, new sites incorporate this feature into their sites daily. RSS looks set to become a dominant force. Numerous news sites including BBC, Yahoo! and Wired, currently use RSS to provide their subscribers with the latest headlines. Indeed the websites of many mainstream 'giants' also incorporate RSS in a bid to keep their subscribers notified of announcements, events and advertisements. As yet, only sites which currently offer news in RSS format may be read using a news aggregator. To ascertain if a site utilizes RSS is generally simple. Sites make no secret of the fact and proudly display RSS feed pictograms such as ("🔊") throughout their pages indicating which sections are available in RSS format. Right clicking on such an icon, copying the shortcut (URL) and adding it to an aggregator, creates a feed. This establishes a subscription to that particular website for the desired information. Channels to numerous sites can be created, maintained and removed if desired using most aggregators with minimal effort.

A RSS text file contains both static and dynamic information. At a high level, a RSS document is an rss element, with an obligatory attribute called version, this attribute specifies the version of RSS that the document conforms to. Here an element is a piece of data within a document that may contain either text or other subelements describing the RSS data. Succeeding the rss element is a single channel element, which contains information about the channel (metadata) and its contents. Metadata is commonly defined as "data about data" or data describing context, content and structure of records and their management through time. A channel may in turn contain any number of items. Items are sub elements which are enclosed in matching XML start and end tags and appear as sub elements of channel, listed before the closing /channel tag. Each item is identified with an opening item tag, and concluded with a closing /item tag. All child elements of an item are optional, however at least one element must be present, either title or description. An item may be a snippet of information which represents a larger article, much in the same way as a headline represents a newspaper article. If this is the case, the item's description is a synopsis of the story, and the link points to the full story. An item may also be complete in itself, if so, the description contains the full text, and the link and title may be omitted. In this way, an RSS channel can contain many items which in turn may incorporate many differing sub elements. When design and coding is complete, the validated RSS file can be registered with various aggregators allowing the feed to be 'sucked up' by discerning subscribers. Any amendments or updates made to the RSS file will automatically be relayed to all subscribing clients.

RSS Enclosures

RSS version 2.0 encompasses a powerful feature; it allows an item to have an enclosure. This can, in simplistic terms, be likened to an email having an attachment. In reality, enclosures hold huge potential and represent another step in the evolution of content syndication (Kerner, 2004). By incorporating an enclosure sub-element into an item any RSS element can then describe a video or audio file. The enclosure feature has three attributes, the first, 'url' says where the multi-media file is located, the second 'length' determines the size of the file in bytes, and the last 'type' describes the Multi-purpose Internet Mail Extension (MIME) type of the multi-media file. In this way an aggregator can determine the payload attributes prior to any communication, and can then apply the appropriate scheduling and filtering rules. Primarily, the most attractive feature of RSS is that it enables information from numerous websites to be viewed simultaneously, all on one page; consequently, numerous sites can be scrutinized in seconds rather than having to be tediously downloaded independently. A free newsreader is *RssReader*. Like other aggregators, the RssReader aggregator can sustain numerous channels, scouring each of the user's designated websites for updated feeds at regular intervals. When RssReader gathers updated headlines from the various sites, it displays an amalgamation of such in a list box positioned in the bottom right of the user's desktop (see Figure 31; which displays headlines from Yahoo's entertainment news feed).

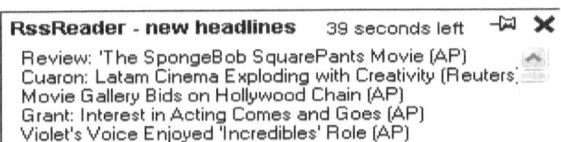

Figure 31: RssReader's 'headline alert' screen

If a user wishes to select a headline from the list, aggregators will provides features to open and provide a synopsis of each news article, if the user wishes to read further on any given topic a link is provided to the specific article on each of the initiating websites. This way, web publishers are able to channel tremendous traffic towards their sites. No longer having to wait for passing traffic, RSS bestows a means of advertising ware on a much wider stage indeed. This way, by employing a news aggregator, a client can subscribe to any sites of their choosing that provide RSS feeds. The websites that do not offer this facility may be disadvantaged, and must wait for the client to visit their page directly if at all, see Figure 32.

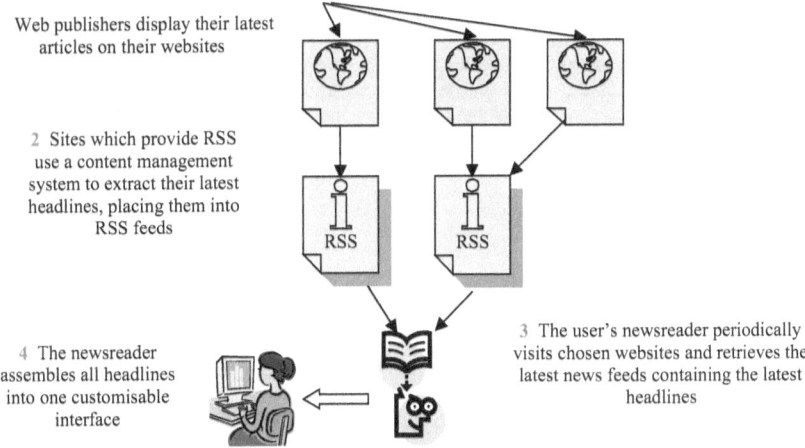

Figure 32: How RSS feeds work

Perhaps the most compelling feature of RSS feeds is the ability to keep track of changes on the web. It is not difficult to ascertain what websites are available today, what is difficult, is to ascertain when such sites make crucial changes. RSS feeds provide us with the necessary aptitude to overcome such problems.

Podcasting

Podcasting is a term derived from Apple's portable MP3 player i.e. the iPod. Podcasting is the preparation and distribution of predominately audio for download to digital music players, such as the iPod player. A podcast is created from a digital audio file which must be saved in an MP3 format and then uploaded to the web site of a service provider. The MP3 file then receives its own URL, which is inserted into an RSS XML document as an enclosure within an XML item tag. Once a podcast has been created, it is usually registered with content aggregators, such as podcasting.net or ipodder.org, for inclusion in podcast directories. Interested parties can then browse through these categories, or subscribe to specific podcast RSS feeds which will in turn download to their audio players automatically when they next connect. Although podcasts are generally audio files created for digital music players, the same technology can be used to prepare and transmit images, text, and video to any capable device, this is the approach taken for this project. Podcasting could be described as the first application based on RSS enclosures to capture the imagination of users and developers. Podcasting allows users to listen to selected podcasts whenever they like, similar to the way time-shifting allows viewers to watch television programs when it suits them. The cultural milieu supporting podcasting is sometimes referred to as the podosphere, just as the cultural environment surrounding the blog is called the blogosphere. Anyone using RSS to distribute information can potentially make use of enclosures, for example a company currently distributing a newsletter using an RSS feed could upgrade this completely with the inclusion of a promotional video clip as an enclosure in the feed.

RSS Systems

There are an increasing number of websites which offer RSS format producing software. Two of the more popular are Nooked and Radio Userland.

Nooked (Nooked, 2008) is an online service which enables users to create, publish and maintain their own RSS channels, with the minimal amount of effort and at low costs. Nooked makes RSS potentially available to users of all abilities by shielding the technical intricacies of how RSS is configured. They have a FeedWizard on their site which is web based. It allows a feed to be created quite quickly and support podcasting and flashcasting similar to the system described here.

Radio UserLand is one of the most popular weblogging tools. Radio supports the publication of weblogs which can optionally include enclosures and also allow customers use of its own built-in news aggregator. Users can subscribe via this aggregator to feeds, allowing Radio users to achieve more than is possible with similar services which offer only weblog hosting. Radio comprises features such as the 'category' feature that supports blogging on varied topics, and a 'multi-author weblog tool' which permits multiple authors to contribute to a community weblog.

The Future for RSS

It should not be forgotten that one of the main objectives of all RSS modules is to extend the basic XML schema which was established for more robust content syndication allowing for wider ranging yet standardized, transactions without modifying the core RSS specification. This can be achieved with an XML namespace which give names to concepts and relationships between those concepts. We can expect to see an increasing number of RSS 2.0 modules with established namespaces appearing in the near future such as Media RSS Module - RSS 2.0 Module (MRSS, 2007).

Really Simple Syndication is central to some of the leading companies such as Google, Yahoo and Microsoft (Rubel, 2006). Yahoo, has stated in the past that almost 3 out of 10 Internet users consume RSS syndicated content on personalized start pages without knowing that RSS is the enabling technology (Hrastnik, 2005). We expect that feed reading will become even easier than it is now, and should be incorporated into all kinds of connected devices especially mobile phones and home media units. We can expect to see it become more embedded into bit-torrent-based peer-to-peer applications where even now, feeds (also known as *Torrent/RSS-es* or *Torrentcasts*) allow client applications to download files automatically from the moment the RSS reader detects them. The term for this currently is Broadcatching. News site such as the Guardian (www.guardian.co.uk) will continue to increasingly provide RSS feeds for a selection of news services and sites automatically updating as stories are added across the network, flagging up what's new as it breaks (Guardian, 2008) .

We also expect to see diverse uses of RSS such as the encoding of location in RSS as performed by georss.org. Here location is described in an interoperable manner so that applications can request, aggregate, share and map geographically tagged feeds. This site was created to promote a relatively small number of encodings that meet the needs of a wide range of communities in the hope that building these encodings on a common information model would result in an "upwards-compatibility" across encodings.

Conclusion

Email suffers from an increasing number of problems as a medium for delivering information to the correct audience in a timely manner due to the volume of spam and viruses arriving in our inboxes on an hourly basis. RSS is a way of receiving constantly updated links to selected websites. Once a connection is setup to a website, then a list of all the stories currently shown on a certain page or section of that site can be retrieved. There are several ways of receiving RSS feeds, but a common method is to download a program called a 'News Reader' which can then be setup to receive RSS information from websites offering it, and browse headlines and story summaries that link through to the full story on the website. Alternatively, newer web browsers offer similar functionality already built-in which will detect whether the website one is currently browsing offers an RSS feed and will then let you create a constantly-updated list of links in the 'bookmarks' menu. Perhaps the most compelling feature of RSS feeds is the ability to keep track of changes on the web as it can be difficult to ascertain when sites make crucial changes. RSS feeds however provide us with the necessary aptitude to overcome such problems.

References

BBC (2008) News feeds from the BBC. http://news.bbc.co.uk/1/hi/help/3223484.stm
Byrne, T. (2003) Content syndication: Ready for the masses? All Business Magazine, June 2003
http://www.allbusiness.com/information/internet-publishing-broadcasting/955591-1.html

Guardian (2008) http://www.guardian.co.uk/webfeeds

Hrastnik, R. (2005) *Analyzing the New Yahoo RSS* - Whitepaper for Marketers, *RSS Statistics,* October 10, 2005
http://rssdiary.marketingstudies.net/content/analyzing_the_new_yahoo_rss_whitepaper_for_marketers.php

Kerner, S (2004), *The RSS Enclosure Exposure* - It's really simple stuff: audio feeds and the rise of RSS.
Internet News – Realtime IT, November 2004 http://internetnews.com/xSP/article.php/3431901

King, A. B., (2004), *Webref and the future of RSS, Introduction to RSS , WebRef and RSS,*
http://www.webreference.com/authoring/languages/xml/rss/intro/3.html,

MRSS (2007) Media RSS Module - RSS 2.0 Module. http://search.yahoo.com/mrss:

Netscape (2005) http://my.netscape.com

Nilsson, M. (2001) The semantic web: How RDF will change learning technology standards, Center for User-Oriented IT-design, Royal Institute of Technology, Stockholm September 27, 2001

Nooked (2008) http://www.nooked.com

Oasis-open, (2004), *Technology Reports, RDF Rich Site Summary (RSS)* http://www.oasis-open.org/cover/rss.html,

Patch & McKinlay-Key, (2004), *Netiquette Notes,* http://www.synergywise.com/internet.html,

Radio Userland (2008) http://www.userland.com

Rubel, S. (2006) Trends to Watch Part III: "RSS Inside", Micropersuasion blog, December 2006, http://www.micropersuasion.com/2005/12/2006_trends_to__1.html

RSS Reader (2007) http://www.rssreader.com

Van der Vlist, E. (2001) Building a Semantic Web Site, XML.com, May 2001

Wikipedia (2008) http://en.wikipedia.org/wiki/Aggregator

12 Javascript, XML, E4X and AJAX

Kevin Curran, Karen Lee, David McClenaghan

Asynchronous JavaScript and XML (AJAX) is a web development technique for creating interactive web applications. The intent of AJAX is to make the web experience interactive, faster and more user friendly, AJAX makes this possible by exchanging small amounts of data with the server behind the scenes which results in the web page on the client side not needing to be reloaded when a user makes a chance thus resulting in the once slow and painful Web application experience as one more similar to that of desktop applications.

Introduction

Ajax, which consists of XML, JavaScript technology, DHTML, and DOM, is an approach that helps developers transform clunky Web interfaces into interactive Ajax applications (McLaughlin, 2005). Consider the choice of applications that developers are writing such as desktop applications or Web applications. Desktop applications usually come on a CD or can be downloaded from a Web site and installed completely on any computer. They might use the Internet to download updates, but the code that runs these applications resides on the desktop. Web applications on the other hand run on a Web server somewhere and can access the application with a Web browser. More important than where the code for these applications runs, though, is how the applications behave and how they can be interacted with. Desktop applications are usually quite fast as they are running on a computer, therefore Internet connection speed is not an issue, and they have great graphical user interfaces which usually interacts with the operating system. All and all they are incredibly dynamic. Desktop applications are extremely interactive these days, they can be clicked, pointed & typed with almost no waiting around (McLaughlin, 2005).

On the other hand, Web applications are usually up to the second updated and they provide services which could not be got on a desktop, a really good example of this is eBay. However, with the power of the Web comes waiting, waiting for a server to respond, waiting for a screen to refresh, waiting for a request to come back and generate a new page. Again with the example of eBay, how frustrating when an auction is nearing its end and the current bidder is being outbid because of the length of time the page is taking to refresh before they can enter a new bid again, most times they have lost the item they were interested in (McLaughlin, 2006). Ajax attempts to bridge the gap between the functionality and interactivity of a desktop application and the always-updated Web application. This technology uses dynamic user interfaces and fancier controls like that which are found on a desktop application, but now has become available on a Web application.

AJAX is also a key component of Web 2.0 applications such as Flickr, now part of Yahoo!, 37signals' applications basecamp and backpack, as well as other Google applications such as Gmail and Orkut (O'Reilly, 2006). Another definition of AJAX coined by Jesse James Garrett was that Ajax was not just one technology, but several, each flourishing in its own right, each coming together in powerful new ways. AJAX incorporates several technologies including Standards-based presentation using XHTML and CSS, dynamic display and interaction using the Document Object Model, data interchange and manipulation using XML and XSLT, asynchronous data retrieval using XMLHttpRequest and JavaScript binding everything together.

The classic web application works by a user triggering a HTTP request, which would be generated from the users action. The user then waits while the server performs its processes say it be retrieving data, calculating numbers or talking to various legacy systems and then returns a HTML page to the user. Figure 33 illustrates the classic web application model and the AJAX web application model. Although the AJAX appears more technical, it offers a solution to what most users loath, which is having to wait during a web session.

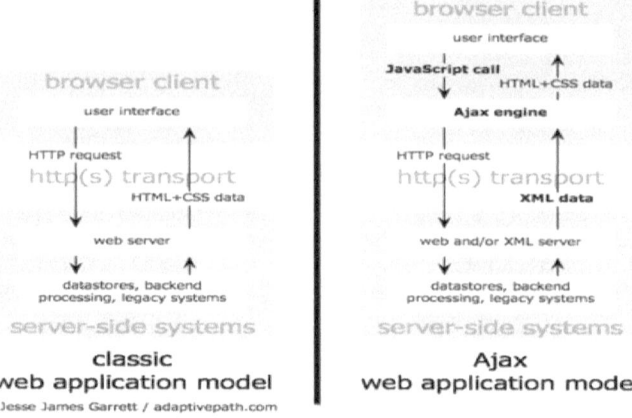

Figure 33: AJAX versus the classic Web Application Model

There is some initial wait for the AJAX engine to load up in a frame at the start however once this period is over – each AJAX site becomes speedier in response. The remainder of this chapter introduces the components involved in AJAX and related technologies JavaScript Object Notation (JSON) and ECMAScript for XML (E4X) with regards their role in creating social software.

JavaScript and XML

Essentially taking each part of the acronym in isolation Asynchronous, means that when you a request is sent, the user must wait for a response to come back, but is free to do other things while they wait. The response probably does not come back immediately, so the developer can set up a function that will wait for it to be sent by the server, and react to it once it happens. The next stage is JavaScript. This code is the core code running Ajax applications. It is used to make a request to the server. Once the response is returned by the server, the developer will generally use some more JavaScript to modify the current page's document object model (DOM) in some way to show the user that the submission went through successfully. JavaScript is the scripting language of the Web, it is used in millions of Web pages to improve the design, validate forms, detect browsers, create cookies, and is the most popular scripting language on the internet and works in all major browsers, such as Internet Explorer, Mozilla, Firefox, Netscape, Opera among others. A big advantage for developers is the fact that it is easy to learn (W3Schools, 2006). JavaScript is a prototype based scripting language with a syntax loosely based on C. Like C, the language has no input or output constructs of its own. Whereas C relies on standard I/O libraries, a JavaScript engine relies on a host environment into which it is embedded. There are many such host environment applications, of which web technologies are the most well known examples. One major use of web based JavaScript is to write functions that are embedded on or included from HTML pages and interact with the Document Object Model of the page to perform tasks not possible in HTML alone. The final component in AJAX is XML. XML stands for Extensible Markup Language which is used as a way of describing data. An XML file can contain the data too, similar to that of a database. The primary purpose of XML is to facilitate the sharing of information across different systems, particular those connected to the internet. AJAX passes data to servers packaged up as snippets of XML code, so that it can be easily processed with JavaScript. This data can be anything which is needed, and as long as required. It is not a new technology as this is already how the web works, the only difference is that now these requests can be made from JavaScript. In short a file is requested and a page is received in response.

The AJAX Model

Ajax is not a technology but rather a family of technologies that have been available for years, each flourishing in their own right and coming together in significant new ways (Garrett, 2005). Ajax incorporates standards-based presentation using XHTML and CSS, the former is a stricter and cleaner version of HTML, which is used to build Web forms and identify fields for use in applications. The latter is CSS which stands for Cascading Style Sheets which define how to display HTML elements in a web application. These standards are W3C Recommendations which describe the communication protocols of HTML, XML and other building blocks of the Web (Garrett, 2005). Also incorporated in AJAX is dynamic display and interaction using the Document Object Model, data interchange and manipulation using XML and Extensible StyleSheet Language Transformations (XSLT), asynchronous data retrieval using XMLHttpRequest and JavaScript binding everything together which gives faster access, better support, and acceptance as a data structure in a Web application. The preferred way to communicate with the server is by sending data as XML but other methods can be used. Although XML provides two enormous advantages as a data representation language, as it is text based and is position independent. Unfortunately, XML is not well suited to data interchange as it carries a lot of baggage, and it does not match the data model of most programming languages. However there is another text notation that has all of the advantages of XML, but is much better suited to data interchange. That notation is JavaScript Object Notation (JSON). JSON is a lightweight computer data interchange format. It is a subset of the object literal notation of JavaScript but its use does not require Javascript. JSON's elegance and simplicity has resulted in its widespread use, especially as an alternative to XML in Ajax. One of the claimed advantages of JSON over XML as a data interchange format in this context is that it is much easier to write a JSON parser. JSON parses ten times quicker than XML, which is quite expensive to parse. In JavaScript itself, JSON can be parsed trivially using the `eval()` procedure. This was important for the acceptance of JSON within the Ajax programming community because of JavaScript's ubiquity among web browsers.

For that reason JSON is typically used in environments where the size of the data stream between the client and the server is of paramount importance hence its use by Google, Yahoo, etc, which serves millions of users and the source of the data can be explicitly trusted, and where the loss of fact access to client-side XSLT processing for data manipulation or UI generation is not a consideration. While JSON is often positioned against XML, it is not uncommon to see both JSON and XML used in the same application. For example, a client-side application which integrates Google Maps data with SOAP weather data requires support for both data formats. (JSON, The Fat Free Alternative To XML). Comparing XML and JSON on the attributes which are considered important, the first is how simplistic JSON is, it has a much smaller grammar and maps more directly onto the data structures used in modern programming languages therefore less coding is required compared to XML. It it also easier for humans to read and for machines to read and write. Secondly JSON is not extensible because it does not need to be. JSON is not a document mark-up language, so it is not necessary to define new tags or attributes to represent data in it. JSON has the same interoperability potential as XML and lastly is at least as open as XML, perhaps more so because it is not in the centre of corporate/political standardisation struggles (Kelly, 2005). Whatever is used XML or JSON, for developers to get the right look for an AJAX application, Cascading Style Sheets (CSS), a World Wide Web Consortium (W3C) standard is a crucial weapon in the AJAX developer's arsenal. CSS provides the mechanism for separating the style and design of an application from the content itself. Although CSS plays a prominent and important role in AJAX applications, it also tends to be one of the bigger stumbling blocks in building cross browser compatible applications since there are widely varying levels of support from different browser vendors (Johnson, 2006)

Therefore the real complexity in JavaScript programming results from the incompatibility of Web browsers' support for varied technologies and standards. Building an application that runs on different browsers e.g. IE and Mozilla's Firefox is a difficult task to say the least. To that end, several AJAX JavaScript frameworks commercial and open source either generate JavaScript code based on server side logic or tag libraries, or provide a client side JavaScript library to facilitate cross browser AJAX development. Some of the more popular frameworks include AJAX.Net, Backbase, Bitkraft, Django, DOJO, DWR, MochiKit, Prototype, Rico, Sajax, Sarissa, and Script.aculo.us. The browser wars from a few years ago are still going on albeit on a much smaller scale. Therefore the effect on Ajax applications as regards the XMLHttpRequest finds itself one of the victims of this war. Consequently a few different things are necessary to get an XMLHttpRequest object going. The key is to support all browsers. No developer wants to write an application that works just on Internet Explorer or an application that works just on non-Microsoft browsers. It's a poor answer to write an application twice, therefore code should combine support for both Internet Explorer and non-Microsoft browsers in a multi browser way. Modern browsers offer users the ability to change their security levels, and to turn off JavaScript technology, disable any number of options in their browser. Therefore, developers need to handle the problems associated with these changes without letting the application fall over. Writing robust code is a challenge for Ajax developers.

E4X and JSON

As of 2008, the latest version of the JavaScript language is JavaScript 1.6, which corresponds to ECMA-262 Edition 3 similar to JavaScript 1.5, except for Array extras, and Array and String generics. ECMAScript is a standardized version of JavaScript. The ECMA-357 standard specifies E4X, a language extension dealing with XML. E4X is basically an extension on the ECMAScript (JavaScript) it adds native XML support to the language which in turn means that along with the types already useable in the ECMAScript, that is the number type, the string type, the Boolean type and the object type, a XML type is also implementable for representing XML elements, attributes, comments, processing-instructions and text nodes. There is also the added functionality of having an XMLList, which allows a list of XML objects. Presently there are two ECMAScript implementations that have been extended to implement E4X they are the Mozilla Javascript engines Spidermonkey and Rhino. E4X is much simpler since an XML document can be declared as an XML object therefore it is easy to parse and manipulate XML. Without E4X an XML library or an XML component is necessary to work with XML. It does this by providing access to the XML document in a form that feels natural for ECMAScript programmers. The goal is to provide an alternative, simpler syntax for accessing XML documents than via DOM interfaces. Additionally, it offers a new way of visualizing XML. Up to the release of E4X, XML was always accessed at an object level. E4X changes that, and thinks of XML as a primitive as a result implies faster access and better support

JavaScript Object Notation (JSON) is defined as a lightweight computer data interchange format[2]. It is a subset of the object literal notation of JavaScript but its use does not require JavaScript. JSON is independent from other languages but uses conventions that are familiar to that in C-family of languages. The JSON is built on two structures, a collection of name/value pairs and an ordered list of values. The main benefit of JSON is that it is not that it is smaller on the wire, but that it better represents the structure of the data and so requires less coding and processing. One of the most important advantages of JSON is that bypasses JavaScript's same source policy, which is that JavaScript does not allow you to access documents sent from another server. However with JSON you can import a JSON file as a new script tag. Another advantage is that JSON data are slightly simpler and slightly more in line with the rest of the JavaScript language than scripts for XML data. JSON however can be difficult to read and each single comma, quote, and bracket should be in the correct place. While this is also true of XML, JSON's welter of complicated-looking syntax, like the }}]} at the end of the data snippet, may frighten the newbie's and make for complicated debugging. JSON is relatively a lot younger than XML and of course needs time to grow. As the older kid on the block XML has wider support and offers more development tools in both client side and server side. However client side parsing for JSON is supported natively with JavaScript's eval() method. The main benefit of JSON is not that it is smaller on the wire, but that it better represents the structure of the data and so requires less coding and processing.

Social Interaction Technologies and AJAX

There has been a lot of talk about social interactive technology, but only a little on the impact these technologies will have on user experience apart from Ajax. The first "Real-World AJAX" event, held in New York City, featured 15 speakers in 11 sessions, including many of the world's most renowned AJAX experts, and more than 400 delegates attended while more than 15,000 SYS-CON.TV viewers tuned into the simulcast on March 13, 2006. At this seminar Jesse James Garrett (Adaptive Path publications) declared 'The biggest challenges in creating Ajax applications are not technical. The core Ajax technologies are mature, stable, and well understood. Instead, the challenges are for the designers of these applications: to forget what we think we know about the limitations of the Web, and begin to imagine a wider, richer range of possibilities'. The impact of Ajax for Web applications covers a wide range of issues, business strategy, technology, design, team structure and processes are all potentially affected by the move to Ajax. (Garrett, 2005)

This middle of the road approach as opposed to screen based approaches which mimic the sophistication of desktop applications, with Java, Flash or a similar technology or page based approaches which force developers to deal with the load-reload effect of normal web pages. Resulting in users who enter and manipulate information in page based applications sitting through a page refresh in order for their changes to take place. The Amazon.com checkout sequence, Google search, and the eBay selling sequence are common examples of the page based approach. While both approaches have proven successful, each has drawbacks. Ajax on the other hand marries the benefits of both screen and paged based approaches by allowing more sophisticated functionality using easier to implement web standards. Ajax is a solid alternative for new interface development and experts have already affirmed the viability of the web as a standalone software development platform. Its popularity is certainly helped with large companies like Google creating amazing applications using the Ajax technology eg Google Maps, Google Gmail, and Google Suggest and another reason is the continuing adoption of standards compliant browsers that support Ajax technology, Firefox, Safari, Opera, and Internet Explorer 6 (Porter, 2005). Most notably Firefox, for their support of Ajax software, eg ajaxWrite, ajaxTunes which are all small rich web based applications which run on a computer. These programs launch in 3-4 seconds and have all the interactivety of Writely or Microsoft Office applications. Ajax13[1] has just 6-8 servers and serves millions of people with their "service from servers" web based applications. Their goal is to show all core applications from the Internet. They believe that consumers don't need to know anything about version compatibility with their existing computer or operating system.

ajaxOS[2] is a fully functional AJAX-aware operating system. Features in ajaxOS include the ability to store to a remote server, with full access to file navigation on this remote server as well as a computer's hard disk. As easily as documents on a local machine can be saved and opened, users will be able to do so, on the company's secure servers. With the trend steering towards Ajax, it looks like this new approach to web applications is here to stay, assisted by indispensable ubiquitous broadband it seems everything will soon be in the 'cloud'. With the simplicity of using Ajax applications coupled with the fact that they are built using nothing more than current web standards, which makes them relatively easy to create therefore most web designers familiar with building paged based applications can migrate an interface to Ajax quickly. Also, enterprising Ajax developers have created easy to use building blocks that allow developers unfamiliar with the approach to migrate their applications over without having to write code from scratch, and there is also an abundance of articles in magazines, Ajax related weblogs and Ajax tutorials on the Web for developers who want to start building these dynamic Web applications, therefore as a result Ajax is becoming a commonplace tool.

Conclusion

AJAX allows the user to interact with the current page with little or no communication with the server. The resources to enable AJAX to function are already available on all major browsers on most existing platforms. The most widely voiced concern regarding the usability of AJAX is that when a user selects the back button on the browser, they will not undo the recent AJAX imposed changed but the last page stored in the history of the browsers. Developers have tried to overcome this by using IFRAMES to store the status of a page at specific times. AJAX is currently being used by Google. Google groups, Google Suggest and Google maps are all based on AJAX, which proves not only that AJAX is technically sound but also that it is practical for real world application. The simplicity of JSON may in fact replace XML as first choice for sending data. E4X just seems a natural progression from the ECMA standard.

References

Garrett, J.J. (2005) Ajax: A New Approach to Web Applications. Adaptive Path Publications, February, 2005
http://www.adaptivepath.com/publications/essays/archives/000385.php

Johnson, D. (2006) Ajax: Dawn Of A New Developer, Java World, October 2005

Kelly, S. (2005) Speeding up AJAX with JSON, Developer.com, October 2005
http://www.developer.com/lang/jscript/article.php/10939_3596836_2

McLaughlin, B (2005) Mastering Ajax, Part 1: Introduction to Ajax, December 2005
http://www-128.ibm.com/developerworks/web/library/wa-ajaxintro1.html

---

[1] http://www.ajaxlaunch.com/
[2] http://www.myajaxos.com/

McLaughlin, B (2006) Mastering Ajax, Part 2: Introduction to Ajax, January 2006
http://www-128.ibm.com/developerworks/web/library/wa-ajaxintro2/

O'Reilly, T. (2005). What is Web 2.0 – Design patterns and business models for the next generation of software,
http://www.oreillynet.com/pub/a/oreilly/tim/news/2005/09/30/what-is-web-20.html

Porter, J. (2005) Using Ajax for Creating Web Applications. Proceedings of User Interface 10 Conference,
Cambridge, MA, July 2005

W3Schools (2006) Ajax, Json & E4X tutorials. http://www.w3schools.com/ajax/default.asp

13   The Semantic Web

Kevin Curran, Gary Gumbleton

The Semantic Web (SW) is a vision of the Web where its information is more efficiently linked up in such a way so that machines can more easily process its information. Tim Berners-Lee, inventor of the World Wide Web (WWW), is credited with created the Semantic Web. Currently there is a large team of people at various academic institutes across the world working on improving and extending the system to make the goal come true. They are doing this by creating applications for the Semantic Web, making publications and creating languages for the Semantic Web to be published with. This chapter provides an overview of the semantic web.

Introduction

The Semantic Web has for some time now being generating interest and not just because Tim Berners-Lee is advocating it but also because it aims to solve the largest problem faced by the web at present. This problem is that information is hidden away on it in HTML documents, which are easy for humans to get information out of but are difficult for machines to do so. But the question has to be asked how it will work? As already mentioned there is a large group of people working on this coming up with different solutions, for representing the data and storing it. But there is a general consensus that says it should be built out of the current technology of the Web, in general using Universal Resource Identifiers (URI's) and the eXtensive Mark-up Language (XML). The semantic web is not a completely new form of the WWW instead it is an extension of the current web aimed at overcoming some of the disadvantages of the current web. In particular it is concerned with making the Web more readable for computers so they would be able to interpret it better and as a result be better able to assist us. Tim Berners-Lee, Director of the World Wide Web Consortium (W3C) states that "The Semantic Web is not a separate Web but an extension of the current one, in which information is given well-defined meaning, better enabling computers and people to work in cooperation" [W4]. To achieve this goal the authors of the report "The Semantic Web" suggested that four components were needed.

- Expressing Meaning - The Semantic Web will bring structure to the meaningful content of Web pages, creating an environment where software agents roaming from page to page can readily carry out sophisticated tasks for users. [W4].

Knowledge representations (KR) are needed for the semantic web to function; the computers and software agents using it need to have access to structured information and inference rules in order to perform some reasoning. Also the rules and information must be powerful enough to describe complex terms. Languages like the Extensible Mark-up Language (XML) and Resource Description Framework (RDF) are already in place and helping to make this happen along with newer languages such as here and here, which shall all be described in more detail later on. Ontologies are a document or file that formally defines the relationship between terms. On the web the most commonly used type of ontology used is taxonomy (subclass–super class) hierarchy, though they may not just be limited to this form. These taxonomy's work on classes and descried the relationship between them together with their inference rules, they play a vital part in the semantic web. For example if a salary class is associated with a currency class and the currency class is then associated with a county class. The inference rules could then say that if an employee gets paid in British pounds then they work in the UK. Also you could have different ontologies pointing to each other so your ontology for "person" could point to someone else's that is describing the same thing but using different terminology this would then increase the scope of the inference rules and make then more reliable.

Agents are the programs that will gather the contents of the semantic web process them and exchange them with other agents. Off course for the agents to exchange information with each other there will have to be some degree of proof between them that the information they gathered is true. Digital signatures and proofs can overcome this.

The Architecture of the Semantic Web

In the XML 2000 conference[1], Tim Berners-Lee gave a talk at which he described the architecture of the semantic web as illustrated in Figure 34. In it he described the Semantic Web as being build upon the current web using some of the already existing technology to improve the functionality of the Web and to help enable it to its full potential. The bottom layer is made up of Uniform Resource Identifier (URI). URI's are a fundamental component of the web and are also the foundation of the SW. URI's are a compact string of characters for identifying an abstract or physical resource" [Berners-Lee98b]. It is not a set of direction that tells a computer how to get to a specific site on the web (though it can also do this). Because anyone can create a URI and their ownership is clearly delegated they are the ideal building blocks for the web. Also because URI's are not tied to a specific protocol, they can be used to access different ones. So when a new protocol is invented the same URI can be used to address the same resource.

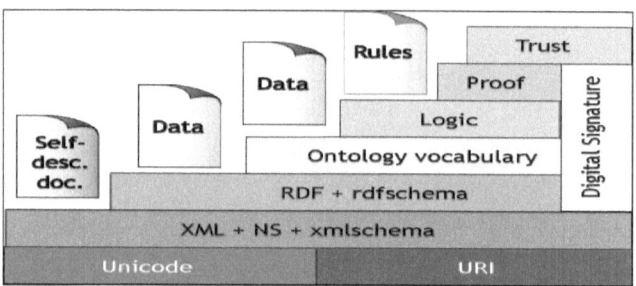

Figure 34: The layered architecture of the SW

The next layer is the XML and xmlschema layer. XML is a system for defining specialized markup languages that are used to transmit formatted data. This markup is used to encode instructions that can tell applications what to do with the information it refers to. It was created to make a version of SGML (Standard Generalized Mark-up Language) that would be as widely used on the Internet as HTML. The problem with HTML being that it did not allow machines to easily extract information from it as it was mainly designed to present information to humans and SGML was considered too difficult to implement just for a web browser. XML however is a text based language it is platform and software independent this also has the knock on effect of making XML documents transmittable over networks using existing protocols. In addition, because it is a hierarchical structure it allows for powerful data constructs from databases and other applications. The syntax of XML is similar to that of HTML, this is because both of them are derived from SGML with the exception that in XML we are describing the data not the format of the document. An example of a XML document is shown in Figure 35. XML allows authors of documents to create their own mark-up language, where the meaning of the information is placed in the document. The information placed into the document is called "elements"; these elements are encapsulated by start (<) and end tags (/>). Tag names are the word inside the start and end tags of elements for example dataBaseFootball would be an example tag name in Figure 35. Elements can contain attributes, other elements (giving the document a hierarchical structure) or a combination of the both. These tags tell the computer that (in the case of Figure 35) "Ferguson "is a "Manager" but they do not tell the computer what a "Manager" is. Since XML cannot express the meaning of the tags it can cause problems for machine processing. As most processing applications require tag sets whose meanings have been agreed to some standard or convention.

---

[1] http://www.gca.org/attend/2000_conferences/XML_2000/default.htm

```
<? Xml version="1.0"? >
<dataBaseFootball>
<team>
<manager> Ferguson </manager>
<name>Manchester United</name>
<leagueposition>3</leagueposition>
</team>
<team>
<manager>Venger, Arsen</manager>
<name>Arsenal</name>
<leagueposition>2</leagueposition>
</team>
<team>
<manager>Gerald Hupea</manager>
<name>Liverpool</name>
<leagueposition>1</leagueposition>
</team>
</dataBaseFootball>
```

Figure 35: Example XML structure

To help with this, "document type definition" (DTD) was created allowing for grammar to be defined. DTDs specify elements; the context of elements and which attributes in elements can be changed. Although DTDs allow for syntax in XML documents the semantics are still implicit. Meaning that a human infers the meaning of a DTD element by the name given to it as a comment in the DTD or it is described in a separate document. This makes it easy to exchange XML documents between people on a small scale as they can get together beforehand and design DTDs that will meet there combined needs. But it runs into problems when you scale it up and for example you want to integrate your DTD with similar one's from multiple sources. One of these problems is exchanging representations of the same idea structure. As XML allows the author of the document to represent that data in there own way. This can lead to a simple thing like a name structure, being represented in different way as shown in Figure 36, causing a lack of semantics.

```
<Person>
  <Name>Gary</Name>
</Person>
<Peron>
  <Name><Forename>Gary</Forename></Name>
</Peron>
```

Figure 36: Example of person structure represented in different ways

XML Schema is an XML language for describing and constraining the content of XML documents. This gives us greater flexibility when defining a XML document. For example, Figure 35 could now be rewritten as in Figure 37.

```
<? Xml version="1.0" encoding="utf-8"? >
<xs: schema xmlns: xs="http://www.w3.org/2001/XMLSchema">
<dataBaseFootball>
  <team>
<Xs: element team="character" minOccurs="0" maxOccurs="unbounded"
    <manager> Ferguson </manager>
    <name>Manchester United</name>
    <leagueposition>3</leagueposition>
  </team>
</dataBaseFootball>
</xs: schema>
```

Figure 37: Example XML structure Version 2

In this new version the mark up elements have been uniquely identified by use of a URL, doing so is called XML Namespacing. [W 10] define namespaces as "An XML namespace, is a collection of names identified by a

URI reference [RFC2396]. Which are used in XML documents as element types and attribute names. XML namespaces differ from the "namespaces" conventionally used in computing disciplines in that the XML version has internal structure and is not, mathematically speaking, a set." By using namespaces everyone can create their own tags for XML documents and mix and match then with others created by different people. But XML Schema still suffers from the same semantic flaws as DTD.

Resource Development Language (RDF)

Though XML is good at letting you invent tags it can have problems with scalability. For example often the order in which elements appear in XML is significant, so keeping the correct order of data items on something as extensive as the Web could prove impractical. To help solve this RDF was developed by a number of different metadata communities under the umbrella flagship of the W3C, with the aim to develop a flexible architecture for supporting Metadata on the web. Its history derives from 1995 when the W3C developed PICS (Platform for Internet Content Selection), which was a mechanism for communicating the ratings of web pages from a server to a client (mainly with the aim to tell the client if a particular Web page was or wasn't suitable for children) by using metadata. However for whatever reason PICS did not take off but it was clear that other metadata communities could use some of the infrastructure that had been developed. So the W3C created a working group to bring together the requirements of several different metadata groups and in 1998 they released these recommendations. In its essence RDF is a method to express and process a series of simple assertions, such as "Ora Lassila created this page (Home/Lassila)". This is called an RDF statement and illustrated it looks like Figure 38 comprising of nodes, labeled arcs and values. It consists of three parts a subject (Resource); predicate (Property) and an object (Literal) as shown in Table 3 with their corresponding values.

Figure 38: An example RDF diagram (Triple)

Predicate (Property)	Creator
Object (literal)	Ora Lassila

Table 3: Figure 38 broken up into consistence parts

RDF provides also provides a model for describing resources The basic concept behind it is that an object (a resource) is described throw a collection of properties called an RDF Description which itself consists of a property type and value, as long as that object has a unique URL address. In RDF values may be text, strings, numbers and so on, but they may also be other resources which themselves can have properties of their own. Figure 39 shows Figure 38 as an RDF description with some additional descriptive information.

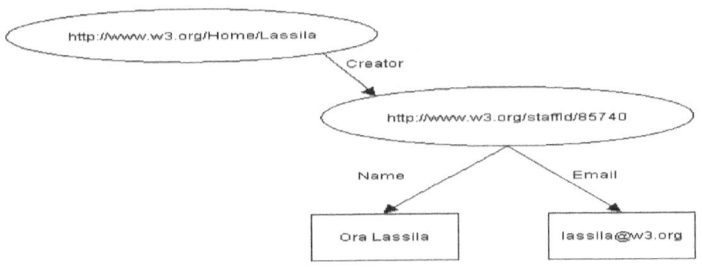

Figure 39: An RDF Graph [W6]

Because more descriptive information is provided in Figure 38 a unique identifier has to be provided about Ora Lassila, in Figure 39's case Ora Lassila is given an staff number. This can be something like an employee number. This is needed for the unambiguous association of properties on resources. As the person Ora Lassila may be value of different property types. E.g. he may be the creator of index.html but may also be a value in a table "employees" for a company. This allows for the reuse of descriptive information.

```
<? Xml version="1.0"? >
<RDF xmlns = http://w3.org/TR/1999/PR-rdf-syntax-19990105#>
   <xmlns: DC = "http://purl.org/DC#" >
    <Description about = " http://www.w3.org/Home/Lassila.html  " >
    <DC: Creator> Ora Lassila </DC: Creator>
   </Description>
</RDF>
</xml>
```

Figure 40: Example RDF Syntax

RDF Schema is needed for the creation of controlled, sharable and extensible vocabularies. It extends RDF to include a larger reserved vocabulary with more complex semantic constraints allow users to create schemas of classes and properties using RDF. RDF then uses XML Namespaces in order to avoid confusion between two separate definitions of the same term, which could have conflicting meaning. RDF can easily be marked up into XML as Figure 40 shows. You can also see the use of XML namespaces as RDF relies heavily on XML namespaces for disambiguating names.

Ontologies

The next Layer proposed for the SW is ontologies. Ontologies as already mentioned are fundamental to the SW, providing the mechanisms for the interchange of data between different Knowledge representations. Ontologies are a specification of a representational vocabulary for a shared domain of discourse - definitions of classes, relations, functions, and other objects [W2]. Today there is a great deal of research going on into this area, carried out by such groups as the DAML group, who in conjunction with the European initiative came up with DAML + OIL which is an extension of the RDF language. Other ontology languages include Simple HTML Ontology Extensions (SHOE) and the Ontology Exchange Language (XOL). The reasons of developing ontologies are:

- To share common understanding of the structure of information between people or machines
- To enables the reuse of knowledge
- To make it clear the domain assumptions
- To separate domain knowledge from the operational knowledge
- To analyze domain knowledge

To share common understanding of the structure of information is one of the more common reason for developing ontologies. Doing so allows will allow computer software agents to extract information from different sites that share the same ontologies and then go on to possibly use this information to answer queries on to use them as inputs to other queries. Enabling the reuse of knowledge allows us to save time in developing our own ontology. For example if a group of researchers develop a complex ontology and publish it other researcher can simply copy this again saving both time and money. Also if a large ontology needs to be built the researchers developing may be able to group together several smaller ones in order to achieve their goal. There are already lots of reusable ontologies on the web such as the DAML ontology library [W5] or Dublin core [W13]. By making clear the domain assumptions made about knowledge and it structure makes it easier to change these assumptions if our knowledge about the domain changes. This also makes it easier for new comers to the area that the ontology was written about to pick it up and continue on the work. With the separation of domain knowledge from operational knowledge we can develop applications that use the same knowledge base but require different operational knowledge to carry out their own respective tasks. This again helps in the reuse of already existing ontologies. Once an ontology has been defined formal analyze of it can of the terms can begin. This can result in valuable information for when exciting are being attempted to be reused or updated. However for the SW to truly take off in the way the way that the original web has there must be software agents cheaply available in not free too people in order for them to construct new web sites. As creating ontologies or indeed using already existing one requires a great deal of fore knowledge about the knowledge domain. And to expecting everybody who wants to publish to the SW to posses this knowledge would prove unfounded.

DAML + OIL

RDF was developed at about the same time as XML with the aim to provide a language for modeling semi-structured metadata and enabling knowledge management systems. And it has proved to be successful because of its simplicity. But as RDF scope has expanded to include things like the SW, the limitations of its RDF Schema have become clear, as it lacks for catering data typing and a consistent expression for enumerations as well as other facilities. In response the DAML (DARPA Agent Mark-up Language) was set up and grouped its efforts with OIL (Ontology Inference Layer) another group working in the same area to provide a more sophisticated classification, who were using constructs from frame based AI (Artificial Intelligence). This resulted in a language that was able to express far more sophisticated classifications and property of resource than RDFS. The W3C is making the DAML + OIL specifications and its relationship with RDF and RDFS as a series of notes and have commissioned the WOWG (Web Ontology Working Group) to produce a new ontology language which is to be based upon DAML + OIL. DAML + OIL makes a separation between properties that relate object to object (called Object properties) and those that relate objects to datatype values (Datatype properties). There is also some change to the semantics of rdfs: domain and rdfs: range such as now a property can have multiple value ranges. In RDF and RDFS there is limited expression allowed on property declarations. E.g. somebody looking at Figure 41 would think that personal number properties were numbers. There were even declared as a literal. But literals can be any string including those that cannot be interpreted as numbers.

```
<rdfs:Property rdf:ID="PersonalINumber">
 <rdfs:Label>Personal Number</rdfs:Label>
 <rdfs:domain rdf:resource="#PNumber"/>
 <rdfs:range rdf:resource="http://www.w3c.org/2000/01/rdf-schema
  #Literal/>
</rdfs:Property>
```

Figure 41: Example RDFS statement

DAML + OIL overcomes this by restricting property values to data types that a defined in XSDL (XML Schema Definition Language) as-well as to user defined data types. So Figure 41 could be rewritten as shown in Figure 42.

```
<daml:DatatypeProperty rdf:ID="PersonalNumber">
  <rdfs:label>Personal Number</rdfs:label>
  <rdfs:domain rdf:resource="#PNumber"/>
  <rdfs:range rdf:resource="http://www.w3.org/2000/10/XMLSchema#
    nonNegativeInteger"/>
</daml:DatatypeProperty>
```

Figure 42: Example DAML + OIL statement

Properties in DAML + OIL can also be defined as being identical to each other by using daml: equivalentTo or daml: samePropertyAs. Other more expressive terms can be obtained with properties such as daml: UniqueProperty, daml: TransitiveProperty and daml: UnambiguousProperty. The most important facilities DAML + OIL provides is allowing designers to increase the expressivity's in classifying resources. The daml: Class is defined as being a subclass of rdfs: Class and it new facilities. An example of this is the built in support for enumerations, which was lacking in RDF. An enumeration defines a class by giving an explicit list of its members. In RDFS you could define a class and then have instances of this class. But the problem was that someone could come along and add new instances. An example of one such enumeration in DAML + OIL is shown in Figure 43.

```
<daml:Class ID="Position">
  <daml:oneOf parseType="daml:collection">
    <daml:Thing rdf:ID="1st">
      <rdfs:label>1st position</rdfs:label>
    </daml:Thing>
    <daml:Thing rdf:ID="2nd">
      <rdfs:label>2nd position</rdfs:label>
    </daml:Thing>
    <daml:Thing rdf:ID="3rd">
      <rdfs:label>3rd position</rdfs:label>
    </daml:Thing>
  </daml:oneOf>
</daml:Class>
```

Figure 43: An example DAML + OIL enumeration

In Figure 43 a DAML + OIL agent will be able to interpret the body of a property element as a special form of list, which is made up of each of the instances that appear in the element body. In this type of list you cannot add an item to the list without replacing another item. With DAML + OIL it is possible to say that one class is disjointed from another, so that the two classes will have no instances in common. This is achieved by using daml: disjointWith. DAML + OIL also allows for property restrictions which is a way to restrict classes to a set of resources based on particular properties of theirs, the number or the value of these properties.

```
<daml:Class rdf:ID="Fish">
  <rdfs:label>Types of Fish</rdfs:label>
  <rdfs:comment>A type of animal that lives in water</rdfs:comment>
  <rdfs:subClassOf>
    <daml:Restriction>
      <daml:onProperty rdf:resource="#anatomy"/>
      <daml:hasValue rdf:resource="#Fins"/>
    </daml:Restriction>
  </rdfs:subClassOf>
</daml:Class>
```

Figure 44: Example DAML + OIL property restriction

For instance, Figure 44 defines the fish class as a subclass of another class that is defined as a DAML + OIL restriction. These types of classes are defined by rules that specify what conditions of a resources properties has to be met for a resource to be a member of that class. Daml: onProperty identifies which property is to be checked. Daml: hasValue then declares that the property in question must have a particular value. So this states that a fish is a subclass of all resources, which has at least one-piece anatomy property whose value is fins.

RDF VCards

Some years ago, a number of companies got together to define a standard for electronic business cards, which was later developed by the International Mail Consortium and standardized by the IETF in RFC 2426 and became known as VCards. VCards consist of different property types describing different properties a person may want to put on a business card. The majority of these properties have strings or numbers as their values. Some of these include: First Name, Last Name, Full Name (FN), Birthday (BDAY), Role, Title, Phone number, E-Mail Address and URI. A full list of the property types available can be viewed at [W14]. A VCard may have multiple values for a property type. To allow for this RDF provides three mechanisms. These are Bags, Sequences and Alternatives. An RDF Bag is to be used when there is no relevance to the order in which the values appear. But if the order is important RDF Sequence may be used. RDF Alternatives is used when there is a choice of values available for a property with each value being valid but dependent on some other externally defined factor the first value is the default. RDF uses XML name spaces to uniquely identify the metadata schema and version and the name space for VCards is www.w3.org/2001/vcard-rdf/3.0#. Which is the current version of VCards. Using a prefix, which contains the current version number, has the advantage that there is no need to provide a special version number amongst the property tags. It also means that there is no need for the "begin" and "end" types as XML encoding of RDF automatically tells when the description starts and ends. Various VCard properties have the ability to one or more parameter types for a value. This may be needed for example, if it is wished to show that a telephone number is a home not a work telephone number or that a particular address is the preferred one. To achieve this in RDF the <RDF: type> property is used. This allows for the speciation of the type of the resource by indicating a URI that represents that type. This URI will be: www.w3.org/2001/vcard-rdf/3.0#<type>. Where the "<type>" will be substituted for one of the officially defined VCard parameter types, an example of this is shown in Figure 45.

```
<vCard:ADR rdf:parseType="Resource">
  <rdf:value> 12 New Street </rdf:value>
  <rdf:type rdf:resource="http://www.w3.org/2001/vcard-rdf/3.0#work"/>
</vCard:ADR>
```

Figure 45: Example RDF VCard showing use of Properties with Attributes

Some VCard properties can define sub-structures. For example the ADR property has post office box, region and postcode as some of its sub-structures. Thus allowing for a more defined and detailed description of attributes. Jena is a java API written in Java for manipulating RDF models it was created by Hewlett Packard (HP) semantic web research group, based in Bristol. Jena was developed to provide an API that was easier for the programmer to use than alternative implementations and to be conformant to the RDF specifications. Jena is open source and is available for download from [Jena]. Jena has a number of features that make it an ideal tool for carrying out research into the SW as it allows for: -

- ARP parser compliant with latest working group recommendations
- Integrated query language (RDQL)
- Support for storing DAML ontologies in a model
- Persistent storage module based on Berkeley DB (BDB) or in relational databases

The ARP parser is a standards compliant parser for the full RDF/XML syntax for RDF. It has a modular design based on XML Info set and is capable of parsing large files. Jena's query language is an implementation of an SQL-like query language for RDF derived from another query language called SquishQL (Squish Query

Language) which itself is derived from rdfDB (RDF Database). It treats RDF as data and provides query with triple patterns and constraints over a single RDF model. The target usage is for scripting and for experimentation in information modeling languages. However Jena's query language is considered to be "data oriented" as it only queries the information held in the models; that is there is no inference being done. Figure 46 shows an example Jena query that looks for a resource that has a property age with a value greater than 24.

```
SELECT ?resource
WHERE (?resource, <info:age>, ?age)
AND ?age >= 24
USING info FOR <http://somewhere/peopleInfo#>
```

Figure 46: Example Jena Query

Jena can also handle DAML+OIL by using its DAML model. This is a Jena model with some additional functionality to support the programmer in creating DAML ontologies. Each DAML ontology is encoded as RDF triples that can be stored within a Jena model. All of the operations of the DAML API get translated into adding, deleting and navigating the triples of this model. The BDB storage module allows Jena Models to be persistently stored using the Sleepy cat Berkeley dB storage manager. Offering a high performance implementation of the fine-grained RDF API. The relational database storage also allows for Jena models to be persistently stored but is slower than the BDB facility. However the relational database option does allow for use of such things as connectable to many different relational databases though configuration files support for My SQL. Jena also provides various methods to write out RDF/XML this is aided by the fact that the syntax of RDF/XML is flexible, allowing the same RDF graph to be written in many different ways. However this introduces the notion of style. Jena's basic RDF/XML writer takes no advantage of RDF/XML features that allow more compact and elegant expression, but it can write graphs of large sizes. Jena's Pretty Writer, however can take full advantage of the available syntax to produce compact output, but on the down side it has limited scalability.

Conclusion

The Semantic web is a vision of what the web of the future will be. Offering a web, which is not just designed for navigation by humans but also by machines, where information will not just be hidden away on text documents but will be structured in a manner that will make the discovery of documents and facts far easier. To support the Meta data describing the resources the authors of the semantic web proposed the use of ontologies, with the aim of providing the "semantics" for the semantic web. .

References

Bennett, S, (2002) Object – Oriented System Analysis and Design using UML, 2nd edition, McGraw Hill, p.301

Lee, T. (1998) http://www.w3.org/DesignIssues/Semantic.html, September 1998

RFC2396. Uniform Resource Identifiers (URI): Generic Syntax, http://www.ietf.org/rfc/rfc2396.txt, Eds. T. Berners-Lee, R. Fielding, L. Masinter. August 1998, August 1998

Lee, T. (2001) The Semantic Web, http://www.scientificamerican.com/2001/0501-issue/-0501- berners-lee.html

Cara (2005) http://zoe.mathematik.uni-osnabrueck.de/RDF/parser.html

Jena (2004) http://www.hpl.hp.com/semweb/

Pressman, R, (2000) Software Engineering a practitioner's approach, 5th edition, McGraw Hill, p.288

[W1] http://www710.univ-lyon1.fr/~champin/rdf-tutorial/node4.html

[W2] http://ksl-web.stanford.edu/KSL_Abstracts/KSL-92-71.html

[W3] Eric van der Vlist, James Hendler, Using W3C XML Schema, October 2001

[W4] DAML ontology library, http://www.daml.org/ontologies/

[W5] http://www.w3.org/TR/1999/REC-rdf-syntax-19990222/

[W6] www.TopicMaps.org

[W7] www.y12.doe.gov/sgml/sc34/document/0129.pdf

[W8] Lars Marius Garshol, What are Topic Maps, http://www.xml.com/lpt/a/2002/09/11/topicmaps.html

[W9] http://www.w3.org/TR/REC-xml-names/

[W10] World Wide Web Consortium (W3C) http://www.w3.org

[W11] http://www.semanticweb.org

[W12] Dublin Core www.dublincore.org

[W13] http://www.w3.org/TR/vcard-rdf

14   VoiceXML

Kevin Curran, Ashlean McNulty

Until recently, Internet applications have primarily been dependent on visual interfaces to provide access to information or services. Now advances in speech recognition technology are allowing the creation of voice applications; the user interacts with these applications by speaking to them through a telephone rather than by using traditional input devices. Driving this technology is Voice Extensible Markup Language, or VoiceXML. VoiceXML is a standard language for building interfaces between voice recognition software and Web content. Just as HTML defines the display and delivery of text and images on the Internet, VoiceXML translates XML-tagged Web content into a format that speech recognition Software can deliver by phone. With VoiceXML, users can create a new class of Web sites using audio interfaces, which are not really Web sites in the normal sense because they provide Internet access with a standard telephone. This has a great impact on people who are very mobile, who move from one location to the next on a regular basis and always have access to a telephone. It also has a profound impact on people with disabilities, especially the blind and visually impaired, where all that is necessary is their own voice to acquire the information they need. By applying voice technology to mobile phones, information transactions can take place verbally. Hence, by allowing voice access to information anytime, anywhere, from any device, voice recognition can provide a more effective way for companies to communicate with customers, save money and facilitate those with disabilities.

Introduction

HTML is the original language used to power the Web. It has served its purpose and without it the Web would not be possible. However, due to the Webs rapid growth and popularity HTML has begun to experience limitations. These limitations are evident with regard to structuring and retrieving data as the actual Web documents have increased and are more diverse than before. Obviously, a new approach was needed to overcome these limitations and hence a new language known as XML (Extensible Mark-up Language) was developed in February 1998 (Hocek and Cuddihy, 2003). This meant that developers could create applications in the language and environment with which they are already familiar. XML is an industry standard, it is simple in that any computer can read it, making communications with other systems in the Internet simple. The Internet was designed as an information medium but it is rapidly becoming a communications medium. Being able to talk to someone on the other side of the world via e-mail or even purchase a product from the comfort of your own home. However, knowing how rapidly technology and the Internet has evolved it has one major drawback, voice recognition technology.

The Internet has raised public expectations, with people growing used to having information at their fingertips when they want it. Mobile phones and WAP (Wireless Applications Protocol) technology have bridged the gap between mobility and access to the Internet. However WAP has recently highlighted many limitations, such as slow speeds and limited graphics. Due to these limitations of WAP the emergence of voiceXML, a derivative of XML, was developed in March 2001. This Mark-up language allows developers to bridge the gap between vast amounts of Web content and a purely voice-interface. VXML converts human speech to data that is usable by applications and servers. The XML based standard for voice browsing will significantly reduce the amount of time and effort needed to develop and deploy speech applications, because developers can use the same technology that they use for developing web sites. One segment of the population that will benefit from the advances in this voice technology is people with disabilities, including the blind and visually impaired. The technology advances in handheld devices and voice portals will reduce many barriers for these people leaving them to participate in society more fully. Interestingly, a datamonitor report suggests that 2008 will be an inflection point for VoiceXML-based interactive voice response (IVR), with the number of shipped ports utilizing the technology expected to surpass traditional IVR ports for the first time (Datamonitor, 2008).

The Importance of Voice Recognition

The emergence of voice recognition technology gives businesses a competitive edge and allows achievement of higher operational efficiency. It will free the user of limited navigation and confusing touch-tone menus, resulting in greater customer satisfaction. Navigation is now given a new dimension, allowing the user to move in any direction and at a desired speed all with the use of the most natural user interface – voice [2]. Since first being introduced in the late 1980's, voice recognition technology has become more efficient and less expensive, and the commercial market has expanded rapidly. The adoption of the standard voice scripting language, VoiceXML, is expected to fuel voice portal services, just as HTML fueled development of the Internet. Many researchers [3] believe that the 'cost of creating a speech-based portal platform continues to decline'. The reason for the decline in costs is due to the increasing densities and decreasing costs on the voice processing and the network interface hardware. These form a central part of a voice portal system and allow service providers to cater for more users at a lower price. One segment of the population that will benefit immensely from the advances in voice recognition technology than any other are people with disabilities.

Technological advances and the continuing convergence of computing and the telecommunications are reducing barriers, but for many people with disabilities the impact is more profound. Computerised voice recognition provides even further opportunities, particularly for those with severe arthritis or those who are visually impaired and blind. The capacity to communicate with, and collect information from almost any point on the globe or from one's home, has already expanded the ability of persons with disabilities to participate in an information oriented society more effectively than before. People with disabilities meet barriers of all types. However, computers are helping to lower many of these barriers through voice recognition. For blind people voice output can be used to read screen text to the blind computer users. Voice input provides another option for individuals with disabilities. Voice recognition systems allow users to control the menus on computers by speaking the specified words and letters. Sometimes different disabilities require similar accommodations. For instance, someone who is blind and someone who cannot use his/her hands both require full keyboard equivalents, since they both have difficulty using the keyboard and a mouse but can speak fine and hence can use voice recognition software.

Examples of barriers that people with blindness may encounter on the Web can include:

- Images that do not have alt text – this way a blind person cannot understand what the image is because it can not be described in braille or read out by a text screen reader.
- Complex images, for example: graphs and charts, are usually not adequately described.
- Video that is not described in audio.
- Tables that do not make sense when read serially – in a cell by cell mode.
- Non-standard document format that can be difficult for a screen reader to interpret.

Examples of barriers that people with physical and motor disabilities affecting the hands and arms may encounter include:

- Time-limited response options on Webpages – they will normally not be able to respond in the specified period.
- Browsers and authoring tools that do not support keyboard alternatives for mouse commands.
- Forms that cannot be tabbed through in order.

These web barriers may be overcome if more Web sites were developed primarily in voice and where no visual aids like images are needed. Voice recognition software and voice browsers make it possible for people to navigate the web site by their voice, some both with voice-input and voice-output, and some allowing telephone based web access. This would eliminate many of these barriers, for example, filling in a form would be simple, with the voice activated software asking the questions and presenting the specific options. The users can then simply choosing the options that are most suited to their particular needs.

The W3C are working to expand access to the Web to allow people to interact with Web sites via spoken commands. This should will allow any telephone to be used to access Web based services, and will be a boon to people with visual impairments or needing Web access while keeping their hands and eyes free for other things (Shukla et al., 2002). The focus of the W3C has naturally been on auditory interfaces, and hence all of the work has a positive impact on the user groups facing the most access challenges on the visual World Wide Web today – namely the blind and low vision users. Severe visual impairment is one of the rarest disabilities, affecting less than 1 percent of the population and it is one of the most difficult to overcome when using information Technology (Hocek and Cuddihy, 2003). When the Internet became graphical it left blind people struggling to catch up. But with voice recognition it has helped to liberate blind users from specially designed keyboards and mice, which can be inconvenient. The Internet is more likely to improve the quality of life for adults with disability than adults without disabilities. According to a recent survey carried out, forty eight percent of adults with disabilities believe that the Internet has greatly improved the quality of life, compared to only twenty seven percent of adults without disabilities. The Internet allows people with disabilities to be more informed and more connected to the world, and it also provides them with communication with people who have similar interests and experiences. If technology is designed to be useable by people with disabilities, it will increase their ability to participate in the workforce and lead independent lives.

VoiceXML

VoiceXML is an emerging standard that has been defined by the VoiceXML Forum, an industry organisation founded by AT&T, IBM, Lucent Technologies, and Motorola and consisting of more than three hundred companies. VoiceXML 1.0 is a specification of the VoiceXML Forum. It was released in March 2000, and accepted by World Wide Web Consortium (W3C) two months later as a standard for voice Mark up on the Web. Voice Extensible Markup language, is designed for creating dynamic, Interent- powered phone applications that feature synthesized speech, digitized audio, recognition of spoken DTMF (Touch tone)key input and telephone. Its major gaol is to bring the advantages of Web based development and content delivery to interactive voice response applications. VoiceXML is a web-based markup language based on XML. Its uses are somewhat similar to HTML, but while HTML assumes a Web-browser such as IE or Netscape, display screen, keyboard, and mouse, VoiceXML uses a voice browser with audio output (TTS, or pre-recorded prompts). It must be pointed out that XML is designed to represent arbitrary data and VoiceXML describes grammers, prompts, event handlers, and other data structures useful in describing voice interaction between a human and a computer. Until recently, the World Wide Web has relied exclusively on visual interfaces to deliver information and services to users via computers equipped with a monitor, keyboard and mouse. In doing so, a huge potential customer base has been ignored, for example people who due to location, time and disabilities do not have access to a computer. However, many of these people do have access to a telephone, so users will benefit from the convenience of using the mobile internet for self service transaction, while companies enjoy the Web's relatively low transaction costs.

VoiceXML is similar to HTML in that VoiceXML is a Mark up language for creating distributed voice applications, much as HTML is a Mark up language for creating visual applications. Just as HTML defines the display and delivery of text and images on the Internet, VXML translates any XML tagged Web content into a format that speech recognition Software can deliver by phone. With VoiceXML, users can create a new class of web sites using audio interfaces which can access the Internet with a standard telephone. Phones are everywhere in the developed world, in far greater numbers than the Internet-connected computers. They are more portable and accessible than computers. So with VoiceXML, these common devices can be used for applications such as voice activated weather forecasts, restaurant listings and other location based services that are not feasible on computers. The best suited applications for VoiceXML are information retrieval, electronic commerce, personal services, and unified messages. The value of moving applications and content to XML means that you're really positioning yourself to take advantages of VoiceXML as its emerging. It is apparent that basing VXML on the XML standard yields some important benefits. The most important is that it allows the reuse and easy retooling of existing tools for creating, transforming and parsing XML documents. VoiceXML and XML are similar in that that they both provide advance features such as, local validation and processing but VoiceXML provide slightly more advanced features such as playback and recording, and support for context-specific and tapered help.

Voice applications are applications in which the input/output are through spoken, rather than a graphical user interface. The application files can reside on the local system, an Intranet, or the Internet. A voice application is a collection of one or more VoiceXML documents (Lucas, 2000). Each VoiceXML document contains one or more dialogs describing a specific interaction with the user. These dialogs may present the user with information or prompt the user to provide information. When this is complete, they can redirect the flow of control to another dialog in that document, to a dialog in another document in the same application, or even to a dialog in another application entirely. A user can then access the assembled applications anytime, anywhere, from any telephone-capable device. The designer can also design the application to restrict access only to those who are authorised to receive it. These voice applications provide a simple and novel way for users to surf or shop on the Internet – browsing by voice. Hence, there is no need for a keyboard/mouse, just voice.

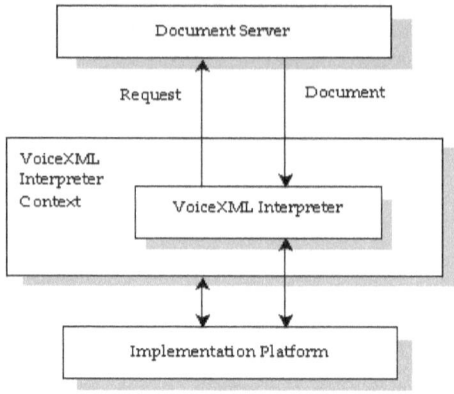

Figure 47 : Components of VoiceXML

As illustrated in Figure 47, a document server (e.g. a web server) processes requests from a client application, the VoiceXML Interpreter, through the VoiceXML interpreter context. The server produces VoiceXML documents in reply, which are processed by the VoiceXML Interpreter. The VoiceXML interpreter context may monitor user inputs in parallel with the VoiceXML interpreter. For example, one VoiceXML interpreter context may always listen for a special escape phrase that takes the user to a high-level personal assistant, and another may listen for escape phrases that alter user preferences like volume or text-to-speech characteristics.

The implementation platform is controlled by the VoiceXML interpreter context and by the VoiceXML interpreter. For instance, in an interactive voice response application, the VoiceXML interpreter context may be responsible for detecting an incoming call, acquiring the initial VoiceXML document, and answering the call, while the VoiceXML interpreter conducts the dialog after answer. The implementation platform generates events in response to user actions (e.g. spoken or character input received, disconnect) and system events (e.g. timer expiration). Some of these events are acted upon by the VoiceXML interpreter itself, as specified by the VoiceXML document, while others are acted upon by the VoiceXML interpreter context.

VoiceXML implements a client server paradigm, where a web server provides VoiceXML documents that contain dialogs to be interpreted and presented to the user; the users responses are then submitted to the Web Server, which responds by providing additional VoiceXML documents, as appropriate. Unlike proprietary Interactive VoiceResponse (IVR) systems, VoiceXML provides an open application development environment that generates portable applications. This makes it a more cost effective alternative for providing voice access services. Moreover, most IVR systems today accept input from the telephone keypad only, in contrast, VoiceXML is designed predominantly to accept spoken input, but, if desired, can also accept telephone key pad (DTMF) input (Phillips, 2000). VoiceXML supports local processing and validation of user input and playback of prerecorded audio files.

Conclusions

VoiceXML is a standard language for building interfaces between voice recognition software and Web content. Just as HTML defines the display and delivery of text and images on the Internet, VoiceXML translates XML-tagged Web content into a format that speech recognition Software can deliver by phone. With VoiceXML, users can create a new class of Web sites using audio interfaces, which are not really Web sites in the normal sense because they provide Internet access with a standard telephone. With Voice recognition becoming more 'mainstream', significantly simpler to work with, and less expensive, it is possible that users will become receptive to this technology and be willing to try it out. Voice command input can be more natural and much faster. People can speak in a natural voice to interact with their computers. Thus, combined with affordable pricing, and increased consumer demand, is leading to the evolution of transparent computing, where human/machine interaction is so natural that it is almost invisible.

References

Datamonitor (2008) VoiceXML tipped to become the dominant platform for IVR technology in 2008
1 Jan 2008, http://www.cbronline.com/article_feature.asp?guid=3AA03978-E715-49C2-A314-6D3AF5BE7703

Hocek, A., Cuddihy, D. (2003) Definitive VoiceXML, Prentice Hall, ISBN-10: 0130463450

Lucas, B. (2000). VoiceXML for Web-based distributed applications. Communications of the ACM: New York, Vol 43, pp53-57

Phillips, L. (2000) VoiceXML: The new standard in Web Telephony, Web Review Magazine, http://www.webreview.com

Shukla, C. Dass, A Gupta, V. (2002) *VoiceXML 2.0 Developer's Guide*, California USA: McGraw-Hill/Osborne.

15   Web Services

Kevin Curran and Padraig O'Kane

The online community steadily grows each year and with this escalation, the number of services provided increases in an attempt to meet the demands of a computer literate audience. There is a progression from a human-oriented use of the web to an application driven concept referred to as web services. We discuss the factors leading to this development and the inspiration behind web services. We detail the languages, platforms and systems involved in these services.

Introduction

The term 'Web Services' was initially employed by Bill Gates, Chairman of Microsoft, at the Microsoft Professional Developers Conference in Orlando, Florida on July 12th, 2000. Fundamentally, the term refers to automated resources accessed via an Internet URL. However a more comprehensive definition is that of the World Wide Web Consortium (W3C)[1], which declare web services as *"providing a standard means of interoperating between different software applications, running on a variety of platforms and/or frameworks."* An Internet connection allows retrieval of software powered resources or functional components and is therefore regarded as an extension of the World Wide Web infrastructure. Web services represent the evolution of a human-oriented utilization of the web to a technology that is application driven. It attempts to replace human centric searches for information with searches that are primarily application based.

The primary elements associated with web services are Repositories (i.e. a location for storage) and Messaging. Web service applications can perform a range of requests or processes yet several characteristics found are common throughout. All web service applications connect over a network i.e. a medium that allows users to share information and resources. The networks frequently associated with web services are Intranet (within an organisation), Extranet (within an organisation including controlled outside partners) or Internet (within the global community). Communication between the applications within the network is performed using a set of standardised protocols; those used include Hypertext Transport Protocol (HTTP) and the Secure Hypertext Transport Protocol (HTTPS). Another common characteristic associated with web services is that the connection between applications is standardized, yet it is operating system and language independent so that disparate or varying systems can benefit. The principal language that conveys the information distributed across the network is Extensible Mark-up Language (XML) and this language is expressed using SOAP Messaging. Web services are often called XML Web Services to emphasize the importance of XML as the underlying language whilst distinguishing such services for other types commonly available on the web. The Interfaces of a web service are often defined using the Web Services Description Language (WSDL). IT employs XML grammar in describing network services as collections of endpoints capable of exchanging messages. Through the use of WSDL, web services can enable applications to use its services once they have found and interpreted its definition. Yet another common characteristic is that of UDDI. Characteristics of a web service including its existence, location and purpose can be published and discovered using Universal Description, Discovery and Integration (UDDI). Web service descriptions and the methods for publishing and discovering them are stored in a repository provided by UDDI.

History of Web Services

Web Services derived from the efforts of a number of businesses that shared a mutual interest in developing and maintaining an "electronic marketplace". In 1975, Electronic Data Interchange (EDI) was launched and was deemed the first attempt to create a medium where businesses could communicate over a network. However EDI was difficult to implement due to its complexity and cost constraints and in the 25 years since its introduction numerous efforts at a global business network technology have been introduced e.g. Distributed Component Object Model, UNIX Remote Procedure Call and Java Remote Method Invocation. Each of the

---

[1] www.webservices.org

applications failed to gain significant market status or enough momentum to succeed, although all of them exist today and are still useful they failed to generate broad industry support. A combination of factors has contributed to the failure of these previous technologies and it was imperative that software vendors accepted this and concentrated on implementing a technology where an "electronic marketplace" was a realisation. Before the introduction of the web, the possibility of ensuring that all major software vendors agreed on a transport protocol for communication across network application services was unrealistic. But when the web was a reality, lower level transports for standardized communication was specified. The standards TCP/IP and HTTP where already integrated by the time the web went global in 1994, all that was required was a messaging and data encapsulation standard and it was essential that software vendors co-operated fully.

The introduction of Extensible Mark-up Language (XML) was instrumental in the rise of web services. It officially became a recognised standard in February 1998 when the World Wide Web Consortium announced that XML 1.0 was suitable for integration into software applications. XML is described as a *"widely heralded, platform independent standard for data description"* (Levitt, 2001). It provided the means of communicating between standardized applications and by early 1998, a number of attempts where made at an XML protocol encouraging interprocess communication. One such protocol, SOAP is regarded as the basis for web services. It proved popular considering the consensus among certain individuals who appeared a little dubious at first due to the fact that Microsoft developed the protocol. SOAP was advantageous in that it was flexible, general purpose and its compatibility across platforms meant that its acceptance was widespread. Surprisingly after private meetings, IBM publicly backed Microsoft's SOAP and in March 2000 both companies began to develop SOAP 1.1. Both companies also began to work individually on protocols, which encouraged connectivity to a web service. They emerged with IBM's Network Accessible Service Specification Language and Microsoft's Service Description Language and SOAP Contract Language. During the autumn of 2000, the protocol proposals were merged and Web Services Description Language (WSDL) was announced. Companies could therefore create and describe their web services using SOAP and WSDL, yet a means of locating and advertising web services was still required. IBM, Microsoft and now Ariba began working on a solution in March 2000, their efforts produced the standard Universal Description, Discovery and Integration (UDDI) which was announced in September 2000. With SOAP, WSDL and UDDI in place it was apparent that the standards to create locate and advertise web services had arrived. However, Software Infrastructure Vendors remained defiant and it was not until the end of 2000 that Oracle, HP, Sun, IBM and Microsoft revealed their intention to support and incorporate the standards into their products.

Web Service Technologies

Web services use a number of inter-related technologies and languages. However we intend to focus on those that have aided the growth of web services and those that where established in an effort to maximize its potential namely XML, SOAP and WSDL.

XML

In order to understand XML (Goldfarb and Prescod, 2006) it is important to realise that it is an outgrowth of Standard Generalized Mark-up Language (SGML), which became a standard of the International Organization for Standardization (ISO) in 1986. SGML had its early origins in IBM, they realised the importance of publishing content in a number of different ways. With a number of organizations struggling with similar problems IBM seized the opportunity to create a standard for document mark-up. The resulting rich document mark-up language allowed authors to separate the logical content of a document from its presentation. This approach involved the introduction of Metadata. Metadata describes the attributes of an information bearing object (IBO) e.g. Document, Dataset, Database, image etc. It is more commonly referred to as *"Data about Data"* (Dick, 2001). Another definition states *"Metadata usually includes information about the intellectual content of the image, digital representation data and security or rights management information"*[1]. With SGML, Metadata was added to indicate the logical structure and to provide shared context. HTML is also a descendant of SGML. However both HTML and SGML where lacing in terms of defining the requirements of Metadata. Yet when companies began to develop a standard addressing the problems associated with these languages they naturally looked at SGML as a starting point. As mentioned previously the World Wide Web Consortium formed a working group to study the issue. Their primary goal was to establish a simplified subset of SGML suitable for use on the web, as SGML is extremely complex and poses problems for automated processing of large volumes of Internet documents. A subset of SGML that would be simple enough for people

---

[1] http://xml.coverpages.org

to understand yet expressive enough to meet the need for shared context on the Internet was what was required. The resulting specification was XML 1.0. The XML approach to Metadata and shared context is simple to grasp. Programmers add Metadata through tags, the syntax is similar to that of HTML with angled brackets (<>) commonplace throughout (See Figure 48).

```
<to>Padraig</to>
<from>Ruairi</from>
<re><customer-name>Joe Bloggs</customer-name>
    <customer-number>0101-0101-010</customer-number>
    <document-type-request>order form</document-type-request>
</re>
<p>Joe Bloggs wants to complain about his order. He feels he has been
overcharged.</p>
```

Figure 48: XML Document detailing a letter regarding an order

Document designers add shared context through Document Type Definitions (DTD's). A DTD uses a collection of rules to specify the allowable order, structure and attributes of tags for a particular type of document, in simpler terms the DTD handles the mark-up language and therefore specifies what tags are valid. Using an Internet Uniform Resource Locator (URL) a document can reference the DTD. XML offers a standard, flexible and data format that is extensible which therefore reduces the burden of organizing a number of technologies needed to ensure web services are a success. The XML syntax is an extremely important aspect as are the concepts of the XML Infoset, XML Schema and XML Namespaces. XML Infoset is a formal set of information items and associated properties that provide an abstract description of an XML document. It attempts to define a set of terms that specifications can use to refer to information within an XML document. The concept of XML Namespaces is extremely important in that it ensures XML documents remain recognizable and are free from 'collisions' that occur when other software packages use similar attribute or element naming conventions. The XML Namespaces mechanism is a collection of names identified by a URL reference, they differ from other naming conventions in that the XML version has an internal structure and uses families of reserved attributes. The XML Schema is a concept that allows machines to process work based on a series of rules developed by people. The structure and content of an XML document can be defined using such a schema.

SOAP

Simple Object Access Protocol or SOAP is a protocol based on XML Messaging and is used to encode the information in web service request and response messages before they can be sent over a network. SOAP is used to gain access to services, objects and servers in a standard way. Its main goal is to facilitate interoperability i.e. the ability of software and hardware located in multiple machines to communicate. They are independent of any operating system and/or protocol and can be sent using a range of Internet protocols however the underlying communication protocol is that of HTTP. When SOAP was first introduced programmers/authors focused on accessing objects, a medium specific to technologies that recognised an object oriented approach. Over time it was felt that SOAP was restricted and that a wider audience was required and therefore the specification moved away from an object-centric one to a generalized XML Messaging framework. As mentioned previously SOAP defines a method of transferring XML messages from one point to the next (See Figure 49).

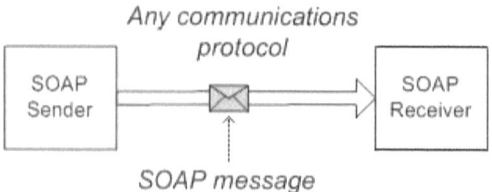

The messaging framework carries this out, as it is extensible, usable over a variety of underlying protocols and independent of programming models. The key to SOAP is its extensibility. Simplicity still remains one of SOAP's primary design goals as is often witnessed with software. SOAP lacks in a number of various distributed system features such as security, routing and reliability, however such features can be added at later stages and with IBM, Microsoft and other software vendors working continually on SOAP extensions, developers remain optimistic. Secondly, SOAP can be used over any transport protocol such as TCP; HTTP etc however a standard protocol required defining in order to outline rules governing the environment. The SOAP specification encourages the definition of absolute protocols by providing such a flexible framework. The third characteristic of SOAP is that it doesn't conform to just one programming model. SOAP defines a model for processing individual, single path messages however it is possible to combine multiple messages into an overall message exchange, SOAP therefore allows for any number of message exchange patterns. The SOAP messaging framework consists of a number of core elements: Envelope, Header, Body and Fault. The Envelope element is always the root element of a SOAP message, making it easy for applications to identify a message by simply looking at the name of the root element. The version of SOAP being used can also be identified from information stated in the envelope element. The envelope element contains an optional Header element, which is followed by a Body element, which represents the majority of the message. The body element can contain varying numbers of elements from any namespace. The data that a user wants to send is placed within the body element. The Fault element highlights errors within the body element in the event that something goes wrong. A standard error representation is paramount in that it insures that applications refrain from inventing their own, therefore making it impossible for the general infrastructure to differentiate between success and failure.

WSDL

The Web Services Description Language (WSDL) provides an XML grammar and supplies a means of grouping messages into operations and operations into interfaces. WSDL is essential to the web services architecture as it describes the complete contract for application communication. WSDL is a machine-readable language and therefore tools and infrastructure can be easily built around it. Developments within this technology have insured that programmers can use WSDL definitions to generate code that interacts with web services precisely. Code generation like this encapsulates details concerned with the sending and receiving of SOAP messages over different protocols and makes web services a lot more approachable. Regardless of the programming language in use be it JAVA, C++ etc, the classes generated from the same WSDL definition should be able to communicate with each other through the WSDL provided interfaces. A WSDL definition contains several elements including types, messages, port Type, binding and service (See Figure 50) all of which come from the same namespace. It is therefore important that when referencing something in a WSDL file that a qualified name is used.

```
<!-- WSDL definition structure -->
<definitions
        name="MathService"
        targetNamespace="http://example.org/math/"
xmlns=http://schemas.xmlsoap.org/wsdl/
>
        <!-- abstract definitions -->
        <types> ...
        <message> ...
        <portType> ...
        <!-- concrete definitions -->
        <binding> ...
        <service> ...
</definition>
```

Figure 50: Basic structure of a WSDL definition

The elements type, message, and portType are abstract definitions of the web service interface. These 3 elements make up the programmatic interface that one interacts with. The last 2 elements (binding and service) describe the concrete details of how the interface translates messages onto the wire.   The underlying infrastructure handles these details rather than the application code.   Several editors are now available allowing the generation of WSDL and thus making the authoring of such definitions a lot easier.

Successful Web Service Implementations

It is fair to comment that successful web service implementations are business driven.   Customers and users alike state that technology will survive due to its impact on business rather than its adoption purely for technology sake.   Companies that pioneered the web service revolution understand the benefits reaped are significant and they plan to insure that continued investment is maintained.   One example is Systinet who are a leading independent provider of web services infrastructure software.   In January 2004 Systinet announced that its revenue for 2003 was 5 times greater than that of 2003, resulting from contracts agreed with 70 new companies.   Systinet developed a selection of products most notably WASP, which is based on the industry standards of XML, SOAP, WSDL and UDDI.   Their products are available for use with a number of languages mainly JAVA and C++, WASP also displays interoperability with other web service implementations e.g. Microsoft. NET.   Systinet's products are also portable across a wide variety of platforms and servers.

Qwest Communications International Inc is another example of a company excelling due to its implementation of a web service infrastructure.   Qwest is a leading provider of voice, video and data services to more than 25 million customers.   The company is a leader in web hosting services, managed solutions, high-speed Internet access and private networks choosing to develop an XML-based system by embracing two platform technologies: the Microsoft.NET framework and Java 2 Enterprise Edition (J2EE).   Qwest worked with Microsoft Consulting Services and Hewlett Packard in order to design a tailored XML web services project. The benefits Qwest experienced where that of increased reliability and availability.   The implementation handles failures without interrupting service on a particular machine.   The critical measure of success was the reduction in time of the development of applications from 1 year to 90 days.   This enabled Qwest to create an increased number of applications faster.

BizDex is a project aimed at using web services to build a national e-business network for small companies in Australia.   Australia's National Office for the Information Economy (NOIE) joined forces with Standards Australia to develop the e-business solution.   To date the solution hasn't been fully implemented although BizDex anticipates that they can reach a large enough scale to ensure that vendors will enter the market due to its economic benefits and therefore making it inexpensive for small businesses to exploit.   BizDex is a registry based on UDDI, a concept discussed earlier in this assignment.   The registry provides a means of classifying and identifying data into a common format.   BizDex also uses WSDL files to populate models representing public and private processes and ebXML provides the messaging function critical to the success of any web service. BizDex has secured the support of both Intuit and Microsoft, which highlights the project as one of great status. The developers behind BizDex claim that it has the *"structure and stability of a public service combined with the entrepreneurial energy of the private sector"* [1].

Future of Web Services

Web services have established themselves and have found a critical mass. In order to maintain this momentum, web service standards need to progress quickly and efficiently and the concept of interoperability must be achieved.   The choices evident within the world of web services are of an extremely delicate nature especially during such a formative period.   The factors that will determine the success of web services technology are those concerned with the variety of scales and whether the technology can be used with simple, small projects as well as more complex developments.   Both SOAP and WSDL are complementary to projects of varying sizes and it is these technologies that will ensure continued support from businesses and organizations as these standards are now globally accepted.   Integrated environments such as Microsoft Visual Studio.NET already provide a framework to create and control web services in a seamless fashion.   Other web service product developers such as IBM are extending their environments to encourage an easy to use development platform.   It is predicted that as the number of businesses publishing web services grows they will seek to provide services alternatives to guarantee 24/7 availability and aid the monitoring of web services as well as validating service providers and offering one-stop shopping for web services.   It is also felt that a centralised web services repository will be created to encourage real time processing of data form multiple systems in the correct format and this may be a

---

[1] http://xml.coverpages.org

fundamental stage in ensuring the future of web services (Kotok, 2004).

Conclusion

Since the introduction of XML in 1998, the web service technology has steadily gathered momentum. Both Microsoft and IBM were pioneering forces behind its implementation and their work together has seen a number of developments most notably SOAP and WSDL, gain global status in an effort to firmly establish web services as the key in developing an electronic marketplace. Companies are keen to exploit this solution and the examples of Systinet, Qwest and BizDex highlight this firmly. It is however imperative that companies, vendors and the World Wide Web Consortium agree on standards and that the factors contributing to successful web service growth are harnessed in order to ensure that the future for web services is prosperous.

References

Levitt, J. (2001). From EDI to XML and UDDI: A Brief History of Web Services. Information Week, October 2001

Goldfarb, C. and Prescod, P. (2006) The XML Handbook Second Edition, Wiley Publishers, NY

Dick, K. (2001) XML – A Manager's Guide, Pearson Education, London

Kotok, A. (2004) ebXML And Web Services to Go the Last Mile. BizDex Journal, January 2004

16   Web 2.0

Kevin Curran, David Stephen Norrby, Martin Christian

Web 2.0 is a social phenomenon referring to an approach to creating and distributing Web content itself, characterized by open communication, decentralization of authority, freedom to share and re-use and "the market as a conversation. Web 2.0 is about making sure that users add value to a site as a side effect of what they are actually using the site for. In effect, web 2.0 is making use of the long tail such as Amazon when it collects user reviews of their products. Most of us are used to software being developed, packaged, picked up in the store and kept updated through downloaded and installed patches. In the web 2.0 world, applications are run online, with no installation, updates are constant and continuous and access is instant from any computer with a browser. This chapter provides a clearer definition of web 2.0 and the technologies and web sites which utilise web 2.0 principles.

Introduction

A new term has emerged known as "Web 2.0". Most web surfers will have come across the terms "blog," "wiki," "podcast," "RSS Feed," and "CSS and XHTML Validated." These are all associated with the umbrella term of "Web 2.0," although the actual definition of this term is still hotly debated. "Web 2.0" it was first used by O'Reilly Media as the name of a series of web-development conferences[1] that started in 2004. Wikipedia also define the expression as referring to any of the following:

> "The transition of websites from isolated information silos to sources of content and functionality, thus becoming a computer platform serving web applications to end users.
> A social phenomenon referring to an approach to creating and distributing Web content itself, characterized by open communication, decentralization of authority, freedom to share and re-use and "the market as a conversation."
> A more organized and categorized content, with far more developed deep linking web architecture.
> A shift in economic value of the web, possibly surpassing that of the dot com boom of the late 1990s.
> A marketing term to differentiate new web businesses from those of the dot com boom, which due to the bust now seems discredited.
> The resurgence of excitement around the possibilities of innovative web applications and services that gained a lot of momentum around mid 2005."

Sub-categories of what Web 2.0 encapsulates include usability, economy, participation, convergence, design, standardization and remixability. These categories are further broken down with sub-categories such as blogs, audio, video, RSS, open APIs, wikis, social software and focus on simplicity. This chapter presents an overview of web 2.0 including definitions, technologies involved and sites currently advocated as examples of web 2.0.

Web 2.0

Tim O'Reilly defines Web 2.0 as "Web 2.0 is the network as platform, spanning all connected devices; Web 2.0 applications are those that make the most of the intrinsic advantages of that platform: delivering software as a continually-updated service that gets better the more people use it, consuming and remixing data from multiple sources, including individual users, while providing their own data and services in a form that allows remixing by others, creating network effects through an "architecture of participation," and going beyond the page metaphor of Web 1.0 to deliver rich user experiences."[2]. Tim O'Reilly also posted the following figure to serve as a further explanation[3].

---

[1] http://www.web2con.com/

[2] http://radar.oreilly.com/archives/2005/10/web_20_compact_definition.html

[3] http://www.oreillynet.com/pub/a/oreilly/tim/news/2005/09/30/what-is-web-20.html

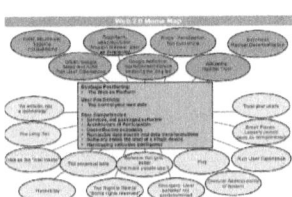

Figure 51: Web 2.0 Meme Map

Figure 51 is a diagram created at the web 2.0 conference which describes the concept of web 2.0 as not having a hard boundary, but rather, a gravitational core. The web is the platform for this concept, while the user gets to control his/her own data.

Figure 52: What is Web 2.0

Figure 52 points out the evolution of services such as "DoubleClick" and "Britannica Online" into the Web 2.0 generation, where the popularity of their Web 2.0 counterparts, "Google AdSense" and "Wikipedia" respectively, has increased massively. A general comparison between Web 2.0 & Web 1.0 is shown in Table 4.

	Web 1.0	Web 2.0
Mode of Usage	Read	Write and Contribute
Unit of Content	Page	Record
State	Static	Dynamic
How Content is Viewed	Web Browser	Browser, RSS Readers, Mobile Devices, etc.
Creation of Content	By Website Authors	By Everyone

Table 4: Difference between Web 1.0 and Web 2.0

There are those (Shaw, 2005) who debate the validity of the term "Web 2.0." claiming that Web 2.0 does not exist and that the term is merely a marketing slogan that is used to convince investors and the media that the companies are "creating something fundamentally new, rather than continuing to develop and use well-established technologies." Whatever the actual definition, the most widely accepted idea of what makes a website Web 2.0 is the following set of criteria:

1. User-generated content, as opposed to content posted solely by the site author(s). One example of this would be the recently developed www.newsvine.com, which allows users to post their own news articles and maintain their own news columns.
2. Treats users as if they are co-developers of the site: The more people that use the service, the better it becomes. User contribution, by means of reviews, comments, etc. is encouraged.
3. Highly customisable content and interface. For example, allowing users to put their own news feeds on their homepage as in www.netvibes.com (See Figure 53), rather than serving content that the user has little to no control over, as in the home page of MSN, BBC or NBC.
4. The core application of the website runs through the browser and web server, rather than on a desktop platform.
5. The incorporation of popular internet trends such as "blogging," "tagging," "podcasting," "wikis," the sharing of media and content and the use of web standards such as validated XHTML and Cascading Style Sheets (CSS).
6. Integration of emerging web technologies such as Asynchronous JavaScript and XML (AJAX), Really Simple Syndication (RSS) and Application Programming Interfaces (APIs)

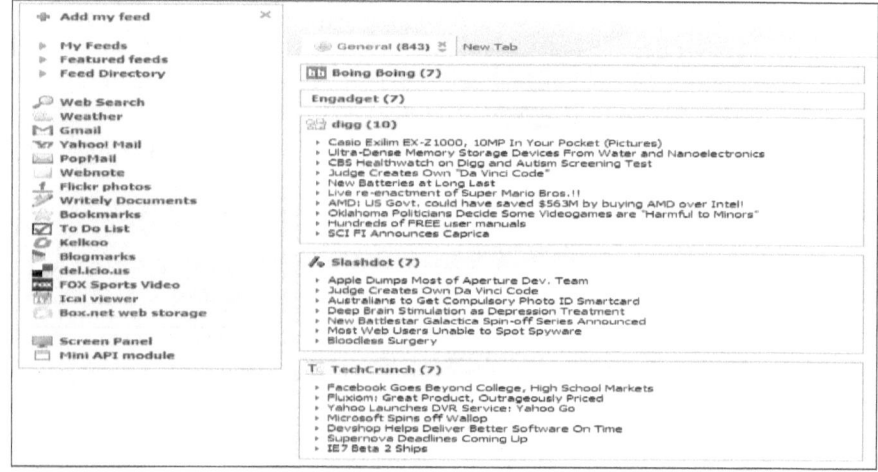

Figure 53: Netvibes.com Customisable Homepage

Quite often, one can recognise a Web 2.0 site based on the following minor characteristics:

1. Clean interface with an extensive use of colour gradients, large fonts and CSS design;
2. Contains a development wiki;
3. Separate RSS feeds for every part of the site;
4. Links to a "meet the team" personal blog maintained by the site authors;
5. The company's name sounds like a character from Star Wars and/or at least one vowel appears to be missing. For example: Renkoo, Gabbr, Meebo, Congoo, Flickr, Frappr, Tagyu, Goowy and Squidoo;
6. Box of "tags" with varying font sizes (See Figure 54).

Figure 54: Most Popular Tags on Flickr.com

The use of Hyper linking on Web pages underpins the 2.0 Web. The high level of connectibility between content on the web has encouraged sustained growth as more and more users add new content. Users can then link to newly discovered sites in a way similar to dendrites forming relationships in the human brain. The success of Google is a result of 2.0 technologies. Google have created a business from linking users of one site to the information or service provided by another. Google has none of the trappings of software provider's products. These trappings are the purchase cost of the software, limited applications to a particular platform and the product life span where the next generation would involve the consumer having to purchase an upgrade or a whole new software package. There are no direct costs to the users of Google; all the business costs are met by advertising and the placing of sponsored links in prominent positions. Continuous upgrades are of very little significance to the end user as they have no direct input either with time or resources. The key to Google's success is the use of PageRank which used web link structure as opposed to the page content to rank search results. This open source operating systems would have been impossible to run with Web 1.0 technologies supporting the argument that Web 2.0 is a platform where the user has control of the information provided (McCormack, 2002). While it is clear that Web 2.0 has no clear and concise definition, one could argue that the term is useful in that it allows non-technical users to the define the complicated set of concepts and technologies that are constantly being developed for use in new websites, and it allows companies to promote their websites to the masses without having to explain the sophisticated array of technologies used to create the application.

Popular Trends

A "blog," short for "web log," is a web-based publication comprising individual articles that are posted periodically and are usually displayed in reverse chronological order. Blogs are often used to create online journals and others may focus on one particular subject, such as technology or politics. Content submission to blogs is usually done on the web server, rather than uploading manually, with templates automatically styling the newly-created content to fit appropriately on the blog home page. Most blog software allows readers to submit comments on each piece of content and it is customary, especially on professional blogs, to provide links to similar articles on different blogs. Blogs have become extremely popular over the past few years. technorati.com, a popular blog search engine, is "currently tracking 36.7 million sites and 2.3 billion links" and, with free blog hosting sites such as www.livejournal.com and www.blogger.com allowing users to create a blog within minutes, that number is steadily increasing. Examples of popular blogs are engadget[1], boingboing[2] and techcrunch[3].

Syndication

---

[1] www.engadget.com
[2] www.boingboing.net
[3] www.techcrunch.com

The use of Really Simple Syndication (RSS) and/or Atom Feeds to allow users to view new site updates without having to visit the actual website, such as by using a news reader (e.g. Microsoft Outlook), downloading onto a mobile device, or integrating the syndication feed into a desktop program (e.g. Google Desktop).

Podcasts

Podcasting is the use of syndication, RSS or Atom, for the distribution of multimedia files such as audio recordings over the internet for playback on mobile devices and personal computers. Usually the podcast is some from of show, like a weekly radio programme.

Tagging

A tag is a word attached to a piece of content that acts as a category. Multiple tags can be assigned to the content and they allow content to be sorted according to category, in the same way that similar files can be located within one directory. The difference, however, is that sorting by tags is dynamic. A piece of content's tags can be easily added, edited or removed with no hindrance to the sorting process as the sorting is done using software on the web server.Tags are often used in Web 2.0 applications. For example, on www.flickr.com, users can assign their own tags to the photographs they have uploaded so that other users can see it when they are viewing photographs with similar tags. This method of open categorisation on the internet is known as "Folksonomy."

Mashups

A "mashup" is a product that incorporates multiple technologies and information from different sources into one application by making use of Application Programming Interfaces (APIs). One example would be the correlation of information with Google Maps, e.g. placing houses to buy and rent on the Google Maps interface, as used in www.ononemap.com.

Folksonomies.

Folksonomy is a combination of the words "Folk" and "taxonomy," literally meaning "people's classification management". Folksonomies allow internet users to categorize web pages, photographs and links. This labelling process is called "tagging" and the result is an improved quality of search results.

Web 2.0 is more interactive than its predecessor. Web pages are now described as "User dependant web portals". These portals require user input and feed back for success. EBay is an online business that depends on transactions conducted by it members to sustain growth. In a way similar to the Web, eBay is a supplier of content that supports user activities with continued market domination almost guaranteed due to its sheer scale of operation. The major high street retailers are now flexing their collective business muscle on the Web. Tesco.com provides all the facilities of their physical store online enabling the customer to shop from home using JavaScript and secure internet connections to facilitate transactions. Other business can now compete with the big retail companies even if they are based solely online. Ryan Air provides agent free bookings removing the middle man and more importantly for the consumer, agent fees from air travel. Web 2.0 applications have helped Ryan Air grow as a company at a time when the general air industry is in recession (MacManus, 2005).

A lot of the people involved in the development of Web 1.0 are today involved in the Web 2.0 industry, this bank of knowledge can only help guarantee the success of Web 2.0 applications. Web 1.0 many companies which were involved in the original dot com era had moved on to join larger companies. This suggests that there is plenty of web experience in the mix. These people will have the knowledge of what works and what doesn't. But more importantly, why something does or does not work. Today's Websites are now dynamic rather than being static, websites have become platforms for web applications for end users. With the use of development systems such as AJAX, there are now many web based applications which imitate standard computer applications, for example word processing, spreadsheets and slide show presentations. These are applications that the general public are familiar with, making it easier for an end user to operate these applications. These new web applications are often much more complicated to design and create creating employment opportunities for it professionals. The way in which communities interact socially has changed with Web 2.0 innovations. No longer do people depend on written letters in the post or telephone calls to communicate. Web 2.0 has helped to create online social networks for public use; some of them provide social software which members can use to connect with each other. Microsoft's MSN and Bebo.com are two of these online communities. Benefits to web 2.0 include the fact that it holds collective intelligence. This makes the work on it collaborative. Also because everything is updated instantly, using RSS feeds, there is an instant gratification. Users have a sense of ownership over the web because it holds their work. This makes them much more passionate about using the web and updating it regularly, meaning everyone who reads the information on the web gets up to date information all the time. The early Web was primarily for the reading of information by users, today on the web the user can still just read but they also now can contribute to a website.

Today's online tasks are more than surfing for information, the now include shopping, down and uploading, blogging and sharing files with web users both known and unknown to the user. There is no argument against the fact that there have been major developments in the way today's Web is run or in the applications and expectations end users now have of the Web. Even when all the previously discussed developments are considered there still is no direct evidence that Web 2.0 exists as an actual methodology or technology. It seems to be a phrase used to describe recent innovations in the natural development cycle, although some older technologies have been included under the Web 2.0 banner (MacManus, 2005).

Web 2.0 Technology

The following is a brief overview of the technology and software used to create the Web 2.0 Experience.

AJAX

AJAX stands for "Asynchronous JavaScript and XML." It is a technique used to create interactive web applications, where small parts of a website can be refreshed with new content without the need to reload the whole page to reflect any change made by the user. AJAX uses the following:

- HTML and CSS, to include formatted information within the webpage
- JavaScript, to dynamically display and interact with the information to be processed
- The XMLHttpRequest object to asynchronously exchange data with the web server

An example of AJAX in action can be viewed on www.flickr.com, where, when one wants to edit the title of a photograph, clicking on the title will automatically change it to an editable text-box and, when edited, the new title will be displayed in regular HTML. This is all done without reloading the page once. The advantages of AJAX are in its ability to present a large amount of interactivity to the user, and its portability, as the technique uses elements that are present in almost all modern browsers. There are a number of complaints concerning the use of AJAX. One is that, if there are network latency issues, a user would not know if there is any information being processed or why there is a delay in the interface unless some sort of indication is given, much like the loading progress bar on internet browsers when a page is being loaded. Another concern is that some browsers will not be able to support AJAX, either because the browser is too old, or JavaScript is disabled. Internet Explorer 6 and below also require ActiveX to be enabled for proper use of the XMLHttpRequest object (Gehtland et al, 2006).

RSS

Really Simple Syndication (RSS) is a method used for Web syndication which delivers information in the form of an XML (Extensible Markup Language) file as illustrated in Figure 55.

```
<?xml version="1.0"?>
<rss version="2.0">
 <channel>
  <title>Liftoff News</title>
  <link>http://liftoff.msfc.nasa.gov/</link>
  <description>Liftoff to Space Exploration.</description>
  <language>en-us</language>
  <pubDate>Tue, 10 Jun 2003 04:00:00 GMT</pubDate>

  <lastBuildDate>Tue, 10 Jun 2003 09:41:01 GMT</lastBuildDate>
  <docs>http://blogs.law.harvard.edu/tech/rss</docs>
  <generator>Weblog Editor 2.0</generator>
  <managingEditor>editor@example.com</managingEditor>
  <webMaster>webmaster@example.com</webMaster>

  <item>
   <title>Star City</title>
   <link>http://liftoff.msfc.nasa.gov/news/2003/news-starcity.asp</link>
   <description>How do Americans get ready to work with Russians aboard the
```

International Space Station? They take a crash course in culture, language
and protocol at Russia's Star City.</**description**>
<**pubDate**>Tue, 03 Jun 2003 09:39:21 GMT</**pubDate**>
<**guid**>http://liftoff.msfc.nasa.gov/2003/06/03.html#item573</**guid**>
</**item**>
</**channel**>
</**rss**>

Figure 55: An example of an RSS file

Wiki
A "wiki" is a type of website allows the easy addition, removal and editing of all content. Wikis are ideal for the
collaborative writing of articles, so it is no surprise that most famous wiki is www.wikipedia.org, a large, free
and up-to-date web-based encyclopaedia. Wikis allow users with little to no knowledge of HTML to create
neatly formatted articles, with pictures and links to other articles, by using a simple and extremely human-
readable syntax. This also makes sure that every article looks similar to the other articles contained on the site.

Extensible Markup Language (XML)
Extensible Markup Language allows us to create custom tags, which can transmit, validate, and interpret data
between applications but also require the Document Type Definition (DTD) to describe the data which is going
to be read. XML has a very descriptive filing system that allows you to label parts of the document relative to
the content it holds. This is extremely beneficial when organising and searching for certain content.

XHTML
"Extensible HyperText Markup Language," or XHTML, is basically HTML done in XML. This means it has a
much stricter syntax, meaning that the document must be well formed with the proper usage of tags. Stricter
syntax encourages standardisation, so that the content is compatible with as many browsers, platforms and
devices as possible.

CSS
A Cascading Style Sheet's most common application is to determine the style of documents created in HTML or
XHTML. The primary advantage of CSS is that all the information about the presentation of a document's
content is contained in one separate file, greatly increasing efficiency and flexibility when one wants to edit any
aspect of the styling. This also means that the document will not be bloated with repetitive coding and countless
"<font>," "<b>" and "<br>" tags, etc. as the styling of individual HTML elements are determined only once in
the CSS file. CSS has become very popular in the design of Web 2.0 websites as it allows for a neat, efficient
and easily changeable interface design. Also, multiple style sheets can be used so that each user of the site can
choose the look they want.

Document Object Model (DOM)
Recently the web has improved through the use of standards. Standards allow us to maintain a credible and
accessible style of designing webpages without alienating possible visitors/users through bad design practice.
The DOM created by the World Wide Web Consortium (W3C) and technically, it provides the XML or HTML
file as a tree structure for accessing objects and its information within that document.

Popular Web 2.0 Sites

Meebo (see Figure 56) enables users to chat using their AIM, ICQ, Yahoo! Messenger, Jabber, GTalk and MSN
Messenger accounts through a neat AJAX interface. The AJAX interface allows the page to act much like a
desktop where multiple chat windows can be open at once.

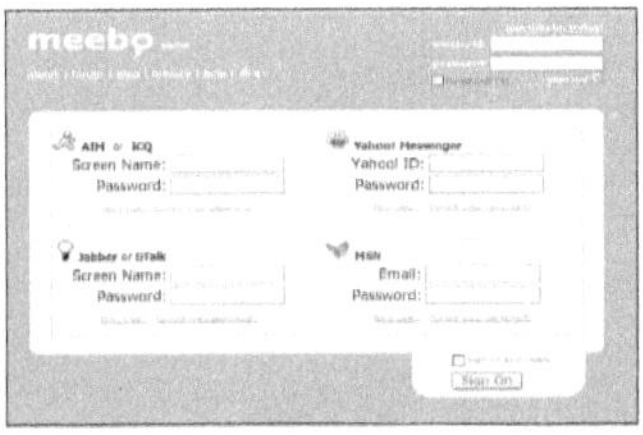

Figure 56: Meebo.com

Flickr (see Figure 57) is an extremely popular photo-sharing site where users can browse photos according to user or category and upload their own photos. Photos are categorised using user-defined tags, and the site utilises an innovative AJAX interface to allow photo information to be easily edited without having to refresh the page even once.

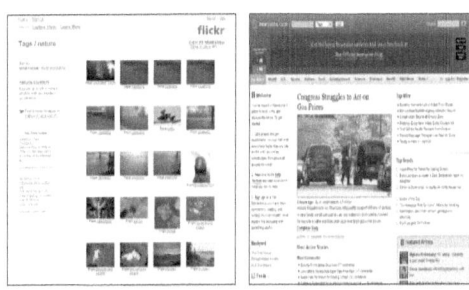

Figure 57: Flickr.com   Figure 58: Newsvine

Newsvine[1] (see Figure 58) is a site consisting of community-driven news. Users write articles and vote, comment and chat on articles created by both users and journalists. Extensive tagging is used to fully categorise every news article, and there are many RSS feeds available for the different news categories.
Gmail[2] is Google's answer to hotmail. It was launched in 2003 with a powerful adaptable interface and multiple functionality. Napster[3] is one of the most widely used music file-sharing network came to fame many years ago,

[1] http://www.newsvine.com/
[2] www.gmail.com
[3] www.napster.com

but was forced shut by lawsuits claiming the service was damaging the music industry unlawfully. Back it came with the new release and its pleasant XHTML / XML interface offering instant download and installation of the service. Del.icio.us[1] is a network of favourite web resources, del.icio.us, allows the sharing of websites, articles, blogs, and reviews with any individual on the planet who is registered. Wikipedia[2] is an online open-sourced encyclopedia allows users to add definitions for words, abbreviations, and just about anything that is searchable. Users can add/edit/delete entries facilitated by a strict AJAX backend architecture and comprehensive content management system.

Site	Valid XHTML?	Valid CSS?	Valid XML?
digg.com	✗	✗	✗
flickr.com	✗	✗	✗
gmail.com	✗	✗	-
rollyo.com	✗	✗	-
napster.com	✗	✓	-
Del.icio.us	✗	✗	-
wikipedia.org	✓	-	-

Table 5: W3C standard compliance

Table 5 shows that most of these websites do adhere to W3C standards due to the implementation of the Strict DTD. A solution to this is importing the transition DTD to allow for a more lenient flow of coding. Although each of these services work without fail across different browsers the closer we are to meeting W3C guidelines, the closer we are to a perfect web.

Other examples include 30Boxes[3] which is an online calendar and event planner. Using the AJAX-built interface, the whole calendar can be browsed without any page-refreshing, and users can easily add, edit and delete events in a pop-up box on the same page. Netvibes[4] is a start page similar to Google's personalised homepage. Netvibes supports RSS feeds, Google Mail, Webnotes, Web Search and Weather. It also allows users to integrate their photographs from their Flickr.com account, as well as their bookmarks from their del.icio.us account. AJAX is used to enable the user to dynamically edit the layout of the content that they add to their personalised homepage.

Conclusion

Making use of web 2.0 is about making sure that, as a side effect to what the user is actually doing that they actually add value. In short, making use of web 2.0 principals is making use of the long tail. A common technique is simply to collect user reviews. Amazon was one of the pioneers when it came to collecting user reviews of their products, and today the numbers of online stores that uses this system has boomed. Google has revolutionized advertising by making it easy for the small "every day" websites (which make up the majority of sites on the net. The long tail, that is) to put adverts on their sites without signing a big contract. Proponents speak of the web as a new platform. Most of us are used to software being developed, packaged, picked up in the store and kept updated through downloaded and installed patches. In the web 2.0 world, applications are run online, with no installation, updates are constant and continuous and access is instant from any computer with a browser. BitTorrent is a good example of web 2.0 ideas put to practice. BitTorrent is P2P software which differs from traditional downloading in that one is also forced to upload in parallel to downloading. This in turn means that the more who download, the faster each transfer will be.

References

[1] Del.icio.us
[2] www.wikipedia.org
[3] http://30boxes.com/
[4] http://www.netvibes.com/

Gehtland, J., Almaer, D., Galbraith, B. (2006) Pragmatic Ajax : A Web 2.0 Primer. Pragmatic Bookshelf; 1st edition, April 2006, ISBN: 0976694085

MacManus, R. Porter, J. (2005). *Bootstrapping the social Web. Digital Web Magazine,* May 2005. http://www.digital-web.com/articles/web_2_for_designers

McCormack, D. (2002). Web 2.0: The Future of the Internet and Technology Economy and How Entrepreneurs, Investors, Executives & Consumers Can Take Ad (Execenablers), Aspatore Books; 1st edition, ISBN: 1587622009, June 2002,

Shaw, R. (2005) *Web 2.0? It doesn't exist.* ZDNet, December 2005, http://blogs.zdnet.com/ip-telephony/?p=805

17   Computer Surveillance

Kevin Curran, Steven McIntyre, Hugo Meenan

Employers have a legitimate interest in monitoring work to ensure efficiency and productivity however electronic surveillance often goes well beyond legitimate management concerns and becomes a tool for spying on employees. Modern technologies are providing unprecedented opportunities for surveillance. Employers can read e-mail, look at workers computer files and eavesdrop on phone calls. Many companies also have cameras monitoring their employees all day. Since employees don't usually have access to their own electronically stored data, they can't correct inaccurate information. Although it's often done without an employee's knowledge, this kind of info-gathering is almost always legal. This is because there are no laws regulating electronic surveillance in the private sector workplace. Employers have a legitimate interest in monitoring work to ensure efficiency and productivity however it can be argued that electronic surveillance often goes well beyond legitimate management concerns and becomes a tool for spying on employees. This chapter examines these and related issues concerning electronic surveillance and privacy.

Introduction

With the amount of information that is freely available on the internet people are becoming more informed of what governments, companies or corporations are doing. The internet also provides an open forum where citizens can voice concerns for civil liberties (Arterton, 1989). The Civil Liberties Monitoring Project (CLMP)[1] is an American based organisation whose mission statement is to monitor, document, advocate and educate about civil rights and human rights abuses by law enforcement and other government agencies. The aim of CLMP, founded by local citizens of Southern Humboldt County, CA, is to encourage public awareness of constitutional rights and encourage involvement of the whole community in preserving and protecting them. The European equivalent is StateWatch[2] which monitors civil liberties, security & intelligence issues. Computer data banks help employers track employees' past employment records, financial status and medical histories. Although there are laws that prevent an employer from sharing intimate employee information with individuals outside the company, there are few restrictions on an employer's right to share it with people on the inside (ACLU, 2004).

In 2002 postal workers in New York City were horrified to discover that management had installed video cameras in the restroom stalls. Female workers at a large North Eastern department store discovered a hidden video camera installed in an empty office space that was commonly used as a changing room. Waiters in a large Boston hotel were secretly videotaped dressing and undressing in their locker room. Although in each of these instances the employer claimed it was concerned about theft, no illegal acts were ever uncovered. But the employees were robbed of their dignity and personal privacy (ACLU, 2004). We are living in a digital world and surveillance is very much part of that. It seems that we have to just get used to that. One of the more intrusive mechanisms at present are speed cameras which pick up and record the vehicle registration numbers of any vehicle traveling too fast along particular stretches of road (Simons, 2003). They do however often serve another purpose, and that is to identify vehicles without 'road tax'. This is done by running the plates against a road tax database.

In a security-conscious world at present, it seems that no activity is off limits to government inspection. Polls show that many people are willing to tolerate increased surveillance, higher encryption standards and other measures for the sake of security (Borland, 2002; Barquin, 1995; Ang, 1996). But civil libertarians worry that the increased investigative powers granted since the attacks, and people's eagerness to comply with them, have needlessly entangled innocent citizens and threaten to undermine constitutional rights to privacy and free speech. Even without explicit limitations, some say that fear of reprisal may have a chilling effect on public

---

[1] http://www.civilliberties.org
[2] http://www.statewatch.org

behaviour. Given the proliferation of log files and massive customer databases, combined with easy access to controversial sites and other information, the Net has accelerated the debate over electronic information and terrorism (Borland, 2002). In the United States since September 11th an unnamed supermarket chain had given shopping club card records to federal investigators and Lexis/Nexis, (the large database containing news articles, legal filings and public records of all kinds), says it is working more closely with law enforcement on several fronts since September 11th, including "authentication" of individuals' identity (Borland, 2002). In early 2005, Google to the dismay of many announced that it had agreed to censor its results in China, adhering to the country's free-speech restrictions in return for better access in the Internet's fastest growing market (Liedtke, 2005). Because of government barriers set up to suppress information, Google's China users have been blocked from using the search engine due to government barriers or when they can actually get through to the site – they experience long delays in response time. China already has more than 100 million Web surfers and the audience is expected to swell substantially (Liedtke, 2005).

Electronic Monitoring

The Canadian Judicial Council[1] states that "computer monitoring involves the use of software to track computer activities. Monitoring may include tracking of network activities and security threats, as well as Internet usage, data entry, e-mail and other computer use by individual users. Monitoring is done by someone other than the user, and may be made known to the user or may be surreptitious. In either case, the user has no control over the monitoring activities and the data that is generated."

Employers want to be sure their employees are doing a good job, but employees do not want intrusive monitoring techniques used throughout the work day. This is the essential conflict of workplace monitoring. New technologies make it possible for employers to monitor many aspects of their employees' jobs, especially on telephones, computer terminals, through electronic and voice mail and when employees are using the internet. Most people have some form of Internet access at work and a lot of them have some restrictions put on them. These may come in the form of Internet access control developed from packages that were used to restrict children using PCs at home but this has proved difficult to implement and administer, often preventing employees gaining access to legitimate sites; although they have developed new technology that enables greater administration capabilities to be incorporated into applications. Thus different levels of protection can be implemented for different employees. Even with these developments companies must trust their employees to use the resource properly. Sometimes this trust can be hard to understand. An employee's productivity, the company's security and liability are all affected by an Internet connection. Take for example some of the figures banded about for the loss of productivity with employees using the Internet during company time. Companies are reported to be losing millions of pounds each year due to employees surfing on the web during working hours. A recent Chartered Institute of Personnel Development (CIPD)[2] report found that UK companies are losing up to £2.5m each year due to non-work-related surfing. Another report claimed that employees posed more problems to businesses than hackers. Viruses can also be downloaded onto their system by the negligence of their employee's. This can happen in a number of different ways. For example an employee may receive a file attachments on a personal Email and when the download it they may not realise that it contains a virus which could cost the company millions if it were to stop operations for any length of time depending on the size of the firm. An employee may take work home with them and work on it on their own PC at home and not realise that they have just brought back in the virus that they did not even realise was on their home computer. Yet again these examples may be accidental but they still cost a lot of money. Email has also made it much easier for information to be passed from one company to another. This in turn makes it much easier for employees to pass information to rival companies as sending attachments by Email is easy to do and with the amount of information that can flow through a company it can be easily missed. This kind of action can be catastrophic for a company such as the case of an employee who came across the plans for a new car design and passed them to a rival which lead to the car design being scraped costing millions. With all these dangers faced by business today people claim that there is no other alternative but to monitor employee's use of computers (Introna, 2000).

Employees however, are given some protection from computer and other forms of electronic monitoring under certain circumstances. Union contracts, for example, may limit the employer's right to monitor. When using the internet for electronic mail, the employee should assume that these activities are being monitored and are not

---

[1] http://www.cjc-ccm.gc.ca/english/publications/ComputerMonitoringGuidelines.htm
[2] http://www.cipd.co.uk/default.cipd

private. Most people would assume correctly that the company's own e-mail system is being monitored because the employer owns it and is allowed to review it. However many employees wrongly believe that by using web based e-mail accounts that these are not being monitored. Indeed, messages sent within the company as well as those that are sent from your terminal to another company or received from another company can be subject to monitoring by employers. Several workplace privacy court cases have been decided in the employer's favour e.g. Bourke v. Nissan[1], Smyth v. Pillsbury[2] and Shoars v. Epson[3]. Technologies to monitor workplaces have become unavoidable facts of life. A survey by the American Management Association in New York found that 77 per cent of major U.S. firms in 2001 recorded and reviewed employee communications and activities on the job - a figure that had doubled in just four years (Immen, 2004). More than one-third of companies surveyed said they do video security surveillance and 15 per cent said they keep tape or digital recordings for review of employee performance. Most of the firms reported they both review and record telephone conversations, voice-mail and e-mail messages, and monitor what websites employees go to. Many said they also routinely record the time logged onto a computer and the number of keystrokes people make in a day (Immen, 2004).

Monitoring Software And Hardware

Keystroke recording software has existed almost since the arrival of the first computers. These programs create a log of all keystrokes typed and store the log file on the computer hard drive. These programs are generally interrupt-driven (from the keyboard interrupt). Thus, it consumes computer time while it reads the keystrokes and writes them to the computer hard drive. Further, the file on the hard drive may be discovered and erased/ modified. *WinWhatWhere* [4]was one of the first professional monitoring programs available, and has continued to evolve. It can even be set up to automatically uninstall itself at a pre-determined date, possibly preventing detection. Users also have the option of being e-mailed the log files and/or storing them locally on the hard drive. Spectorsoft[5] can record the screen images, and play them back similar to a VCR. Some programs can email the keystroke logs to a remote computer.

Anti-spy programs can detect and remove software keystroke recorders. *SpyCop*[6] can detect over 300 available keystroke recording programs. SpectorSoft acknowledges that it is detected by the *SpyGuard* anti-spy software. Some anti-virus programs are also beginning to attack the software keystroke recorders as well. McAfee anti-virus detects some of the popular keystroke recording software. Erasers attempt to cover the tracks of the computer user. Surfsecret Privacy Protector will erase all internet history, and history from over 30 third party applications. SpyGuard combines the anti-spy functions with the eraser functions by both detecting monitoring software and erasing internet history.

Hardware keystroke recorders contain two main components: a simple microprocessor and non-volatile memory. The microprocessor handles tasks such as: interpreting keystrokes, checking for the access password, and displaying menu options. The non-volatile memory is a fairly large sized memory which is used to store the keystrokes. Non-volatile memory retains data even during a power loss. Hardware keystroke recorders come in two different physical forms. Devices such as 4spycameras[7] keystroke recorders are about the size of an AA battery, and plug in to the back of the computer between the keyboard port and the keyboard cable. The InstaGuard[8] computer security keyboard has the hardware keystroke recorder physically built-in to the keyboard case. In both of these cases, the power to the device is supplied by the keyboard port, so that no additional wiring is necessary. Hardware keystroke recorders require no specialized software on the computer system. They are accessed through a "host program", which can be any word processor or text editor. Hardware keystroke recorders are constantly examining the keystroke stream looking for the access password. As soon the device sees the access password, it temporarily shuts down the keyboard and "types" a menu on the screen. This is perhaps the most novel aspect of the hardware keystroke recorder. This technology allows hardware keystroke recorders to be used without installing any software on the computer system, and allows recording to take place without consuming any CPU cycles. Another technology which has governments scared is Pretty Good Privacy (PGP)[9]. PGP allows the encryption of information - including electronic mail - with an encryption algorithm that

---

[1] http://www.loundy.com/CASES/Bourke_v_Nissan.html
[2] http://www.loundy.com/CASES/Smyth_v_Pillsbury.html
[3] http://www.law.seattleu.edu/fachome/chonm/Cases/shoars.html
[4] http://www.winwhatwhere.com
[5] http://www.spectorsoft.com
[6] http://www.spycop.com
[7] http://www.4spycameras.com
[8] http://www.instaguard.com/

has to date, proven to be unbreakable. This software is so strong that the U.S. Department of Defense has formally declared PGP to be a "munition", and has banned PGP's export outside North America. Some believe that a legitimate use for the above systems might be where a parent or guardian has a serious worry about what their child is viewing or communicating with through the internet.

Governmental Surveillance Techniques

The European Council has taken steps to establish a Europe-wide arrest warrant and a common definition of "terrorist crime." Germany's government has loosened restrictions on phone tapping and the monitoring of email and bank records and freed up once-proscribed communication between the police and the secret services. In June 2002, the U.K. attempted to introduce regulations under the pretext of anti-terrorism that would have mandated almost all local and national government agencies to gain access without warrant to communications traffic data. Australia introduced a terrorist law to intercept email (giving powers to the nation's chief domestic spy agency, the Australian Security Intelligence Organization), creating an offense related to preparing for or planning terrorist acts, and will allow terrorist property to be frozen and seized. New Zealand commenced similar legislation in keeping with the bilateral legal harmonization agreements of the two countries. India also passed its Prevention of Terrorism Ordinance allowing authorities to detain suspects without trial, impose capital punishment in some cases, conduct wiretapping, and seize cash and property from terrorist suspects— despite concerns it would be used to suppress political opponents.

The introduction of compulsory identity cards[1] in Britain has moved a step closer with a plan for "entitlement cards". It is suggested they would be used to clamp down on fraud by checking rights to receive NHS treatment, education and state benefits. The computerized cards could store a photograph, finger prints and personal information including name and address. David Blunkett has stated that the main use of the cards would be to demonstrate what entitlement people have to state services and not to identify them. David Blunkett states that "We're not interested in just having another form of ID because people already have a passport or driving licence" (BBC, 2002). It is thought the system could also make it easier for banks to cut down on identity fraud, such as credit card crime or bogus benefit claims however Liberty's (a civil liberties organization) campaigns director Mark Littlewood called on the government to look at alternative ways of tackling identity fraud. Rejecting the idea that people would not be forced into carrying the cards, he said: "If it's going to be necessary to have one to access all types of service it is, for all intents and purposes, compulsory" (BBC, 2002).

Since 11 September 2001, some people it seems have become more prepared to give up civil liberties in order to increase security. Not everyone however is convinced that limiting privacy is a good thing. In 2004, US scuba divers found out just how far the long arm of the law can reach since 11 September. Federal agents concerned about scuba-related terrorist plans requested the entire database of the Professional Association of Diving Instructors (Borland, 2002). Unknown to most of its members, the organisation voluntarily handed over a list of more than 100,000 certified divers worldwide, explaining later that it wanted to avoid an FBI subpoena that would have required far more information to be disclosed[2]. Of late, private databases have found their way into the hands of federal investigators hungry for any scraps of data that might serve as leads in terrorism investigations. Grocery shopping lists, travel records and information from other, public databases have all been caught in the government's antiterrorism net (Borland, 2002).

The Federal Bureau of Investigations (FBI) runs an internet surveillance tool called Carnivore[3], (or DCS1000) which allows law enforcement agents to intercept and collect Email and other electronic communications authorized by a court order. Due to the nature of packet networks it is a lot harder to identify particular target information compared with traditional telephone systems. FBI personnel only receive and see the specified communications addressing information associated with a particular criminal subject's service, concerned which a particular court order that has been authorized. Recently, according to an FBI press release the FBI uncovered a plot to break into National Guard armoires and to steal the armaments and explosives necessary to simultaneously destroy multiple power transmission facilities in the Southern United States. "After introducing a cooperating witness into the inner circle of this domestic terrorist group, it became clear that many of the

---

[9] http://www.pgp.com/
[1] http://www.homeoffice.gov.uk/comrace/identitycards/
[2] http://www.civilliberties.com
[3] http://stopcarnivore.org/

communications of the group were occurring via E-mail. As the investigation closed, computer evidence disclosed that the group was downloading information about Ricin, the third most deadly toxin in the world. It is easy to understand why people feel uneasy about Carnivore. The installation of Carnivore at ISP facilities is carried out only by FBI technicians and all the traffic on the ISP goes through the surveillance system which can leave it open to unauthorized surveillance. The system is reportedly able to track a lot more information than it needs which anyone with the correct passwords can access. Compared with traditional wire tapping systems were the provider of the service gathers the information that is required by a court order and hands it over to the agency that requests it, the FBI system can by-pass this. This leaves them open to the claim that they break one of the American Amendments that prohibits law enforcement agencies from gathering more information than is required although the bureau says that future systems will have audit trails and features to guard against abuse.

Privacy Rights Organisations

There are those who oppose the invasion of privacy and fight for the rights of victims of internet abusers. Two of these organisations who oppose privacy invasion are the Privacy Rights Clearinghouse and the Electronic Privacy Information Center (EPIC).

The Privacy Rights Clearinghouse is a non-profit consumer education and research program which educates on controlling personal information by providing practical tips on privacy protection. The majority of people on a daily basis give away information. "Junk mail" is among the top five consumer complaint topics each year. Wireless phones have become very popular the last number of years and the number of people who use them is steadily growing. Although wireless devices have many advantages, privacy isn't one of them. Depending on the type of phone being used, other people can listen into conversations. Scanners can zoom in on devices as diverse as baby monitors and walkie-talkies, and can intercept any transmission from emergency and police calls to aircraft to weather reports to user maintenance reports, among others. Wireless phones that operate on a higher frequency (900MHz to 5.8GHz) are more secure but not immune to monitoring. Pager messages are also not immune to monitoring, as networks are generally not encrypted. They transmit in lower frequencies that radio scanners and baby monitors, etc operate on, although messages cannot be deciphered without special equipment attached to the scanner. It is still unclear on whether text messages, or short message services (SMS) from mobile phones can be intercepted (Kamien, 2006). A person's chance of landing a job or getting promoted may depend on the information revealed in a background check. Background checks can be random as current employees may be asked to submit a check, but they are often asked from a job applicant. For certain areas of employment, screening is compulsory, for example au pairs and teachers need to have a clean record to stand any chance of a job and employers will scour through their employment history to ensure they have no previous history of ill-treatment of children. In short, employers are being cautious, although applicants and current employees may fear that employers will dig through their history for other reasons than the job. The things an employer needs to know about the applicant can vary with the nature of the job. Negligent hiring lawsuits are rising, and if there is an accident the employer can be liable, which is a good reason to be cautious about potential employees (Thuraisingham, 2002).

The Electronic Privacy Information Centre (EPIC) EPIC is a public interest research centre, which focuses public attention on emerging civil liberties issues. In January 2004, their Alert newsletter[1] mentioned an agreement between the US and the EU concerning the disclosure of passenger name records of Europeans travelling to the US. The European Parliament criticised this agreement, and urged the European Commission to broker another agreement, which offered genuine privacy guarantees for air passengers. Pending conclusion of this new agreement, the European Parliament's resolution asked European countries to immediately comply with European and domestic data protection laws. The Spanish government put forward a proposal suggesting airlines which operate within Europe would be required to provide passenger data to governments in the EU country of arrival. In regards to SPAM, EPIC supports the creation of a Do Not E-mail Registry to prevent spam, which supports enrolment at the domain-level, so that individuals can enjoy whatever benefit it gives without revealing the individuals e-mail address. EPIC also encouraged anti-spam principles endorsed by a coalition of privacy groups, which urged regulators to adopt a clear definition of spam as unsolicited, bulk, commercial mail, to establish opt-in protections, to establish private rights of action for individuals, to enable technical solutions for spam, to support international anti-spam co-operation, and to oppose pre-emption of state efforts to curb spam (Danchev, 2005). EPIC and a coalition of privacy and consumer groups have put pressure on Google to suspend its plans to deploy G-mail[2]: a web mail system that will scan user's communications in

---

[1] http://www.epic.org/alert/
[2] https://gmail.google.com

order to target advertisements. This is regarded as an unprecedented invasion into the privacy of communications. The system keeps communications for an extended period of time, causing users to have less privacy protection in their communications. EPIC launched a page on its site on the privacy of diplomatic in the aftermath of United Nations Secretary Kofi Annan and other UN officials personal conversations' and telephone communications being bugged by the US National Security Agency and the British Government Communication Headquarters (BBC, 2004).

In January 2003, European governments forced Microsoft to modify Passport - an online authentication system which identifies internet users and enables the transfer of personal information between various websites around the world- in order to protect the privacy rights of computer users in the European Union. It was found that Passport violated several EU data protection rules. Instating this rule meant Microsoft had to make more clear privacy rights under European laws and to collect and process personal data fairer. It also gives users the right to indicate on a site-by-site basis which personal information they wish to disclose. This rule has waited almost 18 months since EPIC and a coalition of privacy and consumer groups initiated a complaint against Microsoft at the Federal Trade Commission in July 2001, which alleged that Passport violated a section of the Federal Trade Commission Act and constituted an "unfair and deceptive trade practice". EPIC provides an extensive range of secure communications tools on its site[1] such as CryptoAnywhere, Ensuredmail, Hushmail and Mutemail. These tools all basically allow secure e-mail traffic through encrypted connections (Gordon, 2005).

Conclusion

Governments are seeking to control the internet and monitor computers because of the current threat of terrorism. In the US, the Patriot Act[2] has been introduced. This brings into question civil liberties of privacy versus security for a government or employer or indeed another individual (MOR, 2004; McClure, 2003). Indeed, the current trend of information gathering is growing and without proper restrictions leaving it open to abuses and mishandling. The freedom of information act entitles us to know exactly what information is being held on us by businesses and even the police. There is a very small amount of people who actually know this or who take of advantage of this opportunity. There is always a chance that incorrect information gathered about us is being used in decisions that affect us adversely in the future. Simon Davies (Davies, 2002) sums this topic up and splits the beliefs of citizens into just two groups. "A sceptic would call this censorship; a patriot would call it cooperation." This is true to a certain extent but it is in everyone's interest to ask the difficult questions of our governments and to preserve our civil liberties today, but for the future generations.

References

ACLU (2004) American Civil Liberties Union. *Privacy in America – Electronic Monitoring.* http://archive.aclu.org/library/pbr2.html

Ang, P., Nadarajan, B. (1996). Censorship and the Internet: A Singapore Perspective, Communications of the ACM, Vol. 39, No. 6, June 1996, pp. 72-78.

Arterton, C. (1989) Teledemocracy: Can Technology Protect Democracy? Naebury Park, CA: Sage, 1987. Portions of this work are excerpted as Teledemocracy Reconsidered, in T. Forester, ed. Computers in the Human Context. Cambridge, MA: MIT Press, 1989, pp. 438-450.

Barquin, R., LaPorte, T., Weitzner, D. (1995) Democracy in Cyberspace, a panel discussion at the 4th National Computer Ethics Institute Conference, Washington, DC, April 28, 1995.

BBC (2002) BBC News Online. Move towards compulsory ID cards, 5th February, 2002, http://news.bbc.co.uk/1/hi/uk_politics/1802847.stm (Accessed 25/5/2004)

BBC (2004) BBC News. UN bugging scandal widens. 27th February 2004 http://news.bbc.co.uk/2/hi/asia-pacific/3492146.stm

---

[1] http://www.epic.org/privacy/tools.html
[2] http://www.lifeandliberty.gov/

Borland, J., Bowman, L. (2002)   E-terrorism: Liberty vs. security, ZDNet.com, August 27, 2002. http://zdnet.com.com/2100-1105-955493.html

Danchev, D. (2005). Cyberterrorism - don't stereotype and it's there!, Mind streams of information security knowledge blog, December 19th 2005, http://ddanchev.blogspot.com/2005/12/cyberterrorism-dont-stereotype-and-its.html

Davies, S. (2002). *A year after 9/11: where are we now?* Communications of the ACM, Volume 45, Issue 9, Pages: 35 – 39, ISSN:0001-0782, September 2002

Gordon, L. Loeb, M. (2005). Managing aging Cybersecurity Resources: A Cost-Benefit Analysis, McGraw-Hill; 1st edition, September 2005

Immen, W. (2004) Workplace privacy gets day in court. The Globe and Mail, Wednesday, April 28, 2004. http://www.theglobeandmail.com

Kamien, D. (2006). The McGraw-Hill Homeland Security Handbook, ISBN: *0-07-144665-6*, McGraw-Hill, 2006

Introna, L. (2000). *Workplace Surveillance, Privacy and Distributive Justice.* ACM SIGCAS Computers and Society, Volume 30, Issue 4, CEPE 2000, Pages: 33 – 39, ISSN:0095-273, December 2000

Liedtke, M. (2005). Google Agrees to Censor Results in China. BREITBART.COM, January 24th 2005

McClure, S., Scambray, J., and Jurtz, G. (2003) *Hacking Exposed: Network Security Secrets and Solutions*, 4th Edition, Osbourne McGraw-Hill

MOR (1996) Ministry of Research. The Global Short-Circuit and the Explosion of Information, 1996. http://www.fsk.dk/fsk/publ/info2000-uk/chap01.html

Simons, B., Spafford, E. H. (2003). Inside Risks 153, Communications of the ACM, Vol. 46, No. 3, March 2003

Thuraisingham, B (2002). *Data Mining, National Security, Privacy and Civil Liberties,* ACM SIGKDD Explorations Newsletter, Vol. 4, No. 2, pp:1-5, December 2002

18   Mobile Social Software

Kevin Curran, Jason Downey, Danny Otterson

Developments in the communications in recent years have created a new era in which online communities can share information and socialise in different ways. Communication information systems have been connected to the strong emergence in social software. This chapter discusses their uses and the applications of mobile social software and their risks and disadvantages.

Introduction

Mobile Social Software (MSS) is software that supports user group interaction in online communities. MSS overlays a place and time element to the idea of digital networking. It enables users to find one another, in a particular vicinity and time, for social or business networking. Mobile social software have been largely targeted to cities, on the assumption that urban areas provide a sufficient density of people that users may serendipitously encounter as they go about their everyday lives (Thom-Santelli, 2007). Social software is defined by three characteristics one or more of the three criteria must be met to be considered social software[1].

1. Support for conversational interaction between individuals or groups ranging from real-time instant messaging to asynchronous collaborative teamwork spaces. This category also includes collaborative commenting on and within blog spaces.

2. Support for social feedback which allows a group to rate the contributions of others, perhaps implicitly, leading to the creation of digital reputation.

3. Support for social networks to explicitly create and manage a digital expression of people's personal relationships, and to help them build new relationships."

Almost one in five people who log on to the internet has signed up to a social networking site like Facebook, Bebo or MySpace. In addition, the majority of teens today own a mobile phone. The merging of these trends harkens the arrival of mobile social networking. The technology in mobile phones is advancing year on year. 3G uptake today is still an expensive notion but it has been predicted that by 2012 80% of phone users will in fact be 3G users (Hirsch and Henry, 2005). With these technologies in place there will be opportunities for developers to design software to take advantage of these developments that exist.

E-mail was the first major online socialising network which allowed users to communicate with people they knew but has now been superseded for socializing by instant messaging programs such as MSN Messenger or AIM and online networks like Bebo and MySpace. MySpace was created by Tom Anderson and sold to the News Corp, which is owned by Rupert Murdoch for $580 million and has an active user count of 43 million with over 100 million accounts registered on it. MySpace, Face Book, Yahoo and Bebo are currently targeting all mobile phone users.

Mobile Social Software Providers

Slam (Social, Location, Annotation, Mobile)

Slam[2] supports real-time communication between groups of people. It works on the basis of people joining a group which can be a person's friends, family, colleagues, classmates or even just a group of people with shared

[1] http://www.stoweboyd.com/
[2] http://www.msslam.com/About.aspx

interests. The messages on each group discussion or chat are uploaded onto web pages. When there has been a new posting on the page each member of the group will be alerted of the updates automatically.

Enpresence

Enpresence[1] is mobile phone software that uses Bluetooth technology. Personal information, likes, dislikes, hobbies are all requested by the software and this information is used to scan against other users of the software in a 100 meter radius using Bluetooth. When certain similarities are matched between users then the phone informs the user. If the third party does not wish to reciprocate, then they discard that profile. If they do in fact want to send a message they can do so.

Dodgeball

Dodgeball[2] is popular mobile social software available in over 22 cities in America. Dodgeball aims at helping users plot a social life. Friends are added to a users list by visiting the website. Dodgeball Social allows one to find out if they have any friends within a 10 block radius. This feature is useful for finding people after a time apart and also could be helpful in the case of emergency. The Dodgeball system works through sending a message to friends letting them know of the new location. A unique feature within Dodgeball is "crushes" which allows each member to pick five people on Dodgeball and when they are in range, they will receive a SMS with details, picture and location, so they will have the choice of meeting the third party. The shout feature of Dodgeball allows users to send all their friends a message and the check-in feature allows users to let people know where they are. Google has recently bought Dodgeball.

Jambo Networks

Jambo Networks[3] is mobile social software for matching people with similar interests. Users need a wireless device (cell phone, PDA or laptop) with Jambo installed to get started. Next, they enter interests and social groups (school, a conference attended etc.) upload pictures and then Jambo will notify them when people from their pre-defined network or similar interests are nearby so that they can meet

Wavemarket

Wavemarket[4] is a suite that can turn a mobile phone into an on-location broadcaster. Information and commentary about items such as restaurant reviews to safety tips can be added. One can find a buddy using the friend finder which gives user information on where friends are located using interactive maps. The resource finder function can be used to track a truck, inspect a neighbourhood for real estate or child safety.

Peepsnation

Peepsnation[5] is social software for interacting with groups at nearby locations. Filters can be activated in order to downsize the number of people one wishes to contact. Peepsnation provides groups that one can join such as 1. seeking friends, 2.seeking activity partner and 3. looking to date.

Risks of Mobile Social Software

The blue tooth/Wi-Fi hack is one of the most popular anti-MoSoSo devices. Wi-Fi is not as secure as blue tooth as it uses a fixed connection between the node and the network. Blue tooth is like a sonar connection between devices. Bluetooth exploits are well known and the four main areas are:

1. Bluesnarfing – unauthorized access of information from a wireless device through a Bluetooth connection, often between mobile phones, desktops, laptops, and PDAs. This allows access to a calendar, contact list, emails and text messages, and on some phones users can steal pictures and private videos. Currently available programs must allow a connection and to be 'paired' to another phone to steal content.

2. Blue Bugging – this is when a hacker gains access to the Bluetooth device to use the function and features of the phone. A hacker could read personal texts and listen into your phone calls.

---

[1] http://www.enpresence.com/
[2] http://www.dodgeball.com/
[3] http://www.jambo.net
[4] http://www.wavemarket.com/news_press.php?newsid=18
[5] http://www.peepsnation.com/

3. Blue Jacking – this is when a hacker gains access to your phone to send out mainly offensive or abusive sms.

4. Denial of Service – this is when a hacker repeatedly sends and invite to the users phone therefore wasting the users time and denying him from using other functions on the device.

This can be avoided by updating software as frequently and keeping it turned off when not in use. A problem with MoSoSo is the location software as it allows people to see where a person is located in real time. This could lead to a situation with a stranger or stalker. 25% of 8-11 year olds that have internet access have made a profile on social networking sites such as Bebo, MySpace and Face Book. Although the sites claim to have a minimum age of 13, there simple sign up forms allow under 13's to sign up. Within the age bracket 8-17 41% percent admit they do not use any privacy features, such as blocking everyone but friends from seeing your account. For children of such ages, having a social networking account could be dangerous as many users post there address, date of birth and other private details that could be used in fraud or other circumstances. The other problem with social networking sites is that people do not have to put in their real details. Sites like these can attract sexual predators; many of the sites have had issues with older men and women grooming children by pretending to be a child of the same age. A job advertising site call Craigslist was recently used to lure a victim to their death, when they went to meet their potential employer.

Conclusion

Mobile social network software seeks to facilitate social connection and coordination among friends in urban public spaces. With the expected upgrade of phones to 3G and 4G, mobile social network software will become more pervasive, allowing more and more websites to provide mobile software support. This will connect people with new contacts. A downside might be the security issues associated with mobile social software and social networks.

References

Thom-Santelli, J. (2007) Mobile Social Software: Facilitating Serendipity or Encouraging Homogeneity? *IEEE Pervasive Computing*, vol. 6, no. 3, pp. 46-51, Jul-Sept, 2007

Hirsch, T. and Henry, J. (2005) TXTmob: Text Messaging for Protest Swarms, *Extended Abstracts of SIGCHI Conf. Human Factors,* ACM Press, 2005, pp. 1455–1458.

Artin, N. (2007) Facebook, Bebo, Myspace dominate web, Daily Telegraph, 24th August 2007
http://www.telegraph.co.uk/news/uknews/1561090/Facebook,-Bebo,-Myspace-dominate-web.html

19   The Long Tail

Kevin Curran, Danielle McCartney, Karen Elder

The long tail is the colloquial name for a long-known feature of statistical distributions. The feature is also known as "heavy tails", "power-law tails" or "Pareto tails". The long tail gets its name from the shape formed on a graph with the number of plays (or sales) on the vertical axes against the rank (popularity) on the horizontal axes. The companies who use the power of the long tail to exist are working by three main 'rules': 1. Make everything available, 2. cut the price in half and then lower it, and 3. help the user find it. Google and eBay make most of their revenue from the long tail – Google from small advertisers and eBay from niche and collectible items. Their sites are easily accessed, easily browsed, and everything is well laid out, straight forward and in the main, user-friendly. What we mean by user friendly is that, even someone who is not confident using the web could search for and find something (Rule 3). Rule 1 however one can argue is what the long tail is about – make everything available. This chapter discusses the long tail phenomenon.

Introduction

The long tail is the theory that customer buying trends and the economy are moving away from the small number of hit products widely available in offline stores and towards the huge number of one off and niche products that are only available on-line. The reason that it gets its name is because when a graph of sales against products sold is plotted as shown in Figure 59, we can see that only a small number of products sell in large quantities "the hits" and there are a large number of products which only sell in small quantities "the misses". These misses are the one off and niche products that are not available in the high street due to the expense of shelf space and therefore form the long tail. The main reason that it has become possible for the long tail to become profitable is the fall in production and distribution costs through the Internet. Customers are now able to find products that are of special interest to them rather than the "one size fits all" products that are well marketed and available in most offline stores.

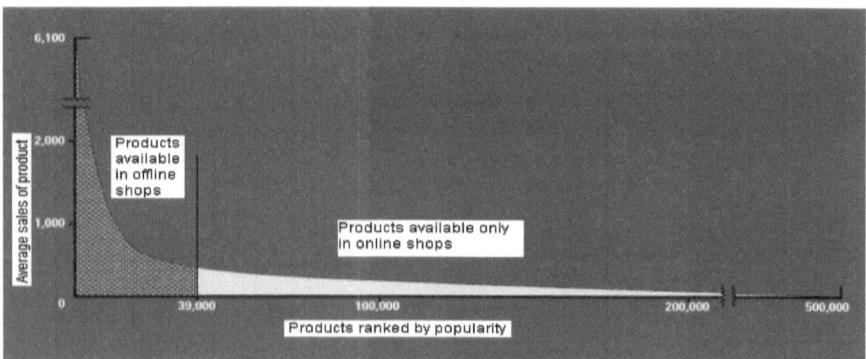

Figure 59: The Long Tail Effect

In 1988 a book by a British mountain climber Joe Simpson – which did not do exceedingly well, was promoted by Amazon alongside a book written by John Krakauer, released a decade later, which was also about a mountain-climbing tragedy. Amazon recommends products of similar interests to a customer when they are purchasing from the website, i.e. 'Other customers buying this product have also liked….' It was this that led to the great success of Simpson's book. It went on to outsell Krakauer's 1998 book by 2-1 (Anderson, 2004). This was possible due to the public being able to leave positive feedback about the book – so that the consumer knew before they tried it how many other people had already found it interesting. This is not just true for online book stores, the same happens in online music & media centres. The long tail is also about online retailers making products available to the public that high-street stores or cinemas cannot due to limited demand for the products. (Anderson, 2004) highlights this fact by stating that the average movie theatre will not screen a film unless it can attract at least 1500 people during a 2 week run. This is basically the rent for a screen. Also a typical record shop needs to sell at least two copies of a CD per year to make it worth carrying. This is equivalent to the rent for a half inch of shelf space. This model also applies to DVD rental shops, videogame stores, booksellers, and newsstands.

The Long Tail and the Internet

Although many people have not yet heard of the long tail it is clear that many of the large Internet companies are already using this strategy in order to make their profits. For example eBay uses the long tail by selling one-off and niche products through their auctions, which helps them to bring in new customers who are looking for a specific item, and cannot find it in the high street. This is profitable for eBay as they can make the same amount of money from the hit products as they do from the misses due to the fact that they are always paid for listing time regardless of the final price of the product. Google also makes a large percentage of its profits through small advertisers that want to advertise to as many people as possible and cannot afford to do so through the offline mediums such as newspaper and television advertisements.   Three of the leading companies that use the long tail theory are Amazon, rhapsody and Netflix. These three companies all make huge profits every year from selling products that are considered long tail products. Amazon offers its customers the choice of around 2.3 million books compared to the 130,000 "hit" books that are available in the average Barne's and Noble store. Needless to say they make a huge 57% of their profits from selling the books that are unavailable in any high-street store. The reason that they can do this is because if Barne's and Noble were to stock books that only sold once a month they would be loosing money due to the expense of shelf space whereas Amazon pays nothing to advertise an extra book on their site. Rhapsody offers its customers around 735,000 songs with offline competitors offering around 30,000 songs. This along with the fact that customers only have to buy the one or two tracks that they want means that rhapsody makes huge profits of which 22% come from long tail products. Rhapsody benefits in the fact that it costs them nothing to store old and niche music on a server somewhere so that it can be located when needed and doesn't take up necessary space when it is not in use.

Netflix offers customers the chance to rent of buy 25,000 DVD's of which only 3,000 are available in the typical blockbuster store. This gives customers a chance to see films that maybe never made it to cinemas near them or films that are of special interest to them. 20% of the company's profits come from products unavailable in offline stores. The fact that the companies' customers can watch a short clip before purchasing and the low cost of delivery of products means that Netflix has also been successful. The companies that are setting the standards for long tail products all follow three rules:

1. Make everything available.
2. Cut the price in half then lower it.
3. Help people to find what they want.

Some people think that it is not possible to survive in the long tail market if all three of these rules are not carefully followed. If we look at the three big companies from earlier we can see how they all fulfil the first rule by offering a larger number of products to their customers than the offline shops. The reason that this helps to make them successful is that if a customer is offered more choice they are more likely to find a product that they like and will therefore be more likely to become a repeat customer which is needed for a successful business.
        The second rule was tested in an experiment by rhapsody in which they offered tracks at three different prices, they found that the cheapest tracks outsold the most expensive tracks by 300% although the company was making a loss on the lower priced tracks. This proved that by lowering the price of their product they could attract more customers. The other big companies can fulfil this rule as they have low overhead cost due to the fact that they sell their products on the internet and therefore can cut out rent, heating and electricity costs which are more expensive on busy high streets where offline companies need to be located. This rule is important due to the fact that everybody likes to think that they are getting a bargain and as these companies are selling a larger range of products they can afford to make less profit per unit sold and sell more products to make the same amount of profit.

The third rule is one that is fulfilled by all three big companies in different ways. Netflix helps customers to find the products that they want through recommendations of other customers. They do this by letting customers write reviews on the films that they have watched and then making these available when a customer wants to rent the film. This has proved to be successful for Netflix as they are selling a range of products that will appeal to groups of people with similar interests. Rhapsody uses human editors and genre guides in order to add links on their pages which will lead users to artists similar in style to the music that they like. Each page contains links to similar artists, followers and influences therefore leading users to music from all generations. This method helps the customers to explore music that the may never have thought they would enjoy and leads them further down the long tail in search of their own style of music. As rhapsody is a music company this style works for them but may not work for companies selling other products that are harder to categorise.

Amazon uses the information they gain from customer buying patterns in order to guide their customers to other products that they may enjoy. They do this by selecting a few products that have been purchased at the same time as the product a customer is going to buy and showing these at the checkout. They also provide reviews on their books in order to get more sales. This works well as they are using strong marketing which is also used in offline shops by leading the customer to make last minute choices when they reach the check outs. Although all three companies use different methods all three are successful in leading their customers into the long tail products, which are not advertised as widely and may never have appeared on the shelves of any high street shop. Therefore these methods have become very powerful marketing tools for the online market, although there is still a large emphasis on using the right method to suit the product that one is selling.

The Future

One suggestion is that, due to the new powers that customers are gaining through being able to buy products considered long tail, the large offline companies will be forced to offer more choice in their product range in order to be successful, although there are many problems that could arise from this. One of these problems is that due to the additional products sold by the offline shops the costs of running these businesses will increase. This could have three effects the first is that the prices will increase in order to keep profit margins the same and therefore lower the demand for these products returning the market to what it is now. The second effect is that the increase in price would lead many more customers to internet shopping therefore cutting out the large offline companies except for necessity products such as food. Thirdly the large offline companies may keep the long tail products as loss leaders and increase the prices of their necessity products in order to stay profitable. A second suggestion is that due to the large number of long tail products now available to customers the so called "hits" will end up being a thing of the past with the top selling products only slightly out selling those at the bottom of the tail as shown in Figure 60.

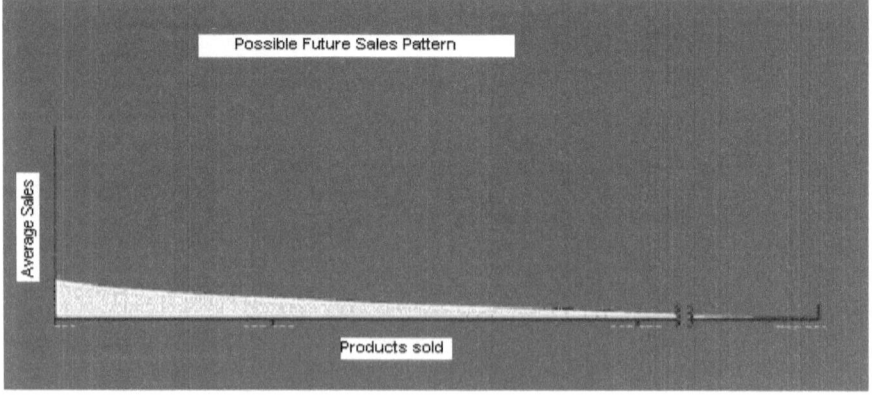

Figure 60: A possible future sales pattern

There is a possibility of this happening if everyone was to decide to buy products that are to their own taste rather than following trends which are currently forced by the large companies. Another suggestion is that with customers having so much choice in every product that they buy few will ever move down the tail and buy the one off and niche items as they are happy to follow the trends and buy the products that are heavily marketed in the off line shops therefore keeping the market in its current state where customers are divided equally between the long tail businesses and the offline "hits" orientated businesses where long tail products never even reach the shelves.

Conclusion

It seems that companies which are currently making their profits using the long tail are set to continue to do so in the future due to factors such as consumers favouring choice and the lower costs of running an online business. Consumers want more variety, choice and selection. This generation is breaking boundaries and exceeding expectations as a rule almost, therefore, why they are not simply putting up with the bands forced upon them by record labels but rather selecting from niche available to them online. This is why the long tail has taken off in the 21st century, because they refuse to accept less than perfect (Anderson, 2004).

References

Anderson, C. (2004). The Long Tail. Wired Magazine, Issue 12.10, October 2004
http://www.wired.com/wired/archive/12.10/tail.html

20   Cyber Terrorism Attacks

Kevin Curran, Kevin Concannon, Sean Mc Keever

Cyber terrorism is the premeditated, politically motivated attacks against information, computer systems, computer programs, and data which result in violence against non-combatant targets by sub-national groups or clandestine agents. This chapter provides a brief overview of previous cyber terrorism attacks and government responses.

Introduction

Terrorism can be defined as "The unlawful use or threatened use of force or violence by a person or an organized group against people or property with the intention of intimidating or coercing societies or governments, often for ideological or political reasons". To date there has been no serious act of cyberterrorism, but computer networks have been attacked in recent conflicts in Kosovo and the Middle East. As terrorists have a limited amount of funds cyber attacks are more tempting as they would require less people, less resources meaning less funds. Another advantage of cyber attacks is that it enables the terrorist to remain unknown, as they could be far away from the actual place where the terrorism is being carried out. As terrorist normally set up camp in a country with a weak government, the cyber terrorist could set up camp anywhere and remain anonymous. A combination of both physical terrorism and cyber terrorism is thought to be the most effective use of cyberterrorism. For example disrupting the emergency services in which case the emergency was created by physical terrorism would be a very effective way to combine both. The possibilities created for cyber terrorism by the use of technology via the internet are vast. Government computer networks, financial networks, power plants, etc are all possible targets as terrorism may identify these as the most appropriate features to corrupt or disarm in order to cause havoc. Manipulation of systems via software with secret "back doors", theft of classified files, erasing data, re-writing web pages, introducing viruses, etc are just a few examples of how terrorism can penetrate secure systems. Terrorist attacks made possible by the use of computer technology could also be demonstrated via air traffic control hi-jacking systems, or corrupting the systems for power grids from a remote destination.

Terrorist groups are increasingly using new information technology (IT) and the Internet to formulate plans, raise funds, spread propaganda, and communicate securely. In his statement on the worldwide threat in the year 2000, Director of Central Intelligence George Tenet testified that terrorist groups, "including Hezbollah, HAMAS, the Abu Nidal organization, and Bin Laden's al Qa'ida organization were using computerised files, E-mail, and encryption to support their operations." Convicted terrorist Ramzi Yousef, the mastermind of the World Trade Center bombing, stored detailed plans to destroy United States airliners on encrypted files on his laptop computer.

Terrorist organisations also make opportunity of the Internet to target their audiences without depending on overt mechanisms such as radio, television, or the press. Web sites are presented as a way of highlighting injustices and seeking support for political prisoners who are oppressed or incarcerated because of their fight for freedom. A typical site will not reveal any information about violent activities and will usually claim that they have been left with no choice but to turn to violence. They claim they are persecuted, their leader's subject to assassination attempts and its supporters massacred. They use this tactic to give the impression they are weak, small, they portrait themselves as the underdog (adl, 2004). This public relations exercise is a very easy way of recruiting supporters and members. Alongside the propaganda aspect terrorists often present web sites for information on how to build chemical and explosive weapons. This allows them to identify frequent users who may be systematic to their cause and therefore is a cost effective recruitment method. It also enables individuals who are acting on their own to engage in terrorist activity. In 1999, a terrorist called David Copeland killed 3 people and injured 139 in London. This was done through nail bombs planted in three different locations. At his trial it was revealed the he used the *Terrorist Handbook* (Handbook, 2004), and *How to Make Bombs* (Bombs, 2004) which were simply downloaded from the internet.

Cyber Terrorist Attacks

Terrorists use cyberspace to cause disruption. Terrorists fight against governments for their cause, and they use every means possible to get what they want. Cyber attacks come in two forms; one against data, the other control systems (Lemos, 2002). Theft and corruption of data leads to servicing being sabotaged and this is the most common form of internet and computer attacks. Attacks which focus on control systems are used to disable or manipulate physical infrastructure. For example, the provision of electrical networks, railroads or water supplies could be infiltrated to have wide negative impact on particular geographical areas. This is done by using the internet to send data or by penetrating security systems. These weak spots in the system were highlighted by an incident in Australia in March 2000 where a disgruntled employee (who failed to secure full-time employment) used the internet to release 1 million litres of raw sewage into the river and coastal waters in Queensland. Actually, it took him a total of 44 failed attempts to breach the system and his 45th attempt was successful. The first 44 were not detected. Following the twin tower attack, 11 September, auditors for public security were concerned that critical infrastructure is owned primarily by private companies, which are not always geared to high security practices (Lemos, 2002).

In 1998, a terrorist guerrilla organisation flooded Sri Lankan embassies with 800 e-mails a day for a two-week period. The messages simply read "We are the Internet Black Tigers and we're doing this to interrupt your communications." Intelligence departments characterised it as the first known attack by terrorists against a country's computer systems. Internet saboteurs defaced the Home Page of, and stole E-mail from, India's Bhabha Atomic Research Center in the summer of 1998. The three anonymous saboteurs claimed in an Internet interview to have been protesting recent Indian nuclear blasts. In July, the leader of a Chinese hacker group claimed to have temporarily disabled a Chinese satellite in 1997 announced he was forming a new global cracker organization to protest and disrupt Western investment in China.

In September 1998, on the eve of Sweden's general election, saboteurs defaced the Web site of Sweden's right-wing Moderates political party and created links to the Home Pages of the left-wing party and a pornography site. That same month, other saboteurs rewrote the Home Page of a Mexican Government Internet site to protest what they said were instances of government corruption and censorship. Analysts have referred to these examples of cyber crime as low-level information warfare [adl04]. Some countries such as the US and Australia have recommended the setting up of a cyberspace network operations centre which will include internet service providers and computer hardware and software developers. Their task is to develop secure technology such as intelligence analysis software which will be capable of sifting through and analysing existing data, both public and private, in order to uncover suspicious activity.

Governmental Responses to Cyber terrorism

The European Commission has pursued a provision requiring all European Union members to make "attacks through interference with an information system" punishable as a terrorist offense if it is aimed at "seriously altering or destroying the political, economic, or social structures." France has expanded police powers to search private property without warrant. Spain now limits the activities of any organization directly or tangentially associated with ETA—the armed Basque Homeland and Freedom group (similar to U.K. legislation). The European Council has taken steps to establish a Europe-wide arrest warrant and a common definition of "terrorist crime." Germany's government has loosened restrictions on phone tapping and the monitoring of email and bank records and freed up once-proscribed communication between the police and the secret services. In June 2002, the U.K. attempted to introduce regulations under the pretext of anti-terrorism that would have mandated almost all local and national government agencies to gain access without warrant to communications traffic data.

Australia introduced a terrorist law to intercept email (giving powers to the nation's chief domestic spy agency, the Australian Security Intelligence Organization), creating an offense related to preparing for or planning terrorist acts, and will allow terrorist property to be frozen and seized. New Zealand commenced similar legislation in keeping with the bilateral legal harmonization agreements of the two countries. India also passed its Prevention of Terrorism Ordinance allowing authorities to detain suspects without trial, impose capital punishment in some cases, conduct wiretapping, and seize cash and property from terrorist suspects—despite concerns it would be used to suppress political opponents.

Risks of Total Surveillance

There are those however who oppose some of the counter terrorism programmes in place by our western governments. One such lobby group is the U.S. Public Policy committee of ACM (USACM) who are concerned that the proposed Total Information Awareness (TIA) Program, sponsored by the Defense Advanced Research Projects Agency, will fail to achieve its stated goal of 'countering terrorism through prevention'. They also believe that the vast amount of information and misinformation collected may be misused to the detriment of the public (Simons, 2003). They recommend a rigorous, independent review of TIA which should include an examination of the technical feasibility and practical reality of this vast database surveillance system. They claim that the databases proposed by TIA would increase the risk of identity theft by providing a wealth of personal information to anyone accessing the databases, including terrorists masquerading as others. Recent compromises involving about 500,000 military-relevant medical files and 30,000 credit histories are harbingers of what may be in store. They also point out that the secrecy inherent in TIA implies that citizens could not verify that information about them is accurate and shielded from misuse. Worse yet would be the resulting lack of protection against harassment or blackmail by individuals who have inappropriately obtained access to an individual's information, or by government agencies that misuse their authority. As the entire population would be subjected to TIA surveillance, even a very small percentage of false positives would result in a large number of law-abiding Americans being mistakenly identified as suspects.

The Federal Bureau of Investigations (FBI) runs an internet surveillance tool called Carnivore, which was changed to DCS1000 to make it more innocuous sounding, that allows American law enforcement agents to intercept and collect Email and other electronic communications authorized by a court order. Due to the nature of packet networks it is a lot harder to identify particular target information compared with traditional telephone systems. FBI personnel only receive and see the specified communications addressing information associated with a particular criminal subject's service, concerned which a particular court order that has been authorized. Recently, according to an FBI press release the FBI uncovered a plot to break into National Guard armoires and to steal the armaments and explosives necessary to simultaneously destroy multiple power transmission facilities in the Southern United States. "After introducing a cooperating witness into the inner circle of this domestic terrorist group, it became clear that many of the communications of the group were occurring via E-mail. As the investigation closed, computer evidence disclosed that the group was downloading information about Ricin, the third most deadly toxin in the world. Without the fortunate ability to place a person in this group, the need and technological capability to intercept their E-mail communications' content and addressing information would have been imperative, if the FBI were to be able to detect and prevent these acts and successfully prosecute". With all these potential disastrous scenarios it is strange that anyone could deny that there is a need for monitoring. The problem maybe that the line between monitoring and invasion of privacy becomes very blurred. It is easy to understand why people feel uneasy about Carnivore. The installation of Carnivore at an ISP facility is carried out only by FBI technicians and all the traffic on the ISP goes through the surveillance system which can leave it open to unauthorized surveillance. The system is a risk however as any hacker with the correct password can gain access to sensitive information on the public. Compared with traditional wire tapping systems where the provider of the service gathers the information that is required by a court order and hands it over to the agency that requests it, the FBI system can by-pass this. This leaves them open to the claim that they break one of the American Amendments that prohibits law enforcement agencies from gathering more information than is required although the bureau says that future systems will have audit trails and features to guard against abuse.

Conclusion

Cyber terrorists are creating increasingly clever methods and tools to attack computer systems and governments in order to get their political views across. Issues of national and worldwide safety are at risk here. The reason this risk exists is due to the fact that the internet offers little or no regulation, potentially huge audiences, anonymity of communication and a fast flow of information. These four critical features require father research in order to combat cyber terrorism.

References

ADL (2004) http://www.adl.org/Terror/

Bluemud (2004) http://www.bluemud.org/article/11606

Handbook (2004) http://www.capricorn.org/~akira/home/terror.html

Lemos, R. (2002) What are the real risks of cyberterrorism? ZDNet, Aug 26, 2002

Simons, B. and Spafford, E. H. (2003) Inside Risks 153, Communications of the ACM, Vol. 46, No. 3, Mar 2003

21   Podcasting, Screencasting, Blogging And Videoblogging

Kevin Curran, David Pollock, Ronan McGarrigle, Colleen Ferguson

PodCasting, Blogging, VideoBlogging, and ScreenCasting allow the uploading of personal content to the web. Podcasting allows users to listen to music files from Podcasting websites or indeed any website for that matter. Unlike internet radio Podcasting allows listeners to download the podcast so that they can listen to it later or store it on a mobile device. Screencasting has become popular with individual users who wish to document program bugs or oddities as a visual demonstration showing how a program works can be much clearer than a verbal description. A blog is a website similar to an on-line diary where messages are posted describing items of interest to the blog author. A videoblog is a short video clip with sound posted on a website describing an event. This chapter discusses these new technologies.

Introduction

A podcast is a web feed containing audio and/or video files which is then placed on the internet for anyone to download. What makes the podcast distinct from traditional media like broadcasting and streaming is that the podcast file will arrive in archived form. A Screencast is a digital recording of computer screen output, which contains audio narration. Screencasts are useful for demonstrating simple and complicated new software to others. It is a neat way to show off work, report bugs and show how a task can be accomplished. Screencasting is a term for recording a movie of a computer screen to a file that others can view. Screencasts are mostly used for tutorials, overview/tours, reviews, and demonstrations. Screencasts may also be used as a way to enhance regular movie files. A weblog, or blog which it is also known, is a website were the owner or user of the website posts messages on it so that others can log on and read them. Blogs often focus on one subject, for example if the blogger is a computer programmer, then the topic of his messages is mainly related to programming languages. However many are using the blogs as on-line diaries where they post messages describing their daily news or how they feel about certain subjects. Videoblogging is a new form of blogging, which includes posting videos on the web. It is a new paradigm for people to place aspects of their personal lives on the web. Videoblogging is rising in popularity partially due to the release of the Video iPod and the availability of videoblogs on iTunes. So this means that with the recent boom in iPod sales, they will see this one as the most updated one and this will also hit the computer industry by storm. The rest of this chapter examines the new phenomenon of podcasting, screencasting, blogging and videoblogging.

Podcasting

A factor which is influencing the popularity of Podcasting is cheap MP3 players such as the iPod. A possible reason why Podcasting allows users to keep up to date with items that interest them, e.g. local radio shows, events in a city or region, favourite radio talk shows, sermons, technical talks or simply listening to their music (Farkas, 2005). RSS (Really Simple Syndication) is a type of web format which is widely used with Podcasting. The web feeds that the RSS provide simply link to the podcast. At present, there are is no clear revenue model related to podcasting. There are only a small amount of podcasts which actually make money from subscriptions. Some podcasters are beginning however to place advertisements in their podcasts. The other problem is also the sheer amount of rubbish placed online in podcast directories. Due to the nature of brief podcast (or none) descriptions, one has to generally download the podcast and listen to it to ascertain the actual relevance and quality.

Podcasting started in 2004 when David Winer, a software developer created a program from home to allow him to record broadcasts off the internet radio stations and play them on an iPod. He wanted to be able to save them to his computer so he could return to them later. He released the software online and eventually other software developers improved on the idea and Podcasting gained momentum. The name Podcasting actually comes from two different words - pod came from the iPod and casting came from broadcasting (Morris, 2005). The net caught onto pod casting quickly. For instance, in September 2004 a blogger and columnist - Doc Searls began keeping track of how many people searched Google for the word "podcasts" and the result was 24. A week later, it was 526, and after another 3 days, it was 2,750. It then doubled every couple of days, passing 100,000 on the 18th October 2004. In October, 2005 there was more than 100,000,000 hits on the word "podcasts" on Google.

The production of a podcast is not complex. Equipment needed is a computer with access to the internet along with a microphone to record sound and software to record the sounds to the computer. Fortunately, there is free software available for recording sounds and editing them. One popular package is gold wave[1]. One a podcast has been recorded; it can be uploaded to a podcast directory. Many are free but some such as iTunes charge for adding content. Once uploaded to a directory or to a website, one must make sure that the file is accessible through an internet address. In the next step the file provider then acknowledges the existence of that file by referencing it in another file known as the feed which then reads the list of URL's and is published in RSS format which contains details of the file like the author, publish date, title and description. The third step is for the file provider to post the feed to a known and permanent location and make this feed URL known to the intended audience. A consumer then enters this feed into their desired software program (example: iTunes) which will then retrieve the data. This then allows the audience to do what they want with the file like any other computer file, they can play it to listen or watch and archive it.

In 2004, Musselburgh grammar school in Scotland started handing out Podcasts in class as revision help for foreign language classes[2]. Church's and religious groups are also broadcasting items ranging from church music to sermons, talks and prayers. The number of people that are using what the church would refer to as Godcasts is growing. Many podcasters see it as a hobby. Many podcasts disappear over time as they rapidly find out that it takes a lot more time than initially expected to produce a weekly or daily show. Most of these podcasters do it just to reach others on the web about something they believe in passionately. They do not rely on ratings which often allows them to talk about anything from how to cook an apple tart to just playing music all day long. Many of these take a liberal view on copyright issues.

Screencasting

Screencasting is where a video file of the running of a program is used to help people understand the functions of the desired program. It achieves this by using a narrator and capturing video of the program actually performing different functions. A narrator will talk though the process describing operations mirrored on the video. This can be extremely helpful in the use of training staff on a new system, as it will show them what to do with narrations. This can be more cost effective than normal training. Another use of this is to use it as a presentation, with the Screencast explaining all the information, along with someone answering questions that the viewers may have about what they have just seen. This would be effective in marketing new products to a large audience at once.

The term was created in 2004 by Jon Udell - a columnist who wished to show his readers applications that he found interesting. He noticed that geeks caught onto the computer concepts immediately. Therefore, Jon wanted to transmit this knowledge to regular people as well so he made a screencast. He had hoped that it would attract a wider, less technical and it worked. Screencasting however has been around since 1993 when Lotus introduced ScreenCam. This never gained popularity due to the size of the files and the limited features and indeed the size of the created files (pre-broadband). Modern screencasting produces compact files and possesses more advanced features that which allow more detailed changes. For example there was no sound available with ScreenCam and there were a lot of problems with trying to locate and specify the location that the pointer should reside.

A popular programme for creating screencasts is Macromedia Flash MX. This provides editing features for manipulating even the smallest details on the screen. There are two main types of screencasting, screenshots and fluid movies. Screenshots is just pictures of the screen every time the mouse or a button has been clicked, this is produced by the screencasting tools which saves the location of the cursor and shows it through a series of screenshots. However some offer the ability to manually press a hotkey to take you to a new screenshot. The problem with this is that it can be hard to capture images at the right times to make it look like a smooth flowing movie. It often ends up being a movie with random screenshots like menus that seem to appear out of nowhere.

---

[1] www.goldwave.com
[2] http://en.wikipedia.org/wiki/Musselburgh

Fluid movies work by capturing the desktop and audio at high rates. It is created by basically choosing an area of screen, then recording a narrator's voice to accompany the recorded 'screencast'. When complete, a movie of actions can be edited and then published. A program which supports multiple output formats such as compiled flash, raw flash, video, and standalone exe provides plenty of choice when creating a screencast. The ability to record audio narrations and edit them in order to explain every move being made in the screencast is also desirable. For example how easy it is to remove screens, change cursor position and change audio will be essential for first timers who have never created a screencast and need to constantly edit so that the output is to their standard. The software's ability to record fast changes is a feature to look out for. You want to know how well it handles occurrences of rapid screen changes, because if this is a key feature for the user then he/she must consider it when buying the software. Support for interactive features, an example of this is where users must click in places to continue, interactive features keep the users attention and interested and so would be a good feature. Smart automatic captioning is a good feature in software for novice computer users and most software has tools that can automatically add captions when you perform certain actions like going over the menu button. Some software packages that include all of these features include Camtasia Studio[1], BB Flashback[2], Macromedia Captivate[3] and ViewletCam[4].

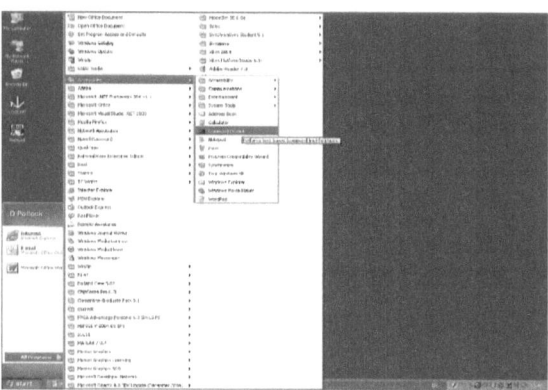

Figure 61: Screencast of a desktop

Figure 61 is what a Screencast might look like of an application being selected from the menu of a Windows XP desktop machine. The user gets the impression that the computer is running programs with no help from them. Screencasts are a powerful means of demonstrating an application's features. There saying "a picture is worth a thousand words" can be applied to screencasting.

People that screencast do it for similar reasons to those that blog and podcast. They basically have a message that they wish to communicate. Screencasting however allows one to speak it, show it and share it. Subscribers can then hear it, watch it and experience it. With a blog you can just write it and the reader can just read it. With a podcast you can just say it and the reader can just listen to it. Interestingly, each copy of Windows XP starts with a popup box asking the user if they wish to take a tour. This is basically a screencast where one can watch the mouse run through features of Windows. There are different types that screencasting appeals to. One group is software providers who want to make a demonstration movie. Screencasts allow the author to post on a website for potential buyers to guide them around the features and how to use the software appropriately and to its full potential. Example screencasts include an animated whiteboard[5] by Troy Stein, product manager for Camtasia Studio who made a screencast for the football team he coaches. It is a picture of a football pitch and Troy Stein is taking you through the basics of football by explaining the rules through audio and drawing on the picture. It is well edited and easy to understand. Jon Udel has produced a screencast-enhanced video about a local flooding scene[6] from downtown Keene NH during October 2005. The screencast takes us through his

[1] www.techsmith.com/
[2] www.bbsoftware.co.uk/BBFlashBack.aspx
[3] www.adobe.com/products/captivate/
[4] www.qarbon.com/presentation-software/vc/
[5] http://www.techsmith.com/community/blog/movies/soccer3.html
[6] http://weblog.infoworld.com/udell/gems/KeeneFlood.html

hometown and visits the worst hit areas of the flood. It is mostly video, with bits of screen animation interspersed to contextualize the scenes.

Blogging

A weblog, or blog which it is also known, is a website where the owner or user of the website posts messages on it so that others can log on and read them. Blogs often focus on one subject, for example if the blogger, which is a person who owns the blog, is a computer programmer, then the topic of his messages is mainly computers. However some people are using the blogs as on-line diaries where they post up messages describing their daily news or how they feel about certain subjects. They typically contain messages containing the bloggers feelings on a topic or if they have an opinion of something, they also have links to websites that they are interested in, other blogs, and more recently they have links to pod casts and screen casts. A person that has a blog is called a blogger and when you are maintaining, adding to or reading other blogs, this is referred to as blogging (Hill, 2005).

As 2004 commenced, blogging really started to make its mark, but it was playing the role of a mainstream news service due to the fact that bloggers began to provide nearly-instant commentary on televised events, instead of the more traditional online diary blog which was not as popular. An example of this is in the December 2004 Tsunami which had people blogging about the events that occurred. Here blogs such as Medecins Sans Frontieres were created, which used SMS text messaging to report from affected areas in Sri Lanka and Southern India so that people could read about the extend of the damage. The term blog came about with the two words *web* and *log* combined together and then shortened by Jorn Barger in 1997. The term was then shortened by Peter Merholz in May of 1999. Justin Hall who began eleven years of personal blogging in 1994 while being a student at Swarthmore College, is generally recognized as one of the first bloggers.

Before blogging came about there were several other similar communities such as Usenet, email-lists and Bulletin board systems. However the blog evolved from the on-line diary where people would keep a blog of their personal lives, the first of these personal blogs started in 1995. Most of the writers called themselves diarists and journalists. After a slow start, blogging rapidly became popular: the site Xanga, started in 1996, had only 100 diaries by 1997, and over 50,000,000 in December 2005. It was the launch of Open Diaries in 1998 that helped blogging become more popular, as this was the first blog community where readers could add comments to other writers' blog entries. Others started blog communities including Pita.com, Diaryland, Blogger.com and Lifelog. The pioneer of weblogging tools is Dave Winer who changed a blog from just a website to frenzy within the computer world. One of his most significant contributions was setting up servers so that blogs could make a sound to indicate when it has been updated. In 2001 Andrew Sullivan's blog[1] and Ron Gunzburger's Politics1.com became one of the first broadly popular American blogs. These blog on US politics. User manuals also started to appear for the novice users. This helped the blog become a modern phenomenon, as people who just heard of them but could not actually figure out how to start their own, could now do so. The importance of the blogging community gained rapid respect and importance, in actual fact journalism schools started to teach about blogging, the difference from blogging to journalism. A year later from this, in 2002, Markos Moulitsas Zuniga started up DailyKos which had up to a million visits a day during peak events, it has now become one of the most trafficked blogs (Hill, 2005).

When the war in Iraq began, it also started the first blog war. Iraqi bloggers started to read other blogs from America and their views on the war in Iraq, they seen that the Americans were naive to what was really going on and so they joined blogging to get their message across. One of the most memorable blogger was a man called Salam Pax, who published a book of his blog to show his views of the war and open others eyes to it. Blogs played an important role in opening up peoples eyes to the brutal facts of war. Blogs were also created by soldiers serving in the Iraq war. Such blogs were referred to as milblogs, which gave readers new perspectives on the realities of war, as well as often offering different viewpoints from those of official news sources.

There are many different types of blogs, from personal to educational. A personal blog is one where the blogger uses it as an online diary, posting views on anything that they consider interesting. A career blog is one which is used to dictate a professional journey, demonstrate expertise, or network out to other professionals. It shows the bloggers career moves through all jobs throughout their lifetime, but has little of no ties to his/her employer. A paid blog is one where a person is employed to blog for a living, this can be done to promote the company, log

---

[1] www.AndrewSullivan.cm

onto other blogs to tell others of the company, or to raise search engine relevancy so that the company becomes more well known. Cultural blogs allow the bloggers to discuss their preferred music, sports, theater, arts, and popular culture. These are among the most read blogs within the blogging community because people like to talk to others with the same interests and it is a great way to meet new people that have the same things in common. Almost like a chat room. Topical blogs focus on just one topic. An example of this is the Google blog which only covers news about Google. These types of blogs need to keep the readers attention and meet the readers needs so that the amount of readers and comments keeps increasing. The business blogs help promote the businesses in which they are created for as they are free and easy to maintain. The stock market is a popular subject of blogging where both amateur and professional investors use blogs to share stock tips. A moblog or mobile blog, consists of content posted to the Internet from a mobile phone. However it may require special software to do this blog.

Collaborative blogs can be created by everyone or limited to a group of people. An example of a collaborative blog is Blogcritics, but now thinks itself as an online magazine more than a blog. Educational blogs were created for students and teachers alike and are growing in popularity. Students can use blogs to record what they learn and teachers can use blogs to record what they teach. For example, a teacher can blog what homework students are required to carry out, including links to Internet resources, and recording each day what is taught. This way if a student is off sick they can quickly catch-up, the teacher can use the blog as a course plan, and finally new teachers can refer to if the teacher falls sick or leaves. This type of blogging can motivate students to do more reading and encourage them to improve their writing style, due to the presence of viewers that will go through the blog, making the students conscience of what they are doing and writing as thousands of people could be reading it. Spam blogs which are often referred to as splogs, are a form of high-pressure advertising. They are generally like spam e-mails, often linked to each other to increase their Internet presence. Political blogs are among the most common forms of blogs. Most political blogs are news driven, and most political bloggers will link to articles from news web sites so that they can add their own views on the subject. Other political blogs feature original commentary, with occasional hyperlinks to back up the blogger's talking points (Holtz, 2006).

Many bloggers support the open source movement, and the free speech nature of the blogs, has helped blogging to have a social impact. An example of this is that blogging makes it easy for employees to irritate their bosses, and a number have been sacked because of this. One in particular was Heather Armstrong who, in 2002, ignited a fierce debate about privacy issues when she was fired from her job as a web designer and graphic artist because she had written accounts of her experiences at the workplace in her blog "dooce.com". Because of this incident the word "dooce" now means to the blogging world, to lose your job as a result of something you wrote in an online journal. Another worry within the blogging community is the open source politics, which gives people the ability to participate more directly and have a role in politics. Some critics are worrying that some of these bloggers have no respect for the copy right laws nor care if they are presenting society with credible news. Another blog which gained media attention was by Simon Ng, who in 2005 posted a blog that helped identify his murderer. Simon was an American student but was born in Hong Kong. In 2005, while a freshman at Queens College, he was murdered, together with his older sister, Sharon Ng. Media attention was drawn to his case by the fact that Ng kept a Xanga weblog during his time at Queens College, and posted an entry just hours before his death. In this, he posted that a former boyfriend of his sister, Jin Lin, was visiting. This helped invalidate Jin Lin's alibi, resulting in Jin Lin being charged with two counts of first degree murder. To think, without this blog entry, Jin Lins alibi might have been accepted and he would have got away with it. So the blog in this case was used as an online diary which came in extremely useful in the end.

Videoblogging

Videoblogging is similar to blogs, with the exception that it presents the blog in a video format. A factor which is influencing the popularity of videoblogging is the video iPod which is capable of playing video files. A videoblog is a video clip that includes sound for users to view much Podcasts (Weynand, 2006). Often, Videoblogs contain text or captions to explain what is happening. Videoblogging has taken a while to gain followers however due to the uptake of broadband, it is becoming more ubiquitous.

Videoblogging became more popular around 2004. One of the main organizations to evangelize was Yahoo! who started a videoblogging group. Users who were creating videoblogs moved to the Yahoo! service as it provided a larger audience where more people were able to view their blogs. In November 2000 Adrian Miles posted the first ever known video blog. It was not until 2004 when Steve Garfield (a videographer and video blogger), brought the concept to a much larger audience. The Yahoo Videoblogging Group was started by Peter Van Dijck and Jay Dedman (Dedman, 2006). They attracted a small group of people calling themselves vloggers. Video blogging then began to receive media attention from outlets such as the New York Times (Boxer, 2005). The first videoblogger conference was held in New York and classes teaching vlogging sprang up. VlogMap.org launched Google maps and Google earth so that they displayed vloggers throughout the entire world. By the end of 2005 Yahoo Videoblogging Group had well over 1000 members and the number is rising rapidly.

Vloggercon is a site where vloggers go to meet and learn from each other. Some of the video topics include community, politics, journalism, music, iMovie, final cut pro, Rocketboom and Blogger. The site owner also has videoblogs about his trips shopping, family days out and work meetings. Chuck Olsen is a US documentary maker & video blogger. He is also the producer of the documentary film 'Blogumentary' This film explores the impact of blogging on media and politics. BBC radio also hosts video blogs. There are video blogs on many subjects relating to entertainment (Stolarz, 2006).

Conclusion

PodCasting, Blogging, VideoBlogging, and ScreenCasting allow the uploading of personal content to the web. Podcasting allows users to listen to music files from Podcasting websites or indeed any website for that matter. Files are mostly in the MP3 format but that's not the only format available they can also be in the form of WAV, WMA, QW or AU files. Unlike internet radio Podcasting allows listeners to download the podcast so that they can listen to it later or even store it on an mp3 player. Screencasting has also become popular with individual users who wish to document program bugs or oddities because a demonstration showing how a program functions can be better than a verbal description. A weblog, or blog which it is also known, is a website where the owner posts messages so that others can log on and read them. Blogs often focus on one subject however some people are using the blogs as on-line diaries where they post up messages describing their daily news or how they feel about certain subjects. Since Apple released the video iPod which allows videos to be viewed on the iPod, there has been an increase in Videoblogging. Smartphones also allow the viewing of videoblogs and indeed the creation.

References

Boxer, S. (2005). Watch me do this and that online, Critic Notebook Column, New York Times, July 25th 2005

Dedman, J., Kinberg, J., Paul, J. (2006). Video Blogging, Hungry Minds Inc, U.S, ISBN: 0470037881

Farkas, B. (2005) Secrets of Podcasting: Audio Blogging for the Masses Peachpit Press, ISB: 0321369297

Hill, B. (2005) Blogging for Dummies, Hungry Minds Inc, ISBN: 0471770841

Holtz, S., Demopoulos, T. (2006) Blogging for Business: Everything You Need to Know and Why You Should Care, Kaplan Professional, ISBN: 1419536451

Morris, T., Terro, E. (2005). Podcasting for Dummies, Hungry Minds Inc, USA, ISBN: 0471748986

Stolarz, D., Felix, L. (2006) Hands-On Guide to Video Blogging and Podcasting: Emerging Media Tools for Business Communication (Hands-on Guide S.), Focal Press, ISBN: 0240808312

Weynand, D., Hodson, R., Verdi, M. (2006) Secrets of Video Blogging, Peachpit Press, ISBN: 0321429176

22   Web Accessibility for Users with disabilities online

Kevin Curran, Nicolle Walters and David Robinson

Irresponsible and inaccessible web design causes unnecessary problems to certain website users. By applying the Web content accessibility guidelines to a web site the amount of possible users who can successfully view the content of that site will increase especially for those who are in the disabled and older adult categories of online users. We present the results of assessing the compliance of a selection of web sites with guidelines set out by the Web Accessibility Initiative (WAI). It was found that most sites evaluated were inaccessible to those with disabilities. Only 1 of the selected sites passed all 3-priority levels set out by the WAI. In many cases, minor modifications to sites will make them accessible to people with disabilities. Therefore it can only be speculated that the reasons for lack of conformance may vary from lack of awareness of the issue, time constraints or the general stress of having to keep up with new technologies. Companies who overlook users with disabilities however may be doing so at long-term risk to their legal position, public image, and ultimately business success.

Introduction

The UK has 1.5 million people with cognitive difficulties, 1.6 million with visual impairments, 3.4 million with disabilities preventing them from easily using a standard keyboard, screen and mouse set-up, and 6 million people with dyslexia (Loiacono, 2004). For those unfamiliar with accessibility issues pertaining to web page design, consider that many users may be operating in contexts very different from our own. They may not be able to see, hear, move or may not be able to process some types of information easily or at all. They may have difficulty reading or comprehending text. They may not have or be able to use a keyboard or mouse. They may have a text-only screen, a small screen or a slow Internet connection. They may not speak or understand fluently the language in which the document is written. They may be in a situation where their eyes, ears or hands are busy or interfered with and they may have an earlier version of a browser entirely, a voice browser or a different operating system.

Internet users who have no sight at all may utilize a screen reader, which reads the content of the web page, or rather the HTML (Hypertext Mark-up Language) code of the page, back to them. These machines sift through the HTML code and the technology deciphers what needs to be read aloud and what should be ignored. To take full advantage of the Internet, users with partial or poor sight may need to be able to enlarge the text on web pages. Text embedded within graphics isn't resizable and may cause difficulties for this group of web users. Users with poor vision may also use a screen magnifier to enlarge the text size. Again, text embedded within graphics may cause difficulties as it can appear blurry and pixilated when magnified.

Deaf web users are often able to access the Internet in much the same way as able-bodied people, with one key exception - audio content. If it's a key function of your website for people to be able to hear a message, then be sure to provide subtitles or a written transcript. An additional disadvantage deaf users may face is that British Sign Language is actually their first language. As such, they may be unable to understand some advanced English words and sentences.

Individuals with mobility disabilities have physical impairments that substantially limit either their movement, such as lifting or walking, or fine motor control like typing. These people face difficulties using computers input devices or handling removable storage media (a floppy disk, an optical disk or other removable devices). Assistive technologies include alternate input approaches, such as voice input or the ability to enter information at the user's own pace. Other people who may access the internet that have disadvantages include epileptic users who must always be careful to avoid seeing flickering between 2 and 55 Hz and users whose first language is not English.

Since 1999, the Disability Discrimination Act (DDA) (DDA, 1995) has required that disabled individuals have effective access to services and information. This should also include web sites. Although no organisation would purposefully bar disabled visitors from on-line services offered to the general public, there are many either not aware of the problem, or don't know what to do to address it. By following a few simple guidelines set out by The Web Accessibility Initiative (WAI)[1], companies can welcome their disabled customers into the virtual world. The WAI has developed guidelines on Web content accessibility. The guidelines, based on the impact of a Web site's accessibility, have three priority's levels – with one being the most serious and three being the least.

Priority 1. "A web content developer must satisfy this criterion"
…Otherwise, one or more groups will find it impossible to access information in the document. Satisfying this checkpoint is a basic requirement for some groups to be able to use the web documents.

1.1 Priority 2. "A web content developer should satisfy this criterion"
….Otherwise, one or more groups will find difficulty to access information in the document. Satisfying this checkpoint will remove significant barriers to accessing the web documents.

Priority 3. "A web content developer may address this criterion"
….Otherwise, one or more groups will find it somewhat difficult to access information in the document. Satisfying this checkpoint will provide access to web documents.

This chapter documents research into a selection of randomly chosen web sites as to whether or not they adhere to guidelines set out by the Web Accessibility Initiative (WAI) guidelines. Each of the 12 web sites are manually tested as to whether they pass the 10 stated guidelines. An accessibility checker, available on the Internet is also used to test the sites. There are 4 categories each containing 3 sites. The categories chosen are Government, Universities, Shopping and Charities.

Users with Disabilities

According to the Disability Rights Commission (DRC, 2005) the circumstances in which a person is "disabled" is if they have a mental or physical impairment that has an adverse effect on their ability to carry out normal day-to-day activities. In representing "day-to-day" activities, at least one of the following activities must be badly affected which include mobility, manual dexterity, physical co-ordination, continence, ability to lift, carry or move everyday objects, speech, hearing and eyesight, memory or the ability to concentrate, learn or understand, and the ability to understand the risk of physical danger. The broader category of disability contains within it: visual impairments, hearing impairments, motor impairments and cognitive impairments. The percentage of people who have to deal with a disability of some kind increases as they become older.

Restricted access on the web is because of the barriers that older adults are encountering. Adults 60 years plus however are encountering usability barriers on e-government sites that may be difficult to overcome (Becker, 2005). The barriers that are preventing ageing users from accessing Web content can be attributed to vision, cognition, and physical impairments all of which are associated with the normal aging process. Vision changes include a decline in visual acuity impacting the ability to see objects clearly, decreased capacity to focus at close range, or increased sensitivity to glare from light reflecting or shining into the eye (AFB, 2003). The American Foundation for the Blind describes visual capacity diminishing in terms of visual acuity, contrast sensitivity, glare sensitivity, visual field, and ability to discern colours. As well as visual decline, older users will experience a decrease in motor co-ordination making it more difficult to move a mouse, scroll down a web page and click on standard – size links. For example people with memory impairments may rely on consistent navigational structure throughout the site to allow them to efficiently navigate within the pages. The ability to perform spatial memory tasks decline with age, as does the ability to discern details in the presence of distracting information. As a result, complex navigation layouts, poorly designed search capabilities, and cluttered web pages will affect an older user's website experience (Becker, 2005). Other potential web usability barriers that effect older adults include:

---

[1] http://www.w3.org/TR/WAI-WEBCONTENT/full-checklist

- **Advertisements**

  Advertisements or images that look like ads, can negatively impact the usability of a site when they add clutter to a page. They often navigate to an external site, which may be confusing to the user. Their clutter may result in a page that is less intuitive in terms of navigation and information content

- **Links**

  Older adults find visual clues that differentiate between visited and unvisited links helpful when navigating a visited site.

- **Search**

  The use of the standard search box location at the top of the page minimises potential confusions that may arise from other designs.

- **Mouseovers**

  Older adults with unsteady hands can find the small movements required for highlighting and selecting objects difficult. Mouseovers may therefore pose a barrier to older adults.

- **Font size**

  Aging vision causes small font using eight to ten point font virtually inaccessible to anyone with poor vision.

- **Patterned background images**

  The readability of a site is negatively impacted if patterned backgrounds are used with small overlaying text.

- **Colour Discrimination**

  The amount of perceived light for a 60 year old is reduced by two thirds when compared to a twenty year old (Weale, 1961). The implication of this is for many older adults, foreground and background colour combinations that are similar in hue or low in saturation may render a web page visually inaccessible.

- **Visual Field**

  Web objects that are placed on the peripheral of a web page such as navigation, search and help may be difficult to find especially if the font size is small and the font colour doesn't contrast enough with the background (Echt, 2002).

Older users may use specialised hardware and software to access the web. These tools are known as assistive technologies and include screen readers and head pointers. A head pointer is simply a stick that is placed in a person's mouth or mounted on a head strap. The user can then use this to interact with a keyboard or a touch screen. Users can also use keyboards instead of a mouse to make use of a site. Some web developers design their site so it is unusable without a mouse this is one of the main reasons why certain sites are inaccessible to old and disabled users. It is very important that essential components of the page can work without a mouse. This implies that rollovers, drop down menus and interactive simulations are all redundant because of their dependence on using a mouse for user interaction. A typical interaction between a disabled user and the website via a keyboard could be the user moving to focusable objects including links, form controls and embedded objects by pressing the tab key and then activating the selected objects by means of pressing the enter key. The user can move between frames by pressing the control button and tab button together. This means that enabling the navigation of the website without the availability of a mouse is important. Meaningful commands, menus and icons, a well-designed navigation system, and comprehensive feedback messages help to reduce the amount of cognitive and physical effort required from the user.

Web Site Accessibility

Web accessibility can be defined simply, as to which degree a site is accessible to the largest possible range of people. The more people able to access a website, the more accessible is the site. At its core, Web accessibility emphasizes making website accessible to persons with disabilities and involves removing potential barriers to access caused by inconsiderate website designs. Today many services are only available, or offered at a discounted rate over the Internet. If a website does not meet a basic level of accessibility then it will be impossible for the many millions of potential visitors who have a disability, dyslexia or who simply can not use a mouse very well to use it.

The most important guideline for any type of design is the implementation of page structure. It is necessary for each page or sub-menu to be relevant to the page content. The structure of a web site is also concerned with some navigation issues. Guidelines state that at any given time users should be able to tell what area of the web site they are currently viewing. A link to the main menu should always be available, so that the user may be able to return to it from any area of the site. Sub-menu content generally should not be any more than 2 clicks away from the main menu of the site to enable users to access information quickly (Nielsen, 1999).

Another guideline for design is to make content understandable and navigable. The language should be clear and simple with easily understood techniques for navigating between pages. The provision of clear and consistent navigational mechanisms on a web site is very important for the user. Links and buttons are another important navigation tool; they may be presented in 2 forms, text and graphics. Text links should be created with the most important key word first. Buttons should provide information where the user will be taken when they are pressed or activated (Fleming, 1998). Each page of a web site should have a consistent design and content layout. Users should be able to access similar information on each page of the site in almost the same area.

Some guidelines state that the colour scheme of a web site should be limited to 3 colours. However the main design issue is concerned with colour-blind people in mind. Therefore it is important to use contrasting colours, which are separated possibly by a black or white border to provide the user with definition to an area. By default text should be a reasonable size, it should be no smaller than 10pt. For web design it should be possible for the user to change the display size of the text using the viewing options on their browser. This is important aspect for those that are partially sighted (Nielsen, 2001). Graphics should be used sparingly as users often interpret graphics as adverts and focus on other parts of the site that seem to be more useful. However images may be powerful communicators if they are meaningful and show items of interest to the users rather than being used for decoration alone (Nielsen, 2002).

HTML documents have common elements as it is a language for describing the structure of a document rather than its actual presentation. HTML also defines character styles as boldface and code examples. These styles are indicated inside HTML documents using tags. Each tag has a specific name and users cannot make up their own tags or create new appearances or features. HTML files contain the following:

<thetagname> affected text </thetagname>.

The tag name itself (here, *thetagname*) is enclosed in brackets (< >). HTML tags generally have a beginning and an ending tag surrounding the text they affect. The beginning tag "turns on" a feature (such as headings, bold so on), and the ending tag "turns it off". Closing tags have the tag name preceded by a slash (/). The three main guidelines to look into the tags on a web page are:

1. Providing alternative text for all images
2. Providing alternative text for all image-type buttons
3. Use mark-up style sheets and do so properly

For guideline 1 and , one should be checking for the tag *Alt* = "... " which is a text string that will be displayed in browsers that cannot support images. For guideline 4, one should be examing for the tag *Style* = "... ". By including the style attribute in a tag, one or more style declarations within a tag itself can be include such as using the <H1> tag in the following way:

<H1 style = "font-family:Verdana,sans-serif"> Heading </H1>

All style declarations follow this same basic pattern. With the property on the left and the value associated with that property on the right. In the above example the property is font-family, and the value is Verdana, sans-serif. This attribute modifies the standard <H1> tag by changing the font to Verdana, and if the user doesn't have that font installed on their system, a sans-serif font is selected (Lemay, 2003).

The increasing amount of older & users with disabilities online has made accessibility a greater issue than it was. Many older users have visual impairments or are disabled and have to deal with and overcome frequent web barriers online. Recent legislation that has been passed in the UK called the Disability Discrimination Act now makes it illegal for websites providing a service to be inaccessible to disabled users. Basic accessibility solutions for Web sites include:

- using the "Alt" tag within HTML to provide the user with alternative text to non-text objects,
- using clear and concise language throughout a web page,
- using clear descriptive wording to make sense to the user when inserting hyperlinks,
- making sure colour is not used to convey information within the site
- allowing text to be enlarged without distortion to the layout of the interface.

Implementing these techniques benefits all users and hence is good design practice. It was found out that most websites do not even satisfy the most basic conformance level. It was found that 55% of the websites did not meet *level A* conformance. A single issue prevented most of the websites from satisfying the minimum set of checkpoints needed for *level A* compliance of the Web Content Accessibility Guidelines. This issue was concerned with correctly providing alternative text for images.

Conclusion

Most sites evaluated were inaccessible to those with disabilities. Only 1 of the web sites passed all 3-priority levels set out by the WAI. One of the best categories was the universities, with all of them passing priority levels 1 and 2 with Cynthia. In many cases, minor modifications to sites will make them accessible to people with disabilities. Therefore the reasons for lack of conformance can vary from lack of awareness of the issue, time constraints, and the general stress of having to keep up with new technologies. Companies who overlook the disability market may be doing so at long-term risk to their legal position, public image, and ultimately business success.

References

Andrew, R., and Turnbull, R., (2004) The Expert's Voice - ASP Web Development with Macromedia Dreamweaver MX 2004.

AFB. American Foundation for the Blind. (2003). Normal changes in the aging eye. http://www.afb.org/info_document_view.asp?documentid=203

AoA. Administration on Aging (1999). Profile of Older Adults. http://www.aoa.gov/aoa/stats/profile/5.html

Becker, S.A. (2005). E-government usability for older adults. Communications of the ACM - Technical Opinion Column, Vol. 48, No. 2, pp: 100-102

Coulson, I. (2000) Introduction: Technological challenges for gerontologists in the 21st century. Educational Gerontology 26, 307 -315

DDA. Disability Discrimination Act, (1995), Disability Discrimination Act 1995, PART III-Discrimination in other areas. http://www.hmso.gov.uk/acts/acts1995/95050--c.htm#19

DRC. Disability Rights Commission (2005). askDRC – What counts as a disability according to the law? http://www.drc-gb.org/askdrc/category/show.asp?id=114

Echt, K. V. (2002) Designing Web based health information for older adults: Visual considerations and design directives for older adults, Health information and the World Wide Web, pp. 61-88, Erlbaum

Fleming, J. (1998). *Web Navigation: Designing the User Experience,* O'Reilly.

Lemay, L. (2003). *HTML and XHTML in 21 days.* 4th Edition, Sams Publishing, May 2003

Loiacono, E. (2004). *CyberAccess- Web Accessibility and Corporate America*, Communications of the ACM, Vol. 47, No. 12, December 2004

Nielsen, J. (1999). *Designing Web Usability: The Practice of Simplicity,* New Riders

Nielsen, J., Tahir, M. (2001). *Homepage Usability: 50 Websites Deconstructed,* New Riders

Nielsen, J. (2002). *Top Ten guidelines for homepage usability,* Useit.com, AlertBox, May 2002, http://www.useit.com/alterbox/20020512.html

Schmetzke, A. (2001) Web accessibility at university libraries and library schools. Library Hi Tech Vol. 19, No. 1

Weale, R. (1961). Retinal illumination and age. Transactions of the Illuminating Engineering Society. 25, 95-100.

25   Introduction

Cities around the world are increasingly installing Wi-Fi internet access so that people can access the web from anywhere. The big selling point for WiFi is wireless freedom, namely allowing devices to communicate without wires at high speeds. Wi-Fi technology uses radio frequencies to allow computers or wireless enabled devices to communicate using IEEE standards for the data communication. Intel and other industry giants are fully behind Wi-Fi introducing new systems which have wireless chipsets integrated. It is becoming more likely nowadays that the future exists in tourists powering up their PDA/Smart Phones and finding city maps or restaurants easily throughout the world (Ohrtman, 2003). In tandem with wifi availabitity, satellites are available for global positioning to civilians from all countries around the world. In order to find your position all you need is a receiver and some software to equate that to a map location. The military and some keen hikers/mountaineers have used the handheld receivers to find where they are and to point them in the direction they want to be for some time.

Both of these technologies have very useful applications, but combining them will allow feature rich applications to be delivered in the context of where you are in the world. For example, suppose you are in London and you want to find a nearby restaurant, currently you would ask someone or walk around trying to find somewhere but if you had a GPS receiver which knew your location and applied that to local maps and lists of restaurants you would have a review, directions and maybe even a menu.

The Global Positioning System (GPS) is becoming more and more integrated into our day to day lives. New cars are coming equipped with the system as it assists drivers with their directions, taxi firms are using it to track their drivers and inform the customer when they have arrived. The number of applications is growing and the receivers are becoming cheaper making them more accessible to ordinary people. The receivers are also a lot smaller than they used to be which means they can be integrated into other electronic devices easily. GPS is a method of determining current position wherever one is in the world, in any weather conditions. It uses a number of satellites in orbit around the earth to triangulate your position. GPS works by calculating the distance of the satellites from the receivers location, where a minimum of three satellites are required for a two dimensional position and four satellites minimum for a three dimensional position (elevation). If you know the distance to one satellite is 11,000 miles you are within a sphere of 11,000 miles around that satellite, if you know the distance to two other satellites you have two other spheres and when the overlap that should be your location. The more satellites you can find the more accurate the position as the point of intersection becomes smaller. The receiver calculates the distances using precise timing. Radio signals travel at the speed of light 186,000 miles per second (Hofmann, 1997).

23 Worldwide Interoperability for Microwave Access (WiMAX)

Kevin Curran, Francis Doherty, Conrad Deighan, Gerard Galway

WiMAX signals the arrival of the next wave of wireless data technologies. Unhampered by the short range and data orientations of WLAN's these technologies will see users having high speed wireless on the road. WiMAX deployments are similar to that used in a WiFi network. WiMAX does not suffer from interference such as mobile phone masts. Once in the residential building the WiMAX base station beams a signal to the WiMAX receiver in a desktop or notebook receiver. This is very similar to the process in a WiFi LAN. Third world countries will greatly benefit from deploying WiMAX networks. African countries are now going to start deploying WiMAX networks instead of cell phone networks and disaster zones could also utilize WiMAX giving them the ability to distribute crisis information quickly & cheaply. This chapter provides an overview of WiMAX.

Introduction

Wireless communications can trace its history back to the start of the twentieth century and to the electrical engineer Nikola Telsa, who pioneered the early development on radio and wireless technologies. Perhaps the most well known of the early developers was Guglielmo Marconi, who developed early wireless communication through telegraphy and radio. During the nineteen sixties the space race between the USA and the USSR allowed for the development of communicating networks, the USA created a number of agencies that required to communicate and share information, the agencies setup a network between there facilities this network was to become more commonly known as Arpanet. In Hawaii, the Aloha net was born allowing for wireless networking (Wikipedia, 2006). The next major step in the evolution was mobile telecommunications. Wireless communication has developed rapidly in the last 10 years in the field of mobile telephone communications and more recently with the wireless network communications through the 802.11 groups of standards, more commonly known as Wi-Fi. The success of Wi-Fi has served only to encourage the development of WiMAX, which with the slow rollout of mobile 3G technologies has only served to confirm the emergence of mobile WiMAX has a viable technology and alternative.

WiMAX development has been driven by the WiMAX Forum, this is an industry-based consortium that was set-up to promote and certify the compatibility and interoperability of broadband wireless access equipment with conformance to the IEEE802.16 set of standards. In particular the technology more commonly known as mobile WiMAX or IEEE 802.16e will be studied, this in some quarters is seen as possibly the most important member of the IEE 802.16 group of standards with the greatest potential. WiMAX transmits data from a single location point within a city to multiple locations throughout that city or cities. WiMAX is a high speed internet wireless technology planned purposely for outsized IP networks providing superior coverage than its rival competitor Wi-Fi. WiMAX will make sure that it will be more cost-effective than other wireless technologies by ensuring compatibility between high speed internet wireless access equipment. WiMAX is available in two different standards. 802.16-2004 is for fixed networks and 802.16e is for mobile. The 802.16-2004 is rigid, moveable and nomadic; the 802.16-2004 can be accessed in two different approaches, Line of Sight and Non Line of Sight. It can reach frequency bands of 5.8GHz.The 802.16e standard supports mobile access in frequency bands of up to 3.5GHz. This chapter provides an overview of WiMAX, the history and evolution of wireless networking and current developments relating to WiMAX.

WiMAX

The Worldwide Interoperability for Microwave Access (WiMAX) is based on the IEEE 802.16 set of standards that have been developed from a need to have a standardized platform on which broadband wireless access could be introduced. The initial scope was that the technology would allow a standardization of technology that was already in use by communications companies who were using the technology to connect between the communication end users and the telecommunications backbone, but these various vendors each had there own proprietary solutions which were not inter-operability, as a local in-house solution this was acceptable but inhibited acceptance and growth in the wider market. Areas of opportunity and growth out with the original remit were then realized and seen as markets to which the technology could be aimed. The market that took a major lead was fixed wireless access, this was seen as an opportunity to allow broadband access to areas that lacked DSL or cable services, and in the past a major obstacle to this was the cost of the "final mile" (Marks, 2005), which is the connection between the infrastructure backbone and the customer's home or place of work.

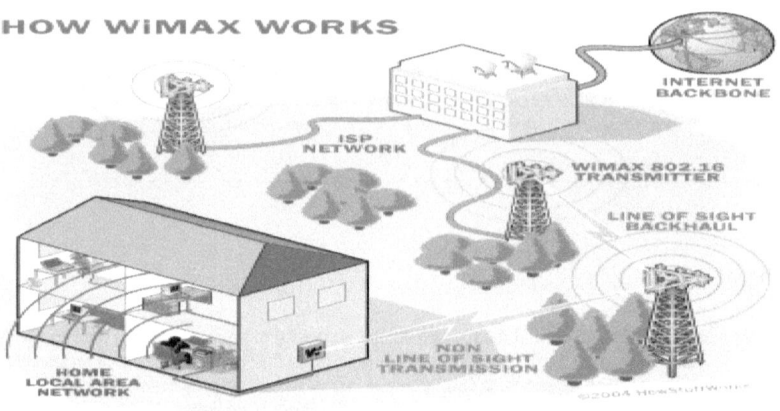

Figure 62: How WiMAX works (Grabianowski and Brain, 2006)

The technology when used in these circumstances has a typical deployment area of between three to ten kilometres without direct line of sight to a base station, which if used in major towns and cities would allow full coverage from a small number of base station, with this the need for expensive and high maintenance fixed wire solutions would be negligible. This is seen as a large growth market in developing and third world countries where current infrastructure is limited and the installation of new systems is prohibitive due to the costs. In remote areas or where the terrain makes fixed solutions difficult to deploy the advantages of the technology can also be utilized, with a range of up to fifty kilometres from emitter to receiver the cost difference between wired and wireless solutions are significant (see Figure 62).

The natural progression of the technology was then to investigate how it would be implemented in a truly wireless situation rather than a fixed wireless scenario, for this a different set of objectives were realized and from this the IEE 802.16e standards were published in December of 2005, these standards would allow for the technology to be developed to allow high speed data access to be available to the mobile market. The mobile WiMAX market is seen as the most lucrative with possible earnings of up to US$45 billion per year from networking equipment only, compared to the fixed market with projected earnings of US$500 million per year (CISCO, 2006). The scope of uses for mobile WiMAX encompasses different technologies from mobile telephones to laptops to PDA's, in the telecommunication market mobile WiMAX is seen as a viable competitor to 3G technologies, currently the rollout and take-up of 3G services has been slower than expected due to high costs.

WiMAX can be used for a number of applications, including "last mile" broadband connections, hotspot and cellular backhaul, and high-speed enterprise connectivity for businesses. Mobile WiMAX (802.16e) is part of a group of broadband wireless communications standards for Metropolitan Area Networks developed by IEEE. It complements the earlier standard of 802.11 for Wireless LANs. The earlier versions of 802.16 a b c and d are only for fixed Wireless connections 802.16e enables connections for mobile devices. WiMAX uses microwaves to transfer data through the air at high speed for a number of miles. The earlier standard 802.11 uses channels to transmit and receive data and voice from a fixed width of the bandwidth spectrum. WiMAX 'condenses' these channels narrowing the bandwidth allowing more users access and to be served. The same spread of the spectrum is used but more channels are available due to the 'narrowing' and more data is sent along the channels. The highway if you like is divided into more lanes and more traffic is packed into each lane. The same core technology underpins both 802.11 and 802.16e but WiMAX exceeds in distance by miles versus feet. This means that you can wander around buildings or areas there are hotspots and maintain your broadband connection. However, since the standard has only recently been ratified commercialization and true mobility will not be available for a couple of years. The 802.16e standard covers data rates from 1.5Mbps to 70Mbps over distances in excess 20 miles, although the farther away the lower the data rate. 802.16e is viewed as compatible with the 802.11 Wi-Fi LAN standards in that it can extend its range and support higher data rates. WiMAX so far can be viewed as a complementary technology to 3G. However the WiMAX Forum and IEEE (both groups work to produce and test the standard) are keen to include greater interoperability in the standard. So when devices that are Mobile WiMAX enabled are actually produced commercially, different manufacturers' equipment and systems will be able to work together. Mobile WiMAX has clearly fixed its crosshairs on wireless data, which means it poses a potential threat to Wi-Fi but it also is aiming to include wireless voice which is perceived by the Telecom operators as a threat to their monopolies particularly with respect to what is know as the Last Mile. Last Mile refers to the last leg of getting broadband technology to the users house, which although is often a relatively short distance from the exchange becomes extremely expensive because of all the costs involved in getting the physical cable to the users house, such as labour, digging up the roads, the cost of the equipment etc, and the return on the investment shows little or no profit. With WiMAX the last mile does not present the same obstacles. Mobile WiMAX also alleviates the problems associated with 'backhaul' which means getting the network data on to the backbone so that it can be redistributed or routed to another location. The current explosion in Wi-Fi means that a lot of investment has been put into deploying and promoting the WLANs (Wireless Local Area Networks) but one of the problems users of Wi-Fi run into is what is referred to as 'no-connection space'. This is where the user basically is 'out of coverage' for about five minutes on average in a Metropolitan Area Network hotspot configuration. What WiMAX aims to achieve in the long-term is for the nomadic user to get a connection anytime anywhere and become a mobile user. The difference between the nomadic user and the mobile user is that the mobile user is connected all the time on the go, while the nomadic user finds a hotspot gets connected, disconnects, moves to another hotspot connects and so on. A similar explosion in Mobile WiMAX to that of Wi-Fi would see an estimated 2-4 million subscribers by 2008, with expected sales and revenue in excess of $1 billion. (Barry et al, 2005).

The type of connection being referred to in the WiMAX specification is high-speed broadband connectivity to the internet or Broadband Wireless Access (BWA). People who experience internet access using broadband tend to leave their connection open, remaining almost always connected to the internet. WiMAX recognizes this could be a major selling point for the new technology; that no matter where you are you will always be connected. Of course there are obstacles to this and the standard must address such things as interoperability, network security and roaming. The interoperability is dealt with in 802.16e and addresses the problem quickly discovered by Wi-Fi operators as they tried to extend their WLANs. They got equipment that was built to extend WLANs but it would not work with their particular brand of Wi-Fi equipment. The maximum transmission range for Wi-Fi is about 50 feet in an urban area so a large number of access points are needed to provide decent coverage for the area and to meet customer expectations. The deployment of Wi-Fi tends to take on a mesh-like topology largely because the Wi-Fi chipsets are very inexpensive and are being built into more and more devices. WLANs are then deployed in close proximity to each other, each Access Point connecting to each other Access Point. This poses a smaller obstacle to WiMAX. Mobile WiMAX has to convince manufacturers to install WiMAX components in their devices either alongside or in place of the Wi-Fi component. If WiMAX can achieve this then it is sure to accelerate the rapid adoption of WiMAX enabled products. This in turn will facilitate the spread of WiMAX. This ratification opens the door for the mass production of 802.16e compatible technology which will result in standard components that will enhance interoperability. WiMAX can deliver high speed broadband internet access over a wireless connection. It does not require Line of Sight between the source and the endpoint and this distance can range up as far as 50 kilometers providing a shared data rate of up to 70 Mbps. This could provide high speed internet access of 2Mbps for hundreds of home on last mile networks. Of course the service suffers degradation the further away the endpoint is from the source. The source, a Base Station, which would probably be on a tower or some high location, connects the users' devices, or Subscriber Stations, through their antenna, which may or may not be part of their device. This then is connected using a high speed wired connection or microwave point-to-point link in to the backbone, which is the main pipe of the internet. The WiMAX connection can also be routed or bridged into a standard LAN. Due to the absence of wires and cables, deployment of a WiMAX solution can be very fast.

In South Korea there has recently been a recent announcement to allow a WiMAX compatible standard called WiBro to be made available for use in the mobile market. WiBro is not exactly the same as WiMAX but it is based on similar technologies and the success of WiBro is seen as critical to the future of WiMAX (Clendenin, 2005). Within the mobile pc market either by use of laptop or PDA's it is seen that one of the opportunities will be for mobile WiMAX to be utilized in a similar but much larger scale to WiFi networking, it is envisaged that there will be the possibility to allow secure roaming. The success of WiFi can also be used as encouragement to the developers of WiMAX, in recent years the growth of WiFi hotspots where users can connect to the internet using their wireless 802.11 device has grown with many businesses such as restaurants, airports and shopping centres installing them to attract customers, small countries and cities have also taken up the mantle setting up regional wide WiFi zones for general use (Marks, 2005). With limited area coverage at approx 100 meters indoor and 150 meters outside the scope for WiFi is limited unless a mesh network connecting users and transmitters to the network can be utilized.

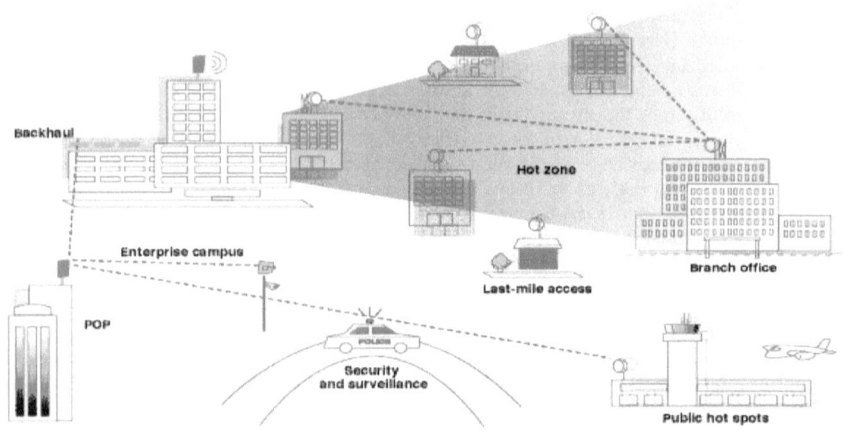

Figure 63: Potential WiMAX application for Service Providers (Kajian, 2004)

Each node acts as a repeater, allowing a large network to be constructed at a very low cost, this system can be quite robust with the network being set-up with more than one connection between nodes allowing nodes to leave and join the network without the integrity of the network being affected. This type of network setup and hotspots can be seen as another opportunity for WiMAX, existing networks could be supplied by a WiMAX signal to allow a central transmitter which could then transmit the Wi-Fi signal to create a Wi-Fi hotspot in area's of limited access or not being supplied by a fixed communications infrastructure. The range of potential uses for WiMAX is constantly growing and Figure 63 shows the breath of potential WiMAX applications for service providers. WiMAX can be used in the enterprise environment and the transportation and security industries (Kajian, 2004).

WiMAX Forum

The WiMAX Forum was formed in June of 2001 with a mandate to facilitate and assist with the deployment of broadband wireless networks using the IEEE 802.16 standards. The forum would ensure that the equipment being developed for the technology by all manufacturers that were part of the forum would be compatible and inter-operability. The forum from the outset was set-up as a non-profit making organisation that would act as an association for the equipment and component suppliers who were members and ensure adequate promotion for the adoption of the new standard.   The forum laid out set principles to which the forum would work towards, they are:

- Support IEEE 802.16 standard

- Propose and promote access profiles for their IEEE 802.16 standard
- Certify inter-operability levels both in network and the cell
- Achieve global acceptance
- Promote use of broadband wireless access overall

With the forum any equipment or component supplier that is a member can ensure that their equipment will be compliant and have full inter-operability with fellow members of the forum's equipment. This certification will ensure that a service provider that is sourcing and or purchasing equipment will have the confidence to know that equipment purchased from different manufacturers who are members of the forum and have their equipment listed as WiMAX Forum Certified will have full inter-operability and will have no major problems inter-connecting the equipment as full testing will have been carried out. The importance of the forum can be seen by reading through the list of the board members, from this list we can see that there is representation from a number of the major manufacturers and service providers on a global scale, this ensured that there would be global acceptance of the technologies and that the forums initiative would be taken serious and be fully implemented to the one standard worldwide.

The list of the board members above highlights the strength of the forum, this strength can be also be verified with the list of member companies who have joined the forum. The current total is 368, this list of members contains companies from all aspects of the communications industry Dell, Nokia, Motorola, Samsung, Nortel, Cisco and Netgear are all members and show the varied interest from the hardware manufacturing industry. Major communication and service providers on the members list include AOL, AT&T, BT, and Sprint- Nextel.

WiMAX Physical Layers

IEEE 802.16 standard has been developed for point to multipoint broadband wireless, for use in the range of sub 11GHz and 10-66 GHz frequency and covers the physical and media access control layers of the ISO model. The first standard was approved in December 2001 and was known as 802.16a, this was primarily developed for fixed broadband access, further development was announced in June 2003 with the 802.16-2004 standard which gave more support for customer support equipment, from then there has been a continual development and in December 2005 the 802.16-2005 commonly known as 802.16e standard was finalized, this is better known as the Mobile WiMAX standard, this allowed the standard to be better utilized and to include mobility in the standard which had been primarily developed for fixed operation.

During the development of the standard a number of critical consideration were included in the requirements, the ability to use various physical types would allow for different operating environments to be utilized. Non-line of site conditions can be used in the sub 10GHz frequencies compared to the higher frequencies in the 10 to 66 GHz ranges, which require line of sight; with this wide channels with high capacity links can be setup. The WiMAX standard has been developed to use the same MAC (Machine Access Control) layer for varying PHY (physical layers), this allows for technology to have a high inter-operability with the hardware for different vendors being compatible. The standard uses 256-point orthogonal frequency division multiplexed carrier (OFDM) compared to a 64-point orthogonal frequency division multiplexed, which is used by the 802.11 technologies giving it a higher range. OFDM is a digital encoding and modulation technology that has been previously used in applications used to access applications in DLS and cable systems, within the WiMAX technologies it will allow for the use in non line of sight environments. These non line of sight environments have been addressed by use of the OFDM that allows the ability to deliver higher bandwidth and data rate by using multiple overlapping carrier signals instead of one as with existing networks.

The recent ratification where 'e' was appended to 802.16 means that mobility is included. The first 802.16 addressed spectrum ranges from 10 – 66 GHz, was focused on multipath Line of Sight issues which were combatted using orthogonal frequency division multiplexing (OFDM) techniques. It allowed for wide channels greater than 10 MHz in the licensed spectrum. Changes were made to the two layers the MAC layer and the Physical (PHY) layer. The MAC layer uses Point to MultiPoint as its foundation for the Downlink from the Base Station to the Subscriber Station. That means all Subscriber Stations with in a given frequency and antenna sector will receive the same transmissions. In other words the Downlink is broadcast to all unless modified otherwise. The MAC connection is geared towards Quality of Service and meeting and managing the services being used. This means depending on the users application the transmission can be continual as is with Voice over IP traffic or in bursts such as MPEG transmissions. When the Subscriber Station connects after satisfying a number of criteria based on the DOCSIS standard (Data Over Cable Service Interface

Specifications) such Downlink channel synchronisation, range and capability agreement, authentication, registration and IP connectivity, bandwidth is allocated based upon the type of service. The Base Station can manage the allocation by resizing the amount of bandwidth needed by the service being used. In the Mesh topology Subscriber Stations can communicate directly with each other with out having to go through the Base Station. ARQ processing maintains Quality of Service by retransmitting dropped or lost blocks. The scheduling service comprising of the Fast Data Scheduler, dynamic resource allocation and frequency selective scheduiling is designed to deliver the broadband services of data, video and voice efficiently and with in Quality of Service parameters. Three handoff methods are supported; Hard Handoff which is mandatory, Fast Base Station Switching and Macro Diversity Handover. The delay of handover is kept to less than 50 milliseconds.

The Physical layer (PHY) is defined for the 10 – 66 GHz licensed range of the spectrum and supports the 2 – GHz band of licensed and unlicensed spectrum bands. The most significant modification to this layer allows the Non Line of Sight environment to send a signal by different routes. This was enabled by adding the Othogonal Frequency Division Multiplexing (OFDM) modulation scheme. The data is transmitted in the signal with forward error correction in place then using an Inverse Discrete Fourier Transform applied to the data the frequency domain is converted, filtered and modulated up to the carrier frequency using Time Division Multiplexing on the Downlink and Time Division Multiple Access on the Uplink. The 802.16e is based on the OFDM system. In this system the signal can be divided into many sub-channels that run at lower speeds. This increases the resistence to interference that would be experienced on the non line of sight multipath routes. As noted previously depending on the distance and services being accessed by the user the allocation of sub-channels is dynamically assigned. When the location is in close proximity to the Base Station, QAM, quadrature amplitude modulation can be used for higher bandwidth across several channels. When the distance from the Base Station is great the number of channels being used drops but the power per channel increases ensuring that even if the data rate goes down the user stays connected. OFDM technology uses Fast Fourier Transform (FFT) algorithms to get the frequencies perpendicular (orthogonal) to each other so that the sub-channels can overlap with out causing interference to one another. This method fully utilises the available spectrum. FFT is a formula that uses a variable N, where N can be 1K, 2K, 128, 256 etc. and The fast Fourier transform (FFT) is extremely useful in analyzing unsteady measurements, because the frequency spectrum from an FFT provides information about the frequency content of the signal. So by using this technique, OFDMA in the PHY layer dynamically corrects and stabilizes the multi path spectrum use by Mobile WiMAX. It is important to note that OFDMA and OFDM are two different modes that have very much in common. Both support high data rates, utilizing multipath methods to increase signal quality in non line of sight environments and the ability to split channels up into many sub channels. Both also support Time Division Duplex (TDD) and Frequency Division Duplex (FDD) in the modulation scheme to dynamically shift the allocation depending on capacity and proximity. OFDMA is also scalable which means it can adapt to the different channel frequencies in different countries, and can use a variety of FFT versions. Deciding on the type of architecture to deploy is dependent on whether to use TDD or FDD. TDD will only transmit or receive at a specified time, reducing interference because the transmitter is off when the receiver is on, however this can create problems when switching modes and reduce throughput and curtailing the number of users supported. It is economical due to the reuse of the local oscillator to generate the frequency which saves in space and costs and components. FDD can be employed in both the Base Station and the Subscriber Stations; it uses two different frequencies to transmit and receive at the same time. This method uses up a considerable amount of the spectrum bandwidth but does give higher throughput and can support a lot more users. All these factors come into play when approving the standard. At least three manufacturers have to agree to provide a basis for interoperability. The choice will affect the mobility and speed of handoff (going from one cell to another), the spectrum range and size of channels available.

A phrase that is commonly associated with WiMAX technologies but not necessarily mobile WiMAX is "The Last Mile", this is described as being the Holy Grail in communications infrastructures, and needs to be explained to understand the demand for this new technology. With the development and rollout of broadband services globally the bottleneck worldwide has been the connection between the infrastructure backbone and the end user customer either domestic or commercial. In the developed world the telecommunications network has been established and in place for a long period of time and totally unsuitable to use with the new technologies, the cost of replacing this has been high with a large financial outlay to the companies that have went ahead with the upgrade, in the developing world the cost of installing this technology is not possible due to financial constraints. It is also seen that major telecommunication companies own and manage the network infrastructure and are therefore in an advantageous position for implementing the broadband technologies, to allow for more competition by means of allowing more service providers to enter the market giving the customer more choice. The wireless networks supplied by WiMAX will allow for low cost installation and maintenance of the network, for both provider and customer.

WiMAX Versus 3G and Wi-Fi

WiMAX can and does give more significant advantages of wireless technology over WIFI. WiMAX presents a superior range and has more bandwidth on offer. WiMAX could eventually take out most of the cabled networks that connect to the internet as it can provide connectivity to whole towns and cities. WiMAX could even replace the WIFI receivers that are built into laptops as WiMAX was built for outdoor mobility. The main challenge now for WiMAX developers is to get more chips (WiMAX receivers) into laptops and PC's.

Wireless Communication Standard	Max Data Rate	Distance Max Range
Wide Area Network		
802.16d Fixed WiMAX	75MBps	6 Miles
802.16e Mobile WiMAX	30MBps	3 Miles
Local Area Network		
802.11a/g WIFI	54MBps	300 Feet
802.11b WIFI	11MBps	300 Feet

Figure 64: WiMAX statistics

Currently Mobile WiMAX is the biggest threat to 3G and they compete as to who offers the better service of wireless connectivity. WiMAX are still trying to market this new technology and "experts" believe that the longer this product takes to get on the market the better chance that 3G has. Intel state that 3G is excellent for voice and WiMAX will take over the market for mobile data services. For providers to stay competitive they may have to start to offer WiMAX and 3G. Figure 64 illustrates the distance range and data rate that each standardisation provides. WiMAX is superior to WIFI in terms of data transfer and the range that it provides.

Wireless had received some bad press in recent years because of a proliferation of security issues and while no system is completely secure Mobile WiMAX is supporting many of the best security technologies available today. Among these are Privacy and Key Management Protocol v2 which manages the EAP authentication, Traffic Encryption and Handover Key Exchange. Extensible Authentication Protocol (EAP) is the main protocol for device and user authentication from the Internet Engineering Task Force (IETF). Advanced Encryption Standard (AES) encrypts data when activated. These features builtin to the 802.16e standard provide the basis for secure networks. The weakest link is also the human factor so it becomes critical that users maintain high security practices when accessing networks. The keystone to the success of Mobile WiMAX will be the development and spread of Smart Antenna technologies. Fortunately OFDMA supports smart antenna technologies in particular Multiple Input Mulitple Output (MIMO) which behaves as if it is many antenna thereby giving large coverage while maximising use of the spectrum. It does this by using adaptive switching and providing coverage where conditions deteriorate. Support is also built into the Mobile WiMAX architecture for a packet-switched framework and IP as well as for a variety of topologies. The network architecture can support voice, data, multimedia and a host of other services. One other exciting development arising from Mobile WiMAX is Voice over IP on mobile phones which will benefit further from the adoption of .IPv6.

The Future of WiMAX

The future implementation of WiMAX technologies and in particular mobile WiMAX seems inevitable. The role of the WiMAX Forum has played a crucial role in positioning the technology in a powerful position. Once the forum was able to list such names like Intel, Nokia, Motorola, Cisco and AT&T amongst its members then acceptance to the wider technology market would be assured, with a large number of similar companies joining the forum. Announcements of testing and plans to rollout WiMAX networks, include the South Korean governments plans to develop a mobile WiMAX compatible telecommunication network (WiBro). In France Iliad have announced plans to offer WiMAX services to a base of 1.6 million users (Gabriel, 2006), previously BT have announced membership of the forum and testing of WiMAX in a number of rural areas of the UK including Northern Ireland (Smith, 2004). Subsequent developments will likely see a new breed of PDA and multifunction mobile phones. With the variety of applications available over Mobile WiMAX the target audience will be as diverse as the Mobile WiMAX enabled products and it has been suggested that with the large scale adoption that has been predicted costs will be driven down with in two to three years. At this point Mobile Wimax products will not be commercially and generally available until about 2007. The main aspect under for consideration for worldwide adoption is to ensure that the same spread from the spectrum is being used and educating users about the benefits of mobile highspeed wireless broadband. With non line of sight high speed and long reach combined with flexible on demand delivery and connectivity Mobile WiMAX looks like having a good future.

These announcements tend to heighten expectation that can only help the acceptance of the technology along with similar type announcements from the WiMAX Forum on equipment being submitted for certification. Another gauge for the market is monitoring start-up companies that are managing to acquire significant amounts of capital from investors with the sales pitch of developing WiMAX networks, a good example is Clearwire a US based company who recently announced that they had raised US$1 billion to build a WiMAX network (Murphy, 2006). Announcements like what have been mentioned previously only serve to establish the technology. With these kinds of investments taking place then the rollout of mobile WiMAX can only benefit from the infrastructure being put together and benefit from the work of the forum guaranteeing inter-operability of the hardware. Intel have recently announced the release in the latter part of 2006 of laptops with integrated 802.16e technology onboard (Wimaxxed, 2006), Nokia have just announced successful testing using 802.16e technologies between two bases and Motorola, and Samsung have published plans for mobile telephones with the technology inbuilt either in 2007 or 2008 (Motorola, 2006), with announcements from companied of this stature the future looks positive and will be further enhanced if the trials in South Korea with WiBro are successful. Samsung have released their first mobile phone with WiMAX capabilities Nokia and Motorola have since broadcasted that they are employing WiMAX for use in these mobile phones[1]. Intel[2] have predicted that the first version of service 802.16d fixed WiMAX will be available to users by the second half of 2006 but this will only be accessible through an external box, possibly a USB interface. The possibility of incorporating WiMAX chips into laptops seems to lack clarification as WI-FI is occupying the PCI Slot of the laptop, this would mean that there would need to be some integration in the compatibility between the two chips.

Conclusion

WiMAX promises cost effective service for both consumer and manufactures as they have all the key components to supply a wider area with high speed internet access compared with wired broadband. WiMAX sends the wireless frequencies directly to the customer avoiding the need for unnecessary costs for underground cabling and physical labour. WiMAX is most certainly a "promising next generation wireless technology" with high data rate transfers (peak rates 20Mbps) over vast distances removing the necessity of having to find a Wi-Fi hot-spot. Telco's, have spent small fortunes upgrading their mobile network but are limited to transfer speeds of approximately 400kbps per second -700kbps per user. WiMAX can operate at environmentally friendly frequencies below 11GHz. Higher frequencies do require line of sight. There are some concerns however regarding the "battery life" for WiMAX and it seems that portable competition from 3G and 4G networks will be the main competitor against WiMAX.

References

Barry, A., Daly, C., Johnson, J., Skehill, R. (2005) *Overview of WiMAX 802.16e.* Proceedings of 5th Annual International Conference on Information Telecommunications and Technology, Cork, Ireland

Cisco Systems, Inc. (2006) *Cisco Position paper on WiMAX and Related Technologies for Mobile Operators.* San Jose, USA. http://www.cisco.com

Clendenin, M. (2005) *South Korea preps deployment of WiMAX variant.* EE Times Online, January 21st 2005 http://www.eetimes.com

---

[1] http://www.channelregister.co.uk/2005/06/10/intel_nokia_wimax/
[2] http://www.whatlaptop.co.uk/YdNQTkpom_3ZfA.html

Gabriel, C. (2006) *Iliad launches WiMAX service amid legal wrangles.* WiMAX Trends Online, Northboro, USA. http://www.wimaxtrends.com/feature.htm

Grabianowski, E., Brain, M. (2006). *How WiMAX Works.* How Stuff Works. http://computer.howstuffworks.com/wimax.htm

Kajian, H. (2004). *WiMAX.* EBizzAsia – Information Technology, Communications and E-Business Magazine, Vol. 2, No. 20, September 2004

Marks, R. (2005) *IEEE 802.16e Mobile Wireless MAN Standard is Official.* New York, USA. Available at: http://standards.ieee.org/announcements/pr_p80216.html

Motorola Inc (2006) *Leading WiMAX Technology* [online]. Illinois, USA. Available at: http://www.motorola.com/networkoperators/pdfs/Wi4-brochure.pdf

Murphy, T. (2006) *Clearwire Casts $1B into WiMAX group.* Red Herring, March 19th 2006 http://www.redherring.com/Article.aspx?a=16166&hed=Startup+Casts+%241B+into+WiMAX

Smith, T. (2004) *BT joins WiMAX standards group.* The Register. 27th April 2004. http://www.theregister.co.uk/2004/04/27/bt_joins_wimax_forum

Wikipedia (2006) *Wireless network*   http://en.wikipedia.org/wiki/Wireless_networking

Wimaxxed (2006) *WiMAX Laptops Coming in Late 2006* March 2006 http://www.wimaxxed.com/wimaxxed_news/wimax_laptops_c.html

24 Hybrid Web Applications

Karen Lee, Joan Condell, Kevin Curran

To date there has been a distinct difference in the way applications are delivered. Applications tend to be either desktop based or Internet based. This has worked for the most part to date however with the wide spread deployment of wireless technology. There is a greater need to offer end users increased functionality which will allow them to work seamlessly on a desktop and on the Internet. Google Gears, is a new open source JavaScript API that allows the building of offline web applications which can meet the demand for 'dual' applications. Adding Gears support to an application enables it to offer functionality offline and provide an experience similar to a native client-side application.

Due to the growing number of people diagnosed with diabetes each year, this chapter outlines a web-based application for diabetics to simply track, monitor and share their blood sugar levels with other key statistics to help them manage their diabetes. The application will showcase the functionality of Google Gears APIs by offering an offline web application. This application is a rich Internet application (RIA) which will allow users to login whether online or offline and use the application. When reconnected to the Internet, the data will automatically synchronise making the application's data up-to-date and available for sharing.

Introduction

Applications tend to be either desktop based or Internet based. Users are currently looking for more functionality especially since the wide spread deployment of wireless technology. This has led to the research and the evolutionary growth of hybrid web-desktop applications. The hybrid web-desktop terminology used simply describes applications which can run seamlessly offline as if online. When in offline mode, users have exactly the same functionality as online users. They will be able to enter and edit data as if online. This is particularly useful when there is a loss of connectivity or travelling by car or air allowing users to manage their time and plan ahead. The application will automatically update the new data once a connection is re-established therefore allowing more effectiveness among users.

Desktop applications typically use thick client architecture as this provides users with more features, graphics and choices, making the desktop applications more customisable. Thick clients do not rely on a central processing server because the processing is done locally on the user system. Also the server is accessed primarily for storage purposes therefore allowing the user more functionality hence making the PC more useful. Desktop applications became popular in the 70s for home use with the revolutionary idea of the electronic spreadsheet application VisiCalc, and then spread to business users. VisiCalc was soon superseded by Lotus and Microsoft Excel, which is one of today's most powerful desktop applications. These applications are technically more robust which allows for a greater uptime. There is more flexibility than running desktop programs on some operating systems e.g. Microsoft Windows as they are designed for personal computers and use their own local resources. An important feature is their ability to integrate with other products, e.g. when a user needs to exchange data with Word or Excel. Automation such as this is very easy in a desktop application, but not so easy with a browser-based interface. The integration process between applications is hard to make generic enough to work across all browsers. Fewer server requirements are needed as a thick client server does not require as high a level of performance as a thin client server since thick clients generally do much of the application processing. This may result in cheaper servers although in practice many thin client servers are actually equivalent to file servers in specifications but with additional memory. Performance is generally quicker on a desktop because the screen is drawn only once on the desktop and only the data changes[1]. This prevents a lot of screen data coming from the server to the client, which increases the time taken to display the data (Microsoft, 2007). A feature common in today's desktop applications is better multimedia performance especially in the field of video gaming as thick clients have advantages in multimedia-rich applications that would be bandwidth intensive if fully served. Games applications also typically need to interact directly with the video card on the users PC which is much simpler to do than through a browser. Additionally desktop

---

[1] .NET Development (General) Technical Articles, Designing for Web or Desktop?, Microsoft 2002

applications are suitable for poor network connections and it may be also possible to work offline with a thick client, although the network oriented manner in which many people work today means that thick client usage can still be curtailed if the network is down. From the software developers' point of view, desktop applications can be difficult to deploy, as they usually come on a compact disc (CD) or are downloaded from a web site and installed directly on any computer. This has problems such as compatibility i.e. an application is not backward compatible etc. Desktop applications may use the Internet to download updates, but the code that runs these applications resides on the desktop. Desktop applications are usually quite fast as they are running on a computer, therefore Internet connection speed is not an issue, and they have great graphical user interfaces which usually interact with the operating system. Desktop applications are extremely interactive these days - they can be clicked, pointed & typed. Additions such as pull up menus and sub-menus can be played around with, with almost no waiting around. Microsoft remains strong with market share based on revenue of at least 95% according to research firm International Data Corp, 2007 however there are competitors such as Google distributing Sun's Microsystems' StarOffice 8, a rival productivity software suite. Google also have a web-based Google Docs and spreadsheets application. Another competitor is Apples iWork application suite, Apple have introduced a new spreadsheet application called Numbers which could compete with Excel. There is also OpenOffice, an open source suite built on the same code as Sun's StarOffice along with several web-based such as ThinkFree and Zoho which has been gaining ground from Microsoft.

In the early days of the web, web sites consisted of static pages, which severely limited interaction with the user. Web portals started to become popular and were the opening point for people surfing the internet. In the early 1990's, the limitation with static pages was removed when web servers were modified to allow communication with server-side custom scripts. No longer were applications just static brochure-ware, edited only by those who knew HTML, therefore with this single change, normal users could interact with the application for the first time. Web applications have an advantage in that they make use of ubiquitous web browser software. The first of these were Netscape Navigator and Microsoft Internet Explorer took the lead in 1999 due to its distribution advantage. Web browsers do not make big demands on the client-side infrastructure as the use of a web application does not usually require any configuration or installation of client-side software (Teamquest, 2007). Web-based applications have one big advantage over the desktop application in that they have far more reasonable demands on end-user Random Access Memory (RAM) memory than locally installed programs. They reside and run off the provider's servers, therefore these web-based applications use in most cases the memory of the computers they run on, leaving more space for running multiple applications at the same time without incurring frustrating performance hits. On the other hand traditional web applications provide limited user interfaces hampered by the stateless nature of HTML applications. A user can interact with one web page at a time, entering information on the page, sending information to the web server, then waiting for a new page as the result. From a developers point of view they are unable to make use of the more sophisticated user interface capabilities users expect from everyday desktop applications. However these web-based applications are less prone to crashing and creating technical problems due to software or hardware conflicts with other existing applications, protocols or internal custom software. Software updates, hot fixes and upgrades can all be dealt with efficiently therefore allowing no user impact. Data is safer than on a desktop application as it need not be concerned with hard disk storage issues. Today companies such as Google can take over the storage of users data, with highly reliable redundant data storage farms such as Gdata[1] becoming the norm rather than the exception, and users will have much less risk of losing their data due to an unforeseen disk crash or computer virus. Increasingly companies providing web-based applications are providing extensive back up services either as an integral part of their basic service or as a paid option. Web-based applications do not require the distribution, technical support and marketing infrastructure required by traditional downloadable software. This therefore allows online applications to cost a fraction of their downloadable counterparts if not being altogether free, while offering additional components and premium services as an option. Web applications are adaptable and can be written in any language using any web technology. Web-based applications do not have to be downloaded, installed and configured, however sometimes the limited capabilities provided by a traditional web applications are sufficient for the task at hand, but as technology evolves we find it is not necessary to live within the bounds of a traditional web application. A further development is the Rich Internet Application RIA[2], which can leverage the ability to run on common browser software while at the same time delivering a user interface on a par with that expected from a thick client.

A Rich Internet application (RIA) is an entirely new kind of web experience that is engaging, interactive, lightweight, and flexible. RIAs offer the flexibility and ease of use of an intelligent desktop application which add the broad reach of traditional web applications. Traditional web applications centred all activity

---

[1] Google data APIs provide a simple standard protocol for reading and writing data on the web.
[2] W3, Rich Web Application Backplane, W3C Coordination Group Note 16 November 2006.

151

around a client-server architecture with a thin client. Under this system all processing is done on the server, and the client is only used to display static content. A drawback with this system is that all interaction with the application must pass through the server, which requires data to be sent to the server, the server to respond, and the page to be reloaded on the client with the response. That said it needs only retrieve the data that is needed making the interface behaviours typically much more responsive than those of a standard web browser that must always interact with a remote server. As with traditional web applications described previously a broadband connection is a requirement to work with all of these web applications hence denoting the downside to the complete success of web applications. Even the most sophisticated web applications need Internet access for users to log on and use the application. This causes inconvenience to users who may be travelling or moving in and out of hot-spot areas.

This advance is linked to the perceived Web 2.0 approach. The concept of "Web 2.0" began with a conference brainstorming session between O'Reilly (O'Reilly, 2005) and MediaLive International in early 2004 however there has been a huge amount of disagreement as to what defines Web 2.0. It is clear that the web has changed since the dot.com era. Figure 65 shows the Web 2.0 mantra described by O'Reilly at the conference. The diagram clearly illustrates how the web is no longer exclusively about companies with websites. It is has now recognisably changed, e.g. communities have emerged on the new Web 2.0 and blogs are the new "homepages".

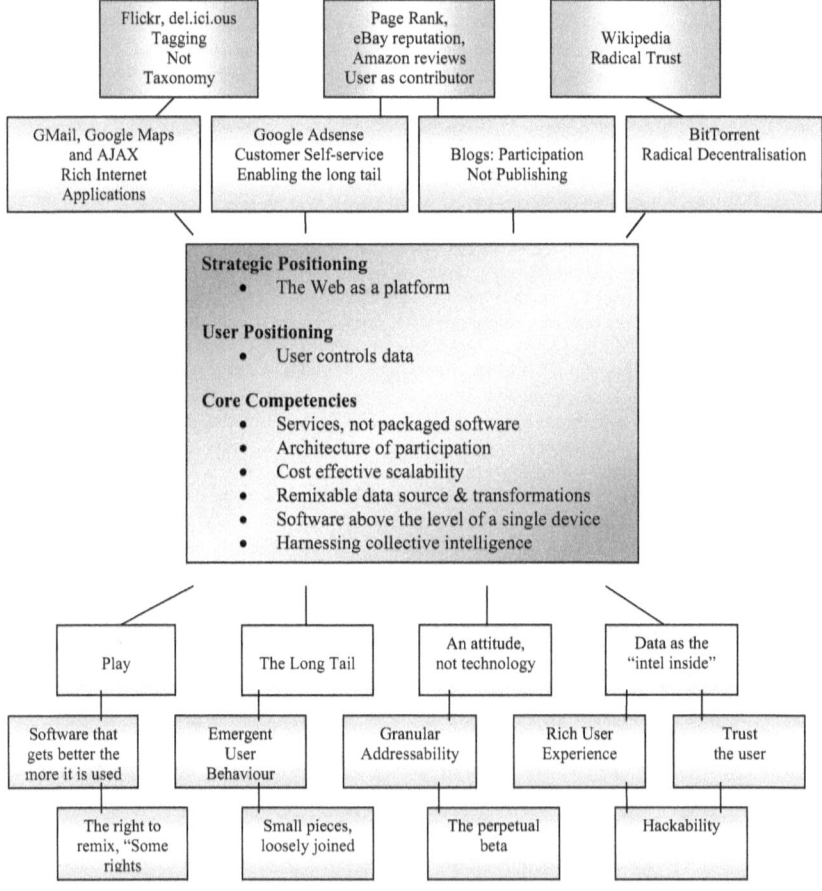

Figure 65: Web 2.0 mantra

AJAX (Asynchronous JavaScript and XML) evolved and is injected into web applications to make them look and feel like a desktop application with the added advantage of convenience. When these technologies are combined in the Ajax model[1], web applications are able to make quick, incremental updates to the user interface without reloading the entire browser page. Where a computer has an internet connection, these 'new' applications can be accessed typically with a username and password. Google is most certainly the standard bearer for Ajax RIAs as they have invested a considerable amount of time and money researching and developing AJAX applications, most notably the free web based Google Docs, Google Reader and Google Maps. Reducing the maintenance burden further is another Web 2.0 concept which can be integrated in RIAs. RSS (Really Simple Syndication or Rich Site Summary) is an Extensible Markup Language (XML-based) format that allows the syndication of lists of hyperlinks, along with other information, or metadata, which then helps viewers decide whether they want to follow the link. Basically the technique reads the summary of the site for general information and presents the key points to the user. Google, Yahoo, and Microsoft have been developing RSS readers which add a richer user experience to these new web applications. RSS can also be attributed to the success of pod-casting and videocasting. It is the RSS feed with audio or video enclosures that makes a podcast visible to search engine spiders. SEO (Search Engine Optimisation) then increases the amount of visitors to the web site by ranking high in the search results of a search engine. The higher a web site ranks in the results of a search, the greater the chance that that site will be visited by a user. Google along with other major 2.0 Web presences Adobe, Microsoft, Java, Amazon, and many more have been developing a new technology that could revolutionise the way business-to-business and business-to-consumer services are provided. The definition peer to peer web services describes a standardised way of integrating rich web-based applications using the XML, SOAP (Simple Object Access Protocol), WSDL (Web Services Description Language) and UDDI (Universal Description, Discovery and Integration) open standards over an Internet protocol backbone. No longer does each application need to copy and maintain external data sources. The user can request and get information in real time, and transform it to their particular format. Individualised software and services can then be delivered, this saves time and money as the maintenance burden is reduced. Amazon, del.icio.us and Flickr (ProgrammableWeb, 2007) offer their information free via a Representational State Transfer (REST) API. It can be seen as direct and indirect advertising as this service opens access to the majority of items in Amazon's product catalog. The API is quite rich and allows manipulation of users, wish lists and shopping carts. However its essence is the ability to lookup Amazon's products. Most applications who build on top of this service drive traffic back to Amazon boosting sales of the fantastic E-Commerce application. These web applications rely on the use of mash-ups, as they overlay traffic data from one source on the Internet for example, over maps from Yahoo, Microsoft, Google or any content provider. This capability to mix and match data and applications from multiple sources into one dynamic entity is considered by many to represent the promise of the web service standard which is also referred to as on-demand computing.

APIs are critical to the success of today's web applications as they often need to request information from third parties in order to perform functions that they may not be able or permitted to do, such as verifying credit card details and buying and selling. It is a virtual interface which is said to grant access to or open an application through a set of function calls or subroutine calls that access functions in a library. Programs that use these rules or functions in their API calls can communicate with any others that use the API, regardless of the others' specifics providing more. The first of the Web 2.0 APIs came from eBay back in November 2000 and they have come a long way in the 7 years since then. They serve over 5.7 billion API calls every month with 60% of all eBay listings listed through eBay services, of which about half come through 3rd parties[2]. The web 2.0 poster child, del.icio.us, is also famous as one of the first companies to open a subset of its web site functionality via an API giving rise to a true API culture. As on-demand computing products are rapidly becoming prevalent in the market place International Business Machines (IBM) see grid computing as the way forward in the advancement of this technology. Grids connect up computers - usually not in the same building or even the same country with the idea of joining up power and resources of disparate machines. The term 'grid', coined by Dr Ian Foster (Scientific American Magazine, 2004), refers to the idea of electricity grids[3]. The theory behind both computer grids and electric grids being that power can be acquired whenever needed, with power going in from any number of disparate sources. Predictions for the future of grid computing are that grid computing could eventually grow either to replace or enhance the internet, with spare computing power distributed around the world when it is needed and where it is needed. However with users unlikely to share their spare capacity with people they do not know and the security implications of this technology, standards need to evolve quickly before large scale implementation could be considered as it is currently only used for solving scientific, mathematical, and academic problems.

[1] Ajax: A New Approach to Web Applications, Jesse James Garrett 2005
[2] eBay serves 5 million API calls each month.
[3] By linking digital processors, storage systems and software on a global scale, grid technology is poised to transform computing from an individual and corporate activity into a general utility, The Grid: Computing without Bounds, (Scientific American Magazine, 2004).

Mobile Computing is a term describing the ability to use technology 'untethered', i.e. which is not physically connected to a local-area network. In practice often mobile computing is connected wirelessly to and through the internet or to and through a private network. This connection ties the mobile device to centrally located information and/or application software through the use of battery powered, portable, and wireless computing and communication devices. Mobile computing can include laptops, mobile phones, personal digital assistants (PDAs) and other mobile devices. Connectivity can include Wireless Fidelity (Wi-Fi), bluetooth, General Packet Radio Service (GPRS) or occasional physical connection. As computers increased in popularity so too have mobile devices such as mobile phones and PDA's. In just 35 years almost the same amount of time as the PC and nearly one-fourth that of the landline phone, mobile device penetration has surpassed the PC and landline phone *combined*, reaching 2.7 billion mobile subscriptions in 2006. In fact, in some of the more developed areas of the world, penetration is at 100% or better. According to a study conducted in January 2007 by Telephia and comScore, two leading research firms for mobile media and internet metrics respectively, **5.7 million people in the U.K.** used a mobile device to access the web compared to 30 million who accessed the web from a PC.

Web-based applications have been applauded for their richness, simplicity and elegant user experience, but only while an Internet connection is available. There are many times when a connection is lost due to a fault on the line, moving home and having to wait on broadband installations, air travel or maintenance issues etc. This is disruptive as users are immediately impacted due to the loss of service from their connection. Today, with applications such as Google Docs and Google Spreadsheets, this is indeed the case. If the user is composing a document and experiences a sudden loss in connectivity, not only will they lose access to Google's word processing logic, they will not be able to save their document or open up other ones. This could also depend on how the browser responds to a loss of connectivity - the user may lose any work done since the last "save" took place. Users will not be able to access work or emails and will have to wait for the connection to be re-established. This could take time, meanwhile users are frustrated and dissatisfied. Business companies will be losing revenue and reputation if users cannot access their portals. The United States (US) based Customer Relationship Management (CRM) giant, Salesforce.com, were plagued with major outages last year and minor outages this year which resulted in the company losing millions in revenue, disappointing their customers and damaging their reputation. The company is currently working with Google to develop a beta version of the application with some offline capabilities therefore thwarting the reoccurrence of outages. Developers appreciate while the Internet is pervasive it is still not truly everywhere and in an offline world desktop applications still have supremacy. Therefore making offline web applications a reality is a vision which many see as the future. Critics of web applications like those served up by web giants Google, Yahoo, and Salesforce.com have argued that those applications can never replace their desktop counterparts because of the so-called "off-line problem."

Hybrid Webified Applications

More and more applications these days are being 'Webified' in that they are made to operate on the web using a browser or made to function in a similar manner. The reason is that the Internet is capable of significantly augmenting human interaction, with its decentralised system of ubiquitous data accessibility. Webaroo is a free software service that gives you the power to search and browse the web on the go. Webaroo's advanced technology enables the user to search web content offline on your laptop, PDA or smartphones. As the Web becomes increasingly interconnected and applications continue to blur the distinction between the desktop and web, we should expect to see more applications that allow web/desktop synchronization. This will happen due to the increasing development of web services that enable applications to work equally well across web and desktop clients. Applications such as the Microsoft Windows Live suite supplement the traditional desktop applications with web-based software and services. Google is very browser-centric so their offerings tend to be online only and are heavily tied to the cloud. Microsoft has years of desktop experience and is leveraging all of that in their RIA push. They see a lot of benefits in keeping a majority of the processing power and storage on the desktop but providing the flexibility and freedom that comes with the web through a number of different online services. By tying those online services such as Office Live Workspace and some of the other Windows Live products to their desktop counterparts, a workflow that transitions pretty seamlessly between web and desktop is accomplished. Adobe on the other hand has always been middle of the road. They have made money on their desktop software but there has always been a presence on the web with things like Flash, Portable Document Format (PDF) and server software like ColdFusion. The current browser-desktop hybrid solutions like Adobe Integrated Runtime (AIR) are representative of that involvement and that said it seems that they have the vision that a hybrid approach is a successful way to go. The future is hybrid, where desktop and web-based software and services become intertwined to the point where users will not know the difference between the two. There is a greater need to offer end users increased functionality which will allow them to work seamlessly on a desktop and on the Internet using a hybrid application which can be developed to be accessed anytime, anywhere regardless of Internet connectivity. Internet applications simply cannot compete at a user interface level with a desktop application so ultimately with these limits and the offline limitation the next step is about creating other web-centric features to bridge the gap. Currently there are a handful of applications which can be accessed regardless of Internet connection, 'Remember the Milk', the popular online to-do list application was the first popular non-Google web application to go offline with Gears technology. Anything that is possible online with 'Remember the Milk' now works offline too. Not only can the user access their lists, but they can add new tasks and notes, edit existing tasks, complete, postpone, prioritise, tag, and change due dates without Internet access.

Google's own application Google Reader is a decidedly simple yet very usable and quite comprehensive web-based RSS feed reader[1]. Google started experimenting with offline capabilities and Reader became the first Google application to benefit. Due to high demand for this functionality Google recently announced on April 1st 2008 that Google Docs has become available with the same offline functionality as Reader. Competitors such as Zoho Writer, the online word processor, launched a new version in August 2007 which lets users work on their documents offline[2]. On November 26th 2007 they added read and write offline functionality which is advantageous as Zoho is really pushing the boundary of what online office applications mean. The Read/WriteWeb notes are a big leap forward from what other office RIAs are providing in that they can work on the document offline and when reconnected to the Internet, the synchronisation will take place for initially sharing files and in the future much more is promised from this application.

With the movement of web applications onto the desktop, Adobe Air[3] lets developers use their existing web development skills in HTML, AJAX, Flash and Flex to build and deploy rich Internet applications to the desktop. It is an out of browser application which uses ActionScript 3 but with all of the traits and features that make for a rich Internet application. What AIR has over a purely web-based RIA depends on what is it required for. Local access to the file structure and the local windowing system is enabled therefore allowing the developer to save and open files in the native window. Drag and drop, plus a SQLite-embedded database add to the overall feeling of permanence. Among other benefits, applications developed with AIR will be operating system OS-independent (Google, 2007).

Mozilla recognise that personal computing is currently in a state of transition and while traditionally users have interacted mostly with desktop applications, more and more of them are using web applications. As a result the latter often fit awkwardly into the document-centric interface of web browsers. Consequently Mozilla Labs are launching a series of experiments to bridge the divide in the user experience between web applications and desktop apps. The first release is Prism the new name for WebRunner. Prism allows developers to create desktop-like applications out of individual websites. Prism looks like it will enable greater desktop functionality much like Adobe AIR. Prism also lets users split web applications out of their browser and run them directly on their desktop (Mozilla Labs, 2007).

Flex is a cross-platform development framework for creating RIAs. Flex enables the user to create expressive, high-performance applications that run identically on all major browsers and operating systems. Adobe Flex is a collection of technologies released by Adobe Systems for the development and deployment of cross platform, rich Internet applications based on the proprietary Adobe Flash platform. Flex is the first and most complete solution for accessible Rich Internet Applications. It combines the responsiveness and interactivity of desktop applications with the broad reach and ease of distribution of web applications, while still creating an experience that all users find accessible, regardless of disability. It includes 23 accessible components that accelerate application development and create a consistent, usable experience for users with disabilities. Using these key components, developers can create RIAs quickly and easily while ensuring a high level of accessibility (Adobe Labs, 2007).

---

[1] Google Reader is a Web-based aggregator, capable of reading Atom and RSS feeds online or offline. It was released by Google on October 7, 2005. Google Reader was the first application to make use of Google Gears
[2] Zoho Writer is a tool to access, edit and share documents from anywhere.
[3] Adobe Air, also known as Adobe Integrated Runtime, codenamed Apollo is a cross OS runtime environment for building Rich Internet Applications (RIAs).

A major competitor for Adobe AIR is JavaFX. The demand continues to grow for secure, interactive content, applications and services that run on a variety of clients. To simplify and speed the creation and deployment of high-impact content for a wide range of devices, Sun is introducing JavaFX, a new family of products based on Java technology designed to enable consistent user experiences, from desktop to mobile device to set-top box to Blu-ray Disc. The JavaFX family of products comprises a set of runtime environments, widgets, development tools, and scripting environments based on Java technology. Sun's widespread install base and highly polished developer network make it a strong contender to expand Sun's horizons in this field. Sun also currently have plans to make it open source which will also have an impact. Sun's motto, *write once, run anywhere* promises to create highly interactive and animated content running on computers, digital TVs, regular TVs and mobile devices, and have the content look the same across all platforms and behave the same way (Sun, 2007). The JavaFX product family uses the Java FX Script tool to create content for Web and Web 2.0-oriented applications. FX Script is designed for content authoring of web and network-facing applications. Developers will be able to access and use all of the Java SE/ME (Standard Edition/Micro Edition) applications and libraries. Therefore unnecessary bridging to libraries will no longer be a problem as Java FX will handle that efficiently. It also offers features for safer use. It does not rely on a constant connection such as JavaScript in the Ajax model. Java FX will need only one new library to be installed along with the standard SE or ME runtime. By having locally installed SE/ME files working with Java FX it has potential to take the Google applications offline and work on them.

Microsoft Silverlight is a cross-browser, cross-platform plugin for delivering next-generation media experiences and RIAs for the web. Silverlight offers a flexible programming model that supports JavaScript, Visual C#, Visual Basic, and other languages. Silverlight directly competes with Adobe's Flash and with the world of RIAs increasing in importance, with Internet users seeking out better experiences both in the browser and outside it, and both online and offline. Microsoft and Adobe are busy battling it out in the 'richer' products - which either extend the browser or utilise the desktop. Silverlight is an impressive package with a seemingly endless array of compatibilities. A full .NET framework means that any .NET languages can be executed, alongside multimedia and text-based content from WMV (Windows Media File Format), MP3 (Media Player3), XML and JavaScript (Microsoft, 2007).

Prior to the arrival of Google Gears, there were other approaches to the same problem. One of them involved a Java-based database that is referred to as the Derby Project by the Apache Foundation (also called JavaDB). However neither the Apache Foundation nor Sun saw the need to drive Derby/JavaDB into the market as a solution to the so-called offline problem. Francois Orsini, a talented engineer at Sun, saw the potential for JavaDB to take web apps offline and proved it with some self-built prototypes. At that time solving the offline problem for web applications was not one of Sun Microsystems' priorities hence the project ended without any further considerations by Sun (Sun, 2007). Dojo Offline is an open-source toolkit that makes it easy to create sophisticated, offline web applications (Neuberg, 2007). It sits on top of Google Gears, which helps extend web browsers with new functionality. Dojo Offline makes working with Google Gears easier, extends it with important functionality, creates a higher-level API than Google Gears provides, and exposes developer productivity features.

Google is also partnering with Norway's Opera Software Adobe AIR, maker of the web browser popular with mobile phone users, and Mozilla, the group behind Firefox, the biggest alternative to Microsoft's Internet Explorer browser. Firefox has currently added offline support to Zimbra, a web-based open source server and client software for messaging and collaboration, email, group calendaring, contacts, web document management and authoring therefore delivering end users increased productivity, flexibility and choice. Firefox have developed their own Greasemonkey extension which works with Gears to customize the way web pages look and function. Firefox have named their mix GearsMonkey and they are advocating all developers to inject Gear code so that all web applications can be used offline (Mozilla, 2007). Phyton with Django are also developing the DjangoKit framework which will take a Django application and turn it into a stand-alone MacOS application with a local database and media files to bring offline functionality. The 'not yet released' Ruby on Rails product, Joyent Slingshot, is a new technology developed by Joyent and Magnetk which provides a Windows and OS X client for specially designing Rails applications. The advantage with Joyent is that the application looks more like a desktop application than other web applications with the online/offline functionality (Google, 2007).

Google Gears

Google has a vision of building web software that runs online and offline to let users work remotely on planes, trains, slow dial-up connections or even the most remote locations in the world achievable. The technology which they recently showcased at Google's global developer day in May 2007, called Google Gears, allows users of computers, phones and other devices to manipulate web services like e-mail, online calendars or news readers whether online, intermittently connected to the web or completely offline. By bridging the gap between new web services and the older world of desktop software, where any data changes are stored locally on users' machines, Google is pushing the web into whole new spheres of activity and posing a challenge to rival Microsoft Corp, the market leader in the desktop software era (Google, 2007). With the release of the open source code, Google Gears JavaScript APIs allows the building of offline web applications which can meet the demand for 'dual' applications. This open source browser extension installs six Google APIs for employment on the user's browser. The first API is a LocalServer which handles the creation of data objects to store application information locally, a SQLite relational database[1] for searching the data, and the third API, the WorkerPool will enable asynchronous JavaScript so applications can synchronise data in the background without overburdening the browser. The HttpRequest API module implements a subset of the W3C XmlHttpRequest specification, and makes it available in both workers and the main HTML page. The two remaining APIs, the Timer module implements HTML 5 Timer specification, and makes it available in both workers and the main HTML page. This is the same timer API that is traditionally available in browsers on the `window` object. Finally the last API is the Factory module which uses the Factory class to instantiate all other Google Gears objects. In addition to making the user's transition from online to offline seamless, this platform has the potential to improve web page performance by allowing larger portions of the computationally intensive tasks like animation, video, complex calculations etc. to be passed onto the local computer. In recent years, we have seen the web and desktop move closer to each other, with web-based versions of desktop software such as the previously mentioned Google applications. Many applications developed using the above technologies will take this direction one step further, falling somewhere in between desktop applications and websites but with the unique offline functionality. Google reported at the Gears launch that not every application would be suitable to have an offline option. Applications such as a stock pricing ticker or a chat application could not have an offline option as these applications need to retrieve the live data every second from the online server. That said general applications such as online word processing, email, calendaring applications etc would be suitable to have an offline option and would be useful for frequent travellers or when a network or Internet connection is unavailable. Then once connected to the Internet, the data will automatically synchronise making the application real time for all users. Applications such as a web portal application which offers staff the option to query a company database, issue sales order or invoices, would also be suitable to provide an offline option. Google's push into the world of web services has given it a much wider reach than its core search business and the rationale behind Google Gears is that they can see there is a demand for Google applications to run without its servers.

Security is a key issue with Google Gears offline functionality as the user's privacy can be breached. In most cases the offline feature is only safe for use on the users own personal computer, laptop or PDA, where they are sure that no one else has access as the information resides on the local computer. Google Gears data files are protected with the user's operating system login credentials however two people could theoretically access each other's Gears data files. Therefore working on a public or shared computer should be avoided at all times thus eliminating the possibility of identity fraud or corruption of the users files. To protect users in general, Google Gears shows a warning dialog when a site first attempts to use the Google Gears API, as user opt-in is important. Users can then grant or deny access for each security origin. When a user grants access to Gears from a particular origin, Gears remembers this decision for the future. Denying access to users is only remembered until the page is reloaded.

Another key issue for users planning to use Google Gears on more than one computer is that each computer synchronises offline separately and for that reason each computer must be synchronised with the offline data as synchronised changes on one computer will not be reflected on another computer. Conflict resolution for situations such as when two users are working on the same offline data and synchronise it at different times requires workarounds not currently available for Gears. Circumstances like these could lead to inaccuracy and confusion for the user resulting in lost data and negative acceptance of the application. Also each browser synchronises offline data separately, i.e. Firefox 1.5 and IE, therefore if a user plans to use Google Gears on more than one browser, they must also remember to synchronise each browser and be aware that uninstalling Google Gears will not clear any offline information the user currently has on their system. This data is not encrypted as Google stores all the data in plain text in the database or local server. Files can not be password

---

[1] SQLite is an in-process library that implements a self-contained, serverless, zero-configuration, transactional SQL database engine.

protected either. This is a major issue if the system was maliciously attacked. This would also be an issue if the user wished to sell or recycle his computer in the future. Synchronisation of the data will also make the browser slow in response as it uses up extra memory to start this process (Google, 2008).

Wireless Google Gears on Windows Mobile 5 and 6 devices

The impact of wireless communications has been and will continue to be profound. Very few inventions have been able to shrink the world in such a manner (Stallings, 2005). The trend towards wireless communications has revealed to professionals and general users the benefits of having their electronic work available at any place and any time spurring a demand for mobile and nomadic computing. Mobile computing is pushing the design and development of RIAs with incredible pace. It is acknowledged that due to the growth in the wireless technology industry that mobile access has far exceeded that of the native PC (Telephia and comScore, 2007).

As a result handheld mobile devices such as PDAs require similar offline capabilities as provided by Google for web applications sitting on other platforms. Since the launch of Google Gears in May 2007, the company have recognised the demand for such and in 2008, they have made available a mobile beta version of the Google Gears browser extension software for use by mobile application developers.

Mobile web application developers accept the Internet is pervasive although it is still not truly everywhere hence prompting the necessity for a similar offline experience whilst accessing and working with mobile web applications. Google software engineer Chris Prince stated at the launch that "the mission of Gears is to extend the capabilities of web browsers as it is clear to Google that mobile browsers can benefit just as much as desktop browsers". Also at the launch mobile product manager Charles Wiles declared the software is currently available to mobile handset owners equipped with Microsoft Internet Explorer Mobile on Windows Mobile 5 and Windows Mobile 6 devices only however he added that versions for other mobile platforms such as Google Android will also be forthcoming in the near future (ibtimes, 2008). Google cite the main reason for not supporting other platforms initially is due to the state of the mobile application development today. Setting the specific device limitations aside for now, developers often need to write native code, and build against different SDKs, using several different compilers. This is a difficult and time consuming task, which explains why so few people write mobile applications. Google Gears for Windows mobile device usage will enable mobile developers to work with their Web-based applications when either online or offline, with data saved to the host handset for further work whenever the user decides to return to it, reports the International Business Times (ibtimes, 2008). Google Gears for mobile devices works in exactly the same way as the Gears API for desktop web applications as is the limitations. Users can log in to web-based applications such as Google Reader or Zoho Reader using their PDA's and work on documents regardless of Internet connection. Gears for mobile devices allows the user to not only download files but also edit them therefore creating new versions of documents or amendments to the data they have worked on. This will then be saved on the local device, and later when a connection is established the data will be synchronised effortlessly. This is advantageous as users can utilise this new functionality as they go about their daily business and need not worry about a permanent connection into the network. With the fundamental nature of mobile computing it is prone to sudden failures in network connectivity such as when a physical obstruction blocks the signal from a cellular modem. Even times when the mobile device is connected, the connection often has low bandwidth and high latency. Lastly the mobile device may be forced to use different transmission channels depending on its physical location. The performance of its network connection can then vary dramatically from one session to another (Cao et al, 2003). Therefore the recent and timely launch of Gears for Windows Mobile devices running on Pocket IE has proved particularly appropriate for the aims and objectives of this thesis. This is good news for the future as an implementation of the proposed web based blood sugar tracker application on a mobile device will be beneficial for many young teenagers. According to The Mobile Life Survey, commissioned by Carphone Warehouse in 2006, nine out of ten teenagers own a mobile phone and 30% access the Internet to download music and contact social networking sites such as Bebo and Facebook.

With almost 20% of all web users accessing the web on their mobile device today, this brings new challenges to developers of mobile devices, as users expect an experience equal to the familiar desktop application experience. The developer for that reason must appreciate that mobile devices involve an entirely different user experience and development technique. Consequently deploying web applications for mobile devices has presented many challenges to small device application developers. Various limitations and constraints are encountered during the software development lifecycle of such devices. *Visually we can see t*he device is smaller. The screen size does prove a major constraint for developers, the average screen size is 240 pixels. One of the most common screen sizes is a square 128 pixels by 128 pixels. Nokia Series 40 devices have this screen size as do most Basic Data Mobile Devices. The Enhanced Data Mobile Device, 02 Trion has a larger screen size of 240 pixels by 320 pixels with 65,536 colours and can be viewed either portrait or landscape view. The actual page size, however, will be smaller than the total screen, since, as with desktop browsers, the browser chrome takes space. But screen size, as apparent as it is, is not the sole limiting factor. Input methods are often much different than that of a QWERTY keyboard therefore with limited ability to input text this may affect the applications. Additionally there are many different smart devices on the market today, which in itself proves to be difficult whilst also maintaining and regulating accessibility for everyone including the disabled on the many different devices. Designers must address issues that fit easily into both schools of thought when targeting screen readers. As a result limitations on development, testing and deployment of applications for smart devices are inevitable. By far the biggest challenge to date is developing for the specified Windows 5 and 6 platforms where developers are limited to using the .NET compact framework as opposed to the large body of pre-coded solutions common to software developers using the full .Net framework. The Windows Mobile platform uses the .Net compact framework and this has access to only 85 of the 400 plus class libraries of the full framework however it brings the benefits of managed code development to mobile devices.

As a mobile device has considerably less data storage capacity, it must therefore be considered. Generally a hand held device is not great as a data storage device as it uses a lot of the device memory resources whilst i.e. storing the local data on the directly on the device as would be the case with going offline with Google Gears. Processing capabilities have been enhanced in the Windows 6 platform and it does have database support which makes it convenient for business users. Memory storage cards can be inserted and data can be stored directly on these cards so as to save memory on the device itself. This can therefore alleviate slow responses or timeouts due to a lack of system memory. Windows Mobile 6 is the latest version of Windows Mobile platform and it was released on 12th February 2007. There were three editions released. Windows Mobile 6 Standard was released for the Smartphone, Windows Mobile 6 Professional for Pocket PCs which have phone functionality, and Windows Mobile 6 Classic for Pocket PCs without cellular radios (Microsoft, 2007). Due to greater support of HTML elements, CSS, the Document Object Model, and the presence of a touch screen in the latter two platforms mentioned, Google recommend these for device or emulator development (IbiTimes, 2008).

Although just launched the personal finance service Buxfer[1] and online application provider Zoho[2] have both demonstrated that with implementing workarounds such as those mentioned it is still possible to give mobile web applications the same Gears enabled offline capabilities as have been achieved with their online counterparts for the desktop. Users of these applications are asked to install Google Gears for mobile. Once it is installed on the device, Google Gears will remain on the Smartphone thus allowing users to retrieve data whether they have network connectivity or not (See Figure 66).

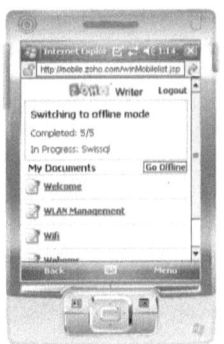 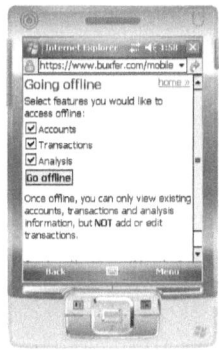

Figure 66: Google Gears enabled Zoho Writer offline and Buxfer Finance offline

Google Gears can be used to take an existing web application offline whereas Adobe Air, Microsoft Silverlight and the other rich internet applications platforms are for new applications that consequently change the way users work with sites and services. Google has used Gears to give Google Reader and Google Docs offline

[1] www.buxfer.com
[2] www.zoho.com

capabilities, while eBay has used AIR to give their well known site a complete overhaul with a new desktop application without the uniqueness which is attributed to Gears. All these new platforms let the developer work with their existing tools however Google has the added advantage as it can be used with any JavaScript editing package, which means developers and designers are not required to learn new languages or tools. This increases productivity, saves money and brings new developers into the industry. Limiting factors for Google Gears are existing browser capabilities, the better the browser, the better Gears will work. Also Gears uses a same origin policy, therefore an application can only access its own database and cannot save files locally as in the case of other platforms. At the present time Google are working with Adobe, Firefox and Opera to develop additional APIs e.g. a more powerful SQLite database, which will have more in common and deliver future applications which can run on various platforms. This open source set of JavaScript APIs will bridge the gap and allow users to take the web with them, creating an offline experience to match the existing Web 2.0 online experience. This concept will be particularly beneficial to existing business and medical applications. The proposed diabetes application which will be developed using Google Gears will be a valuable application for sufferers and carers alike in that it can be accessed via a mobile device or a PC. More people will make use of it due to the fact that most people already own a mobile device. Mobile phones would be the best platform for teenagers to use, especially while at school. Using the concept of this chapter's application as an example, users can be anywhere with a mobile device or their laptop/PC when they need to test a glucose level or inject insulin. As this application will be Google Gears enabled it will allow these users to enter their glucose level offline anywhere. Google Gears is the emergent technology of tomorrow's browsers where offline functionality will be incorporated seamlessly providing true integration and allowing users to take the 'web' wherever they go without the limitations of Internet access.

Conclusion

To date the greatest limitation to using a web application is the need for a constant connection to the Internet. When an Internet connection is disrupted or is unavailable, a web application is inaccessible to the many users who now use and depend on web-based applications for business or personal use. There is now more than ever a greater need to offer end users increased functionality which will allow them to work seamlessly on a desktop or a mobile device using a hybrid application which can be developed to be accessed anytime, anywhere regardless of Internet connectivity. Google have recognised this and are helping to bridge the gap between desktop applications and web-based applications with their set of new APIs. Gears accomplishes what is needed to add this functionality for enabling the offline/online synchronisation of a web based application. With this innovative solution a medical web-based application suitable for diabetics was successfully developed to showcase how the gap between online / offline functionality could be bridged using Google's new open source JavaScript APIs. This system will be particularly helpful for diabetic teenagers accessing the application from a mobile device or when they do not have a connection. When the Internet connection is reestablished Google Gears will synchronize the data with Google's remote servers seamlessly making the medical monitoring application's data available to both the diabetic users and their carers.

References

Adobe Labs, 2007. Adobe Integrated Runtime . http://labs.adobe.com/technologies/flex/

Bellis M, 2007. The First Spreadsheet- VisiCalc. http://inventors.about.com/library/weekly/aa010199.htm

Cao, J., Zhou, J., Chen, D., Chan, A,. Lu, J. 2003. Mobile Agent Technology and Its Applications in Internet Computing, Computational Web Intelligence: Intelligent Technology for Web Applications, World Scientific Publishers

GearsMonkey: Google Gears + Greasemonkey to take Wikipedia offline, 2007. Lisbakken, Ben http://code.google.com/support/bin/answer.py?answer=81101&topic=11982

Google, 2007. "Take Your Web Applications Offline With Google's Gears", Web Designer. Issue 138, 26-28.

Google Data APIs, 2007. code.google.com/apis/gdata/

IbiTimes, 2008. Google Gears heads for Mobile phones, http://ibtimes.com/articles/20080304/google-gear-mobile-windows.htm

Microsoft, 2007, Application Device Overview.

Mozilla Labs, 2007.http://labs.mozilla.com/2007/10/prism/

Mozilla, 2007. http://www.mozilla-europe.org/en/products/firefox/

Neuberg B, 2007. Creating Offline Web Applications With Dojo Offline, Available at:
http://docs.google.com/View?docid=dhkhksk4_8gdp9gr&pli=1

O'Reilly, Tim, 2005. What is Web 2.0?
http://www.oreillynet.com/pub/a/oreilly/tim/news/2005/09/30/what-is-web-20.html#mememap

ProgrammableWeb, API Dashboard, 2007. http://www.programmableweb.com/apis

Scientific American Magazine, 2003. The Grid: Computing Without Bounds
http://www.sciam.com/article.cfm?colID=1&articleID=000B1833-21DF-1E64-A98A809EC5880105

Sun, 2007. http://java.sun.com/javafx/faqs.jsp#1

Stallings, W, Wireless Communications and Networks, 2005.2nd Ed., Prentice Hall, Pearson Education.

25   Website Design for Mobile Devices

Kevin Curran, Winston Huang

Mobile communications is a continually growing sector in industry and a wide variety of visual services such as video-on-demand have been created which are limited by low-bandwidth network infrastructures. The distinction between mobile phones and personal device assistants (PDA's) has already become blurred with pervasive computing being the term coined to describe the tendency to integrate computing and communication into everyday life. This chapter outlines the peculiarities of designing sites for visitors who will be browsing through mobile devices.

Introduction

In ubiquitous computing, software is used by roaming users interacting with the electronic world through a collection of devices ranging from handhelds such as PDAs (Figure 67) and mobile phones (Figure 68) to personal computers (Figure 69) and laptops (Figure 70). The heterogeneity added by modern smart devices is also characterised by an additional property, which is that many of these devices are typically tailored to distinct purposes. Therefore, not only memory and storage capabilities differ widely but local device capabilities, in addition to the availability of resources changing over time.

Figure 67: PDAs   Figure 68: Mobiles   Figure 69: Desktops   Figure 70: Laptops

The Mobile Web refers to the World Wide Web accessible to mobile devices such as cell phones, PDAs, and other mobile devices connected to a public network. Accessing the Mobile Web does not require a desktop computer and since it can be accessed with a number of mobile devices, the Internet can be accessed in remote places previously unconnected to the Internet. For example, medical information could be sent by a mountaineer in difficulty and received by rescuers. Currently, the mobile visitors browsing the web with wireless mobile devices like PDA and Smartphones become the fastest growing community of web users. According to the market data released by market advisory firm IDC (Tilak 2005) , in the opening quarter of 2005, the European handheld devices market (including smartphones and PDAs) grew by 55 % with shipments reaching 2.5m units compared to 1.6m units in the corresponding quarter of 2004 (Tilak, 2005). A large proportion of mobile devices enable wireless internet sold today predicts that they will more crucial in our daily lives. There are three main benefits of the mobile web.

1. Users can access the Internet anytime and anywhere, as long as there is network coverage. In a WIFI hotspot, users can enable retrieve and exchange information more quickly. The web can go where you go (Rabin, 2006).

2. Vast connectivity is offered. Currently, nearly 4% of people have access to the web through a mobile device around the world. The number of PCs connected is only half. It's predicted that, by 2010, 50% of people will have access to the internet via handheld device throughout the world (Rabin, 2006).

3. Location-dependent content is provided. Users can get location-sensitive information by Location technologies. Users can reach useful content in reduced steps to make it accessible with the minimum effort.

Mobile devices are not the same as desktop counterparts; instead they can be limited by slow text input facilities, environment of user, low bandwidth, small storage capacity, limited battery life, and slow CPU speed. Scripting or plug-ins is often not supported by mobile browsers therefore the range of content supported is limited. Other limitations include:

- **Environment of User** - A computer user will generally be in a specially designed office environment and can devote their attention to the screen. Conversely, a mobile device user may be in a noisy, distracting environment and only devoting some time to the device. The content and interface therefore need to be designed for quick and easy reading, without too much detail.

- **Limited Keyboard** - The O2 Mini S and O2-Xda-Exec have a small QWERTY keyboard; other portable devices may have only a few keys and touch screen. As such, the first factor should be considered is to first place the significant content of the web page on obvious area so that the user sees it without need to scroll.

- **Limited Memory** - The typical desktop computer's memory is up to 1 GB; on the contrary the average memory of mobile device is less than 256 MB. In other words, one typically only has 1/5th as much memory in a mobile device as a user would on an internet-enabled desktop computer. For this reason, any solution that attempts to deliver internet content onto a mobile phone must be very space efficient.

- **Limited Electric Power** - Handhelds do not have a limitless supply of electrical power. Great strides have been made in recent years to increase the amount of so-called standby time the cellular phones can stay turned on when they are actually in use. This allows the modern mobile phone to wait for long periods (often as long as multiple weeks) to receive a call. Unfortunately, this ability to exist in standby mode for weeks at a time does not help when you are connected to the internet. For all intents and purposes, a connection to the internet from modern mobile phones is the same thing as a telephone call. If a user can expect one hour of talk time on a single battery with your current phone, then user should expect about the amount of internet connectivity. Compared with a laptop where the battery enables one to access the internet for 3~5 hours or more, the battery of a mobile device allows less than 1 hour on an average (Ferguson, 2002). Other limitation such as display quality, processor speed, available bandwidth, and supported protocols become significant issues as well.

- **Limited Display Screens** - Compared to a conventional PC, Smartphones, PDAs and Ultra-Mobile all have limited screen area. A smart phone may have a screen of only 2.5 inches, a PDA of 4 inches and Ultra-Mobile PC 7 inches, with resolutions from QVGA (240 x 320 pixels) to 800 x 480 or larger for a Ultra-Mobile PC. The web page design therefore needs to be able to adapt to different size and shape screens.

Among these, the screen size limitations require special attention, because this directly affects the interaction of users and web pages. Studies have shown that when browsing on small screens, users follow links less frequently than those with larger displays.. As shown in Figure 71, a traditional web page can be hard to read on a small screen device, such as a PDA. If rendering such a page in a two-dimensional layout like desktop, users have to scroll horizontally and vertical while reading text (Baudisch, 2004).

Figure 71: Original layout on mobile devices

Figure 71 shows that viewing a page designed for the desktop on a small screen device require users to scroll not only vertically, but also horizontally (Baudisch, 2004). Figure 72 shows the homepage of the University of Ulster viewed on both a Sony Ericsson and a Nokia N70. The page has been distorted so that browsing is not a pleasant experience.

Figure 72: K750i and Nokia N70 showing the University of Ulster Homepage.

There are a number of methods for adapting traditional web pages for smaller screens. One solution is to present web pages in full form on mobile screen however, the approach is problematic for battery and bandwidth limitations, even with compression. Further more, the full form view results in excessive scrolling requirements in vertical and horizontal dimensions. Some approaches use single-column views to facilitate the reading process, however, they generate a large amount of vertical scrolling, instead of horizontal scrolling (Buyukkokten, 1999)

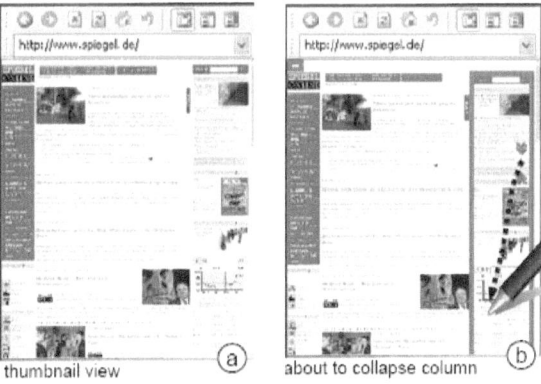

thumbnail view (a) about to collapse column (b)

Figure 73: (a) Thumbnail View on PDAs (b) Collapse-to-Zoom View

To avoid excessive vertical and horizontal scrolling, researchers present a miniature version of the page to users. There are some overviews proposed such as thumbnails and summarized versions of the page. Overviews provide users with visual context, and allow one to zoom in on content for a close-up view. However, as shown on the left of Figure 73, due to the inherent limitation of small screens, users find that the content is reduced and are unable to show which titles hold the relevant information (Baudisch, 2004). The Collapse-To-Zoom technique addresses the earlier problems by offering an alternative exploration strategy. It allows users to collapse areas deemed irrelevant, such as contents like advertising and archive material. Un-collapsed content will need to be redrawn in more detail. Then the full-size view is switched, and the page size reduced significantly, so that users can view the remaining relevant content with little scrolling (see Figure 73(b)). Unfortunately, the collapse-to-zoom requires mobile devices to be equipped with touch-screens. Other popular approaches are to concentrate on minimizing the amount of content on pages and only the relevant piece of content will be sent to the mobile devices. The filtering methods are divided into those based on the structure of the HTML page (Roto & Kaikkonen, 2003), (Buyukkokten et al, 2001) and ones based on user's preferences (Anderson et al, 2001) and (Kaikkonen, 2003). Without specific metadata in the HTML code, however, the relevant content from a page is difficult to be rendered properly by these filtering methods.

The Tate Modern in London launched an interactive audio-visual tour of its Museum for handhelds. It is provided to visitors when they visit and users can see video and still images on the display. Thalys[1] provide leisure and business travelers a high-speed European network that provides travelers the information they need via mobile phones. The site offers train schedules and fare information for the mobile users in four-languages with up-to-the-minute traffic information. The UAA Campus has a guided tour on a PDA using an Avantgo web Channel. The Avantgo service makes the content maintainable and enables the information to be viewed on most PDAs. Tags in the Avantgo helps minimize the impact to the host server by utilizing server caching and helps the web site customize PDA appropriate content and graphics. The system enables any individual with a PDA to be able to download and conduct the self-guided tour themselves. It provided both visual and textual content, and is constructed to allow users to start their guide anywhere and go in any direction they want.

Mobile Web Enabling Technologies

HDML (Handheld Device Mark-up Language) was one of the first popular standards to target the mobile web. HDML contained features to program a mobile phone UI (e.g. soft keys, numeric keyboard) and make the best use of scarce wireless bandwidth (client-side variable, deck/card metaphor). Since 1999, WML can be seen as the first global wireless mark-up language. It retained almost all the features of HDML along with some additional features like timers. HTML 2.0, HTML 3.2 and HTML 4.0 (1997) were defined as the proper formalization of what was just current practice. By the time of the HTML 4.0, XML and XML hype were created and the "xmlification" of HTM became the logical next step. XHTML 1.0 was introduced in 2000 (see Figure 74).

---

[1] Thalys.mobi

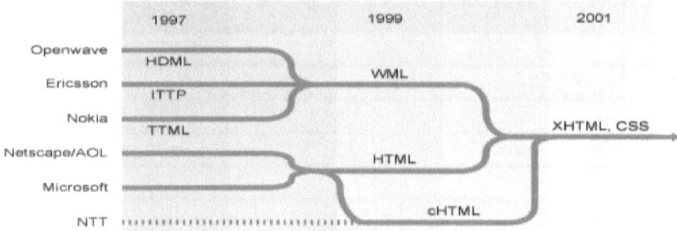

Figure 74: History of Mark-up Language (Passini, 2006)

Extensible Hypertext Markup Language (XHTML)

The Extensible Hypertext Markup Language (XHTML) is a markup language that has the expressive possibilities similar to HTML, but with a stricter, more particular syntax. It is considered as being the current or latest version of HTML. The use of XHTML 1.1, XHTML 1.0, and HTML 4.01 is recommended for web publishing by W3C. HTML is a flexible markup language and an application of SGML However, HTML, is a limited subset of SGML, an application of XML. HTML requires a relatively complicated and custom parser. XHTML can be considered as the intersection of HTML and XML in many respects, since it is a reformulation of HTML in XML. Although the XML suitable for data conversion will replace HTML in the future in all probability, it is too early to adopt the XML as the key language in design web, since thousands of HTML-based websites already exist. For this reason, XHTML is an extension of XML. The goal of XHTML is to provide a smooth transition between HTML and XML. Its extensibility and flexibility cause it to be suitable for mobile web applications. XHTML Mobile Profile 1.0 (XHTML MP) is the official mark-up language of WAP 2.0 created by the Open Mobile Alliance (OMA) (formerly the WAPForum) for wireless devices (Passani, 2006). XHTML MP adds styling information (style attribute and tag plus WCSS) in addition to a handful of style tags belonging to other XHTML 1.0 module s such as b, i, big, hr, big and small. Cascading Style Sheets (CSS) are another mechanism for adding style (like colors, spacing) to web documents. WAP 2.0 brings the power of CSS to wireless by introducing WCSS, which is an abridged version of web CSS for wireless devices (Passani, 2006).

Extensible Markup Language (XML)

Extensible Markup Language (XML) is a simple, flexible text format derived from SGML. It is a subset of standard generalized markup language and supports a wide variety of applications. Its goal is to enable generic SGML to be served, received, and processed on the web in the way now possible with HTML. Originally, its primary purpose is to meet the challenges of large-scale electronic publishing. XML is also playing an increasingly important role in the exchange of a wide variety of data on the Web and elsewhere. It has been designed for ease of implementation and for interoperability with both SGML and HTML. Now, its primary goal is to facilitate the sharing of data across different information systems, particularly ones connected via the Internet. Compared with HTML, XML is a tiny SGML (standard for general markup language), it combine the powerful feature and convenience of HTML into the usage of web. Since keeping the extensible feature, the XML is quite different from the HTML. It allows to defining lots of tags to describe the document in the information, rather than a fixed tag. In other words, HTML is a general method to display data of web, however, the XML provide a general method to deal with web data directly. HTML focuses on the display format in web page, however, the XML focuses on the content on web pages.

Wireless Markup Language (WML)

WML is a content format for devices that implement the WAP specification. It is suitable for mobile devices, such as PDA, mobile phones. WML is optimized for low-bandwidth transactions. One of the optimizations in WAP and WML is that a server can return multiple display pages in a single request. And these display pages are referred to as cards. WML includes advanced features optimized for mobile environment including Card and Deck Structure, Event, Navigation and History Stack, Variables, Presentation of Text and Images, Support for User Input and Context Management. A WML page, which is called DECK, is composed of a pack of card linked to each other. While a mobile device is accessing a WML page, all the cards of a page will be downloaded to a device from WAP sever. The switch among cards is processed by a processor inside the mobile device, rather than accessing the server to get information. Cards include text, tag, link, input control, task, image. The body of the WML document is included in the tag <wml>....</wml>, each card in a document is included in <card>...</card>, then the character paragraph is inserted into the tag <p>...</p>.

Mobile Device HCI

When technology reaches the point that meets user requirements, consumers no longer seek the best technology. They seek the most convenient one, the one with the most satisfactory user experience, the lowest cost, and the highest reliability (Preece, 1994). Human-computer interaction is a discipline concerned with the design, evaluation and implementation of interactive computing systems for human use and with the study of major phenomena surrounding them. HCI aims to produce usable, multifunctional and safe systems. Namely, the goal is to develop or improve the safety, utility, effectiveness, efficiency, and usability of systems that include computers. Here, the 'system' refers not only to the software and hardware but also to the entire environment. 'Usability', a key concept in HCI, is concerned with making systems easy to learn and use. Poorly designed computer systems can be extremely annoying to users. HCI draws from the knowledge and methods of many different disciplines, chiefly computer science, cognitive psychology, social science and ergonomics of human factors. Web sites may be accessed by people for multitudes of tasks so making a site friendlier and more responsive is a problem for HCI design. Because of this, the key principle is that HCI design should be user-centered, integrate knowledge from different disciplines and be highly iterative. In order to produce computer systems with good usability, developers must attempt to:

- Understand the factors that determine how people use technology and systems
- Develop tools and techniques to enable building suitable systems.
- Achieve efficient, effective, and safe interaction and put people first (Preece, 1994)

In summary, the key principle in designing HCI is that understanding how users will interact with them and what approaches will lead to more effective usability. User centred design methods and processes improve the usability of systems (Jones et al, 2000). However, designers often overlook important HCI factors, even with conventional interactive systems. In the case of mobile Web technology, designers in the past have developed many devices with little reference to well-known HCI factors. In fact, applying known HCI guidelines can improve the surfing experience on such devices, owing to the limitations mentioned earlier. The first factor that should be considered is the impact of reduced screen size on reading rate, interaction and comprehension. For example, navigation needs rethinking for small screen situations to provide systematic, direct access mechanisms in a small size screen. In addition, designers should pay attention to past usability experiences but should not assume that everything will transfer effectively from the desktop to the handheld environment. The distinction between mobile device and conventional PCs also should be considered carefully within design. User-centered design focuses on placing users at the centre of web design and development. Developers are encouraged to talk directly to the users about the main aspects of the site design to ensure that the final site meets their requirements. The most important aspects here are that user-centered design requires special attention in order to understand users. It is important to be able to anticipate how users would like to navigate so that efficient site navigation can be provided.

When designing mobile sites, it is recommended to structure a menu in a shallow fashion in order to reduce the cognitive burden, rather than creating a deep hierarchy (Lee & Benbasat, 2003). This means fewer levels but more choices per level. Placing a brief summary with key information on a page can enable users to better understand a body of content which is spread over separate pages. In addition, partitioning information into separate pages will decrease scrolling up and down, while reading the separate pages. Customization is defined as the ability of web site to tailor itself or to be tailored by users, namely, personalization and tailoring. It requires designers to filter the unnecessary information to abate the constraints of the small screen. Due to the limited display in viewing web pages, user still often feel frustrated therefore (Lee & Benbasat, 2003) recommend inserting a brief site map to identify the locations and placing icons linking to the start page. Care should be taken to take into account the capabilities of the requesting device such as designing suitable web pages for various mobile screens, and presenting the most important information first at the top of the hierarchy. There are also other limitations in such as visible navigation bars being impractical along with mouse over type techniques.

Standard web pages are generally unsuitable for mobile devices, which vary considerably in their capabilities. Mobile-specific content is a more suitable approach to developing mobile web content. There are three main categories of mobile web authoring techniques: Multiple Authoring, Single Authoring and flexible Authoring (Hanrahan & Merrick, 2004). Multiple Authoring and Flexible authoring are the approaches for developing different versions for different devices. The associated development and maintenance costs are usually considered prohibitive, although it provides authors complete control over the user experience on each device. Among these, the single Authoring, which is an adaptation solution that translates the single authored content into a form appropriate to a wide range of mobile devices, is the most suitable for our mobile web portal.

The objectives of authoring can be categorized into several aspects, and different authoring techniques can be applied to different aspects. For example, structure refers to the relationship between parts of the delivered page and subsequently delivered page. Navigation allows users to move from the currently perceived unit to some related unit, with the minimum of user effort. Content is intended to convey some information to users by the raw text raw text and other media resources from the delivered content. In addition to these aspects, style, layout, application interaction are also parts of authoring aspects, and each of these aspects can be addressed by authoring techniques. For instance, the Cascading Style Sheets can be applied to Style to separation (Hanrahan & Merrick, 2004).

well-known structures are often used to represent content in mobile web development. They are linear structure, hierarchy and mesh, with different influence on content navigation. The linear structure has many problems such as users having to browse a single page each time. For instance Figure 75 shows a typical "Hierarchy" web page structure. Here the site is represented by nodes which comprises an ordered collection of one or more item (such as N 1 which comprises N 1.1 and N1.2 in Figure 75), and items which may be a piece of content or a node (such as N5.1 and N5.2 in Figure 75).

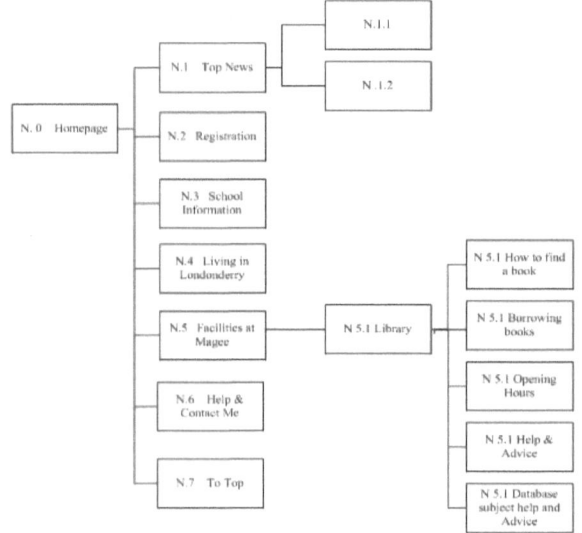

Figure 75: Web Site Map

As shown in Figure 75, a hierarchical structure can be applied to a mobile site with a simple drill-down architecture nesting content into labeled categories. To cater for small screens, information has to be spread out into multiple pages rather than placed on a single page. A well designed click stream requires special attention. This is an effective approach to show what actions users will likely take to reach the content needed. However, to avoid users become disoriented as they go deeper into a site, the levels should be limited as much as possible. Only 3 levels are presented on this portal. In the simple site map (Figure 75), the 1st level is homepage (N1), and the nodes from N1 to N7 are presented on Level 2, and the level 3 contains nodes N2.1, N2.2, and nodes from N.5.1 to N5.3. One limitation during design is to limit links per page. Figure 76 shows a walk through for some of the pages

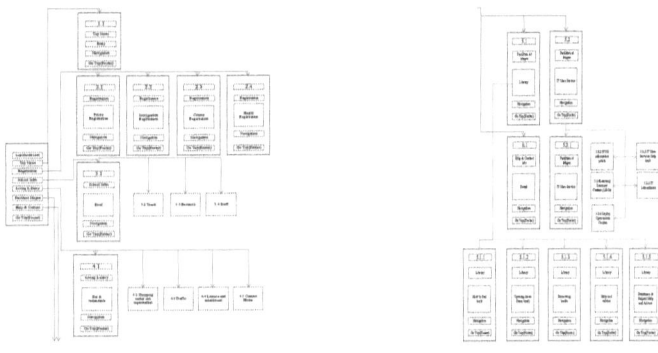

Figure 76: Walk through of typical mobile website pages

Navigation enables users to browse the page in the order intended by the designer, and locate any necessary content. For the mobile devices' limited screen size and navigation capability constraints (for example, some devices do not support script and be not equipped with some desktop inputs like mouse), however, it is difficult to located navigation schemes and menus like web pages for desktop. To create the navigation by author is the easiest approach. Some navigation features are provided to author, such as Menus and access keys. A preferred and most common method of creating mobile navigation schemes is to employ a simple vertical list of menus. As shown on the right of Figure 77, the "body" area lists all the main topics in with a simple vertical list of menus from 1 to 7. Following those topic links, users can reach each sub-topic. For instance, using *Accesskey* in the code, an attribute of XHTML enables users to quickly navigate to areas of the pages via the numerical keypad. Assigning a vertical list of menus on one page creates less disorientation for users as they browse pages. It might also be a consideration to place a link "Go to the Top" on the bottom of each page to allow navigation to the top of page.

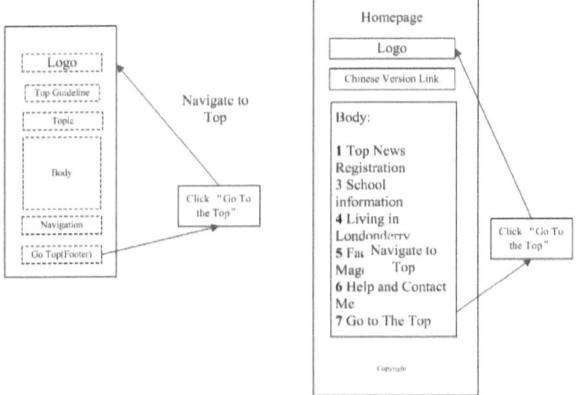

Figure 77: 'go to top' link action

To help users to judge where they are in the web site, a "top guideline" can also be placed on each page. It provides escape points to the parent page, home page or all of the above. As shown in Figure 78, a path is presented on each page except the home page. Node N1 is the N1.1's parent node, and they are both linked to a corresponding page.

Node 1 >> Node 1.1 >> Node1.1.2

Figure 78: Top guideline

169

On each page, a series of navigation bars should also be provided to link to the nodes on the same level. Rather than browsing mobile pages, users in a mobile context are often seeking a special piece of information. Designers should spend time considering what content users are seeking and offer appropriate information. Clear and simple language is essential to enable users to reach the information effectively. Limited Content should also be offered to ensure that users pay less for the experience. Pages should be divided into usable but limited size portions. In addition, due to the memory limitations of devices, authors should ensure that the overall size of page is appropriate so the correct balance between page portion and scrolling is achieved. Scrolling sometimes cannot be avoided (such as maps), so scrolling should be limited to one direction only. Frames are not supported by all mobile devices so use of frames should be avoided.

Mobile browsers identify and treat a document by the HTTP servers sent by MIME Types. Incorrect MIME types with a document may cause the browser to incorrectly interpret and fail to render the document. Also, many mobile devices do not support objects and scripts, therefore – their use is to be avoided. Also, due to the limited bandwidth and high latency often experience by 2G surfers, it is useful to provide caching of information where possible to reduce the need to reload data such as style sheets, pages and images, thus improving performance and lowering cost of use. This especially helps with resources like logos or stylesheets. For instance, to set an expiry times of "200" under the title in the code as follows: <meta   http-equiv="Cache-Control" content="max-age=200" />.

Emulator testing, which uses one or more mobile device emulators, is a common method to test a site designed for the mobile web. Typically, it will mimic the device experience for a particular device or class of devices via a desktop or web-hosted application. They can offer quick verification of how code performs without actually loading it on a device. DotMobi provides a tool[1] which adheres to industry standards set by W3C consortium. The tool simulates mobile devices such as the Sony Ericsson K750i and the Nokia N70. The output from the tool provides assessment scores for web sites ranging from 1 (least mobile ready) to 5 (most mobile ready).

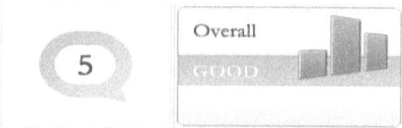

Figure 79: Site overall result

A rating of five for example suggests that a mobile site "will probably display very well on a mobile phone". A more detailed output is presented in Figure 80. The readiness score is also calculated to reach 4.55/5.0. It means that the majority of mobile users can access and view our pages effectively and efficiently. Page size is a significant aspect in the test as it would directly relate to whether the devices can download the page successfully within the limited device's memory and network bandwidth. The figure illustrates that the page tested here is only 12.96k. The size is much lower than the recommended least size by W3C-- 20k per page. Download time is also a major concern in creating a web site, due to users not waiting longer than about thirty seconds for a page to download. Currently, GPRS, 3G and WiFi are the common methods to access internet for mobile devices. The home page being assessed here achieved a result showing that a mobile device will spend 4.14s on access to the page via GPRS, and 1.22s on 3G. The fastest method of access is by WiFi where the page only took 0.53s to load.

[1] http://ready.mobi

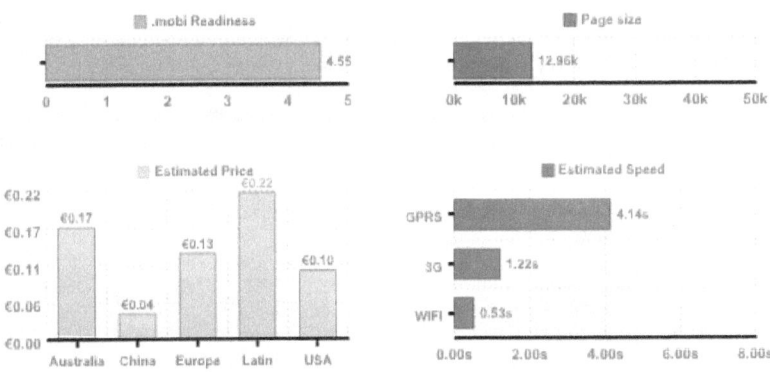

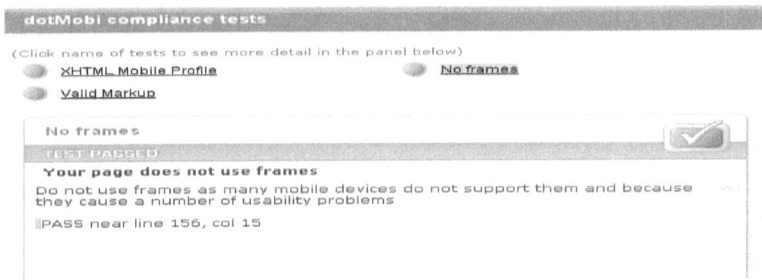

Figure 80: Readiness, Size, Time and Cost from Test

Mobile data transfer often cost money so it is good practice to provide only relevant information. The estimated prices in global regions are calculated as well. We can see in Figure 80 that loading the sample page only costs € 0.13 in Europe and € 0.04 in China. In other regions, it is only €0.17 in Australia, €0.22 in Latin and €0.10 in USA.

Figure 81: DotMobi Compliance Tests

Three key tests in these items are for the XHTML Mobile Profile, Valid Markup and No frames. Frames are not supported by most mobiles therefore it is recommended not to include frames (see Figure 81). The test suggests that the site should use XHTML-MP as the default markup to ensure pages work on multiple mobile devices as well as standard browsers. Non-validating markup might not display correctly or efficiently on mobile devices. In some cases, particularly on older mobile devices, it will cause only error messages in the browser for failing to render. There are other tests that should be performed as well such as compatibility checking for image maps, measures, use of style sheets, objects or scripts, large graphics and table for layout.

Conclusion

The content provided on websites designed for an audience using mobile devices must try to meet all the mobile web design standards due to the inherent limitation of mobile devices. Small screens bring not only convenience but also limitations when viewing sites. Thus, logical web site structure and page layout will influence directly the interaction between users and mobile devices. Navigation becomes more important and it is important to note that images, frames and scripts are not recommended since the bandwidth is limited and plenty of mobile devices do not support scripts and Frames. The development of successful mobile websites is a balance between satisfying the wishes of users and ensuring design conforms to the limitations of the devices.

References

Anderson, C., Domingos, P., Weld, D. (2001) *Personalizing Web Sites for Mobile Users*, Proceedings of the 10th international conference on World Wide Web, Hong Kong, pp: 565 - 575 , ISBN:1-58113-348-0

Baudisch, P., Xie, X., Wang, C., Ma, W. (2004). *Collapse-to-Zoom: Viewing Web Pages on Small Screen Devices by Interactively Removing Irrelevant Content*, UIST '04: Proceedings of the 17th annual ACM symposium on User interface: software and technology, pp: 91--94. ACM Press, 2004

Buyukkokten. O (2000) *Power browser: Efficient web browsing for PDAs*, Proceedings of the Conference on Human Factors in Computing Systems, (CHI 2000), pp: 21-32, 2000

Church, K., Smyth, B. and Keane, M. (2006) *Evaluating Interfaces for Intelligent Mobile Search,* 2006 ACM Proceedings of the 2006 international cross-disciplinary workshop on Web accessibility (W4A), Edinburgh, U.K., pp: 69 – 78, ISBN:1-59593-281-X

Ferguson, D. (2002). *Mobile.NET*, New York, Springer-Verlag, ISBN: 1852335912

Hanrahan, R., Merrick, R. (2004), *Authoring Techniques for Device Independence.* W3C Working Group Note 18 February 2004. Online at http://www.w3.org/TR/di-atdi/

Jones, M., Buchanan, G., Marsden, G., & Thimbleby, H. (2000) *User Interfaces for Mobile Web Devices,* WWW9 Mobile Workshop Position Paper, 9th International World Wide Web Conference, May 2000, Amsterdam, The Netherlands

Kaikkonen A., Roto V. (2003) *Perception of narrow web pages on a mobile phone.* Proceedings of the 19th International Symposium on Human Factors in Telecommunication. Berlin, Germany, December 1-4, 2003.

Lee, Y. E. and Benbasat, I.(2003). Interface design for mobile commerce. *Commun. ACM* 46, 12 (Dec. 2003), 48-52. DOI= http://doi.acm.org/10.1145/953460.953487

Passani, L.(2006) *Openwave developer network: XHTML-MP Style Guide* Chapter 1 - History of XHTML Mobile Profile.   http://developer.openwave.com/dvl/support/documentation/guides_and_references/xhtml-mp_style_guide/chapter1.htm Referenced 24.5.2006

Preece, J. (1994) *Human Computer Interaction*, Addison Wesley, ISBN-10: 0201627698

Rabin, J., McCathie, C. (2006) *Mobile Web Best Practices 1.0,* W3C, Online at http://www.w3.org/TR/mobile-bp/#UserGoals

Roto, V. Kaikkonen, A., (2003) *Navigating in a mobile XHTML application*, Proceedings of the SIGCHI conference on Human factors in computing systems, April 5-10, 2003, Florida, USA

Tilak, J. (2005) *European mobile devices market grew 55% in Q1,* DMEurope,. May 13th 2005, Online at http://www.dmeurope.com/default.asp?ArticleID=7838

26   In-Vehicle Computing

Kevin Curran, Nigel Griffin, James Lee

Telematics is the convergence of telecommunications and information processing. The term has evolved to refer to automobile systems that combine GPS satellite tracking and wireless communications for automatic roadside assistance and remote diagnostics. Satellite navigation has the advantages of showing the driver the route which will have the shortest mileage. It can also however direct a driver along poor quality roads than they normally would not want to use as they can be harmful to their vehicle. Voice enabled sat nav systems are useful as the driver can keep focused on the road as they can be assured that the satellite navigation system will tell them the route instead of them having to glance at the screen every so often. This chapter provides an overview of these technologies.

Introduction

In vehicle computing consists of a collection of multi devices (like sat nav) or just one single unit (on board computer or pc). These may be attached directly to the vehicle or hand-held. Each device can connect to a central node (server), communicating with each other, which may in turn connect to the Internet for uploading of information out on the field (see Figure 82). This may arguably help avoid car accidents as the driver can focus on what he or she is doing instead of focusing on following an on screen map. Telematics services are gradually becoming increasingly popular among drivers. The upsurge in these systems is due to improved reliability, accuracy and decreasing costs of the technologies involved. Many vehicles now come with integrated navigation systems, and Microsoft has targeted the area with its Car .NET strategy and Windows CE for Automotive platform. A brief overview of current in-car navigation systems identifies two main variations of commercial in-car navigation systems:

1) A dedicated terminal, usually relying on CD or DVD based map data which is combined with input from a Global Positioning Satellite (GPS) antenna. These terminals may have optional displays and voice interfaces.

2) Add-on kits for Personal Digital Assistants (PDA) running Microsoft's PocketPC operating system or PalmOS by Palm. These systems typically consist of a 'jacket' comprising a GPS antenna & additional slots for memory cards for storing map data.

Computing is defined by the Compact Oxford English Dictionary *as the use or operation of computers*. Today computers are used in many different environments. They are no longer restricted to the office or home but can be used anywhere and everywhere. Computers have originated from the desktop, to the laptop, to the Personal Digital Assistant (PDA), to the Ultra-Mobile PC (UMPC) and now to the in-vehicle computer. The In-Vehicle Computer is the latest type of computer to be developed. It is just like a desktop computer and laptop in that it has all the same components and a chassis for storing these components. In addition to this it requires a monitor just like a desktop computer and laptop in order to *present the output from the compute*. An In-Vehicle Computer is small in size and is like a miniature horizontal desktop computer.

In-Vehicle Computing can be therefore defined as the use of computers in vehicles. There are several other names for In-Vehicle computers: Vehicle Computer, Car PC, Carputer, Auto PC or Bus PC, Mobile Data Terminal (MDT) or Vehicle/In-Vehicle PC. Each of these is similar in that they are all in-vehicle computers but they are different in their features and their setup.

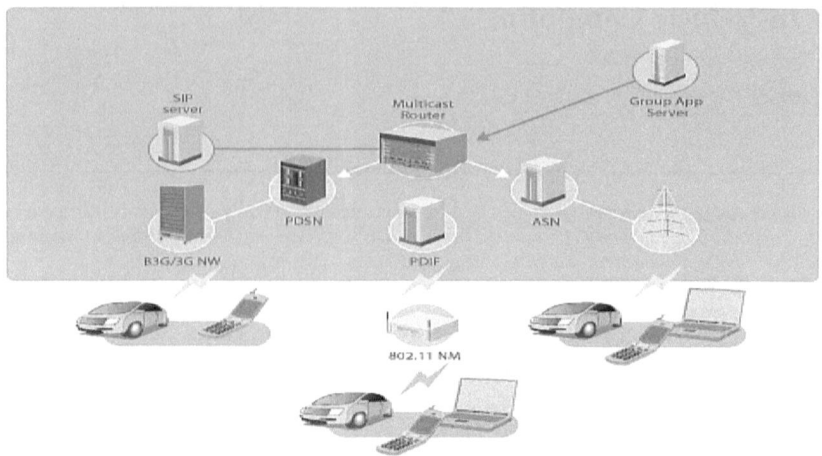

Figure 82: Typical Vehicle Computer Network

As the modern workforce becomes increasing mobile, it is important to have access to information. Computer systems can provide the functions of almost any application that electronic devices can perform within the vehicle. The dominance of in-vehicle computer systems comes not only from its capability to achieve all functions from single hand held devices, but also from the fact that one can perform tasks quickly as if using any desktop pc (see Figure 83).

Figure 83: PC being used instead of multiple devices

Many commercial fleet forces deploy a rugged yet semi rugged computer systems, the ability to keep on the move is critical in order to profit time efficiently, to cut costs on transportation and better communications within the company. Many businesses such as Courier Services, Water Services, B.T and public safety (Police, Fire, and Medical Services) deploy ruggedized portable computers such as the Panasonic Tough book. These laptops are rated for severe vibration associated with large service vehicles and off- road driving. They are designed to cope with drops, splashes, severe temperatures and other rough handling. Many applications for fleet computing are designed for touch screen control with keyboards, only be used for a lot of data input. Advanced vehicle PCs will also deploy on screen applications controlled systems. Fleet computing is common in vehicle security, field operations, vehicle diagnostics, vehicle navigation, mobile surveillance, mobile Office, mobile entertainment, mobile networking and mobile telecommunications.

Figure 84: In-Vehicle Computer in radio   Figure 85: In-Vehicle Computer in boot

There are different setups for In-Vehicle Computers. The most common option is to install the computer into the radio slot on the vehicle's dashboard (see Figure 84). This would is used by car manufacturers and manufacturers of In-Vehicle Computers. The amateur installer however would opt for the more straightforward installation technique which involves mounting the monitor to the dashboard while screwing the computer into the boot (see Figure 85).

Applications of Mobile Computing

In-Vehicle Computers can perform a wide range of tasks due to the extensive number of features they obtain. There are basically two different sets of features, the first set are for general users and the second set is for emergency service workers. The first set of features includes: Satellite Navigation, Hands-free Phone System, Skype (VoIP), Music, Internet, Movies and TV, Speech Pack, Rear-view Camera, view and edit documents. The second set of features includes: Automatic Number Plate Recognition (ANPR), Automatic Vehicle Location System (AVLS), remote database access, light bar control (siren control). There are generally two types of in-vehicle computers – the personal and the emergency services as shown in figure 2 and 3.

Figure 86: Personal In-Vehicle computer   Figure 87: Emergency Services In-Vehicle computer

In-Vehicle computers make life much easier due to the wide-range of functions they can perform. Business people can now have an office in their car, as the In-Vehicle computer allows them to email clients, write up reports and surf the internet. Parents no longer have to worry about keeping their children entertained as the in-vehicle computer can play DVD's. They also make the jobs of emergency service personnel less demanding. As a police officer no longer has to go back to the police station to write up incident reports but they can do it instantly on the computer and it is available to other officers immediately. They can also run an instant check on a suspect themselves rather then having to use their radio through the direct access to the police national computer that the In-Vehicle Computer provides. The fire service can use In-Vehicle Computers to identify any potential hazards an area contains and receive details of safety equipment needed at a particular site. Among the most possible operations that have be thought up for Mobile Computing within vehicle and fleet are the extreme cost saving and utilization of resources (staff) and the impact of site maintenance and improved communications throughout the network. The signification of mobile computers has being focused below:

- **Emergency Services**
  The ability to check up personal addresses and information, regarding accidents or convictions, Can be done with ease and at the touch of a screen via a CDPD system.

- **In Companies**
  The ability to select Jobs through schedules and daily planners, management can access the latest stock information. And be able to track goods delivered to customers etc.

- **Taxi/ Truck Despatch**
  The ability to give drivers full details of dispatched jobs, which appear on the system, allowing drivers to communicate their location. It can be used in courier services as the whereabouts of drivers, and can be used also for securing deliveries.

- **Vehicle Navigation**
  Used for navigation of fleets of vehicles or emergency services, via GPRS and self-sensory navigation systems with visuals and voice.

- **Mobile Entertainment**
  Used for playing, recording and managing, local and remote digital media wirelessly. Delivering Internet radio (DAB).

In the road haulage industry today it has become a European Union law for all lorries to be fitted with electronic Tachographs so information about the lorries usage can be recorded and stored on smart cards that are not as vulnerable to tampering. Tachographs were introduced to stop companies forcing their drivers to drive without taking a break therefore risking there own life but the lives of other motorists. With new technology such as fleet cards companies can send out their drivers with these cards the drivers can use then to fill with fuel but the companies can track how much fuel is being put on board and how much fuel is needed for each journey this way they can keep track of what their drivers are doing it also saves them money as the drivers of the vehicle can not claim they have used more fuel than they did and the company can pay for the fuel by themselves.

Social Issues

In-Vehicle Computers can face adverse conditions. The conditions they face include shock, vibration, humid and freezing temperatures. In-Vehicle Computers require a number of safety features in order to operate efficiently in all situations. The major concern is ruggedness, as In-Vehicle Computers operate in an environment which is constantly unstable. They face road bumps, sudden stops and starts, and potholes. The hard drive, DVD/CD drive are the components of the computer that are most affected, due to these being the components that have moving parts (BAPCO, 2007). Therefore both the hard drive and DVD/CD drive have to be able to handle shock. Issues arising could also include:

1. Operating temperature: Computers must be able to withstand different temperatures throughout the year from -20F to + 140F to be able to function correctly.

2. Daylight/sunlight readability: The visibility of the VDU comes an issue in complete sunlight, user interface.

3. Vibrations: Vehicles typically vibrate, which can reduce the life of computer components, particular hard drives.

4. Network challenges: The bandwidth and delay factors accessing data and information could be an issue.

5. Device challenges: The Memory and processing power of the system could be slow.

6. Battery life: 6 cell or 9 cell battery's, rechargeable, or high temperature battery settings could be an

issue for long periods on a stand-alone basis when out on the field.

7. Noise or dead spots

Further safety features for an In-Vehicle Computer include the Operating Temperature and Storage Temperature. The computer will be in direct contact with the temperature, so it needs effective protection. Both the operating temperature and the storage temperature provide this protection. The operating temperature will allow the computer to function in extreme temperatures, both hot and cold. Then the storage temperature will mean the computer is protected from extreme temperatures.

The monitor of an In-Vehicle computer faces a problem again due to its environment. The monitor faces direct exposure to sunlight and this causes poor screen visibility. In order to prevent this, the monitor has to have both the high brightness and the sunlight readable features (see Figure 88). This will ensure that the glare caused by the sun does not affect the viewing on the screen. The monitor also needs to be able to operate effectively and legally at night time. This is generally provided by the Night Mode feature offered by the software used on the computer (see Figure 89).

Figure 88: Monitor glare   Figure 89: Night Mode feature

In addition to this, the temperature itself is of huge importance to the monitor. Just as the temperature can cause catastrophic problems to the computer, it can seriously damage the monitor. In order to prevent this and ensure maximum efficiency, the monitor has to have both an appropriate operating temperature and storage temperature. In-Vehicle Computers are small because they have to fit into small spaces. Vehicles already have a lack of space due to the excessive amount of accessories they acquire. Desktop computers and laptops have space in abundance available to them compared to vehicle computers. This limited space available affects and determines their design. In-Vehicle Computers can face problems with power supply. In-Vehicle Computers are powered by the vehicles battery. This means that they always have a limited amount of power available, as they have to share a limited amount of power. In addition to this many In-Vehicle Computers will carry out an organised shut down when the battery is drained. Therefore the computer is inactive until the battery is recharged. A further feature that an In-Vehicle Computer needs to have in order to enable satisfactory performance, and which is related to the power supply, is the ability to not to reboot while the engine is cranked.

The advantages of all these technologies often outweigh the disadvantages. The advantages of cruise control is that on long and tiring journey the car driver can set a speed that is below the sped limit and can relax knowing that the car will control its own speed all the driver has to do is steer. It also is simple to turn of cruise control in the case of an emergency by either touching the brake or clutch pedal. In modern designs sensor have been added so that the car will slow down if there is another car in front of it. This is to prevent sudden breaking by the driver or a collision. The disadvantages of cruise control is that drivers can often lapse in concentration as they are not driving the car manually this can lead to driver falling asleep and causing accidents. Other disadvantages are that it is not fuel efficient in rolling terrain or on hills than a skilled driver is for example a skilled driver will keep the throttle steady when coming to an incline allowing a certain amount of deceleration and when going down the other side a driver can let the car accelerate due to gravity more so than using the power of the engine. Whereas cruise control will accelerate to keep the speed the same whilst going uphill, and use the engine management breaking systems to hold the car back when going down the hill. Some cruise control system will actually go over the speed limit on downhill's that are steep enough to accelerate with the engine idling.

The advantage of having engine management systems in many motor vehicle today especially in cars is that they are more fuel efficient and can be serviced by the manufacturers more efficiently. Today many service teams work with laptops so as they can plug them into the cars ECU. They then process all the data stored on the ECU and can use the laptop to find the problem that the car has. This in turn speeds up breakdown recovery times as the service team doesn't have to search the whole engine to find faults that are very small and usually uncommon. The problems with the ECU in cars nowadays are that there is not enough trained staff to use the technology involved and as well as this a lot of the systems are not accurate enough. This cause vehicle owners greater expense as they sometimes have to have their cars put through the same fault finding techniques numerous times as the fault cannot be found. Engine management systems now cause older garages to lose out on a lot of revenue as they do not have the technology or the authority to work on modern cars. Since there are fewer and fewer older cars on the road now, many garages have seen a reduction in business. The field navigation system in use in the agricultural sector today are a great benefit to farmers as they can increase production whilst using the minimum amount of input like seeds and sprays. They can also prevent sowing on the ground where the tractor is going to trample the planted crops. This increase overall profit margins so as the farmers can be more competitive from international markets and many of the foreign imports that can be found in the United Kingdom today. It can also save on fuel use as it can figure out what would be the fastest way to work across the field as the tractor will be more efficient whilst working on long straights rather than spending time turning on already prepared ground. But there are also a few disadvantages with these systems as the field boundaries which they work with are constantly changing with farmers being given grants to create more natural habitat by planting hedgerows or leaving a certain boundary of the field untouched. As well as this the technology which has mainly stationary receivers sometimes does not have a strong enough frequency so it sometimes does not work over long distances away from the farm where the receiver is often mounted. This technology is not available in all new tractors and since it only recently has been introduced, there has been relevantly little experience in fixing any problems that these new engines have.

Fleet computing is a good way for large haulage companies to keep track on their delivery vehicles. They can use computers to track vehicles from destination to destination. They can also keep track on the driver to make sure they are not driving illegally and driving for longer hours than they are permitted by law. It gives the advantages to river if they are trying to claim for loss of earning as the data stored cannot be tampered with. The main disadvantage is that drivers are always trying to find ways to get round the systems by short circuiting the device or replacing fuses with fuses that are broken.

Conclusion

Many people obtain an In-Vehicle Computer today as standard in a new car. In-Vehicle Computers not only face problems but may cause them too as they can escalate driver distraction. It presents drivers with a single object that can do many interesting things, and through this it can easily obtain the drivers attention. Current legislation in the UK helps in minimizing this distraction. It is against the law for a driver to watch a DVD in a moving vehicle. Therefore In-Vehicle Computers are generally installed in a way which allows backseat passengers to watch films while the vehicle is in motion, and at the same time allows the driver to use the computer for other applications such as satellite navigation and MP3 playing.

The second problem that In-Vehicle Computers cause is Electromagnetic Interference (ECI). ECI produces poor radio reception and poor performance from wireless receivers. It occurs when Electromagnetic fields are produced. These fields are created by the joining of an electric field produced by a voltage and a magnetic field which is produced by a current. The fields affect the operation of other objects or devices that use electricity. Any object that touches this field will receive interference (Anon, 2008). All producers of In-Vehicle Computers whether professional or amateurs have to adhere to the EMC Directive (89/336/EEC). This is a ruling which is law throughout Europe that requires electrical equipment that is sold to not create unacceptable interferences and have sufficient immunity from interferences (CASES, 2006). In-Vehicle Computers can also be affected by ECI (RA, 2008). However the metal casing inside the computer chassis prevents this. There have been immeasurable advancements in the field of robotics in the past from the simple artificial intelligence that could play chess to the advanced ones that can navigate a car through a race and adapt to different situations without the intervention of a user. There may indeed be numerous autonomous vehicles sooner than we think.

References

http://www.microsoft.com/automotive/cardotnet/cardotnetnews.pdf

http://www.microsoft.com/automotive/cardotnet/EnablingCarNet.doc

What is an In-Vehicle PC, Microbus, Date Retrieved: March 12, 2008,
http://mobile-data.microbus.com/products/in-vehicle_pc.php

Features, In-Car PC, Date Retrieved: March 12, 2008,
http://www.in-carpc.co.uk/Features/Features.htm

Home, Microbus, Date Retrieved: March 12, 2008,
http://mobile-data.microbus.com/

Hard Drive Crash Recovery by SalvageData UK, SalvageData UK, Date Retrieved: April 3, 2008,
http://www.salvagedata.co.uk/hard-drive-crash/

BAPCO (2007) In-vehicle workhorses, Bapco Journal, 29 November, 2007
http://www.bapcojournal.com/news/fullstory.php/aid/1051/In-vehicle_workhorses.html

Verwoert, C. (2007) What is electromagnetic interference?, SearchMobileComputing.com, 28 May, 2007,
http://searchmobilecomputing.techtarget.com/sDefinition/0,,sid40_gci213940,00.html

Anon (2008) A basic introduction to electricity, EMFs and the terminology used, Electric and Magnetic Fields,
http://www.emfs.info/what_TermTuto.asp

RA (2008) Frequently Asked Questions, Radiocommunications Agency EMC Awareness,
http://www.ofcom.org.uk/static/archive/ra/topics/research/RAwebPages/Radiocomms/pages/faqs.htm#WhatisEMC

CASES (2006) Computer Cases, Electronic Information Online, Thursday, 19 October 2006,
http://www.electronics-manufacturers.com/info/computers-and-laptops/computer-cases.html

27   Body Area Networks

Kevin Curran, Eoghan Furey, Mary Kelly

Recent technological advances in integrated circuits, wireless networks, and physiological sensing have enabled miniature, lightweight, low power, intelligent monitoring devices to be integrated into a Body Area Network (BAN). This new type of technology hold much promise for future patient health monitoring. BANs promise inexpensive, unobtrusive, and unsupervised ambulatory monitoring during normal daily activities for long periods of time. However, in order for BANs to become ubiquitous and affordable, a number of challenging issues must be resolved, such as integration, standardisation, system design, customisation, security and privacy, and social issues. This chapter presents an overview of many of these issues and indeed the background and rationale of body area networks.

Introduction

A Body Area Network (BAN) is a collection of advanced nano and micro-technology components. They are designed to improve the speed and accuracy of how data is recorded. In general a Body Area Network has sensors and actuators that are used to monitor and log data, this data is then transmitted and stored to a base station. When the data has reached the base station it is possible for it to be sent on to devices via the internet for others to access. Body Area Networks are a relatively modern invention and are primarily being designed for use within the health industry. Their main purpose is to enable doctors and other medical staff to safely monitor the health status of patients. One of the benefits of Body Area Networks is that those patients with chronic diseases such as Alzheimer's, Asthma and Diabetes can be monitored much more closely. Doctors will have the power to update patient records quickly and efficiently and they will be able to store information on the patients' general health.

Hospitals throughout the United States and in Europe have been running pilot programmes to experiment with monitoring patients' health. They have introduced ID bracelet's that contain chips and antennas, which can follow the patients' whereabouts. The system will also use antennas to track individuals as they walk about the hospital and send alerts if a patient begins to collapse. A company called Zarlink[1] are currently working on a project named 'Healthy Aims' which is focusing on in-body devices that will help millions of people world-wide. Body Area Networks take advantage of the low power radio frequencies (RF) and enable the Body Area Network to supply the patients' data in real time. There is a frequency range dedicated to Body Area Networks, known as MICS (Medical Implantable Communication Service) band, it operates between 402 and 405 MHz and is specifically for implanted devices to communicate with other external devices.

Not only will doctors be able to monitor patients' general health but they will also have the ability to change the settings for specific implanted devices so that they perform much better, thus improving the patients health. Currently individuals requiring pacemakers have to endure the pain and stress of surgery in order to have their pacemaker device fitted. The very first implantable pacemaker invented was produced in the 1960's and has evolved tremendously since. The pacemakers set up as part of a Body Area Network wirelessly send the patients' health status to a near-by RF transceiver. From this RF transceiver the data is transmitted to a doctor. The fact that the patients health status is regularly being forwarded to the doctor means that their health record is always up-to-date and the information reaches the doctor in real-time. If at any stage in life a patient encounters problems with their current pacemaker then it is quite possible that they will have to endure more surgery simply to alter the settings on the pacemaker. Therefore the added benefit of the 'Healthy Aims' project is the fact that the patient will only ever need to have surgery performed once and this is only to have the device fitted. Doctors and medical staff will be able to monitor the health status of many patients without their need to visit the clinic. Doctors can stay in their office and work their way through the patients' records; if they discover that a patients' health status is below normal they will be able to prepare a prescription or make an adjustment without the patient being aware. The doctor will then simply have to contact the patient to inform them of the

---

[1] http://www.zarlink.com/

outcome. The doctor is able to do this because of the fact that the patients Body Area Network independently transmits data to the doctor, therefore crisis information will reach the doctor much quicker than if somebody discovered the patient unconscious on their bathroom floor and made an emergency call to the ambulance service.

Having a Body Area Network in place would mean that individuals would not have to travel to the clinic, which means that there would be less pollution made to the environment. Also, the clinic will then have fewer visiting patients to check, which will mean that the waiting times for those patients in the waiting area would be reduced immensely. This complex method of communication between the patient and the doctor is made possible by a two-way RF link. The sensors of a Body Area Network are extremely compact and complex in design. The fact that the sensors are so minute means that the patients will be able to lead a normal life, as the sensor devices are very unobtrusive. All sensors produced will contain the same basic elements such as a power supply and wireless transceiver as well as a control mechanism, a sensor and the casing that will hold all of the components together. The sensors will be designed in a way that allows them to be self-governing for the entire lifetime. These sensors are designed to "measure and monitor events and physical properties such as temperature, movement, pressure, and location"[1].

BAN's work through a process of data being transmitted from an implanted device to an external device. The sensor that is implanted inside the patient's body wirelessly interacts with other sensors and actuators. An actuator is the mechanism by which an agent acts upon an environment. The agent can be either an artificial intelligent agent or any other autonomous being. An autonomous being can be a human being or an animal. The Body Area Network functions by passing data from each sensor to a main station. The main station then fuses the data passed from each of the sensors and it is then sent to a recipient via the internet. The IMEC (Interuniversity Micro Electronics Center) has stated that "At the system level, it is concentrating on wireless communications in and around the human body; ad-hoc networking of wireless nodes; reliability, accuracy and sensitivity issues; position determination; and design technology for a fast reproducible design cycle"[2]. Ad hoc networking is the best suited networking type for Body Area Networks because of the fact that it is comprised of small wireless electronic devices. The IMEC is working on implementing the ability to monitor the location of the patients within the hospital. This means that the patients will have the freedom to walk around the hospital or go outside for fresh air; the sensors within the Body Area Network will be programmed to detect the patients' temperature and other vital signs. Therefore, if a patient suddenly collapses the doctors and medical staff will be notified; and can rush to the patient's aid and provide treatment. Next we examine in more detail the field of wireless body area networks.

Body Area Networks

A BAN consists of a collection of small sensor nodes that are placed around the body. These may be attached directly to the skin or as part of special clothing. Each node has either a small power source or takes power from the body. The nodes can collectively communicate with a central node (like a PDA) which can in turn connect to the internet and in doing so can relay the data from the sensors to a particular application or person. There should be no wires involved, making the BAN as unobtrusive as possible as illustrated in Figure 90.

---

[1] http://csrc.nist.gov/manet/
[2] http://www.electronicstalk.com/news/ime/ime114.html

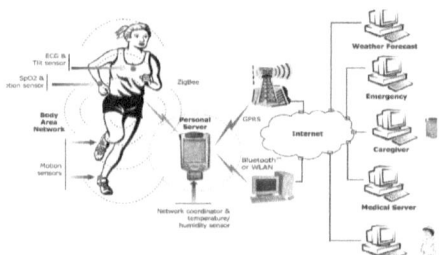

Figure 90: How a Body Area Network is linked to the Internet (Jovanov, 2005)

To engineer a successful BAN, a number of challenges exist which must be overcome. New methods need to be developed to address the following such as:

- The lifetime of the power sources in the sensors needs to be increased and/or methods to get energy from other sources (e.g.: body heat) need to be perfected.

- The interaction of the sensors (nodes) and the main node (PDA) needs to be designed in such a way so as to allow specialist applications to be written to do particular functions (e.g.: disease management).

- The device needs intelligence (memory and processing capabilities) to allow it to process, transfer and store data.

- Chemical, Physical and Biological measurement needs to be integrated with the sensors to give a clear picture of human physiology and the BAN components need to be integrated in a reliable and cost effective way.

History of Body Area Networks

The development of the PAN (Personal Area Network) grew out of the work being done by a number of different groups working in MIT (Massachusetts Institute of Technology) on the 90's. The original groups wanted to interconnect information appliances that were carried on the body. Also they wanted to measure positioning using electric field sensing and they realised that they could send data through the body by modulating the electric field. Thomas G. Zimmerman was one of the main players in the development of the PANs. He developed technology that has the effect of allowing the body to act like a copper cable, basically like a conductor. The other main player in those early days was Neil Gershenfeld who was in charge of the Physics and Media Group in MIT. His group applied a method known as "near-field coupling" to particular problems. This allows them to determine the accurate position of one part of the body in relation to another. They placed pairs of antennas on parts of the body (e.g.: on the hand and elbow). By running an electric current between them they noted that as the parts moved (i.e. flex of the elbow) the capacitance of the circuit was changed. By measuring the capacitance they were able to determine the positions of the antenna.

Zimmerman solved a problem they encountered. If a hand was placed between the antennas then the measurement was no longer accurate. He was able to show that some of the current was passing through the body, therefore affecting the measurement. Another group working at the media lab then asked these two to develop a network to connect together all the electric gadgets that a person might carry on their person. Many people carried around a number of digital devices but none of them could communicate with each other. A person might have a mobile phone, a pager, a PDA and a digital watch all about their person at the same time. This person might receive a page, then type the number into the PDA to see whose it is, then dial it on the mobile phone. Too much effort is being wasted on a very low-level information exchange. Zimmerman and Gershenfeld noticed that if they modulated the electric field flowing through a person's body, they could make it represent a 1 or 0, thus allowing the body to carry digital information. The discovered that if the frequency and power used were both kept very low then the signal would not propagate far beyond the body. This would mean that only devices on the body or in direct contact with it could detect the signal. The current used is very small and is totally unnoticed by the person. These ideas of how a PAN developed were the early attempts at creating a BAN.

Applications of BANs

Among the many possible applications that have been thought up for BANs are communication in hospitals, communication on aeroplanes or spaceships, monitoring of patients at home (post operative care), modern Warfare, monitoring of babies, interlinking of components in home entertainment products and athlete monitoring and sports analysis

Medical Applications
BANs can provide interfaces for diagnostics, for remote monitoring of human physiological data, for administration of drugs in hospitals and as an aid to rehabilitation. In the future it will be possible to monitor patients continuously and give the necessary medication whether they are at home, in a hospital or elsewhere. Patients will no longer need to be connected to large machines in order to be monitored.

Sports Applications
In the sporting arena is will be possible to take many different readings from an athlete without having them on a treadmill in a laboratory. The ability to measure various levels during real life competition, a race for example, would give coaches a more accurate picture of their athlete's strengths and weaknesses. Another application of using BANs in sport to monitor athletes closely.

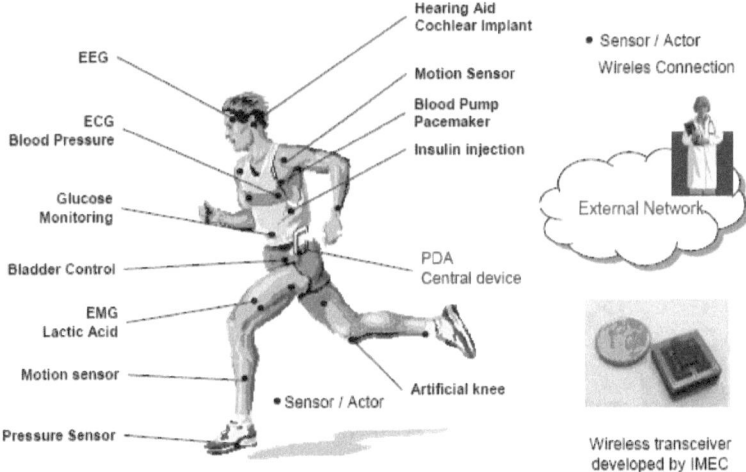

Figure 91: A BAN on an Athlete (Latré, 2005)

Military Applications

The opportunities for using BANs in the military are numerous. Some of the military applications for BANs include monitoring health, location, temperature and hydration levels. These readings can then be used to administer Casualty care (e.g.: morphine), knowledge of when to enhance strength, concentration, accuracy (e.g.: drugs) and possibly to reduce friendly fire incidents (tell them who each other is and where).

Sensors and Actuators

In a BAN two main types of non-computer device can be identified known as sensors and actuators. The Sensors measure certain human body parameters such as temperature, heart rate, EEG, pressure on joints, etc. These measurements can be taken inside or outside of the human body. Actuators take particular actions depending on the information received by the sensors and instructions given via the PDA and the web. Administration of insulin for diabetics would be an example of something that the actuators could control. (Jovanov, 2005) lists some of the specific sensors that could be used in their version of a wireless BAN such as:

- An ECG (electrocardiogram) sensor for monitoring heart activity.
- An EMG (electromyography) sensor for monitoring muscle activity.
- An EEG (electroencephalography?) sensor for monitoring brain electrical activity.
- A blood pressure sensor.
- A tilt sensor for monitoring trunk position.
- A breathing sensor for monitoring respiration.
- Movement sensors used to estimate a users' activity.

Most of the sensors that are in use are of an electronic or electrical nature. These types of sensor may sense a change in current or resistance in a body (a muscle for example). When the muscle is contracted it would give a different reading to a small voltage applied to it than if it was relaxed. It is these differences that are measured by the sensor. In a very simplistic version a totally relaxed state (i.e.: laying down) might correspond to a value of 0, but a tensed state (i.e.: standing on one leg) might give a value of 10. Any readings in between 1 and 10 will correspond to the state of relaxation/contraction of the muscle. When this information is sent back to the PDA and then on to the main computer it would be possible to know at all stages the activity state of a muscle. For instance, if a large number of sensors were placed on the legs of a runner and all the data was recorded over an 800m race, it would be possible to determine at exactly what point the runner was getting tired or was losing form. Training could then be tailored specifically; i.e. strengthen calf muscles because the runner becomes flatfooted at 650m and therefore slows down.

An actuator is a device that transforms an input signal into motion. If one was used to control the amount of insulin that a diabetic was receiving, then an instruction given by a computer could control the amount of the chemical released into the body. A medical person could send this instruction directly to the BAN that the patient was wearing no matter where they were located; via the Internet, WiFi, Bluetooth or some other means of communicating the signal to the PDA, which in turn would control the actuator. Along with the sensors, the actuators are engineering components, which allow the human body to be influenced, monitored or controlled by the computer system.

Networking Body Area Networks

When creating a BAN, a number networking issues need to be addressed. Direct communication is where a node sends data directly to a central device. If a node were on the foot, its data would have to pass other nodes on the way to the PDA meaning that a number of data pathways would exist in the same tissue at the same time. This could cause interference and could also cause unnecessary temperature rise in the tissue however with Multihop communication, data is sent through the intermediate nodes on the way to its destination. Each of the nodes acts as a small router. This would eliminate internal interference. This is also more energy efficient than the direct route. IEEE 802.15 oversees the standards for how Wireless PANs communicate. These standards are essential to ensure that all of the different groups who are involved in designing the BANs make sure that everything will work with everything else. The 802.15 standard has 4 task groups, each of which has authority over the development of a certain type of technology which will be used in BANs such as WPAN/Bluetooth, WPAN/

Wireless Local Area Networks, WPAN High Rate (20Mbit/s or higher) and WPAN Low Rate (long battery life – Zigbee). They are at different stages of development and will eventually ensure that BANs created in one country will work with those in another.

Software

One of the main options that is available and in use (and development) is "Tiny OS" which was developed by UC Berkley in California. This is an open source operating system for wireless embedded sensor networks. It is an extremely small OS (Operating System) in terms of code and memory resources. This is what makes it suitable for sensor networks where memory is at a minimum. A lot of the groups that are currently using Tiny OS are involved in research using sensor networks to monitor some phenomenon or other. Some examples include sensor networks to monitor volcanic eruptions in Ecuador and tracking of fire fighters in buildings. Another option in control software is to use MSR Networked Embedded Sensing Toolkit (MSR Sense) from Microsoft. This is a collection of software tools that allow users to collect, process, archive and visualise data from a sensor network Other options are available and in development so it remains to be seen which will come to the fore. At the moment Tiny OS and MSR are freely available to download.

Social Issues

A number of issues exist regarding the creation of BANs include system design issues and human issues. System Design Issues include (Jovanov, 2005):

1. **Sensor Types**
   What type of sensor should be included in the BAN? This will depend on where it is to be used and for what purpose

2. **Power Sources**
   If the BAN is designed to be used for a long period of time then the power sources must be appropriate. If it is going to be used for some short intense activity then a different source could be used.

3. **Wireless Communication Range**
   Is the person using the BAN likely to remain within a particular area? e.g.: a hospital, or are they likely to be outdoors? E.g.: a soldier in the desert.

4. **Sensor location and mounting**
   Could they be woven into the uniform of a solider or might they need to be small unobtrusive implants in the skin?

5. **Weight and size of sensor**
   If the person is confined to bed at home then the sensors could be of a different type from those used on a runner.

6. **Coexistence Issues**
   Will the system interfere with other systems that are in place such as a pacemaker or the hearing aid of a patient.

A number of major trials are being conducted all over the world such as the MobiHealth trial (Bults, 2004) which is being carried out in four European countries. MobiHealth was used by medical personnel to monitor a range of conditions in patients outside of hospitals. The 9 trials that were carried to date were[1]:

1. Germany: Telemonitoring of patients with cardiac arrhythmia.
2. The Netherlands: Integrated homecare for women with high-risk pregnancies and tele trauma team
3. Spain: Support of home based healthcare services and outdoor patient rehabilitation.

---

[1] http://www.mobihealth.org

4. Sweden: Lighthouse alarm and locator trial; Physical activity and impediments to activity for women with RA.; Monitoring the vital parameters in patients with respiratory insuffiency and Homecare with remote consultation for recently released patients in a rural area.

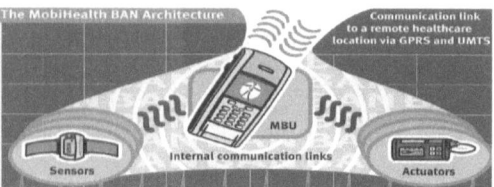

Figure 92: MobileHealth BAN Architecture (http://www.mobihealth.org/)

As a result of these trials a number issues arose such as data rates fluctuating, operator errors, handover errors (e.g.: changing from one network to another), bandwidth issues, IP address allocation and power supplies insufficient. Other issues regarding BANs in general include privacy & security, legal issues and control issues. For instance, will the data that is being transferred remain private? Is it secure and would it be possible for someone to send false information to a BAN and tell it to perform some dangerous function? e.g.: make you warmer or make you overdose. Is it legal to hold all information about a person in case a company could detect from records that a person had a weak heart. Finally, in an advanced BAN important functions might be controlled by a computer such as the ability to fall asleep or stay awake being controlled by an actuator that regulated the flow of a certain chemical in the body. All of these issues will need to be addressed and before Body Area Networks become a part of everyday life.

Conclusion

A major issue with Body Area Networks is security. As data that has been logged is transmitted over the internet there is always the possibility of someone else hacking into it. Therefore, in order to prevent a hacker from gaining access to the network and corrupting the data, it is vital that there is adequate encryption in place. In order to ensure that it is impossible for anyone to hack into a Body Area Network thorough testing must be carried out. Also, because each patient is unique and requires different treatments the data held on one patient will be completely different to the data held on another patient. Therefore, it is extremely important that each patients individual Body Area Network is not confused with one another. The use of chips that can wirelessly communicate via a Body Area Network is an excellent idea, but only if they are used in an ethical manner. Body Area Networking can be used to allow an individuals personal details to be stored on a chip, which can then easily interact with other devices.

References

Jovanov, E. Milenkovic, A., Otto, C. and de Groen· P (2005). *A wireless body area network of intelligent motion sensors for computer assisted physical rehabilitation*. Journal of Neuroengineering Rehabilitation. 2005; 2: 6., 2005 March 1. doi: 10.1186/1743-0003-2-6.

Latré, B., Moerman, I., Dhoedt, B, Demeester, P. (2005) *Networking in Wireless Body Area Networks*, http://www.ibcn.intec.ugent.be/css_design/research/topics/2005/Networking%20in%20Wireless%20Body%20Area%20Networks.pdf

Bults, R., Wac, K, Van Halteren, A., Konstantas, D., Jones, V., Widya, I. (2004) *Body Area Networks for Ambulant Patient Monitoring Over Next Generation Public Wireless Networks.* Prroceedings of the 3th IST Mobile and Wireless Communications Summit 27-30 June 2004, Lyon, France

28   Mobile IP and Cellular IP

Kevin Curran, Martina Quinn

Fourth generation mobile networks will have large numbers of mobile users utilizing a single wireless device that will send and receive numerous services and applications over high-speed micro-cellular wireless networks. An important issue in these micro-cellular networks are user handoffs. Mobile location deals with the process of finding the current location of the mobile user (MU) for the delivery of the call. Also required, as the networks themselves evolve, are more intelligent system management. Additionally cell sizes will decrease, resulting in Micro-cells in urban areas and Pico-cells within buildings and campuses. Mobile IP represents a simple and scalable global mobility that is optimised for macro-level ability and relatively slow moving hosts. Cellular IP (CIP) is known as a local mobility protocol. It uses some basic principles of cellular systems such as mobility management, passive connectivity and handoff support but also allows routing IP datagrams to a mobile host. The CIP networks are linked using Mobile IP. Mobile IP is optimized for what is known as 'macro-level mobility 'where slow moving mobile hosts do not need to migrate often. Conversely Mobile IP does not work well in small geographic areas where the hosts migrate frequently. CIP provides fast and smooth handoffs within restricted geographic areas e.g. a LAN. The CIP architecture relies on this separation of local mobility from wide area network mobility. This chapter provides an overview of Mobile IP and Cellular IP.

Introduction

In today's wireless environment people expect to be always connected, using mobile phones, PDA's or other digital mobile devices. An increase in multimedia applications for these portable devices means providing seamless mobility has become a critical issue. Seamless mobility is the ability of the network to support fast handoffs between base stations, with low latency and minimum or zero packet loss. Mobility itself can be categorised as either micro-mobility or macro-mobility (Campbell et al, 1999). In a Wireless LAN (WLAN) micro-mobility is defined as mobile nodes moving within an IP domain while keeping connected with the network during an ongoing session. Macro-mobility is defined as mobile nodes moving between IP domains while keeping connected with the network during an ongoing session (Li, 2004).

Mobile IP, which is a standard communications protocol designed by the Internet Engineering Task Force (IETF), is optimized for macro-mobility and slow moving hosts. It was created to allow users to retain the same IP address even when moving to a different network. So Mobile IP is an extension to the Internet Protocol and makes mobility transparent to higher level protocols like Transmission Control Protocol (TCP) (Perkins, 2002). It allows a mobile host (MH), to maintain the communication with another wired or wireless host, called a remote host (RH), even when moving and passing by different base stations belonging to diverse WLANs (Palazzi et al, 2007). However at a micro-mobility level and with fast moving hosts, problems exist. These include registration delay and handoff latency (Campbell, 2000). Providing fast and reliable handoffs is a major obstacle to enabling seamless micro-mobility in wireless access networks (Nurvitadhi et al, 2005). This chapter provides an overview of Mobile IP.

Being able to achieve network access anywhere, anytime, is driving the demand for wireless access. Cellular technology is the foundation of mobile wireless communication and facilitates a whole range of devices such mobile phones, PDAs, PCs scanning the airwaves for the best possible method of connectivity. As described by Forouzan (2004), the components of a cellular system consist of mobile stations (MSs), a mobile switching centre (MSC) and a base transceiver station or base station (BS). The mobile unit communicates with the MSC via the base station, and each hexagonal cell has one base station (a hexagonal pattern provides for equidistant antennas within the cells unlike a square cell would provide). The network provides communications between one mobile unit (MS) and another (MS) or between one mobile unit and one stationary unit (wired). Each cellular service transmits voice or data by radio frequencies. The service area is divided into cells each served by a transmitter and each cell is allocated a set of frequencies. The transmitters operate in a low power range, in the order of 100watts or smaller. This helps prevent interference or crosstalk in adjacent cells. The cells are connected to the mobile switching centre which is connected to a worldwide network, e.g. Internet/ telephone network (Figure 1). The service provider must be able to locate and track a caller, assign a channel to the call, and transfer the channel from base station to base station as the caller moves out of range (Forouzan, 2004).

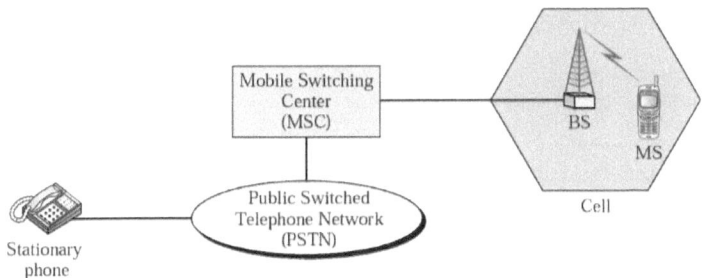

Figure 93: Cellular systems (Forouzan, 2004)

The number and size of cells within a service providers area is dependent on the population density of the area. Therefore an area with a high population requires a large number of smaller cells whereas an area with a sparse population only requires a smaller number of larger cells. Multiple frequency bands are assigned to a given cell. But neighbouring cells should not use the same set of frequencies for communication because this can cause interference between the cells. The set of frequencies available are limited and so need to be reused. So a solution would be to use the same frequency band in multiple cells which are at some distance from one another thus reducing the possibility of interference. When a mobile unit moves out of the range of one cell and into the range of another during a connection, the traffic channel has to change to the one assigned to the base station in the new cell (Forouzan, 2004). Handoff may be network initiated or mobile initiated. Either way network/mobile measurements of the received signal and also different performance metrics determine whether a handoff should occur. Usually if the signal strength from one base station to the mobile unit becomes weak, then the mobile unit will look for a base station with a stronger signal and trigger a handoff.

IEEE 802.11 (WiFi)

IEEE has defined the specifications for a wireless LAN, called IEEE 802.11, which covers the physical and data link layers. The demand for WLANs, at different frequencies and data rates, has exploded. Therefore the IEEE 802.11 working group has issued an ever expanding list of standards. WLANs are generally categorised according to the transmission technique that is used. All current wireless LAN products fall into one of the following categories:

- Spread spectrum LANs: In most cases these LANs operate in the Industrial, Scientific and Medical (ISM)) bands so that no Federal Communications Commission (FCC) licensing is required. Spread spectrum techniques will be discussed later.

- Infrared LAN (IR): Infrared cannot penetrate walls so a cell in this case is contained within one room.

Currently the most popular type of wireless LAN uses spread spectrum techniques (Stallings, 2007). Spread spectrum is a form of encoding for wireless communications. The idea of spread spectrum is to modulate the signal and therefore increase the bandwidth (spread the spectrum) of the signal being sent (Stallings, 2007). Spread spectrum was developed by the military because the wide spreading of the signal made it difficult to detect and jam, so this improved the security of the signal. On spread spectrum networks, channels can be reused without causing interference in adjacent cells because different Pseudorandom Number (PN) codes are used in each cell site. The three basic types of spread spectrum techniques according to Stallings are:

- **Frequency Hopping Spread Spectrum**
  Frequency Hopping Spread Spectrum (FHSS) is the oldest of the spread spectrum techniques. The sender transmits at one carrier frequency for a short period of time, and then hops to another carrier

frequency for the same amount of time and so on. After N hops the cycle is repeated. This random pattern of hops between frequencies is known only to the transmitter and receiver. The FHSS operates at 2.4 GHz ISM band. If a large number of hopping channels are required then this will increase the required bandwidth. If the bandwidth required by the original signal is b then the required spread spectrum bandwidth becomes Nxb.

- **Direct Sequence Spread Spectrum**
  Direct sequence spread spectrum (DSSS) is used in most of the latest systems e.g. 802.11b WLANs. Each data bit in the original signal is represented by multiple bits in the transmitted signal. DSSS multiples the data bit by a pseudorandom bit pattern which spreads the data into a large coded stream. If an 11 bit spreading code is used then this will spread the signal over a frequency band which is 11x times greater than a 1 bit spreading code. DSSS requires greater bandwidth than FHSS but provides good performance and reliability. DSSS operates in 2.4 GHz ISM band.

- **Code Division Multiple Access**
  Code Division Multiple Access (CDMA) is a multiple access method in which one channel carries all transmissions simultaneously. It enables multiple users to use the same bandwidth with very little interference.

IEEE 802.11 uses a collision avoidance technique rather than the collision detection method, carrier sense multiple access with collision detection (CSMA/CD) used in wired Ethernet LANs. Carrier sense multiple access with collision avoidance (CSMA/CA) waits for an acknowledgement from the other end to determine whether the packet was sent properly. Collisions need to be avoided on wireless networks as it is difficult to detect them. CSMA/CA avoids collisions by having all nodes signal their intention to transmit before transmitting. If two nodes send intentions to transmit messages at the same time, both nodes wait for a random amount of time before trying again (Lillian, 2006). Because the protocol waits for acknowledgements the throughput is affected, so the expected speeds are often quite a bit lower. Also the speed of a WLAN is determined by the distance of the remote device from the wireless access point.

IEEE 802.11 allows for two modes, the ad hoc and the infrastructure mode. The Basic Service Set (BSS) is the building block of a wireless LAN. The ad hoc architecture has no access point (AP), which is a base station in a BSS. The devices communicate with each other on a peer to peer basis and agree to be part of a BSS. There are two types of BSSs (Figure 2). The first is a stand alone or ad hoc network. The second type has an AP or base station. The AP is equipped with an antenna and provides access to a wired LAN and the internet.

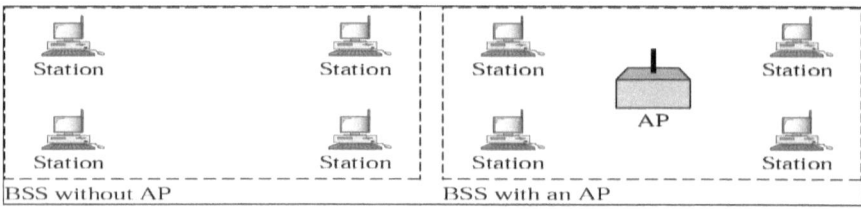

Figure 94: Basic Service Set (BSS) (Forouzan, 2004)

Another type of service set is called the Extended Service Set (ESS). In this case the BSSs are connected in the Infrastructure mode (Figure 3). An ESS is made up of several BSSs and APs. The access points and therefore the BSSs are connected to each other through a wired LAN. Communication between mobile stations can be done within the BSS without the access point. But if two mobile devices residing in different BSSs wish to communicate then this is usually done through the access points in the two BSSs. Comparing this set up with a cellular network the AP is acting as the base station and the range of the BSS is acting as a cell. The wired LAN is known as the distribution system.

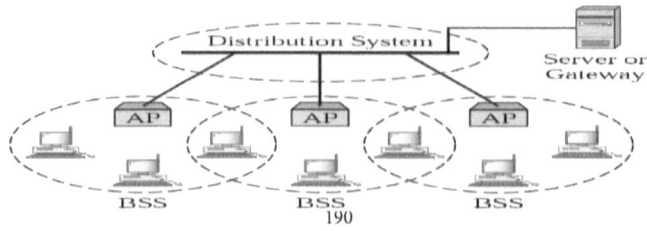

Figure 95: Distribution System (Forouzan, 2004)

Usually within a large WLAN a number of access points are used with overlap of their cells. This permits roaming between the cells and the percentage of overlap affects the handoff quality within the LAN. Because of this overlap a mobile device can belong to more than one   BSS   simultaneously.   Access   points   with overlapping coverage areas operate on different frequency channels to avoid interference between their cells or BSSs (Forouzan, 2004).

Handover Procedure

There are three types of frames defined by IEEE 802.11 which are management frames, control frames and data frames. Management frames are used for the communication between access points and mobile stations, whereas control frames are used for acknowledgement and access onto the channel. Three types of control frames are the clear to send (CTS), request to send (RTS) and acknowledgement (ACK) frames, used in the handshaking period. Basic transfer of data in IEEE 802.11 includes these frames. The first frame used is a RTS frame sent from the source to the destination and the destination then responds with a CTS frame. Once the source receives the CTS frame the data frame is transmitted and the destination responds with an ACK frame. To help avoid collisions the RTS frame also alerts stations within the source's range that data transfer is in process. The CTS frame also alerts stations within the destination's range that data transfer is in progress. This process involving control frames for data transfer helps prevent collisions but increases the latency of the transfer. There are two logical steps in a handoff, the discovery step and then the reauthentication step.

If a mobile station experiences degradation of the signal from the access point it is associated with, it will begin to search for an AP with a better quality signal to associate to. This is known as scanning, which can be active or passive. Passive scanning occurs when mobile devices listen to beacon frames sent by the APs (beacon signals are sent out periodically at a rate of 10ms). If the mobile device receives a beacon that contains the service set identifier (SSID) of the network it is trying to join, then an attempt is made to join the network. SSID is a label that distinguishes one wireless LAN from another. In active scanning as well as listening to beacon packets the mobile host sends probe broadcast packets with the SSID of the network it wishes to join. Then an AP with the correct SSID will send a probe response (Anuresh et al, 2002). So the mobile host actively probes for APs. The reauthentication step involves the transfer of credentials from the old AP to the new AP. This can be achieved using a protocol such as Inter Access Point Protocol (IAPP). Next is a detailed description of the IEEE802.11 handoff procedure followed by most network interface (NIC) cards (Vatn et al, 2003).

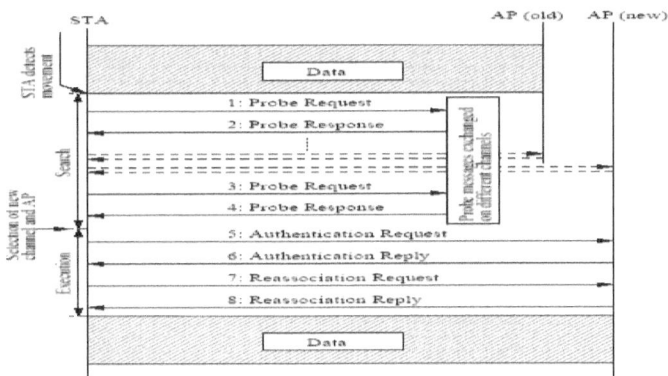

Figure 96: Handover Procedure (Vatn, 2003)

Figure 4 shows the sequence of messages typically observed during a handoff process. The handoff process starts with the first probe request message and ends with a reassociation response message from an AP. We divide the entire handoff latency into three delays which is detailed below.

1. **Probe Delay** - Messages 1 to 4 are the probe messages from an active scan. Consequently we call the latency for this process, probe delay. The actual number of messages during the probe process may vary from 3 to 11.

2. **Authentication Delay** - This is the latency incurred during the exchange of the authentication frames (messages 5 and 6). Authentication consists of two or four consecutive frames depending on the authentication used by the AP. Some wireless network interface cards (NICs) try to initiate reassociation prior to authentication, which introduces an additional delay in the handoff process and is also a violation of the IEEE 802.11 state machine.

2. **Reassociation Delay** - This is the latency incurred during the exchange of the reassociation frames (messages 7 and 8). Upon successful authentication process, the station sends a reassociation request frame to the AP and receives a reassociation response frame and completes the handoff. Future implementations will include additional IAPP messages during this phase which will further increase the reassociation delay.

Mobile IP

Mobile IP is used most often in wireless WAN environments, where users need to carry their mobile phone devices across multiple LANs with different IP addresses. So it is optimised for a macro-level approach in comparison with Cellular IP which is optimised for a micro-level approach. Mobile IP is a standard communications protocol designed by the Internet Engineering Task Force, (IETF). It is designed to allow mobile device users to move from one network to another while maintaining a permanent IP address. So MIP allows a mobile host (MH) to maintain the communication with another wired or wireless host, called remote host (RH), even when moving or passing by different base stations and still maintain a permanent IP address (Perkins, 2002). The internet is built on top of a collection of protocols called the TCP/IP protocol suite. IP requires the location of any host connected to the internet to be uniquely identified by an assigned IP address. To understand how Mobile IP works, the structure of an IP packet must be examined. An IP address is a 32-bit binary number (Figure 97). The first part of an IP address identifies the network, on which the host resides, while the second part identifies the particular host on the given network. This creates a two-level addressing hierarchy. The destination address is read by routers to determine the next hop.

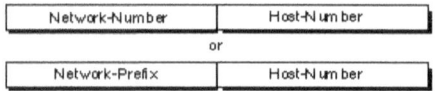

Figure 97: Two-Level Internet Address Structure (www.cisco.com)

Mobile IP allows each host to have two IP addresses, a permanent home address and a care of address (COA). The permanent home address is assigned at the home network and is used to identify communication end points. The temporary COA address is associated with the network the mobile node is visiting. The aim is to make mobility transparent to upper level protocols (Figure 98).

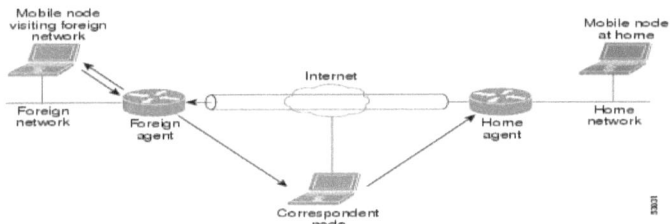

Figure 98: Diagram of Mobile IP[1]

There are two types of mobility agents which essentially are specialised routers, used to transparently bind the home address of the mobile node with its COA. They are called home agents (HAs) and foreign agents (FAs). A home agent stores information about mobile nodes whose permanent address is in the home agent's network. This information is stored in a mobility binding table, an example of which is in Table 6.

Home Address	Care-of –address (COA)	Lifetime (secs)
190.128.154.5	130.173.5.3	140
190.128.154.8	110.45.67.3	250

Table 6: Mobility Binding Table for home agent 190.128.67.36

The entries include the permanent home address, temporary COA and association lifetime. The table maps a mobile nodes home address with its COA and hence can forward packets. A foreign agent (FA) stores information about mobile nodes which are visiting its network. The FA maintains a visitors list, an example of which is shown in Table 7.

Home Address	Home Agent Address	Media Address	Lifetime (secs)
190.128.154.5	190.128.67.36	00-11-43-08-07-6F	140
156.37.29.134	135.49.23.89	00-03-BA-26-01-B0	250

Table 7: Visitor List for Foreign Agent 130.173.5.3

Entries include the mobile node's permanent home address, the home agent address, media access control address (MAC) and association lifetime. Usually the COA of the mobile nodes is the FA's IP address but not always. Sometimes another COA address called a co-located COA is used. This co-located COA is acquired by the mobile node locally by some external method e.g. Dynamic Host Configuration Protocol (DHCP). In this case the end point is the mobile node and not the FA. The advantage of this method is that the mobile node can function without a FA (Ghosh, 2000).

Operation of Mobile IP

The basic steps for the operation of Mobile IP are Mobile Agents Advertisements, registration and movement of nodes between networks. Mobility Agents advertise their presence using Agent Advertisements Messages (AAM), which are broadcast periodically (beacons). These advertisements agents contain a list of COAs. Once a mobile node receives an AAM it can determine whether it is on the home network or a foreign network. The

---

[1] www.cisco.com

mobile node as well as receiving and responding to these beacons can also send out an Agent Solicitation Message which the mobility agent will respond to.

A mobile node that determines it is on its home network does not require any mobility services. If the mobile node returns to its home network after it was registered to a foreign network, it will deregister by sending its home agent a registration request and receive a registration reply from the HA. If a mobile node discovers it is on a foreign network, it registers with the FA by sending a registration request message. In this message will be the mobile nodes permanent IP address and the IP address of the HA. The FA will then send a registration request to the HA, containing the mobile node's permanent IP address and the IP address of the FA. The HA then updates its mobility binding table, associating the COA of the mobile node with its home address. The home agent then sends an acknowledgement to the FA. The FA will also update its visitors list with the entry for the mobile node and relays a reply to the mobile node (Figure 7).

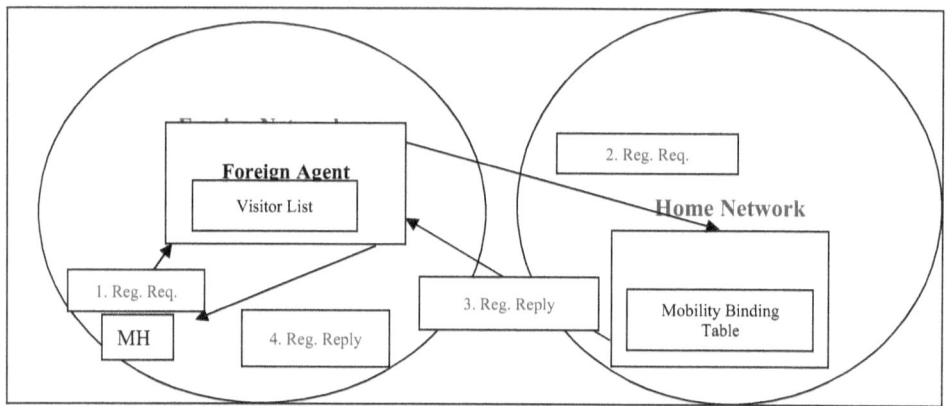

Figure 99: Registration process in Mobile IP

Datagrams destined to the mobile node's home address are intercepted by the HA, which consults its mobility binding table to determine if the mobile host is visiting any other network. If the mobile node is on another network the HA uses the mobile node's COA. It then constructs a new IP header with the COA as the destination IP address. The original IP packet is encapsulated into another IP packet, known as IP- within -IP encapsulation or tunnelling. The encapsulated packet reaches the foreign network where the mobile node is currently residing. The FA decapsulates the packet and finds the mobile nodes home address. The visiting list is consulted to see if any entry for this mobile node exists, if an entry exits then the datagram is delivered to the mobile node. If the mobile node wants to send a message (reverse direction), the datagram is sent to the FA, which uses standard IP routing. In the mobility binding table and the visiting list table there exists the lifetime for each mapping. So if a mobile node wants to continue being serviced by a FA, it must reissue the registration request. If a mobile node wants to drop its current COA then it sends a registration request with the lifetime set to zero to its home agent. One problem exists however, if the mobile node has moved to another foreign network, the old foreign network does not know its new COA. So any datagrams already forwarded by the HA to the old FA will be lost (Perkins, 2002).

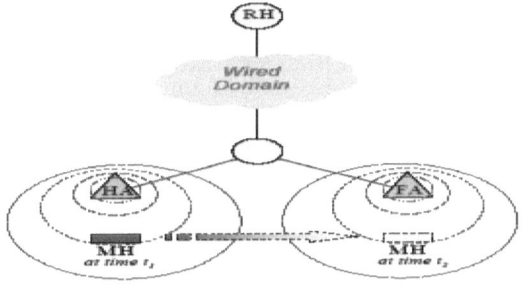

Figure 100: Simplified handoff in Mobile IP (Palazzi, 2007)

Looking at a simple handover procedure as shown in Figure 100, the Mobile Host (MH) is initially registered with it's HA and so packets from the Remote Host (RH) will simply pass through the wired domain to the HA and onto the MH. But if the MH moves towards the FA the MH may decide to switch association. If the MH decides to switch to a new agent FA, this is achieved using tunnelling. So packets destined to the MH from the RH will continue to route through the HA, which will then pass the packets to the FA and finally to the mobile node. The data packet is encapsulated by the HA and decapsulated by the FA. If now the MH wishes to send a packet to the RH this is done simply by sending the packet to the FA and directly through the wired domain to the RH (Palazzi, 2007).

Cellular IP

Cellular IP specifies a protocol that allows routing IP datagrams to a mobile host. The protocol is intended to provide local mobility and handoff support. It can internetwork with Mobile IP to provide wide area mobility support. Cellular IP is known as a local mobility protocol. It uses some basic principles of cellular systems such as mobility management, passive connectivity and handoff support but also allows routing IP datagrams to a mobile host. The CIP networks are linked using Mobile IP. Mobile IP is optimized for what is known as 'macro-level mobility 'where slow moving mobile hosts do not need to migrate often. Conversely Mobile IP does not work well in small geographic areas where the hosts migrate frequently. CIP provides fast and smooth handoffs within restricted geographic areas e.g. a LAN. The CIP architecture relies on this separation of local mobility from wide area network mobility (Valko, 1999).

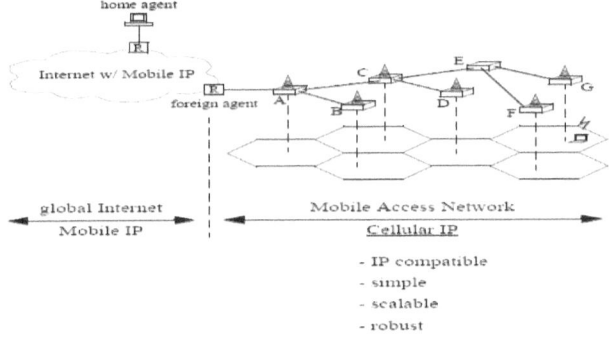

Figure 101: Mobile IP (Valko, 1999)

CIP therefore provides micro-mobility within a LAN supported and interworking with Mobile IP for macro-mobility between the CIP wireless access networks (Figure 102). In Mobile IP after each migration a local address must be obtained and communicated to a distant home agent. But CIP uses a distributed database where location information is obtained from the mobile hosts. This reduces network overhead such as increased delay, packet loss and significantly less signaling is required. Hence CIP handles local movement of mobile hosts without interaction with the Mobile IP enabled internet (Campbell, 2002).

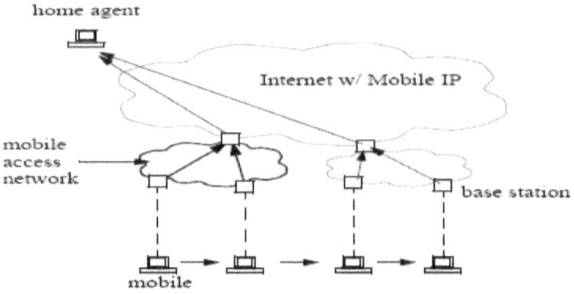

Figure 102: Mobile Access Network (Valko, 1999)

The primary role of micro mobility protocols is to ensure that packets arriving from the internet and addressed to mobile hosts are forwarded to the appropriate wireless access point in an efficient manner. To do this micro mobility protocols maintain a location database that maps mobile host identifiers to location information (Campbell, 2002). Hence CIP maintains distributed caches for location management and routing purposes.

Handoffs within CIP Protocol

Packets routed in a CIP network use a shortest path hop-by-hop algorithm. Cellular IP supports two types of handoff techniques, hard handoffs and semi-soft handoffs. A handoff is where a mobile host moves out of range of one cell and into the range of another during a connection. The traffic channel then has to change to the one assigned to the base station in the new cell. Handoffs are initiated by mobile hosts in CIP, so a change of access point during connectivity is typically called a handoff. A hard handoff is a fast and simple handoff where potentially some packets may be lost. It is not suited to real time applications. Mobile hosts listen to beacons transmitted by base stations and initiate a handoff based on the signal strength from the base stations. So when an active host approaches a new base station and wants to perform a handoff it must tune its radio to the new base station and send a route-update packet. This creates route cache mapping on route to the CIP Gateway and it follows that a downlink route is created to the new base station. But this type of handoff means a rough transition from the old base station to the new base station. The mobile host has switched in one step, all at once to the new base station. This opens up the possibility of packet loss since any packets travelling on the old path to the old base station will be lost (http://www.comet.columbia.edu/cellularip). Handoff latency is the time that elapses between the handoff and the arrival of the first packet through the new route.

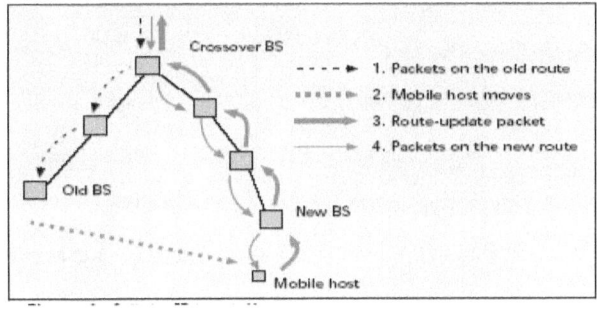

Figure 103: Handoff in Cellular IP (Campbell, 2000)

This is equal to the round trip time from the mobile host to the crossover point, i.e. where the old path and new path meet. To help prevent loss of packets and hence improve performance of the handover procedure there is the second type of handoff called semi soft handoff. In this handoff an active host can communicate between two base stations at the same time. During a semi soft handoff a mobile host can set up routing to the new base station while still in contact with the old base station.

Packets that are now transmitting to the mobile host take two paths, the old path to the old base station and the new path to the new base station. When handoff takes place the route to the new path has been established and packets are already following this route so this will reduce packet loss. To stop packets continuing to the old base station a normal route update packet is sent to the crossover base station. This packet will clear any mapping to the old base station and the remaining mappings will point only to the new base station. But some packets may still be lost if the path to the new base station is longer than to the old base station, or if the switching time to the new base station is extremely small. To help prevent this, packets that are being sent to the new base station can be delayed during the handoff process. Duplication of packets to the mobile host may occur but this is preferable to packet loss which would definitely degrade the performance of the throughput (Nurvitadhi, 2007).

References

Campbell, A., Gomez, J., Wan, C., Turanyi, Z., Valko, A. (1999) Cellular IP, October, 1999)

Campbell, A., Gomez, J., Wan, C., Turanyi, Z., Valko, A (2002), Comparison of IP Micromobility Protocols, February, 2002

Campbell, A., Gomez, J., Wan, C., Turanyi, Z., Valko, A, Kim, S. (2000), Design, Implementation and Evaluation of Cellular IP, August, 2000

Fengping Li, (2004) A study of mobility in WLANs, Helsinki University of Technology, Telecommunication Software and Multimedia Laboratory

Forouzan, B. (2007) Data Communications and Networking, 4th Edition, Publisher Mc Graw Hill

Ghosh, D. (2006) Mobile IP (http://www.acm.org)

Goleniewski, L. (2006) "Telecommunications Essentials" 2nd Edition, Publisher Addison Wesley

Mishra, A. (2002) An empirical analysis of the IEEE 802.11 MAC layer handoff process, University of Maryland Technical Report, UMIACS-TR-2002-75, 2002

Nurvitadhi, E. (2005) "Adaptive Semi-Soft Handoff for Cellular IP Networks" Vol. 1 Issue 4

NS-2, (http://www.isi.edu/nsnam/ns/)

Perkins, C. (2002) IP Mobility Support for IPv4

Palazzi, C. (2007) High Mobility in a Realistic Wireless Environment: a Mobile IP Handoff Model for NS-2,

Stallings, W. (2007) "Data and Computer Communications" 8th Edition, Publisher Pearson Prentice Hall

Valko, A. (1999) Cellular IP – A New Approach to Internet Host Mobility, January 1999

Vatn, J., (2003), An experimental study of IEEE 802.11b handover performance and its effect on voice traffic.

29   Adaptive Mobile Applications

Conrad Deighan, Joan Condell, Kevin Curran

The area of computing incorporates a vast range of devices with different capabilities in terms of battery life, network connectivity, processing power and disk management. An endless battery life and flawless connectivity to multiple wireless access points are increasingly essential for the mobile device user. Nevertheless the battery life and the capability of being able to connect to wireless networks will fluctuate greatly between each device. Portable multimedia devices such as Personal Digital Assistants (PDA's) and Smartphones with restricted memory will also vary greatly; however, users of these devices will expect optimal multimedia delivery. Therefore there is a need an intelligent middleware application that will take a critical role for the coordination between the devices hardware and software so that the user can get the full potential from the device. This chapter outlines the quest to provide mobile devices with the abiltity to detect and respond appropriately to changes in network connectivity, network connection quality and power consumption.

Introduction

Mobile devices such as Ultra Mobile Personal Computer's (UMPC's), laptops, Personal Digital Assistants (PDA's) and Smartphones are becoming an increasingly frequent element of any IT orientated business. Business users need their applications to work just as well while on the road as they do when they are within the office. This means that developers of mobile applications face complex tasks of extending existing or developing a new range of mobile applications that target multiple platforms to meet the requirements of the users in the mobile environment (Vick, 2007). The Intel Mobile SDK is an open source library which enables the creation of context aware applications by taking advantage of the mobile features on Ultra Mobile Personal Computers (UMPCs), notebooks and Personal Digital Assistants (PDA's). In addition it also allows the creation of applications with the platform and the environment in mind by leveraging information about the platform's configuration and context. This means that developers can provide more expressive interactions and better user experience for applications, especially on mobile platforms where intermittent connectivity and limited power are common issues. For instance, if applications could be aware of the platform they are running on and the environment, then they could leverage multi-core power to provide more immersive user interfaces, postpone certain tasks during low power situations, avoid network traffic over low bandwidth/high latency connections and delay saving files back to network drives while not connected to the network.

Currently there are various versions of media player available for consumer use, on both mobile and PC based environments. Popular media players include Windows Media Player, QuickTime and Real Player. Although these media players carry out their intended functionality; playing audio and video, they lack the ability of being aware of their context. For example, they will not have the ability to inform the user if they try to retrieve a media file from an unavailable location or if they have disconnected from the power supply. The mobile environment has very limited resources compared to the traditional desktop computing environment. Applications for mobile devices have lacked innovation due to the fact that the device in which they are installed has strict limitations in terms of memory capacity, processing power and battery power compared to the desktop computer. The screen size aspect is a very challenging area for developers as most devices vary in size therefore resulting in the need of an application being re-designed and re-coded to suit the target device. Most mobile users will use their device frequently but only for a brief amount of time and will have a different usage paradigm i.e. for input, output, e-mail and calendar scheduling. Mobile applications must be dynamic and adapt to changes in environment in which they exist. Meaning the application must be self organising and able to accommodate new sets of requirements and functionality when it is deployed in the context that it will exist. Mobile device users are expecting much more as technology increases. Instead of them dealing with the device working for a limited time scale in restricted environments, users are now expecting developers to come up with applications that will enable them to:

> Manage connections
> Balance power and performance
> Work offline
> Work across multiple platforms

Users want their connections managed transparently where their main focal point is the task in hand without having to worry about managing a connection to one or more networks. They expect to get optimal performance from their available battery life while there is no available power source. When they are out of the range from a network or server they want to be able to locally store their data and information so they can continue to work with clients and then synchronize their data with the server when they re-connect to the network (Vick, 2007).Working across multiple platforms is essential for users as then they can choose a device that suits them rather than having to use a device that they are unfamiliar with just because it has the relevant software installed on it (ISN, 2005). When developers are either creating or extending mobile applications they face two important obstacles:

> Creating applications that are aware of platform context and resources that can efficiently adapt when changes occur. This is a new paradigm, and not well supported by current software solutions.
> Developing cross-platform and runtime solutions to enable applications to be deployed over multiple clients is challenging, given that there is no standard way to implement this functionality across a wide range of mobile devices.

Unfortunately it is not as simple as that, as most people do not take into consideration the fact that the three devices use different software and have different screen sizes. Here developers run into problems as they need to change a great deal of code to transfer from one device to another device. Therefore if there was a method for developing software that is aware of which device that it is being implemented on, then the re-design and re-coding process would be made significantly easier. The application would know how to adapt to the environment on which it has been implemented. Each mobile phone, PDA or Smartphone that is available to consumers has an emulator released so that applications can be developed for that device. So in order to develop a mobile application, the developer has to design and code each application to target each emulator's specification. This means developers needing a common development interface with consistent naming criteria; parameters and object model so that developers can minimize extensive re-coding in order to get an application operational on a range of devices.

Heterogeneity is a major problem for developers developing any type of application regardless of whether it is for the mobile or desktop environment. For example, if an application was developed on a Windows platform; there could be runtime and compatibility issues if deployed into a Linux based environment. The interoperability of current devices is largely untapped due to the fact that heterogeneity exists. This means that devices with different contexts cannot operate and communicate effectively and efficiently with each other. In order for these devices to interoperate with each other, developers must come up with a solution that will make this possible. A middleware layer primarily hides the underlying complexity of the environment by insulating the applications from explicit protocol handling, disjoint memories, data replication, network faults, and parallelism. Moreover, it masks the heterogeneity of computer architectures, operating systems, programming languages, and networking technologies to facilitate application programming and management (Bernstein, 1996). Currently there are several middleware projects such as Gaia [Roman, 2002], M3 System (BEA, 1998) and Aura (Harkes, 2000) for efficient ubiquitous computing. The Gaia project aims to aid humans by making physical spaces like homes and buildings intelligent. The M3 system uses a component-based modelling paradigm and employs an event-based mechanism that provides significant flexibility in dynamic system configuration and adaptation. The Aura project aims to provide the user with a distraction-free computing environment and minimize intrusion of systems. CORBA (Common Object Request Broker Architecture) enables applications to dynamically select the components that best met their requirements and to verify that the requirements are appropriate for the services that are in use. CORBA is a trading service to support dynamic component selection. An extensive monitoring facility within CORBA supports the use of dynamically defined requirements.

The fact that a mobile device must be aware of its power and network connectivity status is no secret to developers and users of these devices. This chapter documents an adaptable middleware architecture which allows high flexibility by probing a platform's configuration, e.g. display, storage, processor, and the platform's context, e.g. bandwidth, connectivity, power and location, etc. within a mobile application. A challenge in distributed system design is to cope with the dynamic nature of the execution environment. We present a model-driven development approach for adaptive component-based applications running on mobile devices. The aim is to use the Intel Mobile Platform SDK to develop a context aware mobile media player application which will know how to adapt to platform state changes. If mobile applications could be aware of the platform they are running on and the environment they exist within then they could detect and respond appropriately to changes in network connectivity, network connection quality and power consumption optimization and then gracefully handle intermittent connectivity. We combat heterogeneity by incorporating specific runtimes and libraries from the Intel Mobile Platform SDK into applications to make them aware of their context. Middleware applications stress modularity which encourages decoupling of applications into modules. By incorporating these runtime and libraries into mobile applications it will still enable them to have a minimal footprint and lightweight on system resources, which is a must, if they are to be implemented onto PDA's and Smart Phones.

Dynamic Mobile Applications

We have become accustomed with a computation model in which applications require only a single or a small number of devices. One distinct characteristic of ubiquitous computing, however, is the attempt to break away from the traditional desktop interaction paradigm, making computational power available to the end-user whenever and wherever possible. Furthermore, ubiquitous computing involves a wide range of devices of different capabilities in terms of processing power, screen display, input facilities, middleware, and network connectivity of various wired and wireless links. Among them, middleware takes a crucial role which consists of remote procedure call, file service, and directory service reflecting dramatic advances in hardware technology, fast networking, and workstation systems. A middleware layer primarily hides the underlying sophistication of the environment by insulating the applications. Recently, applications (desktop and web based) have been moving from the static environment to a more dynamic adaptive application. An adaptive application has the ability to predict changes in context and automatically handle these changes in a runtime environment without the need for a programmer. It would be classed as a component based middleware, where the middleware can re-organise components by insulating the application. Non-adaptive software can also be described as 'fragile', if it is used outside the context in which it was developed. One of the key implications with developing software is that it can be an expensive and a time consuming process. This is the main objective behind dynamic applications - that the software can adapt to the non-functional requirements properties of their components and their execution environment. With this objective being met, it can result in the re-use of an application and not require a time consuming re-write to meet a new set of requirements.

If an application has not been specifically designed for the mobile environment the mobile user may be disappointed. An example of this would be excessive necessary power that the system needs when running on a battery power source. Therefore this will decrease the length of time that a user can use their device in between battery charges. Another example is long running or power-hungry operations such as writing to a CD or DVD when the power is at a low level. By using intelligent adaptation in applications, we could for instance, suspend non-critical operations or processes whenever the device is running on a battery power supply. The main problem with applications is that they are not developed to save system power and suspend non-critical processes when running on battery power and then continue the operation when the device is connected to an AC power supply. In order to add this functionality into the application without asking the operating system for power connection status we need to by-pass the operating system.

Managing resources such as runtime and platform state changes is vital on mobile devices. Therefore we need to efficiently manage these resources and adapt applications to act on these changes. With the use of some kind of intelligent middleware these programs can become aware of their context and adapt gracefully to the change. For example, if a mobile application was developed specifically for a mobile device then in order to get the application fully functional on other devices there would be a need for re-coding of the application. The need for re-designing and re-coding of the application would be necessary as these two devices are not similar in terms of screen size, memory size, processing speed and battery power. This would result in the user not getting the full functionality and potential from the application. This is why developers need to access information regarding the target device so that it can gracefully adapt to the context of the device. Developers need a common environment to develop applications that can self-manage and adapt effectively to changes in platform context and take advantage of the capabilities of the runtime platform.

Screen size can vary from device to device therefore if mobile applications are not aware of which device that they are going to be deployed on; then the user's application may end up unusable due to the fact that the application does not complement the display of the target device. Incorporating tools from the Intel Mobile

SDK will enable an application to retrieve the target device's screen information, process that information and then adapt the application to meet that size of display (ISN, 2007).

Modern day mobile systems such as laptops and UMPCs are equipped with multi-core processors. This means processing power has been doubled, so in turn we need applications taking advantage of the extra cores. This is why developers would need to access information regarding the processor of the target device so that the application can adapt to the processor that is available (i.e. single core, dual core and quad core). With the use of an intelligent middleware between device and application, it can redesign the application to take advantage of the extra available cores. For example, if an application was developed for a single core processor and then deployed onto a multi-core processing device, it would only take advantage of one of the available cores. This is when the middleware would redesign the application and take advantage of the multiple cores and result in processing time being decreased.

There is also a need for applications to be designed specifically for the mobile environment as most mobile applications require a steady connection to remote resources to access information. This is where there is a clear need for network connections to be managed seamlessly. If applications are not designed for the mobile world then the user will have a very tedious task at hand as they must manually manage their network connections in order for their application to run. Some applications may require a 'restart' in order to become functional again if these connections are not managed.

The middleware application of Gaia (Roman, 2002) was developed to manage network communication connections within active and physical spaces. Gaia is a distributed middleware infrastructure that coordinates software entities and heterogeneous networked devices contained within physical spaces. The main aims and objectives of the Gaia (a meta-operating system) middleware are to maintain the development and execution of mobile applications for active spaces. For example, if a boardroom was hosting a presentation where it had different guest speakers with their own mobile devices running on different platforms attempting to connect to either audio or visual devices, there could be communication problems due to the fact that heterogeneity is present. If the application within the boardroom has been developed with the Gaia Application Framework then there will be no problem with a user who wants to connect to the audio or visual aids.

SenSay (Siewiorek, 2001) and MIThrill (Devaul, 2001) are two projects that enable the mobile phone to determine the context in which it exists. This information can then be used to change and adapt the phone's behaviour to suit the user. Once the context of the phone is known there can be a predefined set of rules that can produce behaviour to the phone which can appear very intelligent. For example, a phone with the context awareness enabled could automatically switch profiles when a person enters the driving seat of a car, a chapel, restaurant or university.

SATIN (System Adaptation Targeting Integrated Networks) is a component based meta-model, a purposed built lightweight local component that gives flexibility for use of logical mobility to reconfigure software systems by dynamically transferring and changing code. A meta-model, in theory, is a model about a model; the meta-model is implemented into SATIN that can reconfigure both itself and applications that it hosts. SATIN was developed to experiment with concepts of Reflection and logical (software) mobility. Reflection enables application to observe and modify their structure and behaviours. The mobility of software allows SATIN applications to send, receive and process any part of an application i.e. objects, classes and components. This means that systems built with the underlying architecture of SATIN, regardless of runtime or platform, can communicate with each other. SATIN was built with Java 2 Micro Edition which facilitates implementation on handheld device such as PDA's and Laptops.

Energy-aware processors are now being manufactured tackling the problem of power consumption; these processors will be designed to consume much less power than what a normal processor would. Intel's XScale (IST, 2000) architecture has been designed to optimize on low power consumption; XScale has become a major building bock of Intel's PCA architecture. In addition to XScale architecture, SpeedStep is a technology that enables the processor to drop to a lower frequency and voltage while still maintaining a high level of performance, resulting in the conserving of battery life (Intel PCA, 2008). Software application techniques are becoming more significant for power management on mobile devices. Ellis (Ellis, 1999) states that the gains from a high level power management level are significant at the application level as well as at the operating system level. With the advancements of these energy-aware processors developers can enhance their applications to take advantage of the power saving techniques that are implemented into these processors. This will result in the hardware and software becoming power aware and giving a longer battery life to the mobile device.

Auto Switch is a newly developed network aware application that automatically disables the wireless card whenever you connect to a LAN (hard wire) connection, and re-enables the wireless card when there is no LAN connection present. This ensures the user is always using the fastest possible connection for network traffic. Within the office this will help reduce redundant network connections, while still helping employees seamlessly transfer from wired to wireless network connections. For offices that are wireless security conscious, this application ensures that the laptop's wireless card is off when the user is wired into your network (Sham, 2008).

Managing resources such as battery power, screen size, hard disk and connectivity is essential on mobile devices as most devices have different specifications to one another. This can result in the need for applications to be re-designed and re-coded to manage resources differently. Since mobile devices have certain limitations compared to the desktop PC, there is a need for their resources to be managed much more efficiently. This is where the application must monitor the resources and change state when necessary in order to get the full potential from the devices limitations. In order for more mobile applications to become aware of their context and available resources there must be some sort of active middleware to communicate efficiently between the application and the device. The Intel Mobile SDK is going to play a major role in the development of new applications as it can effectively manage and adapt applications where necessary.

Intel Mobile Software Development Kit (SDK)

The Intel Mobile Software Development Kit (SDK) version 1.2 is a free open source library which enables the development of applications which attempt to overcome the mobile features of mobile devices significantly easier. The Intel SDK is made up of multiple libraries and runtime components with a built in interface which is familiar to programmers across various supported platforms. Also, the Intel Mobile SDK would be similar to Object Orientated languages as the main aim of it is to maximise code reuse with the feature of mobility in mind. When developing applications for mobile devices, developers must take connectivity into consideration. In theory, users want 100% connectivity. Unfortunately in the real world this is un-realistic, therefore applications must have the ability to determine the current status of connectivity and make a decision based on the change in circumstances (Chabukswar, 2007).

The most significant feature of the Intel Mobile SDK is that it facilitates software functionality with mobile devices. Mobile device users expect their applications to adapt whenever they leave the office in order to get the same type of performance and power combined as they would whilst in the office. The effective balance of power and performance, the ability of working across multiple platforms, the adaptation of screen types and the capability of managing network connectivity and bandwidth within mobile devices and applications are major areas in which developers must tap into (ISN, 2007). This is why the Intel Mobile Platform will be a key development tool for developers - it provides them with the ability to manage these areas with minimal knowledge of the hardware architecture of mobile devices.

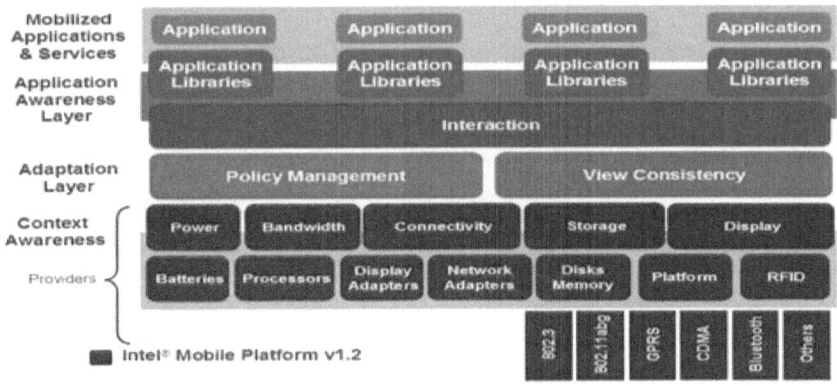

Figure 104: Overview of the Intel SDK[1]

Figure 104 demonstrates the Context Awareness area of the mobile device that Intel Mobile SDK provides and manages. The Intel Mobile Platform SDK supports the development of context aware mobile applications with the use a of multi-platform and multi runtime development kit. The Intel SDK supports three different object-orientated development languages: these are C++, C#.NET and Java. With the addition of the Intel Mobile SDK libraries incorporated into one of these development environments, developers have the ability to develop context-aware mobile applications without the burden of having to gain knowledge of a new development environment.

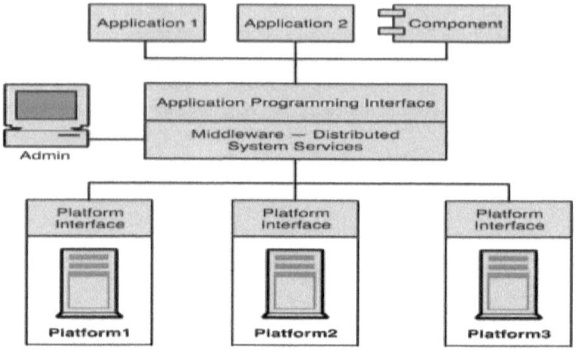

Figure 105: Use of Middleware[1]

Figure 105 demonstrates where the middleware layer is situated between the application programming interface and the platform interface so that applications can communicate with each platform's interface. With the availability of the Intel Mobile SDK developers can include an active middleware into a new range of applications to combat the heterogeneity aspects of the mobile environment. To run the Intel SDK system, laptops and UMPC's need additional software such as the .NET Framework and the Intel Mobile Platform SDK. PDA's and Smartphones will need the .NET Compact Framework and the Intel Mobile Platform SDK installed. There is generally a two-tier architecture approach to developing the system which identifies each layer with its own distinct properties and functionality.

➤ Client – Users will use the windows based application and be able to select from available media.

➤ Application – The middle layer will provide a service that will enable the mobile device to reach its full potential of battery life and connectivity status.

The Intel Mobile Media Player involved three main distinct areas of development:

     ➤ User interface
     ➤ Power monitor middleware
     ➤ Network monitor middleware

When the user initially loads the application the middleware layer does not become active until the user starts to view video clips or listens to audio. When the selection is confirmed and the media starts to play this is when middleware becomes active and constantly monitors the battery power and network connectivity status of the target machine. Figure 3 illustrates the system architecture of the Intel Mobile Media Player.

---

[1] softwarecommunity.intel.com/articles/eng/1164.htm

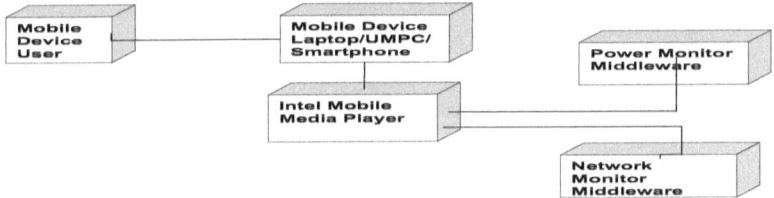

Figure 106: The Intel Mobile Media Player System Architecture

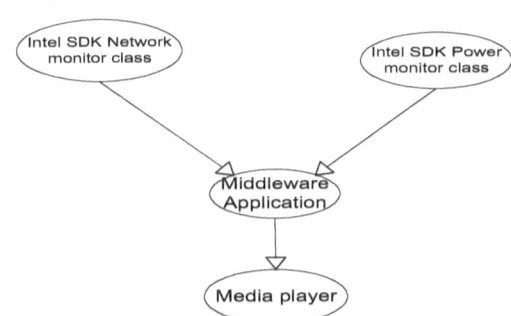

Figure 107: Middleware Application

Figure 106 shows the hierarchy of how the middleware application is implemented by incorporating the appropriate classes from the Intel Mobile SDK. The middleware aspect is made up of the Network Connectivity and Power Monitor classes. Figure 107 shows one key difference from standard media players which is the addition of the power and network status info box.

Conclusion

With the technology advancements in the world of computing, mobile devices are getting smaller, faster and more powerful; it is clear they are becoming increasingly popular. Consequently, resulting in a gap in the market for a new range of mobile applications - applications built with mobility as the main objective. Currently there are few development environments available in order to build this new range of applications needed for the mobile world. We documented here mainly the Intel Mobile SDK that can save power and dynamically allow applications to adapt themselves to seamlessly deal with the context in which they exist. Consequently if these features can be targeted and dealt with appropriately, then mobile devices can be just as powerful, if not more powerful in comparison to the traditional desktop computer. Applications on mobile platforms are becoming more popular and are being used more frequently used with mobile device users. However, if the applications are not correctly managed and aware of the environment in which they exist, then this can lead to problems where intermittent connectivity and power sources are limited to the user. In order for developers to resolve this problem they must use a common API which can monitor the device and applications so that it can address these problems and deal with them gracefully.

References

BEA, (1998). "BEA Begins Shipping BEA M3 Middleware on Schedule to Enterprise Customers Worldwide" http://www.bea.com/framework.jsp?CNT=pr00137.htm&FP=/content/news_events/press_releases/1998

Bernstein Philip A, (1996) "Middleware: A Model for Distributed Services." Communications of the ACM 39, 2 (February 1996): 86-97. 96 http://www.sei.cmu.edu/str/descriptions/middleware.html

Bhola, H S (1990), "Evaluating literacy for developing projects, programs and campaigns. http://www.sil.org/lingualinks/literacy/referencematerials/glossaryofliteracyterms/WhatIsFormativeEvaluation.htm

Bluetooth, (2007). "Get technical"   www.bluetooth.com

Bowman, B. (2002). "Making the Wireless Home Network Connection in Windows XP Without a Router" http://www.microsoft.com/windowsxp/using/networking/expert/bowman_02april08.mspx

Cameron, M. (2007). "2.7 billion Mobile users in context" http://cameronmoll.com/archives/2007/01/3_billion_mobile_users_in_context/

Chabukswar, R. (2007). "Intel® Mobile Platform SDK: Monitor Connectivity Status" http://softwarecommunity.intel.com/articles/eng/1111.htm

COMTEC, (2007). "GPRS Tutorial". http://www.comtechm2m.com/m2m-technology/gprs-tutorial.htm

Datasynopse, (2007) http://www.datasynapse.com/glossary.aspx

Derick, (2007). "WIMAX" http://techcapsules.blogspot.com/2005/08/wi-max.html?gclid=CPKv7P6SxoQCFRN5MAodARcZKw

DeVaul, R and Dunn, S, (2001). "The Context Aware Cell Phone Project". http://www.media.mit.edu/wearables/mithril/phone.html

DeVaul, R. (2001). "MIThril project overview" http://www.media.mit.edu/wearables/mithril/overview.html

Ellis, C., Lebeck, A. and Vahdat, A. (1999). System support for energy management in mobile and embedded workloads: A white paper. Tech. rep., Duke University, Department of Computer Science, Oct 1999.

Gillespie, Matt. (2007). "Developer Tools from Intel Help Build RFID into Digital Health Software" http://softwarecommunity.intel.com/articles/eng/1164.htm/ (incorporating RFID Functionality)

GSM World, (2007). "The wireless evolution" http://www.gsmworld.com/index.shtml

Harkes, (2000). "Real Time Distributed Objects for Interactive Multimedia" http://www.cs.cmu.edu/~auraRT/

Hutchison 3G UK, (2007). "What can it do" http://www.three.co.uk/hygiene/aboutnetwork.omp

Intel PCA, (2008), "Intel PCA Developer Network" http://www.intel.com/support/processors/sb/cs-028855.htm

ISN - Intel Software Network, (2005). "Introducing the Intel Mobile Platform Software Development Kit (Intel Mobile Platform)" http://cache-www.intel.com/cd/00/00/20/47/204798_204798.pdf

ISN - Intel Software Network, (2007). "Mobile Platform Software Development Kit - An Open Source Project for Windows and Linux" http://softwarecommunity.intel.com/articles/eng/1331.htm

ISN - Intel Software Network, (2007). "An Overview of the Intel Mobile Platform SDK 1.2 Running open source solutions.

IST, (2000), "Intel XScale Technology"
http://www.intel.com/design/intelxscale

Jaffe, J. (2006). "Sony VAIO UX180P: a first look"
http://reviews.zdnet.co.uk/hardware/notebooks/0,1000000333,39270047,00.htm?r=1

Jon, J (2006). "Setting up a Bluetooth Personal Area Network for Internet Connection Sharing"
http://www.jonsguides.com/bluetooth/lanshare.html

Penn C, (2000). "Laptop Computer Purchasing Guide"
http://www.upenn.edu/computing/arch/standards/supportingdocs/99-00/laptop-99-00.html

Perfect XML, (2004). "Guide to Perfect XML"
http://www.perfectxml.com/glossary.asp

RFID Centre, (2006). "Mobility Technologies and Standards"
http://www.rfidc.com/docs/introductiontomobility_standards.htm

Roman M et al, (2002). "Gaia: A middleware Infrastructure to Enable Active Spaces Research Paper"

Sham, S (2008), "Wireless AutoSwitch"
http://software.techrepublic.com.com/download.aspx?docid=238025

SATIN Portal, (2001). "SATIN Overview"
http://www.isoc.org/seinit/portal/index2.php?option=com_content&do_pdf=1&id=12

Scriven, M (1991). Evaluation Thesaurus. 4th ed. Newbury Park, CA: Sage Publications.

Sobel, J et al (2000). "An Introduction to Reflection-Oriented Programming"
http://www.cs.indiana.edu/~jsobel/rop.html

Siewiorek, D et al (2001). "SenSay, A Context-Aware Mobile Phone"
http://www.cs.cmu.edu/~aura/docdir/sensay_iswc.pdf

Sun Microsystems, (2007). "Learn about Java"
http://www.java.com/en/about/

Vick, CV et al (2007). "Making Applications aware of their Mobile Contexts using the Intel® Mobile Platform SDK" http://softwarecommunity.intel.com/articles/eng/1457.htm

Zone NI, (2007). "Concepts and Overview of IrDA"
http://zone.ni.com/reference/en-XX/help/371361B-01/lvconcepts/overview_of_irda/

30   Cryptography

Kevin Curran, Niall Smyth, Bryan McGrory

One of the main methods of security is cryptography – encrypting data so that only a person with the right key can decrypt it and make sense of the data. There are many forms of encryption, some more effective than others. This chapter discusses a little of the history of cryptography, some popular encryption methods, and also some of the issues regarding encryption, such as government restrictions.

Introduction

The history of Cryptography dates back to the early 20th Century, where various devices and aids where used for encryption. During World War II, several mechanical devices were invented for performing encryption, this included rotor machines, most notably the Enigma cipher. The Ciphers implemented by these machines brought about a significant increase in the complexity of cryptanalysis. The art of Cryptography reaches back as far as far as 1900 BC when an Egyptian scribe, used a derivation of hieroglyphics to communicate. Throughout history there have been many people responsible for the growth of Cryptography. Many of these people were quite famous and one of these was Julius Caesar. He used a substitution of characters and just moved them about. Another historical figure who used and changed cryptography was Thomas Jefferson. He developed a wheel cipher that was made back in 1790. This cipher was then to be used to create the Strip cipher, which was used by the US Navy during the Second World War. Encryption methods have historically been divided into two categories: substitution ciphers and transposition ciphers. Substitution ciphers preserve the order of the plaintext symbols but disguise them. Transposition ciphers, in contrast, reorder the letters but do not disguise them (Tannenbaum, 1996). Plaintext is the common term for the original text of a message before it has been encrypted.

What is possibly the earliest encryption method was developed by a Greek historian of the 2nd century BC named Polybius, and is a type of substitution cipher (Burgess, 2000). This method worked with the idea of a translation table containing the letters of the Greek alphabet. See Figure 108 for an example of such a table using English letters.

	1	2	3	4	5
1	S	Y	D	W	Z
2	R	I	P	U	L
3	H	C	A	X	F
4	T	N	O	G	E
5	B	K	M	Q	

Figure 108: Translation table containing the letters of the Greek alphabet

This was used for sending messages with torch telegraphy. The sender of the message would have 10 torches, 5 for each hand. He would send the message letter by letter, holding the number of torches representing the row of the letter in his left hand, and the number of torches representing the column of the letter in his right hand. For example, in the case of the letter "s", the sender would hold 3 torches in his left hand and 4 in his right hand. Polybius wrote that "this method was invented by Cleoxenus and Democritus but it was enhanced by me." (Dénes, 2002). This method, while simple, was an effective way of encrypting telegraphic messages. The table could easily be changed without changing the method, so as long as both the sender and receiver were using the same table and no one else had the table they could send messages that anyone could see being sent but which would only be understood by the intended recipient. This is a form of private key encryption – where both the sender and the recipient share the key to the encrypted messages. In this case the key is the letter table.

Another type of substitution cipher is the Caesar cipher, attributed to Julius Caesar (Tannenbaum, 1996, p. 582). In this method, the alphabet is shifted by a certain number of letters, this number being represented by k. For example, where k is 3, the letter A would be replaced with D, B would be replaced with E, Z would be replaced with C, etc. This is also a form of private key encryption, where the value of k must be known to decrypt the message. Obviously this simple form of encryption is not difficult to crack, with only 26 possible values of k; it is only a matter of shifting the encrypted message with values of k until you get a comprehensible decrypted message. There are also more complex methods of cracking such encryption, such as using letter frequency statistics to work out some likely letters from the message – for example, 'E' is the most common letter in the English language, so the most common letter in the encrypted message is likely to be 'E'. Replacing the most common letters in the encrypted message with the most common letters of the language may help to make sense of some words. Once a word is partially decrypted, it may be easy to guess what the word is, which will then allow more letters to be substituted with their decrypted versions. For example if 'E' and 'T' had been used to replace the most common letters and one of the partially decrypted words is "tXe", then the X is likely to be H forming the word "the", so replacing all occurrences of "X" in the message with "h" may provide some more words which can be guessed easily.

A common transposition cipher, the columnar transposition, works with a private key. The private key is a word or phrase not containing any repeated letters, for example, "HISTORY". This key is used to number columns, with column 1 being under the letter closest to the start of the alphabet, etc. The plaintext is written in rows under the key, and the encrypted text is read in columns, starting with the column numbered 1. An example is shown in

Figure 109.

H	I	S	T	O	R	Y
1	2	5	6	3	4	7
a	_	p	r	i	v	a
a	t	e	_	p	h	r
a	s	e	_	t	o	_
b	e	_	e	n	c	r
y	p	t	e	d		_

Original Message:
   a_private_phrase_to_be_encrypted

Encrypted Message:
   aaaby_tsepiptndvhoc_pee_tr__eear_r_

The recipient of this message will then put the encrypted message back into the table with the key providing the column numbers.

Figure 109: Common transposition cipher

Cryptanalysis is the study of methods for obtaining the plain text of encrypted information without access to the key that is usually required to decrypt. In lay-man's terms it is the practice of code breaking or cracking code. The dictionary defines cryptanalysis as the analysis and deciphering of cryptographic writings/systems, or the branch of cryptography concerned with decoding encrypted messages. Cryptanalyst's are the natural adversary of a cryptographer, in that a cryptographer works to protect or secure information and a cryptanalyst works to read date that has been encrypted. Although they also complement each other well as without cryptanalyst's, or the understanding of the cryptanalysis process it would be very difficult to create secure cryptography. So when designing a new cryptogram it is common to use cryptanalysis in order to find and correct any weaknesses in the algorithm. Most cryptanalysis techniques exploit patterns found in the plain text code in order to crack the cipher; however compression of the data can reduce these patterns and hence enhance the resistance to cryptanalysis.

Popular Encryption Methods

Cryptography works by taking the original information and converting it with ciphertext, which encrypts the information to an unreadable form. To decrypt the information we simply do the opposite and decipher the unreadable information back into plain text. This enciphering and deciphering of information is done using an algorithm called a cipher. A cipher is basically like a secret code, but the main difference between using a secret code and a cipher is that a secret code will only work at a level of meaning. This basically means that the secret code could be made up with the same letters and words but just rearranged to mean something else. Ciphers work differently; they can target individual bits or individual letters and design a totally unrecognisable representation of the original document. Another interesting thing about ciphers is that they are usually accompanied by the use of a key. Depending on the type of key, different forms of encrypting procedures can be carried out, without the key the cipher would be unable to encrypt or decrypt[1].

One-Time Pads

The previous traditional forms of encryption discussed can be broken by someone who knows what to look for, but there is another method known as the one-time pad that can create unbreakable encrypted messages. A random bit string is used as the key. The message to be encrypted is then converted into a bit string, for example by using the ASCII codes for each character in the message. Then the EXCLUSIVE OR of these two strings is calculated, bit by bit. For example, take the key to be "0100010" and the message to be "A". The ASCII code for "A" is 1000001. The resulting one-time pad would be "1100011".

A one-time padded message cannot be broken, because every possible plaintext message is an equally probably candidate (Tannenbaum p. 585, 1996). The message can only be decrypted by someone who knows the correct key. There are certain disadvantages to this. Firstly, the key must be at least as long as the bit string to be encrypted. Since the key will be a long random bit string, it would be very difficult to memorise, so both the sender and the receiver will need written copies of the key, and having written copies of keys is a security risk if there is any chance of the key falling into the wrong hands. Also, if the sender and the recipient both have a previously agreed key to use, the sender will be limited as they will not be able to send a message too long for the key. With computer systems, the one-time pad method is more useful, as the key could be stored digitally on something like a CD and could therefore be extremely long and relatively easy to disguise.

DES

IBM developed a method of encryption known as the Data Encryption Standard (DES), which was adopted by the US government as its official standard for unclassified information in 1977. According to Tanenbaum (1996, p. 588) the standard "is no longer secure in its original form, but in a modified form it is still useful." When IBM originally developed DES, they called it Lucifer, and it used a 128 bit key. The NSA (National Security Agency) discussed the system with IBM, and after these discussions IBM reduced the key from 128 bits to 56 bits before the government adopted the standard. Many people suspected that the key was reduced so that the NSA would be able to break DES on encrypted data that they wished to view, but organisations with smaller budgets would not be able to (Tannenbaum, 1996, p. 593). It was also suspected that IBM kept the design of DES secret to hide a trapdoor which could make it even easier for the NSA to break DES.

As with all forms of encryption, it is possible to break DES encryption by means of a brute-force approach, where a computer is used to attempt to decrypt the data using possible keys one after the other until the correct key is found. Due to the constant speed increase of computers, it becomes faster to break DES encryption with every passing year. The key size of DES is no longer big enough for it to stand up to brute-force attacks long enough to make the attacks pointless, so in its original form DES is no longer safe for use. Many other encryption methods which work on similar principles to DES have been proposed since, including IDEA (International Data Encryption Algorithm) which uses a 128 bit key and is still safe from brute force attacks due to the length of time required to find the correct key from the huge key space.

All of the encryption methods discussed so far have been private key methods – meaning they depend on data being encrypted with a key known both to the sender and the recipient. This means that an unencrypted key must somehow be transferred between the sender and the recipient, and finding a secure method of doing that can present a problem in many situations. For example, there is no point in encrypting an email to a business partner, and then emailing him the encryption key, as this defeats the purpose of making the original email secure. Next we discuss another type of encryption which solves this problem – known as public key encryption.

Public Key Encryption

[1] http://en.wikipedia.org/wiki/Cryptography#Terminology

The idea of public key cryptography was first presented by Martin Hellman, Ralph Merkle, and Whitfield Diffie at Stanford University in 1976 (Burgess, 2000). They proposed a method in which the encryption and decryption keys were different, and in which the decryption key could not be determined using the encryption key. Using such a system, the encryption key could be given out publicly, as only the intended recipient would have the decryption key to make sense of it. A common use of this system is for a person to give out a public key to anyone who wishes to send them private information, keeping their private key to themselves. Of course, the encryption algorithm will also need to be public. There are 3 important requirements for a public key encryption method:

1. When the decryption process is applied to the encrypted message, the result must be the same as the original message before it was encrypted.

2. It must be exceedingly difficult (ideally impossible) to deduce the decryption (private) key from the encryption (public) key.

3. The encryption must not be able to be broken by a plaintext attack. Since the encryption and decryption algorithms and the encryption key will be public, people attempting to break the encryption will be able to experiment with the algorithms to attempt to find any flaws in the system.

The RSA Algorithm

One popular method for public key encryption was discovered by a group at MIT in 1978, and was named after the initials of the three members of the group: Ron Rivest, Adi Shamir, and Leonard Adleman (Tannenbaum, 1996 p. 599). Shortly before the details of RSA encryption were to be published, the US government reportedly "asked" the inventors to cancel the publication. However, copies of the article had already reached the public - A.K. Dewdney of Scientific American had a photocopy of the document explaining the algorithm, and more photocopies of this quickly spread. The RSA algorithm was patented by MIT, and then this patent was handed over to a company in California called Public Key Partners (PKP). PKP hold the exclusive commercial license to sell and sub-license the RSA public key cryptosystem. They also hold other patents which cover other public key cryptography algorithms. This gives them absolute control over who may legally use public key cryptography in the US and Canada (Menage, 1994). Since the RSA patent was not applied for until after publication of the algorithm, the patents are only valid inside the US and Canada.

There is a recognised method of breaking RSA encryption based on factoring numbers involved, although this can be safely ignored due to the huge amount of time required to factor large numbers. Unfortunately, RSA is too slow for encrypting large amounts of data, so it is often used for encrypting the key used in a private key method, such as IDEA. This key can then be transferred in public securely, resolving the key security problem for IDEA.

The Knapsack Algorithm

This algorithm was invented by Merkle and Hellman, who first proposed the idea of public key encryption, in 1978. The idea is that someone owns a large number of objects, each with a different weight. The owner encodes the message by secretly selecting a subset of the objects and placing them in the knapsack. The total weight of the objects in the knapsack is made public, as is the list of all possible objects. The list of objects in the knapsack is kept secret. With certain additional restrictions, the problem of figuring out a possible list of objects with the given weight was thought to be computationally infeasible, and formed the basis of the public key algorithm (Tannenbaum, 1996). It turns out that it was not computationally infeasible, as when Merkle offered a $100 reward to anyone who could break the encryption, Adi Shamir (one of the inventors of RSA) did so and collected the reward. After strengthening the algorithm, Merkle offered a $1000 reward to anyone who could break this, and Ron Rivest (another of the inventors of RSA) did so and also collected the reward. Merkle offered no further rewards. Although the algorithm was strengthened again, it is not regarded as secure and is not used widely.

Pretty Good Privacy

Published for free on the internet in 1991, PGP (Pretty Good Privacy) was a public key email encryption software package. It was originally designed by Philip R. Zimmermann as a human rights tool, allowing human rights activists to protect sensitive information from the prying eyes of opposed forces (Zimmermann, 2004). At the time of its development there were laws against the export of cryptography software from the US, so when PGP spread worldwide after its release on the internet, Zimmermann came under criminal investigation. Despite this, PGP spread to become the most widely used email encryption software in the world. PGP used a combination of IDEA and RSA encryption to allow emails to be transferred securely under public key encryption. There were some disputes over patent issues. As I mentioned earlier, PKP were the patent holders for the RSA algorithms. PKP, however, avoided legal action – they did threaten Zimmermann, but did not actually take action. They did refuse to license RSA for use in PGP, until MIT (the original patent holders) forced them to license MIT PGP 2.6. Another US company named ViaCrypt licensed the RSA algorithm from PKP, and were then able to sell a fully legal version of PGP using RSA. MIT later released their own version of PGP, and PKP threatened them with a lawsuit, but MIT refused to give in, and later distributed a legal freeware version of the program (Menage, 1994).

Eventually in 1996 the US government dropped its case against Zimmermann, and so he founded PGP Inc. to continue development of the software. PGP Inc. bought up ViaCrypt and began to publish new versions of PGP. Since the US export restrictions on cryptography software were not lifted until early 2000, PGP Inc. used a legal loophole that meant it was legal for them to print the PGP source code and export the books containing the code outside the US, where they could then scan it in using OCR (Optical Character Recognition) software and publish an international version of the software legally. In 1997, PGP Inc. was acquired by Network Associates Inc. (NAI), where Zimmermann stayed on for 3 years as a Senior Fellow. In 2002, the rights to PGP were acquired from NAI by a new company called PGP Corporation, where Zimmermann now works as a consultant. The PGP Corporation carries on the tradition of publishing the source code of their software for peer review so that customers and cryptography experts may validate the integrity of the products, and satisfy themselves that there are no back doors in the software allowing easy decryption (PGP Corp, 2005).

Steganography

Steganography refers to hiding a secret message inside a larger message in such a way that someone unaware of the presence of the hidden message cannot detect it. Steganography in terms of computer data works by replacing useless or unused data in regular files (such as images, audio files, or documents) with different, invisible information. This hidden information can be plain text, encrypted text, or even images. This method is useful for those who wish to avoid it being known that they are sending private information at all; with a public key encryption method, although the data is safe, anyone viewing it will be able to see that what is transferring is a private encrypted message. With steganography, even this fact is kept private, as you can hide a message in a simple photograph, where no one will suspect its presence. This leads onto an important issue of cryptography: the involvement of governments.

Governments and Cryptography

We have mentioned issues between the US government and those involved with cryptography previously – the government having IBM provide them a less secure version of the DES algorithm, reportedly attempting to stop the RSA algorithm being published, and taking legal action against the creator of PGP.

Many governments try to suppress usage of encryption, as they wish to be able to spy on potential criminals, and if these criminals use secure encryption to send information between each other, law enforcement agencies will not be able to tap in to what is being said. The US government at one point developed what is known as a key escrow system, and the UK government were rumoured to be working on a similar system, which never came to fruition. The idea of a key escrow system is that you can use it as a public key encryption system, with the addition that certain government agencies will hold a "spare key", allowing them to decrypt your private messages if they are suspicious of illegal activities being discussed in the contents of the messages. There are some obvious flaws with such a system; for one, the only people who would use the key escrow encryption would be those with nothing to hide from the government. People wishing to keep something private from government agencies would continue to use something like PGP. Unless all forms of strong encryption other than the key escrow system were banned, in which case a person using another method would be in breach of the law to begin with, then the development of such a system is a waste of time. If the government tried to restrict encryption in such a manner after it has been legal and widely used for so long, there would obviously be a lot of complaints from the cryptography-using public. Another problem is that people may worry about the security of the spare keys held by the government agencies. All it takes is one corrupt employee with access to the keys and their information is no longer secure.

The US Government has made moves into the cryptography field with the development of the clipper chip that the NSA developed in the hope that the company's would install them in their fax machines, phones and various other communication devices. However although the clipper chip had each its own unique key there was a catch that required the government to get to keep a copy of it. But for this to work effectively it would require that everyone is forced to use this method of cryptography over others. If privacy is outlawed, only outlaws will have privacy (Zimmerman, 2005).

After World War II the USA sold German Enigma Ciphering machines to third-world governments, without telling them that they were able to crack the enigma code during the war. Many UNIX systems around the world still use enigma cipher to encrypt files, and can't change to better, stronger more secure algorithms because of legal barriers that the governments have put in place. The government's clipper chip was widely opposed on technical and political grounds. The key escrow method means that the government has the key to decrypt the codes of anyone who uses this system. They do however still need to meet some legal requirements, although there is still the opportunity for abuse of this system[1].

The British Government have also tried to introduce the method of key recovery (key escrow). It is very hard for people to trust this kind of system when we think back to the US Governments illegal use of surveillance by the FBI against political opponents of the government in the 1950's through 1970's. Although there have been put in place certain measures to ensure this kind of thing doesn't happen in some countries, there are still cases appearing where the higher authorities are breaking laws in order to obtain information they want. Another disadvantage/flaw of a design like this is the central storage of keys would make an irresistible target for intruders or terrorists. There is also the human factor involved in such a system where people will be susceptible to temptations of bribes or blackmail in order to share these keys with unauthorised parties.

The Benefits of the government key escrow or key recovery program seem to benefit them solely in that they can track who they want when they want. It can however if used properly and without abuse, aid law enforcement. It has the potential to meet the needs of user's confidentiality (Denning, 1996). The most obvious downside of key escrow or the clipper chip is that its main purpose is for law enforcement but why would a criminal or terrorist use a technology that the government can decipher. This could only lead to the terrorists turning to stronger forms of cryptography and then all the benefits of the model are gone. It is only likely to be successful to capture or monitor petty criminals (Zimmermann, 2005).

Conclusion

Cryptography is a powerful tool, both for keeping important information private, and, when in the wrong hands, for keeping illegal activities hidden from government agencies. As computers grow faster and methods for breaking encryption become more viable, encryption algorithms will need to be constantly strengthened to stop them becoming insecure. There is little that can be done about the usage of cryptography to keep illegal activites hidden – short of making all forms of strong encryption illegal, which would create an outrage in western countries used to freedom in such matters, and would still not guarantee that usage of strong encryption would stop, with steganography allowing even the usage of encryption to be kept hidden. It is a problem that will likely become more and more pertinent as time goes by, with more criminals and terrorist groups making use of encryption to organise crimes, no easy solution is currently visible.

References

Burgess, J., Pattison, E., Goksel, M. (2000) Public Key Cryptography. Stanford University. http://cse.stanford.edu/classes/sophomore-college/projects-97/cryptography/history.html

[1] http://www.philzimmermann.com/EN/essays/WhyIWrotePGP.htm

Dénes, T. (2002) Cardan and cryptography - The mathematics of encryption grids. Hungary.
http://www.komal.hu/lap/2002-ang/cardano.e.shtml

Denning, D. (1996). Comments on the NRC Cryptography Report
http://www.cs.georgetown.edu/~denning/crypto/NRC.txt

Menage, M. (1994). Pretty Good Privacy - Legal Issues. http://193.125.152.107/pub/msdos/crypto/pgp/pgp-legal/

PGP Corporation. (2005) PGP Corporation Source Code. Silicon Valley, California.
http://www.pgp.com/downloads/sourcecode/index.html

Tannenbaum, A. (1996) Computer Networks – Third Edition. Prentice Hall.

Zimmermann, P. (2004) Philip Zimmermann – Creator of PGP. Silicon Valley, California.
http://www.philzimmermann.com

Zimmermann, P. (2005). Why do you need PGP? http://www.pgpi.org/doc/whypgp/en/
Accessed

31   Universal Authentication

Kevin Curran, Jennifer Caldwell, Declan Walsh, Marcella Gallacher

Authentication is the process of determining whether a user is to be granted access and verifying that they are whom they claim to be. This is generally done via a login system; typically consisting of a user ID and a corresponding password. An intrinsic weakness of this system of authentication is that passwords are easily forgotten, accidentally revealed, can be second guessed or even stolen. Users today have multiple email accounts, manage their financial affairs, buy and even sell regularly online. Many sites offer the opportunity to 'sign up'. This can be problematic for managing usernames and passwords and it encourages insecure practices such as writing them down, storing them electronically or reusing the same login data on multiple websites repeatedly. One of the most common online security issues faced today is that every website has its own diverse authentication system that significantly heightens the probability of online crime such as fraud and identity theft and furthermore can comprise the privacy of the individual. A common network identity-verification method is Universal authentication which allows users to roam between sites without having to repeatedly enter identifying information. Privacy of user's information should be maintained as only relevant details are passed on to other sites. A number of organizations are already taking universal authentication on board and have had successful outcomes using this type of system. Some companies such as Microsoft Passport have used a single sign-on password system but they have had security and privacy issues after the launch of it. The future for most if not all users may be a secure and private single logon to access different sites and accounts on the Internet via Universal Authentication. This chapter discusses universal authentication.

Introduction

Plain old authentication can be defined in many ways but perhaps the simplest and most relevant definition to most computer users is a security measure for checking a network user's identity. Even in today's world of digital certificates and biometrics, authentication most typically takes the form of a username and password. Figure 110 shows a standard authentication process. Note that this is "Basic" authentication, wherein the web server prompts for a username and password.

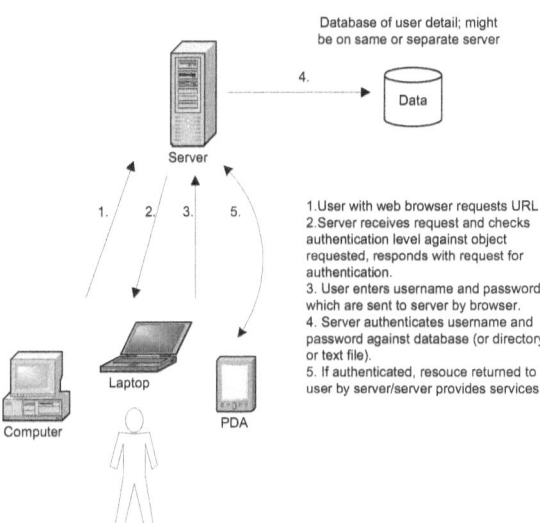

Figure 110: Authentication on the web

Other common web authentication types are "Anonymous" (no authentication required) and "Integrated" (currently logged in authentication details automatically checked to see if the user can access the resource). Universal Authentication is the concept of allowing users to move from one web site to another on the web without having to enter identifying information numerous times (see Figure 111).

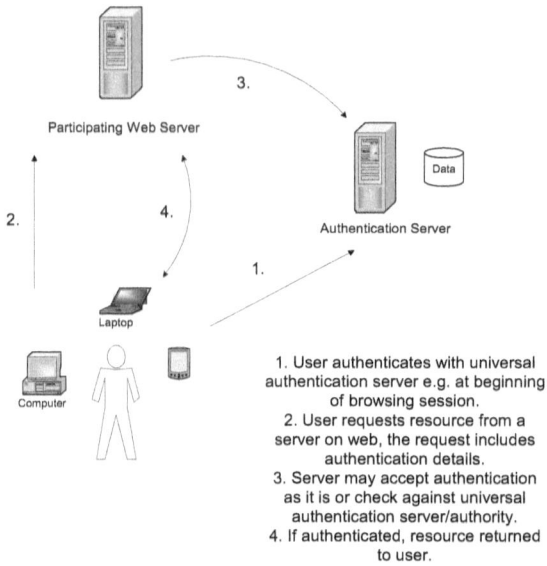

1. User authenticates with universal authentication server e.g. at beginning of browsing session.
2. User requests resource from a server on web, the request includes authentication details.
3. Server may accept authentication as it is or check against universal authentication server/authority.
4. If authenticated, resource returned to user.

Figure 111: Universal Authentication on the web

A person would enter, for example, a username and password, at the start of a network session and this authentication information would be automatically passed to/each web site they visit thereafter. (A network session might be when a user connects to the internet or opens a web browser). The rationale behind universal authentication is obvious; the growth of the Web has led to people having to manage a host of usernames and passwords for web sites. An average web user now shops online, pursues hobbies online, manages their bank accounts online, communicates online using email, instant messaging, photo-sharing etc. The list is lengthy, and almost all of these require authentication, usually in the form of a username and password. For many users a "single sign-on" would be welcome. There are obvious benefits of universal authentication which include:

➢ More convenient for the user as they have to remember only one username and password
➢ Security issue should be reduced as the user should not have to write down the one username/password
➢ With only one authentication system it should lessen the chance of having the password stolen
➢ As the user has to logon only once there is faster access to different sites
➢ There should be a continuous link to different sites
➢ System managed centrally

As well as speed and convenience, universal authentication also offers improved security too. Web users no longer have to remember and manage countless logons (making them more vulnerable to fraud) and organisations have less responsibility for the security and privacy of peoples' authentication (and personal) information. The balkanization of today's online identity-verifying systems is a big part of the Internet's fraud and security crisis. Improving and maintaining people's "trust" in the internet is critical to its survival as a useful, thriving entity (Talbot, 2006). Also, if authentication is consolidated in one session or authority, web users only need to share their personal information once instead of giving numerous copies of that information to multiple third parties. This means greater privacy for users and less risk of personal information being accessed. Many companies have already encountered these issues on an organizational scale; workers use numerous systems and have to manage authentication for each of them. This causes a lot of inconvenience to users, I.T. resources are eaten up resetting passwords and administering user accounts, and security can be compromised by users writing down usernames and passwords because they cannot remember them all. As a result many organisations have implemented universal authentication that allows workers (or students, or customers) to log in once, in order to access all the systems they use. Scaling this kind of solution up to something as vast and heterogeneous as the web is a challenge.

Universal Authentication Implementations

Most web surfers have encountered universal authentication, albeit on a relatively small scale at sites like MSN Hotmail and Windows Live Spaces. To date there are a small number of players which we list here.

Shibboleth

Shibboleth is an open-standard authentication system which allows users to "hop securely from one site to another after signing on just once" (Talbot, 2006). Figure 112 shows Shibboleth being used to authenticate a university student when accessing another university's resources.

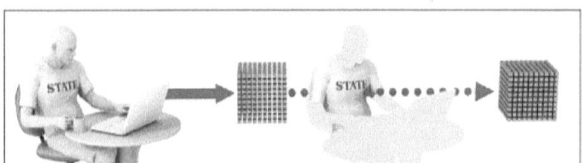

Figure 112: Shibboleth (Talbot, 2006)

Figure 113 illustrates a Shibboleth implementation for a project involving seven U.S. universities "to create cross-institutional authentication and authorization services on the Web" (Gettes, 1999). Shibboleth is currently deployed at over 500 sites worldwide, predominately educational institutions. The science and medical division of publishing conglomerate "Reed Elsevier" has allowed university-based subscribers to access its online resources using Shibboleth, and this progress into the private sector is apparently advancing with the "Liberty Alliance". The Liberty Alliance is composed of companies such as America Online, France Telecom, Novell, Sun Microsystems, Ericsson, Intel, Oracle Corporation, Hewlett Packard, NTT and Fidelity Investment. The design is based on the XML standard Security Assertion Markup Language (SAML) created by an industry group called OASIS. It is worth noting that other players such as Windows "Card Space" also use SAML.

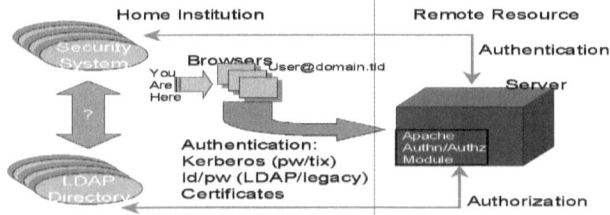

Figure 113: Shibboleth – Middleware Web Authentication Project (Gettes, 1999)

217

Shibboleth is interoperable with Windows Active Directory Federation Services (ADFS). This allows federation agreements among companies and organisations regardless of the underlying technical solution they choose to deploy (Rotman, 2005). Such "tie-ins" with Microsoft could do Shibboleth no harm in its bid as a web universal authentication standard. Microsoft may be cooperating with and publicly supporting systems like Shibboleth but there are two Microsoft systems addressing universal authentication. These are MS Passport.NET and Infocard/Windows Card Space which we detail next.

Microsoft Windows Live ID

Most users of Microsoft web sites and services like MSN, hotmail, Windows Live Web Spaces are likely to have encountered Microsoft .NET Passport which is now renamed "Windows Live ID". Under the umbrella of its ".NET" initiative, Microsoft launched a set of web services; .NET Passport is a user authentication and single sign-in service. Users set up an email account, register with this email address and password for a ".NET passport", and have a .NET Passport profile created. They are then assigned a personal identification number, which is sent to the user's computer in the form of a cookie. The cookie allows users to visit participating web sites without having to sign into each site. .NET Passport and its SSI service have been criticized for poor security and privacy. Its centralized nature makes it possible that other problems and security breaches will occur (Oppliger, 2003).

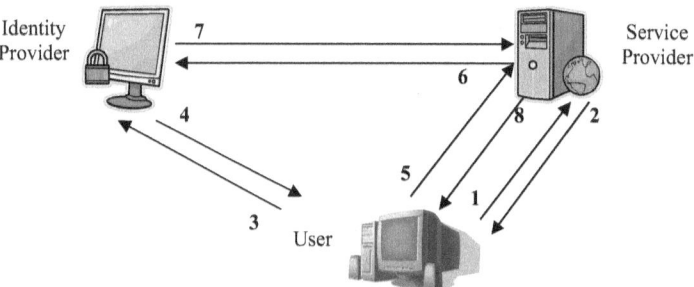

Figure 114: Single Sign-On and Federations interactions

One similar system in the form of single sign on is the *Microsoft* Passport authentication service (see Figure 114). The Microsoft and Windows Live websites promote this service. Once signed in using an ID, which usually takes the form of a hotmail address, users can then interact between a number of different services such as Windows Live accounts and Windows Live messenger. The single sign on (SSO) works by directing users to a login screen where they must supply correct credentials. Once they have been verified, the user is then sent back to the restricted page along with an authenticated cookie which is proof that they have successfully logged in. When changing to a different site that has this system enabled, the user still has their authentication cookie, allowing them to browse these sites, for the duration of the session.

Microsoft Windows Card Space

Windows Card Space (originally named "Infocard") was released as an Application Programming Interface (API) in .NET Framework Version 3.0. At the core of Windows Card Space lies the idea that users set up a set of digital identities, known as "information cards", which they use for authentication/identification. Card Space has a user interface for managing these information cards. The system sits on top of security tokens (a security token could be a simple username, a digital certificate, SAML token etc.). This overcomes the security weakness of username/password authentication in Passport/Live ID as illustrated in Figure 115.

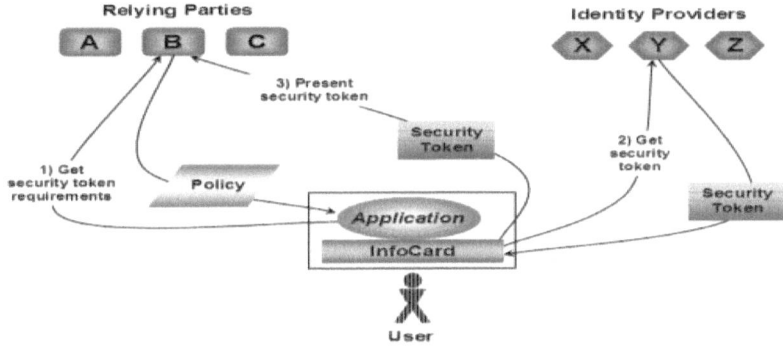

Figure 115: Interactions the user, identity provider, and relying party roles" (Chappel, 2006).

In
Figure 115, "Identity Provider" is the system which provides a digital identity. However a provider could also be a credit card company i.e. to make payments online, or an employer, when they supply a username and password to access systems. "Relying Parties" refers to online services, like shopping sites or online auctions that use digital identities to authenticate a user (and often to authorise what a user has access to /can do). Windows Card Space can also be used to provide identities for web sites and web services applications, thereby tackling the other end of the identification/authentication conundrum; how to identify authentic web sites to users and to prevent phishing (getting information fraudulently) using fake sites. In addition, as the identity metasystem underlying Card Space is based on open protocols, Card Space-compatible software for identity providers, relying parties, and other identity selectors can be built on any platform or device (Chappell, 2006).

Project Higgins

Project Higgins is an open source initiative, originating from the Berkman Centre for Internet & Society, a research programme based in the Law School of Harvard university in the U.S. It is being managed by the Eclipse open source foundation and in 2006 IBM, Novell and Parity Communications announced they were contributing code to spur swift adoption of Higgins by the broadest community of software developers and IBM plans to incorporate Higgins technology within its Tivoli identity management software, with added support by independent software vendors and IBM's consulting services division (Becker, 2006). Like Microsoft's Card Space, "user-centric" identity management is a central concept in its Project Higgins; it is intended that users manage their online personal information and decide what they want to share (by breaking their identity into pieces or "services") with trusted web sites that use the software. The developers believe it will support any technology platform and identity management system (Becker, 2006). The route Higgins' is taking; that of using open and standard code/protocols (as are Shibboleth and Windows Card Space) works in its favour. Arguably it is the only feasible way to go with a system you want vast numbers of users and companies on the Internet to adopt anyway. Strong authentication is a must for the future but people may not feel as safe as many websites will already know various things about the user, "Essentially and eventually, authentication will result in the Web becoming one huge interconnected site where everyone who you want to do business with already knows who you are and what you like...... It will be as if the Web was custom-designed just for you... Universal authentication will only be widely used if people feel safe and feel they are getting fair value for giving up some privacy." (Delio, 2002).

Universal Authentication Issues

Consolidating all, or at least a large segment, of authentication on the internet may reduce inconvenience to users but there is a worry that the "single sign-on" can become compromised. The question is whether concentrating everything in one authentication session becomes a massive security risk in itself. There is a responsibility for security on both the organization that took on the considerable challenge of providing the authentication, and on the web users themselves. If universal authentication becomes a reality, this risk will have to be accepted, and as much done to mitigate it as possible; it seems inevitable that the standard username and password will be deemed too weak. Realistically biometrics, smartcards, digital certificates and the like will be necessary in an implementation of universal authentication. Universal authentication systems operating at a business level already support multiple authentication methods e.g. ID's/Passwords, dynamic passwords, certificates, biometrics, or security tokens. This entails some investment. In addition to these issues, the levels of agreement, cooperation, standardization etc. needed to achieve universal authentication, even among a section of organizations and companies on the web, are considerable. The disadvantages of universal authentication include:

- ➢ Potential security risk as a potential hacker has only one username and password to obtain
- ➢ Potential hacker would have access to all users' accounts
- ➢ Password can be forgotten by the user and they therefore do not have access to any of their accounts
- ➢ Would have to include numerous layers of authentication between organisations
- ➢ System will need more robust security and require powerful encryption

Conclusion

Authentication is the procedure of deciding if a user or something is, in fact who they are declaring they are. The internet and private computer networks mainly require authentication. This is normally done through the use of usernames and passwords. Business and personal transactions require a strict authentication process therefore a digital certificate verified by Certificate Authority (CA) is the standard way to perform authentication. Authentication precedes authorization although they are commonly misguided to be the same. The commonly known problem that arises with authentication is that most users now have more than one username and password to use, for work, the internet, University, e-mail, bank etc.

The proposed solution to this problem is Authentication Systems where each user enters their ID and password only once so that they can securely access other sites thus speeding things up. Shibboleth is an open standard authentication system mainly used by Universities with a high level of security and guarantee for each transaction. The system also provides a guard for privacy for example when a student logs on to the University's network all their information is on their account and when they go to the library to request books only the necessary information will be available to view by the librarian as the librarian will not need to view the students test results. Microsoft also launched a similar system named Passport System which allows Windows users to access specific websites with their hotmail address and password. If we assume the development of universal authentication follows that of many technologies, we can imagine that leaders will emerge and much universal authentication will converge on their standards, with the result of a level of homogeny. It is also likely that there may always be some scattering of technologies and companies who offer/manage universal authentication, with some resulting interoperability and incompatibility issues.

References

Becker, J. (2006) Open Source Initiative to Give People More Control Over Their Personal Online Information – IBM Press Release, http://www-03.ibm.com/press/us/en/pressrelease/19280.wss

Chappel, D. (2006) Introducing Windows Card Space Online, Windows Vista Technical Articles, http://msdn2.microsoft.com/en-us/library/aa480189.aspx

Delio, M. (2002) Sun Shines Light on ID Alliance, Wired Magazine, February 2002 http://www.wired.com/news/business/0,1367,53859,00.html

Gettes, M.R. (1999) Shibboleth - Middleware Web Authentication Project http://shibboleth.internet2.edu/docs/shibboleth-project.html

Oppliger, R. (2003) Microsoft .NET Passport: A Security Analysis. Computer, Vol. 36, No. 7, pp: 29-35, July 2003, http://csdl2.computer.org/persagen/DLAbsToc.jsp?resourcePath=/dl/mags/co/&toc=comp /mags/co/2003/07/r7toc.xml&DOI=10.1109/MC.2003.1212687

Rotman, L. (2005) Internet2 collaborates with Microsoft to Enable Interoperability of Federated Authentication Software, I2 News Archive, http://lists.aarnet.edu.au/pipermail/middle-l/2005-December/000074.html

Talbot, D. (2006) Universal Authentication. MIT Technology Review, March/April 2006. http://www.technologyreview.com/read_article.aspx?ch=specialsections&sc=emerging&id=16474

32   Honeynets

Kevin Curran, Mairead Feeney

Worms, Viruses, DDos and many other varieties of attacks are an everyday occurrence and pressuring today's security professional to raise the bar in order to prevent or minimise their impact. There is a requirement for real time systems to analyse the data we receive and examine the contents for possible Malware contents. The possibilities of using such a function would aid an organisation to detect inconsistencies in data and function as a potential early warning system that an attack could be possibly imminent. A honeypot is one such solution. It is a sweet smelling server of temptation which lures the hacker under the pretence of infiltrating a nice juicy server, but instead of the hacker gathering the spoils the queen bee gathers honey in the form of information from the hacker. It is this information that provides us with the vital clues as to what services, ports and potential security holes the hacker is attacking and in doing so allows for the security personnel to ring fence those areas in the production environment.

Introduction

The lowly computer which sits on a bedroom desk, in an office cubicle or in a boardroom is becoming quite frequently a crime scene location for the 21st century. Law enforcers are being confronted with the increased need to investigate crime perpetrated through the use of the internet or some other electronic media. The need to be able to access, trace, interrogate and retrieve information from any electronic device has become a sought after expertise by both law enforcers and commercial organisations alike as both are keen to build up a portfolio of evidence to help either solve crimes that have been committed or pre-empt potential crimes or weaknesses before they occur. Forensics applied to the computer environment is where techniques are used to investigate and analyse what the computer systems are being used for. Tools include IDS, Network Protocol Analysers, the Coroner's Toolkit[1], Netstat[2] and Fport[3] to name just a few (Honeynet Project, 2004). All of the above mentioned tools are good propriety tools available for purchase or come built in to operating systems.

Intrusion is any action that attempts to comprise the integrity, confidentiality or availability of a resource (Lodin, 1998). Intrusions can come in many varied forms (Sherif, 2003) defines six different types of computer attacks these include:

- Worms – Programs that spread across a computer environment by self replicating.
- Virus – programs that replicate as a result of a user taking some particular action. For example, opening a file.
- Server Attacks – A hacker exploits vulnerability within a server and uses this to perform an unanticipated action.
- Client Attacks – A hacker exploits vulnerability with a client and uses this to perform an unanticipated action.
- Network Attack – An attacker exploits a weakness in the network and uses this to cause, for example, servers or routers to deny execution of a particular service.
- Root Attacks – This is where the root password is compromised, learned and used to carry out activities that would otherwise be restricted (Sherif, 2003)

Intrusion can be caused by individuals from both outside and inside an organisation. We commonly assume when in conversation that intruder means outsider but in fact the intruder from within the organisation poses a much greater threat. They may have access to confidential security data such as passwords or be aware of known vulnerabilities that exist within the computer systems. To this end they can land more deadly blows. Intruder knowledge and sophistication each year is expanding, thanks in part to the large number of tools at their

---

[1] A set of programs developed for analysis of a UNIX system after an attack. http://www.porcupine.org/forensics/tct.html
[2] Command line tool for displaying network communication and configuration. http://www.netstat.net
[3] Reports all open UDP and TCP ports and to which application they belong. http://www.foundstone.com/us/resources/proddesc/fport.htm

disposal. The sophistication of a hacker's tools is allowing hackers to exploit systems without having a good technical knowledge base (see Figure 116).

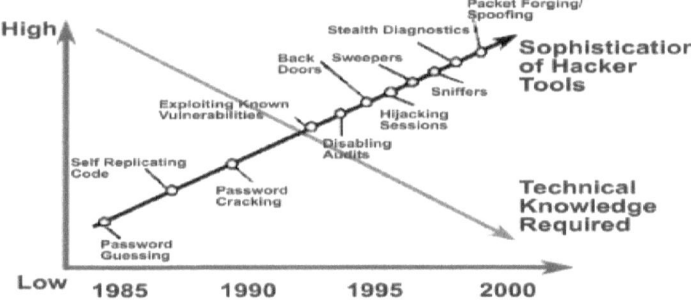

Figure 116: Sophistication of hacker tools (Sherif, 2003)

All organisations have security policies in place to help combat intruders actions such as, logical access, audit trails, firewalls, authentication and the use of encryption and decryption. These techniques are not enough, with the new release of every computer application there will always be bugs and vulnerabilities that will give hackers the back door means of entry to our systems. For many years, intrusion detection systems have been employed by organisations but these systems have limitations as will be discussed later in section 2. It is only in medium to large organisations that we can find dedicated security administrators. In most companies, security could be just one of many tasks on a person's work schedule. Due to this fact, administrators may find themselves consistently playing catch up to the hacker who has only one task. Many organisations are turning to honeynet technology to supplement or help fortify the computer systems by providing the means to be proactive about restraining the intruder rather than reacting to the consequences of the attacker's actions.

Attack Types

Unsolicited mail or spam is a common compliant of many internet users. Spamming means that an attacker sends out huge amounts of emails to miscellaneous email addresses to attack or compromise a specific website. If an attacker uses a botnet made up of thousands of machines this could lead to serious consequences. A machine can be used for spamming once the SOCKS proxy (RFC 1975) is enabled on a machine. Spamming is an illegal activity; the problem is sourcing the originating email or messenger. A Denial of Service (DDoS) attack results in a user losing the services of their computer system or network. The more common DDoS attacks are on network connectivity where bandwidth is consumed or the user's computer resources are overloaded (Honeynet Project, 2005). This is a common technique used by script kiddies. Any service available on the internet is open to a DDoS attack.

Identity Theft involves a user being presented with a fake email or website that is masquerading as a legitimate source in order for the user to provide personal information and more typically personal finance information such as credit card details (Honeynet Project, 2003). We have seen a huge growth in this area, for example some AIB bank internet banking customers received an email supposedly from the bank itself looking for the customer to verify their internet banking details, such as registration and pin codes. Many customers of many organisations have fallen foul to this tactic, as attackers create totally realistic copies of genuine websites such as those used by banking or financial based organisations. Authorities are trying to reduce the amount of exploitations by trying to raise awareness of users and make them more vigilant. But just as quick as the authorities' shutdown one fake site another appears. Many other methods can be used for identify theft such as key logging or sniffing where the attacker listens on communication channels for information relating to finance which they in turn can exploit.

The History of Honeynets

Honeynets are the brain child of the Honeynet project[1]. This organisation is a non-profit, dedicated volunteer research body, whose aim is that through research into threats and vulnerabilities that they will raise awareness and gain insight into internet computer security. The honeynet project was originally founded by 30 US based security professional and today is a worldwide organisation with Honey project groups in all five continents. All of these groups share the same goals to raise awareness, provide accurate and timely information and provide open source tools to help organisations and individuals better protect their computer environment. Here in Ireland also, a Honeynet project was founded in March 2002 and is sponsored by Deloitte and Espion Ltd. The purpose of this venture was to track and analyse the behaviour of hacker in Ireland and those from other countries who liked to visit. Armed with this information they can keep the Irish Internet community aware of the tools, techniques and advances of the hacker community and in response have us all better prepared when they try and strike.

A honeynet is a network of honeypots. A honeypot is a system that is purposely built to attract hackers and analyse how they try to compromise the systems. A honeypot can provide any systems administrator with alerts to potential vulnerabilities or misconfigurations within their computer systems. A honeypot is an information systems resource whose value lies in unauthorised or illicit use of that resource (Spritzer, 2004). When a computer system is attacked, one jumps into reactive mode, trying to minimise the amount of damage that could be potentially done. One doesn't have time to analyse the system to investigate how this attack was instigated. Using a honeypot allows us watch or monitor any advances towards our systems from hackers and patch any vulnerabilities they may find before our production machines are compromised. A honeypot is like a mousetrap, anything you catch in it is a problem (Hall, 2004). A honeynet can replicate any type of system, this helps fool the hacker into believing they are accessing a live production area. A honeypot can be anything you want it to be, it can be a decoy to attract a hacker's attention away from your production systems or it can be a learning tool which will allow you analyse the motives of a hacker and use this information to better protect the systems of the future.

Intrusion Detection Systems (IDS) is a common method of vetting whether a computer system has been compromised. These systems work in two ways. Firstly, anomaly based IDS systems compare current behaviour against what was observed in the past and noted as usual activity. If there is any anomalies between the two an alert it raised to notify whoever is in charge of a possible attack in motion. This functionality can lead to a lot of false positives. The second main type of IDS system is a signature based system, where rules are setup and allow identification of known attacks. The problem here is that we then can only recognised an attack if we have a signature to identify it. Honeynets are not seen as a replacement for IDS systems but a supplement to help boost their defences. A honeynet sits, scans and logs all traffic coming past its door. The honeynet is only used for this purpose so any activity on the honeynet can immediately be treated as suspicious. In a production environment there can be a vast amount of data traffic moving across a network at anyone moment in time making it near impossible to sort manually the good and the bad. Honeynets can serve to make threats more visible, maybe act as an early alarm system, giving a company a more proactive approach to security rather than reactive. We need to be able to close the door before any unwelcome guests arrive.

Honeynet Technical Configuration

Intrusion Detections Systems (IDS) are computer based programs that are designed to scan computer systems for evidence of intrusions. Many different models have been created.

- **Generic Intrusion Detection Model**
  As the name suggests it is a generic model that can be applied comprehensively to any computer environment, for example, UNIX or Windows. It does not search or scan for anyone particular intrusion type. It works by monitoring the users of the system, the services and the activities taking place, in doing so it builds up a profile of who does what and uses this to baseline future activities. The model then watches for abnormal behaviour that differs from the baseline and produces reports or sends alerts to notify. This could be defined as a rule based system (Sundaram, 1996).

- **Autonomous Agents Model**
  Several small processes are used independent of each other. They monitor the system and the information is correlated to give an overview of the system as a whole. As there are many processes involved, this model allows greater efficiency as the workload can now be spread, also providing a

---

[1] http://www.honeynet.org

fault tolerance mechanism. The system is not reliant in just one particular program running. This model gives the organisation the ability if they so wish to extend their monitoring services to other computer systems.

- **Network Security Monitor Model (NSM)**
  Developed by the University of California-Davis, this model monitors network traffic. This model sits and listens to network traffic and intruders are unaware of its presence due to its passive nature.

- **Predictive Pattern Generation Model**
  Predication meaning to foresee is what this model sets out to achieve. It tries to predict what will happen in the future based on what has already occurred. This model is good at anomaly detection. It knows the past behaviour of, for example users, so deviations can be detected very quickly and then administration alerted.

- **Behaviour Based Intrusion Detection Model**
  This model is based on the concept of Anomaly detection, detecting certain deviations from a user's normal behaviour. The key word here is normal and what constitutes normal. This is where the challenge lies with this model. A comprehensive picture of potential normal activities can only be built up over time based on user's activities and available resources. A common problem with this model is that there tends to be a high number of false positives of false alarms.

- **Knowledge Based Intrusion Detection Model**
  This model works under the umbrella that all activity is allowable once it previously has not been identified as unacceptable. This model is very time consuming in building up information on known attacks and new vulnerabilities. This can lead to excessive administrative overheads. A substantial amount of time is required to be spent identifying each vulnerability and taking note of where, when and why they occurred and as a further complication can be very type specific to a particular computer environment.

False positives are the main limitation of IDS. Due to their very nature IDSs tend to raise large amounts of false alarms. If systems are weakened to reduce the number of false positives this in turn opens up systems to a greater number of attacks. IDSs are not a 100% infallible means of detection. Attacks still happen undetected. These are called false negatives. IDSs are required to monitor and analyses traffic in real time. If there is a large amount of traffic this can lead to systems performance levels being lowered and packets being dropped.

The use of IDS systems has been the traditional approach to detect unwelcome guests on a computer system and there are many different models or schemas that can be used. We have also looked at the limitations of such systems, they can be rule based, signature based or just trying to detect behaviour that can be observed or categorised as not normal. Hence solely using this method can lead us to having quite a few red herrings and not too much caviar. Honeynets add a new dimension to the area of intrusion detection; they are not a replacement technology for traditional methods but a supplement, an extra layer of security, a little bit of honey on the toast. Honeynets are a proactive step where one hopes to highlight potential threats before it strikes. A honeynet or honeypot can bring extra beneficial information to computer systems personnel. The amount of traffic that traverses a network cannot be feasibly monitored by IT personnel in the hope of spotting a malicious content or activates. A honeypot can watch, listen and report anything dubious to the security administrator leaving them free to carry out other important tasks. A security administrator can put firewalls in place or close certain ports to eliminate or severely hamper the chance of an attack. This may stop the attack from happening but what does the systems administrator learn? They do not know the reason for a potential attack or what the intent of the attacker was or what methods did they used and how they failed to gain admittance. A honeypot can carry out all of these actions. The honeypot can be put on a reconnaissance mission to infiltrate the enemy and bring back the intelligence.

Honeypots can be classified into two categories; those that are setup purely to aid research and gain intelligence and those that are sitting on a live network surrounded by many other production servers. The whole concept of a honeypot was borne to aid research and this is still among many the main objective. Here the focus is on intelligence gathering and learning the technology and methods used by hackers. Production honeypots are used for a duel purpose. Firstly, as an early warning system that an attack maybe imminent or that suspect traffic as been encountered. Secondly, they can be used as bait to distract the hacker from the production system, simple really, lure the hacker to the honeypot where information can be collected and in parallel keeping the hacker away from the real production machines. Depending on the purpose of the honeypot deployment, research or production different levels of honeypots can be used. If a honeypot is placed in a production environment a high interaction honeypot is used. If research solely is of main interest, then a low interaction honeypot will serve instead.

- **Low Interaction**

  Honeypots setups for low interaction have limited involvement with the hacker. They run emulated systems above the server own operating system. This means that the attacker has no interaction with the underlying OS. The worst an attacker can do is to destroy the emulation. Honeypots of this type are easy to maintain and install but on the other hand the amount of information they can get is limited. The attacker may attempt to connect to a port and this will be denied. The value here is the information about the attempted access. Worms and scans can be identified by this type of honeypot. The problem with these types of honeypots is that an experienced hacker may lose interest quickly or discover that it is a honeypot that he is trying to access. This means that a lot of the time it is only script kiddies who interact, who may not provide as valuable information as the more experiences hack. The more a hacker can access and do on a system the more time he will spend trying to control our system and thus leave us more information to work with.

- **High Interaction**

  Honeypots of this type are real systems, running on real or emulated operating systems. The attacker has access to the real, live systems. These types of honeypots are hard to install and maintain and are very high risk. Once an attacker infiltrates the system they can take full control, thus giving them in turn access to potentially other systems on the network or services that interact with the compromised system. As these systems are in the live environment they give a real world view at the activities and behaviour of intruders.

There are two common approaches to honeynet implementations. These are Generation I and Generation II. Depending on the needs and available resources of an organisation or individual and previous attack patterns identified will decide on which generation of honeynet should be employed.

Generation I

The main focus of Generation I honeypots is towards Data Capture, Data Control and Data Collection. They are highly effective in tracking and detecting attacks at a novice level. This implementation has shortcomings in that this approach can be easily detected by a hacker and with the use of default installations of various operating systems it offers little interest to a skilled hacker (Grimes, 2005). Data Control is a containment activity (Honeynet Project, 2005). When a honeynet is compromised it is critical that we can ensure that any other non-honeynet system cannot be harmed by this infiltration. We need to be able to control the flow of traffic to and from a honeynet but also giving the hacker enough freedom to keep their interest. It is getting the right balance in place that proves tricky. Low interaction honeypots only emulate services, so the amount of power a hacker can assume is limited. High Interaction honeypots are the reverse, where real live systems are in play. The balance of power between hacker and organisation is not definable by any one set standard, it is totally organisational dependant. In a Generation I model a number of scripts or filters are used to block or limit the amount of outbound connections per hour, limit bandwidth hence reducing available resources or employing intrusion prevention gateways. The Honeynet Project recommends the use of layering, not just employing one of these techniques but using all in tandem to provide a more concrete foundation to try and eliminate risk.

Data Capture defines tracking and logging all the actions of the hacker without attracting or informing the hacker of the presence of a honeypot. The challenge is to try and capture as much data as is possible about the movements and motives of a hacker. We need to watch their movements at many different levels in order to complete a more conclusive picture into their psychology. As a result, we capture data at many different levels using methods such as logging, packet sniffing, keystroke logging, snapshot software and network device logs. Hackers are becoming more skilled at their attacks and try to attack using a lot of encrypted communications and commands. This tactic needs to be accounted for. Another important concern is detection or lack there of. According to the honeynet project when setting up a honeypot for optimum data capture it is important to make relatively few modifications to the honeypots to ensure a lesser chance of detection. All captured data should not be stored on the honeypot itself but on a remote secure system (Honeynet Project, 2005).

Data Collection is only required if multiple distributed honeynets are in use by an organisation. This implies that all data collected for the various honeynets should be synchronised and held in a central server area for analysis and archiving (Honeynet Project, 2004). Generation I limitations in data control can be made easier for a very skilled hacker to fingerprint the use of a honeypot. To address the vulnerabilities of Generation I in 2002 a new model was developed to address the shortcomings of Generation I in Data Control. Generation I data control lacked flexibility as it blocked outbound connections. This tactic was seen as a tip off to the hacker that they were in the presence of a honeypot. Generation II provides data control by examining each outbound packet and decides whether it should be blocked, passed or modified to remove any malicious content and then allowing it to pass out (Levine, 2003).

Generation II

Generation II was introduced to address the short comings of Generation I honeynets. A typical honeynet can be seen below. The main inclusion is the use of a honeywall. The honeywall separates the network into production and honeynet (Dorseif, 2006). A honeywall has three network cards. The first interface is used to connect to the main network router and does not interact with any honeynet traffic. The other two interfaces have no IP addresses assigned. These interfaces are used for the production and the honeypots. The traffic moves between these two interfaces without increasing the TTL (time to live) and acts as a transparent bridge. The honeywall of Generation II uses bridging technology to hide data control tools (see Figure 117).

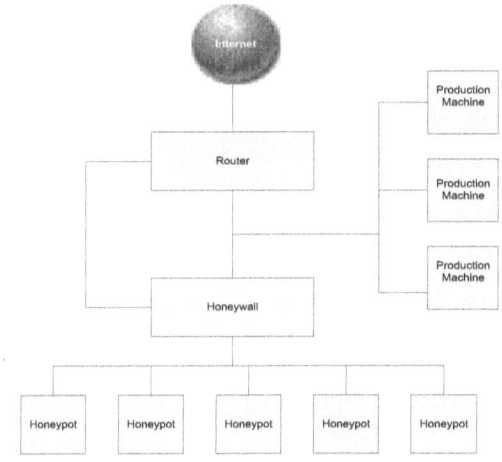

Figure 117: Generation II Honeynet Layout

It is the Generation II honeywall that can change malicious packets into a benign packet to stop the hacker trying to compromise a non-honeynet system. Specific information is collected in Generation II models, these are: firewall logs, network traffic and systems activity (Honeynet Project, 2005). Firewall logs are used to provide summarised information about network activity. Using applications such as Snort, captures network traffic and IDS events as encountered. Syslog and Sebek are used to monitor system activity. Syslog is a built in application that comes included in a honeynets operating system. Sebek is an open source tool developed by the Honeynet Project to monitor hacker behaviour. An abundance of information is gathered by a Generation II honeynet but a number of limitations still exist (Balas, 2005). There are three limitations of a Generation II model (Balas, 2005). The first restriction is that the architecture layers dictate the tools being used rather than using the tools to collect certain toes of data. The second point is that the information collected is very detailed and largely unstructured and the flow of data is not stored so the auditor has to piece this information together. The last limitation identified is that the data being stored is not organised into a defined format and no relationship mapping is in place to link data collected by one tool to data collected by another. This leads to ineffectiveness and inefficiencies as every time we want to examine data we are working with raw data which maybe in many different formats. This implies the need for a conversion programme. To solve these problems the future of honeypots looks to a third generation model.

Generation III

The Generation III approach has four main objectives (Balas, 2005). The data model should be independent of tools used. The use of a new tool should not require a conversion tool to bring the data format in line with that of other tools. The writes acknowledge that this objective is not going to be 100% successful but strive to achieve the need for a reduced amount of modifications to be made. The second aim is that a relationship between the different types of data collected should be achievable. To be able to present a network flow and thus see the relationships between data. The third aim is to have data composited into a central data store in real time as is practically possible. In doing so trying to partially alleviate the amount of time wasted working with information sites in multiple locations over and over again. The final aim is to have a consistent method of accessing data. It is felt that it is not enough just to direct our attention towards the formation of the data itself and d its standardisation but also there is a need for standards to be implemented on access and sharing of data.

Botnets

Malware is one of the biggest problems facing the Internet community today especially if it is specifically constructed to destroy. Hackers are even more interested in gaining access to computer systems using back doors and by controlling the systems from afar. Where we have a network of controlled nodes by a hacker this is called a Botnet. A botnet is a set of machines networked together using programs using a common Command and Control infrastructure (Curran, 2004). Attackers scan networks, especially Class B (128 – 191 address range) for vulnerabilities in such applications as Internet Explorer, misconfigured or vulnerabilities in the firewall or non-updated security patches. Once a machine is located they install and IRC (Internet Relay Chat) bot on the machine. This allows for real time communication with the machine (Alliance, 2005). Various forms or IRC bots are in existence and getting more complex as time goes on. The bot opens a link with a specified IRC channel on an IRC server and awaits commands to be issued by the hacker. Hackers can join many and distributed bots together to form a botnet. As a consequence of the potential of hackers to form huge botnets, this could pose serious threats, such as, denial of service attacks (DDos). According to the paper *Know your Enemy: Tracking Botnets*, it is stated that even if a botnet is made up of only 1000 bots (1000 home PCs with average upstream of 128KB can offer more than 100MBs) their combined bandwidth can be larger than that of an Internet connection of the most corporate systems.

If something of this nature of an attack happens it can be difficult to resolve the situation as many machines belonging to several organisations may be involved. The German Honeynet project analysed traffic and results showed that machines using Windows operating systems carried the highest number of targets totalling 80%. The most common attacks on infiltrates pots were:

- Port 445/TCP – used for resource sharing in Windows 2000+
- Port 139/TCP – NetBIOS session service – as with Port 445 the port is used for resource sharing
- Port 137/UDP – provides information on network devices such as system name and name of file shares
- Port 135/TCP – implement RPC. An RPC allows a computer program running on one machine to execute code on another host.

We have already looked at low and high interaction honeypots and the benefit and limitations of each. Both interaction honeypots can detect a zero day attack and would help in the detection of botnets. However if high interaction honeypots are employed there are a number of disadvantages (Wicherski, 2006). Firstly, some operating system for example Windows 2000 servers can be crashed and this can be exploited by the hacker to force reboots to take place. Medium Interaction honeypots try to patch some of these shortcomings. The main feature of Medium Interaction honeypots is that of application layer visualisation. The medium honeypot does not claim to provide full bells and whistles operating system environment, it provides enough responses to trick the hacker that they are visiting a particular port. Once a connection is made the information is extracted and analysed. The first open source honeypot of this type was developed in 2005 and was called mscollectd, Multiport is a GUI version for Windows (July 2005), nepenthes was released in February 2006 and is a UNIX product. Mwcollectd and nepenthes merged in Feb 2006 and now just go under the name nepehthes. Medium Interaction Honeypots have been proven to be very effective (Wicherski, 2006). Botnets as a tool can be used to cause significant harm in a number of ways. We shall now take a look at some of the potential possible attacks.

The Costs, Risks and Legal Implications of a Honeynet

Although much of the technology that can be employed for setting up a honeynet infrastructure can be sought through open source channels there still are costs involved in setting up honeynets. The cost can be divided up into two main categories: deployment and operating (Dornseif, 2004).

- **Deployment**
  The expense in this area can be compared to an iceberg. The ice on view above the water line reflects the expenses we immediately think of such as hardware and software purchases. But how much ice is hidden beneath the water? Generally the mass of ice below the water is far greater than what is above. Here lies the setup cost. At the outset we may acknowledge that a token amount of technical setup work will be required. This is generally underestimated. Honeynet technology is relatively new with methods; procedures and software are still evolving. To this point the setup of a honeypot on a network is a substantial piece of work. It is very intricate, technical work where time can fly by with little progress to show and this can be difficult to justify.

- **Operations**
  An operating expense refers to the day to day expenses that can be incurred. We can think of the general environmental expenses such as light and heat but these costs are no different to any other piece of hardware in use. Where honeynets are more demanding is the effort required to maintain and monitor. As stated previously, honeynet technology is evolving hence there are always newer, bigger, extras coming to market. These new products, releases or upgrades could provide users with extra functionality or close off known vulnerabilities hence the need also to keep up to date. Honeynets are really labour intensive, it is not the case that once they are up and running that they can be forgotten about. They require monitoring 24/7 both to keep track of any traffic and to do further analysis but also to ensure the honeynet is not being exploited by an attacker to attack another system.

Honeynets allow one to collect a massive amount of information about the information flows across the internet. We create these powerful systems but then as if we had a momentary lapse of conscious we leave the odd window or door open. In doing so we are daring the hacker to come and visit but also we are potentially inviting a hacker into our network where he or she could potentially do damage beyond ones greatest fears. With any system there are always risks involved but it is very important that those risks are measured and inline with what an organisation sees as acceptable. Four different categories of risk are identified, harm, detection, disabling and violation (Honeynet Project, 2005).

- **Harm**
  A honeynet is positioned to bait a hacker so we invite them in and realistically it is expected that they will try and evoke some type of attack on the system. We expect this so we harden the machine. The harm comes from the potential of an attacker to use our gilt edge invite into our party to harm another non-honeynet system either internally or externally of the organisation. Data Control can be put in place to limit the amount of outward connections but this does not guarantee that hacker's wings will be clipped.

- **Detection**
  Huge amounts of resources whether it be time, money or both can be invested into a honeynet project. This investment cannot be assumed to make a good return on investment. Once an attacker becomes suspicious or identifies that he or she has been lured into a honeynet they will be no longer interested and our information gathering will halt. It is generally the more experienced hackers that first identify the presence of a honeypot, they may choose to ignore it or they may go further and set out to destroy the system or provide misleading information. A hacker looks for many clues from the system they are attacking to sense if it's legitimate or not. A crucial part of honeynet technology is ensuring the honeypot is not used to further exploit other systems hence we limit outward connections. The fact that a limit is put in place can alert a hacker that all may not be what it seems. Once alerted a hacker will no longer be interested and may also alert others to its presence making a honeypot worthless and defunct.

- **Disabling**
  If an attacker detect the presence of a honeynet, they may decide to overwrite the Data Control and Data Capture properties in place, thus removing our armoury and leaving the honeynet wide open to

abuse and to be used for the hackers own gain. To this end it is important to have layers of security in place to mitigate the risk.

- **Violation**
  If a hacker compromises ones system they are now freely available to do whatever they wish. They can then launch attacks from a compromised machine on other systems or use it as part of their network to distribute illegal. The honeypot could be a library or data store for the hackers data. This data resides on the compromised system so liability might be on the owner of the machine to prove that it was compromised by a third party.

In order to reduce all of the above risks a security professional should be monitoring and analysing at all times. There is software that can be used to monitor but the supplementary use of human interaction give that extra layer of security and the professional may identify a potential or harmful attack that had never been seen before and hence monitoring software would have no knowledge. It is also required to customise a honeypot. Honeynet technology is open source so it freely available to all persons both good and bad. The hacker will be familiar with the default settings of a honeynet and so they can monitor for these early indications and so detect the honeypot. If we customise it is possible to make detection harder. Honeynets are an emerging technology and so the law also is evolving. One of the main issues is that of honeynet operation liability. Some would state that its possible negligence on the part of the operator to fully secure their system that results in attacks been made, in the case of honeypots we deliberately facilitate the misuse of the machine in question (Dornseif, 2004). From an ethical point of view the approach taken by the majority of honeypot operators is to lure potential attackers to their system thus inviting them is. The bait is given to learn the behaviours of hackers so then the Internet community could be better protected in the future. Another ethical quandary is that we are a big brother to the hacker, inviting them in and watching their tactics in laboratory conditions. (Dornseif et al., 2006) make a comparison to other real life situations where it is generally unacceptable to carry out experiment son non-consenting adults. Ethics are questions and policies for the particular organisation involved. Ethics are quite often fostered from the legal implications that might ensue once an action is taken so legal obligations or consequences can colour ethical behaviour. In Germany to be liable for the actions of an attacker using ones honeypot to attack others the legal system most prove there was the intent on the part of the organisation to attack the third party. The law also comes down on the side of the honeypot operator in the liability for damages. The operator cannot be made liable as long as they have put some measure in place, such as limiting outward connections to prevent attacker abuse. Even though these measures may not be totally secure the fact they have been attempted to restrain an attackers activities deems them not liable to pay damages to the party attacked (Dornseif, 2004).

Honeypot Tools

Many different honeypot software products have been developed, some to work on UNIX, other for Windows and a number have been successful on one platform have been ported to others. We shall now take a look at a number of different products looking at their features and also the limitations they posses.

Honeynet Project – Roo

Honeynets are a valuable source of information about malicious attacks, but the configuration and installation of such systems has considerable demands and risks involved. It is not trivial to install and setup a honeynet and care must be taken on configuration that no weaknesses are left for an attacker to exploit. To tackle this problem the honeynet project developed a piece of software called Honeywall. The older version was called Eeyore and now the newest version with added features is called Roo. The honeynet project put standards in place that defined how Data capture and Control be employed. Data Capture defines the methods of logging all the activity once the hacker enters the honeynet system without their knowledge. Data control defines the procedures for limiting the abilities of an attacker to sue the honeynet to further their own malicious agenda.

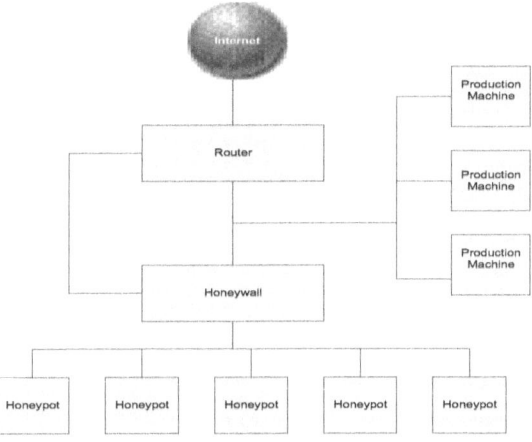

Figure 118: Generation II Honeynet Layout

The core component of this honeynet is the honeywall which is equipped with three interfaces. Two of the interfaces are not assigned IP address, of these two interfaces one is connected to the production system and the other is connected to the honeypots. The information flows directly between these two interfaces without any delay or latency in so doing acting as a transparent bridge. The third interface is connected to the main router on the network and has no interaction with the honeynet. The honeywall implements both the data capture and control policies. As stated already setup, installation and configuration of a honeynet takes a considerable amount of effort. The honeynet project has taken steps to ease this deployment by creating a bootable CD which allows a honeywall to be setup in an easy way. There latest version is a generation III honeynet called Roo. The honeywall is based on Fedora Core 3. The honeywall only creates the honeywall gateway; you are still required to setup the honeypots (Alliance, 2005). This method provides many advantages. Previously, it would be required to download, install and configure all individual pieces. This CD alleviates this entire configuration allowing for faster deployment.

Honey-DVD

The honeynet project Roo CD does alleviate or lessen the setup of a honeynet but it does not automatically setup the honeypots themselves. The honey-DVD solution was developed in the University of Mannheim Germany. It allows for a complete honeynet setup from a bootable DVD. The creators used multiple techniques to devise this technology. The paper 'Design and Implementation of the Honey-DVD' by the German university (Dornseif, 2006) sets out the technologies sued and explains the feature of the DVD. The first technology in use is Live Linux distributions capable of booting from a DVD and running completely within the bounds of memory without interactions with the machines hard disk. The second technique is visualisation, which helps with better performance and instability of different operating systems. The last technique sued it that of remote configuration. The honey-DVD is controlled by a central tool which allows the user to configure every component of the honeynet like the honeypots operating system. The mixture of these three techniques allows the creation of an automatic honeynet with the following features:

- The honeynet can be booted from any PC with a bootable DVD drive
- Fully functioning Generation III honeynet with honeywall and honeypots
- Simplistic setup allows for flexibility in configuring important values
- Allows for all maintenance and traffic analysis to be done from the DVD
- The honey-DVD is independent of the machines underlying hard disk
- Honey-DVD is an open source tool and is freely available to download.

The main areas in which the creators still require improvements are in the trade off between performance and storage space. This would be the main disadvantage of the Honey-DVD. This product in comparison to all other products would be in its infancy and the creators are constantly trying to make it more efficient and more compatible with other third party products is use.

Honeyd

Honeyd is a low interaction honeypot that works with Linux, Solaris and Windows platforms. Honeyd is an open source tool created by Niels Provos of the University of Mannheim and was later ported to Windows by Michael Davis of Security profiling Inc. the strength of Honeyd is in its ability to mimic operating systems IP stacks and offer services and ports for the remote hacker to browse. The main function of Honeyd is to detect unauthorised access within a computer system. It can reply to all TCP and UDP ports and IP addresses and can be configured to emulate a full functioning network. It monitors all unused IP addresses concurrently. When a connection attempt is made to an unused IP address, Honeyd assumes it is an attacker and tries to interact with whoever is making the connection. As a result of this methodology, if Honeyd detects any attackers it can be assumed that the attack is real and not a false alarm. Hence you only get notified of real attacks rather than all connections which dramatically reduces the amount of information that needs to be analysed. Honeyd strength lies in its modular design and the administrator's ability to choose what functionality they wish to implement (Honeynet Project, 2003). Honeyd is one of the more useable honeynet implementations in a non GUI environment but Honeyd is a difficult piece of software to install and configure properly. The user needs good technical and network knowledge and it also takes a significant amount of time to setup.

Honeyd not only detects possible attacks but also allows for services to be emulated. This allows you to see what services interests the attacker and what they are attempting to do. The emulation is created by using scripts to mimic a particular service using a particular port. These scripts can be written in a language of choice, commonly scripts are written in Perl, Shell script or Python. Example two scripts that can be used are those to mimic FTP and Telnet services (Spitzner, 2003). Honeyd can also be used to emulate operating systems adding further in the pretence that the attacker is actually compromising an actual live system instead of a honeypot. Honeyd has many positive features and is freely available open source tool that is continually being improved and increased in functionality. But it cannot be overstated that to get Honeyd installed and configured in any environment required considerable amount of knowledge and time. If it is more preferable to use an easier to install honeynet than a Windows based honeypot could be used such as KFSensor or PatriotBox.

KFSensor

KFSensor[1] is a windows based honeypot system developed by Keyfocus Ltd. It is a commercial product offering standard, professional and enterprise editions. KFSensor simulates system services at the Application layer of OSI network model. The machine running KFSensor does not have to be dedicated to this task solely but conflict can arise if services are being carried out on certain ports that KFSensor wants to simulate. KFSensor emulated ports will not be active if services are being carried out on those ports by other applications on the machine (see Figure 119).

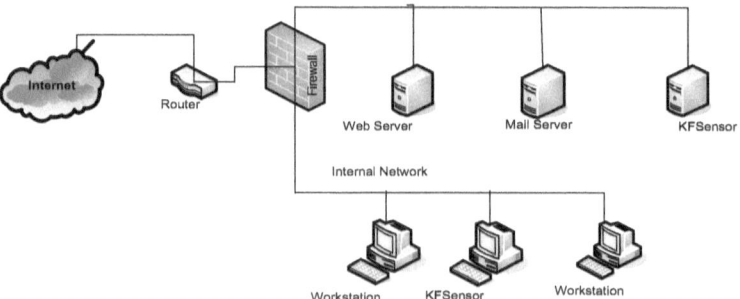

Figure 119: KFSensor Architecture

At the core of the KFSensor application is an internet daemon that has been built to handle multiple ports and IP addresses. Using the features built into the daemon this allows KFSensor to respond to connections in a variety of ways from port listening to complex emulation of system services. For example, KFSensor simulates responses to both valid and invalid request to an IIS Server. This makes it that bit more difficult to be identified as a honeypot. The one disadvantage is that KFSensor works at application layer level and has no IP stack. If a hacker pings a machine running KFSensor, they would identify the KFSensor host machine and not KFSensor

---

[1] http://www.keyfocus.net

itself. This can alert a hacker that something is quite not what it seems. For example, if the KFSensor host machine is running an underlying operating system of XP and the hacker sees Exchange Server supposedly running on the same machine this could alert the hacker. KFSensor supports approximately 256 listeners in comparison Honeyd has an IP stack and this result in Honeyd being able to support thousands of ports. The GUI interface to KFSensor is very user friendly suing colour and icons to donate attack types and their severity. There are two main components of KFSensor the server and the monitor. The monitor provides the interface to the system and is configurable to allow a user to display the granularity of data which they require. The server provides the core functionality, it listens to both TCP and UDP ports and interacts with the visitors and generates responses.

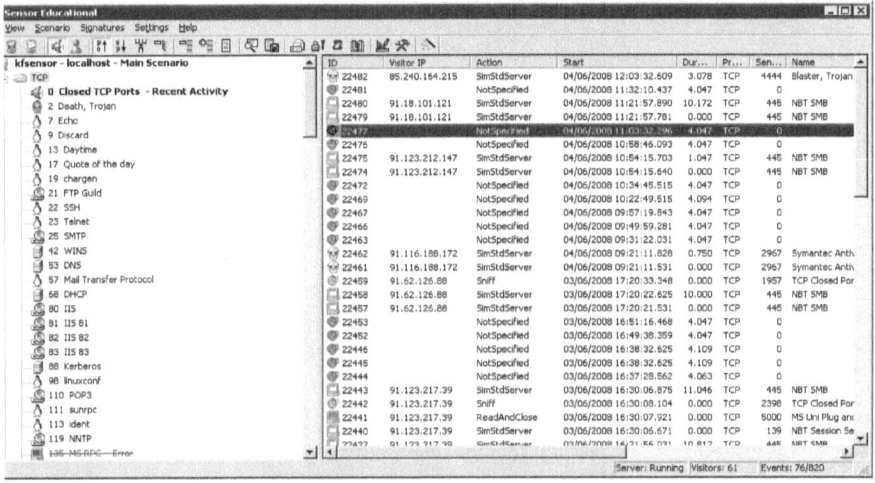

Figure 120: Activity Screen from KFSensor

KFSensor provides a substantial amount of benefits to the administrator and organization in whole. Some of the benefits are as follows:

- Provides both signature attack identification, detection of known threats, responds in real time which allows for identification of known attack patterns. But KFSensor does not rely solely on the signature engine therefore allowing it to detect zero day attacks or internal threats. Once an attack has been identified it is reported and allows for immediate analysis.
- KFSensor has no legitimate users so any connections made to it are treated as suspect thus eliminating the chance of false positives.
- KFSensor is very simple to sue and understand and the configuration of the product is straight forward. Also, the product does not eat up valuable system resources. KFSensor lies dormant until it is attacked so the overheads of having this product installed are very low.
- KFSensor also allows for Remote administration in its enterprise edition and complements the security already in place in an organization such as firewalls, antivirus etc.
- The architecture can be further extended by allowing users to create scripts and load data from log files and data dumps into a database to run numerous queries.
- KFSensor simulates real servers such as FTP, SMB, POP3, HTTP, Telnet, SMTP and SOCKS

PatriotBox

PatriotBox[1] is another GUI based Windows honeypot and is much more affordable than the fore mentioned KFSensor. It does not have the same power as KFSensor in that it has no database capabilities or scripting. PatriotBox provides eight different emulations form which one can choose: Windows 2000, 2003, 98, ME, XP, Linux and FreeBSD. This application allows for some customisation to take place although depending on which emulation is chosen a number of default listeners on certain ports are put in place. The emulations used are not

---

[1] http://www.alkasis.com

233

as professional as KFSensor as the emulations of certain service do not have the accuracy of responses, banners as its counterpart.

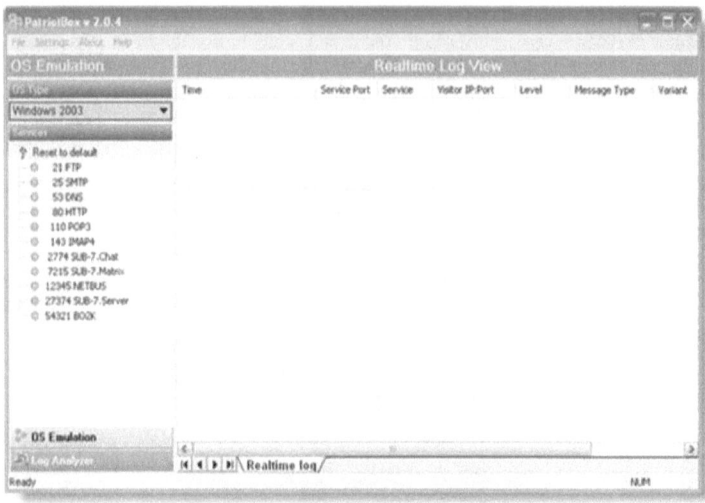

Figure 121: Activity Screen from PatriotBox

PatriotBox offers a good entry level honeypot and is much more affordable but affordability comes at a price and that price is lack of reality or polish. PatriotBox offers all the basic functionality required for a start up project but is still a bit light on the required functionality to implement this honeypot software in a security conscious production environment or to get long term returns in terms of a good information source.

Jackpot

Jackpot[1] is a honeynet dedicated to fighting spam and was developed using a combination of Java and HTML. It operates an SMTP sever decoy system. Jackpot is easy to install and is free of charge. Jackpot allows you to differentiate between spam relay test message and regular spam. Jackpot can be configured to set the number of relay messages you will accept before refusing to relay anymore to other sites. Jackpot fools the spammers into thinking it is relaying their messages when in fact it is sending them to a drop box. If a spammer sends a test spam message to clarify that their spam is being relayed the tester message will be let through but all other message stopped. The tarpit delay can be set very low so as to irritate the spammer waiting for response to return from their commands. Jackpot will save all the information collected on the spam for further analysis and will also trawl the spamming site to see if it can pick up and clues as to the origin of the spam or spammer. The use of honeypot technology is growing rapidly as the benefits of using such systems are revealed. They can emulate an operating system or be a real operating system. We have the ability to mimic a UNIX or Windows environment. Honeypots can add an extra line of defence to an organisations security policy. Honeypots work by logging the attempted exploits of a hacker against them, thus, giving us invaluable information into the objectives of the hacker, are they just snooping around or are they trying to carry out a sinister attack? A honeypot can be a great way to monitor, gather evidence and deflect potential attacks away from a production environment.

Conclusion

Every day it seems, new hackers evolve who strive to find weaknesses in computer systems, infiltrate them and cause havoc. We need to be consistently trying to stay one step ahead. This is a very difficult task. In order to

---

[1] http://www.jackpot.uk.net

234

strengthen security, we need to learn from the hackers; we need to watch them and court them and analyse their activities. Using honeypot technology we can gain the knowledge that helps us defend our systems. The honeypot provides us with insights into the hacker's motivations and movements, thus allowing us the potential to sandbag and harden our production systems against attacks. Honeypots are being deployed globally in an attempt to be the 'recipients' of thousands of exploits from hackers on a daily basis. These honeypots provide invaluable data about hackers all over the world, which is then used to alert the security personnel to the hackers activities. This process basically acts as an early warning system, a means of collecting evidence or at the very least, a tool that can be added to the security arsenal of any organisation.

References

Alliance Research, The Honeynet Project (2005), 'Know your Enemy: Tracking Botnets', http://www.honeynet.org/papers/bots/

Balas, E., Viecco, C. (2005), 'Towards a Third generation data Capture Architecture for Honeynets', IEEE Workshop on Information Assurance and Security 2005, Available at: http://www.honeynet.org/papers/individual/hflow.pdf

Curran, K., Morrissey, C., Fagan, C., Murphy, C., O'Donnell, B., Fitzpatrick, G., Condit, S. (2004),'A Year in the Life of the Irish Honeynet: Attacked, Probed and Bruised but Still Fighting', Information Knowledge Systems Management,pp.201-213

Dornseif M., Gärtner, F.C., Holz, T. (2004), 'Vulnerability Assessment using Honeypots', Praxis der Infromationsverarbeitung und Lommunikation (PIK), vol.4, issue.27, pp.195-201 http://pi1.informatik.uni-mannheim.de/publications/pdf/vulnerability-assessment-using-honepots

Dornseif M., Sascha A. (2004),' Modelling the costs and benefits of Honeynets', http://www.dtc.umn.edu/weis2004/dornseif.pdf

Dornseif M., Holz T., Mathes, J., Weisemoller, I. (2004),' Measuring Security Threats with Honeypot Technology', Available at: http://www.honeynet.org/papers/individual/sane-2004.pdf

Dornseif M., Freiling, F.C., Gedicke, N., Holz, T. (2006), 'Design and Implementation of the Honey-DVD', Proceedings of the 2006 IEEE Workshop on Information Assurance, Available at: http://pi1.informatik.uni-mannheim.de/publications/pdf/design-and-implementation-of-the-honey-dvd

Geer, D. (2006), 'Behaviour Based network Security Goes Mainstream', IEEE, vol.March, pp.14-17

Grimes, R. A. (2005),'Honeypots for Windows', ISBN: 1-59059-335-9

Hall, M. (2004),'Sticky Security',Computerworld, vol.38, issue.3, pp.48

Hamm, S. (2005),'Computer, Heal Thyself', Business Week, issue.3692, pp.74-75

Honeynet Project (2003), 'Know your Enemy: GenII Honeynets', http://www.honeynet.org/papers/gen2/index.html

Honeynet Project (2004),'Honeynet Definitions, Requirements, and Standards' http://www.honeynet.org

Honeynet Project (2005), 'Know your Enemy: Honeynets', http://www.honeynet.org/papers/honeynet/

Horn, P. (2001),'Autonomic Computing: IBM's Perspective on the State of Information Technology', Available at: http://www.research.ibm.com/autonomic/manifesto/autonomic_computing.pdf

Levine, J., LaBella, R., Owen, H., Contis, D., Culver, B. (2003),' The Use of Honeynets to detect Exploited Ststems Across Large Enterprise Networks', Proceedings of the 2003 IEEE Workshop on Information Assurance, Available at: http://www.tracking-hackers.com/papers/gatech-honeynet.pdf

Lodin, S. (1998) Intrusion detection product evaluation criteria,
http://www.cis.udel.edu/~zhi/www.docshow.net/ids.htm

Manzano, Y., Yasinsac, Dr. A. (2003), 'Honeytraps, a Valuable Tool To Provide Effective Countermeasures for Crime Against Computer and Network Systems ',7th World Multiconference on Systemics, Cybernetics and Informatics, Available at: http://ww2.cs.fsu.edu/~manzano/Research/publications/MY_SCI2003.pdf

Sherif, J.S., Ayers, R., Dearmond, T.G. (2003),'Intrusion detection: the art and the practice. Part I', Information Management & Computer Security, vol.11, issue.4, pp.175-186

Sherif, A. (2003),'Intrusion detection: methods and systems. Part II', Information Management & Computer Security, vol.11, issue.5, pp.222-229

Spitzner, L. (2004),' Open Source Honeypots: Learning with Honeyd', http://www.securityfocus.com/infocus/1659

Spitzner, L. (2004), 'Problems and Challenges with Honeypots ',SecurityFocus, http://www.securityfocus.com/print/infocus/1757

Sundaram, A. (1996), 'An Introduction to intrusion detection ',The ACM Student Magazine, vol.2, issue.4

Wicherski, G. (2006), 'Medium Interaction Honeypots ', Available at: http://www.pixel-house.net/midinthp.pdf

33   Wireless 802.11 Security

Kevin Curran and Elaine Smyth

Wireless networks have a number of security issues. Signal leakage means that network communications can be picked up outside the physical boundaries of the building in which they are being operated, meaning a hacker can operate from the street outside or discretely from blocks away. In addition to signal leakage – the Wired Equivalent Privacy protocol is inherently weak. In addition to WEP's weaknesses there are various other attacks that can be initiated against WLAN's, all with detrimental effects. This chapter outlines some of the issues surrounding security on WiFi 802.11 networks.

Introduction

On the surface WLANs act the same as their wired counterparts, transporting data between network devices. However, there is one fundamental, and quite significant, difference; WLANs are based upon radio communications technology, as an alternative to structured wiring and cables. Data is transmitted between devices through the air by utilizing the radio waves. Devices that participate in a WLAN must have a Network Interface Card (NIC) with wireless capabilities. This essentially means that the card contains a small radio device that allows it to communicate with other wireless devices, within the defined range for that card, for example, the 2.4-2.4853 GHz range. For a device to participate in a wireless network it must, firstly, be permitted to communicate with the devices in that network and, secondly, it must be within the transmission range of the devices in that network. To communicate, radio-based devices take advantage of electromagnetic waves and their ability to be altered in such a manner that they can carry information, known as modulation. Information is transferred by mixing the electromagnetic wave with the information to be transmitted. At the receiving end, the signal is compared to an un-modulated signal to reverse the process (called demodulation). There are three main types of modulation techniques; these are Amplitude Modulation (AM), Frequency Modulation (FM), and Phase Modulation (PM). Because FM is more robust against interference, it was chosen as the modulation standard for high frequency radio transmissions (Harte, 2000). Radio devices utilized within WLANs operate in the 2.4-2.4845GHz range of the unlicensed Industrial Scientific and Medical (ISM) frequency band, using either Frequency Hopping Spread Spectrum (FHSS) or Direct Sequence Spread Spectrum (DSSS), which are special modulation techniques used for spreading data over a wide band of frequencies sacrificing bandwidth to gain signal-to-noise (S/N) performance (Harte, 2000).

Wireless devices have the option of participating in two type of networks; Ad Hoc and Infrastructure. An Ad Hoc (also known as peer-to-peer) network is the simplest form of WLAN. It is composed of two or more nodes communicating without any bridging or forwarding capability; all nodes are of equal importance and may join and leave the network at any time, each device also has equal right to the medium. Access Points (APs) are not necessary. For this to work, the devices wishing to participate in an Ad Hoc network must be within transmission range of each other, when a nodes goes out of range it will lose connection with the rest of the devices. The range of this type of network is referred to as a 'single cell' and is called an Independent Basic Service Set (IBSS) (Tourrilhes, 2000).

In an infrastructure network communications take place through an AP, in a many-to-one configuration, with the AP at the single end. In its simplest form it consists of one AP and a group of wireless clients/devices, which must be within transmission range of the AP, and be properly configured to communicate with the AP. This type of network is called a Basic Service Set (BSS) (Sikora, 2003). If two or more BSSes are operated in the same network, by linking the APs via a background network, this is then called an Extended Service Set (ESS). Such a configuration can cover larger, multi-floor, buildings. However, support is required for 'roaming' between different APs on the network, that is the hand-off between a device leaving one APs range and going into the range of another AP (Geier, 1999).

APs can be overlapped if they are each given a different channel, within the 2.4-2.4835GHz, range to communicate on. There are eleven overlapping frequencies specified in IEEE 802.11, which means that with careful planning multiple networks can coexist in the same physical space without interfering with each other (Tourrilhes, 2000). APs must also be configured with a Service Set Identifier (SSID), also known as the network name. It is a simple 1-32 byte alphanumeric string given to each ESS that identifies the wireless network and allows stations to connect to one desired network when multiple independent networks operate in the same physical area. It also provides a very basic way of preventing unauthorised users from joining your network, as all devices in an ESS must have the same ESSID to participate.

Most APs can provide additional, basic, security features, such as WEP and MAC address filtering. WEP, an abbreviation for Wired Equivalent Protocol, is a protocol designed specifically for use on wireless networks and is supposed to provide the security equivalent of the cable in a wired network through the use of encryption. Communicating devices must use the same WEP key in order to communicate. MAC address filtering provides a basis for screening users wanting to connect to a network; for a client device to be able to successfully communicate with the AP, its name must appear on an access control list of MAC addresses held by that AP. However, both these methods have been proven weak in their ability to secure wireless networks; both can be easily broken.

Wired networks have always presented their own security issues, but wireless networks introduce a whole new set of rules with their own unique security vulnerabilities. Most wired security measures are just not appropriate for application within a WLAN environment; this is mostly due to the complete change in transmission medium. However, some of the security implementations developed specifically for WLANs are also not terribly strong. Indeed, this aspect could be viewed as a 'work-in-progress'; new vulnerabilities are being discovered just as quickly as security measures are being released. Perhaps the issue that has received the most publicity is the major weaknesses in WEP, and more particularly the use of the RC4 algorithm and relatively short Initialisation Vectors (IVs).

Signal Leakage

WLANs suffer from all the security risks associated with their wired counterparts; however, they also introduce some unique risks of their own. The main issue with radio-based wireless networks is signal leakage. Due to the properties of radio transmissions it is impossible to contain signals within one clearly defined area. In addition, because data is not enclosed within cable it makes it very easy to intercept without being physically connected to the network. This puts it outside the limits of what a user can physically control; signals can be received outside the building and even from streets away. See Figure 122 below for a view of just how far leakage can go. Signal leakage may not be a huge priority when organisations are implementing their WLAN, but it can present a significant security issue, as demonstrated below. The same signals that are transmitting data around an organisation's office are the same signals that can also be picked up from streets away by an unknown third party. This is what makes WLANs so vulnerable.

Figure 122: Signal Leakage from a WLAN

Before WLAN's became common, someone wishing to gain unauthorised access to a wired network had to physically attach themselves to a cable within the building. This is why wiring closets should be kept locked and secured. Any potential hacker had to take great risks to penetrate a wired network. Today potential hackers do not have to use extreme measures, there's no need to smuggle equipment on site when it can be done from two streets away. It is not difficult for someone to obtain the necessary equipment; access can be gained in a very discrete manner from a distance.

Wired Equivalent Protocol (WEP)

To go some way towards providing the same level of security the cable provides in wired networks, the Wired Equivalent Protocol (WEP) was developed. IEEE 802.11 defined three basic security services for the WLAN environment (Karygiannis & Owens, 2003):

- Authentication (a primary goal of WEP)
- Confidentiality (privacy – a second goal of WEP)
- Integrity (another goal of WEP)

WEP was designed to provide the security of a wired LAN by encryption through use of the RC4 (Rivest Code 4) algorithm. It's primary function was to safeguard against eavesdropping ('sniffing'), by making the data that is transmitted unreadable by a third party who does not have the correct WEP key to decrypt the data. RC4 is not specific to WEP, it is a random generator, also known as a keystream generator or a stream cipher, and was developed in RSA Laboratories by Ron Rivest in 1987 (hence the name Rivest Code (RC)). It takes a relatively short input and produces a somewhat longer output, called a pseudo-random key stream. This key stream is simply added modulo two that is exclusive ORed (XOR), with the data to be transmitted, to generate what is known as ciphertext.

WEP is applied to all data above the 802.11b WLAN layers (Physical and Data Link Layers, the first two layers of the OSI Reference Model) to protect traffic such as Transmission Control Protocol/Internet Protocol (TCP/IP), Internet Packet Exchange (IPX) and Hyper Text Transfer Protocol (HTTP). It should be noted that only the frame body of data frames are encrypted and the entire frame of other frame types are transmitted in the clear, unencrypted (Karygiannis & Owens, 2003). To add an additional integrity check, an Initialisation Vector (IV) is used in conjunction with the secret encryption key. The IV is used to avoid encrypting multiple consecutive ciphertexts with the same key, and is usually 24 bits long. The shared key and the IV are fed into the RC4 algorithm to produce the key stream. This is XORed with the data to produce the ciphertext, the IV is then appended to the message. The IV of the incoming message is used to generate the key sequence necessary to decrypt the incoming message. The ciphertext, combined with the proper key sequence, yields the original plaintext and integrity check value (ICV) (Tyrrell, 2003). The decryption is verified by performing the integrity check algorithm on the recovered plaintext and comparing the output ICV to the ICV transmitted with the message. If it is in error, an indication is sent back to the sending station. The IV increases the key size, for example, a 104 bit WEP key with a 24bit IV becomes a 128 bit RC4 key. In general, increasing the key size increases the security of a cryptographic technique. Research has shown that key sizes of greater than 80 bits make brute force[1] code breaking extremely difficult. For an 80 bit key, the number of possible keys - 10^24 which puts computing power to the test; but this type of computing power is not beyond the reach of most hackers. The standard key in use today is 64-bit. However, research has shown that the WEP approach to privacy is vulnerable to certain attacks regardless of key size (Karygiannis & Owens, 2003). Although the application of WEP may stop casual 'sniffers', determine hackers can crack WEP keys in a busy network within a relatively short period of time.

WEP's major weaknesses relate to three main issues. Firstly, the use of static keys, secondly, the length of the IV, and thirdly, the RC4 algorithm.

Static Keys
When WEP is enabled in accordance with the 802.11b standard, the network administrator must personally visit each wireless device in use and manually enter the appropriate WEP key. This may be acceptable at the installation stage of a WLAN or when a new client joins the network, but if the key becomes compromised and there is a loss of security, the key must be changed. This may not be a huge issue in a small organisation with

---

[1] A method that relies on sheer computing power to try all possibilities until the solution to a problem is found, usually refers to cracking passwords by trying every possible combination of a particular key space.

only a few users, but it can be impractical in large corporations, who typically have hundreds of users (Dismukes, 2002). As a consequence, potentially hundreds of users and devices could be using the same, identical, key for long periods of time. All wireless network traffic from all users will be encrypted using the same key; this makes it a lot easier for someone listening to traffic to crack the key as there are so many packets being transmitted using the same key. Unfortunately, there were no key management provisions in the original WEP protocol.

IV Length

This is a 24 bit initialisation vector WEP appends to the shared key. WEP uses this combined key and IV to generate the RC4 key schedule; it selects a new IV for each packet, so each packet can have a different key. This forms a family of 2^{24} keys. As described, each packet transmission selects one of these 2^{24} keys and encrypts the data under that key. On the surface, this may appear to strengthen protection by lengthening the 40 bit WEP key, however this scheme suffers from a basic problem; if IVs are chosen randomly there is a 50% chance of reuse after less than 5,000 packets (Walker, 2000). The problem is a numerical restriction; because the IV is only 24 bits long, there are a finite number of variations of the IV for RC4 to pick from. Mathematically there are only 16,777,216 possible values for the IV. This may seem like a huge number, but given that it takes so many packets to transmit useful data, 16 million packets can easily go by in hours on a heavily used network. Eventually the RC4 algorithm starts using the same IVs over and over. Thus, someone passively 'listening' to encrypted traffic and picking out the repeating IVs can begin to deduce what the WEP key is. Made easier by the fact that there is a static variable, (the shared key), an attacker can eventually crack the WEP key (iLabs, 2002). For example, a busy AP, which constantly sends 1500 byte packets at 11Mbps, will exhaust the space of IVs after 1500 x 8/(11 x 10^6) x 2^{24} = 18,000 seconds, or 5 hours. (The amount of time may actually be smaller since many packets are less than 1500 bytes). This allows an attacker to collect two ciphertexts that are encrypted with the same key stream. This reveals information about both messages. By XORing two ciphertexts that use the same key stream would cause the key stream to be cancelled out and the result would be the XOR of the two plaintexts (Vines, 2002).

There is an additional problem that involves the use of IVs, more specifically, weak IVs. Some numbers in the range 0-16,777,215 don't work too well with the RC4 algorithm. When these weak IVs are used, the resulting packet can be run through a series of mathematical functions to decipher part of the WEP key. By capturing a large number of packets an attacker can pick out enough weak IVs to reveal the WEP key (PCQuest, 2003). Tools like Airsnort specifically exploit this vulnerability to allow hackers to obtain the above information relatively easily. The crack process within Airsnort works by collecting packets thought to have been encrypted using a weak IV and then sorting them according to which key byte they help expose. A weak IV can assist in exposing only one key byte. The Flurer attack states that a weak IV has about a 5% chance of exposing the corresponding key byte. So, when a sufficient number of weak IVs have been collected for a particular key byte, statistical analysis will show a tendency towards a particular value for that key byte. The crack process makes a key guess based on the highest ranking values in the statistical analysis. Tests conducted by Stubblefield, et al, show that between 60 and 256 weak IVs were needed to recover a key (AirSnort FAQ). In addition to the fundamental weaknesses in the WEP security protocol, (which is the primary security measure in WLANs), there are numerous other attacks that can be instigated against WLANs and their devices. Each of these will be discussed in turn in the next chapter; how they are carried out and what impact they could have. Some of these attacks will be carried out against the test WLAN as part of the primary research; this will assess the relative ease with which these attacks can be carried out and how effective they are.

War-Driving

Not surprisingly a new 'sport' has emerged within the computer hacking world which takes advantage of some of the security weaknesses in WLANs. So called 'War-Driving' is a term used to describe a hacker, who, armed with a laptop, a wireless NIC, an antenna and sometimes a GPS device travels, usually by car, scanning or 'sniffing' for WLAN devices, or more specifically unprotected or 'open' and easily accessed networks . The name is thought to have come from another hacking technique called War-Dialling, where a hacker programs their system to call hundreds of phone numbers in search of a poorly protected computer dial-up (Poulsen, 2001). The concept is made possible by the way these devices interact and communicate with each other. All a hacker needs to do is move about from one place to another and let the devices do the rest. Over time, the hacker builds up a database of logged devices. There is a web site where war-drivers can upload any information they obtain. This site is called Wigle and can be found at http://www.wigle.net (Vines, 2002). Based on US anecdotal evidence just over a year ago, as many as 60-80 per cent of wireless LANs hadn't had the most basic steps taken to secure them, leaving them wide open to unauthorised third parties (Descoeudres,

2002). In November 2001, the BBC took to the streets of London to observe how lax wireless security was. In one short trip around London they found that two-thirds of the networks discovered were wide open (BBC News, 2001). It was noted some of the networks were using DHCP[1], making it even easier for an unauthorised individual to join the network, because they are automatically issued with a valid IP address and other network information.

Due to the increased use of WLANs in recent years, it is quite possible that the number of unsecured devices has also risen in tandem, thus providing potential hackers with more choice. After all that has been written about the insecurities of WLAN, some users/organisations still insist on implementing them with their default settings and no encryption (Ulanoff, 2003). A Worldwide WarDrive, held in August to September 2002, discovered that 70% of APs were running without using any encryption, worse still 27% were doing so while using the default SSID that came with the hardware, leaving them wide open for use by anyone in range with a wireless NIC and a note of all vendor's default SSIDs. These figures are rather disturbing figures; leaving an AP at its default settings is the this is the equivalent of putting an Ethernet socket on the outside of the building so anyone passing by can plug into the network (Griffith, 2002). There is a plethora of hacking tools widely available to download from the Internet for any potential War-Driver to use. Table 8 lists some of the more popular tools and a brief description of their function.

TOOL NAME	DESCRIPTION
Netstumbler (http://www.netstumbler.com)	Wireless AP identifier; listens for SSIDs and sends beacons as probes searching for APs.
Kismet (http://kistmetwireless.net)	Wireless sniffer and monitor; passively monitors wireless traffic and sorts data to identify SSIDs, MAC addresses, channels and connection speeds. Also identifies data with weak ICs that can be used by Airsnort to crack WEP.
Wellenreiter (http://www.wellenreiter.net)	LAN discovery tool; uses brute force to identify low traffic APs, hides real MAC address and integrates with GPS.
THC-RUT (http://packetstormsecurity.nl/filedesc/thcrut-1.2.5.tar.html	WLAN discovery tool; uses brute force to identify low traffic APs.
Ethereal (http://www.ethereal.com)	Network analyser; interactively browses the captured data, viewing summary and detail information for all observed network traffic.
WEPCrack (http://wepcrack.sourceforge.net)	Encryption breaker; cracks 802.11 WEP encryption keys using the discovered weaknesses of the RC4 key scheduling.
AirSnort (http://airsnort.shmoo.com)	Encryption breaker; passively monitoring transmissions, computing the encryption key when enough packets have been gathered with weal IVs.
HostAP (http://hostap.epitest.fi)	Converts a WLAN station to function as an AP (available only for WLAN cards that are based on Intersil's Prism 2/2.5/3 chipset.

(SyDisTyKMoFo, 2003)

Table 8: Wireless Network Hacking Tools

There has been a lot of press globally, and many articles and papers written about wireless networks and their security vulnerabilities. However, despite all the literature, some enterprises still make the mistake of believing that they don't have to worry about wireless security if they are running non-critical systems with non-sensitive information across their WLANs. All information is sensitive information, and what an enterprise may class as being non-sensitive to them may be very useful to a hacker. In addition, most WLANs will connect with the wired enterprise backbone at some point, thus providing hackers with a launch pad to the entire network. The havoc an unwelcome third party could cause from here would be unlimited and very difficult to trace. Aside from the various attacks they could instigate (DoS and viruses); the loss of confidentiality, privacy and integrity that would occur if someone where able to steal, alter or delete information on your customer database is damaging enough. Access to sensitive information would be made relatively easy, perhaps even customer's

---

[1] Dynamic Host Control Protocol; governs the dynamic allocation of IP addresses to network devices/clients.

credit card details. This could have an un-quantifiable affect on business, perhaps resulting in the loss of customers/clients and future revenue (AirDefense, 2003).

Types Of Attack

This chapter deals with the various attacks that can be performed against WLANs (aside from the WEP crack), how they are carried out and what affect they have in relation to authentication, confidentiality and integrity, the three basic security requirements within networks. All of the attacks can be categorised into two general attack types; passive and active.

Passive Attacks

A passive attack is an attack on a system that does not result in a change to the system in any way; the attack is purely to monitor or record data. Passive attacks affect confidentiality, but not necessarily authentication or integrity. Eavesdropping and Traffic Analysis fall under this category. When an attacker eavesdrops, they simply monitor transmissions for message content. It usually takes the form of someone listening into the transmissions on a LAN between stations/devices.

Eavesdropping

Eavesdropping is also known as 'sniffing' or wireless 'footprinting'. As mentioned in a previous chapter there are various tools available for download online which allow the monitoring of networks and their traffic; developed by hackers, for hackers. Netstumbler, Kismet, Airsnort, WEPCrack and Ethereal are all well known names in wireless hacking circles, and all are designed specifically for use on wireless networks, with the exception of Ethereal, which is a packet analyser and can also be used on a wired LAN. NetStumbler and Kismet can be used purely for passive eavesdropping; they have no additional active functions, except perhaps their ability to work in conjunction with Global Positioning Systems (GPSs) to map the exact locations of identified wireless LANs. NetStumbler is a Windows-based sniffer, where Kismet is primarily a Linux-based tool. NetStumbler uses an 802.11 Probe Request sent to the broadcast destination address, which causes all APs in the area to issue an 802.11 Probe Response containing network configuration information, such as their SSID, WEP status, the MAC address of the device, name (if applicable), the channel the device is transmitting on, the vendor and the type, either peer or AP, along with a few other pieces of information. Using the network information and GPS data collected, it is then possible to create maps with tools such as StumbVerter and MS Mappoint. Kismet, although not as graphical or user friendly as NetStumbler, is similar to its Windows counterpart, but it provides superior functionality. While scanning for APs, packets can also be logged for later analysis. Logging features allow for captured packets to be stored in separate categories, depending upon the type of traffic captured. Kismet can even store encrypted packets that use weak keys separately to run them through a WEP key cracker after capture, such as Airsnort or WEPCrack (Sutton, 2002). Wireless network GPS information can be uploaded to a site called Wigle (http://www.wigle.net). Therefore, if wigle data exists for a particular area, there is no need to drive around that area probing for wireless devices; this information can be obtained in advance from the Wigle web site. All that remains is to drive to a location where known networks exist to observe traffic. Wigle currently has a few hundred thousand networks on its database.

Traffic Analysis

Traffic Analysis gains intelligence in a more subtle way by monitoring transmissions for patterns of communication. A considerable amount of information is contained in the flow of messages between communicating parties. Airopeek NX, a commercial 802.11 monitoring and analysis tool for Windows, analyses transmissions and provides a useful node view, which groups detected stations and devices by their MAC address and will also show IP addresses and protocols observed for each. The Peer Map view, within Airopeek NX, presents a matrix of all hosts discovered on the network by their connections to each other. This can make it very easy to visualise AP and client relationships, which could be useful to hackers in deciding where to try and gain access or target for an attack (McClure, 2003). Some attacks may begin as passive, but and then cross over to active as they progress. For example, tools such as Airsnort or WEPCrack may passively monitor transmissions, but their intent is to crack the WEP key used to encrypt data being transmitted.

Ultimately the reasons for wanting to crack the key are so that an unauthorised individual can access a protected network and then launch an active attack of some form or another. These types of attack are classed as passive decryption attacks.

Airsnort, mentioned previously, exploits the key weaknesses and uses this to crack WEP keys, as does WEPCrack. These are tools that put hackers on the first step towards an active attack. However, WEPCrack, unlike Airsnort, must be used in conjunction with a separate packet sniffer as it does not have the ability to capture network traffic. These tools utilise what is known as a Brute Force technique to break codes. Brute Force is a method of breaking a cipher by trying every possible key until the correct key is found. The feasibility of this attack depends on the key length of the cipher, and/or the amount of computational power available to the attacker, and of course time. Another type of passive decryption attack is what is known as a Dictionary Attack, also a form of the brute force technique. A Dictionary Attack refers to breaking a cipher, or obtaining a password by running through a list of likely keys, or a list of words. The term Dictionary Attack initially referred to finding passwords in a specific list, such as an English dictionary. Today, a Brute Force approach can compute likely passwords, such as all five-letter combinations, 'on-the-fly' instead of using a pre-built list. The last Brute Force, passive decryption, attack is called a Table Attack and can be demonstrated with an example that makes reference to IVs. It is a method which involves using the relatively small number of IVs (24 bit) to build decryption tables. Once the contents of a single encrypted packet are known, the hacker can work backwards and build a table of all the keys possible with a particular IV (Franklin, 2001).

Active Attacks

An active attack, also referred to as a malicious attack, occurs when an unauthorised third party gains access to a network and proceeds to perform Denial of Service (DoS) attack, to disrupt the proper operation of a network, to intercept network traffic and either modify or delete it, or inject extra traffic onto the network. There are many active attacks that can be launched against wireless networks; the following few paragraphs outline almost all of these attacks, how they work and what affect they have (Karygiannis & Owens, 2003). DoS attacks are easily the most prevalent type of attack against 802.11 networks, and can be waged against a single client or an entire WLAN. In this type of attack the hacker usually does not steal information, they simply prevent users from accessing network services, or cause services to be interrupted or delayed. Consequences can range from a measurable reduction in performance to the complete failure of the system. Some common DoS attacks are outlined below.

Man-in-the-Middle (MITM) Attack

This attack is carried out by inserting a malicious station between the victim station and the AP, thus the attacker becomes the 'man in the middle'; the station is tricked into believing that the attacker is the AP, and the AP into believing that the attacker is the legitimate station. To being the attack the perpetrator passively monitors the frames sent back and forth between the station and the AP during the initial association process with an 802.11 analyser. As a result, information is obtained about both the station and the AP, such as the MAC and IP address of both devices, association ID for the station and SSID of the network. With this information a rogue station/AP can be set up between the two unsuspecting devices. Because the original 802.11 does not provide mutual authentication, a station will happily re-associate with the rogue AP. The rogue AP will then capture traffic from unsuspecting users; this of course can expose information such as user names and passwords. After gleaning enough information about a particular WLAN, a hacker can then use a rogue station to mimic a valid one. This enables the hacker to deceive an AP by disassociating the valid station and reassociating again as a rogue station with the same parameters as the valid station. Two wireless cards are typically required for this type of attack (Wi-FiPlanet, 2002). Once the attacker has successfully inserted themselves between the AP and client station, they are free to modify traffic, selectively forward or even delete it completely, while logging every packet that comes through it. In addition, the attacker is also free to explore and use other areas of the network as a legitimate user.

Session Hijacking

In this attack the intruder makes it appear to a legitimate user, who has just connected with the AP, that they've been disconnected. Much like the second half of the MITM attack, the intruder then connects with the still active WLAN connection, thereby hijacking the session. The attacker must wait until the client has successfully authenticated to the network, then send a disassociate message to the client on the legitimate APs behalf, using the MAC address of the AP, then send frames to the valid AP, using the MAC address of the valid client. However, this attack assumes that no encryption is present, otherwise the radio perpetrating the attack would not be able to gain access to the network after the hijack because the AP would reject all packets that do not match an encryption key corresponding to a known user, unless of course the attacker has taken the time beforehand to crack the key. When no encryption is present, this attack will easily succeed, allowing the attacker to use the session until the next reauthentication takes place. At the next reauthentication, the attacker would not be reauthenticated and effectively kicked-off, they would then have to hijack another valid session (Proxim, 2003).

MAC Spoofing – AKA Identity Theft

To carry off this attack the intruder impersonates a legitimate device on the network by stealing their credentials. To do this the attacker must change the manufacturer-assigned MAC identity of their NIC to the same value as a legitimate user on the network; they assume the identity of this user by spoofing their MAC address. By analysing traffic, a hacker can easily pick off MAC addresses of authorised users. The hacker then connects to the wireless LAN as an authorised user. Somewhat similar in principal to the initial stage of the MITM attack, where a device impersonates or masquerades as someone they are not. This attack enables the hacker to transmit and receive data within the network as an authorised member; because they are using the identity of an authorised user it will hide their presence on the network and bypass any MAC address-based ACLs (Wright, 2003).

Other MAC Vulnerabilities

A utility known as Interframe spacing can also be utilised to launch malicious attacks. Since every transmitting node must wait at least the Shortest Interframe Space (SIFS) interval before transmitting, if not longer, an attacker could completely monopolise the channel by sending a short signal just before the end of every SIFS period. While this attack could be highly effective, it also requires the attacker to expel considerable energy; an SIFS period is only 20 microseconds on 802.11b networks, leading to a cycle of 50,000 packets per second in order to disable all access to a network (Bellardo & Savage, 2003). However, a more serious vulnerability arises from the virtual carrier-sense mechanism used to mitigate collisions from hidden terminals[1]. For a definition of the hidden terminal problem. Each 802.11 frame carries a Duration Field that indicates the number of microseconds that the channel is reserved. This value, in turn, is used to program the Network Allocation Vector (NAV) on each node. The NAV keeps stations quiet until the first acknowledgement of a transmission is received. Only when a node's NAV reaches zero is it allowed to transmit. This feature is principally used in the Ready-to-Send/Clear-to-Send (RTS/CTS) handshake that can be used to synchronise access to the channel when a hidden terminal may be interfering with transmissions. During this handshake the sending node first sends a small RTS frame that includes a duration large enough to complete the RTS/CTS sequence, including the CTS frame, the data frame, and the subsequent ACK frame. The destination node replies to the RTS with a CTS, containing a new NAV value, updated to account for the time already elapsed in the sequence. After the CTS is sent every station in radio range of either the sending or receiving station will have updated their NAV and will hold all transmissions for the defined duration. While the RTS/CTS feature is rarely used in practice, respecting the virtual carrier sense function indicated by the NAV field is mandatory in all 802.11 implementations. An attacker may exploit this feature by stating a large duration field, thereby preventing stations from gaining access to the channel. While it is possible to use almost any frame type to control the NAV, using the RTS with CTS, legitimate stations will propagate the attack further than it could on its own by passing the large NAV value to all stations within range. To cause a noticeable degradation in network performance, this attack can be carried out again and again, to disrupt network functioning, resulting in a DoS (Bellardo and Savage, 2003).

Malicious Association

Using a freeware tool called HostAP to create what is known as a 'Soft AP', hackers can force unsuspecting stations to connect to an undesired 802.11 network or alter the configuration of the station to operate in ad-hoc mode. The HostAP software enables a station to operate as a functioning AP. As the victim station broadcasts a

---

[1] A problem that occurs when one, or more, stations cannot 'hear' all other stations. These stations cause collisions by transmitting at the same time as another station.

probe to associate with an AP, the attacker's malicious AP responds and starts a connection between the two. At this time, the attacker can exploit the vulnerable victim station. It could be used as a launch pad to the rest of the network, viruses could be unleashed and a so called backdoor could be left for later use. This attack is highlights how vulnerable client stations are; they are not always aware that the AP they connect to is legitimate, this can be attributed to the lack of mutual authentication. (SyDisTyKMoFo, 2003)

De-authentication

Part of the communications framework between an 802.11 AP and client is a message which allows them to explicitly issue a request for de-authentication from one another at any stage. Even if some form of key authentication does exist, this message is not authenticated, which makes it relatively simple for a third party to spoof this message on behalf of either device and direct it to the other party. In response, the AP or client will exit the authenticated state and will refuse all further packets until authentication is re-established. By repeating the attack persistently a client may be kept from transmitting or receiving data indefinitely (Bellardo & Savange 2003).

Association Flood

This is a resource starvation attack. When a station associates with an AP, the AP issues an Associate Identification number (AID) to the station in the range of 1-2007. This value is used for communicating power management information to a station that has been in a power-save state. This attack works by sending multiple authentication and association requests to the AP, each with a unique source MAC address. The AP is unable to differentiate the authentication requests generated by an attacker and those created by legitimate clients, so it is forced to process each request. Eventually, the AP will run out of AIDs to allocate and will be forced to de-associate stations to reuse previously allocated AIDs. In practice, many APs will restart after a few minutes of authentication flooding, however this attack is effective in bringing down entire networks or network segments; if repeatedly carried out, can cause a noticeable decrease in network up time (Wright, 2003).

Power Save Vulnerability

Much like a PC or laptop enters stand-by mode after a period of inactivity, a client station within a WLAN is also permitted to enter a stand-by state, known as power save mode. In this state clients are unable to transmit or receive. Before entering power save mode the client is required to announce its intention so that the AP can start buffering any inbound traffic for the node. Occasionally, the client will awaken to poll the AP for any traffic destined for it. If there is any buffered data, the AP delivers it and subsequently discards the contents of its buffer. By spoofing the polling message on behalf of the client, an attacker can cause the AP to discard the client's packets while it is in power save mode. Along the same lines, it is potentially possible to trick the client station into thinking there are no buffered packets at the AP when in fact there are. The presence of buffered packets is indicated in a periodically broadcast packet called the Traffic Indication Map, or TIM. If the TIM message itself is spoofed, an attacker may convince a client that there is no buffered data for it and the client will immediately revert back to stand-by state (Bellardo & Savage, 2003).

Jamming

Jamming is a ridiculously simple, yet highly effective method of causing a DoS on a wireless LAN. Jamming, as the name suggests, involves the use of a device to intentionally create interfering radio signals to effectively 'jam' the airwaves, resulting in the AP and any client devices being unable to transmit. Unfortunately 802.11b WLANs are easily jammed – intentionally or otherwise – due to the crowded frequency band that they operate in. This provides a would-be attacker with plenty of opportunity, and tools, to jam wireless network signals (Computer Associates, 2003).

The Michael Vulnerability

This attack exploits a weakness in the Wi-Fi Alliance's Protected Access Protocol (WPA). Michael is the codename for a security function within the TKIP encryption system used by WPA; this security function triggers the AP to shutdown if more than two packets of unauthorised data are received during a one-second period. The rationale behind the shutdown is to protect the network from attack; the AP assumes it is under attack and takes the proactive measure of shutting down to prevent any potential attacker from entering the network (Stone, 2002). This shut-down is supposed to thwart attack, but in itself it is a means of attack. An attacker could send vast quantities of unauthorised data, thus triggering an ongoing series of shut-downs. This type of attack is unique to WPA, is easy to mount, and is very stealthy in that only two packets need to be sent every second. Even with sophisticated direction finding equipment it would be difficult to track down the perpetrator.

Attacks that Alter Transmissions

The following attacks describe how it is possible for an attacker to modify messages in transit, without detection. Message modification attacks are made relatively trivial if no message encryption exists, however, even if it does, the hacker can still get around it by first cracking the encryption and then carrying out the attack.

Injecting Traffic

If an attacker knows the exact plaintext for one encrypted message, they can then use this knowledge to construct more correctly encrypted packets. This procedure involves constructing a new message, calculating the CRC-32 checksum, and performing bit-flips[1] on the original encrypted message to change the plaintext to the new message. This packet can now be sent to the AP, and it will be accepted as a valid packet. Because RC4 encrypts data a byte at a time, an attacker can modify one byte of ciphertext and the recipient would not know the data has been changed. RC4 does not detect errors (Borisov, 2003).

IP Redirection

By intercepting and modifying the IP address of the destination in a packet, an attacker can effectively re-route messages. This attack can be used where an AP acts as an IP router with Internet connectivity, which is fairly common. The idea is to take an encrypted packet that has been transmitted, modify it so it has a new destination address, one the attacker controls. The AP will then decrypt the packet and send it off to its new destination, where the attacker can read the packet, now in the clear (Borisov, 2003).

SNMP Attack

The final issue is a threat posed by the Simple Network Management Protocol (SNMP). Some APs can be managed via wireless link, usually with a proprietary application, replying on SNMP. Executing these operations can represent a frightening vulnerability for the whole LAN; because eavesdroppers can decipher the password to access read/write mode on the AP using a packet analyser, this means that they share the same administration privileges with the WLAN administrator and can manage the WLAN in a malicious manner (Me, 2003). The sheer number of attacks, and their affects, would seem to put WLANs at a severe disadvantage over their wired counterparts. However, there are just as many, if not more, security measures that users can utilise to counteract most of the above attacks. Layering one security measure on top of another, to strengthening the overall system to deter any potential attackers, or make their task more difficult, if not impossible. However, as noted in a previous chapter, not all organisations, or indeed individuals, take the time to implement any form of security, or they implement it weakly. The next chapter discusses, firstly, what route the primary research will take, and secondly, the findings resulting from the primary research.

Enterprise WPA and Radius

In the 'enterprise', WPA is used in conjunction with an authentication server to provide centralised access control and management. It is scaleable and suitable for hundreds of users. Authentication can be carried out through a number of credentials, including digital certificates, unique usernames and passwords, smartcards, or other forms of secure ID (Higgins, 2003). WPA for the enterprise makes use of the IEEE's 802.1x infrastructure to standardise the authentication process, originally intended for wired networks. Implementing WPA for the

---

[1] Bit-flipping – changing one or more bits within a message. E.g. change a 0 to a 1, or vice versa.

enterprise will involve, as mentioned, an authentication server, typically RADIUS-based severs, selecting the EAP type that will be supported on all stations, APs and authentication servers, and the software upgrade of client and AP devices to enable them to use WPA (Wi-FI Alliance, February 2003). There are typically four EAP methods in use today; EAP-MD5, EAP-Cisco Wireless (LEAP), EAP-TLS and EAP-TTLS, all of which are unfortunately incompatible with each other. It is important that organisations choose one EAP method and ensure it is applied to all equipment throughout the organisation, otherwise roaming between APs will be prohibited. WPA enterprise provides strong security through authentication, when a device requests access to a network, the AP demands a set of credentials, the information supplied is then passed, by the AP, to a RADIUS server for authentication and authorisation (Dismukes, 2002). In addition, RADIUS allows the existence of a centralised database of user profiles which allows certain network privileges for different users, and also the power to deny participation completely; this is a very powerful network management tool. However, because 802.1x primarily handles authentication, the data is still only as secure as its encryption makes it, therefore if WEP is used, organisations are still caught will all of its associated problems. AES improves upon previous encryption methods by removing use of the RC4 algorithm and using an alternative called the Rijndael algorithm, plus longer keys of 192 and 256 in length, which makes it extremely strong.

Virtual Private Networks (VPNs)

VPNs were originally developed to enable remote clients to securely connect to servers/networks over the public Internet, but are equally useful within the wireless environment. This may be an expensive option, but it is an alternative if not implementing WPA/802.1x. Special VPN software must be purchased and installed on each communicating device, and depending on the number of devices, this could become a huge task in its own. If the number of devices does not run into a few hundred VPN is a feasible option. In addition network administrators are advised to define a VLAN[1] which consists of all APs on the network; then configure a firewall that allows only VPN traffic to access the VLAN. Together, the firewall, VLAN and VPN ensure that wireless users are authenticated and their traffic is encrypted. This requires the skills of a dedicated network administrator, which most medium to large organisations employ (Vernier Networks, 2003). VPNs make use of the IPSec (Internet Protocol Security) protocol suite. This is a set of authentication and encryption protocols developed by IETF (Internet Engineering Task Force). It encapsulates a packet by wrapping another packet around it and then encrypting everything; this double-encryption forms a secure 'tunnel' across an otherwise un-secure network (McDonald, 2003). This means wireless clients can connect securely to the organisational network through a VPN gateway on the organisational network edge. The gateway can be set up to use PSK or digital certificates; additionally user authentication to the VPN gateway can occur using RADIUS. As mentioned, VPNs can prove expensive and scale poorly. If using digital certificates, these must be purchased and tracked; VPN terminators can also become bottlenecks, depending on the level of traffic, thereby degrading network performance. VPNs would work well with a few wireless users, but if the number of users is expected to be large, VPNs are not recommended. They are better utilised for a small section of users who need mobility, but also need to be part of the wired backbone (Vernier Networks, 2003). Using VPNs to secure wireless users is recommended if new users are being added to an already established VPN infrastructure, WPA/802.1x is recommended above the use of VPNs, but if WPA/802.1x is not utilised VPN is also acceptable.

Intrusion Detection Systems (IDS)

This is an option that can be applied in conjunction with, or in addition to any other security measure, but should not be applied on its own. It is recommended that medium to large organisations implement these systems to monitor their network traffic to discover attempts to hack or cause a DoS. Generally speaking, there are four categories of IDS – Network Intrusion Detection Systems (NIDSes), System Integrity Verifiers (SIVs), Log File Monitoring (LFM) and Deception Systems (honeypots). NIDSes, as the name suggests, detects attempts on the network. An example would be to watch for a large number of TCP connection requests to different ports. SIVs monitor system files in an attempt to discover when an intruder changes files, perhaps leaving behind a backdoor for later use. LFUs simply monitor log files (a file that lists actions that have occurred) and looks for patterns that would suggest an intruder is attacking (ISP-Planet). The sole purpose of a deception system is a system designed to be broken in order to lure an intruder way from more valuable systems to log and monitor their activities. Deception systems emulate the type of systems that hackers would normally target, like ftp servers, web servers, etc. This option is an extravagant one and involves the setup of an entire, false, system, purely for deceptive purposes. Many companies may not want to incur the costs of such a system, thus the use

---

[1] VLAN stands for Virtual Local Area Network. Virtual LAN's can only be specified on switch hardware allowing VLAN's to be treated as a separate logical LANs.

of a deception system is recommended to those organisations who feel that their data is highly sensitive enough to merit this (Schoeneck, 2003). IDSes can be further subdivided into passive and reactive systems. Passive systems detect a potential security breach, log the information and signal an alert; reactive systems respond to suspicious activity by actively logging off a user and denying them further access. It is recommended that the medium to large organisations group should implement a reactive NIDS. NIDSes detect an attempt on the network before it becomes successful, whereas SIVs and LFMs are post-event, the damage may already have been done. As mentioned, the deception system option is as an extreme measure and should only be employed if the sensitivity of the data or company operations merits it. However, it must be noted that IDSes are not foolproof, which is why they are recommended as an additional layer of security. Some intrusion attacks can go un-noticed. IDSes should not be utilised where a high amount of traffic overloads the IDS sensor and intrusion traffic is missed. IDSes should also not be utilised where an NIDS needs to see the traffic on each switch segment because in switched networks there is no ideal location to connect an NIDS, and deploying NIDS on each segment is cost prohibitive in many environments, thereby leaving segments unprotected. If a switched network exists with many segments, perhaps an IDS should be avoided completely, or only implemented on a segment that provides access to the outside world, or on a segment that contains a system attractive to attackers, or on the segment where the wireless LAN meets the wired backbone.

Documented Security Policies and Procedures

Like any business function, it is important that policies and procedures for the use of WLANs are defined, mainly to protect the network, but also to protect its users. It is equally important that any policies or procedures are communicated effectively to staff; staff should be in no doubt about what they are/are not permitted to do. Clearly defined policies can protect a network from un-necessary security breaches as well as performance degradation. They are important for medium to large organisations due to the huge number of employees and devices, thus introducing an element of risk into the organisation. There is a need for centralised, management-backed, policies and procedures that are communicated to all staff. Due to its size, this group is at an increased risk of being exposed by a rogue AP; they are easy to install and provide the mobility that employees seek. Employees may think that installing a device which helps them better utilise their PC is harmless, when in reality, if they don't secure their device properly, or at all, it can become a huge security risk. It is issues like this which can be overcome by a defined and enforced security policy.

It is strongly recommended that the use of APs by employees, other than the network administration team, is completely prohibited. This should be strictly enforced as such devices can blow a huge hole in any carefully planned security measures. In addition, policies should be in place which forbid employees to alter the configuration of APs and wireless NICs, especially in relation to WEP and SSID broadcasts. The AP hardware should be placed in a secure room where no one but the network administration team can gain access, this not only minimises un-necessary signal leakage, but means the hardware can be protected from reset to default by an unauthorised individual. Policies which limit transmissions to certain channels, at certain speeds and at certain times make it easier to identify an intruder operating on a different channel from the car park at a lower data rate after office hours (AirDefense II, 2003). However, policies are useless unless a network is actively being monitored for breaches, this may be part of the network administrator's job depending on the size of the network. It is this person's responsibility to report any breaches or peculiar behaviour no matter how trivial it may appear.

Conclusion

Wireless networks have a number of security issues. Signal leakage means that network communications can be picked up outside the physical boundaries of the building in which they are being operated, meaning a hacker can operate from the street outside or discretely from blocks away. In addition to signal leakage wireless networks have various other weaknesses. WEP, the protocol used within WLAN's to provide the equivalent security of wired networks is inherently weak. The use of the RC4 algorithm and weak IV's makes WEP a vulnerable security measure.

References

AirDefense. (2003) *Wireless LAN Security – What Hackers Know That You Don't.*
http://ssl.salesforce.com/servlet.Email/AttachmentDownload?q=00m0000000003Pr00D00000000hiyd00500000
005k8d5. Date Accessed 18th August 2003.

AirDefense II. (2003) *5 Practical Steps to Secure your WLAN.*
http://ssl.salesforce.com/servlet/servlet.EmailAttachnmentDownload?q=00m0000000005af00d0000000hiyd005
0000005k8d5. Date accessed 28th January 2004.

AirSnort FAQ. *How the crack process works.* http://airsnort.shmoo.com/faq.html, article undated, date accessed,
25th October 2003.

BBC News. (2001) *Welcome to the era of drive-by hacking.* http://news.bbc.co.uk/1/hi/sci/tech/1639661.stm.
Date accessed 29th October 2003.

Bellardo, John, Savage, Stefan. (2003) *802.11 Denial of Service Attacks: Real Vulnerabilities and Practical
Solution.* http://www.cs.ucsd.edu/users/savage/papers/UsenixSec03.pdf Date accessed 5th November 2003.

Borisov, Nikita, Goldberg, Ian and Wagner, David. (2003) *Security of the WEP algorithm.*
http://www.isaac.cs.berkeley.edu/isaac/wep-faq.html. Date accessed 6th November 2003.

Computer Associates. (2003) *Who's Watching Your Wireless Network?'*
http://wp.bitpipe.com/resource/org_943197149_209/wireless_network_wp_bpx.pdf Date accessed 27th
September 2003.

Descoeudres, Oliver. (2002) *Wireless: Wide Open to Attack.*
http://techupdate.zdnet.com/techupdate/stories/main/0,14179,2895306,00.html. Date accessed 29th October
2003.

Dismukes, Trey "Azariah". *Wireless Security Blackpaper.* July 2002.
http://arstechnica.com/paedia/w/wireless/security-1.html, Date accessed 18th September 2003.

Franklin, Curtis (2001). *A Cracked Spec.* http://www.internetweek.com/reviews01/rev031201-2.htm. Date
accessed 7th November 2003.

Geier, Jim. (1999) *Wireless LANs, Implementing Interoperable Networks,* MacMillan Network Architecture and
Development Series, 1999, MacMillan Technical Publishing, USA.

Griffth, Eric. (2002) *Mapping the Lack of Security,* http://www.wi-fiplanet.com/news/article.php/1488541. Date
accessed 19th September 2003.

Harte, Lawrence, Kellog, Steven, Dreher, Richard and Schaffinit, Tom. (2000) *The Comprehensive Guide to
Wireless Technologies: Cellular, PCS, Paging, SMR and Satellite.* APDG Publishing, 2000, NC USA.

iLabs, Wireless Security Team. (2002) *What's Wrong with WEP?*
http://www.nwfusion.com/research/2002/0909wepprimer.html. Date accessed 23rd October 2003.

Karygiannis, Tom and Owens, Les. (2003) National Institute of Standards and Technology, Special Publication
800-48, Draft, http://csrc.nist.gov/publications/drafts/draft-sp800-48.pdf. Accessed Aug 18th 2003.

McClure, Stuart, Scambray, Joel and Jurtz, George. (2003) *Hacking Exposed: Network Security Secrets and
Solutions,* 4th Edition, Osbourne McGraw-Hill

Me, Gianluigi. (2003) *A threat posed by SNMP use over WLAN,* http://www.wi-fitechnology.com/Wi-
Fi_Reports_and_Papers/SNMP_use_over_WLAN.html. Date accessed 18th November 2003.

PCQuest. (2003) *WEP Security Cracked.* ttp://www.pcquest.com/content/topstories/wireless/103081102.asp.
Date accessed, 7th November 2003.

Poulsen, Kevin. (2003) *War Driving by the Bay.* http://www.theregister.co.uk/content/archive/18285.html . Date accessed 23rd October 2003.

Proxim, Wireless Networks. *Wireless Network Security.* http://www.proxim.com/learn/library/whitepapers/wireless_security.pdf. Date accessed 7th November 2003.

Sikora, Axel. (2003) *Wireless Personal and Local Area Networks*, John Wiley & Sons Ltd, West Sussex.

Stone, Adam. (2003) *The "Michael" Vulnerability*, http://www.wi-fiplanet.com/columns/article.php/1556321. Date accessed 18th November 2003.

Sutton, Michael (2003). *Hacking the Invisible Network.* iDefense, iAlert White Paper, http://www.rootshell.be/~doxical/download/docs/misc/Idefense_Hacking_the_invisible_network_(wireless).pdf. Date accessed 18th August 2003.

SyDisTyKMoFo (2003) *Wireless Attacks Explained.* http://www.astalavista.com/library/wlan/wlansecurity.htm. Date accessed 7th November 2003.

Tourrilhes, Jean. (2000) *Wireless Overview – The MAC Level.* http://www.hpl.hp.com/personal/Jean_Tourrilhes/Linux/Linux.Wireless.mac.html. Accessed on 10th October 2003.

Tyrrell, K. (2003) *An Overview of Wireless Security Issues.* http://www.giac.org/practical/GSCE/Kevin_Tyrrell_GSEC.pdf. Date Accessed 19th October 2003.

Ulanoff, Lance. (2003) *Get free Wi-Fi, while its hot. PC Magazine, Ziff Davies, July 2003*

Vines, Russell Dean. *Wireless Security Essentials, Defending Mobile Systems from Data Piracy.* Wiley Publishing Inc, 2002, Indiana, USA.

Walker, Jesse. (2000) *Unsafe at any Key Size; An analysis of the WEP encapsulation.* http://www.dis.org/wl/pdf/unsafe.pdf. Date accessed 23rd October 2003.

Wi-FiPlanet (2002). *Minimising WLAN Security Threats.* http://wi-fiplanet.com/tutorials/article.php/1457211. Date accessed 5th November 2003.

Wright, Joshua (2003) *Detecting Wireless LAN MAC Address Spoofing.* http://home.jwu.edu/jwright/papers/wlan-mac-spoof.pdf. Date accessed 5th November 2003.

34   The Problem of SPAM Email

John Honan and Kevin Curran

As a communications medium, email has become very useful and practically universal. However, the usefulness of email and its potential for future growth are jeopardized by the rising tide of unwanted email, both SPAM and viruses. This threatens to wipe out the advantages and benefits of email. An important flaw in current email standards (most notably SMTP) is the lack of any technical requirement that ensures the reliable identification of the sender of messages. A message's domain of origin can easily be faked, or 'spoofed'. This chapter investigates the problem of email spam and provides an overview of methods to efficiently minimize the volumes.

Introduction

Spam can be defined as unsolicited e-mail, often of a commercial nature, sent indiscriminately to multiple mailing lists, individuals, or newsgroups. Spam can be categorized as follows:

- **Junk mail** - mass mailings from legitimate businesses that is unwanted.
- **Non-commercial spam** – mass mailings of unsolicited messages without an apparent commercial motive including chain letters, urban legends and joke collections.
- **Offensive and Pornographic spam** – mass mailings of "adult" advertisements or pornographic pictures.
- **Spam scams** – mass mailings of fraudulent messages or those designed to con people out of personal information for the purpose of identity theft and other criminal acts.
- **Virus spam** – mass mailings that contain viruses, Trojans, malicious scripts, etc.

Spoofing (Templeton and Levitt, 2003) is a technique often used by spammers to make them harder to trace. Trojan viruses embedded in email messages also employ spoofing techniques to ensure the source of the message is more difficult to locate (Ishibashi et al, 2003). Spam filters and virus scanners can only eliminate a certain amount of spam and also risk catching legitimate emails. As the SoBig virus has demonstrated, virus scanners themselves actually add to the email traffic through notification and bounceback messages. SMTP is flawed in that it allows these email headers to be faked, and does not allow for the sender to be authenticated as the 'real' sender of the message. If this problem can be solved, it will result in a reduction in spam email messages, more security for existing emails, and allow email viruses to be tracked down and stopped more effectively (Schwartz, 1998). This approach is known as 'Trusted Email'. The Simple Mail Transport Protocol is the basic protocol used by servers to send email messages to each other (Schwartz, 1998). It defines how the conversation should take place, and the format of the data that is exchanged during the conversation. The email is composed in the senders Mail User Agent (MUA), this is usually a piece of software on the senders PC such as Outlook or Eudora, but can also consist of a web-based email system such as Yahoo or Hotmail. The message might look as follows:

```
Date:    Thursday, 1 Apr 2004 12:40:30 -0000
From:   you@yourhost.com
To:      John & Kevin < jhonan@silveronion.com>
Subject: Party on Sat night

There's a party on Saturday night, would you like to go?
```

There are two parts to the above message, the header and the body. The header contains information about the message, such as who it is to be sent to. The body contains the actual text of the message itself. When the sender clicks the 'Send' button in their MUA, some additional headers are automatically added to the message by the MUA. For example (the new headers added by the MUA are in bold);

```
Date:    Thursday, 1 Apr 2004 12:40:30 -0000
From:   you@yourhost.com
```

```
To:      John & Kevin < jhonan@silveronion.com>
Subject: Party on Sat night
Message-Id: <002d01c444ca$bdaa3e70$5b92cbc1@yourhost.com>
X-Mailer: Microsoft Outlook Express 6.00.2800.1409

There's a party on Saturday night, would you like to go?
```

The message Id is a unique identifier added by the MUA, the X-Mailer is the name and version of the MUA software used to compose the email. To deliver the email, the MUA needs to contact a Mail Transport Agent (MTA). The MTA is responsible for routing and delivering email. In the example above, the MTA at yourhost.com (the senders' domain) needs to establish an SMTP conversation with the MTA at silveronion.com (the recipients' domain). The SMTP conversation takes place as follows. When silveronion.com receives the email, it adds a header of its own, the *Received* header. This is like a postmark. Every MTA that handles a message adds this received header (Tserefos et al, 1997), (Clyman, 2004). This is how the message might look after silveronion.com has received it;

```
Received: from yourhost.com (HELO yourhost.com) (193.203.146.91) by silveronion.com with SMTP;
1 Apr 2004 12:40:40

Date:Thursday, 1 Apr 2004 12:40:30 -0000
From:         you@yourhost.com
To:           John & Kevin < jhonan@silveronion.com>
Subject:      Party on Sat night

Message-Id: <002d01c444ca$bdaa3e70$5b92cbc1@yourhost.com>
X-Mailer: Microsoft Outlook Express 6.00.2800.1409

There's a party on Saturday night, would you like to go?
```

The Received header shows from which server the message was received, it often includes the IP address, in case the server supplied an incorrect or a faked hostname (yourhost.com). Other information stored in the Received header includes the name of the receiving MTA server, and may include other information such as the version of the MTA software the server is running. Each server involved in forwarding the message will add its server information to the received portion of the message thus a message may have many received headers. They are read in reverse order. The header at the top indicates the last server which added its received header. Finally, if the email message has reached its eventual destination, an SMTP From header is added, so the message looks like this;

```
From: you@yourhost.com Thurs Apr 1 2004 12:40:30
Received: from yourhost.com (HELO yourhost.com) (193.203.146.91) by silveronion.com with SMTP; 1
Apr 2004 12:40:40

Date:Thursday, 1 Apr 2004 12:40:30 -0000
From:         you@yourhost.com
To:           John & Kevin < jhonan@silveronion.com>
Subject: Party on Sat night

Message-Id: <002d01c444ca$bdaa3e70$5b92cbc1@yourhost.com>
X-Mailer: Microsoft Outlook Express 6.00.2800.1409

There's a party on Saturday night, would you like to go?
```

The From header lists the address as supplied by the sender in the MAIL part of the SMTP conversation. Some MTA agents store this in a 'Return-Path:' header instead. This final message is how it looks when it reaches the inbox of jhonan@silveronion.com. The recipients email client software parses the header and presents the mail to the user in a more readable format (the final recipient often doesn't see all the headers in their email software, being mainly interested in the 'From', 'Subject' lines, and the body.) The headers as described above are standard SMTP headers. Any header beginning with 'X-' (such as X-Mailer) is a freeform header, and can be used for any purpose (Clyman, 2004). Spammers exploit SMTP through a number of flaws in the SMTP protocol such as;

1) No verification of identify, the server accepts who you say you are without question
2) No consequences for dishonest addressing ('From' line can be anything you want)
3) Content filtering requires delivery (the email has to be received by the server before it can be filtered)
4) Nothing on which to base delivery routing options (no generic flags in the header or elsewhere to allow an email to be flagged as an advertisement, adult content, newsletter, or otherwise)
5) No consequences for dishonest content (the actual message contents do not match the subject line)

The main flaw in SMTP is that it allows 'untrusted' communications to take place (Tserefos et al, 1997). There is no requirement to prove you are who you say you are when an SMTP communication is instigated. SMTP is also very effective at sending email as quickly as possible to its destination, meaning the spammer is only slowed down by the speed of his connection to the internet. These problems offer the spammer two main advantages which allow them to continue spamming unhindered; anonymity and volume of spam (Simpson, 2002).

Apart from the obvious methods of supplying incorrect information in the email header, many spammers go to great lengths to remain anonymous. Anonymity is important to a spammer, because if spammers can be tracked down to an ISP spammers risk having their email servers' shut down or their web-hosting account terminated. In light of the new 'Can-Spam' anti-spam legislation, spammers are even more determined to remain unaccountable. One additional technique used by spammers is exploitation of open email relays. These are SMTP servers that are mis-configured and which allow email to be forwarded to addresses outside of the server's domain. On inspecting the email headers, it appears as if the relay server is the source of the email (Hastings and McLean, 1996). In order to trace the spammer, the owner of the open relay needs to be made aware of the activity. However, some sites are either reluctant to act or willingly abet spammers. Furthermore, even when spammers are identified and an ISP removes their account, spammers will often open a new one immediately and carry on their activities. Many system administrators are aware of tricks that spammers use and have configured email servers correctly and securely. However, spammers have discovered the capability of using common web mail form handling software as open relays. Many websites provide form applications such as mailto and the FormMail Perl scripts to allow users to construct forms, the input to which can be forwarded to a specified email address for collecting information. Spammers write software which exploits security holes in FormMail scripts to enable them to forward email to a specified address. This results in the spam appearing to originate from the website of the FormMail software, a most undesirable outcome (Simpson, 2002).

Spammers email in bulk using automatic email-sending programs. Spammers must first obtain email addresses and sources for email addresses include joining mailing lists to gather addresses from the mailing list software, purchasing mail lists from other spammers on CD-ROM (which can contain millions of addresses) and spambots (or harvesters) which scan internet newsgroups and web pages for email addresses. Spammers ensure their spam is not blocked by spam-filtering software by making the spam look like legitimate email, by avoiding excessive use of HTML or exclamation marks, or by misspelling commonly used spam phrases and words (Goodman and Rounthwaite, 2004).

Existing anti-spam methods

This section discusses a number of technical anti-spam methods currently in use along with the advantages and disadvantages of each method. There are also industry proposals which attempt to address the shortcomings of the current anti-spam approaches. The industry proposals suggest a more robust, future-proof, and all-encompassing solution to stopping spam. These proposals often comprise hybrid approaches i.e. combinations of a number of methods to stop spam, and are generally more complex to implement as they require changes to the email infrastructure.

Requirements of anti-spam systems

Ideally, the system should block all spam. In practice this may not be achievable, as there may always be a small quantity of spam that bypasses whatever system is in place. The number of messages getting through should be perhaps 1 in 1,000. If a person is sent 200 spam emails a day, then if 1 spam gets through to their in-box per 5 day working week, this equates to 0.1%, which should be acceptable to most email users.

The system should not block legitimate email. Not receiving email you are expecting, or important email getting blocked by a spam filter is considered worse by many people then receiving large quantities of spam. It is important therefore that any anti-spam system ensures that 100% of legitimate email gets through.

The system should block spam with little or no user interaction. The spam blocking ideally should happen before the email even reaches the client computer (any filtering that happens on the client computer means the spam has to be downloaded, which results in additional network traffic for the user, and possibly a noticeable delay while the spam is filtered). The system should ideally exist on the email server itself, not on the client computer.

Finally, the user should not be aware of any delays in either sending or receiving and filtering email. Users may be tolerant of certain performance issues if they know it is preventing spam reaching their inbox, but they will not be so accepting if this starts affecting their normal day-to-day operation of their PC to send and receive emails (Bass and Watt, 1997).

Existing methods used to minimize spam

Here are the main methods being used to prevent spam, together with their pros and cons (Graham, 2003).

Complain to the Spammer's ISP

When spam volumes were quite low, it was often effective enough to send a complaint email to the ISP of the spammer. The ISP could then investigate and close down the spammers account.

The advantages of this approach are that it can achieve direct action from the ISP to get the spammer shut down fairly quickly. The disadvantages are that the volumes of spam are now too high to allow a complaint to be sent and followed up on for every spam that is sent. In addition, it is often difficult to determine from the headers who the ISP of the spammer actually is. Spammers shut down in one ISP or hosting company will just open accounts with someone else. The spam blocking efficiency of this method is medium. It may block one spammer, but others will get through. False positives however do not occur (Goodman and Rounthwaite, 2004).

Mail Server IP Blacklists

An IP blacklist is a list of the IP addresses of spammers' mail servers, or relay servers (unsecure servers which allow spammers to forward email). These lists are maintained by volunteer groups and anti-spam organizations. ISPs can then subscribe to these lists and refuse to accept email from any listed IP addresses. This is a very precise method of blocking potential spam however these blacklists can never hope to list every single IP address that spammers use. Spammers often end up listing legitimate IP addresses, or blacklisting an entire domain (1,000 ordinary users could get blacklisted for the actions of one spammer). The source IP is spoofable by the spammer, which means the spammer can bypass the blacklist. The Spam blocking efficiency is high. IT blocks all spam from given IP addresses however false positives are quite likely. If a legitimate sender uses a blacklisted IP block, their email will get stopped.

Signature Based Filtering

This method compares incoming emails against a signature database of known spam emails. The system calculates a checksum signature of an incoming spam message, and adds it to the database. Any incoming emails are then compared to this database to see if the email is spam. The advantages of this are that it is an accurate way of matching spam. It can achieve very low 'false positives' since only definite spasm are matched based on the hash signature of their contents. The disadvantages are that in order to be detected as spam, the message will have to exist in the database of pre-sent spam messages. If the spam is new, it may not exist in the database at this stage, and therefore won't get blocked. The database must be kept up to date (Graham, 2003). The main problem however is that signature filtering is easily bypassed by making minor modifications to each message to avoid signature matches so this technique is not that useful anymore, therefore the Spam blocking efficiency is low.

Bayesian Filtering

This method uses a statistical analysis technique to analyse the words contained in each received email. It uses predefined lookup tables to determine the probability that an email is spam. For example, the word 'Viagra' would have a high weighting, since it commonly appears in spam. Bayesian filtering is a new approach to spam prevention. This approach seems to trigger less false positives than other types of filtering, as it is self-training based on spam it receives. In some cases the user can update the filter if it misclassifies an email, thus improving the detection accuracy. Spammers however often bypass these types of filters by making the spam look less spammy, using less spam-related words (often making the email read like a personal email from a friend), or putting random non-spam words at the end of the message to cause the Bayesian calculation to misclassify them as non-spam. Another technique spammers use is to misspell spam related words. Spam blocking efficiency is high. Bayesian filters are quite accurate but false positives are quite likely (Graham, 2003).

Rule-Based Filtering

Rule-based filters look for patterns that indicate spam: specific words and phrases, lots of uppercase and exclamation points, malformed headers, dates in the future or the past, etc. This is how nearly all spam filters worked until 2002. Until Bayesian filtering was introduced, this was probably the most flexible method to help identify spam but this method is very easy for the spammer to bypass. The clever spammer even runs their spam through rule-based filters before sending it to ensure it doesn't trigger the spam alert. Many spammers have now learnt how to make their email not 'look' like spam to the filters, and use techniques to ensure it is at least opened by the recipient when it reaches their in-box. (e.g. making the 'From' look like a normal persons name, and making the 'Subject' something like 'Hi' or 'Long time no see'). This method is often used in conjunction with Bayesian filtering. The Spam blocking efficiency is high. False positives are quite likely as an email which contains certain words or formatting can be mistakenly flagged as spam. Performance can suffer as each email needs to be scanned (Graham, 2003).

Challenge-Response Filtering

When you get an email from someone you haven't had email from before, a challenge-response filter sends an email back to them, telling them they must go to a web page and fill out a form before the email is delivered. Once the sender has verified themselves, they get added to a senders 'whitelist' to ensure any future emails get through without requiring verification. This method ensures you only receive email from people who really want to correspond with you. The chances are that a spammer is not going to spend the time filling out the web form. However, this can be quite inconvenient for the sender, as they have to remember to fill in the form before the recipient gets the email. In some cases the sender might not bother, and this method will always result in email being delayed. This approach has not been widely adopted. The spam blocking efficiency is medium. Spammers can fill out the forms too, and may use automated scripts. There may be false positives. If the sender doesn't accept the challenge then their email stays in the 'spam' box.

Legal Approach (Can-Spam Act)

In 2003 the US Senate passed into law the 'Can Spam' act as an attempt to cut down spam (Baker, 2003). The main points are:

- Allows businesses to continue to send commercial emails to their customers and prospects, but gives consumers the right to require that a sender of unsolicited commercial email cease sending commercial emails to them. This is known as the "one free shot" approach;
- Requires senders of commercial email to include a functional "opt-out" mechanism in commercial emails. This is not required in "transactional or relationship messages;"
- Requires senders of commercial email messages to provide "clear and conspicuous" identification that the message is an advertisement or solicitation, unless the recipient has given prior "affirmative consent' to receipt of the message;
- Generally allows the sale or rental of email lists, subject to certain restrictions, including that an email address of a recipient who has "opted out" of further commercial emails cannot be transferred to a third

party;

- Creates criminal and civil sanctions (up to $2 million, which can be trebled) for a number of common practices of spammers, including the use of deceptive or misleading origins information, headers, sender identity, transmission information, subject lines, and falsely registered IP addresses;

This should have been an effective deterrent against spammers but weaknesses exist in the CAN SPAM legislation. A loophole in spam laws however is usually in the exact definition of spam. Most spam laws allow the sending of unsolicited email to recipients who have a prior relationship with the sender. This is reasonable, but it must be defined carefully what a prior relationship consists of. There is a type of spammer ("permission-based email marketers") who obtain email addresses by buying them from websites with unethical privacy policies. By calling the site a spammer bought your email address from a "partner" or "affiliate", the spammers can claim that they too have a "prior relationship" with you, and are therefore exempt from spam laws.

In November 2004, (Levine, 2004) the USA held it's first criminal trial concerning spam in Leesburg, Virginia with a conviction of Jeremy Jaynes. The case was brought under Virginia's state anti-spam law, not the weaker Federal CAN-SPAM act. Virginia's law makes it a crime to send unsolicited bulk mail using forgery, so the Commonwealth had to show first that Jaynes sent lots of unsolicited mail and second that it was sent using forgery. The mail in question was sent on three days in October to AOL, which is why the case was heard in Leesburg, the county seat of Loudon county in which AOL's mail servers are located. While most of society welcomes rulings like in Virginia, it must be noted that spammers are often based in different countries, which have different internet laws. Applying a law on an international basis, or prosecuting spammers in other countries is full of difficulties. The Spam blocking efficiency with this method can be said to be high as it stops spam being sent at source.

Slow down spammers (proof of work)

Spam has low response rates (on the order of 15 per million) but spammers make up for it with high volumes, sending millions of emails per day (Schwartz, 1998). If you could slow down the rate at which spammers send email, you could put them out of business. One way to do this would be to make any computer used to send email perform an easily verifiable time-consuming computation before you would accept that email. Whatever these computations are, they should be within acceptable, controllable levels of complexity, because legitimate corporate email servers have to be able to send high volumes of email. And corporate email servers would be running on standard hardware. Many computations can be made hundreds or thousands of times faster by custom hardware.

This is the first approach that directly attacks the spammers' profitability model, instead of trying to block or filter spam that has already been sent, it makes it more costly for the spammer to send each message. Also helps reduce false positives caused by other types of spam filtering. It is likely that if an email has a 'proof of work' stamp, then it has been sent by a genuine sender, and can bypass the standard Bayesian filters. For this idea to work, you'd need to figure out a kind of computation that couldn't easily be speeded up by custom hardware. Even with a suitable computation, this idea would require new email protocols. Any new protocol has a problem: no one is inclined to adopt it till everyone else does. As a result, it is practically impossible to get a new protocol adopted for anything. How are you going to get system administrators who don't even bother to install patches for years-old security holes to switch to a new email protocol? Spammers already have highly tuned systems and would not be deterred by the need for custom hardware. The Spam blocking efficiency here would be medium. If spammers actually performed the proof-of-work test, then the email would get through. False positive may still occur. If a legitimate sender doesn't perform a proof-of-work test to stamp their email, then it could get flagged as 'possible spam'. Performance would be bad on the sender end, as it requires CPU cycles for proof of work but good on the recipient end.

Proposed Industry Solutions

Most of the above approaches take a 'technology only' approach to the spam problem. What is required is an approach which encompasses technology with a policy-based solution. Any approach also needs support from the major ISPs (such as Yahoo, Hotmail, and AOL), and should be aligned with existing anti-spam laws. There are a number of industry proposals, most of which encompass hybrid multi-layer spam blocking/filtering technologies with trust-based systems and often cover the areas of policy as well.

TEOS – Trusted Email Open Standard

On April 30, 2003, ePrivacy Group announced the Trusted Email Open Standard (TEOS) to fight spam, spoofing, and email fraud (Schiavone et al, 2003). TEOS is a staged approach towards a trusted email system built upon and extending the SMTP protocol. TEOS takes a two-track approach comprising an identify verification system, content assertions (flags in the subject line which identify the type of content) in conjunction with a policy-based trust and accountability process. TEOS creates a framework of trusted identity for email senders based on secure, fast, lightweight signatures in email headers, optimized with DNS-based systems for flexibility and ease of implementation. TEOS also provides a common-language framework for making trusted assertions about the content of each individual message. ISPs and email recipients can rely on these assertions to manage their email (ePrivacy Group, 2003).

Microsoft Coordinated Spam Reduction Initiative

Microsoft's proposal covers a number of areas, but the main focus is on a system called Caller ID (Microsoft, 2004). Microsoft and the Internet Engineering Task Force have proposed changes to the way SMTP verifies the sender of an email by looking up the source via DNS. This involves modifications of DNS standards (a central part of the internet itself). Caller ID allows Internet domain owners to publish the IP (Internet Protocol) address of their outgoing email servers in an XML (Extensible Markup Language) format email "policy" in the DNS (Domain Name System) record for their domain. Email servers can query the DNS record and match the source IP address of incoming email messages to the address of the approved sending servers. This results in email being verifiable as coming from who it says it is from.

Domain Keys and Sender Policy Framework (SPF)

These proposals (supported by Yahoo and AOL) are essentially the same as the Caller ID proposals. They use a DNS challenge/response mechanism to allow look-up and verification of the sender of the email to ensure they are who they claim to be. Weaknesses are already becoming apparent in this system. This approach has been implemented by Yahoo in recent months (First quarter, 2004), but it has resulted in no reduction in spam volumes to Yahoo email addresses. The spammers are validating themselves as legitimate email senders to ensure their emails get through, and legitimate emailers are sending from servers who have not actually implemented the Domain Keys technology. Although the spammers no longer have anonymity on their side, there is no solid legal framework in place, or even a way to prevent spammers from continuing to send spam if they are using Domain Keys. Systems like Domain Keys and Caller ID only offer a part of the anti-spam solution. They ensure the email sender can be identified but they do not offer a way to stop a spammer sending spam (Geer, 2004).

Spammer profitability

At the moment, a spammer is only limited by the speed of their uplink and their available hardware as to how many spam messages a spammer can send per day. Spammers are usually specialists in their field. They are employed on a cost per email or sometimes a response commission basis (Boutin, 2004). In order to make it unprofitable for the spammers to stay in business, it is necessary to reduce the amount of spam spammers send, or make it costly to send each message. It should be possible based on existing knowledge about spammers' business models to calculate how much the rate of spamming needs to be slowed down. There are two approaches to calculating spammer profitability and breakeven points; Based on economic calculations, and a simpler model based on a 'slowdown rate' (Goodman and Rounthwaite, 2004).

Computation Time Per Message

The key fact is the observation that the solving of a spam deterring puzzle is *both* an expenditure of actual money (in the form of the amortized yearly cost of a CPU) *as well as* the expenditure of a certain amount of clock time. As there are only so many seconds in a day, these two ideas can be connected. Consider the following four variables:

• *secondsPerMessage*, the amount of CPU time spent per message in solving the puzzle (actually of course this is per message per recipient, but for brevity in the sequel we will simply say "per message")

• *messagesPerResponse*, the number of messages that must be sent to get one actual successful response. For example, if only one in ten thousand spam messages generate a successful response, then the value of this variable is 10,000.

• *revenuePerResponse*, the amount of revenue generated by each successful response. In our analysis here, this should be thought of as the revenue net of both the actual cost of goods and any amortized overhead.

• *cpuCostPerYear*, the burdened cost of a CPU: the amount of money necessary to acquire, house, power, air-condition, maintain and administer a CPU for a year.

With those definitions in hand, we can derive a formula to indicate spammer breakeven points. This calculation is illustrated in the following function.

$$SecondsPerMessage = 31557600*revenuePerResponse/cpuCostPerYear*messagesPerResponse$$

What this says is that given values in hand for the three variables *messagesPerResponse*, *revenuePerResponse*, and *cpuCostPerYear* that one considers reasonable, the expenditure of an amount of CPU time per message beyond the threshold indicated is *guaranteed* to deter a profit-driven spammer. (Note that this equation is independent of any particular currency: it simply requires that *revenuePerResponse* and *cpuCost-PerYear* be denominated in the same units). This equation can be understood in one of two ways, depending on when one considers a response to have occurred. Specifically, *messagesPerResponse* is an indication of either

1. the *click-through* rate, the rate at which the content of spam messages are actively acted upon by their recipients, or

2. the *conversion* rate, the rate at which spam messages actually result in a sale or other transaction involving a transfer of money.

Actual figures for response rates to spam emails are rare, although there is a lot of "what if" speculation. In 2002 the Wall Street Journal (Schryen, 2004) gave real-world examples of spam response rates of 0.013% and 0.0023%. If the rate per email did indeed return to 0.1 cents then at a 0.0023% response rate then advertisers would need to be selling goods with a profit margin of at least $4.35. This is not implausible: mortgage leads are worth $50, cell phone sales about $85 and there are examples of companies selling fake medicines worth $2.50 for $59.95. Hence we would suggest that a price of 0.1 cents per email could return, especially if the senders of spam were to improve response rates by learning lessons in presentation from legitimate marketers. Thus we must look to restrict spammers to just 1,750 emails per day per machine. Of course this would also limit legitimate senders to the same level of sending. Depending on the viewpoint one chooses, the *revenuePerResponse* must of course be adjusted accordingly. Rough real-world estimates for each of the two interpretations of the *messagesPerResponse* rate together with their corresponding profit levels can be gleaned from various and sundry sources, especially the many press interviews of spammers that have appeared. These sources indicate with high probability that the following are not unreasonable estimates for these parameters for the majority of spammers as shown in Table 9.

	Low	High
Click-through rate	1-in-2000	1-in-10,000
Revenue per click	USD $1	USD $2
Conversion rate	1-in-50,000	1-in-100,000
Revenue per conversion	USD $1	USD$80

Table 9: Parameter Approximate Value Range

In order to get a sense of the implications of what this means in concrete terms, if we assume for the moment that *cpuCostPerYear* is for the average spammer in the ballpark of USD$200, then using equation (2) we can conclude that:

• At a 1-in-2000 click-through rate, 78 seconds of computation deters $1 per click.

•At a 1-in-10,000 click-through rate, 31 seconds of computation deters $2 per click.
•At a 1-in-50,000 conversion rate, 78 seconds of computation deters $25 per transaction
•At a 1-in-100,000 conversion rate, 63 seconds of computation deters $40 per transaction.

All in all, given the uncertainty in our parameter estimates and the fact that our model here actually omits several factors of cost to the spammer, it seems reasonable to believe that around one minute of computation is a very significant spam deterrent, and likely a level that will guarantee that a majority of spammers are not profitable. Moreover, for these values the numbers illustrated are an absolute *upper bound*: it is very possible that significantly smaller thresholds are also quite effective deterrents. It is worthwhile to recall that in deployed systems puzzles need not be solved if the sender of a message is on his recipient's known-sender list. The average machine will only need to send about 75 emails, this gives some headroom for legitimate activity, but when one starts to consider variations in sending activity and differences in puzzle-solving speeds, this method of estimating computation times does not give much insight into the value of how much spam will continue to arrive. The difficulty is that the effect will be to suppress the least profitable forms of spam and we have no idea what proportion this might be. However, if spam is more convincingly presented, or the spammer can make a profit from not only emailing but owning other parts of the marketing chain, then it will certainly not be possible to raise the computation time enough to have an impact without starting to affect legitimate email (Goodman and Rounthwaite, 2004).

A slightly different approach to the spammer profitability model, is to work out how much email a spammer can send per day, how much a spammer can be slowed down by, and therefore how much their profitability will be reduced by (Juels and Brainard, 1999). This is an alternative way to work out an acceptable 'breakeven' point for any stamp calculations. If the spammer has an uplink speed of 1.5Mbit = 1,536Kbps and the average email size = 3,000 bytes then this will allow them to transmit (1,536 / 8) * 1,024 / 3,000 = 65.536 emails per second which equates to them taking 0.0153 seconds to send email. This means they can send a maximum of (65.536 * 60 * 60 * 24) = 5,662,310 emails per day as illustrated in Table 10.

Uplink speed (Kbps)	Email Size (bytes)	Emails Per Second	Seconds to send 1 Email	Emails per day
1536	3000	65.536	0.0153	5,662,310

Table 10: Rate of Sending Spam

So, based on this we can work out the 'slowdown rate' for any proof-of-work approach. Therefore, with a stamp calculation time of say, 15 seconds, the spammer will be slowed down by a factor of (15 / 0.0153) = 983.

Hashcash Proof of Concept

Hashcash (Dwork and Naor, 1992), (Back, 1997, 2002) is a method of adding a textual stamp to the header of an email to prove you have expended a certain amount of CPU time calculating the stamp prior to sending the email. In other words, as you have taken a certain amount of time to generate the stamp and send the email, it is unlikely that you are a spammer. The stamp can be validated quickly at the recipient end. If the stamp is valid, then it is possible to flag the message as 'not spam' and direct it straight to the recipients inbox. Hashcash comes in the form of plug-in software for MUAs which adds hashcash stamps to outgoing email. Hashcash inserts a X-Hashcash: header into the email headers section of the email the user sends. The following is an example of an email addressed to me with a hashcash stamp in the email header:

```
From: Someone <test@test.invalid>
To: John Honan jhonan@silveronion.com
Subject: test hashcash
Date: Thu, 24 Jun 2004 11:59:59 +0000
X-Hashcash: 0:040624: jhonan@silveronion.com:1fea2abb184ebf0a
blah blah
 - Someone
```

If the email sender wishes to send a hashcash stamped email to someone, their email address is supplied to the hashcash minter program together with how many 'bits' the stamp should be (larger bit stamps take longer to calculate). The minter program, after a certain amount of calculation time, will return a valid hashcash stamp in the format shown above. The stamp is then attached to the header of the email, and the email is sent as normal. This process should happen automatically as a background job so the sender is not even aware a stamp is being generated and attached to their outgoing email. On the recipient end, the server reads the hashcash stamp and performs the following verification;

1) Is the stamp is the required number of bits?
2) Is the address in the stamp the person the email is intended for?
3) Is the date in the stamp today's date?

If the above three tests are passed, then the stamp is valid, and the email is directed to the recipients in-box. The important point here is that is takes a lot longer to calculate a stamp than to verify it. It could take a number of minutes for the senders PC to calculate a valid stamp, but it only takes a few milliseconds for the recipient's email server to check the stamp is valid. Therefore the 'CPU cost' of calculating a stamp is borne at the senders end. Hashcash is based on the SHA-1 hashing algorithm. SHA-1 generates a unique 160 bit number to from any input text. It is easy to validate the input text generates the output hash. This method is often used to check that executable files or documents which are downloaded from the internet are intact and not tampered with when they reach their destination (by validating their SHA-1 hash signature is correct at the receiving end). Even if one character of the input text changes, this results in a drastically different SHA-1 hash. Hashcash makes use of the fact that it is highly unlikely that any two input strings will generate the same output hash signature (160 bit hashes give 2^{160} possible hash combinations)

Computing hash-collisions

A full-collision is where all bits of SHA-1(x) match SHA-1(y), but a k-bit partial collision is where only the k most-significant bits match. Hashcash looks for partial bit collisions on strings based on the recipient's email address and the date such as "0:040624: jhonan@silveronion.com: 1fea2abb184ebf0a" against an all '0' string. The stamp contains a date (040624= Jun 24th 2004), and an email address (jhonan@silveronion.com). The first field (the 0:) is the stamp version number. The last field, a string of random letters, is some random text used to in the collision detection part of the stamp generation process. Lots of different random strings must be tried to find the required bit-collision, approximately 2^{16} attempts for a 16 bit collision. One of the powerful features of hashcash is that it is defined using SHA-1, a commonly used and effective hashing algorithm. The above stamp hashed gives:

> echo -n **0:040624: jhonan@silveronion.com:1fea2abb184ebf0a** | sha1
> 00000000c70db7389f241b8f441fcf068aead3f0

It can be seen that the first 8 hex digits are 0. Each hex digit is 4 bits. This means the above stamp has a collision on (8*4 bits) = 32 bits. So the above stamp is a 32-bit collision. This is a big collision which would take a high-end 2Ghz PC many hours to compute. But for normal email it is expected to use stamps in the range of 20 - 25 bits (which will take under a minute to calculate on most hardware). The nature of a hashcash stamp means that once the stamp is generated, then any tampering to the stamp will result in the collision bit count changing, and thus rendering the stamp useless. This is very important, as it means a spammer cannot just generate one stamp and slot multiple email addresses into it. They also cannot generate hundreds of stamps in advance for a single email address, as the date forms part of the stamp. For example, assuming a spammer legitimately generated the following 20-bit stamp '0:040624: jhonan@silveronion.com: r7rk+dl/34'. This stamp can only be attached to an email being sent to 'jhonan@silveronion.com' on the 6th April 2004. Any other recipient will reject this stamp (as it doesn't contain their email address), and if it is sent on any other date to jhonan@silveronion.com, then it will be rejected as the date is incorrect. Now, the spammer decides they want to use the same stamp, but doesn't want to spend the CPU time generating it. So they change the stamp slightly to '0:040624: someone@yahoo.com: r7rk+dl/34'. Now the email address has been modified to read 'someone@yahoo.com'. However, if this stamp is validated with SHA-1, it is no longer a 20-bit stamp;

SHA1 (0:040624: someone@yahoo.com: r7rk+dl/34)
= 155DD9CAD53322C7FA119A3AFB6851501D06A7E8 : 3 bit collision (unacceptable)

This is because changing the stamp itself actually results in a different SHA-1 hash output. Once the stamp has been generated, it cannot be tampered with.

Partial hash-collision

As computing a full hash-collision (finding two text inputs that generate the same 160-bit hash output) is computationally infeasible - there isn't enough computing power on the planet to create one in the next 100 years – Hashcash instead works on the basis of partial-collisions. A full-collision would be that all bits of SHA-1(x) must match SHA-1(y), a k-bit partial collision would be where only the k most-significant bits match. The only way to attempt to calculate these partial collisions is by using a brute force method. Taking the hash we need to find a match on, loop through a process of appending randomly generated text until checking the output hash gives the required number of collision bits as shown in Figure 123.

> Take input text to generate stamp for "*0:040624: jhonan@silveronion.com:*"
> Start loop
> Add random string to text "*0:040624: jhonan@silveronion.com:r7rfjs0fsa*"
> Check for collision (Does new string cause X bits collision?)
> No collision found, continue loop
> Yes ,collision found! output final string
> "*0:040624: jhonan@silveronion.com:r7rk+dl/34*"

Figure 123: Pseudo code for Partial Hash-Collision

The loop above can take millions of attempts before it finds a matching collision. And it is because of this brute force iterative approach that it takes so much computational effort to find a collision and therefore generate a valid stamp. There is no other mathematical way of quickly finding hash collisions, this brute-force looping method is the only way. If one could see the output of this loop, it would look something like Figure 124.

Attempt 1
Try "0:040624: jhonan@silveronion.com: r7rfjs0fsa" (iterate through characters)
SHA1(0:040624: jhonan@silveronion.com: r7rfjs0fsa) =
155DD9CAD53322C7FA119A3AFB6851501D06A7E8 : 3 bit collision (unacceptable)

Attempt 2
Try "0:040624: jhonan@silveronion.com: r7rfjs0fsb"
SHA1(0:040624: jhonan@silveronion.com: r7rfjs0fsb) =
036048B1A1AA5FF78EE35965EB37C45A7E9A626C : 6 bit collision (unacceptable)

Attempt 3
Try "0:040624: jhonan@silveronion.com: r7rfjs0fsc"
SHA1(0:040624: jhonan@silveronion.com: r7rfjs0fsc) =
07E18141DACC9A9F2F39419BA36823CB1F420271 :   5 bit collision (unacceptable)

.
.continue looping and testing strings until a 20-bit collision is found...
.

Attempt 1,048,000
Try "0:040624: jhonan@silveronion.com: r7rk+dl/32"
SHA1(0:040624: jhonan@silveronion.com: r7rk+dl/32) =
00016EACE3E12A186394D5AA2FBC8FA0177AAFC6 : 12 bit collision (unacceptable)

Attempt 1,048,001
Try "0:040624: jhonan@silveronion.com: r7rk+dl/33"
SHA1(0:040624: jhonan@silveronion.com: r7rk+dl/33) =
0A581544F62B8C7EACCA37A0AAE2D495F78B4587 : 4 bit collision (unacceptable)

Attempt 1,048,002
Try "0:040624: jhonan@silveronion.com: r7rk+dl/34"

```
SHA1(0:040624: jhonan@silveronion.com: r7rk+dl/34) =
00000B6D7BDF8F3DF424A24F1B2BC4BBFCBF3EDE :20 bit collision
20-bit Collision Found on string "0:040624: jhonan@silveronion.com: r7rk+dl/34"
```

Figure 124: Brute-force looping method

If we take a 20 most significant bits collision for example, a 20-bit partial hash-collision is a practical target. A 2GHz P4 can compute one in about 1.6 seconds, but this equates to about 1,048,576 (2^{20}) iterations, on average, through the loop. Because Hashcash uses a brute-force algorithm to find hash collisions, there is no guarantee as to exactly how many iterations it will take before finding a collision. It might be 'lucky' and start the loop close to a successful collision, and thus calculate the collision in a matter of milliseconds. Or, it might randomly start the loop to cause a large number of iterations, and actually take longer than expected to achieve the required collision.

On average, it will take $2^n - 1$ attempts to find a collision, where n is the number of collision bits required. If we know how long each iteration takes (we can calculate this by timing how long one iteration takes), then we can work out on average how long it will take to calculate the required hash on that particular hardware. The goal of introducing a proof-of-work system like hashcash is to reduce the amount of spam the average person receives to below some fraction of their legitimate email. Independent testing of the best commercial spam filtering solutions shows that they currently achieve an spam-to-legitimate ratio of 0.06. If one is going to improve the email infrastructure to incorporate proof-of-work one might hope to reduce this ratio to say 0.01 (where 1% of email is spam) or, given the significant effort and disruption involved in such a project, 0.001 (one email in a thousand).

There are some[1] who say that hashcash will only slow down much spam sent through large collections of zombie computers, which run malware that send e-mail at the command of a spammer. These large networks have a large total computational power, which can be used to generate legitimate hashes for the spam emails they send. It can be argued however that the extra CPU usage will often be noticed by the owners of the machines, who will be more likely to fix them. (Laurie & Clayton, 2004) argue that while Hashcash for email is attractive, nonetheless spammer profit margins per sale mean that they well be able to afford the PCs to do the proof of work required. We believe however that their economic analysis of spammer charge per email and hardware costs are weighed in favour of the spammer (i.e. lower than we would state them) and they themselves mention that spam response rates to date are badly documented.

Conclusion

It is becoming increasingly clear that a single technology isn't going to solve the problem (Roberts, 2004), (Ishibashi et al, 2003). An intelligent combination of technologies would be much more effective. There are a quartet of complementary technologies to consider which are *proof of work, signatures with whitelist, domain certificates and content filters*. This cocktail of anti-spam measures is known as the 'hybrid' system. A combination of anti-spam solutions which are inadequate when used individually, but when used together can compensate for the inadequacies inherent in each part of the system. An all-encompassing anti-spam system needs to address a number of additional areas however, and ideally consists of a multi-layered approach:

-    Policies, mass-mailers agree to conform to certain standards
-    Accountability – If spammers don't conform, then some sort of internet 'sanctions' should be applied
-    Traceability – Email should be verifiable as coming from who it says it is from, to ensure senders can be traced
-    Legal – For repeat or spammers who refuse to comply with any of the policies, then legal discourse can be used as the fall-back position
-    Technical – Proof-of-work stamps to minimise spam volumes. Traditional Bayesian filters to trap anything that gets through (this is the point where false positives could occur – so whether Bayesian filters are still required in this model is debatable).
-    Whitelists and signatures to ensure ease of communication and establish trust between verified correspondents.

---

[1] http://en.wikipedia.org/wiki/Hashcash

Domain certificates are good as a first line of defence for reducing forgery. This is a highly recommended goal in any case. They can be implemented at the SMTP level, separately from the remainder of the filters, which must operate at the message level. The two reasons for going to a key (whitelist signature) system instead of proof of work systems is to give a mechanism which will allow stamp size to be set to a level to really hammer spammers without hurting ordinary users, as well as giving a mechanism for mailing lists to be able to deliver traffic to all users quickly and efficiently. Signatures for whitelisting are far easier to specify and implement than signatures for message body verification (e.g. PGP) or certificates for blacklisting. There is no need for a 'web of trust', which is burdensome to maintain - in fact, it is possible (and ideal) to make it completely transparent to the user. In this way, they are also applicable to mailing lists. Proof of work can be used as either a substitute or a foundation for signatures. Obviously, it is cheaper for a sender to add a signature than a proof-of-work token, but if a signature relationship hasn't yet been set up, the proof-of-work token is the way to go. Hashcash is a good candidate for the proof-of-work part of a hybrid solution. Content filters are the last line of defence. They should only come into play if a message passes the domain certificate stage but gets an inconclusive result from the signature and proof-of-work filters (perhaps because neither are present). This is the last chance for a message to 'go legit' before it is dropped.

The point of the content filter is to allow the status quo to be gradually phased out, rather than instantaneously becoming obsolete. It also allows senders to be partially ignorant of the quantitative requirements of the sender (ie. Proof-of-work value), without necessarily requiring a message feedback mechanism to avoid excessive false positives. Finally, any hybrid anti-spam solutions such as these discussed in this chapter go far beyond the technically 'simple' anti-spam solutions currently in use, in that to be successful they need to be adopted on a global scale. This means the main industry players have to reach agreement on the type of solution to implement, and how it should be implemented. Currently the main stumbling block in any of these proposed industry solutions is achieving agreement between the industry partners on the best way forward. Spammers have learned to adapt to overcome many of the anti-spam measures used against them thus the greater urgency for industry partners to work together sooner to implement a global hybrid solution.

References

Back, A. (1997). Hashcash. Published at http://www.cypherspace.org/hashcash/.

Back, A. (2002). Hashcash - A Denial of Service Counter-Measure. Technical Report at http://www.cypherspace.org/adam/hashcash/hashcash.pdf

Baker, W. Kamp, J. (2003). Summary of Can Spam Act, December. http://www.wrf.com/publications/publication.asp?id=1623481222003

Bass, T, and Watt, G. (1997). Simple Framework for Filtering Queued SMTP Mail (Cyberwar Countermeasures), Proceedings of IEEE MILCOM '97, Nov. 1997.

Boutin, P. (2004) Interview with a Spammer. InfoWorld, 16 April 2004 http://www.infoworld.com/article/04/04/16/16FEfuturerichter_1.html?s=feature

Clyman, J. (2004). The Problem with Protocols, PC Magazine, Ziff Davies Publishers, February 2004

Dwork, C. and Naor, M. (1992) Pricing via Processing or Combating Junk Mail, Crypto '92, pp.139 -- 147, 1992.

ePrivacy Group (2004). http://www.eprivacygroup.net/teos/TEOSwhitepaper1.pdf

ePrivacy Group (2003). http://www.eprivacygroup.net/teos/ - TEOS proposal document

Geer, D. (2004). Will New Standards Help Curb Spam? IEEE Computer Magazine Feb 2004 http://www.computer.org/computer/homepage/0204/TechNews/index.htm

Goodman, J. and Rounthwaite, R. (2004). Stopping Outgoing Spam. ACM Conference on Electronic Commerce, EC'04, New York, pp: 20-39, ISBN: 1-58113-7110, 2004.

Graham, P. (2003). Different methods of stopping spam. October.
http://www.secinf.net/anti_spam/Stopping_Spam.html

Hastings, N. and McLean, P. (1996). TCP/IP Spoofing Fundamentals. IEEE IPCCC'96, IEEE International Phoenix Conference on Computers and Communications, March 27-29, 1996, Phoenix, Arizona, USA IEEE 1996 0-7803-3255-5/96 pp.218-224

http://www.itsecurity.com/papers/mime6.htm

Ishibashi, H., Yamai, N., Abe, K., Matsuura, T. (2001). Protection Method against Unauthorised Access and Address Spoofing for Open Network Access Systems, IEEE 0-7803-7080-5/01 pp.10-13

Juels, A. and Brainard, J. (1999). Client puzzles: A Cryptographic Countermeasure Against Connection Depletion Attacks. Proceedings of NDSS '99 (Networks and Distributed Systems Security), pp. 151-165.

Laurie, B. and Clayton, R. (2004). Proof of Work proves not to work. The Third Annual Workshop on Economics and Information Security (WEIS04), May 13–14, 2004, University of Minnesota, Digital Technology Center

Levine, J. (2004). Putting a spammer in jail. CircleID, November 16th, 2004,
http://www.circleid.com/article/804_0_1_0_C/

Microsoft (2004). The Coordinated Spam Reduction Initiative – A technology and policy proposal. Microsoft Corporation. February 13th 2004. http://www.microsoft.com/downloads

Roberts, P. (2004). Experts Question Microsoft's Caller ID Patents. InfoWorld, March 2004.
http://www.infoworld.com/article/04/03/05/HNcalleridpatents_1.html

Schiavone, V., Brussin, D., Koenig, J., Cobb, S., Everett, R. (2003). Trusted Email Open Standard – A Comprehensive Policy and Technology Proposal for Email Reform. An

Schryen, G. (2004). Approaches Addressing Spam, Proceedings of IPSI, Hawaii 2004

Schwartz, A., Garfinkel, S. (1998). Stopping Spam. O'Reilly, ISBN:156592388X

Simpson, Pete. (2002) Putting Spam Back in the Can. ITsecurity.com, 13th May,
Templeton, S., Levitt, K. (2003). Detecting spoofed packets. IEEE DARPA Information Survivability Conference and Exposition - Volume I , April 22 - 24, 2003 , Washington, DC, pg. 164-177, 2003

Tserefos, P., Smythe, C., Stergiou, I., Cvetkovic, S. (1997) A Comparative Study of Simple Mail Transfer Protocol (SMTP), POP and X.400 Email Protocols. 22nd Annual IEEE Conference on Local Area Networks, Minneapolis, USA, 1997, pp.545-55

35   Computer Hacking

Kevin Curran, Peter Breslin, Kevin McLaughlin, Gary Tracey

Many self proclaimed hackers would actually consider themselves to be performing a service to businesses as they claim they are simply showing businesses the flaws within their systems so that they can implement ways of prevention. They state that if it was not for hacking then security software would not be where it is today. An ethical hacker will tell you that someone who hacks into a system for purposes of self benefit would be best known as a cracker rather than a hacker for it is them that give cause for security software in the first place. This chapter reviews the role of tools, methods and rationale of hackers.

Introduction

"Access" is defined in Section 2(1)(a) of the Information Technology Act[1] as "gaining entry into, instructing or communicating with the logical, arithmetical, or memory function resources of a computer, computer system or computer network". Unauthorised access would therefore mean any kind of access without the permission of either the rightful owner or the person in charge of a computer, computer system or computer network. Thus not only would accessing a server by cracking its password authentication system be unauthorised access, switching on a computer system without the permission of the person in charge of such a computer system would also be unauthorised access. Eric Raymond, compiler of *The New Hacker's Dictionary* (Raymond, 1996) defines a hacker as a clever programmer. According to Raymond a *"good hack"* is a clever solution to a programming problem and *hacking* is the act of doing it. Raymond lists five possible characteristics that qualify one as a hacker:

1. A person who enjoys learning details of a programming language or system
2. A person who enjoys actually doing the programming rather than just theorizing about it
3. A person capable of appreciating someone else's hacking
4. A person who picks up programming quickly
5. A person who is an expert at a particular programming language or system, as in "Unix hacker"

Raymond, like a lot of hackers condemns someone who attempts to crack someone else's system or otherwise uses programming or expert knowledge to act maliciously. This type of person, according to most hackers would better be described as a *cracker*. A cracker is someone who illegally breaks into someone else's computer or network by bypassing passwords and licences etc. A cracker could be doing this for purposes of maliciously making a profit. On the other hand, a hacker (according to a hacker) would break into a system to supposedly point out sites security problems. Therefore we must carefully distinguish between a hacker and a cracker. Although hacking according to a lot of hackers themselves, is beneficial to the development of systems security, it is still known as a crime under the computer misuse act. Categories of misuse under this act, include: Computer fraud - Unauthorized access to information, Computer hacking, Eavesdropping, Unauthorized use for personal benefit, Unauthorized alteration or destruction of data, Denying access to authorized user and Unauthorized removal of data.

The law does not distinguish between a hacker and a cracker. In relation to this, reformed hacker John Draper states that:

> *"Hackers are very important for the Internet community as a whole because they are the ones who will be buttoning up the holes in the system. Governments should be a little more tolerant of what is going on and hackers should be willing to contact a company and say "I found bugs in your system"."*

---

[1] http://www.stpi.soft.net/itbill2000_1.html

He believes that without hackers, security would not be where it is today, he believes that hackers are playing a valuable part in the development of highly effective security systems, and that the government and the law should recognise this and try to distinguish more carefully between a hacker with intent of displaying security flaws for the company, and a cracker who's intent is truly malicious.

Crackers use various methods to maliciously attack a computer systems security, one such method is a "virus". A virus is defined as a piece of programming code usually disguised as something else that causes some unexpected and usually undesirable event. A *computer virus* attaches itself to a program or file so it can spread from one computer to another, leaving infections as it travels. The severity and effects of a computer virus can range much the same as a human virus. Some viruses have only mild affects simply to annoy the host, more severe viruses can cause serious damages to both hardware and software. Almost all viruses are attached to an executable file, which means the virus may exist on your computer but it cannot infect your computer unless you run or open the malicious program. It is important to note that a virus cannot be spread without a human action, (such as running an infected program) to keep it going. People continue the spread of a computer virus, mostly unknowingly, by sharing infecting files or sending e-mails with viruses as attachments in the e-mail.

Another method is to use a "Worm". A worm is similar to a virus in both design and in the damage it can cause. Like a virus, worms spread from system to system, but unlike a virus, it has the ability to travel without any help from the user, it does this by taking advantage of the files and information already present on the computer. The biggest danger with a worm is its ability to replicate itself on your system, so rather than your computer sending out a single worm, it could send out hundreds or thousands of copies of itself, creating a huge devastating effect. For example, it is common for a worm to be sent through e-mail, if you receive a worm via e-mail, it is possible for the worm to use the information in your e-mails address book to send duplicates of itself to your contacts, and their contacts etc. Due to the copying nature of a worm and its ability to travel across networks the end result in most cases is that the worm consumes too much system memory (or network bandwidth), causing Web servers, network servers, and individual computers to stop responding. In more recent worm attacks such as the much talked about Ms.Blaster Worm., the worm has been designed to tunnel into your system and allow malicious users to control your computer remotely.

To combat viruses and worms there is a lot of measures that can be taken. Measures such as anti-virus software and firewalls. The firewall is the software that will prevent the attacks from entering your system whist if a virus or worm manages to get through, then the ant virus software (A utility that searches a hard disk for viruses and removes any that are found.) can scan your system to remove the pest. Most anti-virus software has an auto update feature that can automatically update the programs virus definitions etc to gain greater security.

Eavesdropping

Eavesdropping can be thought of as another form of hacking. In a lot of cases it involves unlawfully accessing a computer system in order to listen to (gather) information. This is invasion of privacy. Eavesdropping can be used by a hacker to gain information on the victim such as passwords and bank account details, although not all forms of eavesdropping is used for malicious purposes, some governments look to use computer eavesdropping as a way of surveillance. They look use this to catch paedophiles and other people who could be holding illegal information on there computers. More and more employers are investing in surveillance software (Eavesdropping software) that allows them monitor or eavesdrop on everything their employees type on their computers, be it e-mail, website surfing, or even word processing. Therefore not all forms of eavesdropping may be illegal. More and more eavesdropping software is being developed.

The FBI has been known to be developing eavesdropping software called "magic lantern". The Magic Lantern technology, part of a broad FBI project called ``Cyber Knight,'' would allow investigators to secretly install over the Internet powerful eavesdropping software that records every keystroke on a person's computer. Magic Lantern could be installed over the Internet by tricking a person into double-clicking an e-mail attachment or by exploiting some of the same weaknesses in popular commercial software that allow hackers to break into computers. It's uncertain whether or not Magic Lantern software would transmit keystrokes it records back to the FBI over the Internet or if it would store the information that later could be sized in a raid. The reality of Magic Lantern was first disclosed by MSNBC.

This kind of surveillance (Eavesdropping) software is very similar to so-called Trojan software already used illegally by some hackers and corporate spies. Trojan software is a very common hacking and eavesdropping tool used by a lot of hackers. Trojan horse software would allow the hacker to enter your system and even take control of it. It gives the hacker remote access to your computer. The Trojan Horse, at first glance will appear to be useful software but will actually do damage once installed or run on your computer. Those who are at the receiving end of the Trojan will have to activate (by opening it) it for the hacker to gain access; they are normally tricked into doing so because they appear to be receiving legitimate software or files from a legitimate source. Once the Trojan is activated on your computer, the hacker can then gain access. The affects of the Trojan can vary much like a virus; sometimes the affects can be more annoying than malicious (like changing your desktop, adding silly active desktop icons) and sometimes they affects can be severe as Trojans can cause serious damage by deleting files and destroying information on your system. The Trojan opens a "back door" on your system, which allows the user to view personal and confidential files, this kind of information can then be used for purposes such as blackmail.

Electronic eavesdropping is perhaps the most sinister type of data piracy. Even with modest equipment, an eavesdropper can make a complete transcript of a victim's actions - every keystroke, and every piece of information viewed on a screen or sent to a printer. The victim, meanwhile, usually knows nothing of the attacker's presence, and blithely goes about his or her work, revealing not only sensitive information, but the passwords and procedures necessary for obtaining even more. In many cases, you cannot possibly know if you're being monitored. Sometimes you will learn of an eavesdropper's presence when the attacker attempts to make use of the information obtained: often, by then, you cannot prevent significant damage. There are different methods to eavesdropping I have listed a few below and described what they are.

Electrical wires are prime candidates for eavesdropping (hence the name wiretapping). An attacker can follow an entire conversation over a pair of wires with a simple splice - sometimes he doesn't even have to touch the wires physically: a simple induction loop coiled around a terminal wire is enough to pick up most voice and RS-232 communications. Ethernet and other local area networks are also susceptible to eavesdropping; unused offices should not have live Ethernet or twisted-pair ports inside them. You may wish to scan periodically all of the Internet numbers that have been allocated to your subnet to make sure that no unauthorized Internet hosts are operating on your network. You can also run LAN monitoring software and have alarms sound each time a packet is detected with a previously unknown Ethernet address. Some 10Base-T hubs can be set to monitor the IP numbers of incoming packets. If a packet comes in from a computer connected to the hub that doesn't match what the hub has been told is correct, it can raise an alarm or shut down the link. This capability helps prevent various forms of Ethernet spoofing.

Key loggers

Another method of computer systems eavesdropping is to use what is know as a key logger. A Key logger is a program that runs in the background, recording all the keystrokes. Once keystrokes are logged, they are hidden in the machine for later retrieval, or sent automatically back to the attacker. The attacker can use the information gained by the key logger to find passwords and information like bank account details.
It is important to remember that a key logger is not just used as a hacking tool. Many home users and parents use key logger such as Invisible Key logger to record computer and Internet activities. These Key loggers are helpful in collecting information that will be useful when determining if your child is talking to the wrong person online or if your child is surfing inappropriate website content and it again can be used by businesses to monitor employees' work ethics. Normally their may be many files to key loggers and this means that it can be difficult to manually remove them, it is best to use anti-virus software or try to use methods such as firewalls to prevent them form getting onto the system in the first place.

On Thursday March 17th 2005 it was revealed that one of the largest bank robberies in Britain was foiled by Police in London. The target was the London branch of the Japanese bank 'Sumitomo Mitsui'. The bank robbers planned to steal an estimated £220 million pounds. The stolen money was to be wired electronically from the bank into 10 different offshore bank accounts. This planned robbery was unlike any traditional bank robbery in Britain's history. It didn't involve running into the bank with handguns, taking hostages and leaving in a getaway car. This bank robbery was much more high-tech[1]. The bank robbers uploaded a program onto the bank's network that recorded every keystroke made on a keyboard. This type of program is known as 'keylogging software'. The program recorded the websites that were visited on the network, the passwords, bank account numbers and PIN numbers that were entered on these websites and saved them to a file. This file was accessed by the robbers and when they visited the same sites as the people in the bank they could use their

---

[1] http://news.bbc.co.uk/2/hi/technology/4357307.stm

login information to logon. The site wouldn't have any reason to think that the person logging on wasn't authorised to do so.

Keylogging software can record all sorts of computer operations not just keystrokes. It can also record emails received and sent, chats and instant messages, websites, programs accessed, peer-to-peer file sharing and it also takes screen snapshots. Keylogging can occur in two ways. A specially coded program can be uploaded onto a network from anywhere in the world. The other is a piece of hardware that is about the size of a battery. This piece of software is plugged into the computer from the keyboard and records the keystrokes made. This has to be physically installed onto the machine by a person and in order to retrieve the information gathered by the mini-hard drive the person also has to physically remove the hardware.[1] The keylogging software was uploaded to the network more than 6 months prior to the planned robbery. It was first noticed that the keylogging software was on the network in October 2004. It was then that the National Hi-Tech Crime Unit (NHTCU) kept a close eye on the situation. This was the biggest and most high profile coup in the Unit's short history.

Password grabbers however are useful to the owners of systems as well as the crackers as it provides them with the capabilities of monitoring transactions carried out by the users for security auditing purposes. There are several types of password grabbers available such as Keycopy which copies all the keystrokes to a file using timestamp, Keytrap which copies all the keyboard scan codes for later conversion to ASCII and Phantom which logs keys and writes them to file every 32 keystrokes.

Spyware

The most common form of computer systems eavesdropping is the adware and spyware software. Spyware can be defined as software that covertly gathers user information through the user's Internet connection without his or her knowledge, usually for advertising purposes. Spyware applications are typically bundled as a hidden component of freeware or shareware programs that can be downloaded from the Internet; however, it should be noted that the majority of shareware and freeware applications do not come with spyware. Once installed, the spyware monitors user activity on the Internet and transmits that information in the background to someone else. Spyware can also gather information about e-mail addresses and even passwords and credit card numbers (Winopedia, 2005).

Spyware software is quite similar to a Trojan horse in that the user will unknowingly install the software themselves. The software can also cause a decrease in bandwidth as it runs in the systems background sending and receiving information from the software's home base. The most common way in which spyware software is installed to a machine is when the user has downloaded certain free-ware peer to peer file swapping software such as "WarezP2p" or "Kazaa". Spyware software can be used by companies for advertising purposes as well as being used by hackers to gain incriminating information. Adware is extremely similar to spyware. It affects your computer in much the same way, the main difference being that adware is used more for advertising purposes. Adware can cause a lot of pop ups to appear once you have connected to the internet, also it can allow icons to be added to your desktop and add web sites to your internet favourites. Both adware and spyware can be tricky to remove, as they will attach themselves to various parts of your systems registry. Adware and spyware can be removed by downloading variours software tools from the Internet although the best advice is prevention through a firewall.

The law looks down upon unauthorized computer access and computer eavesdropping, but in actual fact in a lot of cases, eavesdropping is not used for incriminating purposes rather it can simply just be a set of parents logging on to their childs computer in order to view their web history and the content of the sites in which they have visited, it could also be that an employer is using certain eavesdropping software to simply check that the employee is working and is doing his or her job. Although again there is also those that would use eavesdropping and unauthorized access for purposes of self benefit.

Packet Sniffing

Packet Sniffing is a technology used by crackers and forensics experts alike. Data travels in the form of packets on networks. These packets, also referred to as data-grams, are of various sizes depending on the network bandwidth as well as amount of data being carried in the packet in the measure of bytes. Each packet has an

[1] http://searchsecurity.techtarget.com/sDefinition/0,,sid14_gci962518,00.html

identification label also called a 'header'. The header carries information of the source, destination, protocol, size of packet, total number of packets in sequence and the unique number of the packet. The data carried by the packet is in an encrypted format, not as much for the sake of security as for the sake of convenience in transmitting the data. This cipher text (encrypted form) is also known as the hex of the data. When a person say 'A' sends a file to 'B' the data in the file gets converted into hex and gets broken into lots of packets finally headers are attached to all packets and the data is ready for transmission.

When being transmitted, the packets travel through a number of layers (Open Systems Interconnection (OSI) Model). Amongst theses layers, the network layer is responsible for preparing the packet for transmission. This is the level where most hackers and adversaries like to attack knowing that the packets are usually not secured and are prone to spoofing and sniffing attacks. Now when an adversary (a person trying to hack into a system) to the whole process - 'C' wishes to intercept the transmission between 'A' and 'B', he would have intercept the data packets and then go on to translate them back from hex to the actual data. For doing this he would normally use a technology called "Packet Sniffing". When he uses this technology he is able to intercept all or some of the packets leaving the victim (sender) computer. The same deception can also be practiced at the point of the intended recipient of the message before it can actually receive the packets. To use the sniffing technology the adversary only needs to know the IP address e.g. (202.13.174.171) of either of the parties involved in the communication. He would then instruct the sniffer to apply itself to the network layer of the victim IP address. From then on, all packets leaving the IP address will be 'sniffed' by the Sniffer and the data that is being carried out will be reported to the adversary in the form of logs. The sniffed data would still be in the hex format however most Sniffers nowadays provide the facility of conversion of the stolen hex into actual human readable data, with varying amount of success.

Tempest attack

Tempest is the ability to monitor electromagnetic emissions from computers in order to reconstruct the data. This allows remote monitoring of network cables or remotely viewing monitors. The word TEMPEST is usually understood to stand for "Transient Electromagnetic Pulse Emanation Standard". There are some fonts that remove the high-frequency information, and thus severely reduce the ability to remotely view text on the screen. PGP also provides this option of using tempest resistant fonts. An appropriately equipped car can park near the target premises and remotely pick up all the keystrokes and messages displayed on the computer video screen. This would compromise all the passwords, messages, and so on. This attack can be thwarted by properly shielding computer equipment and network cabling so that they do not emit these signals.

Hacking

The more experienced, professional hacker will choose a target that will have a significant reward and which appeals to them. They will be willing to work persistently for a long period of time to achieve their goal and it is almost certain that the hacker will gain access to the system at some stage. If a cracker is embarking on a long term attack within a system, he or she will avoid any unusual patterns appearing on the logs. This is achieved by spreading their attacks throughout different remote sites and time patterns, to ensure that any systems administrator will be unable to detect an intrusion if an unusual pattern showing up (Dr-K, 2000). System backdoors are used to gain access. Here an attacker will significantly increase the chance of gaining access by learning the IP network protocols, odd switches on user and system commands. In addition, knowledge of underlying design features is essential. Access is achieved by researching the best way to secure a site by reading through different security manuals to establish the recommendations they offer, and why these are necessary. When the hacker gains access to a system they gain administrative privileges which make the attack worthwhile. This also gives them the freedom which a basic user will not experience, for example, when it comes to privileges the system administrator is at the top of the hierarchy, so access to such capabilities give the attacker major advantages such as access to all types of files, whereas the basic user with set basic privileges can only access the files associated with the work that the particular employee carries out. The attacker is also capable of editing the computer logs of the system in order to cover up their tracks and these capabilities could be used to set up bogus user accounts allowing the attacker to gain easy access to the system upon re-entry.

An important aspect of hacking into a system is the ability to cover up any trace of the intrusion. This is possible via a variety of methods, the most important of course being, that the cracker approaches the attack cautiously however there are "Rootkits" to aid the cracker to do this. This is the hacker's toolkit and is essential for covering tracks. Within this toolkit is a piece of software which when compiled in the targets systems will perform many of the routine tasks needed to hide their actions. However, it is important that the attacker understands the software, making sure to run in the right locations of the system i.e. the Log Files (Dr-K, 2000). Other tools available include password grabbers and key loggers which are tools which assist cracker activities by intercepting and storing away keystrokes of a legitimate user of the system, into a file from which the attacker acquires valid login details to gain entry.

Web Server Hacking

Web Server hacking is when a hacker detects and takes full advantage of web server software's or add-on component's vulnerabilities, an example of this occurred previously when worms "Nimba" and "Code Red" exploited the vulnerabilities of Microsoft's ISS web server software. Source Code Disclosure allows the cracker to view the source code of application files on a vulnerable web server and together with other techniques gives the attacker the capabilities of accessing protected files containing information such as passwords (McClure, 2003). Computer and network resources can often be addressed by two representations Canonicalization resolves resources name to standard form. Applications that make their security decisions based on the resources name can be extremely vulnerable to be duped into executing unexpected actions known as Canonicalization attacks. Web Distributed Authoring and Versioning is an extension to the http protocol that enables distributed web authoring through a set of http headers and methods which allows such capabilities as creating, copying, deleting, and searching for resources as well as set and search for resource properties such ability would cause a major threat to a company if it was available to an attacker. Web Field Over Flow is where an attacker through the use of a web browser can bring down a web server. This vulnerability exists because the web developer often prefers to concentrate on functionality rather than security. A solution would be for the developers to employ an input sanitization routine in every program. The developer could move the administration page to a separate directory. There is web server vulnerability scanners available to scan through a system to find vulnerabilities and has the capabilities of detecting a wide range of well known vulnerabilities (McClure, 2003).

Password cracking

To crack a password means to decrypt a password, or to bypass a protection scheme. When the UNIX operating system was first developed, passwords were stored in the file "/etc/passwd". This file was readable by everyone, but the passwords were encrypted so that a user could not figure out what a person's password was. The passwords were encrypted in such a manner that a person could test a password to see if it was valid, but couldn't decrypt the entry. However, a program called "crack" was developed that would simply test all the words in the dictionary against the passwords in "/etc/passwd". This would find all user accounts whose passwords where chosen from the dictionary. Typical dictionaries also included people's names since a common practice is to choose a spouse or child's name. Password crackers are utilities that try to 'guess' passwords. One way, also known as a dictionary attack involves trying out all the words contained in a predefined dictionary of words. Ready-made dictionaries of millions of commonly used passwords can be freely downloaded from the Internet. Another form of password cracking attack is 'brute force' attack. In this form of attack, all possible combinations of letters, numbers and symbols are tried out one by one till the password is found out. Brute force attacks take much longer than dictionary attacks.

Viruses

A virus provides hackers with the ability to cause damage to a computer system by being destructive. It is initially a program that copies itself within the operating system of a computer. Hackers that develop viruses to plant in their targets system must write the viruses in assembly code specifying them around their potential target's operating system, forming protection for themselves while the viruses spread through the system. Protection from viruses comes in the form of anti-virus software which will detect and remove any suspected viruses. It does this by looking out for "viral signatures" embedded in the programs and also "viral behaviour" which can detect any potential attacks before they occur. This software has the sophistication of being aware of the behaviour adopted by the virus that proves invaluable. The types of destruction caused from these viruses range from non-destructive behaviour like pop ups and banners which basically only cause a general nuisance to random destruction that carries out such actions as altering the users key strokes to heavy destruction which will affect files through such activities as removing data (Dr-K, 2000).

Wireless hacking

Wireless networks, broadcast signals throughout an area, which allows hackers easy connection to their network, by simply being physically within their range. Hackers can access the network by war-driving, provided that they are within range and have the use of hardware such as a large antenna, a small laptop, a wireless card and other palm sized computing devices such as iPAQ. This can be done by simply walking through the hall of an office block or driving through a business centre (McClure, 2003). A hacker will initially locate the wireless device, using either the passive method of listening for access points and broadcast beacons or the aggressive method of transmitting client beacons in search of a response. Through the use of GPS systems, the wireless hacker then has the ability to pinpoint the precise location of the network. Wired based network hacking, requires the hacker to have an in depth knowledge, so that they can apply the most appropriate tools, know what to look for and how to cover their tracks. In contrast to other systems, however, wireless networks are easily located and poorly protected[1]. One method of security which is applied widely is WEP (wireless encryption protocol). By using a key it encrypts the data shared by all users of the network, however with the correct software WEP can be easily bypassed[2]. Another method involves MAC address filtering, which allows only specific wireless network adaptors to connect to the networks. This is facilitated by using a unique identifier, however, this method is both time consuming and requires greater networking knowledge. To overcome this type of obstacle, hackers have been known to monitor the traffic of packets within the network to capture an approved MAC address. This is then imitated to gain access[3]. Wireless routers, commonly come with firewalls, to control access to the computer from outside. However, anyone with the ability to access the wireless portion of the network will be able to bypass the firewall.

Conclusion

Computer eavesdropping and hacking can both be considered forms of the general term Unauthorized Computer Access. Unauthorized access can be described as an action in which a person accesses a computer system without the consent of the owner, this may include using sophisticated hacking/cracking software tools to gain illegal access to a system or it could simply be a case of a person guessing a password and gaining access. There are a lot of methods to be taken in an attempt to prevent unauthorized computer access, such as regularly changing your password, ensuring anti-virus software is up to date and ensuring that an up-to-date firewall exists on each system.

References

Dr-K (2000) Complete Hacker's Handbook, Carlton Book Limited, London

McClure, S., Scrambray, J., and Kurtz, G., (2003) Hacking Exposed: Network Security Secrets & Solutions fourth Edition, USA, McGraw-Hill/Osborne

Raymond, E. (1996). The New Hacker's Dictionary. The MIT Press; 3rd edition, October 1996

---

[1] http://news.bbc.co.uk/1/hi/sci/tech/1639661.stm
[2] http://www.pcstats.com/articleview.cfm?articleID=1489
[3] http://www.pcstats.com/articleview.cfm?articleid=1489&page=2

36   Internet Fraud

Kevin Curran, Laura Mc Elwee, Shubhanker Upadhyaya

Examples of fraud include the unauthorized obtaining of information from a computer e.g. 'hacking', taking unauthorized copies of company records, trade secrets, etc. The 'Salami' fraud this is when the perpetrator carefully 'skims' small sums from the balances of a large number of accounts in order to bypass internal controls and escape detection. Software theft is also becoming more common with the comparative ease of making copies of computer software which has led to a huge illegal market, depriving authors of very significant revenues. This chapter provides an overview of some aspects of computer fraud.

Introduction

Cyber crime is defined by British police as the use of any computer network for crime and the high-tech criminals of the digital age have not been slow to spot the opportunities. The term hacking was originally used to describe an audacious practical joke, but has become better known as a term for the activities of computer enthusiasts who pit their skills against the IT systems of governments and big corporations. The handiwork of some hackers, or "crackers" as they are known in the computer industry, has had disastrous results. The love-bug virus crippled at least 45 million computers worldwide and caused billions of dollars worth of damage. Information systems managers have long been aware of the need to maintain system security, particularly against computer fraud and sabotage. However, Information system managers may not consider their own programmers and analysts as possible perpetrators of computer fraud and sabotage. In addition, other programmers and analysts may be in prime positions to initiate other forms of security problems, such as computer hacking, viruses and software copyright violations. Yet it is tempting for managers to believe that most such security problems come from outside the organisation (Harrington, 1995).

Electronic commerce is about doing business using electronic technologies. It can involve the transmission of data, transactions and payments, or marketing and value adding to existing products of databases. That data can be as simple as an invoice or as complex as an EDI message. It can also represent the exchange of tokens that represent value or the exchange of credit card numbers that represent purchases made by consumers. In all these cases there is an acceptance that the integrity and safety of the exchange has been secure from capture or interference from hackers or others wishing to gain information illegally. Website security is about keeping strangers out but at the same time allowing controlled access to a network. Sometimes achieving both of these elements can be very difficult. According to Lawrence (Lawrence, 1998), there is a great deal of debate about security on the internet. However there can be as much concern about security of transmission using other electronic forms. There is a concern by consumers about sending their credit card details over the Internet. They fear that their transaction information will be intercepted and used by someone else. On the other hand though, people now readily telephone their credit card details when paying accounts. And there is probably not any more security in doing this.

The Law

In the past, the Criminal Law in relation to computers was unreliable as often legislation lagged behind the increasing changes throughout the advent of modern technology. 1980's saw an increase in the use of computer systems and networks. It soon became apparent that the existing laws such as the Theft Act and the Criminal Damage Act were inadequate as a deterrent or suitable remedy. From the industry, businesses and lobbying by some MP's to curtail such problems resulted in the Computer Misuse Act (1990), a vital piece of legislation that provided new offences of unauthorised modification of computer material. At present, computer-enabled crimes, involving the use of computers to commit forgery, fraud, obscenity and hate speech, criminal damage or copyright violation, are all covered by the following UK laws:

- The Theft Act 1968 (on fraud)
- The Telecommunications Act 1984 (section 42 relating to deception and section 43 relating to obscene material)
- The Forgery and Counterfeiting Act 1981
- The Protection of Children Act 1978, the Criminal Justice Act 1988 and the Criminal Justice and Public Order Act 1994 (all on child pornography)
- The Public Order Act 1986 (on racist material)
- The Criminal Damage Act 1977 (to cover physical damage to computer systems)
- The Copyright, Designs and Patents Act 1988

There is an anomaly under current legislation that means that although it is unlawful for you to be defrauded by a computer-related system, it is not unlawful for you to defraud a computer. The courts do not regard a machine to be 'deceivable', because it is automated. In cases involving the use of machines, including use of the Internet, as part of a deception or fraud, it has been judged that a deception cannot take place where a machine is manipulated by others to obtain a service for example giving a false credit card number when signing-up for an online service. The one exception to this is where the deception involves a licensed telecommunications service, such as dial-up chat lines or pay-per-view TV cards in which case it would be an offence under the Telecommunications Act 1984. The Law Commission has recommended that new legislation should be drawn up to deal with this anomaly. The Computer Misuse Act 1990 covers offences related to the penetration, alteration and damage to computer systems, namely:

- cyber-trespass – that is, unauthorized access to systems or intent to gain such access;
- cyber-theft – securing access to a computer in order to commit an offence or with the intent to do so;
- Cyber-violence and 'malware' software that intentionally causes harm such as viruses, worms or Trojans – modifying a system in a manner that impairs its operation.

Computer crime may raise issues of data protection. In this context, unauthorized access to a computer, and authorized access for unauthorized purposes, comes under the Data Protection Act 1998. The European Cyber crime Convention also covers computer intrusion, forgery, copyright and pornography, but extends current law to:

- define offences related to 'aiding and abetting' other offences covered in the treaty;
- formalize the procedure for the search and seizure of computers
- incorporate many of the features of the Regulation of Investigatory Powers (RIP) Act 2000 in relation to forcing the disclosure of decryption keys;
- incorporate UK proposals for the monitoring of networks under proposals for the acquisition and storage of traffic data

Protection from Online Fraud

The Internet Fraud Complaint Center (IFCC) was set up in 2000. The IFCC's primary mission is to address fraud committed over the Internet. This is done by facilitating the flow of information between law enforcement agencies and the victims of fraud, information that might otherwise go unreported. The IFCC Internet Fraud Report is the first annual compilation of information on complaints received and referred by the IFCC to law enforcement or regulatory agencies for appropriate action. The results provide an examination of key characteristics of 1) complaints, 2) perpetrators, 3) complainants, and 4) the interaction between perpetrators and complainants. One complaint that the IFCC continues to receive in high volume, and thus merits special consideration, is the well-known Nigerian Letter Scam. The Nigerian Letter Scam is defined as a correspondence outlining an opportunity to receive non-existent government funds from alleged dignitaries that is designed to collect advance fees from the victims. This sometimes requires payoff money to bribe government officials. While other countries may be mentioned, the correspondence typically indicates "The Government of Nigeria" as the nation of origin. This scam has run since the early 1980's and is also referred to as "419 Fraud" after the relevant section of the Criminal Code of Nigeria, as well as "Advance Fee Fraud". The scam works as follows:

1. A letter, e-mail, or fax is sent from an alleged official representing a foreign government or agency.
2. The letter presents a business proposal to transfer millions of dollars in over- invoiced contract funds into your personal bank account. The recipient is offered a certain percentage of the funds for help and is encouraged to travel overseas to complete the details.
3. The letter also asks for blank company letterhead forms, banking account information, and telephone numbers.
4. Next, the recipient receives various documents with official looking stamps, seals and logos testifying to the authenticity of the proposal.
5. Finally, they ask up-front or advance fees for various taxes, processing fees, license fees, registration fees, attorney fees, etc.

Credit card fraud is more of a problem for electronic commerce for several reasons: Since credit card companies will not hold the defrauded consumer liable, and, due to high risk of credit card fraud on the net, banks may not cover fraudulent expenses charged to electronic commerce vendors. Banks covering fraudulent "chargebacks" often charge significantly higher fees for the service (Coral, 1999). Unlike in person transactions, when an Internet vendor detects fraudulent credit card information, that credit card cannot be confiscated, and the fraudster and the credit card are free to try alternative sites. Since actual cards and signatures are not required, fraud perpetrators are free to use stolen numbers or even attempt to manufacture numbers for use. Michael Vatis, deputy assistant director and chief of the national infrastructure protection centre for the federal bureau of investigation indicates that a sophisticated understanding of computers and internet is no longer required to successfully crack a company's computer [4]. ID numbers, passwords, credit card numbers, and fraud instruction guides are all available on Internet chat rooms. At the same time, hackers are getting more sophisticated and are finding better and faster hardware and software resources at their disposal. Ramiz Saffouri, a consultant with advanced software applications Corp, claims that many electronic commerce sites do not adequately protect customer databases and are vulnerable to hackers seeking customer information [5]. Cyber sources, a developer of software systems that detect fraud, estimates that as much as 5 to 6 percent of the average Internet retailers transactions involve consumer fraud [3]. Others estimated that credit card fraud on the Internet is as high as 30 percent [4].

An Internet firewall is a security mechanism that allows limited access to your site from the Internet, allowing approved traffic in and out according to a thought-out plan. Today's Internet security threats range from curious prowlers to well-organised, technically-knowledgeable intruders. Without the ability to protect your entire network at its connection point, a network is only as strong as its weakest link, and securing each and every system is a complex and cumbersome job with no guarantee of the success, because of the variety of different operating systems, releases, vendor patches, and administrative domains. It is vital that all employees' passwords are changed at least every month. This helps prevent any part timers or contract staff using their knowledge of the computer to there own advantage. A record should be kept off all activity on the computer is important as it shows which users have used what file, who was logged into the computer system. Today's Internet-based payment mechanisms based on SSL are roughly as secure as existing mail order/telephone order (MOTO) credit card transactions (Lucas, 1998). Clearly, many businesses are comfortable with this level of risk and are, therefore, moving ahead and deploying e-commerce. SET (Morgan, 1999), however, can potentially provide an even more robust e-payment infrastructure, resulting in lower fraud rates. Secure electronic standard was published as an open specification and applicable to any payment service. It address several security needs specific to electronic commerce (Furnell & Karweni, 1999):

- Privacy of payment and confidentiality of order information transmissions;
- Authentication of a cardholder for a branded bankcard account using digital signature and cardholder certificate;
- Authentication of the merchant to accept credit card payments using digital signature and merchant certificate;
- Payment information integrity is ensured by the use of digital signature;
- Special purpose certificates;
- Non-repudiation for dispute resolution.

The significance of SET over other Internet security protocols is the use of digital certificates that associate the cardholder and the merchant with a financial institution and the visa and master card payment system. The use of this digital certificate will prevent a level of fraud that the existing systems do not have and gives the cardholders and merchant confidence that the transaction will be handled in the same manner as credit card transactions today. While such technologies are clearly necessary, they do not represent a complete resolution of the trust issue. The difference is that lacks a basis for trust in electronic systems from the outset and, therefore, requires proof of its security before being willing to use it. An example of the need to establish trust is the experience of the credit card operator VISA in relation to the internet-based transactions and instances of fraud. While only around 2 percent of their credit card transactions are currently conducted via the Internet, this accounts for 50 per cent of disputes and discovered frauds (Tadjer, 1999).

Neural networks can be employed to combat computer fraud. The National Health Service (NHS) in the UK investigated 503 cases of fraud in 2003 leading to 45 prosecutions. The software silently monitors all transactions and processes looking for unusual variations and discrepancies compared to the expected normal transactions. Statistical techniques play a major part in this technology which is yet far from accurate and still hasn't been fully become operational in the NHS. Another company using Neural Networks is NTL which has a system in place to monitor telephone lines for excessive activity.

Conclusion

Computer Fraud is any activity which results in deliberately sabotage or stealing of information or data present on a computer. Many companies do not understand the potential seriousness of the problem until they are affected themselves. A company using IT systems determine the impact of a security violation of the organisation's assets and also determine the level of trust that can be placed in the users of the organisation's IT systems. If the business must be connected to the Internet than a firewall is essential as it is an up-to-date virus scanner. Once a company has taken measures against computer fraud they should become complacent about their security systems. Currently approximately 36% of all fraud of fraud is computer fraud. In the future this percentage is expected to fall because of better legislation and internet policing. Most credit card companies are now following the French approach by assigning a pin number to each card which should make it more difficult for fraudsters.

References

Harrington, S. (1995) Computer Crime and Abuse by IS Employees: Something to worry about. Journal of information systems, March/April, 1995

Lawrence, E. (1998) Internet commerce - Digital models for business. 1st edition. John Wiley, 1998

Coral, C. (1999) Online security, payment services aid E-tailers Stung by Fraud. Discount store news. April 19th, p20-25, 1999

Lucas, P. (1998) A security blanket for the Internet. Credit card management, August, pp.33-37, 1998

Morgan, C. (1999) Protecting your web site against credit card fraud. Computerworld March 8th, p. 71, 1999

Furnell, S. & Karweni, T. (1999) Security implications of electronic commerce: a survey of consumers and business. Vol. 9, No. 5, pp.372-382, 1999

Tadjer, R. (1999) Safeguard Your IT Assets - You can prosecute a hacker, if you have the right systems in place. Internet Week, May 31, 1999

37   The Invisible Web

Edwina Sweeney, Kevin Curran

A web crawler or spider crawls through the web looking for pages to index and when it locates a new page it passes the page on to an indexer. The indexer identifies links, keywords, and other content and stores these within its database. This database is searched by entering keywords through a interface and suitable web pages are returned in a results page in the form of hyperlinks accompanied by short descriptions. The Web, however, is increasingly moving away from being a collection of documents to a multidimensional repository for sounds, images, audio, and other formats. This is leading to a situation where certain parts of the web are invisible or hidden. The term known as the "Deep Web" has emerged to refer to the mass of information that can be accessed via the Web but cannot be indexed by conventional search engines. The concept of the Deep Web makes searches quite complex for search engines. Google states that the claim that conventional search engines cannot find such documents as PDF's, Word, PowerPoint, Excel or any non-HTML page is not fully accurate and they have taken steps to address this problem by implementing procedures to search items such as academic publications, news, blogs, video, books, and real-time information. This chapter provides an overview of the 'hidden web'.

Introduction

Eighty-five percent of Web users use search engines to find information about a specific topic. However, nearly an equal amount state that their inability to find desired information as one of their biggest frustrations (Kay, 2005). The fact that so much information is available on the Internet and that the inadequacies of search engines are denying us access, is why search engines are an obvious focus of much investigation. With conventional search engines, indexing a document so that it can be found by a search engine means that the crawler must follow a link from some other document. Therefore, the more links to your document the more chance a document has of been indexed. This leaves a major loop hole for documents that are generated dynamically. Because no links exist to these documents, they will never be located to be indexed. Also, for web sites that host databases, subscriber information or registration information are sometime required before access is given to their resources. Typically, this type of information is never accessed because the crawler does not have the capability to submit registration or subscriber information. Million of these documents exist on the Internet and because of this a substantial amount of valuable information is never read by Internet users. Steve Lawerence of the NEC Research Institute writes that *"Articles freely available online are more highly cited. For greater impact and faster scientific progress, authors and publishers should aim to make their research easy to access. Evidence shows that usage increases when access is more convenient and maximizing the usage of the scientific record benefits all of society"* (Lawerence, 2001).

The [1]Surface Web contains an estimated 2.5 billion documents, growing at a rate of 7.5 million documents per day (Kay, 2005). The Deep Web is estimated to be well in excess of 307,000 Deep Web sites, with 450,000 online databases. Furthermore the content provided by many Deep Web sites is often of very high quality and can be extremely valuable to many users (Ntoulas et al, 2005). Some researchers will point out the fact that the problem is with the database owners, who need to adopt an approach which makes it easier for search engines to gain access. This research is concerned with the problem of accessing the deep web. There are a number of projects (Lin & Chen, 2002; Kabra et al, 2005; Ntoulas, 2004; Raghavan & Garcia-Molina, 2001) which have investigated differing aspects of the Deep Web and later we examine each of these in more detail and outline how we intend to utilize aspects of the research in an innovative custom deep web search engine prototype. Lin & Chen (2002) implement a system which primarily creates a database of Deep Web search engines and subsequently submits queries to specific

---

[1] A term which is used to describe information that is indexed and accessible through conventional search engines.

search engines to find the relevant results. Kabra et al (2005) examine user queries with regard to the Deep Web sources. They attempt to find the most relevant Deep Web resources from a given imprecise query by employing a co-occurrence based attribute graph which captures the relevance of attributes. Based on this relevancy, web pages can be ranked. The key insight underlying this study is that although autonomous heterogeneous sources are seemingly independent, the information that they provide is revealed through the query user-interfaces. Ntoulas (2004) devised a Hidden Web Crawler which uses an algorithm to identify relevant keywords which can be used to query web sources which cannot be indexed by conventional crawlers. Results are downloaded and indexed at a central location so that the Internet user can access all the information at their convenience from a central location. They provide a framework to investigate the query generation problem for the Hidden Web and propose policies for generating queries automatically. The results of their experiments were notable where they claim to have downloaded more than 90% of a Deep Web site after issuing fewer than 100 queries. (Raghavan & Garcia-Molina, 2001) propose a wrapper and alignment program which will work in conjunction with a Web crawler. It extracts data objects from multiple Deep Web sources and integrates the data together in one table. Their research contributes largely to fully automating the data annotations of web sites. Many techniques can be adopted to preclude the Deep or invisible Web problem and a number concentrate on improving a user's query to obtain more relevant results. A user's query has been shown to be extremely effective when searching for relevant information. In addition, directing the user to appropriate search engines or Deep Web sites could ensure a more fruitful search.

The Deep Web

General search engines are the first place a typical user will go in order to find information. There are common approaches implemented by many indexed search engines. They all include three programs such as a crawler, an indexer and a searcher. This architecture can be seen in systems including Google, FAST etc. Some search engines also offer directory categories which involve human intervention in selecting appropriate web sites for certain categories. Directories naturally complement search engines. There is now a trend developing towards the use of directories because, in addition to their classification, their content is pre-screened, evaluated, and annotated by humans (Lackie, 2006). Search engines do not search the WWW directly. In fact, when searching for a Web page through a search engine, it is always searching a somewhat stale copy of the real web page. It is only when that page's URL is returned via a results page that a fresh copy of the page is made available. A web crawler or spider crawls through the web looking for web pages to index. Its journey is directed by links within web pages. Through the process of following links from different web pages, the spider's journey can become infinite. When a spider locates a new page it passes the web page to another program called an indexer. This program identifies links, keywords, and other content and stores these within its database. This database is then searched by entering keywords through a search interface and a number of suitable web pages will be returned in a results page in the form of hyperlinks accompanied by short descriptions (see Figure 125).

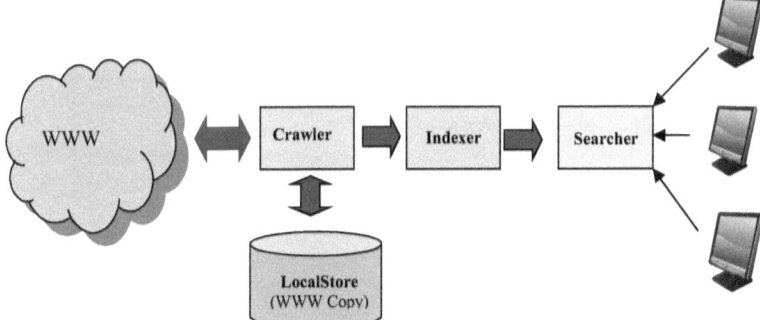

Figure 125: Conventional Search Engine Configuration

Chang et al claim that although *"The surface Web has linked billions of static HTML pages, an equally or even more significant amount of information is "hidden" on the deep Web, behind the query forms of searchable databases"*. (Chang et al, 2006). Conventional search engines create their indices by crawling static web pages. In order to be discovered, the page must be static and linked to other pages (Bergman, 2001). It is thought that web crawlers cannot browse or enter certain types of files for example, dynamic web pages, and therefore cannot index the information within these files. However, claims have now been made that conventional search engines have the capabilities to locate dynamic web pages, pages that are generated in an ad-hoc manner (Berkeley, 2007). Index web crawlers cannot index pages that are in non-HTML format for example PDF's, spreadsheets, presentations, and some word processing files, script-based pages which include Perl, JavaScript, CGI', pages generated dynamically by active server pages for example, Database files and images, video and music files.

The biggest problems faced by search engines to date are their inability to login, to subscribe or enter relevant keywords to specialized databases or catalogs. When you use a search form to query a back-end database, the information generated is just in response to your particular query. It is much more cost effective to use these web resources in this manner as opposed to entering all possible queries and then storing all the generated content in some repository. There are also pages that the search engine companies exclude for specific non-technical reasons. Some pages would not provide a financial benefit to store while other pages would not be of great interest to many people. There are thousands of public, official and special purpose databases containing government, financial, and other types of information that is needed to answer very specific inquiries. This information may include a stable link, however, many search engines don't warrant them important enough to store (Berkeley, 2007). The Web is increasingly moving away from being a collection of documents and becoming multidimensional repository for sounds, images, audio, and other formats. This has lead to a situation where certain parts of the web are invisible or hidden. The term known as the "Deep Web" has been used repeatedly by many writers to refer to the mass of information that can be accessed via the WWW but can't be indexed by conventional search engines. Most people accessing the WWW through a search engine assume that all documents available on the Internet will be found through an efficient search engine like Google for example. In August 2005, Google claimed to have indexed 8.2 billion Web pages (Kay, 2005). This figure sounds impressive. However, when it is compared with the estimated size of the deep or hidden web, it becomes apparent that a whole wealth of information is effectively hidden to Internet users. Extensive research was carried out by a corporation called BrightPlanet in 2001 (Bergman, 2001). Its comprehensive findings concluded that:

  I. Public information on the Deep Web is currently 400 to 550 times larger than the commonly defined WWW
 II. The deep web contains nearly 550 billion individual documents compared to the one billion of the surface web
III. More than 200,000 deep Web sites exist
 IV. Sixty of the largest deep web sites collectively contain about 750 TB of information which is sufficient by themselves to exceed the size of the surface web forty times
  V. On average, deep Web sites receive 50% greater monthly traffic that surface sites
 VI. The deep Web is the largest growing category of new information on the Web
VII. Total quality content of the deep Web is 1,000 to 2,000 times greater than that of the surface Web
VIII. More than half of the deep Web resides in topic-specific databases
 IX. A full 95% of the deep Web is publicly accessible information and is not subject to fees or subscription.

Figure 126 represents the subject coverage across all 17K deep Web sites used in their study. The table shows uniform distribution of content across all areas, with no category lacking significant representation of content illustrating that that Deep Web content has relevance to every information need and market (Bergman, 2001).

Deep Web Coverage			
General	**%**	**Specific**	**%**
Humanities	13	Agriculture	2.7

Lifestyles	4	Arts	6.6
News, Media	12.2	Business	5.9
People Companies	4.9	Computing	6.9
Recreation, Sports	3.5	Education	4.3
Travel	3.4	Government	3.9
Shopping	3.2	Engineering	3.1
Employment	4.1	Health	5.5
Science, Math	4	Law	3.9

Figure 126: Distribution of Deep Web sites by subject area (Bergman, 2001)

The Deep Web also withholds greater "quality" of documents. The BrightPlanet Corporation conducted a series of tests to measure the quality of documents returned from the Deep Web. Using computational linguistic scores, they posed five queries across various subject domains to the Surface Web and the Deep Web. The table in Figure 127 indicates the five queries that were issued to three search engines, namely, AltaVista, Fast and Northern Lights and three well known Deep Web sites. The results show that a Deep Web site is three times more likely to provide "quality"[1] information than a surface Web site. Professional content suppliers typically have the kinds of database sites that make up the Deep Web; static HTML pages that typically make up the surface Web are less likely to be from professional content supplier (Bergman, 2001).

Query	Surface Web			Deep Web		
	Total	Quality	Yield	Total	Quality	Yield
Agriculture	400	20	5.0%	300	42	14.0%
Medicine	500	23	4.6%	400	50	12.5%
Finance	350	18	5.1%	600	75	12.5%
Science	700	30	4.3%	700	80	11.4%
Law	260	12	4.6%	320	38	11.9%
Total	2210	103	4.7%	2320	285	12.3%

Figure 127: "Quality" Documents retrieved from Deep and Surface Web (Bergman, 2001)

The concept of the deep web makes searches quite complex for search engines. Even Google have attempted to integrate the deep Web into their centralized search function. Google provides specific searches for example to academic publications, news, blogs, video, books, and real-time information. However, even a search engine such as Google provides access to only a fraction of the deep web (Cohen, 2006). When the Internet evolved, web pages were structured HTML documents. Managing such static documents was quite achievable. Since then, the growth rate of the Web has been 200% annually (Bergman, 2001). Since 1996, three developments within the WWW have taken place. Firstly, database technology was introduced to the Internet; secondly, the Web became commercialized; and thirdly, web servers became capable of delivering dynamic information through Web pages. It is now quite common for most organizations, public and private, to transfer, seek and provide information through a database-driven application. Governments at all levels around the world have made commitments to making their official documents and records available on the Web through single-access portals (Kay, 2005). Lately, an increasing amount of the deep Web has become available on the Web. As publishers and libraries make agreements with commercial search engines, undoubtedly more content will be searchable through a centralized location. Also, as the amount of on-line information grows, the amount of dynamically generated web pages will grow. Search engines cannot ignore and exclude these pages.

State of the Art in Searching the Deep Web

Currently many tools exist that allow Internet users to find information. However, a large number of web pages require Internet users to submit a query form. The information generated from these query forms is not indexable by most search engines since they are dynamically generated by querying backend-

---

[1] Quality is a metric value that can be difficult to determine or assign.

databases (Broder et al. 1997). The majority of these resources are within the Deep Web and therefore are rarely indexed (Lackie, 2006), (Kabra et al, 2005). When examining the contents of the Deep Web, it became very obvious that much of the information stored here is very accurate and relevant, for example, scientific, historic, medical data which would dramatically improve communication, research and progress in these areas (Lawerence, 2001). This section provides an overview of research addressing the Deep Web problem. Each project proposes a different method; however there are some similarities between them.

Automatic Information Discovery from the Invisible Web

Lin & Chen (2002) propose a process of examining search engines, to select the most appropriate search engine to query. Information was discovered that is not found by conventional search engine. This system maintains information regarding specialized search engines in the Deep Web. When a query is submitted, a selection is made as to the most appropriate search engine and then a query is redirected to that search engine automatically so that the user can directly receive the appropriate query results. The system maintains a database of specialized search engines, storing information such as URL, domain, and search fields. The system utilizes the search engine database to automatically decide which search engine to use and route the query to. It also applies a data mining technique to discover information related to the keywords specified so as to facilitate the search engine selection and the query specification. This would enable more relevant results to be returned. The system is divided into various components (Lin & Chen, 2002). A crawler is used to populate a database with information regarding specialized search engines. A search engine database stores the information regarding the specialized search engines is stored. A Query Pre-Processor receives user input and finds phrases associated with the query keywords. These phrases form the basis of the search engine selection. A search engine selector is finally sent the keyword phrase and with access to the search engine database, it selects the specialized search engine to send the query to. It also proceeds to send the actual query to the selected databases. The search engine database is populated by a crawler. It visits every page, but only extracts the portion that corresponds to a search engine by identifying form tags. The search engine's URL and other information are also stored. This becomes essential when constructing the query string to send to the search engines.

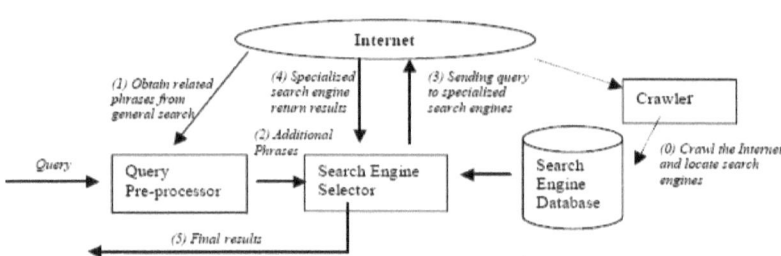

Figure 128: Architecture of system

In order to select the most appropriate search engines, a query pre-processing stage is carried out to determine the best query to send. This will supplement the keywords supplied by the user with other information i.e. keywords and phrases returned from an episode rules discovery technique. Each keyword phrase generated from the pre-processing stage is matched with the three fields of each search engine within the database. The results are ranked and those search engines with the most matches are returned. The system now sends the user query to each of these search engines and the results are returned through a user interface (see Figure 128). The main objective of this system is to use specialized search engines to discover information that cannot be retrieved from a conventional search engine. To measure the effectiveness of this system, the web pages returned from a typical query was compared against results obtained from the Google search engine (Lin & Chen, 2002). Only in 3% of the cases do both systems return similar or related results. While a majority of the time, the system was able to access web pages that are not directly accessible through Google.

Query Routing: Finding Ways in the Maze of the Deep Web

Although autonomous heterogeneous sources are seemingly independent, the information that they provide is revealed through the query user-interfaces. A search form within a book sales website like Barnes & Noble for example, contains attributes like author, title, ISBN, edition etc. This would indicate that this site is about books. Within an airline site, attributes like from, to, departure date, return date etc. would reveal that the site is about flights. (Kabra et al, 2005) have built a *source selection system which* examined user queries with regard to "deep" web sources. Given the huge number of heterogeneous deep web sources, Internet user may not be aware of all the sources that can satisfy their information needs. Therefore, it attempts to find the most relevant deep web resources from a given simple imprecise query. It designs a co-occurrence based attribute graph for capturing the relevance of attributes. It employs this graph to rank sources in order of relevance to a user requirement. The system counteracts the impreciseness and incompleteness in user queries. It assumes that the user may not be aware of the best attributes to enter as a query and so therefore limits themselves in the results that will be returned to them. The main contributions of the work by Kabra et al are an attribute co-occurrence graph for modeling the relevance of attributes and an iterative algorithm that computes attributes relevance given just an imprecise query. A methodology was created in which the relevance of an attribute was determined using the relevance of other attributes. There may be some attributes that are not included in a user's query but which do appear in many of the data source query interfaces. These attributes that co-occur with the input query attributes will also be relevant to the search. Also, there are similar attributes that co-occur with the other attributes that are likely to have some relevance to the query in question. Therefore, any relevant attribute shall lead to increasing the relevance of its co-occurring attributes. In order to quantify this approach, a relevance score was associated with each attribute which represented how likely a query interface containing this attribute will provide appropriate information to the Internet user. A graph was constructed which is similar to the graphs used by search engines to determine the ranking of pages. Each graph contains nodes and edges. Each node corresponds to an attribute and the edges connect two co-occurring nodes which have associated weighting. The weighting indicates the relevant scores, where given an attribute A that is known to be relevant and which co-occurs with attribute B, the more frequently the attribute B occurs with attribute A as compared with other attributes co-occurring with attribute A, the higher the degree to which it gets relevance induced from attribute A (Kabra et al, 2005). Consequently, web sources that contain more attributes with higher relevancy are going to have a higher probability of being more relevant to user requirements. During its experimental evaluation it manually collected a deep set of web sources which contained 494 web query interfaces and a total of 370 attributes. These web sources included a set of diverse domains including airlines, books, car rentals, jobs, music, movies and hotels.

Query 1	(from, to, departure date, return date)
Query 2	(author, title, ISBN)
Query 3	(make, model, price)
Query 4	(song, album, artist)
Query 5	(title, actor, director)
Query 6	(from, to)
Query 7	(from, to, adult, child)

Rank	(Index)	Name
1	(6)	departure date
2	(7)	return date
3	(18)	to
4	(4)	from
5	(9)	adult
6	(10)	child
7	(16)	trip type
8	(8)	class
9	(19)	return
10	(12)	infant
11	(1)	city
12	(14)	departure
13	(15)	senior
14	(28)	airline
15	(2)	destination

Figure 129: Queries used to evaluate the algorithm

Figure 130: Top 15 relevant attributes for query 1

It constructed a number of queries which are listed in Figure 129 and tested it against the algorithm. The algorithm takes as input the set of attributes in the user query. The algorithm was run against all the different queries. A relevance score was associated with each of the attributes and the top five attributes were identified. Figure 130 shows a listing of the top 15 attributes identified from query 1. Based on the co-occurrence analysis, the algorithm is able to find other attributes that are also relevant. The algorithm then uses the top five attribute relevancies to compute a relevance score for each data source. The results indicated that the system frees users from worrying about finding the right set of query attributes. Even with a set of attributes that might not necessarily best describe the type of information required, the algorithm will direct the Internet user to the most appropriate set of web sources.

Downloading the Hidden Web Content

Much of the deep web sources today are only searchable through query interfaces where the Internet user type certain keywords in a search form in order to access pages from different Web sites. (Ntoulas et al, 2005) produced a Hidden Web crawler which automatically generates meaningful queries to a web site by using an *adaptive* algorithm. Results are downloaded and indexed at a central location so that the Internet user can access all the information at their convenience from a central location. They provide a framework to investigate the query generation problem for the Hidden Web and propose policies for generating queries automatically. The results of their experiments were notable where they claim to have downloaded more than 90% of a Deep Web site after issuing fewer than 100 queries. The challenge undertaken by this project was that the Web crawler must generate meaningful queries so that it can discover and download the Deep Web pages. This project also investigated a number of crawling policies in order to find the best policy which could download the most pages with the fewest queries. It proposed a new policy called the adaptive policy which examines the pages returned from the previous queries and adapts its query-selection policy automatically based on them (Ntoulas et al, 2005). The experiments were carried out on real web sites and the results noted for each crawling policy. The proposal focuses on textual databases that support single-attributed keyword queries. The main objectives of this crawler are to gain entry to a Hidden Web site, generate a query, issue it to a Web site, download the results page, and then follow the links to download the actual pages. This process is repeated until all the resources are used up i.e. the crawler has limited time and network resources. The most important decision that the crawler has to make is what query to issue with each iteration. If the crawler issues meaningful queries and returns many web pages, then the crawlers will expose much of the Hidden Web in the least amount of time. However, if the crawler issues inappropriate queries then very few pages will be returned, which will result in a minimum amount of the Hidden Web pages being exposed. Therefore, how the crawler selects its next query greatly affects its effectiveness. There are three different methods to select meaningful queries.

- o Random: Selecting random keywords from an English dictionary and then issuing them a database.
- o Generic-Frequency: Analyzing a generic document body collected elsewhere and obtaining the frequency distribution of each keyword. Based on this selection, the most frequent keyword was selected first and issued to the database and then the next most frequent keyword and so on. The hope was that the list of generic keywords obtained would also occur frequently in the Deep Web databases, returning many matching documents.
- o Adaptive: Analyzing the returned documents from the previous queries issued to the Deep Web database, and estimating which keyword would most likely return the most web pages. The adaptive algorithm learns new keywords from the documents that it downloads and its selection of keywords is driven by a cost model. This cost model can determined the efficiency of each every keyword with regard to the number of links that it returns and select the candidate that will return the most unique documents. This efficiency measurement is identified by maintaining a query statistics table.

The query statistics table is updated with every new query where more documents are downloaded. Using the above algorithms, an experimental evaluation was conducted. It should be noted that with these algorithms the initial keyword chosen has minimal affect on the performance overall. The experiment focused on three Deep Web sites; The PubMed Medical Library, Amazon, and the Open Directory Project. The first observation made was that the generic-frequency and the adaptive policies perform better than the random algorithm. The adaptive policy out performs the generic-frequency algorithm when the site is topic specific .i.e. Medical, Law, Historical topics. For example with the PubMed site, 83 queries were issued by the adaptive algorithm to download 80% of the documents stored at PubMed. While the generic-frequency algorithm required 106 queries for the same coverage. The adaptive algorithm also performed much better than the generic-frequency algorithm when visiting the Open Directory Project / Art site. Here, the adaptive algorithm returned 99.98% coverage by issuing 471 queries while the generic-frequency algorithm discovered 72% coverage with the same number of queries. Obviously, as the adaptive algorithm iterates through the web site material its keyword selection for queries becomes more accurate. It searches through the downloaded pages and selects keywords which occur most frequently, while the generic-frequency algorithm works from a large generic collection (see Figure 131).

Iteration	Keyword	Number of Results
23	departments	2,719,031
34	patients	1,934,428
53	clinical	1,198,322
67	treatment	4,034,565
69	medical	1,368,200
70	hospital	503,307
146	disease	1,520,908
172	protein	2,620,938

Figure 131: Keywords queried to PubMed exclusively by the adaptive policy

Results from the random algorithm performance were not encouraging. It downloaded a 42% from the PubMed site after 200 queries while the coverage for Open Directory Project /Art site was 22.7% after 471 queries. In conclusion, the adaptive algorithm performed well in all cases. However, the generic-frequency algorithm proves to be effective also, though less than the adaptive. It is able to retrieve a large proportion of the Deep Web collection, and when the site is not topic specific it can return the same coverage as that of the adaptive algorithm. The random algorithm should not be considered because it performed poorly overall.

Information Discover, Extraction and Integration for Hidden Web

(Wang & Lochovsky, 2003) explore methods which discover information sources within the hidden web. These methods locate the web site containing the structured data of interest to the Internet user, induce wrappers to extract relevant data objects from discovered web source pages, label the fields of extracted data, and integrate the various data objects from multiple sources with or without the knowledge of the schema. To integrate data from different web sites, Information Extraction systems are utilized. That is, wrappers have been developed which will extract data from a web page based on their HTML tag structure. Their system called DeLa (Data Extraction and Label Assignment) comprises four components; a form crawler, a wrapper generator, a data aligner, and a label assigner. A form crawler called HiWe is adopted for the first task (Raghavan & Garcia-Molina, 2001). This crawler collects labels of the search form and sends queries to the web site. The wrapper generator is then applied to the retrieved web pages.

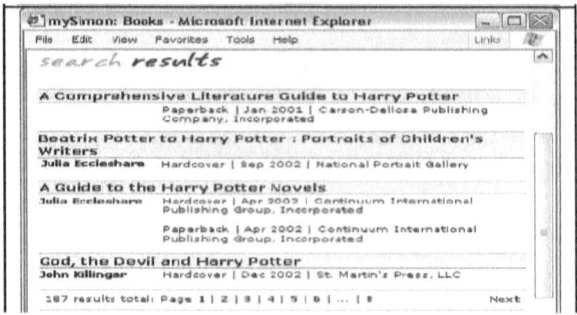

Figure 132: Results Page from a Book Search (Wang & Lochovsky, 2003)

In this results page each book has a book title, zero or more authors, and one or more edition information. The symbols <> represent an unordered list tuple, the symbol { } represent a set and the ? symbol represents an optional attribute (see Figure 132). A data aligner then extracts data objects from the web pages according to the wrapper induced by the wrapper generator. It then filters out the HTML tags and arranges the data instances into a table like format. After data objects are extracted from the results page, it is re-arranged in a table format so that each row of the table represents a data instance, and each column represents a data attribute.

Title	Author	Format	Date	
A Comprehensive Literat...		Paperback	Jan 2001	Carson-D...
Beatrix Potter to Harry Pot...	Julia Eccleshare	Hardcover	Sep 2002	National...
A Guide to the Harry Pot...	Julia Eccleshare	Hardcover	Apr 2002	Continuu...
A Guide to the Harry Pot...	Julia Eccleshare	Paperback	Apr 2002	Continuu...
God, the Devil and Harry ...	John Killinger	Hardcover	Dec 2002	St. Martin'...

Figure 133: The table format which was utilized with the given book search

Each web site's data is represented as a single table to allow easy integration during the later stages (see Figure 133). The data aligner must also separate multiple attributes which are represented as one single string, and it must also separate multi-valued attributes into two separate rows. A label assigner then labels the column of the table by matching them to the form labels retrieved by the form crawler. The system performance had 90% precision in inducing wrappers and over 80% correctness with assigning meaningful labels to the retrieved data. Anticipating the correct type of queries to enter through search forms has been extensively studied (Kabra et al, 2005). However, discovering the actual Deep Web would be at a nascent stage (Wang & Lochovsky, 2003). Many systems would assume that the Internet user is aware of the appropriate Web resource and would ignore the need to help users to find the desired Web site that they want to extract information from. Finding the most relevant Web site to a given user query is the main objective of most search engines. Manually administered measures seem to have the highest percentage of success. Google has always favored the algorithmic approach to search because of the obvious scaling advantages over the human editorial approach. Computer algorithms can evaluate many times more web pages than humans can in a given time period. "Of course the flip side of this argument is that machines lack the ability to truly understand the meaning of a page" (Seth, 2006). The fact that Internet users are now aware of the "Deep Web" should have a profound effect on the development of search tools. Search engines like Yahoo integrate categories into their user-interface which aids in the selection of appropriate Web resources. The Google search engine, which indexes 8 billion pages approximately have created a development forum which allows access to Google APIs. In essence this allows developers to interact with the Google database and search engine to retrieve web pages which can be filtered using a number of different techniques. It also enables developers to create custom search engines which direct their search to specific sites. Coverage of the "Deep" Web is not easily accessed through conventional search engines therefore an invaluable amount of information is never accessed by many Internet users. By directing specific or well defined queries to a Deep Web resource, users can make their own determination of "quality" documents. The implementation of a system to achieve this could be done through use of Google APIs and the Google Custom Search Engine tool.

Google Custom Search Engine

Google recognizes that there are inherent limitations in the use of link based ranking schemes to provide optimal search results (Seth, 2006). In 2006, Google launched a new development tool which enables web users to create their own search engine. The Custom Search Engine (CSE) provides a form-based interface for building a specific search engine on top of the Google search platform. This means that the web user gets to focus on selecting valuable trusted content, while Google does the crawling, indexing, ranking, and displaying of results. The main function of building a CSE is to determine which sites are searched, and to define a set of rules that guide the ranking of results. Specifically, the CSE program allows four major methods for altering the search results; 1) which sites will be included in the displayed results; 2) sites whose ranking should be raised; 3) sites whose ranking should be lowered; 4) sites which should be excluded from the results. Theoretically, this program is about enabling knowledgeable experts the capacity to provide editorial oversight of the CSE results. Google recognizes that there are limitations in the use of link based ranking schemes to provide best possible search results. Knowledgeable experts can now define search engines whose results are manually tweaked. Web designers can also use more than one knowledgeable expert to build a CSE. The program includes a collaboration feature, where other experts can be recruited to contribute their expertise to the CSE. When a user performs a search, they are brought to a web page that looks like the traditional Google results page. However, there are significant differences in that the site owner can choose to have the search results appear on their own web page or, alternatively, they can be hosted by Google on Google.com. The CSE owner can customize the look and feel of the page to make it look more like their existing site. The implication of introducing such a tool is that Google has effectively recruited a number of "knowledgeable experts" to help improve their search results. The potential exists for a substantial amount of search volume to take place through highly trusted resource sites across the web, where trusted and recognized experts put together vertically oriented CSEs that provide superior results in their area of expertise (Seth, 2006). Google offers the designers of these CSEs revenue based on the number of visitors to the site. Google shares in this ad revenue; therefore, there is an incentive for them to promote third party custom search engines. This practice is significant to the whole notion of Google creating a distributed search platform, while distributing the work of CSEs, it still retains its ability to monetize search. To design a Custom Search Engine (CSE), one has to decide on the name of the CSE; a description of the CSE; whether to limit the CSE solely to the sites you specify, or prefer to include results from the entire web, but simply improve your sites' rankings and whether you want third party contributions to your CSE to be by invitation only or to be open to anyone that's interested.

Conclusion

Conventional search engines, index a document so that it can be found by searchers. This is done through a 'crawler' following a link from some other starting point. This means that the more links to yoaur document the more chance a document has of been indexed. This however can mean a problem for documents that are generated dynamically as no links exist to these documents, therefore they will never be located to be indexed. In addition, for web sites that host databases, subscriber information or registration information are sometime required before access is given to their resources. Typically, this type of information is never accessed because the crawler does not have the capability to submit registration or subscriber information. Google is a widely used and reputable search engine. It has released an exciting feature through its Google custom search engine. By allowing Internet users the capability to filter their own search engine is a positive approach to gaining access to the Deep Web. Typically, Internet users will more freely use this technology to search before attempting to subscribe to individual Deep Web sources. Providing a Google technology which can comparably return results as if from a Deep Web site is indeed useful.

References

Bergman, M. (2001) *The Deep Web: Surfacing Hidden Value,* Journal of Electronic Publishing, Publishers: University of Michigan July 2001, http://www.press.umich.edu/jep/07-01/bergman.html,

Berkeley (2007) *What is the Invisible Web, a.k.a. the Deep Web*, Berkeley Teaching Guides, http://www.lib.berkeley.edu/TeachingLib/Guides/Internet/InvisibleWeb.html

Broder, A., Glassman, S., Manasse, M., and Zweig, G. (1997) Syntatic Clustering of the Web, In *6th International World Wide Web Conference*, April 1997. http://proceedings.www6conf.org/HyperNews/get/PAPER205.html.

Chang, K., Cho, J. (2006) *Accessing the web: from search to integration.* 25th ACM SIGMOD International Conference on Management of Data / Principles of Database Systems, Chicago, Illinois, USA; June 26-29, 2006. pp: 804-805

Cohen, L. (2006) Internet Tutorials, The Deep Web, FNO.com, From Now on, The Educational Technology Journal, Vol. 15, No 3, February 2006

Kabra, G., Li, C., Chen-Chuan Chang, K. (2005) *Query Routing: Finding Ways in the Maze of the Deep Web*, Department of Computer Science, University of Illinois at Urbana-Champaign.

Kay R. (2005) *QuickStudy: Deep Web,* ComputerWorld, June 4th 2007 http://www.computerworld.com/action/article.do?command=viewArticleBasic&articleId=293195&source=rss_dept2

Lackie, R. (2006) *Those Dark Hiding Places: The Invisible Web Revealed,* Rider University, New Jersey, 2006.

Lawrence, S. (2001) Online or Invisible, *Nature*, Volume 411, Number 6837, p. 521, 2001.

Lin, K., Chen, H. (2002), *Automatic information discovery from the invisible web,* Proceedings of the International Conference on Information Technology: Coding and Computing, Washington, DC, p. 332

Ntoulas, A., Zerfos, P., Cho, J. (2004) *Downloading textual hidden web content through keyword queries Tools & techniques: searching and IR*, JCDL'05: Proceedings of the 5th ACM/IEEE-CS Joint Conference on Digital Libraries 2005 p.100-109

Ntoulas, A., Zerfos, P., Cho, J. (2005) *What's new on the web?: the evolution of the web from a search engine perspective,* International World Wide Web Conference, Proceedings of the 13th international conference on World Wide Web, New York, USA, Pages: 1 – 12, October 11-15th 2005

Seth, S. (2006), *Google muscle to power custom search engines,* CRIEnglish.com. http://english.cri.cn/2906/2006/10/24/272@154396.htm

Raghavan, S., Garcia-Molina, H., (2001) *Crawling the Hidden Web,* Proceedings of the 27th Intl Conf. on Very large Database, 129 – 138, 2001.

Wang, J., Lochovsky, F. (2003) Data Extraction and Label Assignment for Web Databases, Wang & Lochovsky, International World Wide Web Conference, Proceedings of the 12th international conference

38   Digital Watermarking & Steganography

Kevin Curran, Xuelong Xi and Roisin Clarke

Digital imaging companies lose revenue each year to people who are illegally copying and using their images. One prevention mechanism is to digitally encode images making it difficult for others to copy. This could be done using digital fingerprinting or simply adding a visible watermark. The information is encoded within a host image, so that the actual appearance of the image does not change, but within the image there is a watermark or secret message, which prohibits the attacker from making an exact copy. The objective with Steganography is not to change the actual message, or make it difficult to read, as cryptography does, rather to hide the existence of the message without distorting the carrier or the actual information. This chapter presents the results of implementing a Least Significant Bit (LSB) digital watermarking system.

Introduction

Steganography is derived from the Greek word Steganos which means *covered* or *secret*, and *graphy* meaning written or drawn. The art of Steganography originated from a Greek man named Histiaeus, who was a prisoner of a rival king. He needed a way of transmitting a secret message to his people. He had the idea of shaving a willing slaves head and tattooing the message onto his scalp. When the slave's hair grew back, he was sent to deliver the message to Histiaeus' army (Cole, 2003).

The objective of steganography is to send a message through some media known as a carrier, to a receiver, while preventing anyone else from knowing that the message exists. The carrier can be one of many different digital media, but the most common is the image. The image should not attract any attention as a carrier of a message and should compare as close as possible to the original image by the human eye. When images are used as the carrier in steganography, they are generally manipulated by altering one or more bits of the byte that make up the pixels of the image. The least significant bit (LSB) may be used to encode the bits of the message. These LSB's can then be read by the recipient of the stego image and put together as bytes to reproduce the hidden message, providing they have the stego key – the password for the stego image (Martin, 2005).

Steganalysis is the art of discovering a message. Breaking a steganographic system involves detecting that steganography has been used, reading the embedded message and proving that the message has been embedded to third parties. Steganalysis methods are also used by the steganographer to determine whether the message is secure and whether the process has been successful (Cheddad et al., 2007). Detection involves observing relationships between combinations of cover, stego media and steganography tools. This can be achieved by passive observation of patterns or unusual exaggerated noise and visual corruption. The patterns visible to the human eye could broadcast the existence of the message and point to signatures of certain methods or tools used. If numerous comparisons are made between the cover images and the stego images, patterns can begin to emerge. Some of the methods of carrying out steganography produce characteristics that act as signatures for that particular steganography method. Detection might involve looking at areas in the image where colour does not flow well from one area to the next. The attacker should obviously not be familiar with the cover image; otherwise it would make it a lot easier for comparison.

Today steganography is used for transmitting data, as well as hiding trademarks in images and music. This is known as digital watermarking. Cryptography and steganography are different in their methods of hiding information. Cryptography scrambles a message and hides it in a carrier, so that if it is intercepted it would be generally impossible to decode. Steganography hides the very existence of the message in the carrier. When the message is hidden in the carrier a stego-carrier is formed e.g. a stego-image. If successful, it would be perceived to be as close to the original carrier or cover image by the human eye. Images are the most widespread carrier medium (Martin, 2005). Images are the most widespread carrier medium (Westfield, 1999). They are used for steganography in the following way:

- The message may firstly be encrypted. The sender (or embedder) embeds the secret message to be sent into a graphic file (Zollner, 1998). This results in the production of what is called the stego-image. Additional secret data may be needed in the hiding process e.g. a stegokey (Pfitzmann, 1996). The stegoimage is then transmitted to the recipient.

- The recipient or the extractor extracts the message from the carrier image. The message can only be extracted if there is a shared secret between the sender and the recipient. This could be the algorithm for extraction or a special parameter such as a key (the stegokey).

To make the stegonographic process even more secure the message may be compressed and encrypted before it is hidden in the carrier. Figure 134 illustrates the principles of steganography where a carrier message has a message is added and put through a Stegosystem Encoder. The Stegoimage is then sent through the appropriate channels to a Stegosystem Decoder (Marvel, 1998$).

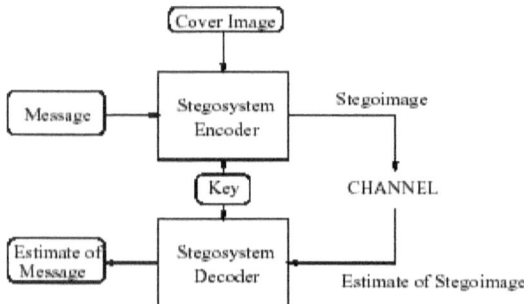

Figure 134: Steganographic System (Marvel, 1998)

For grayscale images each pixel has a value between 0 and 255. The image is broken down into co-ordinates and pixels. The carrier image must be either the same size or larger than the message. The least significant bit of each pixel of the carrier is changed to the least significant bit if each pixel of the message to be hidden. This has the effect of hiding the message but making it appear to be the carrier. The human eye cannot detect and message or any difference to the carrier. It then has to be passed through a stegoimage decoder for the hidden message to be extracted. A username and password is required at this stage. This is where Cryptography and Steganography can be used together. When the message is compressed it takes up less space in the carrier and will minimize the amount of information to be sent. It also limits the chances of being seen or detected in the carrier. The random message resulting from encryption and compression would be easier to hide than a message with a high degree of regularity (Fridrich, 2002). Encryption and compression are recommended in conjunction with steganography, as it offers a higher degree of security and reliability.

There are a variety of digital carriers or places where data can be hidden. Data may be embedded in files at imperceptible levels of noise and properties of images can be changed and used in a way useful to your aim. Features such as luminescence, contrast and colours can be changed according to which one is most useful to your particular application. This chapter focuses on bit values of pixel in the grayscale range which can be altered to embed hidden images inside other images, without changing the actual appearance of the carrier image.

Image Steganography

In Least Significant Bit (LSB) substitution, the least significant bit is changed because this has little effect to the appearance of the carrier message as shown in
Figure **135**:

Image 1:

1	0	0	0	0	0	0	0

The grayscale pixel bit size is: 128

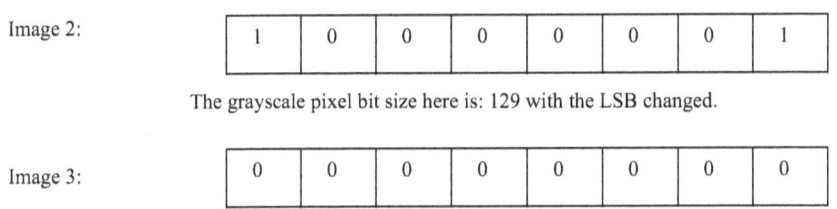

Image 2:

The grayscale pixel bit size here is: 129 with the LSB changed.

Image 3:

By changing the MSB here the bit size has changed from 128 to 0.

Figure 135: LSB and MSB Substitution

This shows that the grayscale image would change significantly if there were any other bit changed than the LSB. It changes more and more the closer you get to the MSB. When the LSB is changed, the pixel bit value changes from 128 to 129, which is undetectable with the human eye. With the MSB changed, the pixel bit value changes from 128 to 0, which makes a significant change to the grayscale view. The theory is that if you take two grayscale images, and change the LSB of image one to the LSB of image two for each co-ordinate or pixel, image two will be hidden in image one as illustrated in Figure 136.

Figure 136: Image Processing Results

When the second image is embedded in the first, there should be no detectable change or alteration to the appearance of the first image. A digital image is the most common type of carrier used for steganography. A digital image is produced using a scanner, camera or other digital device. The digital representation is an approximation of the original source (Hashad et al., 2005). The system used for producing the images focuses two dimensional patterns of varying light intensity and colour onto a sensor. The pattern, in this case a grayscale pattern, has a co-ordinate system with the origin in the upper left corner of the image. The pattern can be described by a function f(x,y). The pattern can be described as an array of numbers that represent light intensities at various points. These are known as pixels. Sampling is the process of measuring the value of the image function, f(x,y) at discrete intervals. Each sample is the small square area of the image known as the pixel. The raster data of an image is the part of the image that can be seen on screen. Pixels are indexed by x and y co-ordinates (x and y are integer values). Dense sampling produces high-resolution images in which there are many pixels, each contributing to a small part of the image. Coarse sampling results in a low-resolution image in which there are fewer pixels.

Application of Steganography to Images

When an image is used as a carrier in steganography, it is generally manipulated by changing on or more bits of the byte, in our case the LSB. If it corresponds to the bit to be hidden or embedded it is left unchanged. Otherwise it is changed to correspond to the hidden bit. These LSB's can then be read by the recipient of the stego image and put together as bytes to reproduce the hidden message. In a grayscale image, each pixel is either black or white and has a level of between 0 and 255, as each pixel has eight bits. Steganography is carried out by changing the low order bit of a pixel, and using it to encode one bit of a character. There are two stages in the steganalysis system:

- Detecting that steganography has been used
- Reading the embedded message

Steganalysis is used by a steganographer in order to determine whether a message is secure and consequently whether the steganographic method has been successful. The aim of a stegoanalyst is to detect stegoimages, find and read the embedded message, and prove that the message has been embedded to third parties. Detection involves observing relationships between combinations of cover, message, stego-media and steganographic tools (Johnson, 2001). Active interference by the stegoanalyst involves removing the message without altering the stego image too much, or removing the image or message without consideration to the stego-image appearance or structure (Pfitzmann, 1996). There are two necessary conditions to be fulfilled for a secure steganographic process. The key must remain unknown or undetectable to the attacker, and the attacker should not be familiar with the cover image (Cheddad et al., 2008). If the cover image is known and it is impossible to keep it unknown from the attacker, the message could be embedded in a random way so that it is secure, as long as the key remains unknown. However, it is preferable that the cover image remains a secret to obtain maximum security.

Digital Watermarking

Digital Watermarking is the process of hiding information in a carrier in order to protect the ownership of text, music, films and art (Hashad et al., 2005). Watermarking can be used to hide or embed visible or hidden copyright information (Wayner, 2002). Steganographic techniques can be used for the purposes of digital watermarking. Often information is hidden about the carrier itself providing further information about the carrier, which is not explicitly, displayed (Johnson, 1998). Watermarks in images are hidden mainly so that the do not disturb or distort the image rather than to avoid detection. They are generally hidden in more significant areas of the image and are not lost by compression. The main aim of watermarking is to prevent unlawful reproduction of a product. The ID of the author can be hidden so that if the image is circulated, the ID of the author still remains embedded in the image. In some cases watermarks are clearly visible. In these cases they are not a type of steganography, but are part of the actual image.

Watermarking does not impair the image. This is a main concern with visible watermarking. Even though the watermark can be seen, it must be inserted in such a way that it does not interfere with the original image. The underlying image must still be legible. If the watermark blocks large portions of the original image or the entire image, it is not an effective watermark. There is also no point in a watermark that can be easily removed. The typical litmus test with the watermark is that if the watermark is removed then the image should be impaired or destroyed. Even though only a small amount of data is to be embedded, it should be inserted in more than one place so that it is more difficult to remove. Someone who is trying to remove the watermark would be unlikely to detect all of the watermarks from the original image.

Figure 137: Visible Watermarking   Figure 138: Invisible Watermarking

There are two types of digital watermarking, visible and invisible. As can be seen from Figure 137 and Figure 138 (Cole, 2003), the two contain watermarks; the first figure contains a visible watermark, whereas the second watermark is invisible. Unlike steganography, it is irrelevant if a digital watermark is detected. Some companies prefer their watermarks to be visible to deter possible thieves. It is essential though, that the watermark cannot be removed or tampered with.

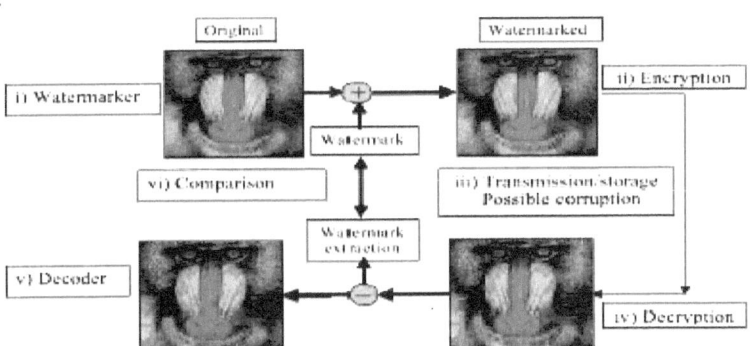

Figure 139: Coloured Watermarking Process

Figure 139 illustrates how an image undergoes the watermarking process and appears at the other side apparently unaltered to the user. In an image such as this, the least significant four bits could be changed without any perceptual change in the resultant image allowing enough space to hide a secret message (Cheddad et al., 2007).

Invisible Watermarks

In visible watermarking, a pattern is applied to a file or image so that it is undetectable by the human eye. With an invisible watermark you can change certain pixels in an image so the human eye cannot tell the difference from the original image. A computer program can however detect these discrepancies. Another factor to consider when applying an invisible watermark is the actual size of the pixels. The smaller the pixel, the less chance there is of detecting the change in colour. The strength of invisible watermarks is that the image quality is not degraded or changed according to the user or consumer. When looking at the image, there is no way of telling there is a watermark, yet the digital image is still protected. Invisible watermarks are effective, though, only while the image is in digital form. If a digital image that has an invisible watermark is printed out, and then rescanned, the watermark is effectively removed.

Visible Watermarking

A visible watermark makes slight modifications to an image. The transformation is such that the image can still be seen, but the watermark is effectively laid over the top of it. One of the advantages of visible watermarks is that even if an image is printed and scanned the watermark is still visible. A visible watermark image will usually make use of a light grayscale tone or simply make the pixels that contain the watermark slightly lighter or darker than the surrounding area. When applying a visible watermark, it is essential that the watermark is applied to enough of the image that it cannot be removed, and the original image can still be seen and is still legible. If you apply too much of the watermark, all you will see is the watermark and little of the actual image. Complex mathematical formula can be used to make watermarks more robust, but at a general level a watermarking program finds a group of pixels and adjusts the pixels in a way that the watermark can be seen but the image is not destroyed. The usual way of performing this operation is to make the colour of specific pixels darker.

Attacks on watermarks

This will involve trying to remove or distort the watermark. The hidden information should be made such an integral part of the image so that it is impossible to remove it without destroying the image. If the watermark is hidden in the LSB, all the individual has to do is flip one LSB and the information cannot be recovered. Various image processing techniques may be used to attack a watermark. It is particularly successful when using the same algorithm as was used to produce the existing watermark. One common problem with watermarks is that their existence is often advertised so that potential users know that the image has copyright information embedded.

Characteristic	Steganography	Digital Watermarking
Amount of Data	As much as Possible	Small Amount
Ease of Detection	Very Difficult to Detect	Not Critical with Visible Watermarks
Ease of Removal	Very Important it cannot be Removed	Important it cannot be Removed
Goal Of Attacker	To Detect the Data	To Remove the Data
Goal of User	To Hide Information so it cannot be Removed	To Embed a Signature to Prove Ownership
Current Uses	Covert Communications	Protecting Rights of Owners

Table 11: Steganography vs. watermarking

Table 11 shows the differences between steganography and digital watermarking. It depends on the use, which one is chosen; each has its advantages and disadvantages. The user will know best which one to choose depending on the application and situation.

Requirements of a Steganographic System

There are a number of ways of hiding information in image pixels. In some methods the objective is to store the message in a random way so as to make it more difficult to detect. These methods typically involve the use of a key – the stego key. The best types of images to use are black and white grayscale or natural photographs. The redundancy of the data helps to hide the existence of a secret message. A cover image should contain some randomness. It should contain some natural uncertainty or noise, as hiding information may introduce enough noise to raise suspicion. Therefore the carrier or cover image must be carefully selected. Once it has been used, the image should not be used again and should be destroyed. A familiar image should not be used, it is better for steganographers to create their own images.

♦ Perceptual Transparency: The Watermark should not affect the quality of the original image. Where possible, the watermark should go undetectable, as this increases security. Attackers find detectible watermarks much easier to remove or manipulate.

♦ Robustness: This is a measure of how well the watermark withstands various methods of image processing. The image may be subjected to filtering, rotation, translation, cropping, scaling etc. as part of image processing. The more robust the watermark is the better it will perform when these methods are applied. If the watermark algorithm is embedded using the spatial or frequency domain, it will withstand the image processing much better. There is also a watermark type called 'Fragile', which is intentionally made non-robust as they are used for authentication of original material rather than tracing it back to the source after processing.

♦ Security: To improve security, it is important that third parties cannot alter the watermark even if they know the algorithm for embedding and recovering.

- Payload of Watermark: The amount of data that can be stored in a watermark depends on the application. For example, in copyright a payload of one bit is sufficient, but for intellectual copyrights such as ISBN a payload of 60-70 bits is required. Watermarking Granularity is a term used to represent the number of bits that are actually needed to represent a watermark within an image.

- Oblivious vs. Non-Oblivious: in copyright and data protection applications, the extraction algorithm can use the original unwatermarked data or image to find the watermark. This is non-oblivious watermarking. In other applications such as indexing or copy protection the watermark extraction algorithm cannot access the original image and therefore makes detection and extraction very difficult for possible attackers. This type of watermarking is known as oblivious.

Implementation of Steganography

An effective way to implement steganography is to use images as the carrier and hidden message and use the pixel values as the method by changing the LSB. A simple method could be to use grayscale images and the effect of transferring the data through embedding images in carriers. Image processing can be done through a program such as Matlab. As mentioned earlier, LSB Substitution involves embedding a watermark by replacing the least significant bit of the image data with a bit of the watermark data. Detection can be done visually or by correlation methods. One of the drawbacks of this method is that if the algorithm is discovered, it is relatively easy for someone to alter it and defeat the purpose. This is why the watermark is often placed in more than one place in the original image.

512x512 pixels

Figure 140: The Image

16x16 pixels

Figure 141: The
Watermark

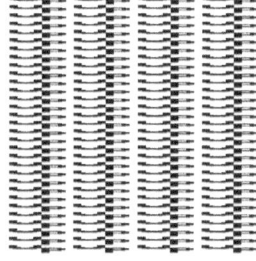

Figure 142: The Recovered Watermark

Figure 140 shows an actual image and Figure 141 shows the watermark that can be used. Figure 142 shows the watermark recovered when the code is implemented with the LSB method. This shows the repetitive nature of this method, making it more difficult for attackers to manipulate. There are however a number of drawbacks with LSB Substitution. LSB Substitution can survive simple operations such as cropping, as it is placed in numerous locations, but any addition of noise or compression of the image is going to overcome the effects quickly. Also, if the watermark is detected, an attacker would only have to replace all LSB bits with a '1' fully defeating the effects. One solution to improve the robustness of the watermark is to use a pseudo random number generator to determine the pixels to be used for the embedding. Security is increased, but it does require effectively a password or key to be sent with the image, or shared among users. Provided the attacker does not receive the password it would be very difficult to manipulate the watermark.

Conclusion

Digital watermarking is used by those who wish to prevent others from stealing their material. LSB substitution is not a very good candidate for digital watermarking, but it is very useful in the art of steganography, due to its lack of robustness. LSB embedded watermarks can easily be removed using techniques that do not affect the image visually to the point of being noticeable. Furthermore if one of the other embedding algorithms is used, the encoded message can be easily recovered and even altered by an attacker. It would appear that LSB will remain in the domain of steganography due to its useful nature and its overall capacity of information.

References

Bailey, K., Curran, K. and Condell, J. (2004) An Evaluation of Pixel based Steganography and Stegodetection Methods. The Imaging Science Journal, ISSN 1368-2199, Maney Publishing, Vol 54, No. 2, June 2004

Cheddad, A., Condell, J., Curran, K and Mc Kevitt, P. (2007) A Comparative Analysis of Steganographic Tools. Proceedings of the Seventh IT&T Conference. Institute of Technology Blanchardstown, Dublin, Ireland. 25th-26th October 2007. pp 29-37.

Cheddad, A., Condell, J., Curran, K., Mc Kevitt, P. (2008) *Securing Information Content using a New Encryption Method and Steganography,* Third International Conference on Digital Information Management 2008, University of East London, London, UK, November 13-16 2008

Cole, E. (2003). Hiding in Plain Sight. John W. Wiley, ISBN: 0-471-44449-9

Fridrich, J., Goljan, M. and Hogeg, D. (2002) Steganalysis of JPEG Images: Breaking the F5 Algorithm. Proceedings of Information Hiding: 5th International Workshop, IH 2002 Noordwijkerhout, The Netherlands, 2578/2003: 310-323, October 7-9, 2002.

Johnson Neil F., Sushil Jajodia (1998), Steganalysis of images created using current Steganography Software, Centre for secure Information Systems, George Mason University, Fairfax, Virginia, information Hiding Second Workshop, IH'98 Portland, Oregon USA, proceedings Computer Science 1525.pp.273-289, April 1998

Johnson Neil F., Zoran Duric, Sushil Jajodia (2001) Information Hiding, and Watermarking - Attacks & Countermeasures, Kluwer 2001.

Hashad, A.I., Madani, A.S. and Wahdan, A.E.M.A. (2005) A Robust Steganography Technique using Discrete Cosine Transform Insertion. Proceedings of IEEE/ITI 3rd International Conference on Information and Communications Technology, Enabling Technologies for the New Knowledge Society. 5-6 Dec. 2005, 255-264.

Martin, A., Sapiro, G. and Seroussi, G., (2005). Is Image Steganography natural? IEEE Trans on Image Processing, 14 (12): pp. 2040-2050, December 2005

Marvel, L., Boncelet, C., Retter, C. (1998) Reliable Blind Information Hiding for Images, Proc. of Information Hiding Workshop, pp.48-62, 1998

Pfitzmann, B. (1996) Information Hiding Terminology collected by Birgit Pfitzmann, Information Hiding First international Workshop, Cambridge, May/June 1996

Vallabha, V. (2001). Multiresolution watermark based on wavelet transform for digital images. MATHLAB Central Document Repository, 2001 http://www.mathworks.com/matlabcentral/

Wayner P. (2002) Disappearing Cryptography, Information Hiding: Steganography and Watermarking, 2nd Edition, Morgan Kaufmann, 2002.

Westfield A. and Pfitzmann, A. (1999) Attacks on Steganographic Systems. Third International Workshop, IH'99 Dresden Germany, October Proceedings, Coputer Science 1768. pp. 61- 76, 1999

Zollner J., H. Federrath, H. Klimant, A. Pfitzmann, R. Piotraschke, A. Westfeld, G. Wicke, G. Wolf, (1998) Modelling the Security of Steganographic Systems, Information Hiding, 2nd International Workshop, IH'98 Portland, Oregon, USA, Computer Science 1525. pp. 344-354, April 1998.

39   Vertical Search Engines

Kevin Curran, Jude Mc Glinchey

This chapter outlines the growth in popularity of vertical search engines, their origins, the differences between them and well known broad based search engines such as Google and Yahoo. We also discuss their use in business to business, their marketing and advertising costs, what the revenue streams are and who uses them.

Introduction

A search engine is a program that will search for keywords in documents and then return a list of the documents that contained those keywords. Typically, it works by sending out a "spider" or "web crawler" that returns all the documents it can find. Each returned document is read and indexed based on its word content by a program known as an "indexer". The indices are created using an algorithm so that in most cases only results that are relevant for the query are returned. The Interactive Television Dictionary & Business Index (ITV, 2007) defines vertical search engines as, *"Web sites which focus on particular topics and which especially allow you to search for information relating to those topics. The "vertical" term comes out of the idea that these are places where instead of searching horizontally, or broadly across a range of topics, you search vertically within only a narrow band of interest."*

A *Vertical Search Engine* can be defined as one that only contains content gathered from a particular narrowly defined web niche therefore the search results will only be relevant to certain users. Vertical search engines are also referred to as vertical portals - vortals, specialty search engines and topical search engines. When we think of a search engine we automatically think of a "broad-based" search engines such as Yahoo, Google, MSN, Altavista, Ask and Dogpile. Currently, these engines dominate the online search market however specialized search engines for niche markets are increasing in popularity. One of the biggest specialized engines at present is LookSmart (see Figure 143).

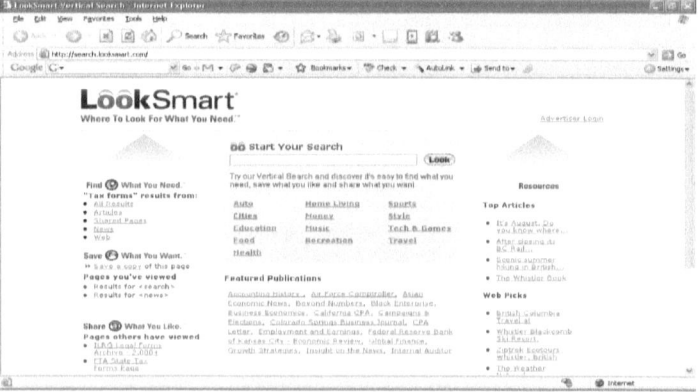

Figure 143: LookSmart

While vertical search engines are not new, what has changed is their increased popularity. Like consumers, businesses use the Internet for a variety of needs. Sometimes they are looking for all the information they can get, and for that the likes of Google and the Yahoo search engines are used. More often however, they are looking for something very specific related to their businesses. That is where vertical search sites come in. Vertical search engines deliver to businesses what the big sites cannot without the use of complex keyword combinations. This results in relevant and essential content rather than an exhaustive return of information. Some examples of vertical search engines include

- **Jobs** - SimplyHired.com, Indeed.com, Eluta.ca , Recruit.net
- **Travel** - Sidestep.com, Kayak.com, Mobissimo.com, Pinpointtravel.com, Farechase.com
- **Health** - Amniota.com, GenieKnows.com, Healia.com, Healthline.com, MammaHealth.com
- **Classifieds** - Edgeio.com, Oodle.com
- **Blogs** - Technorati, Bloglines, Blogger Search, Sphere, Feedster
- **Source Code** - Koders.com, Krugle, Google Code
- **Academic/teen** - Answers.com, Teenja.com, Gradewinner.com, Scholar.google.com.
- **People** - Zoominfo.com, Ziggs.com
- **Shopping** - Become.com; Oodle.com, PinpointShopping.com.

Vertical & Broad-Based Search Engines

Broad based search engines such as Google are not the ultimate for web searching as they are cluttered with all the returned information that matches the words in the requestor's query however relevant or irrelevant they are to what they want. There is a typical search failure rate of 31.9 percent on broad based search engines among business users (Prescott, 2007a). It has also been demonstrated that the professionals using broad based search engines were unable to find important work-related information because they were not trained in their use and the broad based search engines were not designed as business tools. This resulted in a low business user satisfaction rating of forty percent for broad based search engines. Additionally for businesses the broad based search engine has resulted in lower productivity from the failure of users to find critical information, however this has created a gap that is being filled by vertical search engines which the advantage because they can serve highly relevant results Prescott, 2007b). Second generation broad based search engines have tried to overcome this productivity loss by ranking using various human element factors. Yahoo Mindset[1] allows the user to set the bias of commercial vs. non-commercial bias on the returned results by the use of a slide rule (see Figure 144).

Figure 144: Yahoo Mindset

As broad-based search engines are getting broader, so too have their search results, therefore users, particularly business users are starting to make the switch to vertical search engines. Consider the example of a dentist who is looking for information on ceramics, a common material used in dental work. If the dentist performs a Google search on the keyword "ceramics," Google will serve up millions of results, but most of the entries on the first

---

[1] http://mindset.research.yahoo.com/

few pages will concern hobbies like pottery. On the other hand, if the dentist performs the same search on DentalProducts.net Web site, it will return much more relevant results. It would appear that Web users are starting to access / use the Internet the way they do multi channel television namely opting for specialized channels that give them the specialized information that they want e.g. a child wanting to see cartoons will go directly to the cartoon channel.

Vertical Search Engine Advertising

Vertical search engines are attracting professionals and business users searching for niche topics and are providing them with a satisfactory user experience. The high cost of advertising on the mainstream search engines is causing those in marketing to switch to vertical search engines because the space inventory is less crowded and they can negotiate better rates, possibly get better conversions and receive a better return-on-investment (ROI) for their marketing campaigns. Trends to consider include:

- $7.4 billion was spent on search engine marketing in 2005 (16% of which was b2b).
- More than 40% of the average marketer's budget is devoted to search.
- Nearly 38% of Yahoo's and 50% of Google's advertisers are defined as b-to-b.
- Nearly 64% of search engine users search for business information first. [4]

Local online advertising is on the upswing. eMarketer's current estimate shows the U.S. local online ad spend at $1.3 billion in 2006, representing 7.9 percent of a total U.S. online ad spend of $16.7 billion (Prescott, 2007b). A cost-effective way for smaller businesses to compete in pay-per-click (PPC) advertising is through Vertical Search engines. Broad based search engines such as Google and Yahoo! have mainstream advertisers like Amazon who spend millions each week on search advertising, buying every possible term related to their strategic keywords. That prevents smaller businesses from competing for these key terms.

For instance, a search on Google for the term "wholesale toys" will feature results such as AOL and the Discovery Channel. AOL and Discovery are not wholesalers however they will buy every term that people use to buy toys as it attracts traffic and they can quite simply afford it. This creates a problem for smaller advertisers. When companies like AOL and Amazon start bidding on search terms without regulation, the bid price and ability for real businesses to compete get distorted, making it difficult for small businesses to buy these terms. While many small businesses might actually be the most relevant source for a term like "wholesale toys," they can never compete with those 50-million-dollar-a-year search budgets. That is the primary reason why vertical search engines are gaining a toehold and are becoming known as category killers. A vertical in a small niche can become the information super highway on a specialized topic. Many vertical search engines have forums, blogs, fresh content and huge networks set up around a niche topic, providing many attractive promotional opportunities for advertisers. The cost to compete on a VSE is much lower than on general search engines, and marketers can expect much higher clickthroughs and conversions on their search ads, as well as a higher return on investment on their marketing campaigns. There are many benefits of advertising on vertical search engines versus Google AdWords if you pick the right vertical for your product or service. Examples showing how vertical search engines can be used to good advantage (Prescott, 2007a) are:

- **Clickthrough rates**: You can get higher clickthrough rates (CTRs) because the audience is segmented and highly qualified
- **Banner ads**: You can request custom positioning for your banners on vertical search engines. Most verticals offer users highly relevant content with targeted banners.
- **Direct links**: Link directly to the client's site or requested URL which gives the advertisers an SEO benefit because engines can now associate the advertiser with a highly ranked vertical search engine.
- **Special ad placement**: Verticals can accommodate a client's request quickly and on the fly. Vertical search engines are lean and versatile; they can react quickly to changing market conditions and industry trends.
- **User-generated media**: Vertical search engines cover issues related to specific topics or industries. Therefore, they can enable customers to blog on their sites, encouraging industry participation. Blog and story links provide great SEO benefits if a customer is linked to them.
- **Email marketing**: Many verticals have email lists, and these databases consist of recipients interested in the niche. These opt-in email lists can be more relevant than any mass-market offerings. Users look forward to receiving weekly newsletters with stories on the industry.

- **B2B ad advantage**: The big difference is that vertical search engines provide an ad advantage for B2B marketers because their ads are exposed to a highly motivated, targeted audience. Clickthroughs can be fewer, saving you money and conversions can be higher Prescott, 2007a).

Research analysts at Forrester Research, Jupiter Research and Marketing Sherpa have identified a new tier in search dubbed "specialized search," which includes "local," "topical" and "vertical" search (Zillmer and Furlong, 2006).

- **Local** - This is geographic or place based relevance e.g.www.chicago.com

- **Topical** - This is about consumer niches such as travel, golf, hobbies etc e.g. www.kayak.com

- **Vertical or B2B** - This is about search engines designed to serve the needs of businesses in specific industries. In terms of design and implementation, several models are emerging in vertical search they include **The vertical search engine as a destination or** "portal". An example of this is http://www.VetMedSearch.com. Often media companies that own these destination sites optimize them and buy keywords on Google to drive their audience to visit. Another model is **Vertical search as a complementary Web site application**: This model entails embedding a search engine on an existing, already trafficked site e.g. www.CertMag.com. Finally, **Parametric search** is a this tool, more prevalent in engineering and other product-specific, information-intensive, procurement-driven industries which allows for face-to-face product and manufacturer comparison.

In terms of revenue that these vertical search engines generate, a variety of advertising programs are gaining favor, including *cost per click*, in which the advertiser pays only for each time that a user clicks on its ad; *Cost per action*, an emerging model in which the advertiser pays, not on click, or for impressions, but only if the consumer performs a specific action, such as purchases a good and finally, *Flat fee/fixed fee* which is the most popular early ad model for most of the vertical search engines.

With the vertical search engine advertising revenue expected to reach $1 billion by 2009 (Richard, 2006) and their continued growth rate it would not be unexpected that the vertical search engines become more important due to their specialised nature than the broad based engines such as Google unless search engine companies fight back with some form of content control much more advanced. As it is virtually impossible to have a vertical search engine for every speciality, and it is highly likely that vertical search engines specializing in shopping, financial services, media and entertainment, and travel have the best chance of survival, therefore it is not a large surprise to find that advertisers are already spending large amounts of money within these sectors (Kopytoff, 2005).

Conclusion

A Vertical Search Engine contains content gathered from a particular narrowly defined web niche so that the search results will only be relevant to specific users. Vertical search engines are also referred to as vertical portals or topical search engines. Broad-based search engines include Yahoo, Google, MSN, Altavista etc. Currently, these engines dominate the online search market however specialized search engines for niche markets are increasing in popularity. Broad based search engines such as Google are not the ultimate for web searching as they are cluttered with all the returned information that matches the words in the requestor's query however relevant or irrelevant they are to what they want. One of the biggest specialized engines at present is LookSmart. The cost to compete on a vertical search engine is much lower than on general search engines, and marketers can expect much higher clickthroughs and conversions on their search ads, as well as a higher return on investment on their marketing campaigns. There are many benefits of advertising on vertical search engines versus Google AdWords if you pick the right vertical for your product or service.

References

ITV Dictionary – Definition, (2007) http://www.itvdictionary.com/definitions/vertical_portals_vortals_specialty_search_engines_topical_search_engines_definition.html

Prescott, J. (2007a) *Why Google Will Lose Dominance*, iMedia Connection, February 12th 2007
http://www.imediaconnection.com/content/13634.asp

Prescott, J. (2007b) *Find Your Niche with Specialized Search,* iMedia Connection, 26th March 2007
http://www.imediaconnection.com/content/14149.asp

Zillmer, N. and Furlong, B. (2006). *The Emerging Opportunity in Vertical Search*, A White Paper From
SearchChannel & Slack Barshinger, www.slackbarshinger.com/verticalsearch/pdf/0505_vertical_search.pdf

Richard, C. (2006) *Vertical Search Delivers What Big Search Engines Miss*, Outsell White Paper, August 2006
http://www.outsellinc.com/store/products/289

Kopytoff, V. (2005) *New search engines narrowing their focus*, San Francisco Chronicle, Monday, April 4,
2005, http://sfgate.com/cgi-bin/article.cgi?file=/c/a/2005/04/04/BUGJ9C20VU1.DTL

40   Pinpointing the Location of a User or Object

Kevin Curran, Eoghan Furey, Sebastian Hubrich

Location awareness is becoming an important capability for mobile computing; however it has not been possible until now to provide cheap pervasive positioning systems. Wide area coverage is most famously achieved by using GPS which relies on a constellation of low orbit satellites covering the earth's surface. Unfortunately GPS does not work indoors and has limited success in big cities because of the 'urban canyon' effect. There is however a number of wireless positioning systems which attempt to solve the ubiquity issues surrounding wireless based location estimation. Most of these systems require the area to be pre-calibrate in order to predict location later via the known positions of the access points detected by the device. Commonly used systems have a number of drawbacks including cost, accuracy or the ability to work indoors.

Introduction

Over the past two decades a large number of commercial and research location systems have been developed (Hazas et al., 2004). Accuracy systems often require extensive infrastructure, many sensors and time consuming calibration. AT & T Cambridge's Active Bats (Addlesee et al., 2001) system uses ultrasonic badges and requires one ultrasound receiver to be installed every square meter. Wide area coverage is most famously achieved by using GPS. A constellation of low orbit satellites cover the earth's surface. Unfortunately GPS does not work indoors and has limited success in big cities because of the 'urban canyon' effect. Mobile phone companies also have methods of triangulating the position of a user's phone within a particular 'cell'. E911/E112 requirements (Geer, 2001) from the US/EU mean that a phones location can now be discovered to within 100m in Europe and the United States. Microsoft's Research RADAR system uses ambient 802.11 systems to estimate a user's location. RADAR could have accuracy of up to 3 meters but requires calibrating every square meter of the site to be used (Schilit et al., 2003). PlaceLab, like RADAR, uses a device's 802.11 interface, however, it claims not to require the area to be accurately pre-calibrated. It predicts location via the known positions of the access points detected by the device (Hightower et al, 2004). A database cached on the same device provides these positions. The cache can be filled from many different sources of AP databases, including those created by Wardriving [1](also see Wigle.net) and those stored by various organisations. In less dense areas it can use GSM cell towers to establish location.

GPS uses multiple orbiting satellites to triangulate the position of a mobile receiver on the earth's surface. It calculates location by triangulating the time of flight of transmissions from these satellites to the receiver. A user's position can be tracked to within a few meters and it is this accuracy over a wide geographical area that makes GPS so popular. However, it does have some major limitations. Its coverage and accuracy can vary with factors such as the weather, time of day and use in built-up areas. Most notably however, it does not work indoors. Ultrasonic systems use time of flight of ultrasonic sound chips to triangulate position and work well indoors. The university of Bristol has developed a low cost version of this (Randell and Muller, 2001), and an example of its usage is in the 'City Project' (Bronn et al, 2003) where it was used as part of a tour guide system in the Lighthouse museum in Glasgow. Radio Frequency ID (RFID) tags are currently being built into many everyday objects. These tags can give position when they pass close to a reader but they usually need to be a few centimetres away from the reader, making them unsuitable for the purposes of this study. Computer visual techniques are in use in location based systems. One system described by Kata et al (2002) involves the use of special optical markers which a computer can be trained to recognise. Inertia tracking can be used as a means of determining location. Accelerometers can be embedded into mobile devices and these can be used to calculate velocity. Digital compasses can be added to these devices in order to measure orientation. It is important to know what direction you are facing, in order to know what you are looking at (Benford, 2005). Each of these technologies has its own advantages and disadvantages. It is important to note that they are different in a wide ~~variety of ways including: working~~ indoors or outdoors, cost, potential for interference, resolution accuracy and

[1] The term *war-driving* is an allusion to the 1983 movie "WarGames" where the lead character David engaged in *war-dialing* by sequentially dialing blocks of phone numbers in an attempt to establish a modem connection with interesting computers.

whether position is determined by the device itself (greater privacy) or by a centralised technology (network). A number of different systems have previously used 802.11 access points as beacons from which to estimate location. Microsoft research group have developed a similar system called RADAR. (Baht et al, 2000) describe this system as obtaining 1.5m accuracy within a precalibrated area. This was done by constructing a detailed "radio fingerprint" of the 802.11 APs within an office building. The strength of signal detected within a one foot by one foot grid was then used to determine location.

Ekahau[1] has a piece of software for sale that does the same thing as RADAR and claims to be able to pinpoint devices to a room level. Both of these products require intense calibration and only work on the precalibrated area. The data required for *PlaceLab* can be collected while walking or driving. Another system that uses the radio services is the environment was also developed by Microsoft research. RightSPOT uses FM radio signals to determine position (Krumn et al, 2003). The current accuracy of this system is in the order of km. Numerous other indoor location systems have been developed that make use of the sensory technologies discussed earlier but the major drawback with these is that they all require the installation of specialised hardware in the environment to be maintained. The costs of these technologies to date can be expensive for personal use thus making them unsuitable for personal or social applications that are to be used in people's daily lives. They do however offer very high accuracy levels and are therefore used by many commercial organisations. An example of such a system is the LA-200 from Trapeze Networks[2]. This provides a hardware based solution to location tracking. Wireless devices located within the scope of the wireless network may be tracked and located to room level. This system uses the 802.1 network as a means of carrying out the operation and they claim accuracy at 99% with 10 meter precision in fewer than 30 seconds. Many applications utilising location based technologies have recently been developed. There are three major types of these applications. Firstly are those where users do not want to disclose their location to anyone. Mappoint.com is an example of such an application where people may find their own location on a map and be directed to local places of interest. Secondly are those applications that reveal a user's location to a small group of selected friends. Two examples of these include dodgeball.com and AT & T's developed in mMode's Friend Finder. These notify you if a friend is in the area and are becoming popular in big cities.

At a time when 2 billion users already have a mobile phone, there is tremendous interest in having a piece of technology that eliminates the need for an extra device. Hence, location-aware mobile phones could be of interest in a wide area of applications and services; a few examples are friend-finder, restaurant-finder, and routing and tourist information. With the emergence of web-based technologies such as web services, the technical capability of location-based services that can be used from every mobile phone is now available, using technologies such as GPRS or EDGE. In particular, governments in numerous countries have expressed their need to locate mobile phone users, especially for locating the origin of emergency calls. In the US, the Federal Communication Commission stated their requirements in the E911 mandate, which calls for location information at a scale between 50m and 300m in most cases (FCC, 1996). The European counterpart of E911 is E112. Nokia is currently in the early development stages for an indoor analogue to the Global Positioning System used in many of its phones to provide mapping and navigation facilities. Nokia's solution claim to allow for point-to-point directions while inside a mapped building but no details of their method have been released yet (Halfacree, 2008). It is dubbed Indoor Positioning and is currently being trialed in around forty Nokia buildings worldwide, along with some unofficial maps of shopping centres, airports, and university buildings. The team behind the technology sees the Indoor Positioning system being useful for instance in finding seats at football games or when visiting shopping centres (Halfacree, 2008).

Different approaches to the location estimation problem are reviewed here. Although the approaches sometimes differ fundamentally, most of them try to enhance location estimation using the basic properties of the underlying technology, such as signal propagation or Cell broadcasts. Those properties are either determined physically (signal propagation) or architecturally.

GSM Location Estimation Techniques

There are two basic approaches for locating a mobile station; either by using the cellular signalling system, or by using a GPS receiver to provide the location information. The GSM system was not initially designed for positioning. GSM (Global System for Mobile Communication) is a digital system; its operating area (a cellular network) is divided into cells that overlap each other to enable hand-over mechanisms (see Figure 145). Each

---

[1] www. ekahau.com
[2] www.trapezenetworks.com

cell is associated with a unique Base Transceiver Station (BTS), and consists specifically of a group of channels (spread over the frequency band) that is used for communication. A mobile phone (or mobile station, MS) automatically connects to whichever BTS provides the best signal level (Redl et al., 1995).

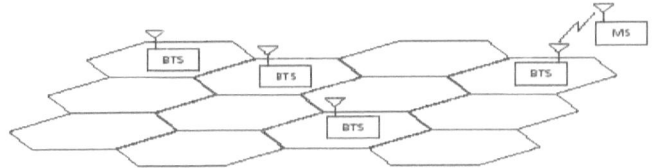

Figure 145: Simplified GSM cell architecture

A variety of location methods that can be used with the GSM networks/technology include:

AOA (Angle Of Arrival): This technique is based on triangulation, where the angle of arrival at the BTS (Base Transceiver Station) is measured by pointing an adaptive phased array antenna in the direction of the arriving MS (Mobile Station) signal (Rappaport, 2001). The position of the MS is calculated from the intersection of a minimum of two bearings. Jami et al. (1999) state that accuracy can be improved by using more than two BTSs; some inaccuracies are caused by multi-path propagation effects.

CellID: In its idealised form, each cell in the GSM network is in the form of a hexagon. The cell broadcasts the following information to each MS in range: MCC (Mobile Country Code), MNC (Mobile Network Code), LAC (Location Area Code) and CI (Cell Identifier). The combination of MCC + MNC + LAC + CI can be uniquely identified. Given a database in which the coordinates of the fingerprint of each CellID are stored, an MS can be localised at the Cell level (LaMarca et al., 2005); Laitinen et al. (2001) state that a cell in the GSM can be between 50m and 30km in diameter. A software package for Microsoft Smartphones that already uses this approach is the freeware CellTrack[1]. Another example of software that is available for Smartphones (and many other platforms) is the Place Lab framework. LaMarca et al. (2005) describe the Place Lab architecture as an open platform for client-side location sensing. Place Lab can use three different beacon types for its location sensing: 802.11 (Wi-Fi), GSM and Bluetooth. While sensing GSM beacons, Place Lab uses their CellID to uniquely identify them.

TA (Timing Advance): This value indirectly indicates the distance between the BTS and the MS. GSM uses time division multiple access technology, which allows several users to share the same frequency by dividing it into discrete timeslots. These timeslots are very short in GSM, meaning that an MS has to send its data package before its assigned timeslot at the BTS actually starts. The TA is the number of units a burst has to be advanced by so as to arrive at the BTS on time; it is proportional to the distance between the MS and the BTS, and can have values ranging from 0 to 63. Each step in TA is approximately 3.69 microseconds, representing a distance of roughly 550m (Willassen, 1998). By combining the TA value with the CellID information, an MS can be tracked within a radius of 550m. Silventoinen et al. (1995) state that the location of the MS can be calculated when the TA is known to at least three BTSs.

TOA (Time Of Arrival): This method works by having all the BTSs within range listen for a burst from the MS. When a base station receives this burst, it records the time it was received and sends it to a server. The server gathers the information from several BTSs and can calculate the position of the MS from the arrival times and the positions of the BTSs, by using triangulation (Jonsson and Olavesen, 2002).

Distance Measurement by Signal Strength: In order to perform a possible hand-over process, an MS needs to constantly monitor the signal strength of each nearby BTS (in view of the hexagonal layout, this restricts the monitoring to the adjacent 6 BTSs). Given the signal strength of the 7 BTSs (6 neighbours plus the one currently serving the MS), statistical calculations can provide an estimated location, taking into account the complex propagation properties of electromagnetic radiation. Tonteri (2001) evaluates this by using a statistical modelling approach. The underlying problem with this approach is that as long as the transmitting power of the BTS is unknown, there is no solid basis for estimating the location. A statistical directional propagation model that uses the measured signal strength was developed by Chu et al. (2004), who later introduced the idea of treating the measured signal strength of Wi-Fi beacons as a weighted property.

---

[1] http://celltrack.spv-developers.com/

Database Correlation (Fingerprinting): Laitinen et al. (2001) state that a key idea is to store the signal information accessible to an MS over the whole coverage area of the location system into a database to be used by a location server. The database should contain signal information samples, called fingerprints, with a resolution corresponding to the accuracy that can be achieved with this method, which may vary in different environments. A location estimate can be made by taking a current reading and performing a database lookup. A system known to use this approach for indoor positioning using Wi-Fi fingerprints is RADAR, introduced by Bahl and Padmanabhan (2000).

Location Estimation Approaches

Different approaches to the location estimation problem are reviewed, with each of the papers providing interesting findings in their respective fields. Although the approaches sometimes differ fundamentally (for example, location estimates initiated or supported by the network, as opposed to those initiated by the mobile), most of them try to enhance location estimation using existing GSM technology, taking into account the basic properties of the underlying technology, such as signal propagation or CellID broadcasts. Those properties are either determined physically (signal propagation) or architecturally (CellID broadcasts), and therefore cannot be changed at will by a single network operator. The following sections will review CellID, Propagation Model or Statistical Modelling broadcasts and Signal Fingerprinting, and will compare the algorithms.

CellID

LaMarca et al. (2005) describe the Place Lab architecture as an open platform for client-side location sensing. Place Lab can use three different beacon types for its location sensing: 802.11 Wi-Fi, GSM and Bluetooth. During field studies, LaMarca et al. (2005) discovered that, because of its smaller cell size, they obtained the best results with the Wi-Fi beacon type as long as the beacon density is sufficient. The 802.11-based location estimates showed a median accuracy of 20.5m in urban areas with 100% coverage, whereas GSM showed a median accuracy of 107.2m with 100% coverage. Due to the limitations of the Nokia cell phone used for the field studies, all GSM-based results were calculated using a single GSM cell reading. Non-mobile Bluetooth beacons have not yet reached sufficient density in the wild for tests to be possible. Place Lab's limitation of investigating only a single cell in GSM-based location sensing is a major drawback. Nevertheless, Place Lab (and POLS in its Dot Net implementation for Microsoft Smartphones) provides a framework to build upon. It is worth noting that the POLS framework for Microsoft Smartphones can retrieve all the GSM cell readings from the phone's memory.

Silventoinen and Rantalainen (1995) provide a rather dated but nevertheless interesting insight into mobile station location using the GSM network. Their focus was on describing methods for locating an MS with minimal changes to the network or the MS. They state that the performance of a locating algorithm relying solely on the CellID is rather poor while pico or nano cells are not being used very frequently. Other methods of mobile station location technologies that they investigated involved design changes (hardware and/or software) at either the BTS, the MS or both. It is also worth stating that Silventoinen and Rantalainen did not perform field tests, but relied on the outcomes of simulations; since both authors were employed at the Nokia Research Centre at the time of their research, it can be assumed that they used a reasonably realistic simulation.

Propagation Model/Statistical Modelling

Willassen (1998) suggests a method for mobile station location using the GSM system, proposing the implementation of a lookup entity as a separate unit not included in the BTS. Particularly interesting is the chapter "Positioning a Mobile Station", in which he gives a good overview of existing technologies and refers to some interesting measurements that Latapy (1996) has provided in his research. These measurements and experiments involved distance estimates based on radio signal strengths and took into account different propagation models for radio wave propagation, such as the Hata formula, the line of sight model or indoor attenuation (empirical). Latapy's ideas on calculating the probability of a location by using different approaches, such as a probability matrix or measurement maps, were also valuable. These ideas were presented in a theoretical manner and still need to be supported by field testing. Tonteri (2001) looks at a statistical modelling approach to location estimation. He describes the propagation properties of electromagnetic radiation and explains signal attenuation, reflection, scattering and diffraction. Tonteri gives descriptions of propagation models and proposes a statistical modelling approach, in which signal properties, such as signal strength, angle of arrival and propagation delay, are treated as random variables that are statistically dependent on the locations of the transmitter and receiver and on the propagation environment. In the traditional geometric approach, the reasoning progresses from the measured signal properties to the location of the transmitter, whereas in Tonteri's (2001) statistical approach, the emphasis is on the propagation model that describes the dependency of the measured signal properties on the location variable, so that the reasoning proceeds from the location to the signal properties. In statistical terms, the propagation model is a sampling distribution whose parameters (in the first phase, the propagation parameters, and in the second phase, the location variable) the study wishes to estimate.

Chu et al. (2004) provide a location estimation method using a statistical directional propagation model. The authors claim that the received signal strength is well handled in all cellular systems and so using this signal property to estimate the location of a MS is a promising general approach. The distance between the transmitter and the receiver can be deduced from the mean signal strength, with reference to a signal propagation model. The DPM (directional propagation model) proposed by Chu et al. (2004) enhances the SPM (statistical propagation model) by adding directional and environmental parameters related to the directional gain of the antenna in the BTS. The experimental results show that the DPM outperforms the SPM with a DPM average error of 340.81m and a SPM average error of 421.07m. Jami et al. (1999) compare methods of locating and tracking cellular mobiles. Although they compare network-based approaches, such as the angle of arrival (AOA), observed time difference (OTD) and time difference of arrival (TDOA), their findings on the impact of errors, as well as multipath propagation issues, are particularly interesting. They mention the possibility of employing a Kalman filter or using a least square technique to improve position estimates.

Zaidi and Mark (2005) look at real-time mobility tracking algorithms for cellular networks based on Kalman filtering, and propose two mobility tracking algorithms. The first algorithm (MT-1) pre-processes RSSI (received signal strength indication) measurements with an averaging filter to obtain coarse position estimates, which are then provided as inputs to a modified Kalman filter that is used only to generate estimates of the discrete command process. A key component of this algorithm is a second Kalman filter that produces mobility state estimates from the raw RSSI measurements and the discrete command estimates. If RSSI measurements from a given BTS are not available for any given timeslot, the averaging process would not have enough samples to perform the averaging properly. To overcome this disadvantage, Zaidi and Mark (2005) propose a simplified mobility tracking algorithm, consisting of only a single (extended) Kalman filter, without a pre-filter (MT-2). The RMSE (root mean square error) results of experiments show some interesting findings in a low-mobility scenario (acceleration levels between -0.5m/s and +0.5m/s), which are more typical of actual cellular networks with a MT-1 RMSE between 2.64m and 6.24m and a MT-2 RMSE between 4.84m and 17.88m. The MT-1 algorithm employs a pre-filter to obtain coarse position estimates prior to the application of the modified Kalman filter and decouples mobility state estimation from the estimation of the discrete command process. The MT-2 algorithm consists of a single extended Kalman filter, treating the discrete command process as additional noise.

Signal Fingerprinting

Otason et al. (2005) present an accurate GSM-based indoor localization system that achieves a median accuracy of 5 metres. They use a modified fingerprint method that they call the *wide* fingerprint, which takes in readings of the six strongest GSM cells and up to 29 additional GSM channels. The higher dimensionality introduced by the additional channels dramatically increases localization accuracy in comparison with the standard fingerprint method. In contrast to the Place Lab philosophy of providing location estimates with minimal calibration effort, Otason et al. (2005) provide a dense grid of fingerprint readings with a granularity of 1.5 metres; for localization, they use the K-nearest neighbours algorithm. Their results demonstrate the advantage of wide fingerprints that include measurements from a large number of channels rather than just the 6 strongest cells. Throughout their test buildings, the channel fingerprinting algorithm achieved a median accuracy of 2.5 to 5.4 metres, which on some floors in their test buildings was even better than fingerprinting done with 802.11 beacons. This accuracy comes at a cost of needing significantly more calibration work.

Cheng et al. (2005) compare various wireless-radio-based positioning algorithms in their study, aimed at providing an understanding of how these algorithms can be adapted for ubiquitous deployment with minimal calibration. Although the comparison was focused on Wi-Fi signals and beacons, their measurements on the performance of each algorithm reveal interesting details about GSM location estimates using them. They compared centroid, weighted centroid, fingerprint radar, fingerprint ranked, particle filter signal strength and particle filter response rates with one another. On the basis of these measurements, the particle filter algorithm performed best, with a median error of 18m in downtown areas. Under certain circumstances (high beacon density, low beacon transmit power), the centroid algorithm came close to that performance. The results of the comparison lead the authors to the conclusion that different algorithms work better for different densities and ranges of access points.

PlaceLab

The PlaceLab architecture consists of three key elements as shown in Figure 146. These are radio beacons in the environment; databases holding beacon location information and PlaceLab clients that estimate their location from this data. PlaceLab operates by listening for transmissions from wireless networking devices such as 802.11 access points, GSM towers and fixed Bluetooth devices. These radio services are collectively referred to as beacons. Each of these are protocols that assign a unique or semi-unique ID to the beacons. Clients' positions can be determined by detecting these ID's. 802.11 access points can be used to determine location. The only interaction between the AP and the PlaceLab enabled device is that the device must detect the unique ID and the signal strength. PlaceLab does not require the client to transmit any data nor is it required to listen to any other network user's transmission with 802.11. This is done entirely passively by listening for the beacon frames that are broadcast periodically by the AP. These frames are sent without any form of encryption and do not employ MAC address authorisation or WEP.

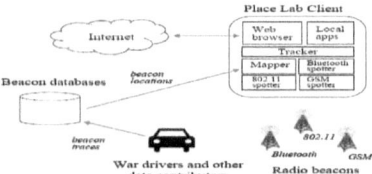

Figure 146: PlaceLab Architecture

The PlaceLab database information is contained in a flat text file with tab separated columns – Latitude, Longitude, SSID and BSSID. This file can be loaded into the PlaceLab database. The client must be able to 'see' a number of these access points to determine location. A minimum of three are required. Merely detecting on AP does not give our client its location. The relevant location information for the AP must be stored in the database. The database plays an essential role in the architecture of PlaceLab. It serves the clients with the beacons location information. The PlaceLab clients determine their location from both the database of APs and from making live observations of the radio signals around them. For reasons of portability and extensibility, the client's functionality is divided into three separate elements: spotters, mappers and trackers. Wigle.com contains a mapping database for the place throughout the world. The tracker is the "brains" of the system and it uses the information from the spotter and the mapper to estimate the client's position. System understanding of signal propagation and its relationship to distance, location and the physical environment are encapsulated in the tracker. A simple tracker is included in PlaceLab that computes Venn diagram-like intersections of the beacons observed. Also included is a Bayesian particle filter tracker that uses range information for specific beacons. Although this requires more computation, it can give a 25% improvement in accuracy and can also give extra information like speed of movement and direction. A number of applications have been developed that use PlaceLab. Some of these have been developed by Intel Research and others by the PlaceLab user community. UC Berkeley has developed a rapid prototyping tool known as Topiary for designing location enhanced applications (Li et al 2004). This allows a prototype to be run on a mobile device while its interactions can be monitored by the designer on another device. The user's location can appear to be changed by the designer by clicking on the map as shown in Figure 147.

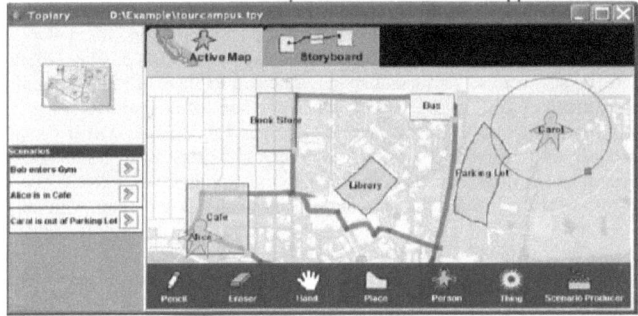

Figure 147: A screenshot of Topiary

Topiary has been adapted to use live location estimates from the device using PlaceLab. As PlaceLab can be used indoors it allows Topiary to be used in a wide variety of settings. A2B[1] is an online catalogue of geocoded web pages (pages tagged with location metadata). Users can add new pages or query for nearby pages. A2B normally discovered its location by the application interacting with a GPS unit. The A2B interface has been extended to support HTTP requests from users who are running the PlaceLab web proxy. Any web browser allows the proxy to talk directly to A2B and to use their location-based lookup services automatically.

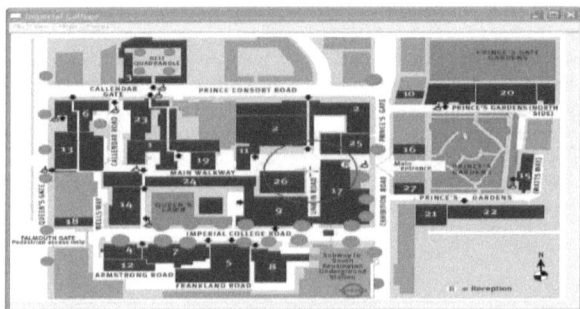

Figure 148: AirWhare with red circle showing users location.

AirWhare is an electronic tour guide of the Imperial College London campus which is built using PlaceLab. A tourist equipped with a wirelessly enabled laptop or PDA may tour the campus and PlaceLab will report an estimate of their location. The program will then give the user information about the location that they are currently in. They claim to achieve accuracy of between 25-50m with almost complete coverage of the campus (Holshausen et al, 2004). Figure 148 is a screenshot from AirWhare with the red circle showing the users location. ActiveCampus is one of the most widely used 802.11-based location-enhanced systems (Griswold et al, 2002). At the University of California, San Diego and at the Georgia Institute of Technology, campus wide installations are already running. Active campus offers students a suite of socially oriented applications. According to La Marca et al (2003) the system is currently being ported to run on top of PlaceLab as this offers more platforms than are currently supported. The 'ActiveCampus Explorer' carries out the same functionality as our proposed system. Fig 11 shows two of its screens. One the left we see a map of the campus with the locations of 'buddies' overlain and on the right we see a clear list of 'buddies' and their locations shown by proximity. One difference between ActiveCampus Explorer and the research proposed here is that while they also use individual 802.11 access point signal strengths, instead they use a 'least squares fit' algorithm to infer location(Griswold et al., 2002) while this project uses PlaceLab's own algorithms.

Radio Frequency Identification (RFID) Location Determination Systems

[1] http://a2b.cc/

Several states in America have employed RFID systems to improve security and automate the monitoring of prison inmates. The Los Angeles County Sheriff Department spent $1.5 million U.S. dollars deploying Alanco Technologies' TSI Prism system at one of their correctional facilities in 2005. The TSI Prism system uses tamper-proof, active RFID tags worn as wristbands by inmates, and RFID readers throughout the jail. Each tag links each inmate to a particular profile in the system, which can be used to restrict them to certain parts of the jail, or keep them away from other particular prisoners. The system alerts prison staff if inmates enter restricted areas or move within a certain range of inmates they are required to stay away from. The ultimate aim is to reduce violence between inmates, deter escape attempts and to monitor their whereabouts at all times.[1] Alanco's TSI Prism system has also been deployed in Minnesota, Michigan, Illinois and Ohio, with other states to follow suit.[2]

In 2005, a trial was conducted in Yokohama City, Japan, to monitor the safety and whereabouts of school children as they travelled to and from school. Each participating child wore a 2.4GHz RFID tag complying with the 802.11 Wi-Fi standard. Software known as AeroScout determined the location of the child based on the signal strength of the tag received by Cisco Wi-Fi access points, acting as RFID readers, around the city. The software then used the tag's unique Media Access Control (MAC) address to record the location in a centralised database. The tags could be read up to one thousand feet away, and location estimation was accurate to within ten metres. Each tag also had a call-button which a child could press if they were distressed or in need of assistance. When pressed, the child's parents or guardian received an email notification along with an image of a map showing the location of the child. The system could be set up to notify parents or guardians if their child passed a certain Wi-Fi access point.[3] The *Legoland* theme park in Denmark introduced the "KidSpotter" system in 2004, where young children are fitted with RFID wristbands when they enter the park. The system tracks these wristbands anywhere within the park's boundaries, meaning that parents can be alerted of a child's whereabouts via SMS if their child goes astray.

Several tracking systems for patients suffering from Alzheimer's disease and dementia exist in hospitals and nursing homes around the world. These patients wear wristbands containing RFID tags that are detected by readers all around the premises. If a patient tries to leave without being discharged, or enters a potentially dangerous area, staff members are alerted to their whereabouts and are able to facilitate their safe return. Another similar system is that used by Project Lifesaver, an American non-profit organisation that employs search teams equipped with RFID readers to scan for and locate RFID tags contained in wristbands worn by patients that wander away from home.[4]

Conclusion

This chapter has described a selection of the literature covering the different approaches used by researchers to improve the accuracy of mobile phone self-locating technologies. Taking into account the results that these researchers have achieved, it can be said that the development of location aware devices built upon the already existing GSM technology is a promising approach, considering the increased interest in location-based services. The beauty of this approach is that the physical properties now being used to provide location estimates are simply those needed to keep the system working (that is, to provide mobile communication). Therefore, most of the abovementioned approaches to location estimation can be done anywhere in the world where there is GSM coverage, independently of the network operator and without any additional cost.

References

Addlesee M. (2001), 'Implementing a Sentient Computing System', *IEEE Computer*, Vol. 34, No. 8, August 2001 http://www.cl.cam.ac.uk/research/dtg/publications/public/files/tr.2001.8.pdf

Bahl, P. & Padmanabhan, V. N. (2000), 'RADAR: an in-building RF-based user location and tracking system', *IEEE INFOCOM 2000,* March 26-30, 2000, Tel Aviv, Israel, pp. 775-784, IEEE.

---

[1] http://www.networkworld.com/news/2007/061807-us-state-turns-to-rfid.html

[2] http://www.rfidjournal.com/article/view/1601/1/1

[3] http://www.rfidjournal.com/article/articleview/2050/1/1/

[4] http://www.projectlifesaver.org/public_html/aboutus.htm

Benford, S. (2005). 'Future Location-Based Experiences'. *JISC TechWatch*. Bristol: JISC.
http://www.jisc.ac.uk/uploaded_documents/jisctsw_05_01.pdf

Brown, B., Maccoll, I., Chalmers, M., Galani, A., Randell, C., Steed, A. (2003). 'Lessons from the Lighthouse: Collaboration in a shared mixed reality system'. In: Cockton, G., Korhonen, P. 2003. *CHI '03: Proceedings of the conference on human factors in computing systems*. New York, NY: ACM Press, pp. 577-584.
http://www.equator.ac.uk/var/uploads/Brown&MacColl2003.pdf

Chen, M., Sohn, T., Chmelev, D., Haehnel, D., Hightower, J., Hughes, J., LaMarca, A., Potter, F., Smith, I. & Varshavsky, A. (2006) Practical Metropolitan-Scale Positioning for GSM Phones. *UbiComp*. Irvine, CA, UbiComp.

Cheng, Y. C., Chawathe, Y., LaMarca, A. & Krumm, J. (2005), 'Accuracy characterization for metropolitan-scale Wi-Fi localization', *Mobisys*, Wednesday, June 8, 2005, Seattle, pp. 233-245.

Chu, K. M. K., Leung, K. & Ng, J. K. (2004), 'Locating mobile stations with statistical directional propagation model', *Advanced Information Networking and Applications (AINA 2004)* March 29 - March 31, 2004, Fukuoka, Japan, pp. 230-235.

Dagon, D., Martin, T. & Starner, T. (2004) 'Mobile Phones as Computing Devices: The Viruses are Coming!' *IEEE Pervasive Computing*, vol. 3, pp.11-15.

FCC (1996) Revision of the Commissions Rules to Ensure Compatibility with Enhanced 911 Emergency Calling Systems, RM-8143, CC Docket No. 94-102

Griswold, W. G., Shanahan, P., Brown, S. W., Boyer, R., Ratto, M., Shapiro, R. B. & Truong, T. M. (2002) ActiveCampus - Experiments in Community-Oriented Ubiquitous Computing, *IEEE Computer*.

Geer, D. (2001) 'The E911 dilemma'. *Wireless Business and Technology*, November/December 2001.
http://www.marconipacific.com/e911Article.pdf

GSM-Association (2006) *GSM Subscriber Statistics* [online], Available from:
http://www.gsmworld.com/news/statistics/pdf/gsma_stats_q2_06.pdf [Accessed 29.07.2006].

Halfacree, G. (2008) Nokia planning Indoor Positioning, Bit Tech Net, 24th September 2008
http://www.bit-tech.net/news/2008/09/24/nokia-planning-indoor-positioning/1

Harrison, G. W. & List, J. A. (2004) 'Field Experiments', *Journal of Economic Literature*, vol. 42, pp. 1013-1059.

Hata, M. (1980) 'Empirical formula for propagation loss in land mobile radio services', *IEEE Transactions on Vehicular Technology*, vol. 29, pp. 317-325.

Hazas M., Scott J., Krumm J. (2004), 'Location-Aware Computing Comes of Age', *IEEE Computer*, Vol. 37, No. 2, February 2004 http://research.microsoft.com/~jckrumm/Publications%202004/lac%20final.pdf

Hightower J., Borriello G. (2004), 'Particle Filters for Location Estimation in Ubiquitous Computing: A Case Study', *6th International Conference on Ubiquitous Computing*, Nottingham, UK, September 2004.
http://www.intel-research.net/Publications/Seattle/100220060958_333.pdf

Hightower J., Lamarca A., Smith I. (2006), 'Practical Lessons from Place Lab', *IEEE Pervasive Computing*, Vol. 5, No. 3, September 2006 http://www.placelab.org/publications/pubs/lessons-ieeeperv2006.pdf

Holshausen D., Li A., Patel S., Turner J. (2004), 'Airwhare – Wireless Tour Guide' Imperial College, London
http://www.doc.ic.ac.uk/~mss/airwhare.html
Hong, J. I., Boriello, G., Landay, J. A., McDonald, D. W., Schilit, B. N. & Tygar, J. D. (2003), 'Privacy and Security in the Location-enhanced World Wide Web', *Fifth International Conference on Ubiquitous Computing: Ubicomp*, October 12 - October 15, 2003, Seattle, WA, USA.

Jonsson, D. K. & Olavesen, J. (2002) *Estimated accuracy of location in mobile networks using E-OTD,* Master's Thesis, Kristiansand, Agder University College.

Krumm, J., Cermak, G. & Horvitz, E. (2003) 'Rightspot: A Novel Sense Of Location For A Smart Personal Object', Paper presented at the *UbiComp 2003.*
http://research.microsoft.com/~jckrumm/Publications%202003/rightSPOT%20publish.pdf

Laitinen, H., Ahonen, S. & Kyriazakos, S. (2001) 'Cellular location technology', *CELLO Consortium, Tech. Rep.*

LaMarca, A., Chawathe, Y., Consolvo, S., Hightower, J., Smith, I., Scott, J., Sohn, T., Howard, J., Hughes, J. & Potter, F. (2005), 'Place Lab: Device Positioning Using Radio Beacons in the Wild', *Pervasive,* May 8 - May 13, 2005, Munich, Germany, pp. 116-133.

Latapy, J. M. (1996) *GSM Mobile Station Locating,* Master's Thesis, Trondheim, Norwegian University of Science and Technology.

Leick, A. (2003) *GPS Satellite Surveying,* Hoboken, Wiley.

Li, Y., Hong, J.I., Landay, J.A. (2004) 'Topiary: A Tool For Prototyping Location-Enhanced Applications'. In *Proceedings of User Interface Software and Technology 2004* http://guir.berkeley.edu/pubs/uist2004/topiary.pdf

Okumura, Y., Ohmori, E., Kawano, T. & Fukuda, K. (1968) 'Field strength and its variability in VHF and UHF land-mobile radio service', *Rev. Electr. Commun. Lab,* vol. 16, pp. 852.

Otsason, V., Varshavsky, A., LaMarca, A. & de Lara, E. (2005), 'Accurate GSM Indoor Localization', *UbiComp 2005,* September 11 - September 14, 2005, Tokyo, Japan.

Rappaport, T. S. (2001) *Wireless Communications: Principles and Practice,* Upper Saddle River, Prentice Hall.
Redl, S., Oliphant, M. W., Weber, M. K. & Weber, M. K. (1995) *An Introduction to GSM,* Norwood, Artech House.

Randell, C., Muller, H. (2001). 'Low Cost Indoor Positioning System'. In: ABOWD, G. (Ed). 2001. *UbiComp '01: Proceedings of the 3rd international conference on Ubiquitous Computing. Springer-Verlag,* pp. 42-48.
http://www.cs.bris.ac.uk/Publications/Papers/1000573.pdf

Schilit, B. (2003) Ubiquitous Location-Aware Computing and the *"PlaceLab"* Initiative, *1st ACM International Workshop on Wireless Mobile Applications and Services on WLAN Hotspots*, San Diego, CA, September 2003. http://*PlaceLab*.org/publications/pubs/wmash-*PlaceLab*.pdf

Sohn T., Griswold Wg., Scott J., Lamarca A., Cheng Y., Smith I., Chawathe Y. (2006) 'Experiences with place lab: an open source toolkit for location-aware computing', *Proceeding of the 28th international conference on Software engineering,* China 2006. http://intelresearch.net/Publications/Seattle/100920061629_368.pdf

Scourias, J. (1995) 'Overview of the Global System for Mobile Communications', University of Waterloo.

Silventoinen, M. & Rantalainen, T. (1995) 'Mobile station locating in GSM', *Wireless Communication System Symposium,* November 27 - November 28, 1995, Smithtown, New York, pp. 53-59.

Tonteri, T. (2001) *A Statistical Modeling Approach to Location Estimation,* Master's Thesis, University of Helsinki.

Willassen, S. Y. (1998) *A Method for Implementing Mobile Station Location in GSM,* Master's Thesis, Trondheim, Norwegian University of Science and Technology.

41   Web Intelligence

Kevin Curran, Cliona Murphy, Stephen Annesley

Web intelligence combines the interaction of the human mind and Artificial Intelligence with networks and technology. This chapter attempts to define and summarise the concept of Web intelligence, highlight the key elements of Web intelligence, and explore the topic of Web information retrieval with particular focus on multimedia/information retrieval and intelligent agents.

Introduction

The Web has increased the availability and accessibility of information to such a large audience that an intelligent system is required to construct a meaningful reply to a query for information. The field of study that is Web intelligence (WI) involves a combination of Artificial Intelligence (AI) and Information Technology (IT) to produce an intelligent system. WI investigates the important roles that these two components have to play on the World Wide Web while being concerned with the practical impact they will have on the new and upcoming generation of Web empowered products, systems, services, and activities (WI, 2003). The study of Web intelligence draws from a range of diverse disciplines such as Mathematics, Linguistics, Psychology and Information Technology (Yao, 2001). The Web intelligence Consortium (WIC) is an international non-profit organization dedicated to the promotion of worldwide scientific research and industrial development in the era of Web and agent intelligence[1]. The Web intelligence Consortium identifies 9 key topics in the area of Web intelligence. One of those topics is Web information retrieval (See Figure 149).

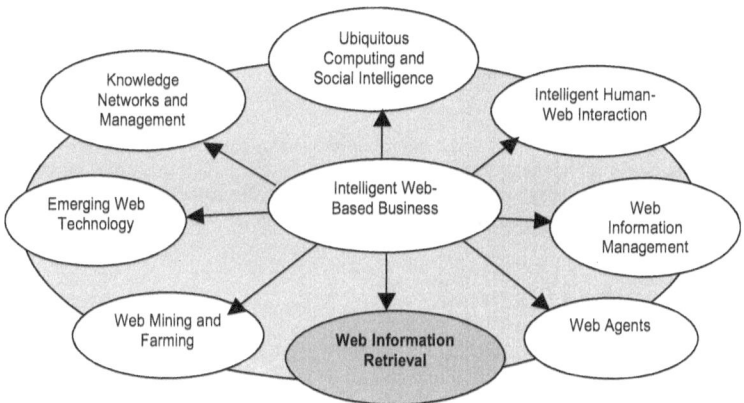

Figure 149: Web intelligence

The 9 key topics are further divided into a total of 75 subsections. Multimedia Retrieval is one of the subsections in the Web information retrieval category (See Figure 150). The following are an attempt to provide succinct summaries of the predominant subjects discussed in this chapter.

Web intelligence is a new direction for scientific research and development that explores the fundamental roles as well as practical impacts of Artificial Intelligence (AI) and advanced Information Technology (IT) on the

---

[1] http://wi-consortium.org/

next generation of Web-empowered products, systems, services, and activities. Goetzel (2002) describes the Web of today as having "an infantile mind" and believes that over the next couple of decades we will see "its growth and maturity into a fully fledged, largely autonomous, globally distributed intelligent system".

Artificial Intelligence (AI) is concerned with the design of intelligent computer programs, which simulate different aspects of intelligent human behaviour. In particular, the focus has been on representing knowledge structures that are utilized in human problem solving. In other words, AI is the simulation of human intelligence processes by machines, especially computer systems. These processes include learning (the acquisition of information and rules for using the information), reasoning (including the rules to reach approximate or definite conclusions, and self correction). Particular applications of AI include expert systems, speech recognition, and machine vision.

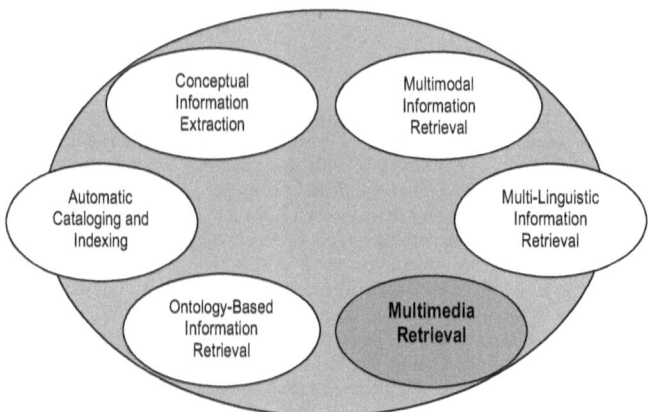

Figure 150: Web Information Retrieval

Web Information Retrieval comprises Conceptual Information Extraction, Automatic Cataloging and Indexing, Ontology-Based Information Retrieval, Multimodal Information Retrieval, Multi-Linguistic Information Retrieval, and Multimedia Retrieval.

Intelligent multimedia information retrieval is a multidisciplinary area that lies at the intersection of Artificial Intelligence, information retrieval, human computer interaction, and multimedia computing (Maybury, 1997). It goes beyond traditional hypertext or hypermedia environments to provide content based indexing of multiple media (e.g., text, audio, imagery, video) and management of the interaction with these materials.

Multimedia Information Retrieval

With the popularity of multimedia technology, contents of the World Wide Web have been a lot more versatile than a few years ago. However, although more information is available on the Web, the efficient and effective retrieval and management of these Web documents are still very challenging research issues [Pringle98]. Intelligent Multimedia information retrieval involves much more than retrieving free text, it "involves systems that enable users to create, process, (e.g., index, profile) summarise, present (e.g., visualise, customise), interact with (e.g., query, browse, navigate), and organise information within and across heterogeneous media such as text, speech, non-speech audio, graphics, imagery, animations, and video." (Maybury, 1997).

With the rapid development of Internet technology, the number of Internet users and the amount of multimedia information on the Internet is ever increasing. Recently, the Web sites such as e-business sites and shopping mall sites deal with lots of image information. To find a specific image from these image sources, we usually use image database engines or Web search engines. But, the feature based retrieval capabilities of these systems are quite limited, especially for the Web images (Hong 2002).

When navigating the Web, with such a vast collection of linked multimedia documents, users can easily get lost in its depths. Multimedia retrieval also poses users problems in finding appropriate resources and extracting information from within multimedia documents. Text and relational databases can be searched on content and indexing terms. However to find information in images, video and speech the user is dependent on the extent of the semantic description of the resource assigned by the database indexer. We need to identify users search methods to develop the technology they will use. And of course the Web needs to become much smarter if it is to optimize its own performance, as well as, package knowledge to answer our ever-increasing questions. Some users know what they are looking for and try to satisfy their needs by following appropriate links. These users may or may not find something of interest, but may easily miss other, more relevant documents far from their current browsing paths.

There exists a great demand for retrieval and management tools for visual data, since visual information is a more capable medium of conveying ideas and is more closely related to human perception of the real world. However, image contents are more complicated to retrieve than say textual data stored in traditional databases. Image retrieval techniques should provide support for user queries in an effective and efficient way, just as conventional information retrieval does for textual retrieval.

Intelligent Agents

Another aspect of WI concerns the study and application of Web agents and intelligent agents. An agent on the Web can be described as a program that assembles information or performs some other service without your immediate presence and on some regular schedule. Usually, an agent program, using parameters provided by the user will search all or some part of the Internet, gather information you're interested in, and present it to you on a predefined periodic basis (Browne, 2002). In general, agents can be defined as programs, used extensively on the Web which perform tasks such as retrieving and delivering information and automating repetitive tasks. Agents are designed to make computing easier and are currently used as Web browsers, news retrieval mechanisms, and shopping assistants. By specifying certain parameters, agents will "search" the Internet and return the results directly back to your PC. In fact, one of the more important roles of information retrieval agents is that of searching and filtering information from distributed web sources. Thus, understanding and developing the correct information foraging behavior for information retrieval is a challenge. It is important to understand how people search for information (Liu, 2003). Liu (2003) presents a foraging agent model which takes into account web topology, information distribution and agent interest profile. They discovered that it is the unique distribution of agent interest that leads to the regularities in agent surfing behavior i.e., a power law distribution of agent surfing depth. The power lay of link click frequency is largely due to agent purposeful surfing behavior demonstrating that web regularities are interrelated. They also categorize foraging agents according to their interests and familiarities: random, rational and recurrent agents. They discovered that the regularities of agent surfing depth on pages and domains still remain the same, while a power law of click frequency distribution will disappear as we move from recurrent to random agents. This result shows that the order existing in link click frequency comes from agent's content prediction ability, that is whether or an agent can determine the next step according to its own interest and current information. Research of web agents by The Web Intelligence consortium can be broken down into a number of subcategories of agents. Examples include Semantic agents, Information filtering agents and Remembrance agents, amongst others. Intelligent Web agents can use the problem solver mark-up language (PSML) (Menasalvas, 2003) to specify their roles, settings, and relationships with any other services. An intelligent Web will have the ability to process and understand natural language. It must understand and correctly judge the meaning of concepts expressed in words, such as "good," "best," and "season." Further, the intelligent Web must grasp the granularities of these terms' corresponding subjects and the location of their ontology definitions (Liu, 2003). In addition to the semantic knowledge that an intelligent search can extract and manipulate, intelligent Web agents will incorporate a dynamically created source of *metaknowledge* that deals with the relationships between concepts and the spatial or temporal constraint knowledge that planning and executing services use allowing agents to self-resolve their conflicts. To solve specific problems, intelligent Web agents must be able to *plan*. The planning process uses goals and associated subgoals, as well as constraints (Liu, 2003).

Research of Web agents by The Web intelligence consortium can be broken down into a number of subcategories of agents. Examples include semantic agents, information filtering agents and remembrance agents, amongst others.

Semantic Agents

Semantic agents operate on the Semantic Web. The Semantic Web operates on the Object orientated model of classes and objects each with their own properties. It is an extension of the current Web in which information is given well-defined meaning (Hendler, 2002). A semantic agent introduces the concept of ontology. Ontology is a means of describing information. It is a set of descriptors, including the vocabulary, the semantic interconnections and some simple rules of inference and logic, for some particular topic. Ontologies let information on the Web to be precisely defined. This better enables computers, using agents, to return a more meaningful set of results to the user. Conversational agents, or 'chatterbots', such as Microsoft Agent (MsAgent, 2002) or Virtual Personalities Inc. (Verbots, 2001) are basically speech-activated agents that can direct a computer generated facial animation and that includes a learning element (Sammut, 2002). For such a system to operate a means of understanding natural language is required. This is undertaken roughly, in three stages of analysis: syntax, semantics and pragmatics. Syntax analysis is concerned with the structure of a sentence in terms of the relative positions of words and their parts of speech. Semantic analysis examines the meaning of words and begins to build an internal representation of the meaning of the sentence. This task cannot be completed without the pragmatics, that is, knowledge about the domain of discussion. An understanding of the pragmatics is needed to resolve uncertainty and fill in assumed knowledge about the domain. They can be used as front ends for database products allowing the user to provide a query in a more natural context although their use is limited.

Information Filtering Agents

A bot - an abbreviation for *robot* - is a relatively small and focused computer application that runs continuously, in the background as other programs is being run, and responds automatically to a user's activity. Current research into Agents is also being undertaken in the field of email Filtering and Automatic Handling agents/bots. These include such innovations as the approach being taken by A-Life BotMail[1]. They have developed a product that allows senders to deliver an interactive and intelligent bot that can converse with the recipient of the email and intelligently present the contents of the message instead of sending a plain document. Snoop[2] is another type of email agent that can automatically inspect and evaluate your incoming mail messages and based on what it finds it can take certain actions such as generate an auto response to an incoming email. It can also forward emails, control your PC by email by launching certain applications in response to an email and parse messages and log information to text files for storage. Other examples of Web agents include 'Copernic Agent'[3] for information retrieval on the Web, 'Emailrobot'[4], an email manager and automater, allowing you to process, route, track and manage messages, and 'NewsRover'[5], a tool for extracting information from Usenet newsgroups automatically. The large number of information sources on the Internet present users with the hard task of gathering relevant and useful information from a query. Such a task is too difficult to solve without some form of high-level filtering of information (Lesser, 1998). Intelligent agents can aid in this area, passing on to the user only those items that they are interested in (Harper, 1996). One solution to this problem is to integrate different Artificial Intelligence technologies such as scheduling, planning, text processing, and interpretation problem solving, into a single information gathering agent, called BIG (resource-Bounded Information Gathering), that can take the role of the human information gatherer (Lesser, 1998). Agents have evolved to the point that complex Web agents now exist that can learn their user's preferences and actively seek out Web pages that could be of interest to them To provide personal assistance, an agent needs information about the user's interests and needs (Payne, 1995). Agents can suggest information sources and products to users based on learning from examples of their likes and dislikes. Such an agent is termed a 'Reccomender Agent'. Two modes of operation exist for recommender agents. Most existing recommender systems use social (collaborative) filtering methods that base recommendations on other users' preferences from Web sites. By contrast, content-based methods use information about an item itself to make suggestions. This approach has the advantage of being able to recommended previously unrated items to users with unique interests and to provide explanations for its recommendations.

Remembrance Agents

---

[1] http://www.artificial-life.com/v5/Website.php
[2] http://www.smalleranimals.com/snoop.htm
[3] http://www.copernic.com/index.html
[4] http://www.gfisoftware.com/
[5] http://www.newsrover.com

A remembrance agent is a program that aids human memory by displaying a list of documents that might be relevant to work the user is doing. Unlike most information retrieval systems, the agent runs continuously without any user intervention. Its unobtrusive interface allows a user to follow up or ignore the agents suggestions as desired. The front end of the agent program continuously watches what the user types and reads. It then sends this information to the back end. The back end finds old email, notes files, and on-line documents that it thinks relevant to the user's context. This information is then displayed by the front end, in such a way as not to distract the user from their current task (Bradley, 1995). Agents called 'Shop Bots' can aid the user in their purchase of an item of interest over the Internet. They compare prices from a number of online stores but currently are not very comprehensive, except in the computing Industry. PriceSCAN[1] offer a service allowing the user to compare the price of any tem from a number of different online stores before making a purchase. Shopping agents can compare prices on a number of different items or they can be specific to the field that they search in. Dealpilot[2] searches over 20 online bookstores for the lowest price and then returns the results to the user.

Profiling Agents

Profiling agents are used to build dynamic sites with information and recommendations tailored to match the individual taste of each visitor. The main purpose of the agent software is to build customer loyalty and profitable one-to-one relationships. Learn Sesame[3] learns about users automatically from their browsing behaviour, adapting to changes in the users interests over time. Agent programs can allow the user to have data sent automatically or 'pushed' to their computer at regular intervals, such as every hour, or when triggered by an event, such as when a Web page is updated. This is accomplished using what is known as 'push technology'. Desktop News[4] keeps the user informed by delivering a continuous stream of news and information from chosen Web sites direct to their desktop in a compact ticker toolbar. Push technology is an alternative to the way the World Wide Web currently operates in that information is presented to the user without their intervention, where ordinarily the user goes online to search for information.

Navigation Agents

Navigation agents are used to navigate through external and internal networks, remember short cuts, pre-load caching information, and automatically bookmark interesting sites. IBM's Web Browser Intelligence (IBM, 2000) pronounced Webby is an example. In addition, agents can help in the development and maintenance of a Web site. CheckWeb[5] scans user generated HTML pages and explore all the links for errors. When finished the program generate a log file with all errors it has found. IseekTraffic[6] submits a site to over 157,000 search engines, directories and links pages in its database. The software will submit all URL's to all of the top Search Engines and Directories. The categories of agents discussed up to now have been engineered to operate in one particular field or mode of information retrieval. Agents can also undertake a variety of features, not being restricted to just one function. Agents such as Ultra Hal[7] can cover a range of functions such as remind you of important dates, start programs on your behalf, browse the Internet and answer emails.

Many image retrieval systems have been developed; such as QBIC[8], VisualSEEK[9] and Photobook[10]. For instance, MultiMediaMiner (Zaiane, 1998) is a prototype of a data mining system for mining high-level multimedia information and knowledge from large multimedia databases. Some systems rely on keyword only retrievals and others support image content-based retrievals. In the latter approach, they support image retrievals based on the image feature information, such as average colors, color histograms, texture patterns, and shape objects. However, most of them are developed for image database applications. Multimedia applications, such as video conferences or Web collaboration, bundle several means of communication (language, text, image). Speech recognition, or speech-to-text, involves capturing and digitizing the sound waves, converting them to

---

[1] http://www.pricescan.com/
[2] http://www.dealpilot.com/
[3] http://www.aminda.com/mazzu/ls.htm
[4] http://www.desktopnews.com/
[5] http://www.algonet.se/~hubbabub/how-to/checkWeben.html
[6] http://www.botspot.com/Intelligent_Agent/1986.html
[7] http://www.agentland.com/
[8] http://wwwqbic.almaden.ibm.com/
[9] http://www.ctr.columbia.edu/VisualSEEk/
[10] http://www-white.media.mit.edu/vismod/demos/facerec/

basic language units or phonemes, constructing words from phonemes, and contextually analyzing the words to ensure correct spelling for words that sound alike (such as write and right). The multimedia revolution brings a challenge for us to create an intelligent Web capable of interacting and even understanding the user. This chapter only skims the surface of the topic of Web intelligence however as it is still in the early stages of research; we all have a part to play in its definition.

Conclusion

The success of Web intelligence will not hinge on available technology alone, but rather on the widespread acceptance of the medium to meet the needs of the user at large. Web intelligence developers will essentially need to combine teams of people with varied perspectives to develop and design an intelligent Web that will effectively address the ultimate requirements of the user. In doing so we may witness a growth and adoption of Web intelligence, encompassing every area of commercial enterprise and every aspect of human endeavor, resulting in the proportional displacement of conventional methods of communication. All categories of intelligent agents discussed in this chapter, although diverse, have one thing in common. They are all constructed to allow the user to query the Internet and its vast array of back end databases and bring back a meaningful set of results which are relevant to the user and allow them to carry out their tasks more efficiently and effectively. Intelligent information retrieval is a small part of Web intelligence that gives us the opportunity to improve the quality and effectiveness of interaction for everyone who communicates with a machine in the future.

References

Bradley J. Rhodes and Thad Starner. (1995) *Remembrance Agent. A continuously running automated information retrieval system.* MIT Media Lab,Cambridge, MA. Proceedings of The First International Conference on The Practical Application Of Intelligent Agents and Multi Agent Technology (PAAM '95), pp. 487-495

Browne, C. (2002) *Web Agents.* Report online at http://cbbrowne.com/info/agents.html, 2002

Goertzel, Ben. (2002) *The Emergence of Global Web intelligence and how it Will Transform the Human Race.* http://www.goertzel.org/papers/Webart.html, 2002

Harper, N. (1996) Intelligent Agents and the Web. Online http://osiris.sunderland.ac.uk/cbowww/AI/TEXTS/AGENTS3,

James Hendler, Tim Berners-Lee and Eric Miller.(2002*) Integrating Applications on the Semantic Web.* Journal of the Institute of Electrical Engineers of Japan, Vol 122(10), October, 2002, p. 676-680.

Hong, S. Lee, C., and Nah, Y. (2002) *An Intelligent Web Image Retrieval System.* Department of Computer Engineering,Dankook University, Seoul, Korea. Technical report available at http://dblab.dankook.ac.kr/SPIE2.pdf, 2002

IBM, (2000). *Web Browser Intelligence - Agent Software,* http:/lwww,raleigh.ibm.com/wbi/wbisoft.htm.

Lesser, V. Horling, B. Klassner, F. Raja , A.Thomas Wagner Shelley XQ. Zhang. (1998) *BIG: A Resource-Bounded Information Gathering Agent.* UMass Computer Science Technical Report 1998-03, http://dis.cs.umass.edu/research/big/big.html

Liu, J. (2003) Web Intelligence (WI): What makes wisdom web?. 18th International joint conference on Artificial Intelligence, Acapulco, Mexico, August 9-15, pp. 1596-1601, 2003

Maybury, M. (1997) *Intelligent Multimedia Information Retrieval.* AAAI Press/MIT Press, London, 1997.

E. Menasalvas, J. Segovia, P.S. Szczepaniak. (2003). Advances in Web Intelligence: First International Atlantic Web Intelligence Conference AWIC 2003, Springer-Verlag Heidelberg Madrid, Spain, May 5-6, 2003.

Microsoft Agents. (2002) http://www.microsoft.com/msagent/

Payne, T. and Edwards, P. (1995) *Learning Mechanisms for Information Filtering Agents*. Proceedings of the UK Intelligent Agents Workshop, SGES Publications, Oxford, UK, November, 1995, pp. 163-183.

Pringle, G., Allison, L. Dowe, D. (1998) *What is a tall poppy among Web pages? Proc. 7th IWWWC*, Brisbane, Australia

Sammut, C. (2002) *Conversational agents*. University of New South Wales, Australia. Report online at http://www.cse.unsw.edu.au/~claude/projects/nlp.html, 2002

Verbots. (2002) http://www.verbots.com/ Virtual Personalities Inc.

The Web intelligence Consortium (2003). http://wi-consortium.org/

Yao, Y. (2001) Web intelligence (WI) *Research Challenges and Trends in the New Information Age*. Knowledge Information Systems Laboratory, Japan, Technical Report online at http://kis.maebashi-it.ac.jp/wi01/pdf/wi_intro/wi-intro-new.pdf

Zaiane, O., Han, J., Chee, S. (1998) *MultiMediaMiner: A System Prototype for MultiMedia Data Mining,* Proc. Of SIGMOD98, USA, 1998

42   Ambient Intelligence

Kevin Curran, Christopher Temple, Danielle Doherty

Ambient Intelligence (AmI) is an evolution of technology, communication and awareness towards human-computer interaction. AmI is the environment of computing, networking technology and interfaces. It has the awareness of specific characteristics of human presence and personality. It deals with the needs of users and should be capable of responding intelligently and may even engage in intelligent dialogue. Ambient Intelligence should not be visible to the user unless necessary. It is also crucial that interaction should be of minimal effort to the user, understandable and enjoyable. This chapter discusses Ambient Intelligence.

Introduction

Ambient Intelligence refers to the environment of computing which is aware and responsive to the presence of human interaction. Its aim is to place great emphasis on the aspect of being user friendly and efficient and provide support for human interaction. It is anticipated that in the near future, people will be surrounded by intelligent interfaces that are to be placed in everyday objects. These objects will then be able to recognise but also respond invisibly to the presence of people. The interaction between the technology and the users should be natural (Ahola, 2001). Ambient Intelligence is said to be sensitive and responsive to our needs. The aim of this new technology is to use the space surrounding us in the form of movement, shape and sound recognition. It also aims to create a system that will be able to recognise all the different scents that are in the environment.

Ambient Intelligence has been influenced by user centred design which is an approach to design which regards the user's needs as the most important determinant of the content and structure of the design (Friedewald et al., 2005) Here the user is asked to give feedback to help to improve the design which can be then corrected. This should lead to technology which is able to learn behaviours from the user and is capable of adjusting to their requirements. Although the technology will be embedded in objects they will still be able to interact. The Ambient Intelligence concept builds upon ubiquitous computing and user-centric design. Ubiquitous computing (calm technology) is the shift, where technology becomes virtually invisible in our everyday life. The technology is now said to be embedded in our environment whereas it is made typically invisible. For this concept to be made successful organizations need to rethink their user interfaces, displays, operating systems, networks, and wireless communication. In ubiquitous computing, technology will be used in our lives and built into the things we use. Mark Weiser is regarded as the founder of what we now know as "ubiquitous computing". In his article "The Computer for the 21st Century", Weiser described multiple computers in a room as tabs, pads and boards, which roughly correspond to post-it notes, sheets of paper, white boards and bulletin boards (Weiser, 1999). His main thought behind this was that computers serve many functions as people come in and out of rooms. Computers can deliver important messages much more efficiently than those methods described above through e-mail. Ambient Intelligence also builds upon Moore's Law which stated that the number of transistors on a chip will double approximately every two years[1]. Electronics are now so small and powerful that they can be adapted to fit into every possible type of object no mater what the shape or size. There are three basic functions of Ambient Intelligence which are:

- Context Awareness – This is where the sensors are placed into the environment. They then communicate and help to identify movements and actions.

- Audio, video and data can be transferred wirelessly to any of the devices within the Ambient Intelligent system, therefore enabling access to information and entertainment wirelessly.

- By doing everyday and natural things such as talking, moving and gestures the users of this Ambient Intelligent environment can interact with their surroundings. By doing these everyday things they are enabling a hands free interactivity with the surrounding environment (Aarts and Marzano, 2003).

---

[1] http://www.intel.com/technology/mooreslaw/index.htm

The key to delivering ambient intelligence to users is being able to provide what is wanted, when, were and how it is wanted. All aspects are important so that the user receives the right information, at the right time and in the right way so that the person can make use of the information. Ambient Intelligence also can cater for those people who may have a disability such as the requirement of a hearing aid. However, user control is voluntary so they can decide what information they want and whether or not they want to receive it at any point (Basten et al., 2003).

Objectives of Ambient Intelligence

Ambient intelligence originated at Philips. In 1998, the board of management of Philips commissioned a number of internal workshops to study different scenarios that would transform the high-volume consumer electronic industry from the current "fragmented with features" world in 2020 where user-friendly devices support ubiquitous information, communication and entertainment. "This is our vision of 'Ambient Intelligence': people living easily in digital environments in which the electronics are sensitive to people's needs, personalized to their requirements, anticipatory of their behaviour and responsive to their presence."[1]. Philips joined Oxygen alliance, an international consortium of industrial partners within the context of the MIT Oxygen project, in 1999. The aim of this was to develop technology for the computer of the 21st century. It was in 2000 that the plans were put into action when a feasible and usable facility dedicated to Ambient Intelligence was built (Riva et al., 2005). Due to the complexity and importance of ambience intelligence, firstly the objectives must be realised before any further continuation into the design phase. Firstly the person or team carrying out the research must rethink the human-machine interaction experience that they are focusing on. The fact that ambience intelligence strives on designing interfaces that are more intelligent and interactive, teams designing interfaces will need to create systems that are more responsive to people's needs and actions, whereas the systems become true assets for expanding our minds. Below are a few technologies that need to be acknowledged before Ambience Intelligence can become a reality:

- Unobtrusive Hardware (use of miniaturisation, smart devices etc.)
- Fixed communication and computer infrastructure
- Device networks which are widely distributed, dynamic, easy to use and program
- Human Centric Computer interfaces (efficient and effortless)
- Dependable and secure system devices

The convergence of computing with telecommunications and multimedia resources will ensure that the means of communicating will increase and help to bring form to the Ambient Intelligence scenarios.

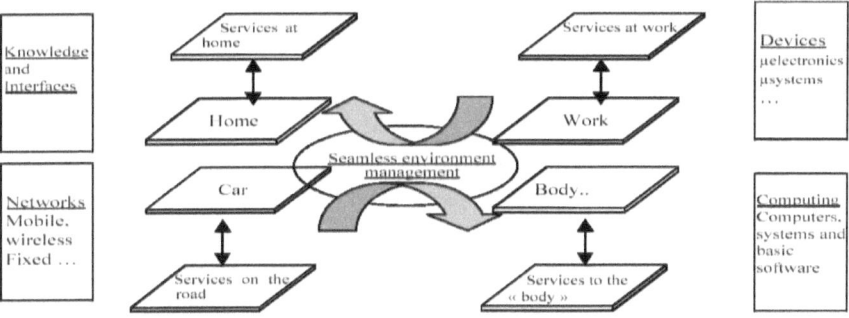

Figure 151: The Ambient Intelligence Space (Riva, 2005)

The Ambient Intelligence Space was introduced by ISTAG Information Society Technologies Advisory Group). Ambient Intelligence is a direct extension to the concept 'ubiquitous computing'. However this new technology

[1] http://www.research.philips.com/technologies/syst_softw/ami/index.html

will have to be more advanced than 'ubiquitous computing', it will actually have to be able to adapt to the users needs and emotions and activities. A few of the characteristics that will help in the social acceptance of an Ambient Intelligence system are (Weber et al., 2005):

- It should be able to facilitate human contact.
- The technology should be controllable by the users. They should be easy to use for those who are weary of technological devices, for example the system should be easy to turn on and off.
- It should help to build up techniques and skills as well as knowledge which in turn will ensure that the quality of work that is produced will be to a higher standard.
- People should be able to trust the system and they should be confident that it works correctly.

The idea of Ambient Technology is to integrate sensors networks into other wireless communications systems, thus allowing these sensors to capture the user's interaction and environmental behaviour and act upon it. For instance, there already are a number of houses equipped with sensors to read users temperature and mood (through other physical factors). Every visitor is also given a PIN chip that has information about the users requirements, the sensors then react to the information from the PIN and the user by increasing/decreasing the temperature in the room, changing the pictures on the wall, changing the music in the room, televisions changing to a certain station and all this happening simultaneously for each person to meet the perfect requirements of the users. Although this technology is attractive, there are still a few implications surrounding its development. Ambient Technology must be miniaturised to go unnoticed by the user, it must be data-secured, have flexible network protocols and also have more efficient wireless network infrastructures. These constraints alone are making ambient technology harder to become a reality, but the biggest constraint involved in all of these other constraints, is the cost of the technology.

Predicting the technologies that will shape the future ambient Intelligence world is difficult however, it is expected that Ambient Intelligent technology will develop considerably. Technology trends certainly have momentum and due to this have paved a way for Ambient Intelligence through such elements as computing, communication, software, sensors and displays. In accordance to Moore's law, data density on integrated circuits is continuing to double every eighteen months. Other related disciplines such as computer storage and CPU speeds also show considerable rates of change. The concept of Ambient Intelligence requires severe technological advances in sensor technology, micro actuator technology, ultra-low power radio and in smart materials to create the adaptiveness and responsiveness to the Ambient Intelligent environment. All of the technological elements have to be integrated into the architectural framework of an Ambient Intelligent System; these will then form a library of building blocks for general Ambient Intelligent System architectures. With ambient technology being related to meet and adjust to user environments and requirements, it has also been applied to many different aspects to suit all of the requirements of today's society. Some of the ways ambient intelligence has been applied has been through entertainment, advertising and home-automation.

Ambient Intelligent Entertainment

Philips has created a new experience through colours that change whilst watching a movie to intensify the mood of the scene. This is known as Ambilight (see Figure 152). This is a form of ambient intelligence which attempts to increases the users senses to provide a more entertaining experience without the user knowing it. The concept behind applying this ambient technology in this form is to reduce eye strain in 60 – 90% of people, improve relaxation and attention levels and improve fatigue.

Figure 152: Example of Ambilight being implemented[1]

Philips have taken the Ambilight concept and developed another ambient technology known as AmBX. It is able to take the concept of the Ambilight lighting and add more multi-sensory to the experience through adding a new type of surround sound, vibration, air movement and some other effects. AmBX is currently being added to PC games and PC gaming peripherals. AmBX is shorthand for 'ambient experiences'. AmBX attempts to deliver an immersive experience for gaming through the integration of games and peripherals providing surround lighting, sound, vibration, air movement and other effects work in harmony together (see Figure 153). Oliver Welsh from EDGE magazine said *"It's going to make games a lot bigger and a lot more intense. It takes over all your senses"*, *"There was a great moment in [computer game] Broken Sword were you could feel the force of the plane's wake from the fans"*[1].

Figure 153: Example of AmBX implemented on a Desktop PC

Note the multidirectional speakers which determine what sound is going to be played from what direction. The Ambilight effect is added to intensify the AmBX experience and multidirectional fans determine what direction air needs to be blown. To use this AmBX technology in games requires game developers to code it into games. Gaming companies such as Ubisoft and EA have already signed an agreement with Philips to get involved in this ambient. Philips have designed their own scripting language to embed the AmBX's instructions into the console. The AmBX engine acts as the middleware between the game code and external AmBX hardware i.e. fans. Figure 154 shows how the AmBX scripting language is embedded to allow the engine to perform the tasks to the external AmBX hardware.

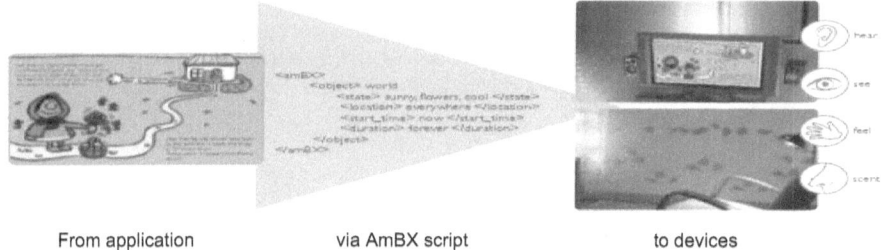

| From application | via AmBX script | to devices |

Figure 154: Example of AmBX scripting interacting with hardware[2]

AmBX technology aims to provide gamers with value added deeper gaming experiences. Philips desire to see AmBX penetrating the home cinema market; and for it to be the domestic LED lighting control and home ambient experience 'mood' solution.

[1] http://www.research.philips.com/password/archive/31/pw31_04_ambilight.html
[1] http://www.research.philips.com/password/archive/27/pw27_ambx.html
[2] http://www.research.philips.com/password/archive/27/downloads/pw27_ambx_16.pdf

Advertising

Ambient intelligence because of it interactivity with the user is an attractive medium to advertisers. Intelligent Earth[1] are applying ambient intelligence in a number of ways including:

- Magic Pen - a piece of software that enables a web camera to monitor 3D trajectory and orientation to display 3D drawings using the pen,
- Face Detector – Face detection software,
- Doki - Artificially intelligent gender recognition robot
- Intelligent Advertising.

Intelligent Advertising is composed of different types of ambient intelligent projects such as AdSwitch and AdWatch. AdSwitch is designed to change to meet the users requirements in watching advertisements. When someone approaches the advert, their gender and age will be determined to evaluate an advertisement suitable to the user. The user approaching it provokes the software to change to meet the environment surrounding it and the user's needs. For instance, as the elderly woman moves to the head of the queue, she is shown the advert for retirement homes and Mills and Boons novels, then the teenage boy heads the queue and some computer games adverts and perhaps appropriate teenage music will play. As he leaves the queue, the young woman comes to the head of the queue and is shown the appropriate lifestyle adverts for her age and gender."[2]. This will be a large step forward for the advertising industry as not all adverts are able to reach their potential customers; for example, there is no point in advertising NiQuitin in an area where not all people smoke. This use of ambient intelligence will allow advertisers to target the correct market no matter what the situation. The advert will adapt to the changing environment. AdWatch works alongside AdSwitch to gather the statistics as a result of the ambient technology. If and when the advert changes, AdWatch is able to record statistics such as gender, age, length of time viewing, when and where the advert is being viewed. This aims at being a tool for marketers and advertisers to pinpoint their target market.

Home-Automation

The most anticipated outcome in the development of ambient technologies is the application of home-automation. Technology is available to create a full automated home, but the cost benefit ratio is much too high to mass-produce it and apply it to a number of homes. The idea of ambient technology in the home, whilst technology it is growing more complex, rather than reduce it, simply allow it to disappear into the environment surrounding us without having to notice it carrying out the complex instructions that would make our lives easier. The technology will only be presented to us in the home through the intelligent user-friendly interfaces. There are a number of methods currently being designed on how to interact with the interfaces including touch screen mobile control panels and the voice recognition systems.

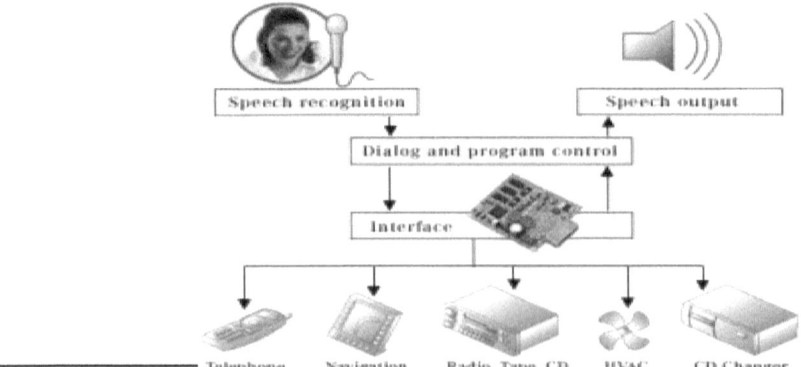

[1] http://www.intelligent-earth.com/
[2] http://www.intelligent-earth.com/products/i_a_adswitch.php

Figure 155: Home-automation using voice recognition[1]

Voice recognition systems work through miniature microphones installed in the home that respond to instructions rather than users carrying the panel around. Figure 155 shows an example of how the ambient technology of the voice recognition can contribute to home-automation.

A user wishing to watch a movie on an Ambilight television could speak to the intelligent user-friendly interface giving it instructions to execute the preset 'Movie' setting that was already customized to close the curtains/blinds, dim the lights, apply climate control (heating, moisture), increase volume etc. The interface will then respond by following instructions and asking, "is that everything?" through the speech output.

The Future of Ambient Intelligence

The reason that ambient intelligence has not been implemented vastly today is due to the constraints that come with it. For ambient technology to be developed, a number of factors have to be considered, such as nanotechnology, self-changing and security.

Nanotechnology is complex and hard to work with, the time it takes to develop devices with nano technology is much longer due to the fact that everything that is in the design must be built on a very small scale. Each tedious component must be carefully applied using a microscope, which is very time-consuming, especially when developing the prototype. Even when nano products are being mass-produced, they take much longer than ordinary scale products due to the precision that must be taken for each nano component.

Part of the experience of ambient intelligence is not being able to notice the complexity of the technology around your environment. But how is the ambient intelligence going to detect changes to the environment without the user having to submit changes through the interface? If this is the case, that the must amend all changes to the environment for the technology to recognize it then it is no longer ambient intelligence. This method of constantly keeping the ambient technology up to date with every change will be very repetitive and becomes more noticeable to the user. Ambient technology should be able to detect changes to the environment and update itself to suit our requirements without us knowing. A successful piece of ambient technology available to consumers is the wireless weather forecast ambient device which connects to the internet in order to update the device to display the most recent weather.

Security

One of the fears surrounding ambient intelligence is security. If people are not willing to trust the ambient technology then it will fail. If ambient technology is to make all of our lives easier by being able to identify us for security reasons, will it contain all of our identity and financial details or credit card details? If it can identify us, will it contain all of our personal details? If someone hacked another's ambient network, will they be able to commit identity fraud with the information? Will they have access to the person's sensitive information on their ambient network? Plus, if AdSwitch has the ability to recognize faces, genders, age and also keeps track of faces to identify a recurrence with a viewer of the advert. Will they be able to keep this sensitive information e.g. image of our image, age, gender? Will there be laws past to ensure peoples privacy through ambient technology in the public and in their home?

Author of 'Safeguards in a World of Ambient Intelligence', David Wright states that "if companies are not careful with the technologies they install or the security measures they employ, once it becomes known that their systems, technologies or services are impacting (on) privacy or have led to a data breach, the company

---

[1] http://www.usautoparts.net/bmw/technology/speech_display.jpg

could suffer damage to its reputation" (Wright et al., 2008). With so much fraud and criminal acts already following the trends of advancement in technology (internet fraud, identity theft), what's to stop it recurring with ambient technology where criminals will be able to gather even more sensitive information? With so much disadvantages of security, there are a few advantages already implemented using ambient technology to the security sector to attempt to even the balance. It will be able to make homes more secure by being able to identify the owners of the ambient network before allowing them access to the home. It will also be able to keep track of all the recent instructions the interface has received as a way of monitoring activity. It will be able to enable/disable certain instructions to different members of the family i.e. administration and user accounts where one account will be able to control heating, cooker and other dangerous actions that will be disabled to the children of the home. With all of these constraints going against the security side of this technology compared to the advantages, it's obvious security is the main concern about ambient intelligence interfering with our lives in the future (Espiner, 2008).

Privacy and trust are vital because if people do not trust the technology then they will not want to use it, particularly in all aspects of their lives. In Ambient Intelligent environments, information not only resides in one node but is distributed between many. This means that if the system is attacked then the entire system should not fail or disclose all the information. A node can be described as 'a connection point in a network, either a redistribution point or an end point for data transmission. Having said this, the disadvantage of an Ambient Intelligence system is that every single node within the system needs to be protected. This can happen when the system is flooded with requests which will result in energy draining from the nodes, which in turn makes the performance of the system weak.

Conclusion

Ambient Intelligence has been described as a 'paradigmatic shift in computing and society'. For a system to be classified as an Ambient Intelligent system the development process has to be potentially very promising for users. The idea of Ambient Intelligence is to make computers/electronics much smarter, in a sense that they will be able to interact and change to suit our immediate requirements through intelligent user-friendly interfaces. It is said that an Ambient Intelligent system has to fulfill the following criteria. It has:

- To facilitate human contact
- To be oriented towards community and cultural enhancement
- To help to build knowledge and skills for work, citizenship and consumer choice
- To inspire trust and confidence
- To be controlled by ordinary people and have long-term maintainability

The future of ambient intelligence depends on how the public reacts to the technology because if they find it too complex then it will not sell. This is why it is important to develop intelligent and user-friendly interfaces for the technology. The key to delivering ambient intelligence to users is being able to provide what is wanted, when, were and how it is wanted. All aspects are important so that the user receives the right information, at the right time and in the right way so that the person can make use of the information. Ambient Intelligence also can cater for those people who may have a disability however; user control is voluntary so they can decide what information they want and whether or not they want to receive it at any point.

References

Ahola, J. (2001). Ambient Intelligence, ERCIM News, No. 47, October 2001
http://www.ercim.org/publication/Ercim_News/enw47/intro.html

Aarts, E. and Marzano, S. (2003) The New Everyday: Visions of Ambient Intelligence. 010 Publishing, Rotterdam, Netherlands, 2003.

Basten, T., Geilen, M. and de Groot, H. (2003) Ambient Intelligence: Impact on Embedded System Design. Kluwer Academic Publishers, Boston, 2003

Espiner, T. (2008) Privacy Experts Warn of 'Ambient Intelligent' Risks, ZDNet.co.uk, February 2008
http://news.zdnet.co.uk/security/0,1000000189,39292582,00.htm?r=2

Friedewald, M., Da Costa, O., Punie, Y., Alahuhta, P. and Heinonen, S. (2005) Perspectives of ambient intelligence in the home environment, Telematics and Informatics, Volume 22, Issue 3, August 2005, Pages 221-238

Riva, G., Vatalaro, F., Davide, F. And Alcaniz, M. (2005) Ambient Intelligence: The Evolution of Technology, Communication and Cognition, IOS Press, US, 2005

Weber, W., Rabaey, J.M., Aarts, E. (2005) Ambient Intelligence, Springer, 1st Edition, 2005

Weiser, M. (1999) The Computer for the 21st Century, ACM SIGMOBILE Mobile Computing and Communications Review, Vol. 3, No. 3, July 1999

Wright, D.; Gutwirth, S.; Friedewald, M.; Vildjiounaite, E.; Punie, Y. (2008) Safeguards in a World of Ambient Intelligence, Vol. 1, 2008, ISBN: 978-1-4020-6661-0